THE COUSINS' WARS

THE COUSINS' WARS

Religion, Politics, and the
Triumph of
Anglo-America

KEVIN PHILLIPS

BASIC
BOOKS

A MEMBER OF THE
PERSEUS BOOKS GROUP

To my father, William E. Phillips (1911–1983),
whose own university days in England led him
to take a young son to all of the 1940s and early 1950s
movies about Elizabethan sea captains, Bengal lancers,
Tories in the Mohawk Valley, the fall of Fort William Henry,
and the Highlanders' relief of Fort Pitt.

Copyright © 1999 by Kevin Phillips

Maps by Mark Stein Studios, New York, NY
Maps 13.1 & 13.2 Copyright 1998 Rodger Doyle
Maps 10.1 A & B Courtesy of James L. Sundquist, *Dynamics of the Party System.* (Washington: the Brookings Institution, 1973)

Published by Basic Books, A Member of the Perseus Books Group

Library of Congress Cataloging-in-Publication Data
   The cousins' wars : religion, politics, and the triumph of
Anglo-America / by Kevin Phillips.
    p.   cm.
   Includes index.
   ISBN 0-465-01369-4
   1. United States—History—Revolution, 1775–1783—Religious
aspects. 2. United States—History—Civil War, 1861–1865—Religious
aspects. 3. Great Britain—History—Civil War, 1642–1649—Religious
aspects. 4. United States—Politics and government—1775–1783. 5.
United States—Politics and government—1861–1865. 6. Great
Britain—Politics and government—1642–1649. 7. Religion and
politics—United States—History. 8. Religion and politics—Great
Britain—History. 9. Politics and war—History. I. Title.
E209.P48   1999
973.3'7—dc21   98-49935
                                                                                                          CIP

Design by Heather Hutchison

The paper used in this publication meets the requirements of the American National Standard for Permanence of Paper for Printed Library Materials Z39.48-1984.

10   9   8   7   6   5   4   3   2   1

CONTENTS

MAPS AND FIGURES

Figures

PREFACE

THIS IS A BOOK ABOUT a famous trio of English-speaking civil wars—the English Civil War, the American Revolution, and the American Civil War. It is also a book about religion—about the interaction of creed, politics, and war during three centuries when faith played a much larger role than now.

But most of all, it is a book about how three great internal wars seeded each other and, in so doing, guided not only politics but the rise of Anglo-America from a small Tudor kingdom to a global community and world hegemony. The English Civil War laid the groundwork for the American Revolution and the political breakaway of North America's English-speaking Low Church Protestants. This gave the English-speaking nations the dual framework so important to their long term future. The American Revolution, in turn, laid the groundwork for a new independent republic split by slavery and an American civil war in which cotton-starved Britain came close to pro-Southern intervention. The American Civil War, when it was over, reformed and framed modern Anglo-America—the principal English-speaking nations.

The emergence of England and then Great Britain during these three centuries was extraordinary. The same can be said of the formation and eventual ascendancy of the United States. What has been unique is the division of the English-speaking community into *two* major nations and successor great powers: one aristocratic, "chosen," and imperial; one democratic, "chosen," and manifest destiny–driven. Lacking equivalent sweep and strength, Spain, France, and then Germany failed in their successive political and military contests with Anglo-America.

This book's pursuit of Anglo-American evolution through the prism of wars, political constituencies, and electoral alignments, some repeating down through the centuries, becomes strikingly revisionist. The pervasive role of religion in eighteenth- and even nineteenth-century American politics comes to the surface much more clearly, as does the relentlessness of Puritanism, in its older and newer forms, on two continents and in three wars. So do the underappreciated (and stimulating) effects of the 1775–1783 and 1861–1865 American wars on Britain.

The importance of religion surprised me, as it probably will many readers. After four years of study and writing, the triangle of religion, politics, and war is unmistakable during the three centuries. I would not have thought so when I began, so hopefully readers will bear with me as the evidence unfolds, war after war.

Religion, politics, war, and their interrelationships are what this book is about. It is not a narrative of campaigns, battles, or decisive maneuvers. I went to each of the pivotal battlefields—Naseby, Saratoga, and Gettysburg. But when I walked where Oliver Cromwell's cavalry charge shattered the Royalists, where the New England militia held the British regulars, and where Joshua Chamberlain's 20th Maine Infantry successfully defended Little Round Top, these individual battles and regiments dissolved into a larger historical panorama. Something bigger, something more important, was emerging. This, hopefully, is that story.

The importance of religion and war in the shaping of nations should not even be debatable. Back in the sixteenth and seventeenth centuries, they were the principal instruments of world affairs. They were also principal instruments of English, then British and American nationalism. From the birth of Protestantism in the sixteenth century, no Western nation has matched the English-speaking peoples in asserting their destiny as God's Kingdom. The newly Protestant Tudors and early seventeenth-century Puritans were the most intense in this respect, echoed later, and more sedately, by Britain's Hanoverian kings, who became chorists and hymnalists of parliamentary supremacy and the Protestant Succession. George Frederick Handel, their court composer, used ceremonial music built around biblical themes from *Judas Maccabeus* to *Zadok the Priest* to celebrate Hanoverian rule with the analogy begun by the Tudors: *The British were the new Chosen People.* Then came the eighteenth-century American colonists, who, from the pulpits of Boston to the tobacco manors of Virginia, confidently predicted that *their* New Israel would stretch to the Mississippi or even the Pacific. And, like the Tudors and Hanoverians, they shouldered muskets to make it come true.

From the beginning, Anglo-American exceptionalism has had its prophets in both nations. There was John Winthrop, who drew on English thinking when he described the new Massachusetts Bay settlement of 1630 as "a city on a hill." There was England's James Thomson, so theologically assured in 1740 in his drumroll opening of *Rule Britannia*: "When Britain first at heaven's command, arose from out the azure main . . ." And Horace Walpole, the English essayist, predicting in 1775 that "the next Augustan age will dawn on the other side of the Atlantic. There will be, perhaps, a Thucydides at Boston, a Xenophon at New York. . . ."

Purplish prose, to be sure, but fair historical prediction. And over quite a time span. The English language, the principal vehicle of global communication in the year 2000, was the same one used in 1719 by Isaac Watts when his immodest translation of the Psalms replaced references to Israel with references to Great Britain. And the same one employed by the bombastic Yankee colonel, Ethan Allen, named like his brothers Heman, Heber, Levi, Zimri, and Ira for a biblical warrior, when he boldly announced the capture of Fort Ticonderoga "In the name of the Great Jehovah and the Continental Congress." Such English-speaking self-assuredness has held up much better, say, than the old German insistence "Gott Mit Uns," or the earlier invocation on the sacred silk banner of the Spanish Armada, which urged "Arise O Lord, and vindicate thy cause."

Unsheathed swords have shone repeatedly in the Anglo-American evolutionary process. "Our God," said his English-speaking Protestant soldiers of the seventeenth century, "is a God of Warr," which, in its coupling of "God" and "war," is one of this book's central points: The great formative events in the rise of England and then of the United States were not steam engines, Conestoga wagons, the canals of the English Midlands or New York, Bessemer's steelmaking process, or J. P. Morgan's gift for corporate finance. They were wars—bitter, fratricidal wars—accompanied by Puritan and abolitionist sermons and battle hymns and principally fought to change the shape of internal politics, liberty, and religion. It was through these three cousins' wars—the English Civil War of 1640–1649 (and its follow-up in 1688), the American Revolution of 1775–1783, and the U.S. Civil War of 1861–1865—that the English-speaking world critically reshaped itself. Broadly, the result was to uphold political liberties, commercial progress, technological inventiveness, linguistic ambition, and territorial expansion.

Let me underscore: Directly and indirectly, each conflict—and all three of them combined revolution *and* civil war—rescripted society, economics, and government on *both* sides of the ocean. And why not? Historians agree that revolutions and civil wars have been watershed events for nearly every power in modern Europe—the Netherlands of the late sixteenth century, the France of the 1790s, the Italy of the mid-nineteenth century, and the Russia of 1917–1921. So, too, for the great civil wars discussed in this book: the internal strife of an England soon to become Britain, the convulsions of George III's overstretched Atlantic Empire, and finally the bloody North-South showdown of the emerging, adolescent United States. All three stand among the most powerful convulsions, clarifications, and political watersheds of the Anglo-American global emergence and achievement.

War is not simply, in the words of von Clausewitz, "a continuation of politics by other means." It has also been an anvil on which some of the most lasting arrangements of English and American politics have been hammered out. Bloodshed, arguably, is to lasting electoral alignments what carbon has been to steel-making. British historian George M. Trevelyan, identifying revolution as "the historian's touchstone, by which to try the quality of a race or age," has called the English civil war "the decisive event in English history." Comparable claims for the United States have been made about the American Revolution and Civil War. Together, the three constitute the central staircase of modern English-speaking history, not least the division into two great powers with pointedly different characteristics—not sister or brother nations, but *cousins*. However unforeseen, this duality proved to be the Anglo-American genius.

The grand framework of *The Cousins' Wars* has already been stated: *putting a new political, religious, and war-based perspective around the dual emergence of America and Great Britain.*

This framework, in turn, yields the following thesis: that from the seventeenth century, the English-speaking peoples on both continents defined themselves by wars that upheld, at least for a while, a guiding political culture of a Low Church, Calvinistic Protestantism, commercially adept, militantly expansionist, and highly convinced, in Old World, New World, or both, that it represented a chosen people and a manifest destiny. In the full, three-century context, Cavaliers, aristocrats, and bishops pretty much lost and Puritans, Yankees, self-made entrepreneurs, Anglo-Saxon nationalists, and expansionists had the edge, especially in America.

There is also an unmistakable thread of ethnocultural continuity: First, East Anglia led the Parliamentary side in the partly successful English Civil War. Later, New England, East Anglia's seventeenth-century Puritan offshoot, was the most aggressive formulator of the American rebellion (and this time, instead of Puritanism being crushed by the Restoration of 1660, New England Yankeedom triumphed and expanded). Finally, in the 1860s, Greater New England—a cultural region now stretching west through New York, Ohio, Michigan, and Minnesota to Oregon and Puget Sound—won the battle to control the expansion and orientation of the United States into the mid-twentieth century.

Several historians and writers have posited a sequence of three "Puritanisms"—the first cresting in mid-seventeenth-century Civil War England, the second in mid-eighteenth-century New England not long before the American Revolution, and the third in nineteenth-century New England before the U.S. Civil War (although England, too, had some parallels). The idea is intriguing because it helps differentiate the revivals in these cultures—invariably reform-minded, communitarian, and commercial as well as strictly religious—from the impacts of the revivals and great awakenings in the American South (and some would add the seventeenth- and eighteenth-century north of England), which were more emotional and less tied to middle-class reform or commercial values. The three cousins' wars, in many ways, overlap the three puritanisms, although this book will leave the theology to others.

While the two paragraphs above have some oversimplifications, they still convey an important essence of this book. Without Greater New England, moreover, the United States—one can imagine an enlarged, more Germanic Northern Hemisphere version of Argentina—might have been neutral in World War I and preoccupied by Pacific considerations in World War II.

Beneath the war-based, religious, and political overviews, this book has several important subfocuses: first, how the republican majority brought about between 1775 and 1783 within the new United States was critically aided by a wartime mosaic of allies, sympathizers, and collaborators in England, Ireland, Scotland, Canada, and the Caribbean (possibly including several senior British military officers). In parts of the British North Atlantic in 1775–1776, there was virtual civil war. The North American colonials in search of independence were at first a shaky plurality; they became a majority and built their new nation only with the important help of a minority of English-speakers elsewhere in the empire. The American Revolution was broader and much more complex than its name implies.

Second, the book will also develop the central significance of wars, civil *and* foreign, but especially the former, in British and U.S. party alignments. In the United States, since 1775, wars and their aftermaths have been the single most important recurring factor in national electoral divisions. The victorious generals and collateral acrimonies of a full half dozen conflicts—the Revolution, that of 1812, the Mexican War, the Civil War, and both world wars—parade, almost literally, across the pages of American election strategy.

Third, it is hard to overstate the importance of the eighteenth- and nineteenth-century division of the English-speaking world into two distinctive political cultures. The societies of Britain and British (Loyalist) Canada, relatively deferential, were complemented by the more democratic (and sometimes radical) societies of the United States and Australia, peopled by transported convicts, indentured servants, and political and religious refugees, as well as by large ethnic diasporas from Ireland and Scotland. The effect of the division in 1783 was to secure smug, conservative, but economically innovative England in its own sceptered islands, an antirevolutionary bulwark of the 1790s and 1840s that became the preeminent empire of the nineteenth and early twentieth centuries. The second impact came as the westward redistribution of

European population built the United States as a more egalitarian English-speaking successor power for a later, democratic age.

Four years ago, this book started growing from the original seed of a narrower query: Could the British army, with its scarlet regimentals and its gleaming eighteen-inch bayonets, have skewered the American Revolution—and then hanged a few of its leaders—with a tougher version of the strategy that failed in 1777 when General John Burgoyne finally surrendered his army at Saratoga? Could history and the vital division of Anglo-America have been stopped in their tracks?

Many Americans, albeit fewer Britons, will remember the famous battle plan from school: Burgoyne's strategy, plausible enough, was to split the uncertain middle states from the buzzing hornets of New England with a three-pronged attack. The principal target was Albany, New York, the onetime Dutch fur-trading center at the confluence of the Hudson and Mohawk Rivers, the new state's controlling water highways. The main invasion force of eight thousand men was to push down the Champlain-Hudson corridor from Canada; a second, smaller army was to drive east through the Mohawk Valley; and a third, never very precisely described, was to sail up the lower Hudson from New York City. Converging, they would conquer.

That, by itself, was to have been this book: Saratoga as a campaign that the British might have won, making it the linchpin of the Anglo-American future. However, the project's scope quickly began to widen. My own revulsion with the politics of the United States in 1995–1996 drew me farther and farther into the intricacies of an altogether different era. Yet the political strategist in me couldn't help consider what Howe, Burgoyne, and Lord George Germain, the American secretary, could or should have done in broader strategic terms. I even found myself putting a new eighteenth-century twist on an old, familiar yardstick from my earlier career: Was there an emerging republican majority in the thirteen colonies circa 1775–1777, as the eventual outcome at Saratoga suggested? Or was there only a minority of committed independence-seekers, one that could have been splintered, outweighed, or overwhelmed by a better-coordinated British political, cultural, and military blueprint? How did it all come about?

Amid this research, a still-larger relationship started to beckon. For over three decades, my writings on politics, beginning with *The Emerging Republican Majority* in 1969, have elaborated the differences within the United States that have repeatedly set Greater New England—the Yankee settlements that soon extended across upstate New York, through the Great Lakes, and eventually to the Pacific Northwest—at cultural, religious, and political odds with the Greater South. Far from beginning in the New World, much of this polarization can be traced back to the Old—to divergent regional, religious, and cultural patterns within seventeenth-century England and later Great Britain and their partial recurrence along the Atlantic Seaboard. Many early settlers of New England came from the Puritan south and east of England. The influx into the American South, however, hailed in much larger ratios from Scotland, Ireland, and the upcountry north and west of England. Kindred divisions within the British Isles had underpinned the political geography of the English Civil War of 1640–1649. Transplanting elements of this framework to the New World turned out to be incendiary.

When Puritan-descended New England launched the Revolution in 1775, some of its words and aspects echoed the old-country cleavages of the 1640s. The early years of the English Civil War can be reread, from a transatlantic perspective, as almost an American Pre-Revolution. This is why I found myself adding an earlier cousins' war and a new early chapter to this book. One hundred and thirty years after the key battles of the English Civil War, Revolutionary New England seethed with seventeenth-century memories, suspicions, and analogies. Connecticut patriots named the flagship of the state navy for Oliver Cromwell, and Governor Jonathan Trumbull castigated supporters of the King as "inimicals" and "malignants" in long-ago Commonwealth fashion. Many American military commanders even bore the same biblical names so prominent a century earlier in Cromwell's New Model Army—Ezekiel, Gideon, Obadiah, Israel, and Ebenezer.

Nor was this any coincidence. The heartland of the Puritan side in the English Civil War had been the Eastern Association—the military confederation of East Anglia (Essex, Suffolk, and Norfolk) with the adjoining shires of Hertford, Cambridge, Huntingdon, and Lincoln. Six generations later, the powder keg of the American Revolution was also located in counties called Essex and Suffolk (Massachusetts Bay), as well as in places like Boston, Norwich, Chelmsford, Billerica, Dedham, and Braintree, named by Massachusetts and Connecticut settlers for East Anglian hometowns.

Beyond Yankee New England, however, from New York to Georgia, two-thirds of the remaining colonies that were debating independence in 1775 and 1776 had major concentrations of loyalists and would-be neutralists. Here were the places where the colonists' struggle might have been lost. Here were the locales in which the fighting became a bitter *civil war*.

Two centuries of American history have submerged this discordant note in a blaze of glorious mythmaking: the united colonies linking arms against the tyranny of George III, followed by the War of 1812 as a heroic reprise to protect American ships and sailors from British search and impressment and maintain the integrity of the Republic. The U.S. Civil War, in this star-spangled illusion, becomes yet another moral battlefield, a successful crusade to end slavery in the South. The disquieting truth, however, is that if history books were to include detailed nationwide maps of internal sympathy or support for the major U.S. conflicts, *the state-by-state portrait of which counties, towns, districts, or regions were loyal, disloyal, neutral, or unwilling to contribute or to draft troops would resemble ethnoreligious maps of the modern-day Balkans.*

In writing this book, I found that a similar pattern could be constructed, albeit much more loosely and without comparable voting data, for the internal divisions of the British Isles in the conflicts of 1640–1649, 1685, 1688, 1715, 1745, and even 1775–1783. These battles, too, have an ethnic and religious continuity, and to a surprising extent, the United States *inherited* its pattern of civil wars fought around a patchwork of regional, religious, ethnic, and economic differences from seventeenth- and eighteenth-century Britain.

Three decades ago, when I began the political analysis published in 1969, one of its central emphases was on how much the existing U.S. party system even then continued to mirror the distant fratricide of 1861–1865—and on how much electoral significance the accelerating collapse of that century-old war-based framework must inevitably have. To explain this, I drew on history, economics, geography, religion, ethnicity, and also the lesser divisions periodically imprinted on the United States by other domestic and foreign wars. From Fort Sumter to Appomattox, the trauma of the Civil War had been powerful enough to etch, in blood and gunpowder, a Republican-Democratic electoral map that lasted a full century. Nothing in the U.S., before or since, has equalled this sectional enmity for political fallout. Even as late as the 1950s, rural and small-town Americans were still broadly voting as their great-grandfathers had shot. The extent to which the cultural, religious, and ethnic quilt of Civil War and post–Civil War politics, four generations old, was finally unravelling in the 1960s was the basis for my prediction of a new, dominant, trans–Mason-Dixon line, conservative coalition.

The predictive success of this methodology has left me convinced that the best dissection of political loyalty and behavior, two or three hundred years ago or today, must be *multidimensional: cultural, ethnic, religious, economic, sectional, and local.* The application of these yardsticks to the cousins' wars makes their alignments—and the basis of their considerable continuity— a lot clearer.

One point cannot be made strongly enough: The English Civil War is the necessary starting point, not just for a piece of Britain's history but for America's. This is where the events and alignments leading up to the American Revolution began. The latter was really a second English-speaking civil war, drawing many of its issues, antagonisms, and divisions from the seventeenth- and eighteenth-century British Isles. Small wonder that the broad origins of the American Revolution, as discussed in U.S. history books, don't do a very good job of explaining the actual wartime loyalties and politics. British religious and ethnic tribalisms from the 1640s and 1690s fill in many important gaps.

No exit polls, obviously, were taken at the Boston Tea Party, at Pennsylvania militia drills, or at Anglican church services or Quaker meetings up and down the Eastern Seaboard. Nevertheless, it's possible—tedious, but doable—to pour through the materials about the colonies in the 1760s and 1770s and figure out which religious, ethnic, vocational, and economic groups lived where and how they believed, fought, skulked, or migrated during the years from 1775 to 1783. Thirty years ago, in writing *The Emerging Republican Majority,* I had been surprised at the impact of religion and sectarian cleavages on U.S. national voting patterns. But there they had been—central to party divisions within the North over slavery and the U.S. Civil War, critical (along with ethnicity) in explaining the national electorate's shifts in response to both world wars, and then at the heart of the sectarian shifts in each of the two elections (1928 and 1960) in which the Democratic Party had nominated a Catholic for president. If you didn't know the religious map of the United States, you couldn't understand the electoral map.

Delving into the cousins' wars took me back to these old tensions, because any serious investigation of the patterns of rebellion and loyalty during the 1775–1783 fighting in the United States leads to religion. Skeptics need only peruse the old county histories and records in Connecticut, New Jersey, or North Carolina. Differences over legal rights, taxes, or livelihoods turn out to be much less mentioned and much less mobilizing. And this makes sense: Back in the seventeenth century, religious faiths had been battle flags, not just belief systems. Church attendance in the colonies was not necessarily high—many locales had more Saturday night inebriates than Sunday worshippers—but the broader reach of religion was pervasive.

After several more secular centuries, this influence on seventeenth- and eighteenth-century British and American life is not easily imaginable. Interest rates, for example, were still a matter of theology in the decade leading up to the English Civil War. Doctors were licensed by the Church of England. Religion, politics, and economics weren't even separable in Tudor and Stuart times; it was all God's province. John Buchan, the famed novelist and biographer of Oliver Cromwell, observed of that century that "no age has been more deeply moved by ideas, but these ideas are not to be hastily identified with modern notions, which they may at first resemble, since they derive from a mood and an outlook far different from our own. Religion, as in the Middle Ages, was still interwoven with the texture of men's minds."

In many parts of the thirteen colonies, the eighteenth century was not too different. Edwin Gaustad, the principal historian of religion in the United States, has emphasized that "in the colonies and settlements, the trading posts and military forts, the interests of church and state could not be readily distinguished. Nor was anyone particularly interested in doing so. The prevailing pattern of religion in colonial America combined political and ecclesiastical interests so intimately that we still have difficulty defining precise limits of and making clear distinctions among the respective roles of governors, legislators, ministers, teachers and the voting members of the public."

Still another chronicler has described how religious rhetoric infused and justified America's call to arms: "Ministers everywhere compared America's break from Britain with the division of Jewish tribes under the tyrant Jereboam, or with the misunderstanding between the Canaanites and the Gileadites. The slavery from which the colonists were being delivered was of course like that of the Israelites under Pharoah, and as early as 1776, George Washington was cast as Moses." At its most intense, religion could be politically annoying or militarily confusing. English officials wryly observed how much more Scots or Ulster Covenanters knew about the geography of Palestine than about that of the British Isles. And during the Saratoga campaign of 1777, officers on both sides were confused by troops approaching in the distance singing indistinguishable hymns and Psalms: Were they Hessian Lutherans or Massachusetts Congregationalists?

The lingering antipathy of Catholics and Protestants, as well as the divisions between Protestant sects, was still explosive. To many eighteenth-century Britons and British colonials, Roman Catholicism was a Pope-led conspiracy on behalf of idolatrous religion and autocratic, tyrannical government. Its ambitions were an automatic threat to the rights and freedoms of Englishmen. Protestantism and liberty went together and had since the Reformation. British historians have pursued this religious insistence with much more candor than their American colleagues, but both countries have been affected. The foremost chronicler of conspiracy-mindedness in American politics, Richard Hofstadter, has profiled colonial anti-Catholicism—fear of every imaginable Popish plot—as an early example of the paranoid style, and a few scholars have ventured to identify a similar role for anti-Catholicism in English politics by the late sixteenth century. Much more was involved than paranoia, of course. The Protestant religion was at the core of English nationalism, and the Catholicism of France and Spain menaced both. Thus the triangle of religion, war, and politics. In the United States of the Civil War era, this ingredient was to some extent fading, although many in New England saw the 1861–65 conflict as yet another battle for faith and liberty in the traditions of 1642 and 1775.

As English-speaking civil wars, the cousins' wars—even those principally fought in North America—invariably divided opinion on both sides of the Atlantic, although with different effects and consequences. British scholars have generally glossed over the sympathy within England for the American cause in 1775, despite its documentation in popular petitions, military recruiting difficulties, and parliamentary opposition speeches. And anyone who doubts how divided London was need only review the pro-American expressions of Middlesex, Westminster, and Southwark. Yet the American war may have been a godsend for Britain, as chapter 7 argues, because it forced an unnerved British elite into new arrangements, attitudes, and reforms vital to the nation's ability to beat Napoleon little more than a decade later. Britain also had powerful internal divisions over the U.S. Civil War, and the victory of the more egalitarian North in 1865 helped bring about the British Reform Act of 1867. Effects of these wars—direct or indirect—were always felt in *both* countries. This is part of the justification for calling them cousins' wars.

Emigration is also part of the dual equation. The founding Puritan exodus to New England is the centerpiece: Witness its importance in shaping America. Numerically, however, it pales next to the eighteenth-, nineteenth-, and early twentieth-century emigration by which roughly two-thirds of the world's population of substantially English, Welsh, Scottish, or Irish descent wound up in the United States, Canada, Australia, and New Zealand. Scots and Irish left the British Isles in such numbers that three-quarters of that descent now live elsewhere. The effects of this migration within Britain—the voluntary and involuntary exodus of religious dissenters, political radicals, and discontented Celts—bolstered English influence and reinforced the United Kingdom's internal balance of antirevolutionary sentiment and commercial preoccupation.

We can only guess the probable politics of late nineteenth- and twentieth-century parliaments had Britain retained its high Irish and Scottish population ratios. Much less Conservative, certainly. Meanwhile, receiving much of this dispersal made the United States a notably different English-speaking, great world power: more democratic in its politics, more egalitarian in its culture, and more revivalist rather than traditionalist in worship. The new republic became a mecca for discontented populations from Catholic as well as Protestant Europe, a role that nineteenth- and twentieth-century Britain could never have played.

Also in the ethnic arena, I found myself appalled by some of the material developed in chapter 11 about the losers of the cousins' wars, particularly the blacks whose trauma from two civil wars and two postwar breaches of national faith over two centuries may provide a partial explanation for one of America's central societal problems. The thrust of chapter 12 that World Wars I and II were also "cousins' wars" of a sort for the American German and Irish populations has been raised elsewhere. But not, so far as I know, the two-war circumstances with respect to blacks.

This book draws heavily on many schools and groups of historians, geographers, political scientists, and military experts. Rather than discuss them here, a bibliography is attached to explain the book's sources, theses, and syntheses in various areas. For those who would pursue some of my points further, a number of footnotes will include additional paragraphs of amplification.

Academicians often take great pride in laying out their original research. My search for the emerging republican coalitions of the 1640s and the 1770s and the brand-new Republican party's emerging majority of the 1860s was essentially the same as my pursuit three decades ago of that era's emerging Republican presidential coalition: pouring over voting returns, local and county histories, maps, religious data, ethnic settlement patterns, cultural geographies, wartime chronicles, and anything else in print that would fill in the gaps and uncertainties of who sided with or opposed whom. Picking sides in civil wars drew on similar antecedents and causations.

These pages are aimed at both British and American audiences, a challenge in itself. Any American has read British books that mix up the two Dakotas or put Pottstown, Pennsylvania, where Pottsville ought to be. And very few Americans could draw a half decent

county-by-county map of Britain (especially now that old boundaries have been changed to make way for historic fakes like Avon
and Cleveland). The confusion of Bridgwater, Bridgnorth, and Bridport makes all too clear how British writers can mix up the various
Springfields and Middletowns. These, of course, are only the tip of
the interpretive iceberg. With rare exceptions, we have all grown up
thinking British or American. Very few think biculturally, even if we
have spent several years or two or three dozen visits on the other
side. You can see it in the history books. Americans generally do
British history only in manageable (short) chronological chunks.
And although dozens of British-born historians are presently at U.S.
universities, not least Yale, most of the books they write continue to
be about Britain. Which is all well and good, since for at least a
hundred millon Americans, the British Isles are our Old Country.

The drawback is that the reverse is not true. How many British
see the United States (with Canada, Australia, and New Zealand)
as the New Country? By this, I mean the current principal entity
charged with our common economic, cultural, and political interest: to keep much of the rest of the world speaking English, the *lingua anglica* of global communications, for at least part of the
twenty-first century? Some Britons look to the United States, to be
sure—certainly the million or two who are increasingly transatlantic. But my use of the term "Anglo-America" is probably more
wish than hard analysis. Too few Americans and Britons have
looked at history with a mind to pursue the extraordinary interre-
lations of these two nations. That, too, is part of the story I have
tried to tell in linking the cousins' wars and positing Anglo-America as something we—*we* includes Washington and Westminster—
should take seriously.

This history, then, is unusual for several reasons. First, because it
tries to encompass both countries. Second, because it tries to do so
through the concepts of war, politics, and an interrelationship that
sometimes verges on indivisibility, and through a conceptual framework—Anglo-America—that has an inevitable tilt toward the millennial flag-bearer: *the United States*. The third unusual angle is that
attention to the principally religious character of wartime loyalties
and allegiances during the American Revolution is aimed at proving
a vital point: the importance of dissenting Protestantism in spurring

the breakaway of the thirteen colonies and in underpinning their divergent politics and civil culture.

Dissenting Protestantism, in turn, despite its seventeenth- and eighteenth-century primitive streaks, by the nineteenth century was an essential foundation of American tolerance and ecumenicalism. It had too many competing strands for any other result.

As the millennium concludes, the principal English-speaking nations, the United States, the United Kingdom, Canada, and Australia, instead of being uplifted by these past glories, look to the uncertain future—cultural, economic, and governmental—with widespread skepticism. This concern is not implausible. Yet for related reasons, the occasion is even more appropriate to look back on extraordinary success: a four-century Anglo-American trajectory that surpassed all but the most extravagant predictions.

In examining America's own great power circumstances, two of my recent books, *Boiling Point* (1993) and *Arrogant Capital* (1994), have looked at the continuum of Britain and the United States as successor leading world powers, the first two ever to have a common language yet speak it in two different hemispheres. This volume will examine that four hundred–year emergence and hegemony—the two nations' interrelated rather than coincidental success and continuity in world leadership. Assembling the mutuality involved may rub against self-preoccupied historiography on both sides of the Atlantic. Fine. It is time to build some more bridges.

A book with these objectives probably had to be written by an American because the concept and denouement are American. But my family origins span the British Isles. The first to come to America was Edward ffoulkes, a Welsh Quaker who emigrated to Pennsylvania in the 1680s. He was a descendent of Sir Owen Tudor, who founded the House of Tudor (and, therefore, helped to put America on the map). There was a Jamison from the southwest of Scotland by way of Ulster; the Deppens or DePews were French Huguenots; and there was an array of English from Bucks County, Pennsylvania. On my father's side, I was the first eldest son not to be named William Edward Phillips for seven or eight generations, back to the time in Ireland when a distant ancestor, refusing to turn Protestant in order to keep some parcel of land, made certain that future eldest sons kept the rightful heir's name, at least. Presumably my ancestor would be disappointed to know that the first renamed heir-to-nothing-but-memories wound up attending summer Bible school at the First Congregational Church of Cornwall, Connecticut, and writing a book about Anglo-America. He would also no doubt be astounded to know that Kevin has become one of the most popular boys' names among Chinese-Americans in suburban California.

In the first months, as I started this book, it never occurred to me how much my own ancestors' tribulations and traumas would confirm the importance of religion in the British Isles and American colonies of the seventeenth and eighteenth centuries. Yet, in a small way, they seem to. Moreover, as one interested since boyhood in U.S. politics and political coalitions, I found researching this book to be a fascinating, "Roots" type of experience. The roots of American political behavior certainly go way, way back. Also, personal connections I had never paid much attention to came alive in visits to Pennsylvania, to the old towns of East Anglia and the west of England whose names live on in Massachusetts, Connecticut, New York, New Jersey, and Pennsylvania, and to the battlefields of all three cousins' wars from Vermont and South Carolina to Northamptonshire and Somerset. These travels had the added benefit of being marvelous medicine for political ennui.

Ennui, however, is an understatement. In September 1994, I published a book, *Arrogant Capital: Washington, Wall Street and the Frustration of American Politics*, which argued that Washington had entrenched, via second-rate leadership and special interests, into a politics of venality, and that Wall Street was building a speculative bubble into the U.S. economy through derivatives, mergermania, and bail-outs that stymied marketplace corrections. The Republican takeover of Congress in November 1994, principally in response to the President's scandals, changed little and prolonged much. And bail-outs continued to protect the bubble as speculation only grew. With nothing further to say, I decided to edge away from Washington and to pursue a new topic while I waited, and this book took on its shape in 1995. It was appealing—uplifting, in fact—to be reading and writing about George Washington, Abraham Lincoln, Elizabeth Tudor, and William Pitt instead of the current cast of characters. As I finish this foreword in October 1998, Washington, Wall Street, and the frustration of American politics are, for the moment, an interactive triangle again. But I am glad I spent the four years increasingly focused on a different challenge. The rise of Anglo-America, despite its splotches, was a therapeutic watch.

Where British and American terminologies differ, I have generally used the American, but with some eclecticism. Finally, a number of specific acknowledgments are in order. Michelle Klein, Rebecca Redman, Joan Arciero, and Janet Magnifico helped with the never-ending word-processing. My sons Andrew and Alec made the library connections. In Mark Stein I found a skilled mapmaker. Professors Byron Shafer of Nuffield College, Oxford, and Anthony Goodman, Chair of the University of Edinburgh history department, went out of their ways to be helpful during 1995 and 1997 visits, respectively. Michelle Trader at Basic provided project-managing skills essential in turning a huge manuscript into a book. My wife, Martha, helped in many ways; my editor, Don Fehr, was an excellent introduction to the new Basic Books; and Bill Leigh, agenting me for a fifth book, shaped as he agented, both to my benefit.

Kevin Phillips
West Goshen, Connecticut
October 1998

PART ONE

The Beginnings of Anglo-America and the Setting of the First Cousins' War

I

THE PROTESTANT BACKGROUND OF ANGLO-AMERICAN EXPANSION AND THE COUSINS' WARS

The colonization of North America has been the decisive fact of the modern world.
—Otto Von Bismarck, 1815–1898

The most important arena [in the rise of capitalism] is England, because it is in England, with its new geographic position as the entrepôt *between Europe and America, its achievement of internal unity two centuries before France and two and a half centuries before Germany, its constitutional revolution, and its powerful bourgeoisie of bankers, shipowners and merchants that the transformation of the structure of society is earliest, swiftest and most complete.*
—R. H. Tawney, *Religion and the Rise of Capitalism,* 1926

English settlement of the new world was a Protestant activity. . . .
—A. L. Rowse, *The Expansion of Elizabethan England,* 1955

THREE HUNDRED AND SEVENTY YEARS ago, before the language of George Washington and George III was confirmed as the *lingua anglica* of global communications and finance, there was another Atlantic community, much smaller, where it all began: five million people in England and Wales, forty thousand on the seaboard of North America, mostly in New England.

In this patch of time and place, in the decades leading up to the English Civil War, finance and communications were relative backwaters, the domain of goldsmiths, moneylenders, and clerks. Palaces, castles, and cathedrals were still the architecture of power. Religion shaped the principal texture of men's minds. Protestantism, in turn, was the particular banner Englishmen carried onto the moral and physical battlefield.

By the 1630s, English Protestantism itself was splitting—into ranks of Anglicans, Puritans, and separatists, High Churchmen and Low Churchmen, conformers and dissenters, advocates of episcopacy and inveterate haters of bishops. Religious divisions, under many labels, will preoccupy us for several chapters because they so clearly preoccupied *both* English-speaking peoples, in America and the British Isles, for several centuries. More than anything else, they were the seedbed of the cousins' wars, especially the English Civil War, which provided much of the framework for the *second* English-speaking civil war fought in North America 130 years later.

However, to understand how the three wars and their outcomes, lessons, and warnings helped to move Anglo-America toward its eventual eminence, we cannot simply begin with the opening clash of steel and armor at Edgehill in 1642. The gestation goes back farther: to late medieval England in the 1480s and the emergence of the House of Tudor which would turn England's mind and faith to Protestantism and its commercial face and settlement toward the Atlantic and the New World.

From Angles to Anglos

Early Tudor England, on the verge of a great change, had its center of gravity in the eastern counties that faced across the Channel and the North Sea to France and the Low Countries. Before the New World shaped a new economic equation, England's greatest wealth was in London, Kent, Sussex, and East Anglia. As Map 1.1

shows, East Anglia was the bulge of English seacoast, fens, and flat farmland that had taken its name from the Angles, sixth-century invaders from western Denmark. They also imprinted their name on England—the land of the Angles—and then, through another settlement wave in the seventeenth century, on New England. Even the county names of East Anglia reflect these origins. Norfolk was the county of the North Folk—the Northern Angles. Suffolk, just below, held the South Folk. Essex, between Suffolk and London, was the home of the East Saxons.

Queen Elizabeth's greatest counselors, Lords Burghley and Cecil, lived in the core area northeast of London. The great "wool churches," built with the profits of the fourteenth-century clothing trade, were in East Anglia. Local ports like Boston, Harwich, King's Lynn, Great Yarmouth, and Colchester ranked with Dover and Folkestone on the English Channel. The famous Cromwells—Thomas, who served Henry VIII, and Oliver, who dominated the English Civil War—came from the east.

Ultimately, the emigration stream from this region encircled the globe—and that, plus the extraordinary cultural legacy of the Angles, is what warrants such attention to its geographic cradle. *Anglican* churches and cathedrals girdle the globe from the North Atlantic to the South Pacific, from St. John, Newfoundland, to Te Ana and Christ Church in New Zealand and Nandi, Fiji. Cultural *Anglophiles* crowd the libraries of Bombay and the polo grounds of Buenos Aires. In California, projected to be America's first Third World state, pre-medieval folk descriptions have become broad ethnic nouns. The word *Anglo*—as distinct from Asian, African-American, or Hispanic—now includes Greeks, Sephardic Jews from North Africa, the Armenian melon growers and truck farmers of the great central valley, and Southern California's quarter-million expatriate Iranians.

Fin-de-siècle Anglo-America, transcending its early outlines, is increasingly a linguistic community and decreasingly a bounded political, religious, or ethnic one. The vital role that Protestant religion played in the earlier expansion of the sixteenth to nineteenth century has ended. If the Anglicization of Norman warlords and Welsh borderers, and, more recently, of French Huguenots and Scots Highlanders, cannot happen again with the Yemeni of New

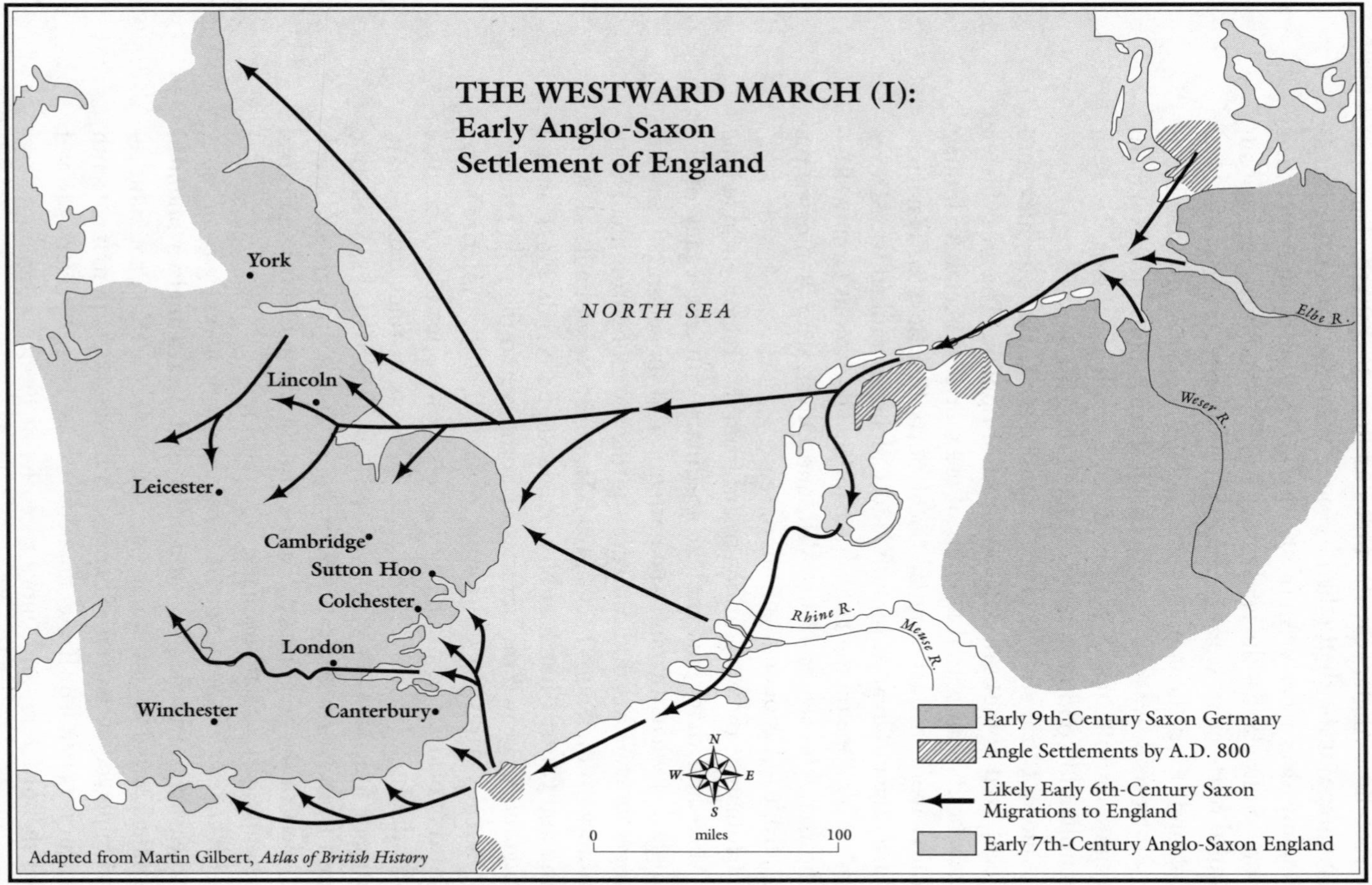

THE WESTWARD MARCH (I):
Early Anglo-Saxon
Settlement of England

Early 9th-Century Saxon Germany

Angle Settlements by A.D. 800

Likely Early 6th-Century Saxon
Migrations to England

Early 7th-Century Anglo-Saxon England

Elbe R.

Weser R.

Meuse R.

Rhine R.

NORTH SEA

York

Lincoln

Leicester

Cambridge

Sutton Hoo

Colchester

London

Canterbury

Winchester

0   100
miles

N
W   E
S

Adapted from Martin Gilbert, *Atlas of British History*

MAP 1.1

York and Bangladeshi of East London, that hardly matters. Language, more than ethnicity or religion the last legacy of the Angles, is the slowly emerging bond, which is not without precedent. Rome—or, more accurately, its language—played a similar world role in A.D. 200, at which point Rome's evolution was many centuries removed from its parochial beginnings.

However, long before the late twentieth-century English linguistic and communications hegemony, to which we will return many chapters hence, religious and nationalistic forces drove English-speaking expansion during the critical era when Anglo-America outdistanced its rivals. Mere narratives of exploration or colonialization do not cut to the imperial core: how these peoples, *internally* divided and bickering, sorted their tensions and forces so advantageously in the earlier centuries of modern Europe that they were able to prevail in the nineteenth and create the commercial and linguistic hegemony of the twentieth. Narratives of religion, sectarianism, politics, and the great internal wars provide better explanations. The setting of the cousins' wars was itself a grand backdrop: England's expansion into North America, following the political unification of the British Isles, was the decisive fact of the modern world. While the twenty-first century may see Anglo-America fade, for over four centuries its commercial, political, and military prowess succeeded in overwhelming all challengers.

The Atlanticization of England: A Protestant Undertaking

Simply put, any broad context for the English Civil War must emphasize two interlaced phenomena: Protestantism and Atlanticization. Anglo-America, the English-speaking community of the Atlantic, developed out of the westward reorientation of England, which itself began with the Tudors and the Protestant Reformation. Between 1485 and 1642, England avoided serious internal warfare while much of continental Europe was being trampled by marching armies, torn by religious conflict, and bankrupted by reckless rulers. The Tudor monarchs, from Henry VII to Elizabeth, turned their kingdom away from old territorial preoccupations on the continent and toward the *Atlantic*. The political unification of the British Isles, shown in Map 1.2, which included English resettlement in parts of Ireland, Wales, and Scotland, furthered the new westward mind-set. This, in turn, pulled England toward North America.

The annexation of Cornwall and Wales, England's two western Celtic-language neighbors, was complete by 1536. The 1560s saw Elizabeth I begin the modern conquest of Ireland. And when her cousin, King James VI of Scotland, succeeded in 1603 as James I of England, the two Crowns were united. As ruler on *both* sides of the perpetually strife-torn Anglo-Scottish border, the new King promptly cracked down on its folkways of border raids, cattle-stealing, family feuds, and "reiving"—a Celtic-flavored lawlessness that would live centuries longer in the ethnically kindred eighteenth- and nineteenth-century borderlands of the United States.

By the seventeenth century, an increasingly Atlantic England was moving into position to accomplish four essential transformations: to grow into *Great Britain*, not the mere land of the Angles; to secure North America's future as a largely English-speaking continent; to become Europe's most politically and commercially advanced nation (during an era in which Spain, France, Austria, and others were in some ways *regressing* toward autocracy); and then to assume center stage as the world's leading maritime and industrial empire. By the late eighteenth century, this had been achieved.

The analyst must ask why: *What forces over two centuries transformed Tudor England into the leading world empire and turned thirteen small North American colonies into the successor empire, the United States?* Of the many ingredients, from commerce and individualism to sea power and parliamentary government, the most important initially was *Protestantism*. The talk about God being an Englishman only began when He—with some political assistance from Henry VIII in 1533—established the Church of England, eliminating the Pope in Rome as an intermediary. Protestantism quickly became one of England's strongest self-identifications. Religion and English nationalism began what would be a memorable convergence.

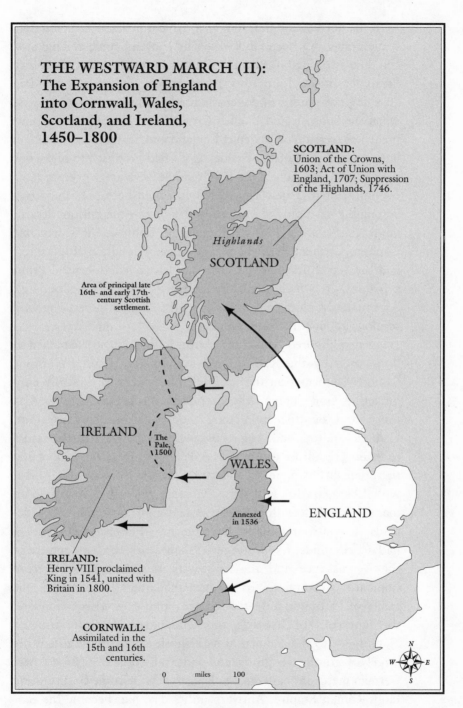

THE WESTWARD MARCH (II):
The Expansion of England
into Cornwall, Wales,
Scotland, and Ireland,
1450–1800

SCOTLAND:
Union of the Crowns,
1603; Act of Union with
England, 1707; Suppression
of the Highlands, 1746.

Highlands

SCOTLAND

Area of principal late
16th- and early 17th-
century Scottish
settlement.

IRELAND

The
Pale,
1500

WALES

ENGLAND

Annexed
in 1536

IRELAND:
Henry VIII proclaimed
King in 1541, united with
Britain in 1800.

CORNWALL:
Assimilated in the
15th and 16th
centuries.

0   miles   100

N
W E
S

MAP 1.2

To the north, Scotland, too, was moving in a kindred direction. If the prayer "O Lord God, save Thy chosen people of England" could be attributed to Edward VI in 1553, the founder of Scottish Presbyterianism, John Knox, was only a few years behind in claiming continuity in covenant for Scotland with Israel.[1] And when the Scottish and English Crowns were united, enthusiastic preachers were quick to depict England and Scotland as Judah and Israel, which the Lord in Ezekiel 37:22 had promised to make one people with one king. One hundred and seventy-two years later, commitment to a new United States would be especially strong among the diasporas of *both* chosen peoples—the Puritan descendants in New England, still naming Connecticut towns for Canaan, Goshen, Bethlehem, and Sharon as late as the 1730s, and the Scotch-Irish of the American Ulster (south-central Pennsylvania), in which ministers of towns named Londonderry, Antrim, and Coleraine sent soldiers off to fight *another* king with sermons about Kirk and Covenant.

For two hundred years after Martin Luther, Europe remained so dominated by the Reformation and by the ensuing Catholic Counter-Reformation that politics, like war, was typically conducted in God's name. And despite the enthusiasms of English kings and Scottish ministers, God was hardly Protestant. Catholicism, too, had been a conquering army from the Crusades to Spain's recapture of the Iberian Peninsula from the Moors and the Spanish-Portuguese exploration of the New World. And it would be again for His Most Christian Majesty, Louis XIV, on many late seventeenth-century German and Low Country battlefields. Innovative republican governments—Florence and Venice—had arisen amidst Latin liturgies. Likewise for the high culture of the Renaissance and the capitalism that furbished it, from Lombardy to Antwerp. To attribute the latter's rise simply to the riches of its hinterland—the woolens and worsteds of Flanders, the tapestries of Brussels and Oudenarde, and the iron of Namur—or to the acumen of its Flemish merchants sidesteps the largely Catholic religious and cultural context. The earliest German merchant bankers, the Fuggers, had become counts of the Holy Roman Empire. Antwerp, in its day, had become the economic crossroad of Europe under Catholicism, and the Rotterdam of Erasmus its philosophic center, just as Amsterdam and then London would under Protestantism.

There is no need to pursue whether a changing faith is more *accompaniment* to national change than *explanation*. What seems obvious is that Protestantism *did* preside over a vital new political, commercial, and religious momentum in northwestern Europe, and England was in the vanguard. Save for the France of Louis XIV, which profited from its own substantial Calvinist minority for a century before their ruthless suppression and expulsion, Europe's new achiever states were the Atlantic-facing nations converted by the Reformation. The late sixteenth- and seventeenth-century accomplishment of England, in particular, was that of a nation no longer sheltering behind island walls, but mastering its surrounding seas. Under Elizabeth, Oliver Cromwell, and William and Mary, England made the championship of global Protestantism a powerful wind in its international sails, however melodramatic that now sounds.

Authors by the hundreds have recounted just how ready Tudor England was to be stirred. The earlier, Catholic kingdom had been a sluggish economic and maritime power. Pre-1485 internal wars had been a hindrance. That earlier England had also been inhibited by a pre-Reformation acceptance of the Pope's division of the New World between Spain and Portugal, by the constraints of massive church landownership, and by church strictures on economic practices. Protestantism, probably more out of greed than credo, led England to a more active domestic and global economics. The seizure and distribution of the Catholic monastic lands under Henry VIII put new capital to work in agriculture, industry, and on the high seas. Glastonbury Abbey became a worsted manufactory, Rotherham College a malthouse, and the eliminations of saints' days were said to be worth £50,000 each in increased economic activity.[2] By the 1560s, English ship captains, sailing from ports like Southampton, Plymouth, and Bristol, were "singeing the King of Spain's beard," attacking his colonies and seizing his treasure galleons up and down the Spanish Main, the fabled northern coast of South America from the Isthmus of Panama to Maracaibo at the mouth of the Orinoco River.

The extent to which England's fortune was made by Atlanticization and the opening of America is a Protestant sermon and drumroll in itself. A. L. Rowse, the principal historian of the expansion of Elizabethan England from 1557 to 1603, is unrestrained about "how much this country owed its future to the Elizabethan drive across the Atlantic to the New World." Religion was an unmistakable spur. This seafaring and opening-up of the New World, to Rowse, "was a Protestant activity," both in commercial spirit and anti-Spanish motivation.[3] No small part of England's growing mid-sixteenth-century Atlantic expertise was owed to the collaboration of France's Protestant minority: the Huguenots, imperiled at home, already trying to implant colonies in Brazil, Florida, and South Carolina.

Militant Protestant sea captains, together with English volunteers in the fight for Dutch independence, gave English rivalry with Spain a crusadelike character that periodically embarrassed the less belligerent queen, for all her bold nickname of Gloriana. As seventeenth-century France began to succeed a weakening Spain as Europe's mightiest power, England sometimes wound up fighting both Bourbon Catholic monarchies—Spain *and* France. The French also made frequent backstairs attempts to subvert Protestant England by sending subsidies, Jesuit priests, royal princesses in marriage, and secret treaties (which often promised French armies) to a succession of monarchs from the House of Stuart, whose Protestantism and even patriotism thereby became increasingly suspect.

To a considerable percentage of seventeenth- and eighteenth-century English-speakers, as we have seen, Protestantism intermingled with their perceived national mission as a people and as a nation. Before 1776, Catholics were not allowed to vote or hold office in most of the American colonies. England barred them from voting or holding office in the years between the Glorious Revolution of 1688 and the enactment of Catholic Emancipation in 1829. The Catholic kings of France and Spain, with whom the Stuarts corresponded about subsidies, marriages, treaties, and troops, allowed far fewer elections and even less religious tolerance, which helped prolong the Protestant apprehension. Through most of the eighteenth century, Spain and France remained autocracies hostile to the basic notions of parliamentary government and political liberty practiced in England and Holland.

Clerics and historians on both sides employed volumes of theory and self-justification. Spain maintained its Inquisition against heretics—non-Catholics—from 1479 through the eighteenth century. Spanish Jews and Moors were the original targets, but during the sixteenth and seventeenth centuries, hundreds of captured English Protestants were burned at the stake. By the eighteenth century, France had become Britain's principal religious, political, and military foe. The French kings, after allowing freedom of worship to Huguenot Protestants in the Edict of Nantes (1598), rescinded that permission in 1685. Even before the infamous "Revocation," Huguenot emigration accelerated under pressures like the "dragonnades," in which troops of dragoons were quartered in Protestant villages of Languedoc and adjacent sections of southern France to supervise their religious reconversion. By 1686, the cumulative flight of France's Huguenots involved several hundred thousand in a population of 18 million. British North America was a favored refuge, along with Holland and England, drawing the first Fanueils, Bowdoins, Reveres, and Olivers to Boston; the first Delanceys, Jays, Boudinots, and Bayards to New York; and the first Dabneys (D'Aubigne) and Battles (Battaille) to Virginia.

British historians are relatively matter-of-fact about that era's religious animosity. Professor Rowse, shuddering at his own visit to the marketplace in Seville where the Spanish burned Protestant heretics, added that "one must not—in the rational quietude, the skeptical disbelief, of a later age—underestimate the force of the hatred for Spain all this piled up among the Protestants of Europe. It was unrelenting, undying, ubiquitous among them: as such it was an historic force of momentous consequence."[4] Linda Colley, a British historian at the London School of Economics, in explaining Protestant nationalism and anti-Catholic feeling in England and Scotland up through the nineteenth century, has pointed out that the signers of the massive popular petitions delivered to Parliament in 1828–1829 opposing enfranchisement of Catholics "saw themselves, quite consciously, as being part of a native tradition of resistance to Catholicism which stretched back for centuries."[5] What is sometimes forgotten—and should not be—is how much the colonies, created by England's Atlantic expansion, were part of the same tradition.

The "Execrable" Stuarts and the
Beginnings of the Cousins' Wars

The fervor of so many of their Protestant subjects made it unacceptable that several of the Stuart monarchs, Anglican in public, were Catholic in their private sympathies. Fearful Puritans saw a black-robed Counter-Reformation lurking in Stuart palace anterooms. In the words of British historian John Morrill, "Talk of 'popery' is not a form of white noise, a constant fuzzy background in the rhetoric and argument of the time. . . . This falsifies the passionate belief . . . that is the ground of action, that England was in the process of being subjected to the force of Antichrist, that the prospects were of anarchy, chaos, the dissolution of government and liberties."[6]

There was some basis, in the decade before the English Civil War and then again in the 1680s, for the popular fear that the pro-French policies of the Stuarts were aligning the monarchy with what critics summed up as popery and absolutism. James I and Charles I had Catholic queens. In the late 1630s, Charles's court had intervals of Catholic fashionability. Noblemen and privy counselors announced their conversions to the Church of Rome. A half century later, Charles II, who had a Portuguese Catholic consort, converted to Catholicism on his deathbed; and James II, married to Mary of Modena, was openly Catholic on his accession. The Stuart political heritage, moreover, was to envy the continental autocrats, mostly Catholics, who could at will execute critics, install cardinals or bishops as their chief ministers, and disregard base-born parliaments. The male Stuart kings, all four, resented England's being the principal exception in a European trend toward increasingly powerful central monarchies.

Together, the Stuart provocations and Protestant paranoia made religious acrimony a staple of seventeenth-century English politics. Many nineteenth- and twentieth-century chroniclers have portrayed the House of Stuart as a millstone on England's constitutional and commercial emergence. A different twist is that the century-long challenge of removing that weight, besides occupying English politics, government, and economics, also sharpened these sectors.*

---

*Professor George Trevelyan began the introduction to his famous book *England Under the Stuarts* with precisely that ringing value judgment: "England has contributed

This interpretation was especially powerful in the American colonies, where eighteenth-century revolutionaries whetted their rhetoric and constitutional sensitivity on Stuart transgressions. John Adams, the second president of the United States, looked back on the Stuarts as "execrable."

To replace and then keep in exile this one royal family, England had more than a half dozen military confrontations and incursions, beginning with the English Civil War of 1640–1649 and not ending until the failure of the last attempt to restore the Stuart line in 1745. The first and bloodiest of these conflicts commands no real agreement on its name or even its chronology. A few scholars apply the term *First Civil War* to the events of 1642 to 1645. Others refer more sweepingly to the English Revolution of 1640–1649. A few even discuss the *British* Civil War. Those who describe the events of 1642–1645 as a First Civil War usually say that a Second Civil War began in 1647, when King Charles I, after making a military alliance with the Scots, lost first the battle of Preston (1648) and then his own head to the executioner (1649). Appendix III to this book includes a time line that matches the important dates and events. The involvement of the Scots and Irish *does* support, superficially at least, describing the fighting as the *British* Civil War. On the other hand, the battles and internal causations were separate in England, Scotland, and Ireland. Besides, as yet there was no Britain. The simplest label is that of the English Civil War, dated from the crisis of 1640 to the King's death in 1649.

Not that it matters much. *Whatever one calls the English Civil War, its causes, hostilities, and alignments echoed for many gen-*

---

many things, good and bad, to the history of the world. But of all her achievements there is one, the most insular in origin and yet the most universal in effect. While Germany boasts her Reformation and France her Revolution, England can point to her dealings with the House of Stuart."

After Trevelyan wrote those words in 1924, however, Britain's decline fed historians' cynicism—especially after World War II. In this revisionism, the Stuart kings re-emerge as partial agents of progress, centralizing revenue management and modernizing agriculture by enclosure, better forest management, and suchlike. Yet if *Anglo-America* becomes the larger yardstick, with English-speaking hegemony still in effect, Trevelyan's negative assessment of the Stuarts regains credence, given the importance of their dismissal not just to English liberties but to the rise of British North America.

erations. One of England's best-known historians, Christopher Hill, has described *The Century of Revolution, 1603–1714,* as the arena of England's most vital political transformation. After being crowned in 1603, to rule by divine right (or so he claimed), James I, the first of the Stuarts, was able to choose and discharge his own ministers. He could dismiss Parliament at will, commanding revenue and authority enough not to need them for years. In this England, which still had more than a whisper of medievalism, bishops could and did hold high government office. Religious heretics were burned at the stake. The king himself could raise customs duties, fix prices, and create monopolies. Internationally, the kingdom of James I was a second-class power. Colonization of the New World by England was just beginning.

When this profoundly redefining "century" ended with the death of Queen Anne and the upholding of the Protestant Settlement in 1714, a much-changed Great Britain—England and Scotland had united in 1707—had become a leading world empire. The new Protestant monarch, George I, plucked from the second-tier Electorate of Hanover, spoke no English and could rule only through Parliament, which had awarded him the crown over other better-pedigreed claimants. Parliament fully controlled the power of the purse, as well as most royal appointments. Among Protestants, at least, religious dissent was protected. Bishops were no longer employable as civil officials. Church courts scarcely mattered. The principal battlegrounds of the transformation were obvious: the civil war of 1640–1649 and the Glorious Revolution of 1688, its conservative follow-up.

Historians and commentators in the late twentieth-century United States have shrunk from emphasizing religion in their explanations of seventeenth- and eighteenth-century affairs. Ecumenicalism to an extent has suppressed candor. Yet when mid-nineteenth-century British historian Thomas Macauley described Protestant North America as humming with enterprise while Catholic Mexico and Quebec stagnated, his remarks paralleled the observations of equally famous mid-nineteenth-century New England chronicler Francis Parkman. Even the "flowering of New England" in the literature of Emerson, Thoreau, and Longfellow, to say nothing of historians like Parkman and William Prescott, took place on the stem of Puritan tradition.

In Britain, by the time of the American Revolution, anti-Catholic concern was muting among pragmatic *elites*. The Enlightenment broadly nurtured tolerance, but on the fingers of ministerial political calculation, anti-Catholicism was also reduced by the mid-century disappearance of the Stuart political threat in Scotland and Ireland, the Crown's desire to enlist Catholic soldiers, and the increasing numbers of Catholics in the empire—in Quebec, Newfoundland, Gibraltar, British Honduras, and some of the sugar islands. In the 1790s, the anti-clericalism and church ransackings of the French Revolution also worked to create a new rapprochement between Europe's Catholic hierarchies and the British crown. Cardinals and bishops now saw British conservatism as a bulwark against the Robespierres and Bonapartes. Governments in Catholic Europe muted some of their own practices, and Britain's imperial preoccupation now encouraged tolerance as well as jingoism. Anti-Catholicism still remained strong among the British *common people*, witness London's Gordon riots of 1780, as well as the popular outpouring against Catholic enfranchisement a half century later. The era of religious wars, however, was over.

The popular culture of the thirteen colonies leading up to 1775 has been called a warmed-over "Radical Whig" or a "Commonwealthman" viewpoint because of its taproots in seventeenth- and early eighteenth-century ideas and anti-Stuart memories. Below the gentry level, however, political thinking was less an intellectual legacy than a powerful folk memory steeped in the Low Church and dissenting Protestant religious suspicions of 1640 to 1745. Doubts about Catholicism were a given just as they were among the British common people. But after the Revolution, the larger force would be ecumenical. National elites with a more cosmopolitan outlook, in Philadelphia, Richmond, New York, Charleston, and even Boston, would impose religious tolerance on late eighteenth-century state and federal constitutional deliberations.

Practicality pushed in the same direction. The same religious hodgepodge of dissenting Protestantism that had spurred revolution in the 1640s and 1770 would, by its sheer multiplicity, compel tolerance and disestablishment in the new United States. This was especially true of the Presbyterians and Baptists, but after the war, Methodism added its own growing voice. Edmund Burke had not been greatly exaggerating in 1775 when he told Parliament that the people of the northern colonies were Protestants "of that kind which is most adverse to all implicit submission of mind and opinion," so that their religion "is a refinement on the principle of resistance."[7] Ultimately, this made for tolerance rather than a state-supported church, for all that Puritan New England gave ground grudgingly.

While church establishment in Britain would continue, by the 1830s the Congregational church would be disestablished in its three remaining New England bastions, and latitudinarian and ecumenical viewpoints would move to the fore—all absolutely essential to America's attractiveness to immigrants and expanding world role. The duality of the English-speaking nations took hold. In the nineteenth-century United States, democratic politics and religious pluralism would unfold together.

New England and the Puritan Hegira

Worry about the political, religious, and moral course of Stuart England had already made disgruntled Puritans the principal architects and settlers of New England in the two decades before 1640. East Anglia and surrounding old Saxon districts were at the heart of the emigration. Carl Bridenbaugh, the American historian, has identified much of the exodus between 1629 and 1640 as originating within a circle fifty miles in each direction from the East Anglian town of Groton, Suffolk. (Map 1.3 shows the county boundaries of the mid-seventeenth century.) Many who plotted the New World settlements or captained the Parliamentary fight against the king shared these origins.[8] Cromwell's native Huntingdonshire was inside the circle. The Buckinghamshire residence of his cousin, John Hampden, was at its edge.

Groton itself was home to John Winthrop, who led the great movement to Massachusetts Bay in 1630. One early Massachusetts biographer likened him to Nehemiah—the biblical hero who led the Israelites back from Babylon to the Promised Land, this one transat-

ENGLAND AND WALES
UNDER THE STUARTS

SCOTLAND

NORTH-
UMBERLAND-

THE
NORTH

●Newcastle

CUMBERLAND

DURHAM

WESTMORLAND

(NORTH RIDING)

Isle of Man

YORKSHIRE

York●

(EAST RIDING)

(WEST RIDING)

Hull●

LANCASHIRE

ANGLESEY

FLINT

CHESHIRE

DERBYSHIRE

LINCOLNSHIRE

DENBIGH

CAERNARVON

STAFFORD-
SHIRE

NOTTINGHAM-
SHIRE

●Nottingham

Norwich

THE
MIDLANDS

RUTLAND

NORFOLK

MONTGOMERY

LEICESTER-
SHIRE

SHROPSHIRE

WARWICK-
SHIRE

HUNTS

EAST
ANGLIA

RADNOR

WORCESTER-
SHIRE

NORTHANTS

CAMBRIDGE-
SHIRE

SUFFOLK

CARDIGAN

HEREFORD-
SHIRE

Coventry●

Ipswich●

WALES

BEDS

CARMARTHEN

BRECKNOCK

Gloucester●

OXFORD-
SHIRE

BUCKS

HERTS

Colchester●

MONMOUTH-
SHIRE

GLOUCESTER-
SHIRE

ESSEX

GLAMORGAN

●Oxford

●Bristol

MDX

BERKSHIRE

London●

WILTSHIRE

SURREY

KENT

SOMERSET

HAMPSHIRE

THE
WEST COUNTRY

SUSSEX

Exeter●

DORSET

DEVON

CORNWALL

Plymouth●

● Major cities and towns in 1640

N
W ✦ E
S

0   miles   50

MAP 1.3

lantic. So many of the towns in this border area of Suffolk and Essex have names that also live on in Massachusetts and Connecticut that visitors from New England can be forgiven for seeing ancestral ghosts in front of the half-timbered buildings. Thomas Hooker, who in 1635 planted Connecticut's main settlement in Hartford, had been an itinerant preacher in Essex and then a controversial church lecturer in its county town of Chelmsford. Roger Williams, prior to establishing Rhode Island in 1636, had also spent time in Essex—as a chaplain of sorts in the Hatfield Broad Oak household of Cromwell's aunt, Lady Joan Barrington.

In England as a whole, Puritans might have been 10 to 20 percent of the population. But in East Anglia, their great citadel, that strength was probably 30 to 40 percent. The county of Essex itself, to the northeast of London in the territory that would be Parliament's "Eastern Association" stronghold during the civil war, could fairly be called the buckle of the seventeenth-century English Bible Belt. To High Church Anglicans, it was a nursery of heresy. Identified during the reign of Henry VIII as England's most strongly Protestant county, Essex bore a similar reputation for the staunchest Puritanism by the outbreak of the civil war in 1642.[9]

The other new strands of English Protestantism circa 1640—the Quakers, Baptists, Diggers, and Ranters—besides being more radical in their beliefs, were much less numerous and important, although their influence would grow as the war dragged on. Those insisting on separation from the Church of England had been punished in the 1590s under Queen Elizabeth I, but they began to proliferate in the open religious climate of the 1640s. Quakers and Baptists would have numbered only a few thousand even in 1647 or 1648, for all that there might have been half a million of them by 1660. The Ranters, and so-called antinomians in general, believed that their personal relationship with God freed them from normal morality and church rules. Presbyterian congregations were important in Scotland, but not in England. Puritans, of whom there could have been nearly a million, constituted by far and away the strongest opposition to High Church Anglican orthodoxy as the 1640s began to unfold.

Distilling the essence of seventeenth-century English Puritan thinking is more controversial. One well-known historian has wryly described the label as "an admirable refuge from clarity of thought."[10] Others have insisted on its original and very narrow meaning: the religion of all those who wished either to "purify" the established Church of England from what they called the taint of Popery, or to worship separately by new forms so purified.[11] As of 1640, the overwhelming majority were still within the established church, which adds to the difficulty of precise definition.

Godly Puritans, however, shared a distinctive lifestyle in which biblical study, predestinarian theology, and suspicion of Rome were more evident than in the lives of most other Church of England communicants. Sundays were days of intense religious preoccupation. Belief that the English were a Chosen People was especially strong, and those who counted themselves among this elect body worried constantly about losing God's favor through some shortcoming, especially failure to promote moral reformation.[12] By and large, Puritans opposed the apostolic authority claimed by bishops and resisted efforts to enforce doctrinal and liturgical conformity to the Prayer Book and canon law. Virtually all looked to the Bible for daily guidance, which made sermons and the interpretive abilities of ministers all-important. Rare were the Puritans who did not deplore the drunkenness, indolence, debauchery, and revels they saw rife in the land.

Beyond these widely shared basics, their views by the 1630s could differ because of practicality as well as theology. The effects on England of three-quarters of a century of destructive price inflation, rising crime, and social decay caused some men to favor more drastic constraints than others. Puritans, as loosely defined, were especially prominent in law and commerce, and as political reaction against the Stuarts mounted, some of their most notable influence was in Parliament. In this, their ultimate pre–civil war power base, they were a powerful force even in the early seventeenth century.

The unparalleled wave of departures for the New World in the 1630s mirrored more than broad dissatisfaction with Charles I. East Anglia had its own particular problems: poor harvests, gruesome plagues, and lean times in the locally important cloth industry. The persecution of Puritans within the established Church of England, which had increased after High Churchman William

Laud became Bishop of London in 1628 and then Archbishop of Canterbury, was particularly intense in these same eastern shires. They soon had England's highest ratios of dismissed, jailed, and exiled preachers. Nearly a century earlier, the same true-believing area had claimed four-fifths of the "Marian Martyrs"—Protestants executed during the brief English Counter-Reformation under Catholic Queen Mary in the mid-1550s.[13] This, too, was part of the intensity brought to New England.

Emigration from England, a trickle in 1607, deepened into a stream in 1620 and a flood in 1629. Some eighty thousand English—2 percent of the national population—left the country between 1620 and 1640 for the American colonies, the Caribbean, or Holland. Twenty-one thousand went to New England.[14] Assuming that population in the temperate North American colonies more or less doubled every twenty-five years, demographers have suggested that by the mid-eighteenth century, this zealous early emigration was the principal source of pre-Revolutionary New England's half a million people.

Neither of the early Stuarts, James I or Charles I, gave England's fledgling colonies in the Americas particular support. Settlement in the New World was generally connected to the non-Stuart opposition—under James, to Lord Southampton and Sir Edwin Sandys; under Charles, to Lords Warwick and Saye, as well as to Pym and Hampden. Nor was the sea itself a particular interest of Stuart kings. Mariners lamented that Holland was outstripping England at sea; Dutch merchantmen carried more than half the trade in and out of English ports, so that by 1620, London-owned shipping was only half its former tonnage.

The Royal Navy was too weak to protect shipping in the English Channel. Algerian pirates, guided by English renegades, captured 466 English merchant vessels between 1609 and 1616. During a ten-day period in 1625, a thousand English seamen were carried off as slaves and twenty-seven vessels were seized. Voyagers to Virginia and New England were among those taken. "Pirates rode, ravaging and kidnapping, up the wooded creeks of Devon and Cornwall, where Drake and Raleigh had prepared the death of Spain," wrote one chronicler. "Trinity House had the (beacon) light on the Lizard extinguished, because it guided the pirates of Sallee, one of whom was captured in the Thames itself."[15] James was equally supine in failing to avenge the massacre of English at Amboyna in the Dutch East Indies.

Charles I was especially concessionary to the French. As part of the arrangement by which he married Princess Henrietta Maria of France in 1625, England was to provide ships to help Louis XIII suppress the French Protestants of La Rochelle. However, the English crews to be put at French disposal mutinied. Then, in 1632, Charles ceded Canada to France, confirming the North American foothold of the rival power that would bottle up English colonization on the Eastern Seaboard for another 130 years. For New England, the assistance of the Stuarts was principally negative: stirring a discontent among Englishmen and then being unable to hold back the resulting great emigration that laid so much foundation for the future.

In 1634, Charles set up a Commission for the Plantations, which scholars have described as more concerned with selling privileges in the New World than expansion.[16] Population movement to the New World had already become a concern of the Crown, not an ambition. Not long after the King's chartering of the Massachusetts Bay Company in 1629, royal authorities, stunned by the surge of emigration, ordered officials in western seaports from Bristol to Liverpool to block the departure of passengers without licenses, but without much success.

To end such "promiscuous and disorderly parting out of the Realme," the Royal Commission in 1634 handed down an extraordinary order. No emigrants, it said, could leave without *two* certificates—one attesting that the applicant had taken the oaths of supremacy and allegiance, and the second from the minister of his parish vouching for his religious conformity. Within another few months, King Charles forbade any subjects save soldiers, mariners, and merchants to leave the realm without a license from him or his council. The purpose was to stop the emigration, to both Holland and America, by Puritans "whose only end is to live as much as they can without the reach of authority."[17]

In 1635, the Commission, now chaired by Archbishop Laud, foe of the Puritans, directed the attorney general to open suit in the Court of the King's Bench for an even stronger remedy: recision of the charter of the Massachusetts Bay Company. When the Court complied in May 1637, Charles Stuart announced that *he* was assuming management of New England. The colony's leaders were only moderately concerned. Massachusetts had already built forts on Castle Island and at Charlestown, brought in £540 of saltpeter and match from Holland, and ensured that Boston could muster two regiments of militia, "able men and well-armed and exercised." By 1638 and 1639, the King had too many other problems to act. Yet in one historian's view, had a royal governor actually been sent, "It is hard to doubt that Massachusetts would have tried to resist him. The first overt rebellion against Charles I might have taken place in Boston harbor instead of Edinburgh."[18]

In Massachusetts, but also elsewhere in New England, the stamp of East Anglia, its people and ideas, was writ large. Map 1.4 shows the imprint of the eastern counties on Massachusetts and Connecticut. Besides the East Anglian town names that cluster in eastern Massachusetts, even the accent has persisted. Linguists identify unmistakable traces of the nasal "Norfolk Whine" in local intonations. The long, wide public greens of Suffolk, Essex, and Hertfordshire—especially notable examples remain in Writtle and Matching, Essex and Long Melford, Suffolk—were transferred to New England en masse, thereafter migrating westward with New Englanders. Southeast England was the principal region where houses and barns were made of wood, although by the seventeenth century it was growing scarce. Immigrants seeing the potential for lumber in Cape Ann and the Charles River Valley gladly reverted to still-familiar old-country house-building techniques.

Transplanted East Anglians also kept familiar Old World neighbors. Most of the East Anglian coast, from Boston, Lincolnshire, and The Wash south to Harwich and Colchester, facing across the sea to the Netherlands, shows a strong and unique Dutch imprint or resemblance in its land reclamation, engineering, agriculture, art, and architecture. Market gardens are common, even fields of tulips. In 1622, the Essex town of Colchester, facing Holland, had some fifteen hundred people of first- and second-generation Dutch extraction, roughly a third of the population. Fenland southern Lincolnshire, where no small part of today's acreage was reclaimed from the sea with the help of seventeenth-century Dutch

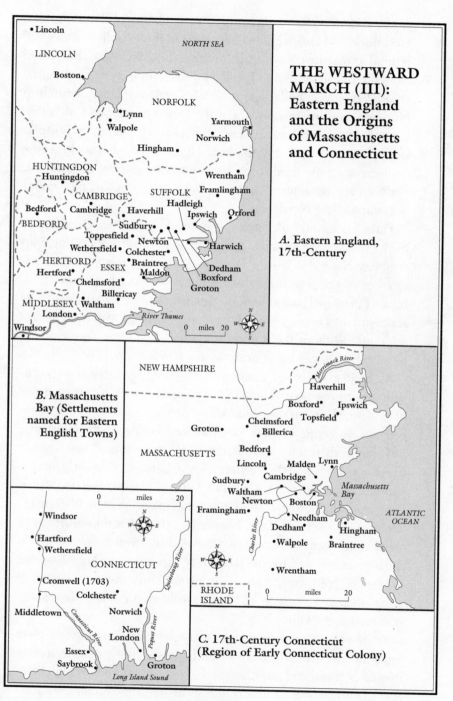

THE WESTWARD MARCH (III): Eastern England and the Origins of Massachusetts and Connecticut

A. Eastern England, 17th-Century

B. Massachusetts Bay (Settlements named for Eastern English Towns)

C. 17th-Century Connecticut (Region of Early Connecticut Colony)

MAP 1.4

engineers, was for many years called the Holland district. Occasional old Dutch gabled houses from there south to Essex still remind the visitor how much architectural style was borrowed from the Netherlands and Flanders. Examples include old brightly colored quayside buildings of King's Lynn, the Dutch church in Norwich, and the row houses of the Dutch quarter of Colchester. Even the most famous school of British art represented by Suffolk-born painters John Constable and Thomas Gainsborough, whose landscapes emphasized lofty dramatic skies and broad horizons, drew on the seventeenth-century Dutch paintings of the similar vistas across the North Sea.

Three thousand miles away, the fledgling New England settlements would have a similar proximity to and cultural overlap with the New Netherlands—for which East Anglian memories and antecedents were presumably an asset, despite occasional squabbles. Like its principal parent region, New England easily assimilated its scattering of Dutch, French Huguenot, Fleming, and Walloon immigrants. Without them, someone other than Paul Revere would have to have made his famous ride.

As befit a region of intensive household industry from yarn-spinning to cheese-making, East Anglia also had a disproportion of craftsmen and tradesmen. Many of the Puritans among them became emigrants to New England, and besides the transatlantic infusion of their religion and culture, their vocational descriptions live on as well-known patronymics: Chandler, Cooper, Currier, Cutler, Draper, Fletcher, Gardiner, Glover, Mason, Mercer, Miller, Sawyer, Saddler, Sherman, Thatcher, Tinker, Turner, Waterman, Webster, and Wheelwright. Names like these remain numerous in the Swamp-Yankee rural townships—and, even more vividly in the nineteenth- and twentieth-century directories of New England university graduates, doctors, ministers, and military officers.[19] They became an elite in the New World to an extent they never managed in the Old.

Yet the most important impact of East Anglia in shaping New England was neither architectural, linguistic, nor patronymic, but instead political and governmental—in a civic culture of high literacy, town meetings, and a tradition of freedom reaching back to Saxon days. The Parliamentary side in the English Civil War upheld this heritage in the early years, but lost its way in the later excesses of the Rump Parliament and the Protectorate. The New England of the 1770s, as befit its origins in liberty-minded but orderly East Anglia, had learned some lessons and spread its influence across America along with its population.

Carl Bridenbaugh, David Hackett Fischer, and others, in setting out the traits and qualities that different English groups brought to different parts of America, have dwelt on the East Anglian origins of New England town government. Centers like Framingham, Braintree, and Dedham—three names that reappeared in Massachusetts—had the equivalent of town by-laws and town meetings. In some, officials were called selectmen.[20] On another dimension of civic-mindedness, Suffolk and Essex were the counties with seventeenth-century England's highest literacy rates, roughly 50 percent. An estimated 85 percent of Puritan men in Massachusetts could sign their names to documents, which was about on a level with yeomen and their wives in East Anglia. Of England's nine "publick libraries" outside London before 1640, five were in Lincolnshire and Norfolk, and a sixth was in Dorchester, the Puritan citadel of the West Country.[21]

From Lincolnshire south to Kent, the eastern counties were distinctive politically as well as educationally. These areas settled by the Angles and Jutes differed from others in having comparatively large ratios of freemen and small numbers of *servi* and *villani*. More than any other part of England, the east was associated with insurrections against arbitrary power—the risings and rebellions of 1381 led by Jack Straw, Wat Tyler, and John Ball in London and most of the eastern counties. Clarence's Rising in 1477 also took place largely within the future bounds of the Eastern Association, whose insurgent cavalry under Cromwell finally did ride down a monarch.[22] Robert Kett's rebellion of 1548 centered in Norfolk. Even Anglo-Saxon opposition to the Normans had lasted longest in the eastern fen country. This was a heritage of liberty New Englanders were proud to share—and would refer to many times in 1774–1775.

John Adams, James Otis, and others cherished the Saxon analogy because it stood for politics more resembling self-determination, free male suffrage, and a consensual social contract—the open-air *folk-moots* and assemblages in places like Spellow, Norfolk (which meant "hill of speech"). New Englanders, like some English republicans of the 1640s, contrasted these practices with the harsher royal authority, edicts, and codes of the Normans, exemplified by the statutory provisions that determined local authority in places like the Channel Islands, Wales, and the Isle of Man.

Otis, extending other theorists, lauded the ancient Saxon origins of the English constitution: Anglo-Saxon England, in Massachusetts eyes, was a kind of pre-feudal elysium until it was conquered and yoked by the Normans.[23] Thomas Jefferson was also an ardent exponent of the Saxon example, but these views were less common in the plantation colonies. By the time the last cousins' war rolled around, the American Southern states had a contrary twist, as chapter 8 will discuss. Northerners were the Saxons, but Southerners were the cavaliers, the knightly Norman stock that conquered them.

From the first, Massachusetts and Connecticut, the principal Puritan colonies, were to be religious and political New Jerusalems. Stuart England, in the eyes of church elders, had been losing its Elizabethan role as God's chosen nation. A new Israel across the sea might have to take up the burden. John Winthrop wrote to his wife in 1629 that "I am veryly persuaded God will bringe some heavy affliction upon this lande" of England. John Cotton, preaching to emigrants bound across the Atlantic at quayside in Gravesend, read from II Samuel 7:10: "And I will appoint a place for my people Israel, and will plant it, that they may dwell in a place of their owne, and move no more, neither shall wicked people trouble them any more as before time."[24] From the start, New Englanders followed in the footsteps of the Puritans in considering themselves a chosen people. Each time—in 1642, in 1775, and in 1861—their ministers sent them off to battle with the requisite assurances that their God was with them.

This, however, is getting ahead of the game. New England historians have correctly called the peak emigration from England in the 1630s the Puritan *hegira*, likening it to the Prophet Mohammed's seventh-century decision to ensure his new religion's future influence by migrating from Mecca to Medina. East Anglia and southeast England were Mecca; after the Stuart Restoration, New

England would indeed be Medina. It would spread the faith, more in a cultural than a strictly religious sense, and ultimately help lead the United States to Britain's support in two world wars and to primacy in the twentieth-century Anglo-American community.

The Advent of Civil War

Puritan voices had been influential at the court of Elizabeth I, among them Lords Burghley and Leicester, two of the Queen's trusted advisers, along with Archbishop Grindal and Bishop Jewel, two of the boldest architects of the new Church of England, and the two Hakluyts, John Sr. and John Jr., preeminent chroniclers of English settlements and prospects in the Americas during the Age of Expansion.

The breadth of Puritan endeavor further expanded in the seventeenth century, despite the wariness of James I. Sympathizers were in the forefront of English seafaring and colonization, of early industrialization—cloth-making, in particular—and almost every kind of small-capitalist assertiveness. Strongest in the larger towns and seaports, London, Bristol, Norwich, and others, the Puritans were correspondingly weak in conservative rural areas. This was especially true in the north and west, most recently brought to heel by the Tudors, where garrisoned castles, Roman Catholicism, and feudal relationships lingered. The aggressiveness of Puritanism, more than any other single factor, may have been the catalyst for the polarization that took over in the 1640s.

R. H. Tawney, in his early twentieth-century masterwork *Religion and the Rise of Capitalism*, argued that "the growth, triumph and transformation of the Puritan spirit was the most fundamental movement of the seventeenth century." Puritanism, he contended, "and not the Tudor secession from Rome, was the true English Reformation, and it is from its struggle against the old order that an England which is unmistakably modern emerges."[25] This seems excessive. The Tudors played an essential role in the political and dynastic success of the Reformation. The Puritans, however, were the principal advance agents of constitutional change and early market capitalism. And they and their heirs would be a catalyst in *each* of the cousins' wars, not just the first one.

Like their Yankee descendants, English Puritans mixed theology and capitalism provocatively and often to great personal profit. The first and second Earls of Warwick, the richest of the Puritan peers, counted warring against Spain not only as patriotism, but as enterprise. Warwick's privateers—on some occasions, *pirates*—pounced on Spanish merchant ships and treasure galleons from bases in England, Holland, and the West Indies.[26] The sun never set on his (and the Puritans') war with Spain. When England made peace with Madrid, Warwick ships fought Spain under letters of marque from Holland, and when the Dutch, too, damped their fuses, his vessels fought under the commission of the far-off Duke of Savoy. In Warwick's shadow, John Hancock and the eighteenth-century New Englanders who made fortunes from smuggling and privateering were small fry.

After Charles I dissolved Parliament in 1629, the Earl and his allies used meetings of their Providence Island Company, founded to establish a Puritan settlement and anti-Spanish privateering base in the Caribbean, as an alternative venue for politicking they had hitherto conducted in Westminster corridors and anterooms. For weeks at a time, the collaborators would visit at Warwick's house in London or Lord Brooke's. John Hampden's famous law-suit against Ship Money, the innovative, irksome royal tax that helped sow the seeds of the Civil War, was plotted at these dinner tables.

Yet despite the undoubted frustrations of Puritans and other critics, as late as 1638 relatively few Englishmen would have felt compelled to take up arms against the King, despite unhappiness over his choice to rule for what would be eleven years without consulting Parliament. What changed this was a succession of re-ligious upheavals in Scotland (1638–1640) and then a rising in Ireland (1641), both of which helped draw England into an internal confrontation of its own. Without these events in Scotland and Ireland, the broader conflict might have been avoided for a while longer.

The specific misjudgment that brought matters to a head in Scotland was Charles Stuart's insistent Anglican orthodoxy. In

1638, after he had for several years demanded unpopular changes in the Scottish Protestant ritual and prayerbooks, the gentry and common people of Scotland, aroused by what they called "plain proofs of popery," united in a Solemn Covenant from which supporters took their name—Covenanters. They also mobilized an army. When the Scots troops marched up to the English border in 1639, many in Parliament and in the English population regarded them as allies, not as threatening foes.

By August 1640, after a second mobilization in which Scots Covenanters—the Presbyterian, nearest north-of-the-border equivalent of English Puritans—crossed the River Tweed and captured Newcastle, the King was in a trap. To obtain money to fight the Scots, he had to call a new Parliament to replace the one he had dismissed eleven years earlier. This "Short Parliament" in the spring of 1640 brought English dissension to a boil. Many in the House of Commons, disliking the previous eleven years as the King's "personal tyranny," preferred to keep the Scots army in place as "a guarantee of English liberties." Cromwell himself is reported to have said that he would rather help the Scots fight the King than vice versa. The Short Parliament was sent home.

In October 1640, Charles agreed to call for a second assemblage and got an even less friendly one—the famous Puritan-dominated Long Parliament. After a year of slow progress on broadly supported reforms, this Parliament wound up in late 1641 confronting the King with the Grand Remonstrance, a lengthy compendium of alleged royal abuses. Parliamentary leaders went so far as to have its sweeping constitutional, religious, and economic charges printed and distributed, a rare appeal to popular opinion. The King, in his famously impolitic response several weeks later, marched soldiers into the House of Commons to seize five Parliamentary leaders on charges of treason. When he failed on that January morning of 1642—all five Puritan blackbirds had flown—civil war became a strong possibility, perhaps a probability. By June, when the King predictably rejected a measure to restrict his powers, Parliament's Nineteen Propositions, the lines were drawn.

Charles, lacking financial resources because the Parliament controlled the purse, took months to gather an army. By the time of the first major battle at Edgehill in October 1642, hundreds of Puritan emigrants were returning from Massachusetts Bay and Connecticut to fight alongside their cousins and to help make history. More than half of those who graduated from Harvard between 1640 and 1650 went back. For Massachusetts, the English Civil War was more than a far-off fight; it was a magnet—and it would be an enduring memory.

PART TWO

The Early Cousins' Wars

2

ANGLO-AMERICA'S FIRST CIVIL WARS

The British Setting, 1630–1763

The First Civil War is the decisive event in English history. . . . defeat in the field would have ruined for ever the cause of Parliament and would have driven the Puritans out of England. The current of European thought and practice, running hard towards despotism, would have caught England into the stream. America, strengthened by the influx of all who could change their country but not their religion, might perhaps have proved unconquerable and gone on her way alone. But England would then have become a mere outlying portion of the State system of Europe, had she not, by the campaign of Naseby, acquired her independent position between the old world and the new, and planted freedom in the deep fruitful soil of antiquity. The flowers of genius and the fruits of life that have since flourished upon that tree, could not have shown their heads under the shadow of tyranny, nor could they have so quickly bloomed to perfection in the thin soil of a newer land.

—George M. Trevelyan,
England Under the Stuarts, 1924

At last, under the execrable race of the Stuarts, the struggle between the people and the confederacy aforesaid of temporal and spiritual tyranny [king and church], became formidable, violent, and bloody. It was this great struggle that peopled America.

—John Adams, second president of the United States

> *The model for the American Revolution should have been the Glorious Revolution of 1688, the revolution honored by all Britons, including colonials, as the culmination of their constitutional development. In that revolution Britain had exchanged one king for another, rather than ending kingship altogether. Yet Americans rejected the Glorious Revolution as a model in 1776 and followed instead the bloody Puritan Revolution, when England had executed its king.*
>
> —Richard Bushman, Gouverneur Morris Professor of History, Columbia University, 1985

O LIVER CROMWELL AND OTHER FUTURE architects of the English Civil War may have been close to moving to America in the 1630s. Even in the 1770s, residents of Old Saybrook, at the mouth of the Connecticut River, named for the Puritan Lords Saye and Brooke, still talked about which prominent Parliamentarian was to have had which town lot.[1]

The clandestine emigration plans of seventeenth-century English political figures, even important ones, are hardly high drama, set against the grander intrigues of British history. But whether the future Lord Protector, along with other prominent Puritans, almost left England for New England in the 1630s has a particular what-might-have-been significance for the Anglo-American future. The cousins' wars themselves could have taken different shape. The American Revolution—and then the American Civil War—might not have occurred. The Puritan and Yankee role, critical in both, might have been different or missing.

Migration to the New World by Cromwell and his associates, in itself, would probably not have greatly rewritten New England's near-term history. The pivot is whether the lack of a Cromwell far off in "Quenecticote," drilling bored Essex and Saybrook militia and fighting Pequot Indians in the Connecticut River Valley, never attending the Long Parliament, never leading his Ironside cavalry through broken Royalist infantry on the battlefield of Naseby, and never ruling England's first and only republic from 1649 to 1658, would have changed Britain's own fortunes. Or whether the similar departure of other Puritan stalwarts like John Pym and John Hampden would have done so. And the answer is: quite possibly. Charles I would have been more likely to keep his throne, and a Stuart dynasty, unbroken from 1603 to, say, 1750, would have held back English political and commercial development, inhibited the growth of British North America, and submerged the radical heritage that helped nurture the thirteen colonies' own rebellion.

This is not to suggest that the rebel side in the English Civil War and Puritanism are synonymous. Many of the early leaders—the Earls of Essex and Manchester and Sir Thomas Fairfax on the 1642 and 1643 battlefields, and Sir Simonds D' Ewes, Lord Saye, and the Earl of Bedford in Parliament—were aristocrats of a more moderate cast. However, many from the political middle, who supported Parliament in 1640 and 1641, swung to the King in 1642 and 1643. The two best-known leaders of the Parliamentary opposition during the decade leading up to the war, Pym and Hampden, were Puritans of a practical sort who might well have been at odds with the later stages of the civil war and revolution had they both not died in 1643—Pym of ill health and Hampden leading his regiment at the battle of Chalgrove Field.

Cromwell's own rise was partly a result of religious and political radicals coming to the fore on the Parliamentary side in those years. Although from a family well known in East Anglia, in 1640 he was only a backbench Member of Parliament for Cambridgeshire. By January 1643, he was a colonel of cavalry and lieutenant-general a year later. By 1646, his prominence in the military victories at Marston Moor and Naseby had made him an important bridge between Parliament and the army. His subsequent emergence reflected the army's growing role in government as well as war, and by the time of the King's execution in 1649, Cromwell could fairly be called the first man in England.

Cromwell, the eventual Lord Protector (1653–1658) of England's only republic, clearly *did* himself consider emigration—in the mid-1630s and then in 1641. What modern historians have rejected is a specific tale first circulated by early, hostile Royalist biographers. In 1638, the story goes, Cromwell, Hampden, and Sir Arthur Haselrig were on a ship in the Thames, waiting to sail. The Privy Council, openly hostile to politically motivated emigration, at first withheld the necessary permission for departure. When clearance came, the tale continues, the three had gone ashore.

The substantial rumors of prominent Puritans being about to emigrate dated back to 1635. Hampden, Haselrig, and Lords Saye and Brooke, along with Pym, were all involved in plans for a new coastal settlement at what is now Old Saybrook on the Connecticut coast. Preparations included sending a ship with an unusual cargo—ironwork for a portcullis and drawbridges, even an experienced military engineer.[2] Saybrook's fort was to be the strongest in New England. Several sponsors were anxious to move, inquiring when houses could be completed. However, they soon "found the countrie [England] full of reports of their going" and became worried that they would not be allowed to sell their estates and take ship.[3] By 1638, the Saybrook plans were moot. Moreover, Cromwell's own financial difficulties had been cleared up in 1636 by an inheritance, and he had moved from Huntingdon to nearby Ely, the fen country cathedral town named, rather commonly, for the abundant eels in the River Ouse.

Yet clearly Cromwell, like his colleagues, had an idealized view of a Puritan New World, and emigration was on his mind again in late 1641. That November, by just eleven votes out of three hundred and after a fierce late-night debate that nearly led to swordplay in the Westminster candlelight, the House of Commons passed the controversial Grand Remonstrance, a landmark of English legal and constitutional history. It warned Charles I against a large catalogue of practices, bemoaned evidence of plots to make England Catholic, and cautioned the King against appointing advisors unacceptable to Parliament. Cromwell himself is said to have whispered to Lord Falkland that "if the Remonstrance had been rejected [in Parliament] he would have sold all he had the next morning; and never have seen England more; and he knew there were many other honest men of the same resolution."[4]

History, having hesitated on its hinge, swung on. The leaders of Parliamentary Puritanism did not leave England to the Stuarts. They fought a civil war and helped bring the Century of Revolution to pass. The merits of the war that began in 1642, one of the great debates of English history, are unlikely to be resolved, but one can argue that within the Century of Revolution that achieved so much in British history, there was a core half century from 1640 to 1690 in which the two armed confrontations—the Civil War of 1640–1649 and the Glorious Revolution of 1688—led to the male Stuarts being finally deposed and to the triumph of both Parliament and the Protestant Succession.

Could England have achieved that result without the Civil War or in the face of a Parliamentary defeat? Probably not. But the importance of the war to America's future seems less debatable. Had Parliament lost its fight with the King in 1643 or 1644, government in England would have turned in a more absolutist direction and some forty, fifty, or sixty thousand additional Puritans might have fled to New England. The latter, instead of slowly maturing and gaining experience and self-sufficiency under the Williamite and Whig regimes that ruled Britain most of the time from the 1690s through 1760, would have been thrust into an embattled and isolated (and probably also radicalized) mid-seventeenth-century prominence. The chances of failure would have been high.

However, because Parliament fought and won the critical battles at Marston Moor and Naseby in 1644 and 1645, crippling the King's cause, the Century of Revolution sustained itself, surviving the Restoration of Charles II in 1660, and triumphing in the moderate, even conservative, garb of 1688. The North American colonies, in turn, enjoyed a drawn-out civic tutelage, along with the protection from France and Spain that they needed from the mother country. The dearth of monuments to Marston Moor and Naseby is perhaps understandable in Britain; it is Boston, New York, Philadelphia, and Washington that should have them.

Culture, Region, and Loyalty in the English Civil War

Little as it mattered at the time, the English Civil War spanned the ocean and involved two continents. Beyond the Puritan stronghold of Boston, a wide range of Parliamentarian-versus-Royalist views prevailed in New England, Maryland, and Virginia among the roughly forty thousand English-speaking colonists. New England was for Parliament, Virginia and Maryland for the King. If in the

1620s and 1630s, Puritan dissidents had migrated to Massachusetts and Connecticut, in 1644 and 1645 as the tide turned against the Stuarts, unhappy Royalists took ship for Virginia, where they were welcomed.

Important groundwork for the future—and for subsequent civil wars—was being laid in the colonies as well as in the British Isles. Yet before examining the England of 1642–1645, its wartime divisions, and their long-range significance, a caution is in order: The twisting, turning political and military confrontations of Parliament and King from 1640 to 1649 created somewhat different constituencies, loyalties, and alignments at various stages. Specific time frames are not just relevant; they are essential.

Revolutionary and civil wars are not static. Loyalties and constituencies on *both* sides keep evolving. The following paragraph is thus broadly useful because it also applies, with different adjectives and dates, to the other cousins' fights:

> The English revolution, like all others we know of, had the habit of devouring its children. The alignment of forces of 1640 was quite different from that of 1642, by which time a large block of former Parliamentarians had moved over to reluctant royalism; it was different again in 1648, when the conservative element among the Parliamentarians, misleadingly known as the Presbyterians, swung back to the side of the King. In 1640 or 1642 virtually no one was republican; in 1649 England was a republic. In 1640 or 1642 virtually no one favored religious toleration; by 1649 wide toleration for Protestants was achieved. One of the major causes of the muddled thinking about the causes of the English revolution has arisen from the failure to establish precisely which stage of revolution is being discussed.[5]

The early divisions of the English Civil War, as noted, constitute an obligatory opening chapter in explanations of America's own War of Independence. Even the confrontations out of which the two conflicts grew have a resemblance. Resentment of Stuart excesses among the English elites in 1640, when a reluctant Charles I had to recall Parliament, was as intense as colonial opposition to the Stamp Act circa 1765 or outrage in the rest of America over the Coercive Acts passed to suppress Boston nine years later. In these early stages, even those who would later be opponents frequently agreed: *The King, his ministers, and his allies had gone too far.* Concessions from the Crown were essential.

The more closely matched divergence of opinion that would give the fighting its civil war intensity developed in the *next* political stage. Reform ceased to be the sole issue. Fear that Parliament was loosing radicalism or even anarchy in the land became an emerging counterforce. In the English Civil War, such a stage came with the breakdown of relations and movement toward open war between the King and Parliament in late 1641 and 1642. Growing concern over Parliament's own ambitions gave the King more support than he had enjoyed a year earlier. The parallel rethinking in the American Revolution, which cooled the enthusiasm of mid-1775, came in the summer and autumn of 1776. This followed the Declaration of Independence, the adoption of a radical new constitution in Pennsylvania, and the success of the British campaign to subjugate Manhattan and the lower Hudson. Each conflict, once transformed, then produced the divisions needed to create the bitter, drawn-out fratricide of civil war.

The relatively equal balance of the English Civil War came in 1642–1644 *after* the broad reformist unity of 1640 and early 1641 had broken down in the face of increasingly controversial Puritan demands, but while the King still held large stretches of territory and *before* the Puritan and Parliamentary military edge became overwhelming after Naseby in 1645. Map 2.1 illustrates the essential contours of loyalty in late 1643; the weight was with Parliament because its territory in the south and southeast included the greatest part of England's population, wealth, shipping, and industry.

Even so, there is too much oversimplification in the common summary that Parliament commanded the progressive, commercially forward-looking, and urban south and east of England while the King drew upon the poorer, still partly feudal north and west. Notwithstanding the would-be neutralist elements in each shire, the *rural* sections of the west and north did hold for the King in the opening years, while the southern and eastern countryside, with only limited exceptions, was Parliamentarian. Urban sympathies, however, were less regional and more national. Parliament

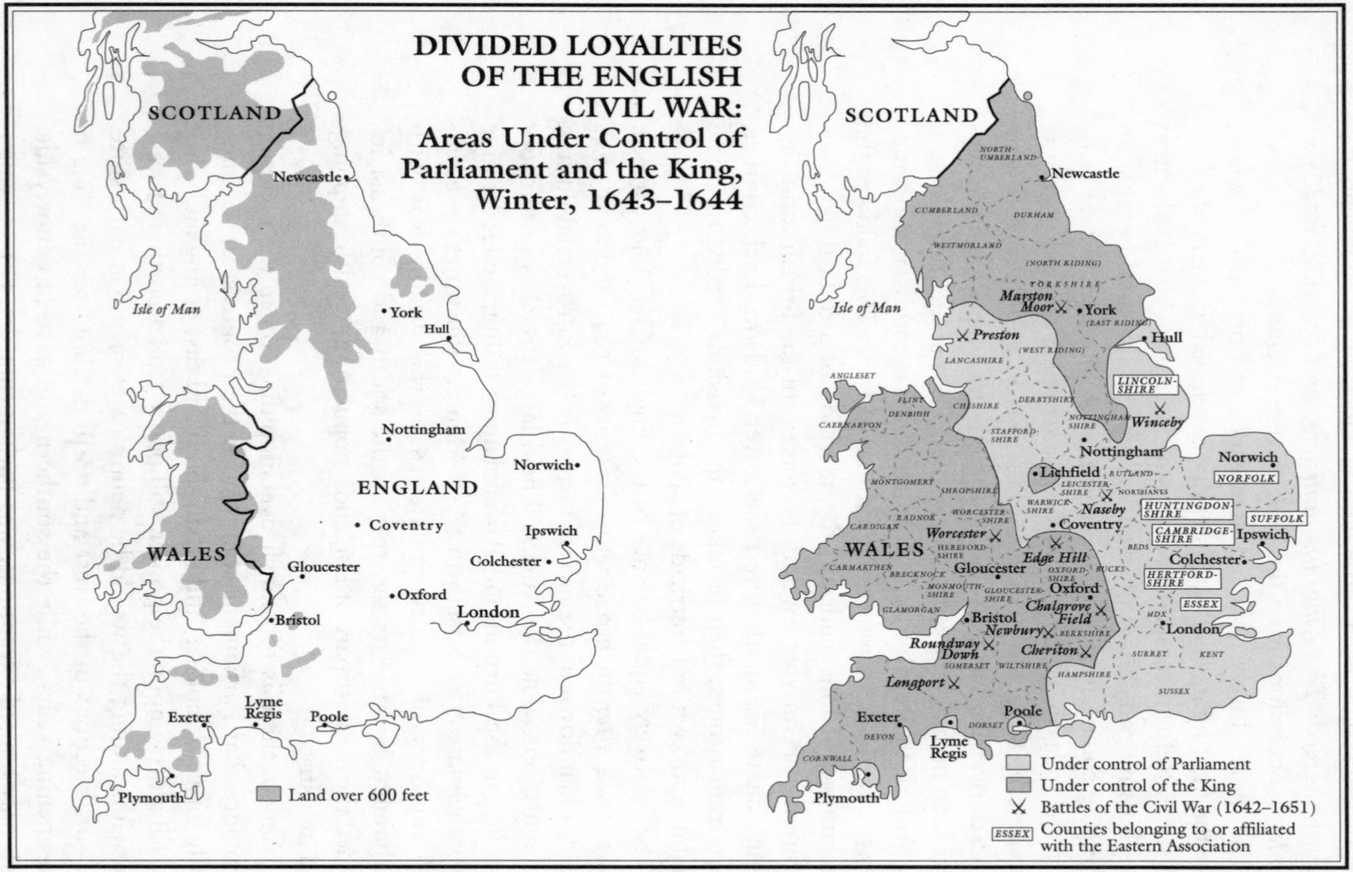

DIVIDED LOYALTIES
OF THE ENGLISH
CIVIL WAR:
Areas Under Control of
Parliament and the King,
Winter, 1643–1644

SCOTLAND

Newcastle

NORTH UMBERLAND
DURHAM
(NORTH RIDING)
YORKSHIRE
Marston Moor ✕ ✕ York (EAST RIDING)
Hull
CUMBERLAND
WESTMORLAND
(WEST RIDING)
LANCASHIRE
✕ Preston
Isle of Man
CHESHIRE
FLINT
DENBIGH
DERBYSHIRE
NOTTINGHAM SHIRE
Nottingham
LINCOLN SHIRE
✕ Winceby
LEICESTER SHIRE
RUTLAND
NORTHANTS
STAFFORD SHIRE
Lichfield ✕
WARWICK SHIRE
✕ Naseby
Coventry
HUNTINGDON SHIRE
CAMBRIDGE SHIRE
NORFOLK
Norwich
SUFFOLK
Ipswich
CAERNARVON
ANGLESEY
MONTGOMERY
SHROPSHIRE
WORCESTER SHIRE
HEREFORD
Worcester ✕
Edge Hill ✕
OXFORD SHIRE
Oxford
BUCKS
BEDS
HERTFORD SHIRE
ESSEX
Colchester ✕
London
KENT
WALES
BRECKNOCK
RADNOR
GLOUCESTER SHIRE
Gloucester
Chalgrove Field ✕
BERKSHIRE
MIDDX
SURREY
SUSSEX
CARMARTHEN
GLAMORGAN
MONMOUTH
Bristol ✕
Roundway Down ✕
Newbury ✕
WILTSHIRE
Cherton ✕
HAMPSHIRE
Langport ✕
SOMERSET
Poole ✕
DEVON
Exeter ✕
DORSET
Lyme Regis ✕
Plymouth
CORNWALL

☐ Under control of Parliament
▨ Under control of the King
✕ Battles of the Civil War (1642–1651)
☐ ESSEX Counties belonging to or affiliated with the Eastern Association

SCOTLAND

Newcastle
ENGLAND
Hull
York
Nottingham
Coventry
Norwich
Ipswich
Colchester
Oxford
London
Gloucester
Bristol
Poole
Lyme Regis
Exeter
Plymouth
WALES

Isle of Man

▨ Land over 600 feet

MAP 2.1

prevailed not only in eastern towns but also in northern and western seaports like Plymouth, Bristol, Bridgwater, Bridport, Lyme Regis, Liverpool, and Hull, together with cloth-manufacturing centers like Gloucester, Taunton, Dorchester, and Exeter in the western shires; Wakefield, Halifax, and Bradford in the West Riding of Yorkshire; and Manchester, Bolton, Blackburn, and Rochdale in Lancashire. The Puritanism of these towns was a thorn in the side for western and northern Royalists.

Puritanism was a tidy, rational, lowland creed, and England's far north, in particular Cumberland and Westmorland, but also upcountry reaches of Durham, Northumberland, Yorkshire, and Lancashire, was a craggy, tribal countryside that startled southern visitors by the "poverty and smallness of the hamlets, the bare feet and uncouth accent of the people."[6] This was the wild, clannish lakeside and hill-country England of Derwentwater, Cross Fell, and the Black Burn, where remote border keeps built of stones carted away from Hadrian's Wall overlooked desolate moors, cultural light-years from the ordered towns and prosperous Puritan burgesses of the south. Support for King Charles also predominated in the higher elevations of Derbyshire, in the shires along the Welsh border, and especially in remote Wales and Cornwall, with old languages, traditions, and lords of their own. Welsh and Cornish troopers bulked large in the Royalist armies, playing major roles in battles like Lansdown Hill and Lostwithiel.

This older England that looked north and west into Celtic uplands and mountains simultaneously faced backward into clan warfare and feudal religion. Catholicism remained substantial, and in the years from 1536 to 1569, these were the locales of risings to overturn the new Protestantism. The northern counties along or near the Scottish border, as well as those edging Wales, had been known as "marches"—armed and mountainous frontiers organized for many years as counties Palatine, local autocracies not far removed from martial law. The neat Dutch churches, town meetings, and selectmen of East Anglia were unheard of in these "dark corners of the land," as the southeasterners called them. The Marches were organized for war, not commerce. In 1640, moreover, border warfare was a living memory—the Welsh Marches were not abolished until the unification of Wales and

England in 1536, and Welsh was still spoken in parts of the three English border counties. The Northern Marches abutting Scotland, where border raids continued fiercely through the sixteenth century, were only tamed by James I in the first decade of the seventeenth.

As the Civil War broke out in England in 1642, loyalties along both the Welsh and Scottish borders ran to the Stuarts and hereditary leaders, not elected ones. Areas closer to London and its commerce—Somerset, Dorset, Wiltshire, Gloucestershire, and Worcestershire—were split. The seaports, cloth centers, and cheese-making districts were strongly Puritan and Parliamentarian. But in the rolling, manor-studded, agricultural countryside where a long-established gentry mostly held for the King, Puritans were few, and traditional religion and the seasons of agriculture still encouraged a tenants' calendar of rustic merriment: Twelfth Night festivities and winter wassailing led through the seasons to spring maypoles, midsummer bonfires, church ales, Michaelmas celebrations of the grain crop, sheepshearings, and harvest homes. Local peasants, resentful of the efforts of lower-middle-class Puritan burgesses and master clothiers to remove church altar rails and to replace this familiar culture with sobriety, sermons, and Sabbath strictness, typically followed the majority of the knights and lords of the shire to serve under the King's banner.[7]

The most riven portion of England was the central war ground that included all but two of the major battlefields of 1642–1645: the East Midlands of Nottinghamshire, Leicestershire, and Northamptonshire; the southern stretch of the West Midlands (Staffordshire, Warwickshire); and, to the south, Oxfordshire and the bitterly contested Cotswolds and Upper Thames Valley (Gloucestershire and Wiltshire). To the west were the prime Royalist recruiting grounds in Shropshire, Worcestershire, and Wales. To the east of this central *champ de Mars*, and both lower in elevation and higher in income, were the grey-worsted Parliamentary and Puritan strongholds: London and its environs (Kent, Sussex, Surrey, Hampshire, Berkshire, Buckinghamshire, and Middlesex) and the seven counties that made up the militant Eastern Association—Essex, Hertford, Suffolk, Norfolk, Cambridge, Huntingdon, and Lincoln.

In late 1643, when the King seemed to be holding his own on the battlefield, he had the largest *geographic* sway. But Parliament's square miles contained, as noted, a larger ratio of England's people, wealth, education, and commerce. The geographic divide was less than precise; the cultural, civic, and religious polarity is more telling and important.

The England of cosmopolitan commerce and Protestant refugees from continental persecution was a particular Puritan and Parliamentary stronghold. The land of the Angles and Saxons has always been a melting pot—the northeastern region settled by the Danes in the tenth and eleventh centuries still displays its Norse heritage in town names ending in "by" (the equivalent of village) or "thorp" (for hamlet) and Norman names still abound in the voters' registers in upper-class precincts of greater London. What seventeenth-century East Anglia, London, and the southeast represented, however, was a new and different kind of English melting pot: a home for entrepreneurs and the Protestant refugees, mostly in trade, who had fled the continental Catholic Counter-Reformation—Huguenot merchants, seafarers, and silkworkers from France; Flemish and Walloon threadmakers, weavers, and artisans from the Spanish Netherlands (now Belgium); Dutch engineers, agriculturists, and scholars; and even a small inflow of Palatine German refugees from an already war-weary Rhineland. Numbering as many as fifty to sixty thousand out of one and a half million people, the foreign Calvinist population in the southeast strengthened the already dominant pro-Parliamentary culture.

The seaport cities were England's other and perhaps even more important ethnic stews. Some coastal towns in Wales or on the Irish Sea were exceptions, but as one historian observed:

> The Protestant zeal of the sea-going population, which during the struggle with Philip had grown into the most constant political sentiment upon which English statesmen could calculate, in no way diminished during the forty years of peace that preceded the Civil War. Along the coasts of Europe and America there was still a freemasonry for defense and offence between all Protestant sailors, whether they hailed from Plymouth, Amsterdam or Rochelle, a fellow-feeling kept alive by forecastle yarns illustrating the pride and extortion of corrupt Spanish officials, and by

stories that stirred the blood, of comrades mysteriously disappearing in the streets of Spanish towns.[8]

Sentiments like these made English seaports—and sailors—pillars of Parliamentary support. As Map 2.1 shows, maritime centers stretched and pocketed the geography of English Civil War loyalty. The westward bulge of Parliamentary territory on the south coast rested on the environs of Portsmouth and Southampton, while the three embattled Parliamentary coastal enclaves beyond were Plymouth, the sallyport of Sir Frances Drake; Lyme Regis, where the Duke of Monmouth would land in 1685; and Poole, a center of the Newfoundland trade. The seaports of Hull and Liverpool anchored Parliamentary peripheries to the north and west.

Students of the American Civil War will already have gleaned a vital parallel. As we will see in chapter 9, the division of England just sketched bears a surprising likeness to the internal geography of the United States in 1865. The two sides ultimately victorious—the Parliamentarians in 1640–1649, the Northern Federals in 1861–1865—each represented the side with the great weight of industry, population, cities, middle-class professionals, entrepreneurs, financiers, seafarers, yeomen (or their equivalents), and foreign-born population. Their politics, culture, and success pointed to the future; the alignments of the English Royalists and the American South pointed to a past that had to be superseded.

The English Civil War, in short, helped set out cultural and economic lines that over three centuries would be threads of England's and America's futures. They would appear in each of the cousins' wars.

The Causes and Dividing Lines of the English Civil War

Such underpinnings cast doubt on abstract theses that dismiss the depth and meaning of the English Civil War. Such explanations include portrayals of an angry mobilization of country gentlemen provoked by an arrogant, effete royal court, or insistence that a tiny minority of zealots, both Puritan and High Church, drew the rest of the nation into an unnecessary conflict. A third contention is that ordinary Englishmen, uncaring about what was fought over in the 1640s, mostly followed their gentry or leaders. Still another disputes the importance of deeply held national viewpoints by emphasizing localism. In most counties, this argument goes, but especially in self-contained places like Kent, men took sides or sought to be neutral in response to *parochial* concerns: county traditions, the role of individual families and inherited feuds, and the local economic hardships brought by the fighting.

While each argument has some merit, what they fail to explain are the English Civil War's larger origins or deeper religious, ethnic, and regional loyalties. This is not to suggest that most Englishmen were caught up in the issues or enthusiastic about the fighting. Surely most were not. Estimates must be guesswork. But a presumption like that for the American Revolution—that 30–35 percent supported it while 20–25 percent were loyalists and 35–45 percent merely wanted to carry on with their lives—may apply just as well to the Revolution circa 1642–1644. For most people, surviving and prospering are always the basic imperatives.

Yet the composition of the two camps was quite different. On the King's side, in addition to his critical support from two-thirds of the nobility and half of the gentry, the royal armies did attract two numerically important nonideological or deferential groups: the countrymen who followed great local Royalist feudatories like the marquesses of Winchester, Newcastle, and Hereford and the Earls of Worcester and Derby, and also the vagabonds, drifters, and lower orders who fought for the pay, the uniform, and the chance to loot a captured town.

However, the appeal of Parliament to its different base of artisan and yeoman supporters and soldiers would have rested less on apathy, deference, or traditionalism. Civic and religious awareness, literacy, and activism would have loomed larger. Scholars estimate that by 1640, one-quarter to one-third of Englishmen, perhaps even 40 percent, were voting in elections for Parliament. Then there was the evidence of petition-signing: For the first time, large compilations were gathered and sent to Parliament. All of which argues for a considerable public political awareness.

Puritan civic involvement was especially intense. The 10 to 20 percent of Englishmen who were Puritans, in particular, often belonged not just to church congregations but to related lecture groups. Roughly a quarter of England's two million households owned a Bible—the most influential indictment of pharisees, courtiers, and tyrants ever printed. We have seen the unusual literacy rates, town-meeting traditions, and bookishness of East Anglia, also true for Puritan towns elsewhere. And as printing presses spread, the Revolution was as much a battle of smudged pamphlets as of roughcast bullets.[9] Celebrations of Protestant political and military successes on the continent also bespoke popular alertness.[10]

Commerce was a second Puritan preoccupation and political motivation. Mid-seventeenth-century merchants, tradesmen, and apprentices sold goods and hired workmen in an economy suffused with lingering medievalism. The extent to which guilds, monopolies, and usury laws stood in the way of would-be entrepreneurs helped to push most of those affected toward the Parliamentary side. As early as 1604, a committee of the House of Commons, already under Puritan influence, declared that "all free subjects are born inheritable, as to their land, so also to the free exercise of their industry, in those trades where to they apply themselves and whereby they are to live. Merchandise being the chiefest and richest of all other, and against the natural right and liberty of the subjects of England to restrain it into the hands of some few."[11] During the 1620s, Parliament began investigating a steady stream of royal patents—the rights to license inns and alehouses, for example—and royal grants of monopolies like the one for gold and silver thread. Even the Root-and-Branch Petition of 1640, largely preoccupied with religion, had a provision criticizing monopolies and patents.

Marxist scholars have erred, not in recognizing economic forces, but in overstating the class tensions and economic causations of the English Civil War. Economic interests and royal favoritisms obviously mattered. Charles I treated the seventeenth-century commerce of England not unlike the Mafia would later treat twentieth-century construction and restaurant activity in New York City and New Jersey: *for whatever could be extorted from it.* When the London Company of Vintners declined to pay the King £4 on each ton of wine sold, he refused them the right to sell food with their wine and hailed them before the Star Chamber. Beaten down, the vintners arranged to pay £30,000 a year for the privilege of serving meals as well as selling wine. In another situation, following the King's sale of an exclusive fourteen-year right to manufacture and market soap of vegetable oil, the grantees further prevailed on him to prohibit the use of a different (fish) oil in soap so that a more successful rival could be shut down. Competing soapmakers found themselves thrown in jail.[12]

Not everyone of "the middling sort" opposed the King. Persons who had bought his favor—his commercial charters, patents, and preferences—took a stake in his rule. Related patterns can also be identified in the American war of 1775–1783. Class was not the issue; *rival economics* was. Among the 507 members of the House of Commons in 1640, for example, were 22 London merchants. A dozen of them were expelled by Parliament because they were monopoly-holders; all were Royalists. Of the ten remaining capitalist Londoners in the House, all were Parliamentarians save one.

In Shropshire, the oligarchies of Shrewsbury and Oswestry drapers, whose Welsh trade had been protected by the Crown, were Royalists in the war. So were the Chester Companies of Shoemakers and Glovers, earlier aided against rivals by the Privy Council, as well as the protected flax merchants of Preston. Mine operators also generally favored the Stuarts who had sold them that privilege.[13] Most favored of all were the "customs farmers," merchants who advanced funds to the Crown against the future royal customs revenues, which they would then gather in.[14] In the American Revolution, some of the greatest loyalty to the Crown came among customs officials, and the producers of indigo, rice, and naval stores enjoying British subsidies under the Navigation Acts.

Whereas "Court" capitalists and monopolists might be Royalists, smaller entrepreneurs, who rose or fell in the marketplace, were much more likely to look to Parliament—to the same House of Commons that by 1642 had passed a half dozen laws and remonstrances touching their interest. Small shipowners, sea officers, and ship's chandlers were in this group; so were many artisans and apprentices, and, most of all, entrepreneurs in four major English industries into which entry was possible with small capital or on a humble scale: cutlery- and weapons-making, cloth work, cheesemaking, and lead-mining. Historians agree that, with few exceptions, the seaports, the ironworking, cloth-making, and cheese-making towns, along with the lead-mining districts, were Parliamentarian.

Metalworkers in the Midlands thrived in part because their craftsmen were not organized in medieval guilds, and avoided serving the seven-year apprenticeships so common elsewhere. For providing sword blades and soldiers only to Parliament, Birmingham was sacked by the King's forces in 1643. Lord Clarendon, the King's counselor-turned-historian, later described the future capital of British steel-making "as famed for hearty, wilful, affected disloyalty to the King as any place in England." Parliamentarian sentiment also thrived in the lead districts of Derbyshire and the Mendip hills of Somerset, unmonopolized and controlled by prosperous, individualistic, and independent small capitalists.[15] Some of the lead mines in the Peak District of Derbyshire had names—Gang, Ball Eye, and Dutchman's Level—that anticipated the nineteenth-century California goldfields. And most of all, there were the clothing centers, damned by the Royalists but romanticized by generations of progressive historians, especially those towns in the north and west that withstood sieges from a hostile Royalist countryside. One fulsome description recalled that "in Lancashire, the clothing towns—the Genevas of Lancashire—rose like Puritan islands from the surrounding sea of Roman Catholicism."[16]

Counterposing Puritan towns against a Royalist countryside can be taken too far. Some of the cathedral cities were Royalist—York, with its dozens of churches, 190-foot minster, and status as the archepiscopal see for northern England; and also Worcester, Shrewsbury, and Chester. Towns with favored municipal corporations, merchants, or guilds took a similar view, as did some market towns serving traditional agricultural districts or sitting in the shadows of great landowners. One survey of the West Country has even alleged a Royalist clothing center—Shepton Mallet, Somerset. But there cannot have been many.

Yet while economic complaints helped to spur and then sort out the loyalties of the English Civil War, class aspects were muted. The "middling sort" were divided, far from monolithic, even if two-thirds did support Parliament in these defining years. And many fiercely Puritan weavers were poor, with incomes no higher than farm laborers. The best explanation probably lies in how a number of economic activities overlapped the country's new individualistic, antifeudal religious preference: *Puritanism*. This is essentially the point made by Max Weber in his classic *The Protestant Ethic and the Spirit of Capitalism*: that capitalism, being more than an economic system, was also a frame of mind closely interrelated with the moral and religious commitments of Protestantism.[17] This religious identification seems to have been the more important, just as it would be among New England's Yankee Congregationalists in 1775. The "Third Puritanism" which mobilized New England in the mid-nineteenth century was another such hybrid of faith, reform, and capitalism. Which brings us to the first war's most important pair of causal forces-cum-loyalties: *religion and sectarianism*.

That religion was not, at first, the contention between King and Parliament was admitted by Oliver Cromwell himself. However, as 1640 became 1641 and then 1642, religious issues and sectarian distrusts moved to the fore. The reforms of 1640 and 1641 that mandated triennial parliaments, restrained royal counselors and prerogative courts, curbed illegal taxes, and reduced royal emergency powers—all curbs on widely disliked abuses seen as personal to Charles I—passed the House of Commons easily. Their majorities reached far beyond the Puritan benches into the opposite tiers of High Church gentry. The more controversial legislation that followed, on issues from control of the militia to religious reform, had a narrower support base. By late 1641, the Grand Remonstrance, which, among its many other provisions, prominently accused Popish sympathizers and agents of plotting to subvert English religion and liberties, carried by only eleven votes.

The gathering religious radicalization of Parliament began in the winter of 1640–1641 in response to a huge inpouring of petitions, from London and the nearby Kent and Essex countryside, demanding root-and-branch reform of the English church. The principal objections were to Catholic ceremonialism, altars and relics, curates' refusal to preach sermons, moral laxity, and the like. Some petitions were orchestrated, but London's submission of fifteen thousand signatures was totally unprecedented for that era, and the House of Commons began to stiffen under the pressure. A

Committee for Scandalous Ministers, established to look into the petitioners' claims, found many of them supported.

With the Lords able to block any legislation, the Commons assumed unprecedented judicial and administrative powers. These were used to incarcerate and silence Archbishop Laud and his allies, to make the parish clergy accountable to committees of the House, to approve and disapprove religious literature, to restore Puritans silenced by the Star Chamber, and even to assume jurisdiction over church furnishings. As open war approached in the summer of 1642, according to Cambridge historian John Morrill, few bishops retained authority in their dioceses, church courts had ceased to function, altar rails were gone, and the liturgy was in retreat.[18] Petitions to Parliament from the shires, although still preoccupied with religion, became more closely divided in their sentiments—urging less reform rather than more—as traditionalists reacted against Puritan successes.

The mobilization for war in 1642 mirrored these later cleavages—a monarchy, bishops-and-altars Anglican party with Catholic allies versus a psalms-and-no-popery Puritan element with country-party Anglican allies. The greatest polarity was between Puritans and Catholics. Some were neutral, but Puritan Royalists and Catholic Parliamentarians were almost unheard of. Mutual suspicion was too pervasive.

Religious historians beg off from stating firm numbers for either camp. If Puritans probably represented 10–20 percent of the national population, most of them still worshiping within the Church of England, Catholics were much harder to count. Open "recusants"—Catholics who paid fines to avoid attending the Church of England—numbered sixty thousand in 1640. Many more, however, reluctantly attended services on Sunday with scowls or for as short a time as possible. The more identifiable of these were called "Church Papists"; the less important, ordinary grumblers who merely talked of preferring the older ceremonies were uncountable. In the north and west, at least half the population outside the towns was Catholic to *some* degree. By this broad definition, Catholics could have numbered 10–15 percent of the total English population. *Practicing* Roman Catholics, however, could not have been more than 2–3 percent.

Catholicism survived most strongly among the nobility, of whom 15–20 percent clung to the old faith, including many leading magnates in an arc from Cumberland, Westmoreland, and Lancashire south to Derby, Worcestershire, and Herefordshire. However, even solidly Protestant East Anglian counties like Suffolk and Essex each had three, four, or a half-dozen aristocratic families holding to the religion of their forebears. This is perhaps one reason why the populace took Catholic "plots" so seriously: What they called popery was especially visible among the powerful and influential.

Open, pitched battles between Catholics and Puritans were rare in the Civil War because moderate Anglicans were split between the two sides and Royalist armies were usually Anglican-led. When such fights occurred, however, the religious wars of Germany found cruel imitation on English soil. For instance, in 1644 when a Royalist force under Prince Rupert, made up of mostly Catholics from the surrounding Lancashire countryside, captured the Puritan cloth town of Bolton, only seven hundred Protestant defenders were allowed to surrender while sixteen hundred were slain. A few months later, when Parliamentarians captured Basing House, the seat of the Marquess of Winchester, Puritan troops retaliated in kind on the Catholic garrison.

Choosing sides in the 1640s could be especially painful for moderate Anglicans. Most disliked the court Catholicism of the Stuart kings, the high ratio of Catholic officers in the King's army, and the repeated evidence of Popish designs and plots. Yet most also disliked the Puritans and the more radical of their church reforms. Even more feared the sectaries—the Quakers, Baptists, Ranters, Familists, and Brownists—to say nothing of the political levelers and anarchists, all of whom seemed to be proliferating and gaining influence under the somber Puritan umbrella of hostility to High Church prelates and practices.

Part of the conundrum of 1642–1645 was the worsening polarization: Each time Parliamentarians seemed to be going too far in favoring radicals, sectaries, and republicans, all anathema to the country gentlemen, something new turned up to tie Charles Stuart to the Pope, the King of France, the Jesuits, the Spanish army, or the Irish Catholics. In 1641, after Protestants were killed during a

Catholic uprising in Ireland, one Irish leader waved a commission from Charles I, forgery though it was. Come autumn 1642, as war broke out, the King's new appointments in his northern army—one-third of the officers and two of the infantry regiments were Catholic—were taken as a vindication of Parliament's suspicions. In 1643, Charles signed a "cessation" with the Irish rebels in order to free up troops for his armies in England, which again struck English moderates as appeasement of Irish Catholicism. Then in 1645, the King's correspondence, captured with his baggage train at Naseby and quickly published by Parliament, documented royal attempts to seek aid from many sources, including the Irish and the Pope.[19]

These fears and tribalisms, more than others, shaped loyalties during the early war years. The *embroidery* was economic and constitutional—the concern over unlawful taxes and over monopolies versus enterprise and even more prominently, the high legal theory of the Grand Remonstrance and the Nineteen Propositions. However, the *fabric* of the conflict was religious: Would England become Popish or Puritan—or remain Anglican? Clearly, the gentry and yeomanry thought a lot about local issues, oppressive war taxes, the billeting of unruly soldiers, or cavalry riding down their crops. But most also pondered the ongoing national dilemma of 1642–1643: Was it better to risk a resumption of Charles's abusive government and Popish plots or the further unfolding of Parliament's predilection for constitutional and political radicalism and the hint of possible military dictatorship?

Nationwide analyses are scanty, but twentieth-century studies of individual English counties have identified religion as the decisive factor in allegiances—in Puritan Essex, Royalist-leaning Herefordshire, divided Lancashire, and also in the West Country, Yorkshire, and the northern Marches.[20] In most shires, Catholics and pro-episcopacy Anglicans accounted for two-thirds to three-quarters of the gentry and nobility active on behalf of the King. Among the same upper strata, those who favored Parliament were mostly Puritans or episcopacy-doubting moderate Anglicans. The centrality of religion was underscored by 1642 riots in Puritan Essex, where the peasantry was almost entirely Protestant, while a number of noble families were Catholics and Royalists. The angry common folk attacked only these *Catholic* aristocrats; a class-based rising would have attacked the Protestant nobility as well. Similarly, England's seaports and cloth towns added up to a display of Parliamentary fidelity, but essentially because these centers were also *Puritan*. A map of England shaded one way for relatively high percentages of Catholics and another for the major Puritan concentrations would most closely capture the underlying polar geography of the 1642–1645 conflict. Its regional contours would resemble the actual loyalties of 1643 set out in Map 2.1.

Religious disagreement, in short, was a principal spur to the war as it developed by 1642—and the principal explanation of the alignments on both sides. Grasping these divisions is essential preparation for understanding the next cousins' war, because many of them would come again in 1775–1783, although Anglicans would constitute a smaller portion of the combatants.

England, America, and the Conservative Reactions to Civil War Excesses

England's first and only republic, declared in 1649, was at best a partial success. Over the next eleven years, its political alignments shifted and sagged until the ultimate decision to restore the monarchy. Much as King Charles's constitutional transgressions and foreign flirtations cost him his throne, the new regime's own republican excesses bred its eventual downfall. However, the effects—and the memories created—were quite different in England than in the still small and sparsely settled American colonies.

While this book is not about those Parliamentary excesses, they became apparent early. In December 1644, leaders of the House of Commons, bolder after 1642 as Royalists were expelled, realized that its next monthly fast observance, normally the occasion for a politically suitable sermon, would fall on December 25, Christmas Day. Their response was an ordinance entitled "For better observance of the Monthly Fast," which deplored how the upcoming Wednesday, commonly called the "Feast of the Nativity of Christ," was a day on which "men took liberty to carnal and sensual delights, contrary to the life which Christ himself led on earth." In 1645, Parliament simply banned Christmas and Easter.[21] In his own town of Ely, Cromwell, although a lover of melody, cleared Ely Cathedral in 1644 because he opposed its choral music. Few applauded save sectarians and stalwart Puritans.

By 1645 and 1646, the reins of power in England were shifting to steel-gloved hands. The Parliamentary side's authority rested less and less on the popularity of its arguments and more and more on smoothbore muskets, pikes, and cannon. Chaplains and Psalm singing notwithstanding, the army was not unfailingly moral; its largest cannon, captured from the Royalists in 1643, continued to be nicknamed "Sweet Lips," after a whore in Hull.[22] Yet in politics and religion alike, many members of the Parliamentary army were well to the left of the legislature itself, most regiments being accompanied by political instructors (called agitators), and officered by a considerable number of religious radicals—Quakers, Ranters, Familists, and other sectarians. Instead of a Puritan Protestant state church, the sectaries, including those in the army, demanded freedom of worship. Instead of a king or Parliament, "Levelers"—an egalitarian movement powerful in the army—wanted a broader democracy, albeit one still dependent on a certain amount of property.

By the end of the eighteenth century, freedom of worship and democracy would stand for progress. Prematurely propounded in the mid-seventeenth, they stood for incipient chaos. Among those most torn, most aware of both the need to suppress liberty of religious conscience and the irony of having to do so, was Oliver Cromwell himself.

Many Englishmen who had supported Parliament in 1642–1644 balked at the new developments of 1646–1647, from the army's new political eminence to the rise of the Levelers and their draft constitution called "The Agreement of the People." So did most of Parliament's former Scottish Presbyterian allies. The Scots, indeed, switched their allegiance to King Charles, although he was once again defeated, this time with finality, at another great battle at Preston, Lancashire, in 1648. Cromwell, now speaking for the army more than for Parliament, assumed even greater control.

East Anglia, with its belief in ordered liberties and relatively conservative middle-class Puritanism, shared some of the displeasure. Many of the Baptists, Quakers, Familists, and other sectaries gaining influence in London came from the more emotional and less bookish, less rational culture in the English north and west.[23] As people chose sides in the years leading up to the war, Puritan leaders in southern and eastern England had described the northern counties, Wales, and Cornwall as "dark corners of the land." They lacked Puritanism, schools, and middle-class sobriety, to say nothing of the neat, commercial influence of the Dutch.

By the late 1650s, the erstwhile dark corners had taken the lead in producing a very different, less sober and more enthusiastic, sort of sectarianism. The Quakers, still given to going naked for a sign and other provocations, started in the north. George Fox, their leader, came from Lancashire. The Baptists, for their part, were especially strong in Wales. Christopher Hill has traced the northern origins of many of the leading Ranters, Diggers, Grindletonians, and Familists. These unorthodox radical sects were either given to searching for revealed truth or inclined to antinomianism—a belief in liberation from moral standards and righteousness. As the Civil War broke down old religious structures and loyalties, the radical sects gained on the cautious Puritans of the south and east, many of whom were appalled. By 1656, the Member of Parliament for Southwark concluded that "those that come out of the North are the greatest pests of the nation."[24]

East Anglia's Puritan diaspora in New England was also disappointed. The settlers of Massachusetts Bay had been pleased by Parliament's early victories. They were also grateful for policies, including liberalization of trade, that looked favorably on New England. But the Quakers and other sectaries gaining prominence in the new English regime were unpopular. Governor John Winthrop had penned a broadside against antinomian sectaries in 1637. He had also driven them out of Massachusetts after whipping and executing several.

The authorities in Boston, while ready enough to drop all formal allegiance to Charles I in 1642, were not quite at one with the Parliament that was emerging in 1643–1644. Occasional Royalist ships were allowed to enter Boston harbor, and in 1643, Winthrop organized a New England Confederation, built around Massachusetts Bay, that included only the other single-church colonies—Connecticut, New Haven, and Plymouth. Their target was Roger Williams, in next-door Rhode Island (then called Narragansett Bay), who was leading a revolt against Puritan orthodoxy in favor of extending free worship to Baptists and supporters of antinomian Anne Hutchinson. The politics were complicated because Williams's religious policies were akin to those also gaining ground in England. Thus, in 1644, Parliament's new Warwick Commission for colonial administration sided with New England's leading maverick, extending recognition to the new colony of Rhode Island and Providence Plantations. In one biographer's words, "it hurt Winthrop to find Parliament sanctioning the religious delusions and civil chaos of the Narragansett plantations."[25]

The chaos briefly threatened to spread. Dissidents in Massachusetts Bay, collaborating with Rhode Island, appealed to Parliament to force the staid Bay Colony to eliminate its religious qualification for voting and to establish religious tolerance. But in 1647, the Warwick Commission declined to act, opting to leave Massachusetts alone. Nevertheless, Governor Winthrop wrote in 1648, shortly before his death, that "the newes out of England is very sad." His son Stephen, a colonel under Cromwell, was mixing in radical army politics and espousing liberty of conscience.[26]

The American colonies were affected by the English Civil War, but not torn by it. Virginia was Royalist and Anglican, New England Parliamentarian and Puritan. (Map 2.2 illustrates the divisions.) Of the American mainland colonies, only Rhode Island was sectarian and tolerant. Pennsylvania did not yet exist, although Maryland, chartered in 1632 for a Catholic, Cecil Calvert, Lord Baltimore, had a considerable Catholic population and partial religious tolerance. The principal fighting in English North America was between Catholics and Puritans in Maryland. In 1645, Captain Richard Ingle, a Parliamentarian, seized the Catholic capital at St. Mary's on Chesapeake Bay, and two Jesuit priests were sent to England in chains. Disgruntled Puritans from Virginia had emigrated to the Severn River shortly before, establishing a settlement at Providence (now Annapolis), which became the center of Parliamentary strength. St. Mary's was recaptured by the Calvert faction in 1646. Maryland Puritans defeated the Calvert forces again a decade later in the "Battle of the Severn" in 1655, but the Calverts came back to full power in 1660 with the Restoration.

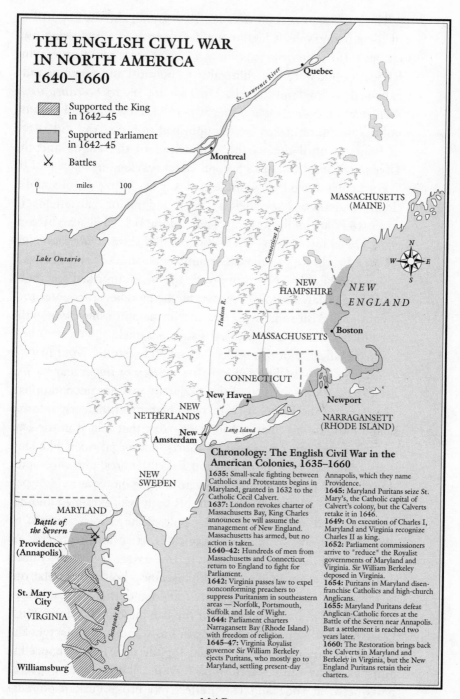

THE ENGLISH CIVIL WAR IN NORTH AMERICA 1640–1660

Supported the King in 1642–45

Supported Parliament in 1642–45

✗ Battles

0   miles   100

Quebec

St. Lawrence River

Montreal

Lake Ontario

MASSACHUSETTS (MAINE)

Connecticut R.

Hudson R.

NEW HAMPSHIRE

NEW ENGLAND

MASSACHUSETTS

• Boston

CONNECTICUT

New Haven •

Newport •

NEW NETHERLANDS

NARRAGANSETT (RHODE ISLAND)

New Amsterdam

Long Island

NEW SWEDEN

MARYLAND

Battle of the Severn

Providence (Annapolis)

St. Mary City

Chesapeake Bay

VIRGINIA

Williamsburg

Chronology: The English Civil War in the American Colonies, 1635–1660

1635: Small-scale fighting between Catholics and Protestants begins in Maryland, granted in 1632 to the Catholic Cecil Calvert.

1637: London revokes charter of Massachusetts Bay, King Charles announces he will assume the management of New England. Massachusetts has armed, but no action is taken.

1640–42: Hundreds of men from Massachusetts and Connecticut return to England to fight for Parliament.

1642: Virginia passes law to expel nonconforming preachers to suppress Puritanism in southeastern areas — Norfolk, Portsmouth, Suffolk and Isle of Wight.

1644: Parliament charters Narragansett Bay (Rhode Island) with freedom of religion.

1645–47: Virginia Royalist governor Sir William Berkeley ejects Puritans, who mostly go to Maryland, settling present-day

Annapolis, which they name Providence.

1645: Maryland Puritans seize St. Mary's, the Catholic capital of Calvert's colony, but the Calverts retake it in 1646.

1649: On execution of Charles I, Maryland and Virginia recognize Charles II as king.

1652: Parliament commissioners arrive to "reduce" the Royalist governments of Maryland and Virginia. Sir William Berkeley deposed in Virginia.

1654: Puritans in Maryland disenfranchise Catholics and high-church Anglicans.

1655: Maryland Puritans defeat Anglican-Catholic forces at the Battle of the Severn near Annapolis. But a settlement is reached two years later.

1660: The Restoration brings back the Calverts in Maryland and Berkeley in Virginia, but the New England Puritans retain their charters.

MAP 2.2

The battles in question were less than grand, and the importance of these paragraphs is less in any details than in a surprising conclusion: *The American colonies of the 1640s and 1650s,* saving Rhode Island, were less vulnerable to political and religious radicalism than England herself. *Most would try to be cautious in their internal policies again in 1775–1783.* New England cultural politics would not resemble the upheaval of the 1640s and 1650s in England until the partial similarities of the 1840s and the 1850s, well into America's Second Great Awakening.

For England, the legacy of the civil war has been painful and difficult to define. The woefully neglected major battlefields of 1642–1645 are an illustration. Those of the U.S. Civil War, by contrast, are hallowed sites—Gettysburg is half shrine, half tourist attraction, with 1,047 separate monuments, statues, and obelisks. Almost nothing has been done with the still-countrified terrain of Yorkshire's Marston Moor, soaked by the bloodiest encounter ever fought on British soil, or Naseby in Northamptonshire, where the site of Parliament's great victory is still an oatfield.

The significance of this neglect is hard to overstate: *What Britons instead chose to celebrate was the restoration of the monarchy under Charles II.* The return of the monarchy was not unconditional. The terms of the Restoration in 1660 reaffirmed the early reforms signed into law by Charles I in 1640–1641 that reined in the Star Chamber and other prerogative courts, extralegal taxes like ship money, the end of monopolies and feudal tenures, and other prewar abuses. Many other changes were undone, however.

Cromwell had died in 1658, but his body was exhumed and decapitated, and his head stuck on a pole. Bishops were restored to office, and a small number of regicides, tried and convicted of complicity in the King's execution in 1649, were themselves put to death. Restoration England quickly became a boisterous polar opposite of the dour Cromwell years: ribald and immoral, and especially gleeful in its suppression of the troublesome Puritans. High Churchmen sought to recast Charles I as Charles the Martyr. The so-called Clarendon Code, named for the new Lord Chancellor and passed by the vengeful new Cavalier Parliament in several parts between 1661 and 1665, effectively broke Puritan political power. These crippling enactments became a chilling symbol in hundreds of towns on both sides of the Atlantic, but they also confirmed the Puritan hegira: New England would indeed be Medina, the new seat of the faith.

The first shackle, the Corporation Act of 1661, reserved to communicants of the Church of England alone the privilege of membership in the municipal corporations that ruled the towns, and in many cases also chose the local Members of Parliament (MPs). Next came the Act of Uniformity of 1662, which reestablished the ritual of the Church of England, after which two thousand Puritan clergy were expelled from the church for refusing to accede. The Conventicle Act of 1664, in turn, punished attendance at religious rites other than those of the established church by imprisonment or transportation. And just to be sure, the Five-Mile Act of 1665 prohibited clergymen and schoolteachers from coming within five miles of a city or corporate town—exactly where most Puritans and their congregations were located—without swearing not to "at any time endeavor any alteration of Government either in Church or State."[27] In fairness to Charles II and the Cavalier Parliament, this was not entirely gratuitous; sectarian provocations continued to be a problem after 1660.[28]

The indirect political impact of the code was also sweeping. Never again would Low Church Anglicans be able to re-create the overt Parliamentary and religious role played by the Puritan squires and nobility in the England of the 1620s and 1630s. As a result, most of the gentlemen of the old Parliamentary strongholds, whatever their earlier inclinations, opted in the 1660s to conform to the established church, thereafter making no great effort to change or secede from it. What they *could do*—and *did*— was seek to limit the church's power in politics.

These efforts were often successful. Not a few of the leaders who banded together in the 1670s and 1680s under the new Whig banner to oppose a new round of Stuart excesses, and whose sons and grandsons would later run England's government during the Whig heyday from 1714 to 1760, came from these old Parliamentary and Puritan-allied families.* They can best be described,

---

*The labeling of the two major factions in Parliament as Whigs and Tories began in 1681, with Whigs as the foes of Stuart practice and prerogative and Tories as the de-

in this new incarnation, as Low Church Anglicans whose politics involved an alliance with what would soon be called middle-class dissenters. In America, this collaboration would be a pillar not just of eighteenth-century Whig politics, but of the effective alliance between Virginians and New Englanders in the Revolution. In Britain, however, the old Parliamentary and Puritan strongholds played a more passive role during the crisis of 1775–1783, as we will see. They signed petitions opposing coercion of the colonies, and many of their MPs were early supporters, especially after 1777, of motions in Parliament for British troop withdrawal. But their doubts were taken no further.

The naivete of the moderates in 1660—their inability to block the Clarendon Code, as well as other weaknesses in negotiating the Restoration—lay in underestimating the vengeance of the high Anglicans and the persistence of the Stuart taste for French gold, autocracy, and personal rule. The extent to which Charles II and especially James II would return to the Catholic faith, to private diplomacy with Louis XIV, and to the Irish, Papal, and army plots of their father constitutes the final chapter in the overthrow of the House of Stuart. After making a secret bargain with Louis XIV in 1670 in which he promised to declare himself a Catholic when

---

fenders, usually, of court and (high Anglican) church. The terms themselves had earlier usages—Tories were Irish Catholic bandits and Whiggamore was a derogatory term for Scottish Presbyterians. However, their employment as abusive political descriptions did not catch on until the late 1670s. Whig views crystallized in the crisis of 1688–1689 around the concepts of limited monarchy and guarantees for liberties and religious freedom. Between 1689 and 1714, under William and Mary and Queen Anne, Tory-Whig rivalry was heated and competitive, but after the accession of the Hanoverian kings in 1714, the Whigs dominated until 1760. George III opposed parties as factions and unnecessary and the old line parties dissolved during the 1760s, despite some re-emergence of what seemed like Tory ideas in the 1770s. By the 1790s, a second Whig-Tory cleavage was emerging around new alignments and issues, and the familiar descriptions were applied again until they were nominally superseded in the mid-nineteenth century by the labels Liberal and Conservative. The use of the terms "Tory" and "Whig" in the American colonies and then in the United States adds a further layer of confusion. Tories were few and far between in colonial legislatures, so the term found its principal application as an epithet for disloyalty—in the Revolution, the War of 1812, and even to a small extent in the U.S. Civil War. Americans of the eighteenth century had been lopsidedly Whig in sympathy, and the name "Whig" was taken in 1836 by the principal opposition to the Democratic Party of Andrew Jackson. This U.S. Whig Party fell apart in the mid-1850s, more or less the same time that British Whigs shifted to the label of Liberal.

English politics permitted, Charles II was given a French subsidy. Within three years, he was appointing a large number of Catholics to high government positions. Parliament, shedding its earlier complicity with the King, passed the Test Act of 1673 to compel their resignation. From 1674 to 1679, the King generally kept Parliament out of session and relied on regular revenues and subsidies from King Louis. The 1680s were about to unfold with more than a hint of the issues of the late 1630s.

The Second Revolt Against the Stuarts

Fraud though he was, the minor adventurer Titus Oates became famous—or infamous—in 1678 by describing a supposed Popish plot: King Charles was to be assassinated, putting the Catholic Duke of York on the throne as James II, which was to be followed with a massacre of Protestants and a French invasion of Ireland. Although fabricated, elements of Oates's tale rang true, prompting the House of Commons to begin what would be an unsuccessful seven-year effort to exclude James from the succession. Each new Parliament passed an Exclusion Act and was dissolved. On his deathbed in February 1685, Charles, somewhat belatedly, did what he had promised Louis XIV a decade and a half earlier by proclaiming himself a Catholic.

The second James Stuart, the former Duke of York, openly Catholic for a decade, took office with a lopsidedly Tory and collaborative House of Commons elected from carefully rearranged districts. However, James II quickly faced other internal suspicions. The Protestant risings by the Earl of Argyll in Scotland and the Duke of Monmouth in the west of England were premature and easily suppressed. More important to Anglicans and nonconformists alike were the events in France where King Louis had just revoked the toleration for Protestants established ninety years earlier in the Edict of Nantes. Fears that James might have something similar in mind mounted when he soon began appointing Catholics to high military positions, the Privy Council, and the Lord Lieutenancy of Ireland, as well as welcoming Franciscan, Dominican, and Benedictine monks to London.

This political and religious commitment to France and Catholicism, surpassing that of Charles I or Charles II, took only three years to produce a second rising against the Stuarts. On assuming the throne, James II had told the French ambassador to "assure your master that he shall always have in me a faithful and grateful servant." England's new monarch even privately apologized for summoning a Parliament without the permission of Louis XIV, because "it is my wish to consult him about everything."[29] English unease grew in June 1688, when the birth of James's first son threatened to ensure a Catholic Stuart succession. Later that summer, word reached London of plans to invade by William of Orange. "Dutch William," as some called him, was the hereditary stadtholder of Holland, leader of Europe's anti-French coalitions, and husband of James's Protestant daughter Mary.

Unnerved by these reports, James started to back down, but it was too late. On Guy Fawkes Day, November 5, 1688, in response to an invitation from a group of English political leaders, Tory as well as Whig, William landed at Torbay and marched on London. Before the month was out, uprisings had secured York, Nottingham, and Chester for William, and James fled. Sailors talked of a "Protestant wind," speeding the Dutch and English ships and bottling up the King's fleet under Lord Dartmouth so it could not interfere.

The invasion itself was worthy of an impresario. William led in the armada's Dutch flagship, and in the words of Thomas Macauley, "more than six hundred vessels, with canvas spread to a favorable wind, followed in his train. . . . His fleet spread to within a league of Dover on the North and of Calais on the South. The men of war on the extreme right and left saluted both fortresses at once. The troops appeared under arms on the decks. The flourish of trumpets, the clash of cymbals and the rolling of drums were distinctly heard at once on the English and French shores." Once ashore, the Protestant army, assembled from a half dozen nations, astounded the country people of Devon with the many faces of England's Protestant deliverance. Parading into Exeter, black colonial soldiers from the Dutch West Indies in embroidered white caps topped by white feather plumes were followed by the King of Sweden's Finnish cavalry in black armor and bearskin cloaks.[30] One wonders what the reaction must have been fifty miles east in the camp of James's army, because within weeks it was melting away.

This is the "Glorious Revolution of 1688," so called because of its ease, speed, and bloodlessness, but something of a spectacle. The central results were lasting: Parliament's supremacy was assured; the future Protestant Succession was laid out; opposition to France was crystallized; and religious tolerance was established for all *Protestants*, although dissenting Protestants were still barred from political office for some years more. Yet in moving against James with reluctance, in only limited numbers, and then partly because the birth of James's son forced their dynastic hand, the English nobility and gentry had been cautious and conservative. Such were the results of how well they remembered the religious, political, and egalitarian Pandora's box that had been opened four decades earlier by revolution and regicide.

By 1688 and 1689, the American colonies were readier to act against their Stuart governors. The hands of Cromwell had not lain so heavily on the New World. He was favorably remembered for suppressing piracy, rebuilding the navy, making overseas trade and development a priority, and passing the Navigation Acts, which ultimately subsidized colonial production of products like tobacco, indigo, and naval stores. Only in the Cavalier sections of Virginia and the Carolinas and among Maryland Catholics were the "Oliverian" years a bogeyman. As dissatisfaction with the Stuarts and their royal governors grew again during the 1670s and 1680s, memories of the 1640s and 1650s, instead of discouraging rebellion, sometimes provided its inspiration. In New York, captured from the Dutch in 1664 and ruled personally by James, Duke of York, Stuart rule was especially autocratic. No permanent elected legislature was authorized until 1691.[31]

Virginia produced the first major insurgency in 1676, twelve years before the Glorious Revolution. It was provoked by the practices of the royal governor, Sir William Berkeley. His family's distinctive twelfth-century castle of pink stone, commanding the lowland corridor between the Cotswolds and the Severn, had been the heart of Gloucestershire Royalism during the English Civil War, and he himself recruited scores of Royalist gentry and younger sons of prominent families to settle in Virginia during the period of Puritan rule in England. As governor, Berkeley recognized Charles II as the rightful ruler after his father's execution and had to be "reduced," albeit without bloodshed, by a Commonwealth naval force in 1652. By the 1670s, he was an aging and corrupt autocrat who governed by dispensing favors to a small plantation elite and taxing everyone else.

The agent of eventual insurrection arrived from England in 1674 in the person of Nathaniel Bacon of East Anglia, educated at Cambridge, the forty-eighth Bacon to read law at Grey's Inn, London. He was a relative and namesake of the Nathaniel Bacon, earlier retired to Virginia, who had been a political theorist for the Parliamentary faction against Charles I and then Master of Requests for Cromwell himself.

Bacon's Rebellion became America's principal pre-1776 insurrection. Near its zenith in June, Bacon sought collaboration between Virginia, the Protestant settlements in Maryland, and the Albemarle settlements of North Carolina. Communications were also opened with far-off Massachusetts Bay. The fighting lasted a number of months, continuing even after the younger Bacon himself died of fever and dysentery. Then it was crushed, although the government in London, aware of Berkeley's own provocation and failures, retired him.

The Commonwealth roots of the insurrection, beyond Bacon's own family, included the hundreds of old Cromwellian soldiers indentured or transported to Virginia. Many still favored a republic, and in the words of historian Stephen Webb, the "revolutionary forms of committee and district, oath and association, convention and ordinance, applied alike in 1642, 1676 and 1776," illustrated the continuity of the revolutionary and republican legacy in America.[32] Given the Royalist character of the plantation elite and Berkeley, it is reasonable to call Bacon's Rebellion a partial, belated extension of the English Civil War.

New England had its own close brush with royal authority in 1676. The initial weakness of the Massachusetts and Connecticut governments against the massive Indian uprising called King Philip's War, which devastated the frontier and brought serious casualties, had all but convinced the Crown that the time was at hand to rescind the several colonial charters, topple Puritan governments, and centralize authority under some kind of New England viceroy appointed by the Crown. Such a show of force could also inhibit the New Englanders from assisting the rebels in Virginia. However, the small English fleet and army that might have cowed Boston was kept occupied putting down Bacon's Rebellion. By the end of the year, the governor of Massachusetts Bay, an old Cromwellian cavalry captain named John Leverett, could breathe easier. The Indians were defeated—the famous Wampanoag chief Metacomet, known as King Philip, was slain that summer—and the hopes of Charles II likewise thwarted.

The succession of James II in 1685, as we have seen, brought matters to a head on both sides of the Atlantic. The hasty challenge by the Protestant Duke of Monmouth, bastard son of Charles II, withered from a fatal lack of support among the English gentry. The Duke himself was callow as well as illegitimate, yet he was popular, and when he landed in the west at Lyme Regis, the yeomen, artisans, and mechanics of the nearby old Puritan districts of Dorset and Somerset flocked to his standard. In Taunton, during a heady, foolish moment, he let himself be proclaimed King. In the ensuing battle of Sedgemoor, Monmouth's untrained local soldiery fought well, but finally broke; he himself was quickly brought to the scaffold. The "Bloody Assize" that followed became a black page of Stuart history. After the King's officers left a trail of hundreds of executions across the West Country, the ships for New England were packed full enough to cause food shortages on the ocean voyages.

Prickly Massachusetts, virtually independent under its 1629 charter, was no more popular with Stuart officials than Monmouth—or a secret Puritan conventicle in Dorset. The Court of Chancery had invalidated the Massachusetts charter in 1684, and two years later, Sir Edmund Andros, a royal administrator based in New York, began to implement a far-reaching plan: to merge the New England colonies into a Royal Dominion of New England. Direct subservience to London was the objective. In 1688, New York and New Jersey were merged into the dominion.

The tinder of transatlantic rebellion now awaited only the spark. Historian Richard Bushman, in his study *King and People in Provincial Massachusetts*, summed up the new Dominion as "the realization of all of Massachusetts' nightmares of oppression and avarice." Not only did Andros govern, in James's name, without an assembly, but "through two and a half years, the colony endured excise taxes, excessive fees or licenses and deed registrations, a requirement to register their lands under the Crown in place of questionable titles from town corporations and the fear of an Anglican or perhaps even a Roman ecclesiastical establishment."[33] Massachusetts leaders knew only too well what had happened to English Puritans under the Clarendon Codes. Not surprisingly, the proclamation of William and Mary in May 1689 following the Glorious Revolution produced "the most joyous celebration the colony had ever seen." Andros himself was thrown in jail.

But colonial political hopes were less than fulfilled. True, the short-lived Dominion of New England, New York, and New Jersey was abolished. Charter government returned to Massachusetts. Officials in Connecticut, who in 1689, rather than turn in their charter, hid the document in what became Hartford's hallowed Charter Oak, were allowed to keep it. New York got a permanent representative assembly. Maryland Protestants, having seized power from the Catholic Calvert family, succeeded in having King William proclaim a royal colony. But the new rulers were practical rulers, not Protestant idealists. William of Orange was a veteran of military campaigns and continental realpolitik; Mary was the daughter, granddaughter, and great-granddaughter of three Stuart kings. Massachusetts got a charter back, but not the old one. The new version disallowed provincial restraints on voting by non-Puritan Protestants. The newly dominant Protestants of Maryland found that their legislature was vulnerable to royal prerogative power, and so was the new assembly in New York.

An even greater caution lay in the mixed fortunes that confronted the organizers of the several rebellions. In Massachusetts and Maryland, where the local power structure was behind them, the ringleaders thrived. Not so in New York, where the 1689 rebellion against the authorities was led by Jacob Leisler. A middling merchant and the son of a Calvinist minister from the German Palatinate, Leisler rallied artisans, farmers, and middle-class merchants against privileged factions in Manhattan and Albany and made himself governor. Popular suspicion of Catholicism was also involved. Thomas Dongan, just retired as governor, was a Catholic, one of several appointed to high positions by James in New York, his personal colony, while he was still Duke of York. Dongan's successor, Francis Nicholson, kept on Dongan's Catholic officials, and Leisler and his militants voiced their distrust of Catholic appointees to carry on the war breaking out with France. War parties were already raiding south from Quebec.

Leisler's fatal illusion lay in relying on the same rhetoric being voiced in England circa 1689: insistence on the rights of Englishmen and distrust of Catholicism and Catholic Stuart officials. Leisler's soldiers, as they expressed themselves, expected to "have parte" of the deliverance obtained by "so happy an instrument" as the new King because they had suffered under the "same oppression."[34] In Massachusetts, where the political elite was all but united, William and Mary accepted the broadly approved overthrow of Andros as an action against the arbitrary government of a Catholic king. Leisler and his lieutenant governor, however, being opposed by much of New York's Anglo-Dutch power structure, were arrested and hanged as rebels by the new Williamite governor shortly after his arrival in 1691. Leisler's name was later cleared. Yet, in a certain sense, the execution remained prophetic.

The essence of the core half century of revolution—the 1640–1690 years encompassing the English Civil War and its consolidating sequel of 1688—was to uphold Parliament and Protestantism, but also to build the framework for an Atlantic political and constitutional divergence. This, we will see, is a continuing characteristic of the Cousins' Wars: to solve one critical problem while also outlining the next one. In the early 1640s, Massachusetts men, led by high ratios of Harvard graduates, flocked to England to fight for a Parliamentary and constitutional cause in which they shared. The rights of Englishmen were not yet categorized geographically. Fifty years later, however, a new division was clear: White, Protestant Englishmen in Massachusetts, New York, Maryland, Virginia, or Connecticut simply did not have the same rights as their uncles and cousins in Devon and Essex.

The Revolution of 1688 was conservative, and also English, with only limited applicability to the American colonies. No rebellion in New York or Maryland could automatically be justified by mere analogy to the overthrow of James Stuart in England. New Yorkers who insisted that their actions were "not only encouraged but invited" by Parliament's and William's own examples found no agreement. Provincials referring to "fellow subjects" in England missed an equally vital distinction. The colonists were not regarded as equal participants in the English Revolution. They could not safely take it upon themselves to jail abusive officials in New York or Boston just as other Englishmen had in Hull and Dover. They were not exactly fellow subjects; their rights were ambiguous. Most of all, colonial legislatures were not little parliaments. When one colony sent to London a proposed charter that borrowed several Parliamentary privileges for its legislators—right of triennial meetings and immunity from arrest—the request wasn't taken seriously.[35] There was only one true Parliament and it was now fused with the King, a lesson Americans would have to learn again in the 1770s.

Within England, the overthrow of James II became a revolution "glorious" for sidestepping the potential chaos of civil war, minimizing popular participation, and institutionalizing an unusual amalgam of conservatism and representative government. These results served *Britain* well in the coming century. The Revolution of 1688 lacked comparable stature in the future United States, though, because it signaled an inevitable political inequality within the English-speaking world. Two rival political traditions were taking shape—and before another century would pass, another gathering rat-tat-tat of drums would send cousins to fight cousins.

The Rival English-Speaking Political Traditions

The politics with which the American colonies entered the 1770s was planted most in the heritage of the Commonwealth and English Radical Whig (and Scottish) interpretations of the seventeenth century. Its principal architects were the New England Yankees who still likened the Stuarts to biblical tyrants, Baptists and sectaries who remembered Cromwell as a patron, Ulster Irish whose own "Glorious" events were the Protestant victories at the Siege of Londonderry and the Battle of the Boyne, and the heirs of Scottish Covenanters, who still told young children to be quiet "or Clavers'll get ye." The reference was to John Graham of Claverhouse, Viscount Dundee, whose Royalist dragoons sabered their way through the lowland Scottish countryside of the 1680s. By the 1760s, even a fair number of the economically pressed tobacco planters of Chesapeake Bay were ripe for a more radical view of politics. As a new British imperialism fanned colonial indignation, the old seventeenth-century embers caught fire again.

A different view held sway in Britain. In late seventeenth-century England, among wearier and more sophisticated elites, the predominant legacy of the English Civil War was to rue the 1640s and to be glad that the upheaval of 1688 had been both successful and restrained. Through the middle of the eighteenth century, this establishment opinion would support Whiggism in upholding the Protestant succession and squelching Stuart pretenders. By the 1760s and 1770s, however, given the needs of the extensive new empire, it was ready for a new and aggressive global policy little concerned with colonial rights and transcending the old Tory versus Whig divisions of the later Stuart years. Only a minority clung to the old Radical Whig viewpoint that enjoyed much greater popularity in North America.

British historians of the nineteenth-century Whig school have long since catalogued the beneficial effects for England of the Civil War. Widely recognized results included modernizing the old guild-and-monopoly-ridden economy of the Stuarts; developing trade, the navy, and the empire; and creating a debate over constitutional and religious liberty that, despite excesses, could be resolved in acceptably moderate form in 1688. Adherents voiced the usual paeans to John Locke and the Glorious Revolution, seeing a great historical progression from the chaos of 1640–1649 to the consummation of 1688.

But antidemocratic perceptions and hostility to innovation better reflected the mood in ruling circles. The regicide and radicalism of 1640–1660, which this book understates by treating only in passing, seared the soul of the English gentry and nobility for at

71

least a century. As a result, the Revolution of 1688, extraordinary in the endurance of its settlement, also had aspects of a conservative preemptive move to ensure that Stuart excesses would not uncork democracy a second time. The rising of artisans and yeomen in the West Country for the Duke of Monmouth in 1685—a rare popular mobilization—must have been as frightening to moderates among the gentry as the open participation of Jesuits in James Stuart's Privy Council. *Both* had to be avoided.

Modernization of the economy aside, the most lasting aftereffects of the Civil War in England itself were conservative, antirevolutionary, and even reactionary. Electoral reforms begun under Cromwell—in particular, the redistribution of seats in Parliament to areas of recent population growth—were reversed during the Restoration era and effectively abandoned for another 170 years. In matters of law, education, prisons, and local government, not only the reforms made under the Commonwealth were swept away. So were further plans for revision. The disturbance unleashed by the Civil War made even modest political change anathema, which explains the persisting discrepancy between England's innovative economy and what remained in some ways ancient, unreformed institutions.[36]

In North America, disparate legacies from the civil war era mattered little in the first half of the eighteenth century. Colonies that had been at loggerheads with the Stuarts turned a corner after 1714. They proved distinctly *unrevolutionary* under the Whig governments basically sympathetic to Protestant dissenters that ruled in England most of the time through 1760. Whig policymaking in London generally ensured the collaboration of essentially Whig elites in Charleston, Hartford, and Philadelphia. And of course, the thirteen colonies were entirely untroubled by—in fact, they were repelled by—the principal insurrectionism that still bothered England and Scotland: the serious Jacobite and Tory-linked attempts to restore Stuart kings in 1715 and 1745, along with several lesser episodes.* Conservative and High Church-

---

*Jacobites were Stuart supporters so named for their adherence to Jacobus Rex—King James II or his son, the putative James III, also known as the "Old Pretender."

linked rebellion was not a threat in America. The Whig ministries of the era could take Essex County, Massachusetts, Suffolk County, New York, and King George County, Virginia, as much for granted as the English home counties of Essex and Suffolk or the anterooms of Kensington Palace. Boston, like Ulster, held annual parades demonstrating against the Pope and the Stuart pretenders living in Paris or Rome.

Indeed, the colonies at mid-century were filling their maps with tributes to the undemanding House of Hanover that replaced the Stuarts—counties named Hanover and New Hanover in Virginia and North Carolina, along with Hanover townships in New Jersey, Pennsylvania, and Virginia. Other counties were named for two more German territories with Hanoverian links: Lunenburg and Brunswick. Virginians waxed especially salutary, naming new counties King and Queen, King George, Brunswick, Frederick (for Prince Frederick, the eldest son of George II), and Prince William. In the early 1760s, North Carolinians and Virginians named several cities and counties Charlotte or Charlottesville, in tribute to Charlotte of Mecklenburg, the new queen of the new young King George III. These christenings amounted to a geographic portrait gallery of the American colonies' shared pride in British nationalism.

Unpopular names put on the lands during those years would be wiped away during the Revolution—for example, Tryon County, New York; Bute County, Virginia; and Dobbs, Bute, and Tryon Counties, North Carolina. These were named for a Tory British first minister, the Earl of Bute, and for two controversial royal governors. The Hanoverian tributes remained, however, along with counties and towns in Pennsylvania, Virginia, New Jersey, Georgia, and North Carolina that saluted another special colonial favorite, William Pitt, Earl of Chatham, a principal figure in the British government during much of the Great War. Like the New England names that recalled Puritan homes in seventeenth-century East Anglia and the Pennsylvania commemorations of the battles and settlements of Northern Ireland, the Whig heritage of 1714–1760 was a connection of which Revolutionary Americans remained proud.

Not surprisingly, the parts of Britain that were still slippery underfoot for the House of Hanover during the first half of the eighteenth century were the polar opposites of Whig America—the northern and western sections of England that had been Stuart-inclined during the 1640s, plus Scotland and Ireland. Nor was this threat vague, quaint, or unimportant. Had the English government, between 1689 and 1745, been less traditionalist, less conservative, more democratic, more radical in removing the Test Act and letting dissenters into high office, then one of the attempts to restore the Stuarts *might* have succeeded.

In 1715, for example, the forces of James III (James Edward Stuart, the Old Pretender, son of James II) moved south from the highlands to the Scottish border and then down the old Stuart invasion highway of 1648 through Westmorland, Cumberland, and into still partially Catholic, rural Lancashire. That army failed to get beyond Preston, Lancashire, a battleground which thereby became twice fatal for Stuart ambitions. But as several historians have noted, the results might have been otherwise: "Had a Scottish rising against the domination of England been properly prepared and judiciously timed with effective English risings in the northern and western counties, 'the Fifteen' might have been the first chapter of a bloody struggle for the throne."[37]

The second major rising in 1745 followed much the same political geography. The grandson of James II, Charles Edward Stuart, the Young Pretender, raised his standard at Glenfinnan and won an important early battle at Prestonpans. But Louis XV of France, who had been assembling an invasion of England in 1744, held back in 1745. When the Prince marched south, following the familiar family invasion path through Lancashire and this time penetrating into Derbyshire, French help was missing. His troops were mostly Scottish, principally highlanders. Just three hundred raw recruits joined him in England, largely Catholics from the Manchester area.

Yet the rising was more than a romantic absurdity, the stuff of Hollywood or Scottish balladeers. The failure of the "Fifteen" had not been a national political or cultural watershed; the defeat of the "Forty Five" would be. Its pain and division, however, ultimately would be liberating for Scotland and Britain alike.

The Stuart invasion, having gathered over several months in early 1745, caught George II visiting Hanover and the British army less than prepared. The early Jacobite success at Prestonpans was doubly important because it forced Scots to choose sides, and in doing so, they defined themselves far more boldly than in 1715—and with great consequences. The highlands generally supported Charles Stuart, the Catholic clans especially. The Anglican gentry, strong north and east of the River Tay, were also Jacobites; their intense hostility to the Presbyterians, who had secured church establishment in Scotland from the Hanoverians, all but ensured their support for the Stuart cause.

Two other important segments of Scotland, meanwhile, rallied to the Hanoverians. The merchants of western seaports like Glasgow, prosperous from trade with the Americas, were under no illusion what a Stuart restoration, with its presumed subservience to France, would mean for the empire. Commercial Glasgow opposed the Stuarts with men and money; its Presbyterian clergy preached sermons of loyalty to George II while armed highlanders occupied the city. To the southwest, Glaswegian support for the Hanoverians was echoed in the old Covenanter strongholds a mere dozen miles across the Irish Sea from Ulster. Just three counties of Scotland, all southwestern, sent loyal addresses to King George: Ayr, Kirkudbright, and Dumfries. A generation later, this same section of Scotland would be the only one to show real support for the Whiggish rebels in America. The role of the Scots in the 1775–1783 American war, already in the making, would be yet another extension of the older fights, as we will see in chapter 5. Images of these earlier British fratricides—from Psalm-singing Puritan militia to kilted highlanders screaming Gaelic curses— would return again on Revolutionary battlefields from New England to North Carolina.

For a few weeks in 1745, however, as the Stuart army passed through Lancashire and entered Derbyshire on December 4, even some Londoners began to worry. Those who understood the marching speed of the Scottish highlanders worried that the Stuart force was closer to the capital city than was the worn-out Hanoverian army. The news reached London on Friday, December 6, causing a bank panic and adding the term "Black Friday" to English usage. Here, too, at least a few historians have suggested the outcome *could* have been different: Had the Prince's army not turned back at

Derby, but marched on London and defeated the small English force available at Finchley, just north of the city, the English Tories might have risen and the French could have intervened.

This seems far-fetched. Enthusiasm for the Stuarts was negligible in the booming western ports, where Scotland's commercial future and growth lay, and mute even in the northern and western parts of England where the Teutonic manners, mind-set, and mistresses of the Hanoverians were still a butt of Tory jokes. Had the Prince kept advancing from Derby, the odds are that his army would have been overwhelmed within weeks. Retreat postponed that fate until the final defeat at Culloden in April 1746.

Defeat brought brutal suppression to the highland clans. Several of their chiefs were executed and clansmen were forbidden to wear their kilts—except as a uniform while serving in the British army, which gained enlistments accordingly. But precisely these imperial uniforms, opportunities, and profits turned out to hold Scotland's future. Indeed, the death throes of the old Stuart cause made possible the emergence of a new imperial coalition which, in the 1760s and 1770s, included yesteryear's Jacobites and looked askance on the increasingly rebellious American colonials as Oliverians. This loose grouping, committed to strong government for a strong and expanding empire, would combine some Whig merchants and conservative Whigs with arch-conservative Tories no longer tainted by Stuart sympathies, as well as with several other English Parliamentary factions, the bulk of the naval and military interest, and the new political machine emerging in Scotland. The Whig and Tory labels of the earlier eighteenth century no longer applied.

This, in turn, meant an end to the era of British politics that held relatively lightly on the reins of colonialism in North America. By 1771, the sympathetic former Whig officials for whom so many American counties and towns were being named—Pitt, Camden, and the rest—were moving into opposition against the ministry of Lord North. George III, who disliked Pitt, had removed him soon after becoming king. The Britain of the 1760s and 1770s had a new internal politics to accompany a changing relationship with its oldest and most populous colonies, which were discovering more and more reasons for frustration. The American provinces' divergent sectarian makeup, along with the constitutional subordination visible even in the 1690s but ignored in the later era of good feeling, was about to come to the fore. The milieu of a new English revolution in North America was now at hand.

3

AMERICA, 1763–1775

The Inheritance of Revolutionary Conflict

Close study of the areas committed to one side or the other supports the view that ethnic and religious differences were important determinants of Revolutionary behavior.

—John S. Shy, *A People Numerous and Armed*, 1976

The effective, triggering convictions that lay behind the Revolution were derived not from common Lockean generalities but from the specific fears and formulations of the radical publicists and opposition politicians of early eighteenth-century England who carried forward into the age of Walpole the peculiar strain of anti-authoritarianism bred in the upheaval of the English Civil War.

—Bernard Bailyn, *The Origins of American Politics*, 1968

At the time of the English Revolution, New England, high and low, shared an identification with Cromwell. In defeat, Cromwell entered popular tradition, where he was stored in folklore—in legend and place lore—for more than a century. By the mid-eighteenth century the high political culture had come to reject the tradition, or at best to bury it; meanwhile the revival of enthusiastic religion invigorated it in popular culture. Beginning in 1765, a time of deep political crisis replicating the dramatis personae *and plot of the seventeenth-century drama, the old political tradition was recovered.*

—Alfred A. Young, *English Plebeian Culture and 18th Century American Radicalism*, 1984

THE THIRTEEN COLONIES, led by New England and Virginia, the oldest among them, revolted in 1775 because they were maturing toward readiness for self-government and well able to imagine a new independent nation reaching to the Mississippi or even beyond. But rebellion came also because their people were inheritors of the spirit of 1640 and 1688 and because the provocations of British colonial policy in America after 1763 resummoned old ghosts of feared plots and tyrannies.

The colonists began the decade of 1764–1774 with a slumbering but powerful political legacy and folk history, British and British-American, to call upon. George III and his ministers were not seventeenth-century Stuarts; nor were their tactics and demands invariably unreasonable, although some were. Yet because the ambitions of imperial Britain and America were diverging, the fuse of insurrection was being lit.

To frame the outbreak of conflict, this chapter will explore five areas of serious disagreement between the colonies and the Crown, the lines of which cut across neat subject-matter categories. North America's critical pre-1775 clashes were hybrids that transcended the modern divisions of scholarship into military science, constitutional law, politics, religion, public finance, geography, and demography.

Each of these disciplines has its own lexicons, statistical approaches, models, or other devices that tend to emphasize one thread of the story, bolstering what become more or less one-dimensional explanations for the Revolution. Among the more important of these are: the Revolution as the self-assertion of American colonies that no longer needed military protection against France; the war as a fight over diverging interpretation of the rights of Englishmen and the British Constitution; the struggle as another Puritan and "Presbyterian" vendetta against bishops and monarchical Anglicanism and Catholicism; the resort to force as an economic rebellion against Britain's post-1763 imperial resubordination of the colonies to the mother country's commerce; and the embrace of revolution as an early version of class warfare in which less prosperous colonists were hoping to topple their own conservative provincial elites as well as the King and his ministers.

No single one-dimensional thesis explains the war, however; not even two or three together. As the foreword has noted, grand abstractions about what caused Americans to rebel in 1775 can appear pompous or even foolish set against the local evidence of how people chose sides or, at least as often, tried to avoid doing so. None of the sweeping theses set out above can satisfactorily include the behavior within all thirteen provinces, given the importance of sectarian, factional, or ethnic variations. Regional differences and parochialisms were significant in the English Civil War. They were even more important in the British Atlantic civil war that we call the American Revolution.

For a lead-in to the events of 1775–1783 and why the fighting started, the theories stated two paragraphs back all have relevance. They were part of the backdrop. Yet to pursue the war's motivations and loyalties, it is better to examine broader areas of developing conflict, the critical disagreements between Britain and America in the decade before Lexington and Concord, how they grew and who they impacted: first, the colonists' changing perceptions of military security and safety—British soldiers and ships as the new threat; second, the importance of religion, from evangelism to anti-episcopacy, as a critical pre-1775 inflammation; third, the fight over the power, politics, and principles involved in the governmental relationship between Britain and the thirteen mainland colonies; fourth, the economics involved, from mercantilism and trade practices to tax burdens and currency regulation; and fifth, the colonial desire for westward expansion and fulfillment of the dream of a New Israel and a new chosen people. From this framework, the four chapters that follow in Part Two will pursue the alignments of the Revolution and the war's broader significance on *both* sides of the Atlantic.

But before tackling these other questions, it is necessary to make brief mention of the war that raged in North America from 1754 to 1763 and in Europe from 1756 to 1763, identified as the French and Indian War by the colonists and as the Seven Years War by Europeans. One of its most prominent chroniclers, Laurence H. Gipson, has called it the Great War for the Empire, and that name, sometimes shortened to the Great War, best conveys its eventual disruption of British relations with the North

American colonies. After 1763, the evolution of British imperialism itself became a provocation.

It makes no sense to contend, as some historians have, that New England, with its heritage of rebellion and its scent of manifest destiny, would have been tame in 1775 if France, beaten in 1763, had nevertheless been allowed to keep Canada. Had King Louis's regiments still menaced the northern border, the argument goes, that would have obliged the American colonials to continue to shelter under British protection. This assertion misunderstands why conflict between Britain and the thirteen colonies intensified so quickly after 1763 and why Americans felt obliged to fight by 1775.

In 1763, Britain's military triumph over France was so complete—in Europe, in North America, and on the high seas—that Parliament and the King's ministers were able to decide what territory they would keep after the peace treaty and what they would return. Gluttony would have been impolitic; ingesting too much would have been unworkable in balance-of-power terms. The practical question was which plum British negotiators should demand: France's West Indian sugar islands, Martinique and Guadeloupe; or Canada, which included not just the St. Lawrence Valley but also former French Louisiana east of the Mississippi, most notably the Ohio Valley. The threefold argument for taking Canada, besides its presumed rich fur trade, was that: (1) The war had begun in North America in 1754 as a struggle for control of the Ohio Valley; (2) the French had been thrashed so decisively, up and down the whole continent—from Louisbourg, Quebec, and Montreal to Forts Duquesne on the Ohio and Detroit on the Great Lakes—that they could not, plausibly, be left in occupation; and (3) the English West Indian sugar planters, a powerful faction in Parliament, feared the new competition within the empire that would come from incorporating France's sugar islands and their lower-cost production.

In theory, Britain could have taken only what had been eastern Louisiana—the territory from the Great Lakes to the Ohio and between the Appalachians and the Mississippi. This would have involved handing back Old Canada, essentially the St. Lawrence Valley with its seventy-five thousand French-speaking Europeans, to France, in which case the reaction in Massachusetts, Connecticut, and New York, where legislatures had voted large amounts of men and money for the campaigns against Old Canada, would have been outrage. Besides, this crippled remainder of sparsely populated New France would not have overawed the English mainland colonies, which by 1765 were approaching a population of two million. To threaten seriously, Paris would have to have sent massive and costly (and unlikely) reinforcements.

To keep the Gallic specter real, British peace negotiators would have had to restore to France not just the St. Lawrence Valley, but the Great Lakes, the Ohio Valley, and the trans-Appalachian South, which would have mocked Britain's enormous sacrifice of men and money, to say nothing of London's ambitions to control the North American fur trade. The New Englanders, one must remember, had been furious in 1697 and 1748, when British peace negotiations returned first Port Royal in Nova Scotia and then the great fortress of Louisbourg to France after each had been conquered by expeditions in which New Englanders played a major role. To restore defeated France's lost North American territory in 1763, thereby raising the ghosts of seventeenth-century Stuart kings, would probably have seeded a different American Revolution. However, reversion to collusion with France was not the problem in Whitehall. The challenge to the easygoing waywardness of the thirteen colonies was developing out of a quite different evolution of British politics and mind-set: a consolidation of imperialism within the now-expanded empire.

The Great War had begun to submerge the turn-of-the-century Tory-Whig cleavages, and the transition accelerated in 1760 when young George III, English-born (1738) and English-raised, and personally aroused against the factionalism of party, succeeded his German-born and German-oriented grandfather, George II, on the throne. The new King had been brought up by his mother in a household and political circle (called Leicester House for the family residence) very much at odds with his grandfather's Teutonic court and Whig advisers. The new King's mother, Princess Augusta, urged her son, in words that became famous, to take firmer hold of the government instead of relying on the Whig leaders who had instructed George I and George II. Imperial insistences were one such lever.

America's Changing Perception of Military Security and Public Safety

By 1775, changing colonial perceptions of American security and public safety had become a major irritant. This was less because the removal of French troops from Canada in 1763 freed otherwise satisfied colonists to rebel than because resentment of British redcoats and Royal Navy vessels grew enough over the next decade to rekindle old fears of an abusive military. Colonists no longer worried about French warships off Nantucket or French Indians whooping out of Pennsylvania forests. The emerging military bogeyman of the pre-Revolutionary decade was British.[1]

The elimination of the French military threat from Canada counted most where it was also most quickly forgotten: in next-door New England. Colonists in Pennsylvania, Virginia, and the southern provinces saw less difference. The Shawnee, Cherokee, and Creek tribes, with American settlers edging into their lands, needed no outside encouragement to make war.

Hitherto, except during the years of actual war with France, peacekeeping in North America had been left to provincial units. Rarely were more than a few companies of British regulars stationed in New York or along the southern frontier in Georgia. The huge cost of the 1754–1763 mobilization had appalled Britain's ruling elite. Skyrocketing debt had meant painful taxes. Now, because the postwar need for regular troops to guard the colonial frontier and Mississippi and Ohio Valley lands surrendered by France promised to continue this unwelcome expense, the government determined to move as much burden as possible to colonial taxpayers.

No sooner had the peace treaty with France been signed than a Royal Proclamation of 1763 prohibited settlers from moving west of a line drawn along the ridge of the Appalachians. Control over these new western lands was consolidated under British rather than provincial authority, even though by the language of their royal charters, the boundaries of Massachusetts, Connecticut, Pennsylvania, and Virginia reached west to the Pacific. The so-called Sugar Act followed in 1764 to maintain the army in North America through revenue from taxing molasses, most of which was being smuggled into the colonies without paying duties. Stricter customs enforcement, another part of the tightening revenue vise, was to be achieved through increased naval patrols and new vice-admiralty courts.

The Proclamation Line was only briefly effective in discouraging new settlements in the over-mountain lands reserved for the Indian tribes, and its provisions were superseded in 1768. But relations between the colonists and the British military had other reasons for deterioration. With the new trans-Appalachian lands needing garrisons, the government decided to increase peacetime regular army strength in what is now the United States from a few units to fifteen battalions totaling seventy-five hundred men. Most were stationed along the frontier or beyond the settlements, but their charge with inhibiting westward movement was unpopular. So was the necessary routing of soldiers through provincial seaports and hinterlands that wanted no part of them.

During the French wars, the King's forces had been economic benefactors as well as popular protectors. Payrolls and purchase orders followed the sound of marching feet. Even in these circumstances, opinion in Boston, Albany, New York, and Philadelphia frayed over the behavior of naval press gangs and demands to house and feed the soldiery. Royal governors might be glad to have more reliable forces than militia at their call, but the colonists, especially in New England, were heirs to English Whig fears of the King's troops as instruments of royal power. The memories of Charles I quartering Irish troops in English towns, of Cromwell's use of major generals to govern counties, and of the concentration of forces by Charles II at Blackheath in 1673 and by James II at Hounslow Heath in 1686 still rankled. Even in 1757, early in the Great French War, prominent Whigs opposed the Militia Bill before Parliament, worrying that it would breed an unwanted military spirit in England.

These issues remained incendiary. Fear of standing armies and suspicion of royal troops had been kept alive in the colonies by politicians and pamphleteers who drew on Radical Whig views that bridged the seventeenth and eighteenth centuries. The two historians who have set out this Anglo-American continuity, Caroline Robbins in *The 18th Century Commonwealthman* and Bernard Bailyn in *The Ideological Origins of the American Revolution,* both emphasize the importance of standing armies in Radical Whig portraiture of despotisms and tyrannies from far-off Turkey to nearby Denmark.[2] As Bailyn has underscored, by the late 1760s, colonists were starting to see the King's troops as part of a larger plot against colonial liberties that even George Washington, John Adams, and Thomas Jefferson took seriously.

The regular battalions being stationed in North America in 1764 were hardly the instruments of a Stuart oppression. Nevertheless, they did justify suspicion of fundamental changes in British policy. Governor William Shirley of Massachusetts had earlier suggested to London that maintaining troops in peacetime would guard against a movement for independence. Also, if Britain needed a larger army to police the enlarged empire, North America might be a convenient station. William Knox, a colonial administrator soon to become deputy secretary of state for the American Department, stated bluntly in 1763 that "the main purpose of sending a large body of troops to America (would be) to secure the dependence of the colonies on Great Britain."[3]

During the Great War, Britain's Mutiny Act, which mandated local assistance to the soldiery, had been held not to apply to the colonies. But to support peacetime military activity, Parliament passed the American Mutiny and Quartering Act of 1765, which required colonial assemblies to provide food and drink, as well as public or private accommodations limited to empty homes and barns.

The Sugar Act, passed the year before to raise revenue for the upkeep of the soldiers, was no great innovation. It replaced the old Molasses Act, with its rarely enforced duty on molasses of six pence a gallon. The new legislation reduced the duty to three pence, but bristled with naval and customs enforcement provisions designed to crack down on its politically charged target. This was the large-scale illicit trade between New England rum producers, who were enormous buyers of molasses, and the sugar growers of the French West Indies, who had large surpluses. There was little home market for molasses because French authorities suppressed rum production to protect wine, cognac, and brandy. Spurned by

Paris, the merchants of Martinique and Guadeloupe gave New England smugglers bargain prices. Yet despite infuriating the New England rum distillers, the new tax enforcement, during its first year, raised a bare one-seventh of the cost of maintaining the transatlantic British army. This shortfall called into play a contingent provision of the Sugar Act: a next-stage imposition of *stamp* duties on the colonies—excise taxes that people in England already paid by affixing stamps to newspapers, legal documents, and the like.

Had the troops been in garrison for the colonists' benefit, constitutional qualms might have been overlooked. But that was not the case. The outcome of the Great War, instead of simply ending America's danger from France, began reconstituting the British military itself as the *new* threat—to westward population expansion, to merchants' vital profits from smuggling, and, more abstractly, to cherished constitutional assumptions.

Until the Sugar Act's inflammatory inclusion of the word "revenue," missing in the old Molasses Act, the government in London had not tried to tax the colonies. Duties on imports were not taxes. Thus the irony: It was to pay for stationing redcoats where colonial Americans didn't want them that Parliament provoked the famous legal protest of "No taxation without representation." This would have occurred even if France had kept what is now *Canada*; this part of the new revenue-and-military crisis was developing over soldiers who were being sent to the existing colonies and to the territory of former French Louisiana beyond the Appalachians.

Trans-Appalachia, no longer a duelling ground of Hanoverians and Bourbons, was now becoming a battleground of British and *American* ambition. Naive officials in London even urged the English-speaking population of the seaboard to spread northward and southward instead of westward: northward to fill up chilly Nova Scotia and to start balancing French-speaking preponderance elsewhere in Canada; southward into malaria country to develop the new colonies of East and West Florida as subtropical plantations. The ministry essentially opposed emigration to where the colonists wanted to go—westward over the Appalachians into the Ohio Valley, the former *belle rivière* of New France.

The purely imperial aspect of British logic was faultless. The endless Indian wars that settlement would provoke, besides being expensive, would disrupt London hopes for a rich fur trade. Ian Christie, a British historian, has pointed out that by 1760, British officials had already begun to detach the Indians from their French alliance by taking over the old French promise to protect their hunting grounds. Over the next year, His Majesty's government intervened with provincial officials to block land grants by Virginia in the Upper Ohio Valley and to bridle New York's encouragement of settlers in the Mohawk Valley. When peace came, military force would be necessary to hold back the surging frontier. "In this context," observed Christie, "the army began to be seen as having a policing role, protecting Red Men against Whites; it was *not* cast for the role of a defense force against the Indians."[4]

The Royal Navy was also becoming an enemy. Illicit American trading with the French had infuriated British officials during the war, and peacetime saw the navy continue to play a central role in interdicting the smuggling that was one of New England's biggest industries—and one of its most lucrative. Only these trading profits, the Yankees claimed, enabled them to pay for the manufactured goods that Parliament required colonists to buy only from Britain.

Unlawful trade was so important economically that colonial courts and juries would rarely convict smugglers. One unpopular provision of the Sugar Act set up a new superior vice-admiralty court in Halifax, Nova Scotia, with jurisdiction over violations of the trade laws up and down the coast. Seized vessels and cargoes were to be sent to Halifax, although other district courts were soon added because of Halifax's distance. To the colonists, the vice-admiralty courts were also an overt threat to liberty. As naval rather than civilian tribunals, these courts dispensed with juries, contrary to the rights of Englishmen. No such practices were allowed in Sussex, Devon, or Cornwall, despite the notoriety of smuggling there, too. "Englishmen" in Massachusetts obviously had a lesser status.

Another bold statute had authorized ships of the Royal Navy to seize vessels engaged in illegal trade while they were still on the high seas. No longer did the navy have to follow merchant barks and brigantines into coastal bays and inlets, where clever captains could hide or quickly unload their cargoes. Forty-four naval vessels were in American waters with orders to pursue suspected smugglers.[5] Colonial leaders, in turn, were determined to fight back, sometimes literally. The fort in Newport, Rhode Island, fired on a British naval schooner as it was trying to seize a smuggler, and in New York, the captain of the sloop-of-war *Hawke* was jailed for an improper seizure.[6] The Royal Navy's new customs-policing role made the senior service as unpopular with merchants, seamen, and ship owners as the regular army was with land speculators, frontier settlers, and traders. In 1710 or 1735, these frictions had been relatively unimportant.

Even after Parliament specifically authorized military officers to require the colonies to provide accommodations, fuel, and food for British troops, Massachusetts refused and New York authorities declined to comply until the order came from the King. Quartering troops was unpopular in itself, but the debate in both provinces also hung on larger fiscal issues and burdens. Strategically located New York contained a disproportionate share of the soldiers stationed in the mainland colonies. The provincial Assembly called it unfair, indeed another unacceptable form of de facto British taxation, to require the one jurisdiction to pay for their supplies and billets.[7] Parliament, unimpressed, replied in 1767 by disallowing the New York Assembly from passing any act until it had complied with the requisitioning order. The ways and means of stationing British military forces in North America were crystallizing into not one, but several, major constitutional debates.

Boston, the epicenter of colonial smuggling, was particularly on edge. The *Liberty*, a large merchant vessel owned by John Hancock, was seized in the summer of 1768 by customs officers within cannon range of the Royal Navy ship *Romney*, a fifty-gun frigate powerful enough to dominate the harbor. Samuel Adams, already a much-heeded agitator, complained in the *Boston Gazette* about "the aid of military power, a power ever dreaded by all the lovers of the peace and good order of the province."[8] Riots followed the seizure, and when customs officials demanded troops, General Gage, the British military commander in North America, ordered four regiments from New York and Ireland to Boston to cope with possible insurrection. By coincidence, they began arriving on the same early autumn day that a special convention of delegates from towns all over Massachusetts met. The delegates' response: to denounce standing armies as dangerous to civil liberty.

That particular crisis produced no further confrontation. But the larger controversy of coercing Massachusetts through a buildup of military forces was just beginning. It would help to ignite the so-called Boston Massacre of 1770, in which troops fired on civilians—a very provocative citizenry, who were at least equally at fault—and, ultimately, the fighting in Lexington and Concord. Parliament's interpretation of the British Constitution and the requirements of post-1763 imperialism were enforceable in New England only by bayonets or the yawning mouths of twenty-four-pound carronades.

Popular antagonism to the British troops stationed in New York and Boston during the pre-Revolutionary decade, by deepening into an important political force, subordinated conflict between the working-class and aristocratic elements of the patriotic movement. Shared opposition to New York's 1769 provincial quartering legislation helped radical leaders reunite with the elite Livingston faction. Bloody fights between soldiers and the populace in lower Manhattan in 1770 even provided lesser local parallels to the "Boston Massacre." Wages in both cities, already depressed because of an economic slump, were reduced in 1770 by the willingness of moonlighting British troops to accept cut-rate employment. In prewar Philadelphia, by contrast, the greater working-class radicalization and emergence of class warfare are partly explained by the absence of British troops to play the unifying role of an external enemy.[9]

As Massachusetts moved toward rebellion, some of British officialdom's vulnerability to the propaganda of men like Sam Adams—his outrage over the Boston Massacre dwarfed his indignation after the seizure of the *Liberty*—could be traced to unprecedented peacetime employment of British military forces in numbers sufficient to outrage the colonists, but not to *control* them. The Boston Tea Party of 1773 finally provoked the critical British counterstrike—the Coercive Acts of 1774, through which a furious Parliament ordered the navy to shut down the port of

Boston, effectively abrogated the Massachusetts charter of 1691, and imposed a new local Quartering Act under which troops could be billeted in private homes. With a malice not applied to recalcitrant Protestant Whigs since the days of James II, Gage was ordered to use his four regiments to achieve "a full and absolute submission."

The transformation of popular attitudes within the thirteen colonies was rare for a single decade. However, something similar had been true in England during the decades leading to 1642 and 1688. Much as the people of Plymouth and Southampton circa 1641 presumably spent little time worrying about yesteryear's Spanish forays, fear of French soldiers and warships was being replaced in the American colonies by popular antipathy to the British army and navy as the new threats to American expansion, prosperity, and liberties. Consider the inflammatory mood of several days in September 1774. After a rumor that six Bostonians had been killed and that the Royal Navy had bombarded the city, thousands of militiamen, perhaps as many as ten thousand, from as far away as Connecticut and New Hampshire, took muskets in hand and marched, turning back only when they heard the news was false. So great was New England's disillusionment with Britain that six years later, Rhode Islanders stood by, with only a small sense of irony, as ships named *Languedoc* and *Tonant* disembarked King Louis's troops—French infantry and cavalry, and even the Irish emigré regiments of Dillon and Walsh—this time back to fight alongside *les Bastonnais* against the forces of King George.

Religion as a Critical Pre-Revolutionary Inflammation

Before sectarian animosities helped to determine which groups fought on what side in 1775–1783, religion in the broader sense helped to bring on the war. The excitement of the religious Great Awakening of the 1730s and 1740s, and its indirect encouragement of a kindred democratic and anti-establishment *politics*, have been widely invoked as a cause of the Revolution by twentieth-century scholars. Many Americans, especially Presbyterians and New England Congregationalists, also believed that as God's chosen people, their fight against tyranny would necessarily enlist divine Providence. Such rhetoric was obviously reminiscent of the 1640s.

King George III and other highly placed Britons, responding in kind, called the colonists' rebellion a "Presbyterian War." One after another, royal governors and Anglican clergy damned Presbyterians and Congregationalists as incipient rebels and "Oliverians." In a twentieth-century introduction to New York Anglican rector Samuel Seabury's 1774 tract, *Letters of a Westchester Farmer*, one American historian concluded that the "religious strife between the Church of England and the Dissenters furnished the mountain of combustible material for the great conflagration, while the dispute over stamp, tea and other taxes and regulations acted merely as the matches of ignition."[10] J. C. D. Clark, an Oxford historian, repeated essentially the same thesis in his late twentieth-century book *The Language of Liberty*, calling the American Revolution "the last religious war."

The English Civil War and the Glorious Revolution of 1688 had been very much about religion—High Church Anglicans and Catholics versus some Low Church Anglicans, Puritans, and sectaries. Similar preoccupations lived on in New England and in the interior settlements dominated by Ulster Presbyterians. Militant Protestants in the American colonies were infuriated by Parliament's passage in 1774 of the Quebec Act, which reestablished the rights of the Roman Catholic Church both in Canada and in the Ohio Valley territory taken from France in 1763, thereby putting French Catholicism in the way of the westward expansion that New England and Virginia believed to have been promised to them. William Pitt shared their indignation. Pauline Maier, a historian of eighteenth-century America, has concluded that subsequent colonial demands for independence grew as much from concern over English "softness" on Catholicism through the Quebec Act jeopardizing colonial liberties as from reaction to unfair taxation or the closing of the port of Boston.[11]

Provincial religious sensitivities had also been aroused during the 1760s and early 1770s by the maneuvers of Anglican clergymen to have the Church of England appoint bishops in the colonies and to strengthen its structure and influence in North America. Here, too, colonists reached back into their seventeenth-century memories and saw a conspiracy. This fear of bishops and what they symbolized is especially hard to convey more than two centuries later. One religious historian notes that "proposals for sending a bishop to America constantly reinforced" not just Puritan but Scotch-Irish and Scots tribal memories of earlier controversies and persecution: "In fact, the drift of American opinion during those years can hardly be explained unless one takes into account the deeply ingrained 'antiprelatical' bias of all but a small percentage of the population."[12] Carl Bridenbaugh has written even more emphatically on the revolutionary thrust of the "great fear of Episcopacy":

> For us of the 20th Century, it is very, very difficult to recover imaginatively a real understanding of the enormous effect of this controversy on the opinions and feelings of a pious, dissenting people grown accustomed to ecclesiastical self-government and currently engaged in a struggle to protect their liberties in the civil sphere. The bad news or threats they read in every week's newspaper produced a cumulative effect like the rising crescendo of a bolero. The agitation over an American episcopate reached its peak by 1770, and the public had grown almost frenzied in the course of it.[13]

Political power was also religious power, witness the Cavalier Parliament's suppression of English Puritanism under the Clarendon Codes a century earlier. Insisting that Parliament had no right to interfere in the religious affairs of the colonies, John Adams, the future president and a close student of seventeenth-century English politics, would recall years later: "If Parliament could tax us, they could establish the Church of England with all of its creeds, articles, tests, ceremonies and titles, and prevent all other churches as conventicles and schism shops."[14] In fact, the Restoration Parliament had done exactly that a century earlier. There was a further correlation, in Whig minds, between pro-High Church or Catholic sentiment and the old Stuart political tendency to constrict religious and constitutional liberties. As the colonists' overall fear of British authority mounted in 1763–1774, the controversies over episcopacy and the Quebec Act both fueled concern.*

To call the American Revolution a religious war is excessive as a *stand-alone* explanation. Religious issues did not overwhelm other discussions as in the 1640s. Yet religion unmistakably *was* a major arena of conflict, not just in these larger senses but also within individual colonies. Small matter that a majority of Americans did not regularly attend church; too many lived on the frontier, or far from churches. Nor is it fatal that anyone who studies colonial life will find the less elevated temptations of taverns equally pervasive. Alehouses outnumbered meetinghouses—and undoubtedly played their own considerable role in generating rebellion. This was especially true in coastal New England, where tavern keepers' ideologies and profits were most bound up with smuggling, the duties paid or evaded on spirits and wine, and the regional politics of rum.

Yet one does well to remember how religion had been the principal reason for the original settlements in New England, Pennsylvania, and Maryland, and how, more recently, the importance of the religious idiom had resurged with the Great Awakening. The enthusiasms of the latter were much more important in the North American colonies than in England. More material was printed in mid-eighteenth-century America about religion than about political science, history, and law combined, and even as the Revolution approached, devotional books outnumbered any single group.[15] The crowd of fifteen thousand that the English revivalist George Whitefield drew in Boston in 1740 was the largest ever assembled in the colonies. By 1776, Congregational ministers in New England were delivering more than two thousand sermons and discourses a week, and just as important, publishing them at a rate that topped *secular* pamphlets from all thirteen colonies by four to one.[16]

---

*Toleration was still a few years from becoming an American theme. The First Continental Congress, meeting in September 1774, expressed outrage to Britons "that a British parliament should ever consent to establish in that country (Quebec) a religion that has deluged your island in blood." J. C. D. Clark argues that "the virulence and power of popular American anti-Catholicism is the suppressed theme of colonial history" (*The Language of Liberty*, p. 273).

In the American colonies, politics and religion remained inextricable. On the eve of battle, as Map 3.1 shows, over half of the provinces had established churches—Anglican in the South, Congregational in New England. In the middle colonies, where no churches were established on a provincewide basis, religious tensions were important enough for politics to develop sectarian alignments. Reference was frequently made to the Quaker party in Pennsylvania, to the Anglican or Church party in both New York and Delaware, and to the Presbyterian party in New York, New Jersey, and Pennsylvania. Henry Melchior Muhlenberg of Pennsylvania, the immigrant Lutheran minister, one of whose sons became a Revolutionary War general, offered this matter-of-fact description of local politics in 1764:

> Never before in the history of Pennsylvania, they say, have so many people assembled for an election. The English and German Quakers, the Hernnhuters, Mennonites, and Schwenckfelders formed one party, and the English of the High Church and the Presbyterian Church, the German Lutheran, and German Reformed joined the other party and gained the upper hand—a thing heretofore unheard of.[17]

The most widely read literature that discussed politics often involved a common context with religion. The only two works of English political reformers reprinted in American versions—the eighteenth-century *Independent Whig* weekly and a seventeenth-century pamphlet by John Milton condemning the Royalist clergy—both emphasized the dangers of church and state combined.[18] When a farmer who had fought at Concord Bridge was asked, years later, whether he had been defending the ideas of English Whig political thinkers, he declared that he had never heard of Locke or Sidney, his reading having been limited to the Bible, the Catechism, Watt's Psalms and Hymns, and the Almanac.[19]

Religion also infused the call to battle in other ways. According to one historian, Reginald Stuart, throughout the colonial era sermons on military occasions reminded New Englanders that struggle held inherent virtue, that war was perpetually likely, and that resort to arms could be morally justified. Too little attention, he

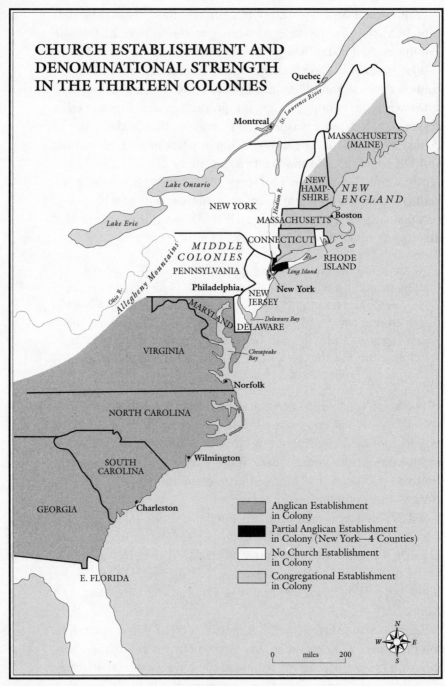

CHURCH ESTABLISHMENT AND
DENOMINATIONAL STRENGTH
IN THE THIRTEEN COLONIES

Quebec

Montreal

St. Lawrence River

MASSACHUSETTS
(MAINE)

Lake Ontario

NEW
HAMP-
SHIRE

NEW
ENGLAND

Hudson R.

NEW YORK

MASSACHUSETTS

Boston

Lake Erie

CONNECTICUT

MIDDLE
COLONIES

RHODE
ISLAND

Allegheny Mountains

PENNSYLVANIA

Long Island

New York

Ohio R.

Philadelphia

NEW
JERSEY

MARYLAND

Delaware Bay

DELAWARE

VIRGINIA

Chesapeake
Bay

Norfolk

NORTH CAROLINA

SOUTH
CAROLINA

Wilmington

GEORGIA

Charleston

Anglican Establishment
in Colony

Partial Anglican Establishment
in Colony (New York—4 Counties)

No Church Establishment
in Colony

E. FLORIDA

Congregational Establishment
in Colony

N
W   E
S

0   miles   200

MAP 3.1

96

contends, has been paid to the complexity of the New Englanders' view of war—one that could simultaneously encourage restraint and urge a crusade against an unrighteous enemy—as an explanation for the coming of the Revolution.[20]

An obvious contagion of antimonarchical arousal was also introduced when "New Side" and "New Light" preachers, who embraced evangelism, revelation, and inner light while assaulting established forms of church government and traditional deference, told their followers not to shrink from challenging tyrannical authority or from abandoning unregenerate "Old Side" or "Old Light" congregations.[21] By and large, the splits within the Presbyterian and Congregationalist churches between the old and new outlooks did not shape alignments in the Revolution a generation later, because compromises and rapprochements developed in the late 1740s and 1750s. Most Old Light Presbyterians and Congregationalists, though more conservative, also supported the patriot cause. It was the *larger* insurrectionist mood of 1775 that owed much to the earlier rebellion in religion.

William Knox, a British undersecretary of state, complained after the fighting started that lack of a prescribed religion in most colonies also stimulated political independence: "Every man being thus allowed to be his own Pope, he becomes disposed to wish to become his own King." Virginia's pro-independence sentiments, despite the local church-establishment of Anglicanism, might seem to contradict Knox, but to religious historian Perry Miller, it was not "genial Anglicanism" or the "urbane rationalism" of the Washingtons, Jeffersons, and Franklins that

> brought the rank and file of American Protestants into the war. What aroused Christian patriotism that needed staying power was a realization of the vengeance God denounced against the wicked; what fed their hopes was not what God promised as a recompense to virtue, but what dreary fortunes would overwhelm those who persisted in sloth; what kept them going was an assurance that by exerting themselves they were fighting for a victory thus providentially predestined.[22]

To the farmer who had been at Concord Bridge in 1775, religion was certainly *coequal* with politics and economics in laying the war's groundwork. As we will see in chapters 5 and 6, sectarian alignments may have been the single most important factor in determining loyalties. On the other hand, one must strain to label an insurgency led—in constitutional assembly and on the battlefield—by Low Church Virginia Anglicans, many influenced by the Enlightenment and even by deism, as "the last religious war." New England began the fighting and provided a stronger religious flavor, as did the fiery Presbyterians of Scotch-Irish Pennsylvanians. But their doctrines did not dominate the new nation or its federal constitution. In those later arenas, urbane rationalism prevailed.

Yet New England's Congregationalist majority did have particular reason to be unnerved, during the decade before 1775, by the petitions of High Churchmen in New England, New York, and New Jersey to have Parliament create American bishoprics. The local ranks of Anglicanism were already expanding in the 1760s, reflecting both English missionary efforts (led by the Society for the Propagation of the Gospel) and the appeal of traditional Anglican ritual to conservative New England Congregationalists offended by the emotionalism and stridency of New Light revivalists. Connecticut saw the strongest Anglican expansion—from thirty churches in 1761 to forty-seven in 1774. The growing ranks of Anglican clergy licensed in London to serve in America made the same point: The church of monarchy, authority, and deference was gaining ground. For New England Puritans, it was not an expansion to take lightly.

The large number of British provincial governors, most of whom were Anglicans, usually tried to build their church, even in New England, as a force for loyalty. From Massachusetts to North Carolina, royal officeholders and Anglican missionaries propounded essentially the same argument: The growth of the church generally meant the growth of loyalty to the Crown. The British cabinets of the late 1760s and early 1770s did not want to pursue the divisive issue of an American bishop. George III, however, liked the transatlantic clerics' proposal. Bishops and monarchs reinforced each other. The already-mentioned Quebec Act of 1774, in which the British government reestablished the local authority of the Catholic hierarchy in Canada and the Ohio Valley, sharpened the colonists' other suspicions of British Anglicanism and its intentions.

Too many histories of the Revolution pass over one of the ways in which religious leaders participated most openly in prewar politics. In 1766, Presbyterians from New York, New Jersey, and Pennsylvania joined with Connecticut Congregationalists to form a loose confederacy against Anglican encroachments. After the first meeting in 1766, meetings were held each year—alternating between New Jersey and Connecticut—with added participation from Delaware, Maryland, and the Carolinas. Members called their group a "Congress," and it, too, established provincial committees of correspondence.[23]

In fact, unhappiness with religion and church organization in the American colonies being controlled from Europe went far beyond Congregationalists and Presbyterians and their hostility to Catholicism and unwanted Anglican bishops. Pressures within churches to localize and Americanize their organization and religious presentment were a powerful pre-revolutionary force. Many sects and churches were affected. In Virginia and Maryland, in particular, local vestries assumed increasing control of Anglican churches during the early eighteenth century, keeping them Low Church in theology and directing their individual loyalties toward colonial interests rather than British hierarchies. Few easygoing tidewater vestrymen were keener than Connecticut Puritans on having a British-ordained bishop. More prophetically, within most churches in the colonies, support for home rule in religion generally correlated with support for home rule in politics.

The Presbyterian church had its own divisions. Traditionally inclined Old Side ministers typically were born in Scotland and Ulster, older in years, and educated there, especially at the University of Glasgow. New Side revivalists, in turn, were often the descendants of seventeenth-century Covenanters or tied to the Popular Party of the Church of Scotland (which faction itself would be pro-American in 1776). Many others were homegrown graduates of William Tennant's "Log College" at Neshaminy, Pennsylvania, and, in later years, of the Presbyterian College of New Jersey (eventually Princeton). In New York and New Jersey, where Presbyterianism had a large component of former New England Congregationalists, many New Side ministers were Harvard and Yale graduates.

Dutch and German churches and ministries were also affected. From the Dutch Reformed Church in New Jersey to the Lutherans in Georgia, individuals and factions were likewise trying to break away from European ordination and guidance. When the fighting broke out, many, though not all, conservative factions, maintaining their ties to Amsterdam and Hallé, would hold for the King. Supporters of a new Americanized Lutheranism or Dutch Reformed religion, more likely to be schooled and ordained locally, mostly took up arms for the Congress.* Relatively unimportant in 1750, these strains, too, were deepening during the 1764–1774 decade.

By 1775, many of America's dissenting pulpits also contained muskets—figuratively, for the most part, but sometimes literally. Edmund Burke was only mildly exaggerating in his remarks to Parliament in 1775 when he described the Protestantism of the northern colonies as unsubmissive and essentially a refinement on the principle of resistance.[24]

The Fight over the British Constitution: Principles, Politics, or Power?

From the West Indies to the House of Commons in Westminster, a significant minority of influential Britons believed that, in some respects, the colonists *were* defending the rights of Englishmen against Crown or ministerial excesses. Members of fiercely involved bodies like the New York Assembly, the Massachusetts House of Representatives, and the Virginia House of Burgesses held these views much more intensely. Yet the same struggle, at bottom, can also be seen as less about rights or principles and more about national emergence and political *power*, which is to say, about Americans wanting to govern themselves.

Nothing about the American Revolution has caused more debates, with one interpretive wave following another. The nationalist school of the nineteenth century, led by historian George Bancroft, demonized George III as a legatee of the Stuarts, over-

*Several of these will be discussed in chapter 5.

stating the war of 1775–1783 as a way station in America's progression toward liberty. This excess begat a correction—the emergence of an "imperial" school which found little to be tyrannical or unconstitutional in the British policies of 1764–1775. America and the burgeoning empire were just growing apart. Clumsy British tightening of what had been a loose colonial system was part of what led to war. So was the emerging conclusion by the colonists and their legislative assemblies that the new relationship was politically and economically unacceptable. This interpretation was spread in twentieth-century America by historians from George Beer to Charles Andrews to Lawrence Gipson, the latter in his epic series about the Great War for the Empire. A related imperial school has been dominant in Britain.[25]

Late twentieth-century explorations of the war's causations have, in general, been less sweeping and more concerned with specific circumstances and evidence. The Neo-Whig view, gathering force in the 1950s and 1960s, moved away from the economic explanations of the early twentieth-century Progressive and New Deal eras to describe the Revolution in essentially conservative terms as a defense of rights and liberties threatened by the mother country.[26] Harvard historian Bernard Bailyn added a new twist in the 1960s, linking American defense of these liberties to a much more radical political mind-set with its roots in the English Civil War and in seventeenth-century conspiracy theories revisited by early eighteenth-century publicists. Then the "Ideological School" of the 1970s and beyond, including Gordon Wood in *The Radicalism of the American Revolution*, not only began to re-ideologize the character of the Revolution, but to resurrect some of the social and economic explanations of the war—to be discussed later in this chapter—that had been submerged by Neo-Whig conservatism.

Still another explanation emphasizes realpolitik over morality—witness historian Theodore Draper's volume entitling the war as *A Struggle for Power* between Britain and the thirteen colonies. Civil wars, of course, are *always* partly about power. Control of government and military resources had been an issue in the English Civil War, was again in 1775–1783, and would be once more in 1861–1865. But the Neo-Whig, Ideological, and Realpolitik Schools would at least agree on the importance of the political and constitutional arena, however differently they might interpret the contesting forces.

The rights and liberties of Englishmen had stirred many a colonist's great-grandfather in 1688, or moved an earlier generation in the 1640s. By the 1770s, however, there was an all-important geographic caveat. Those forebears had, in fact, been Englishmen fighting on home battlegrounds. As the disagreements of 1689–1691 showed, the full applicability of the unwritten British constitution to territorial outliers such as Massachusetts or Virginia was implausible. Other outlying portions or adjuncts of Britain, like Scotland, the Isle of Man, and the Channel Islands, had a special legal status, based on instruments from the medieval statutes to the Act of Union with Scotland in 1707. As for Ireland, its ambiguous circumstances in the 1770s, somewhat like America's, were on the verge of giving the British government a *second* set of political, trade, and constitutional headaches.

Massachusetts's royal governor Francis Bernard neatly summarized the practical dispute in a letter to his friend Viscount Barrington, the secretary at war: The principal colonial legislatures, Bernard observed, had been acting almost independently in passing their own laws for more than a century, which had bred the quasi-constitutional assertion in America that the colonies, having their own legislatures, were united to Britain only through the King. From this perspective, so prominent an American as Benjamin Franklin would contend that London's Parliament, in *domestic* matters, particularly taxation, should legislate only for Britain. Only in broad matters of the *Empire*, issues of war, trade, and suchlike, could it legislate for *all* of the constituent parts. British politicians, however, could not be expected to accept such quibbles. The Parliamentary supremacy secured in 1688 did not establish simultaneous rights for the Jamaica Assembly or the Virginia House of Burgesses; *it established the force of London's Parliament alone.*

Legally and politically, the American colonists were not full-fledged *Englishmen*. In practical terms, however, British North America obviously represented the first overseas colonial settlements of Europeans to reach a size and maturity pointing toward independence. British law probably did not have an answer. The British Constitution furnished no suitable precedents, and the impe-

rialist redefinition of politics in the 1760s worked against concessions. During the years from 1714 to 1755, the population of the
colonies had grown from roughly 300,000 to about 1.5 million.
Colonial government under George I and George II was a loose system run by Whig ministers sympathetic with America and its large
minority of Protestant dissenters. Prior to the Great War, little reason had existed to pressure revenue from the colonies or to doubt
their loyalties. Whether we talk about constitutional rights, about
processes of history, or about raw power, the transition from this relaxed political equation that occurred in the 1760s represents the
third emergent Anglo-American battleground.

When the Treaty of Paris in 1763 confirmed the battlefield gains
of 1759–1762, Britain found itself the richest empire of eigh-
teenth-century Europe, swollen most spectacularly in North
America by the addition of Canada, the eastern part of former
French Louisiana, and Spanish Florida. In the West Indies, St.
Vincent, Dominica, Tobago, and Grenada had been added, and in
Africa, Senegal. The subcontinent of India, while not parceled out
by the treaty, was opened wide to British influence and commerce.
The British victories over France at Plassey and Wandiwash were
decisive. The cost of this new grandeur, however, was painful: a
national debt swollen from £55 million to £132 million. George
III, in turn, was anxious personally to supervise Britain's new imperial role and military requirements.

The charges against him of a return to Tory politics and pursuit
of increased power for the Crown have some substantiation. The
power of the Crown *was* increasing, but the imperialism that arose
triumphant out of victory over France had a much more modern
political texture than the old Toryism of periwigs and toasts to the
King "over the water." Horace Walpole, the essayist, exulted to a
friend that "the Romans were three hundred years conquering the
world. We subdued (it) in three campaigns. . . . Our bells are worn
threadbare with the ringing for victories."[27] These same victories
rang down the final curtain on Tory Jacobitism; Tories were now
true-blue imperialists.

Amid this glow and glitter, Britain's new North American policies of the 1760s make sense. From a desk in London, the
Proclamation Line of 1763 appeared logical in trying to ease the

pressures on the frontier and redirect settlement toward Canada and Florida. The Sugar Act of 1764, the Stamp Act of 1765, and the Townshend Acts of 1767 all pursued revenues needed to help underwrite the British administrative and military presence in North America. The new imperialism, in short, was repositioning the American colonies in just that subsidiary role: *entities maintained to serve the mother country*, now the seat of the new Rome. This misread the colonial mood, and could not have worked for long. But there was no Stuart-Restoration-*ancien-regimist* quality to the failures of the Grenville and Rockingham ministries.

Spoiled for more or less the first half of the eighteenth century, however, the American colonies had grown entirely too big by 1763 to be put back into the political equivalent of short pants. Those on the mainland, by now the richest of Europe's overseas settlements, boasted some 1.8 million people and burgeoning towns. Some visitors rated Philadelphia second only to London among English cities, although the booming West-of-England port of Bristol was larger.

Over the next decades, ballooning emigration from Europe—Scotland, Ireland, and Germany, in particular—would treble and quadruple the population of parts of the Pennsylvania, Carolina, and Virginia backcountry. The new beacon across the ocean had the same name in English, Gaelic, German, or Dutch, and the same pronunciation on the quays of Greenock, Bremen, or Rotterdam as in Bristol: *America*. By the time the first Continental Congress met in 1774, the estimated population of the thirteen colonies was 2.4 million, twice that of Scotland and comparable to or larger than independent nations like Portugal, the Swiss Confederation, and the Netherlands. The imperial future Americans were starting to think about as they crossed the Appalachians or poled flatboats down the Ohio had nothing to do with Royal Navy access to the dockyards of Minorca, trade concessions in Moghul India, or the balance of power on the plains of northern Germany; it was *their own*—the imperative of North America's westward destiny.

With such hopes unfolding, it seems unwise to exaggerate colonists' preoccupation with John Locke's *Second Treatise on Government*, the justifications for revolution set forth by the

Scottish "common sense" school, or even the widely read columns of the *Independent Whig*. To be sure, in 1774 and 1775, as conflicts and tensions grew, the men who would be delegates to congresses, legislatures, and conventions were searching out supportive political philosophy, esteemed thinkers to cite in learned debate, and it was to Locke, to Scots such as Francis Hutcheson and James Burgh, and also to the Radical Whig thinkers James Harrington, John Trenchard, Thomas Gordon, Robert Molesworth, and others, that many turned.

But most ordinary colonials, mulling questions of self-determination and America's future, took their outlook from a less learned framework: the "folk memory" of family and friends, Sunday sermons that compared royal councilors to pharisees and Britain to Babylon, newspaper articles and pamphlets by American dissidents, a rum-flip tavern politics critical of royal officials and far-off aristocrats, the musket-slapping bravado of local militia drills, and the republican camaraderie of groups like the Sons of Liberty. Numerous studies of the 1980s and 1990s have confirmed taverns, newspapers, churches, and militia as the seedbeds of popular revolution. Others have minimized grand political theory in a different way: by detailing the scarcity and small circulation of books by the late seventeenth-century English reformers that historians have grouped together as the Commonwealthmen.[28]

To call the English Civil War as important as the Glorious Revolution of 1688 in laying groundwork for the American Revolution invites controversy, even when the parallels and antecedents have been sketched. It is at odds with the Lockeian tradition. Moreover, as we have seen, even the Massachusetts Puritan elite was somewhat skeptical of Cromwell and the Parliamentarians for being too radical, too Rhode Island–like. Yet memories of the 1640s hung on from Maine to Williamsburg. Thomas Jefferson later recorded that in May 1774, when the British government was about to shut down the port of Boston, he and his allies in the Virginia House of Burgesses took up Rushworth's *Compendium,* "which we rummaged over for the revolutionary precedents and form of the Puritans of that day, (and) we cooked up a resolution, somewhat modernizing their phrases, for appointing the 1st day of

June, on which the Port bill was to commence, for a day of fasting, humiliation and prayer, to implore heaven to avert from us the evils of civil war."[29] John Adams, another future president, was called "John the Roundhead" as a young lawyer. And in 1786, when he was U.S. minister to Britain, Adams made a pilgrimage to the Civil War battlefields at Edge Hill and Worcester, where he lectured indifferent local residents that this was "holy ground."[30]

Dusty corners of libraries all over New England contain old books with notes about American chaplains and officers, about to march off to Canada or the siege of Boston, announcing their political and religious genealogy as the great-grandson of an officer under Cromwell or as a descendant of a minister who exhorted the Puritan troops. Connecticut, in this respect, was more assertive than Massachusetts, naming two ships in its Revolutionary state navy for Cromwell; calling a town after him; boasting that Cromwell, Pym, and Hampden had almost moved to Old Saybrook in the 1630s; and, finally, giving shelter in the 1660s to three of the Regicides flown from England under sentence of death for complicity in the execution of Charles I. Their names are still commemorated by Dixwell, Goffe, and Whalley Avenues in New Haven. But even Virginia extended the practices of the 1640s during Bacon's Rebellion in 1676, in which leaders of the insurrection with Cromwellian antecedents used terms like *committee, convention,* and *association* that had been introduced during the English Civil War and would be used again in the conflagration of 1775–1783.

The lineage between the American War for Independence and the Glorious Revolution is presumed. However, in the years surrounding the bicentennial of the American war, several historians emphasized a three-tier connection: that the fighting in America was a British revolution as well as a war of independence. That British context, in turn, drew not just on 1688 but on the religious and political antagonisms of the 1640s, on the great importance of dissenting Protestantism, and on the inadequacy of the Glorious Revolution settlement to colonies like New York, Virginia, and Massachusetts. These provinces were open to some more radical approaches.

If the American leaders of 1775 drew on the events and philosophies of 1688, which they did, the parallels to the 1640s were also strong. Earlier Hanoverian policies toward colonial America, well-received, generated no muttered analogies to Stuart-era provocations. But by the 1760s, British policy toward America was beginning to anger the colonies in many ways reminiscent of Charles I, Charles II, and James II: abuses by the military, imposition of taxation without representation, high Anglican efforts to establish episcopacy in America, unpopular economic regulation, and commercial favoritism to royal officials. The fight against Charles I and his policies must have seemed increasingly relevant, both in history and in folk memory.

Several scholars have made essentially that case for a major pre-revolutionary resurgence of Cromwellian and English Civil War folk memory in the thirteen colonies. Politics and religion were both involved: increasing public anger at the governing British elite, but also the spiritual effect of the Great Awakening, which resurrected many of the sects, enthusiasms, and excitements of the 1640s and 1650s.

By 1774, a pamphlet, *The American Chronicle of the Times*, appeared in Boston with Oliver Cromwell in full black battle armor on the cover. In its pages, Cromwell accepted the challenge of liberating Massachusetts from the occupying British troops under General Thomas Gage. One American historian, Alfred Young, has suggested that Cromwell's memory, sent underground generations earlier, burst forth again in the 1760s with the revival of enthusiastic religion and a political crisis that replicated the dramatis personae and plot of the Stuart era.[31]

Baptists and other sects that had been favored a century earlier by the former Lord Protector gathered new voice in America during the Great Awakening and spoke well of the Old Cause; Jonathan Edwards commended Cromwell's zeal; and religious historian Alan Heimert has suggested that by 1774, rekindling interest in Cromwell was "a sentiment that one suspects nearly every pietist in New England had secretly shared since the Great Awakening."[32]

Cromwell's legacy survived as a folk tradition in New England to a greater extent than in Old England. And as invocations of "Oliver" were growing in the 1770s, the name itself was becoming more popular in America—especially in New England, and to the greatest degree, according to one study, in four Massachusetts centers named for Puritan towns in East Anglia: Billerica, Dedham, Hadley, and Sudbury. Boston had a tavern called "Cromwell's Head," and anonymous, insurrection-minded letters printed in the Boston newspapers were variously signed Oliver Cromwell, O.C., Goffe and Whalley, and Joyce, Junior (the name of the army officer who seized Charles I in 1647).[33]

In England, Cromwell's memory did not make a serious comeback until the 1840s and 1850s, but his renewed relevance in the American colonies after the middle of the eighteenth century has a logic both in revolutionary politics and in the rekindling of enthusiastic religion. And as we will see in chapter 6, even within Britain the areas that had been most supportive of Puritans, Parliamentarians, and Covenanters back in the 1640s were frequently those most sympathetic with American rebels in the 1770s. Not a few of the most enthusiastically Puritan towns of 1641 repeated on the list of centers that presented pro-American petitions or elected pro-American Members of Parliament from 1774 to 1777.[34]

At the same time, the British Constitution and the rights of Englishmen may not have been as unique a spur to the independence of the thirteen colonies as Anglo-American exceptionalism is wont to claim. The mainland provinces of British North America, with their taproots deep into English liberty and jurisprudence, their relative literacy, and their dissenting Protestant tradition, were indeed the Western Hemisphere's first European settlements to mature and seek independence. Yet the French West Indies by 1775 had "representative" councils strong enough to evoke apprehension from Louis XVI himself: "Let us take care that in our efforts to make our islands flourish we may not give them the means one day, and perhaps soon, to separate themselves from France, for that will one day happen in all that part of the world."[35] A fair prediction, because in 1789, the French Caribbean Islands elected delegates to the Estates-General in Paris, which made them the *first* representatives of American colonies in any European parliament. Unrest among European settlers in Portuguese and Spanish America was not far behind.

The thirteen colonies themselves took up arms because self-determination might not have been achievable peacefully even under Britain's advanced constitution. In 1782, a new Whig government in Britain would give Ireland's parliament seeming independence, but this was retracted in 1800 when Ireland was brought into full union with Britain to keep order during the Napoleonic Wars. Ireland eventually had to fight for independence, as did French-owned St. Domingue and most of Spanish America.

What was arguably more important to Americans than the British Constitution or the "rights of Englishmen," at least in practical terms, may have been the interaction of an Anglo-Saxon sense of justifiable insurrection with a self-perceived readiness for nationhood. Turgot, the French physiocrat, made a related point in likening colonies to fruit; when they ripen they separate themselves from their parent societies to form new ones in accord with their own national geniuses. And Thomas Paine observed that "to know whether it be the interest of this continent to be Independent, we need only ask this easy simple question: Is it the interest of a man to be a boy all his life?"[36] To pursue that evolution, it was not essential—for all that America's English legacy speeded things—to have ancestors who sharpened their swords and their wits against Charles I and James II.

Mercantilist and Colonial Economics: The Fourth Crucible of Independence

The political and military aspects of imperialism, from taxation without representation in Parliament to the assignment of naval frigates as customs enforcers, were hardly its only provocation. Over the first four decades of the twentieth century, historians of the Progressive School blamed the Revolution on the frustrations of colonial economics. "The struggle," said Louis Hacker in *The First American Revolution* (1935), "was not over high-sounding political and constitutional concepts: over the power of taxation and, in the final analysis, over natural rights: but over colonial manufacturing, wild lands and furs, sugar, wine, tea and currency, all of which meant, simply, the survival or collapse of English merchant capitalism within the imperial-colonial framework of the mercantilist system."[37]

Another progressive historian, Charles Beard, argued that the Revolution was about manufacturing and economic self-determination. And Arthur Schlesinger Sr. contended that colonial merchants played a vital early role in the eventual confrontation by organizing resistance to the import duties of 1764–1767, for all that many merchants later began to fear emerging lower-class economic radicalism in Philadelphia and New York as much as they feared Parliament.

Blaming British economic policies for the Revolution lost credibility among American historians during the conservative 1950s. Traditionalist reaction against economic determinism helped promote the change, but new examinations of eighteenth-century data also rebuked previous arguments. The duties and taxes actually collected after 1765 turned out to average just £31,000 a year, a small burden and less than the colonies received in subsidies for indigo, timber, naval stores, and the like.[38] Great revolutions usually do not have such minor triggers. The unprecedented prosperity of the mainland provinces at the end of the Great War provided another implicit rebuttal.* Until the 1750s, at least, the old system had helped to build a thriving group of provinces and plantations.

The better case for mercantilist economics helping to incite the Revolution lay in the new mind-set that intensified after 1763. The lackadaisical administration of the Newcastle era was replaced by fiscal, monetary, and trade policies that represented a clumsy convergence of a recommitted imperialism with a last hurrah of mercantilism—the system that Adam Smith was only a few years away from indicting in *The Wealth of Nations*. Even after 1763, British fiscal policies were more notable for erraticism and inconsistency than for well-calculated malevolence. The Sugar, Stamp, and Townshend Acts gathered so little revenue, in the end, because they were so quickly repealed or reduced. The King and his ministers were not confident about dealing with America; they *were* convinced, however, that the precarious new empire might unravel if they let the thirteen colonies go.

---

*Benjamin Franklin estimated that during the war, Britain was spending an additional £2 million to £3 million a year in America.

Nevertheless, some of the economic pressures and prohibitions catalogued by Hacker, Schlesinger, and their colleagues constituted a fourth arena of American discontent, especially in the decade before war broke out. The various duties and taxes imposed by Parliament to raise money for the defense and administration of British North America were a greater political provocation than real economic burden. The economy itself was more injured by policies that shrank the currency, prohibited many varieties of manufacturing, and paid inadequate prices for commodities, particularly tobacco, that colonial producers were obliged to sell to England.

The Acts of Navigation, first enacted in the seventeenth century, laid out the enduring principles of British mercantilism: The most important commodities produced in the colonies—the so-called enumerated list, which kept growing up through the 1760s—could be exported only to the mother country. British entrepreneurs and merchants would enjoy the profits of processing and re-exporting. On paper, at least, the colonies were also enjoined from operating major manufacturing industries, aside from conspicuous exceptions like shipbuilding. Colonial markets were to be kept safe for British manufacturing. The third premise, equally central, was that because the colonies existed for the mother country, profits and hard currency would be continuously withdrawn from these outliers to the seat of empire.

The "enumerated" list of commodities that the colonies had to sell in Britain had been sweeping in 1750: sugar, tobacco, ginger, cotton-wool, fustic, dye-woods, rice, naval stores, hemp, masts, yards, copper ore, beaver and other furs. In 1764, Parliament added whale fins, hides, lumber, raw silk, potash, and pearl ash, and iron joined the list in 1767. A related form of tightening applied in 1764 required more *non*-enumerated goods to be shipped through English ports. Mercantilism, in short, was spreading its umbrella.

With a few exceptions, British commercial conflicts with America were not serious until the Great War. But then what had been an easygoing relationship—sometimes described as the shoe often not being laced up where it might pinch—proceeded to tighten. And as the shoe pinched, the calculus of who was getting what out of the British-colonial economic relationship became a matter of increasing American complaint.

The burden of new taxes obliged by the war, however, fell hardest on Englishmen—and they protested. Just before Parliament turned its attention to taxing molasses (and thus rum) in America, an equally controversial new levy on cider was imposed in England. *The Oxford History of England* has described the uproar that followed: "The (existing) beer excise could be collected at comparatively few points of supply, the maltsters and breweries. To collect a cider excise meant investigating the affairs of every apple-grower in the west country. It aroused an outcry against increasing the number of government agents and so increasing the power of government by adding to its patronage and influence. It also aroused the cry against invading privacy and the independence of Englishmen's homes."[39] Parliament projected much larger revenues from the tax on British cider (£800,000 a year) than from taxing American molasses imports, but public anger was too great. The apple growers of Devon, Somerset, and Dorset forced the lawmakers to retreat. Indeed, the debate accompanying cider tax repeal in 1766 touched on what Adam Smith, too, would soon underscore: the extent to which taxes weighed more heavily on Britain than on the colonies. Even the stamp duties imposed on the colonies in 1765 and then repealed were only two-thirds as high as the stamp duties that *remained* applicable in the mother country.

One way in which British mercantilism did play economic havoc in the colonies was through the Currency Act of 1764. By prohibiting the further issue of paper notes, this law shrank the money supply in province after province. Currency contraction reduced economic activity and, not coincidentally, stirred a growing radicalism among workers, artisans, and farmers. Since the late seventeenth century, British policy had prohibited the North American colonies from minting their own coinage, which brought about a transatlantic monetary hodgepodge. Virginia made tobacco legal tender, while North Carolina authorized *seventeen* commodities to act in that role. Spanish pieces of eight were often legal tender. But what most colonies, beginning with Massachusetts Bay in 1690, chose was to issue paper currency. In 1740, British gold worth £100 exchanged for £170 in New York or New Jersey currency, but for £800–£1400 in the less acceptable paper money of the Carolinas.[40]

As commerce grew, so did creditors' concerns about inflation. Parliament first restricted New England's currency issues in 1751. Then, following the Great War, it passed the more sweeping act of 1764, disallowing any new paper currency issue in all thirteen mainland colonies. Virginia had printed too much wartime paper, but at least as many provinces had been careful. The New York Assembly reminded the British government, albeit without effect, that it had issued paper bills on an emergency basis ever since the reign of William III, and that one such issue in 1759 had underwritten New York's loan to Sir Jeffrey Amherst of £150,000 to launch his campaign against Canada.[41] Far more than molasses taxes or stamp duties, British regulation that crippled the colonial money supply—shrinking money circulation in some provinces just as immigrants were flooding in—proved the growing incompatibility of British and colonial interests.

British restraint of colonial manufacturing was not a major casus belli. The Navigation Acts *promoted* shipbuilding by requiring that trade be carried in British-built ships including those of colonial construction. The production of crude iron was also encouraged, and subsidies were paid for the gathering of naval stores—turpentine, pitch, and the like. The rub came with Britain prohibiting, save for intraprovincial distribution, the colonial production of woolen goods, shoes, hats, sailcloth, wrought iron, and linen. All of these were to be bought from the mother country. But if ironware was effectively prohibited, some have asked, why did the colonies have more forges than Britain? In Pennsylvania, ironmasters were nevertheless a force on the patriotic side, resentful over the impositions and restraints of the British Iron Act of 1750, even though many managed to evade them.

A further mirror of mercantilism's effects lay in the steadily mounting imbalance of trade and the necessity of smuggling. The northern colonies had to import a wide array of manufactured goods, and unlike the southern plantations, the cool climates of New York and Massachusetts produced few commodities that London, Bristol, or Glasgow merchants wanted. As the population grew fastest in the North, the annual trade imbalance of the thirteen colonies soared. Favorable to Britain by just £50,000 in 1713, the gap increased twentyfold by 1764. At the beginning of the century, seven-eighths of England's colonial trade had been to the commodity-producing colonies: the West Indies, Virginia, Maryland, and the Carolinas. The more northerly provinces were a minor market. But by 1747, the weight was shifting northward, and by the early seventeen seventies the proportion going to the northern colonies was one-half or more. Overall shipments to the colonies, a small part of British global trade in 1700, had risen above one-third of the total volume by 1775.[42]

The ever-more-populous northern provinces, in short, were becoming an enormous market for British goods. As the seventeen-sixties turned into the seventeen-seventies, the export of manufactures across the Atlantic had become the major stimulus of British economic expansion. The early growth of the industrial midlands and western ports owed much to colonial demand. The fruits of England's Atlanticization were being reaped. The rise of west-facing Bristol, Liverpool, and Glasgow confirmed the changing economic center of gravity. Roughly half of Britain's exports of copperware, ironware, glassware, pottery, silk goods, printed cotton, and linen goods and flannels went to colonial buyers, as did two-thirds or more of the cordage, iron nails, beaver hats, and linen shipped overseas.[43] New England, in particular, bought £577,000 worth of goods from Britain in 1774 and sold just £124,000 worth.

This gap became the political crux of economic resentment. New Englanders could buy so much more than they sold only because of large commercial profits—from legitimate shipping and, more importantly, from incessant smuggling. Gold and silver from the illegal trade with the French, Dutch, and Spanish Caribbean purchased British ironware, linen, and pottery. On the day John Hancock of Massachusetts signed the Declaration of Independence—in large letters, he announced, so that the King could read the signature without his spectacles—indictments were outstanding against him for smuggling.[44] In New England, the attempt to eliminate smuggling was where mercantilism rubbed most toward revolution.

Virginia, the other great provincial cockpit of pre-revolutionary plotting, had a different bone to pick: anger over the price, credit arrangements, and enforced marketing through Britain of the colony's all-important tobacco crop. The planters had seen by the 1750s that tobacco's days were numbered; it wore out the soil, labor costs were rising, and prices set by the British frequently fell below the planters' costs. Over two more decades, the tidewater gentry made ends meet by speculating in western lands or by borrowing from their British agents or factors. By 1775, however, Virginia planters' debts to British creditors were over £1.4 million, a huge sum equal to more than twice the value of annual imports from Britain. Although many Virginians had borrowed to pay for unnecessary luxuries, J. H. Plumb, the British historian, has also described the crippling debt as "created very largely through the cupidity and dishonesty of the London factors."[45]

If links to smuggling were common among New England rebels, many Virginia revolutionaries shared tobacco-related debts and commercial complaints. George Washington, a planter himself, complained that "our whole substance does already in a manner flow to Great Britain."[46] In the summer of 1774, with war clouds on the horizon, prominent patriots such as George Mason, Patrick Henry, Richard Henry Lee, and others had pursued a revealing parochialism: a (successful) move to have Virginia's counties close their courts to debt proceedings, thereby halting debt payments to British firms.[47] American historian T. H. Breen, whose book *Tobacco Culture* identifies tobacco economics as a war causation, tabulated important evidence:

> An examination of post-revolutionary (British) debt claims reveals that in 1776 at least ten of Virginia's great planters owed £5,000 or more. This was a huge sum. In the £1,000 to £4,999 range appear such familiar names as Jefferson and Washington. According to one historian who has analyzed British Treasury records, "At least fifty-five of the individuals from whom £500 or more was claimed were members of the House of Burgesses from 1769 to 1774."[48]

The patriots of Massachusetts and Virginia were businessmen as well as constitutional theorists, avid readers of their own commercial ledgers as well as the texts of John Locke. Commercial resentment in New England and the tidewater tobacco region was entirely compatible with political and constitutional resentment. The two sections, more than others, were patriotic bastions because religious, constitutional, and economic annoyances all fitted neatly together, much like the dovetailing religious, constitutional, and economic motivations of English Puritan entrepreneurs circa 1640.

So far, this analysis has only touched on an additional factor, partly economic, partly ideological, to which it is now appropriate to turn: land speculation and the powerful disagreement within most colonies between "expansionists" and "non-expansionists." Just as most of the westward expansionists in seventeenth-century England took the side of Parliament in that civil war, most westward expansionists of the 1770s, save for royal officials with land grants, were on the patriotic side. Both times, national destiny lay in expansion—as it would again in the American Civil War.

America as the New Israel, the Profits of Land Speculation, and the Hint of Manifest Destiny: Expansion or Non-Expansion as a Pre-Revolutionary Battleground

Another seventy years would pass before the term "manifest destiny" came into American use, but its spirit already guided men like Benjamin Franklin, George Washington, and Thomas Jefferson, as well as a considerable ratio of New England's most prominent Congregationalist ministers. Years before the Declaration of Independence, they talked of America reaching the Mississippi or even the Pacific to become the next century's great empire. At first, they assumed that this would take place under the British flag. But the very idea of filling in the continent always carried the seed of independence.

Population pressure was a cause. Worn-out, stony, southern New England farmlands were already driving Yankee settlers north into Vermont, New Hampshire, Maine, and Nova Scotia. Others went west into Pennsylvania's Wyoming Valley, claimed by Connecticut. The Scotch-Irish and Germans of frontier Pennsylvania, in turn, were overflowing southward, down through the Great Valley of Virginia and south into the Carolina Piedmont and the mountain valleys of the Holston, French Broad, and Yadkin Rivers. Scotch-Irish Virginians poured through the same valleys and mountain passes. No colonies had fought the French with more demographic incentive; New England, Pennsylvania, and Virginia all needed growing room.

Seeking the promised land also had religious and ethnic overtones. The Ulster Scotch-Irish having been settled on the seventeenth-century frontier of Northern Ireland to drive back the native Irish Catholics, which they did, made some in London believe that their border-taming skills could be used against America's Indians, which was also true. By the 1760s, Scotch-Irish borderers were expansionist almost by nature. Religion was a related spur, because to the covenanting Presbyterianism that many shared, Ulster had been the first New Israel—and now America would play a grander role. New England Congregationalists also saw North America as the Kingdom of God. In the New World as in the Old, Spain and France were the foes that had to be faced, and overcome, moving west. As New England expanded, so would God's Kingdom. In and around the revolutionary Boston of the early 1770s, ministers like Charles Chauncy, Jonathan Mayhew, and Samuel Cooper voiced powerful visions of a mighty empire reaching across the continent.[49]

Nor is it irrelevant that the great fortunes of eighteenth-century and even early nineteenth-century America were being made in land speculation and furs. The leading families of Massachusetts, Connecticut, New York, Pennsylvania, Virginia, and the Carolinas were heavily involved in western land investments through groups like the Susquehanna, Delaware, Ohio, and Transylvania companies. George Washington may not have confirmed his generalship until the battles of Trenton and Princeton, but he established his land acumen much earlier, betting that the Potomac Valley, not some lesser watercourse, would be the highway west to the Ohio country.

Whatever the balance between sincere politics and economic speculation, the pre-1775 divisions within the provinces between expansionists and non-expansionists turned out to be a predictive yardstick. Canadian historian Marc Egnal, in his 1988 book *A Mighty Empire: The Origins of the American Revolution*, examined the actions of officials and legislators in five provinces—

Massachusetts, New York, Pennsylvania, Virginia, and South Carolina—and found that the alignments of expansionists versus non-expansionists in the years just before 1775 provided a good framework for predicting wartime loyalties.[50]

Part of this predictability, as we have seen, reflected expansionism's overlap with ethnicity and religion—the New England Congregationalists were expansionists, as were the Scotch-Irish Presbyterians of the Pennsylvania and Virginia frontiers. Both groups were mainstays of the patriot side. The Quakers and German pacifist sects, non-expansionists, mostly tried to be neutral in the 1775–1783 fighting.

Geographic orientation within one's province was also relevant. Upper New York's western-focused great landowners—the Livingstons, Van Rensselaers, Ten Broecks, and Schuylers—were mostly expansionists and subsequently patriots. By contrast, the manor lords with property near the city of New York—the DeLanceys and Philipses—were non-expansionists. Their seaboard focus helped keep them loyal to the King. Pennsylvania's non-expansionists, centered in the Philadelphia Quaker and Anglican communities, were Tory or neutral when war broke out. Likewise for the Quaker merchants so important in seaward-looking ports like Nantucket and Newport, Rhode Island. Their view of the world was Atlantic, rather than interior. The least expansionist parts of Virginia and South Carolina, in turn, were the old, established coastal districts settled by the mid-seventeenth century. The Scottish merchants of the Virginia and Carolina port cities circa 1775 were mostly Atlantic-focused non-expansionists (or Indian traders) who wound up returning to Britain.

We should, however, note the principal exception to expansionism's correlation with patriot loyalties in the 1775–1783 war. This involved officials whose large land grants were the fruit of their employment in support of British imperial interests: provincial governors and lieutenant-governors, as well as senior supervisors of Indian affairs and frontier trade like Sir William Johnson in New York, George Croghan in Pennsylvania, and John Stuart in the South. By 1774, most were on the British-Indian side, working to *restrain* colonial expansion.

Beyond Egnal's five provinces, westward dreamers in Connecticut, most of them ardent Congregationalists and many prominent in the Susquehanna Company, led that state's dominant patriotic faction during the war. The state's anti-expansionists, many of them conservative Anglicans, leaned to neutralism or loyalism. In Maryland, Charles Carroll of Carrollton, signer of the Declaration of Independence and probably the state's foremost patriot, was almost as prominent a frontier land speculator as George Washington, his neighbor on the southern side of the Potomac. There can be little doubt: Belief in far-flung national expansion and support for independence usually went hand in hand.

—

The English Revolution of the 1640s and the American Revolution display important parallels in their origins. Both were civil wars that divided the Atlantic English-speaking population—and did so along somewhat similar cultural, economic, ethnic, and religious lines. By following these threads, the greater importance and unappreciated ramifications of the two wars come into view, as the next four chapters will pursue and seek to document. One obvious common thread apparent from the beginning is the leadership of the unfashionable camp—the so-called Roundheads of the 1640s and the Brother Jonathans of the 1770s—by Puritan southeast England, in the first instance, and then by the Puritan-descended Yankees of New England. Each time, Crown officials and High Church Anglicans were disproportionately on the other, fashionable side. Protestant suspicions of Catholicism were spurs both times: to the Puritans and episcopacy-doubting country gentry of the mid-seventeenth century and to the Yankees and Virginians of the eighteenth.

Rebels in both wars were concerned about the rights of Englishmen and the rights of legislatures against the Crown. Yet both Parliament in the 1640s and 1650s and the new American congresses and patriot legislatures of the 1770s were guilty of their own excesses—very substantial, even dictatorial, ones. Rights have always mattered less when they are somebody else's.

Economics was important in both wars. Provocations to rebellion ranged from guilds and monopolies to mercantilism, with recurring indignation against royal grantees and favorites. However, in neither case was economics the principal causation, in part because overlapping cultural and religious denominators usually outweighed it. Most New England smugglers circa 1770 were Yankee Congregationalists, just as most English clothiers circa 1640 were Puritans—and the religious and cultural loyalties seemed to have counted more.

The Americans of 1775 shared the anger of Stuart-era Englishmen at military abuses, billeting, and army plots. Finally, both the Parliamentarians of Cromwell's time and the revolutionaries of George Washington's era displayed a similar combination: a religious sense of being a chosen people and an interrelated pursuit of entrepreneurial economics and land hunger that pushed toward national fulfillment and manifest destinies.

We can also identify two other repetitions from the 1640s: a fear of Popish plots and supposed conspiracies against liberty, as well as the force of a Protestantism that mixed reform and politics into its periodic awakenings.

Chapter 8 and 9, in examining the origins of the American Civil War, will come back to how these shared circumstances rebut the idea of these wars as flukes. The confrontations of 1640–1649 and 1775–1783 both represented a depth of disagreement that probably required combat. But whereas the long-term reaction against the radical revolution of the 1640s left England itself with an essentially conservative tradition, the second legacy was a diverging, partly radical tradition, most powerful in the American colonies, that paved the way for the split that ultimately ensured the duality and long-lasting hegemony of Anglo-America.

Like the 1629–1640 overture to the English Civil War, the American Revolution followed a decade-long prelude. With some oversimplification, colonial antagonism seems to have surged in three waves. The imperialist follow-through of 1763–1765 brought a half dozen new pressures: the restraints of the Proclamation Act, the Sugar and Stamp Acts, the predictable commercial contraction of phasing out paper money, the provocation of using Royal Navy cruisers for customs enforcement, the unpopular tread of peacetime soldiers backstopped by the new Mutiny and Quartering Act, and, by way of countertide, the preliminary intercolonial bonding of future rebels during the Stamp Act Congress. Subsequent waves would not have struck Americans with such little forewarning as this departure from what, in retrospect, began to look like the easy-going accommodation of the past. In most cases, the conflicts that throbbed by 1775 were at least sensitive by 1765.

The next wave brought in the Townshend duties of 1767, the si-multaneous disciplining of colonies such as New York for refusing to quarter British troops, the growing debate in the middle colonies over Anglican bishops being appointed for North America, and General Gage's decision in 1768 to send four regi-ments of British troops into Boston after riots against customs en-forcement. Folk memories of long-ago Stuart parallels started to knit separate complaints into renewed discussion of conspiracies against colonial liberties. The Boston Massacre of 1770 marked a crest.

The years from 1771 to 1773 were mostly prosperous and rela-tively quiet—until the Boston Tea Party in the autumn of 1773. This led to the third and most powerful surge of unrest as an aroused Parliament reacted in the spring of 1774 by passing the Coercive Acts. Britain's hope to make an example of Boston failed as the other colonies instead rallied round. When the First Continental Congress met in Philadelphia, the fighting at Lexington and Concord was only a little more than a half year away. The second half of 1774 and the early months of 1775 re-sembled the 1640–1641 period—an increasingly tense prelude.

Nevertheless, especially among conservatives, memories of the radicalism and periods of near anarchy unleashed by England's Civil War produced a quiet but persistent drumbeat of caution. Absent British restraint, they cautioned, the forces and animosities that divided the various provinces would take over, possibly with enough disequilibrium to tip the continent into civil strife. Jonathan Seawall of Massachusetts, soon to be a loyalist, pre-dicted that separation would produce petty tyrants or that Americans would "live in a state of perpetual war with your neighbors, and suffer all the calamities and misfortunes incident to anarchy, confusion and bloodshed."[51] John Dickinson of Pennsylvania, who aligned with the new republic, nevertheless worried that without Britain, the colonies would degenerate into "a multitude of commonwealths, crimes and calamities—mutual jealousies, hatreds, wars and devastations, till at last the exhausted provinces shall sink into slavery under the yoke of some fortunate conqueror."[52]

There were even times, especially in 1781–1783, that Washington, Thomas Jefferson, and Alexander Hamilton had similar concerns. Jefferson saw unity "going down hill" after the war, with the states likely "to war with each other in defiance of Congress."[53] But in contrast to the radicalism of the 1640s, the civil war aspect of the conflict of 1775–1783, bitter in 1780–1782, was kept from exploding during and after the peace negotiations. Then it was submerged in the excitement of making a new nation work. Eighth-grade history books got their Fourth of July myth. Even so, politics, religion, and society in the United States were left with a reality of divisiveness that would seed yet another civil war and that still lingers just beneath the surface.

However, before returning to parade the two sides of what in 1775 to 1783 became the first full-fledged civil war in America, we must turn to a different kind of overview: the contours of British North America in 1775 and the strategic options by which Britain might suppress or mishandle the rebellion. What became a civil war in the British Atlantic extended far beyond the boundaries of just thirteen colonies into Nova Scotia, Quebec, Bermuda, and the Bahamas—and it might have spread farther.

4

THE BRITISH EMPIRE AND CIVIL WAR IN THE WESTERN HEMISPHERE, 1775–1783

What man living at the beginning of the seventeenth century who had witnessed the sailing of three small ships that carried the first English settlers to the banks of the James River in 1607 would have ventured, even in a moment of the most feverish optimism, to prophesy that within a century and a half England would be the heart of a vast Empire with its outposts scattered from Fort Marlborough in Sumatra in the Far East to the newly acquired French settlements in the Illinois Country in the New World and from the frigid wastes of Hudson Bay to the steaming tropical forests of the Bay of Honduras?
—Lawrence H. Gipson, *The Triumphant Empire*, 1956

In the high eighteenth century, provincial variants of Whig political culture had established themselves in Lowland Scotland, among the Anglo-Irish, in New England, in Pennsylvania, and in Virginia. . . . briefly, there was an Atlantic British political world—rather vaguely termed an empire—which reached from the North Sea to the headwaters of the Ohio. But within this greater Britain there occurred a revolution which must be thought of as the outcome of its common development, but which resulted in the detachment of its English-speaking sector on the mainland of North America, to become a distinct nation and a highly distinctive political culture. The first

*revolution to occur within a "British" political system resulted in
the partial disruption and the pursuit by one of its components of
an independent history.*

—J. G. A. Pocock, *Three British Revolutions,* 1980

$\sim$

T HE BRITISH GLOBAL MILITARY triumph of 1763 was es-
pecially overwhelming on the ramparts of North America.
But within twelve years, the northern half of the Western
Hemisphere would erupt again, this time in a civil war that pitted
Whig against Tory, splintering the great empire almost before the
ink had dried on London's brave new maps.

This new war, like the previous one, would have as its initial
center the well-trodden warpath between Albany and Montreal.
Its breadth—the geographic reach of the complaints and dissatis-
factions just examined in chapter 3—was the uncertainty. The
thirteen rebellious colonies could conceivably have become sixteen
or eighteen, including French Quebeckers, Nova Scotians,
Bermudians, and Bahamians. For months in late 1775 and early
1776, civil war was at hand in the North Atlantic.

*Never, ever, did eighteenth-century Americans fight a simple war
for independence.* Such a conflict would have been impossible.
Besides the internecine warfare within the thirteen colonies, too
many larger political memories, tribalisms, ambitions, and constitutional disagreements—issues that affected *all* Britons—crowded
the Atlantic stage. The battlefield stretched, at various times, from
Barbados and Lake Pontchartrain to Bermuda, the Newfoundland
Straits, and Belfast Lough. Even within the British Isles, important
regional, ethnic, and religious groups were ambivalent or sympathetic to the colonists. This chapter and the three that follow will
look at the divisions within the overall British Empire, at the alignments and loyalties within the thirteen mainland colonies, then at
those within the British Isles, and finally, in chapter 7, at the eventual importance of divided feelings among senior officers of the
British army and the Royal Navy.

These divisions and inhibitions within the expanded empire
were vital to the eventual independence of the thirteen colonies.
Without them, the British élan and momentum that had driven

France from the Hudson-Champlain Corridor fifteen years earlier would probably have prevailed again. Instead, we—Americans, in particular—have all but forgotten that brief North Atlantic *imperium,* the short-lived First British Empire of 1763–1775. Embarrassed in the North Atlantic, Britain after 1783 shifted its attention eastward, to Egypt, India, and the Malaccan Straits. Too little recalls the hugeness of British North America: just three major forts remaining or reconstructed—William Henry, Ticonderoga, and the half-ruins of Crown Point—and minor remembrances like a ferociously scarlet lichen, named "British Soldiers" by local woodsmen, that appears each spring in the granite ridges and hemlock bogs of the Adirondacks, as brilliant in the woods as the jackets of the Royal Americans or the Black Watch must have been in the 1750s.

Yet if Anglo-America has a single corridor of history, this is it. Few contemporary visitors would guess that in 1759–1761, the war trail between French Quebec and English New York was among the most intensely fortified stretches in the world. Its fifty miles of casements, parapets, and counterscarps rivaled northern Italy, the Rhine, and the Low Countries. Bastions like Crown Point and Carillon—the original French name for Ticonderoga, said to describe the sound of the nearby LaChute River tumbling into Lake Champlain—were the stuff of dinner conversations in the Hague and staff reports to Frederick the Great. The surrender of Champlain fortresses could redraw maps on the north German plain, not just in the watersheds of the St. Lawrence and Hudson.

Winston Churchill has correctly summed up the confrontation of 1754–1763 as the first of the world wars. The peace that followed the surrender of the principal French strongholds in North America—those in upper New York, plus Louisbourg, Frontenac, Montreal, and Quebec—promoted the British Empire to first rank. From Portugal to the Ottoman Empire, from Sintra to the Sublime Porte, British ambassadors took diplomatic precedence over their French counterparts as soon as the treaty was signed. Only eighty years before, the last two Stuart kings of England had been the pensioners of Louis XIV.

The imperial transformation, as we have seen, was extraordinary. Only two decades earlier, the British king in 1743, George II, had never visited Scotland, Wales, or even the north of England. His concerns were stolid, parochial, and continental: old friends in petty German states, Swedish ambitions in Pomerania, or the preparations of Louis XV, openly flaunted in French Channel ports, for yet another invasion to restore the exiled Stuarts. The two Georges, while nobody's pensioners, were nevertheless by temperament captives of their German upbringing. Their hearts and minds were usually in Hanover, a pleasant principality no more populous than Wales, where the Harz Mountains met the sandy heaths of north Germany.

George III succeeded to his grandfather's throne in 1760, even as British quartermasters, engineers, and artillerists were putting finishing touches on a three-pronged expedition—from Quebec, Lake Ontario, and Ticonderoga—to overwhelm Montreal, France's last remaining stronghold in Canada. The empire was about to justify George Frederick Handel's "heroick" Protestant percussions. The new King George was just twenty-two. He was also the first male ruler of the United Kingdom of Great Britain and Ireland to be English-born. The third of the Georges would not waste *his* reign worrying about Baltic fisheries or Lutheran church politics.

Simply to look at the revised map would have bred arrogance. Impressive after the Peace of Utrecht in 1713, Britain's overseas domain became truly global in 1763: three dozen colonies, possessions, or spheres of political and commercial influence that spread from the Bay of Bengal to the Arctic Circle, from the Falkland Islands to the Rock of Gibraltar. Two-thirds were in the Western Hemisphere, where their booming commerce was further Atlanticizing the British economy. The east coast of England, with its ancient ports and stately "wool churches" built by the largesse of the medieval cloth trade with Europe, was losing importance not just to London but to the burgeoning west—to ports like Bristol, Liverpool, and Glasgow that owed their teeming quays and swelling fortunes to Britain's American and Caribbean empire. It was, however, an empire with two religious, cultural, and philosophic poles, sceptre and mitre on one side of the ocean, assembly and meetinghouse on the other. No such arrangement could endure.

1775: The First British Empire in Crisis

Too many histories of the United States discuss the events of 1775 as if there were no new and larger British Atlantic empire to take sides, just thirteen united American colonies, chorusing for independence. The reality was infinitely more complicated, as the following chapters will show. Portraits of the 1775–1783 fighting in a global dimension, mostly British-authored, have typically emphasized the naval encounters in European, Caribbean, and Indian waters that followed France's entry in 1778. The notion of a civil war within a larger array of English-speaking territories is not pursued.

In 1775–1776, however, the contours of conflict were anything but fixed. What was occurring was a different war, English-speaking and within the empire, but ranging well beyond America's future boundaries. One of its issues was the very size and direction of those future U.S. boundaries. Clear thinkers in London and elsewhere understood that America's runaway population growth—from about 1.2 million in 1750 to twice that in 1775— promised far greater size, influence, and ambition to come. The thirteen colonies had one-third of the population of England and Wales, a figure that could easily rise to half by 1800. Senior French officials had begun speculating about the British colonies seeking independence as early as the 1740s.

The new British Atlantic empire, meanwhile, was inherently unstable. The King and his ministers had little by way of strategy beyond trying to find new revenues, an admittedly pressing need. Well before the April fighting at Lexington and Concord, New Englanders, as conquest-minded a tribe as any in the Old Testament, had begun pondering how to invade, enlist, or neutralize Canada, the Bahamas, and Bermuda. They counted on sympathetic words, at least, from sugar islands like Jamaica, Barbados, and Grenada, which had a large trade with mainland colonies. Jamaica did cause anxious moments in London with its late 1774 petition supporting the Yankee position on taxation. King George's early fear that losing the American colonies would endanger the rest of the new empire had some basis. The contagion of disaffection eased after 1778, when French entry into the war added reform pressures and restored commitment to the Crown in

Ulster, the Caribbean, and even England. In the opening rounds, though, no one knew how far the rebellion could spread.

Map 4.1 shows the far-flung colonies and territories that made up the First British Empire in the Western Hemisphere. Twenty clustered in or next to eastern North America. Another ten were in the Caribbean, far out in the Atlantic, or along the coast of Central and South America. The Great French War and its aftermath had brought administrative, fiscal, commercial, and military strains. As a result, virtually every colony with representative councils or assemblies—only Newfoundland and a few islands lacked them—had grudges to air against Parliament, the Board of Trade, the War Office, or the Admiralty.

Small grudges, however, were not incitements to a great revolution. Besides the thirteen that broke away, two more colonies, East and West Florida, were ultimately returned by Britain to Spain in 1783. The rest would remain British. The territorial stratagems and subplots of the early 1780s, from creating a loyalist New Ireland in Maine's Penobscot Valley to the possibility of a southern confederation remaining within the empire, could fill another book. The ending is still the same: Only thirteen colonies joined the United States.

The best explanation is that more than dissatisfaction varied from colony to colony. So did culture and preferences in religion. The four New England provinces of Massachusetts, Connecticut, New Hampshire, and Rhode Island, at the core of the insurrection, were as committed to the patriotic side as their East Anglian forebears were to the Puritan and Parliamentary standard. Like all ideological heartlands, New England would not be easy to invade; its militia swarmed on a rumor—or on the approach of an unidentified dust cloud.

Virginia, Pennsylvania, and Maryland were also relatively stalwart. However, the remaining six provinces—New York, New Jersey, Delaware, North and South Carolina, and Georgia—all displayed large loyalist or neutralist minorities during at least one stage of the war. Georgia and the Carolinas might have been detachable. Otherwise, relations clear in twentieth-century history books were not so obvious at the time. The plotting thirteen were surrounded by a larger geographic collar of British-held terri-

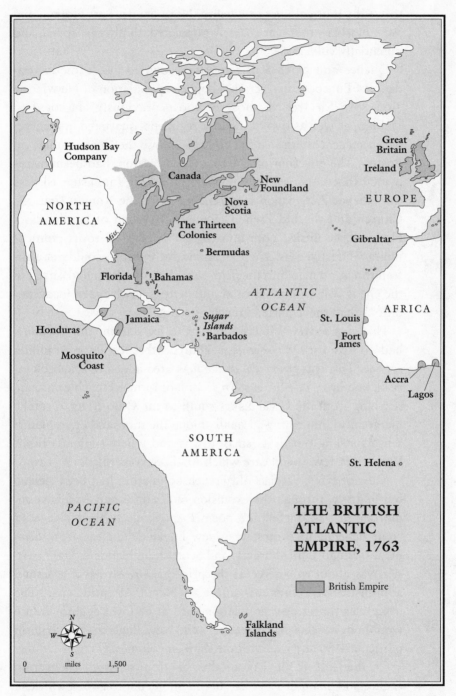

Hudson Bay
Company

NORTH
AMERICA

Miss. R.

Canada

New
Foundland

Nova
Scotia

The Thirteen
Colonies

Bermudas

Florida

Bahamas

ATLANTIC
OCEAN

Jamaica

*Sugar
Islands*

Barbados

Honduras

Mosquito
Coast

Great
Britain

Ireland

EUROPE

Gibraltar

AFRICA

St. Louis

Fort
James

Accra

Lagos

SOUTH
AMERICA

St. Helena

PACIFIC
OCEAN

**THE BRITISH
ATLANTIC
EMPIRE, 1763**

British Empire

N
W   E
S

0   miles   1,500

Falkland
Islands

MAP 4.1

tory—the four colonies of Quebec, Nova Scotia, East Florida, and West Florida—that was sparsely populated, thinly garrisoned, and potentially vulnerable.

Quebec and Nova Scotia together counted just 120,000 residents of European extraction, about the population of New Jersey alone. As for troops, most of those previously stationed in Halifax, as well as two of the four regiments quartered in Quebec, had been sent south in 1774 to help impose the Coercive Acts on Boston. The governor of Quebec, Guy Carleton, had been instrumental that same year in convincing the King's ministers to pass the Quebec Act, which reentrenched both the Roman Catholic Church and the old French seigneurial system of landholding. However, he misled both himself and London as to its politico-military effectiveness. The Canadians, he reported, could put eighteen thousand men into the field, some half of whom had served in the Great War with more valor and better knowledge of local conditions than the departed French regulars.[1]

This was naive. Whatever the 1774 legislation, the *habitants* had no love for their seigneurs, church tithes, or enforced militia service. This was truer still of the new area added to Quebec's jurisdiction in 1774—the eastern section of former French Louisiana reaching from the Great Lakes south to the Ohio River. Catholic hierarchical influence was small among the thousand or so French settlers strung out in its small towns and lonely traders' cabins. Without it, few would care which Anglo-Saxons ruled.

Most of Nova Scotia's old French population had been cleared out in 1755, through the expulsion of six thousand Acadians immortalized by Longfellow's poem *Evangeline*. In their place had come dependable Protestants: New England Yankees, Yorkshiremen, German Lunenburgers, and Scottish highlanders. Halifax itself was about to emerge as the principal British naval base and administrative center on America's North Atlantic coast. The irony was that a new population sure to be loyal against France would not necessarily be reliable—the New England–bred half, in particular—in any war with the thirteen colonies.

On the Gulf of Mexico, another swath of territory taken from France and Spain in 1763 had been remolded into two new British provinces: the virtual garrison states of East and West Florida.

Each had a white population of only three thousand or so, ethnic mixtures laced together by British troops and officials in the provincial capitals. St. Augustine was the seat of formerly Spanish East Florida, which had boundaries much like the present state. Pensacola was the capital of West Florida, much of its territory formerly French. White English-speakers in both were loyal to the British governors, Indian agents, merchants, traders, and military officers for whom they worked, not to the rebellious ideas and politicians a few hundred miles to the north.

The other British colonies in the Americas were peripheral to the civil conflict—barren northern shores or Caribbean sugar islands. In the north, the ten thousand residents of Newfoundland, half of whom were Irish Catholic, cared little for ether side. In the south, the British navy could also be expected to deal with the tropical islands from Jamaica to Barbados. Bermuda and the Bahamas, though, were less dependable because of their close ties to the mainland.

In any case, the early plotters in Boston and Philadelphia had high hopes: Quebec, Nova Scotia, and both Floridas were invited to attend the Continental Congress and a propaganda war for Canada began in 1774. After Massachusetts forces bloodied the British at Bunker Hill in June 1775, rebel ambitions in the North grew. Even after the first military assault on Canada in 1775–1776 collapsed into ragged retreat, further invasions were regularly discussed through 1782.

Neither side, rebel or ministerial, had a true grand plan. Wars of the eighteenth century, like the famous Brown Bess army musket of that era, were typically pointed rather than aimed. Yet in 1774, a political geographer, looking at the new patchwork of empire, would have given the Ministry an unmistakable warning: that a greatly expanded and partly undigested British North America was on the brink of a civil war of hard-to-predict dimension. Canada would be an immediate target. The white population of the sugar islands would not join the rebels, but what if black slave insurrections began in the American South and spread to the Caribbean? In Ireland, where only the Protestant minority could vote, malcontents with Whig antecedents would surely use Britain's American troubles to press for greater self-government. The old Whig political cultures outside England—in Ulster, southwest

131

Scotland, and the American mainland—shared close contacts, often through evangelists and Presbyterian churchmen. To worry about rebellion's spread was hardly far-fetched.

But we've jumped ahead of ourselves. For the moment, it is necessary to leave the broad sweep of the short-lived First British Empire to consider a more specific inhibition: the revealing divergence in size, ethnicity, politics, and dissenting churches between the thirteen insurgent mainland colonies and those remaining loyal.

The Thirteen Colonies as the Center of the Atlantic Revolution in 1774–1776

When Parliament passed the so-called Coercive Acts in 1774, to suppress virtually open rebellion in Massachusetts, the East Coast of the future United States was home to the largest, most densely placed, and best-educated population in the New World. No other European colonies were comparable.

The four hundred thousand European settlers of Portuguese Brazil were spread over an area larger than the entire Atlantic Seaboard of North America. Only a handful of provinces had European concentrations in excess of fifty thousand. Sections of the booming mining district of Minais Gerais might have had a white majority; so might a few thinly settled locales in the south. Spanish America, with roughly the same number of Europeans, occupied three times as much territory. Lima, Peru, had little community with Mexico City, two thousand miles away. French-speaking Canada was thinly populated and remote. For half the year, ships could not even penetrate the icebound St. Lawrence.

The British possessions in America, by contrast, boasted a population of about 2.75 million, of whom 2 million were Europeans. Over 90 percent of this white population was in the thirteen older mainland colonies. Canada, Jamaica, and the Barbados counted not quite 10 percent. The mainland thirteen were particularly distinguished by vital characteristics not conjoined in the others: a predominance of English-speakers, overwhelming Protestantism, literacy rates higher than Europe's, two to six generations of existing settlement, and a culture of religious dissent, political activism, and rebellion against royal authority.

These last attributes were altogether unique. The kings of France had never dared let their own substantial Calvinist minority, the Huguenots who were eventually exiled, settle New France. Had they been given that chance, then the late seventeenth-century New York Huguenot settlement of New Rochelle—called after the French Protestant war stronghold of La Rochelle—might have given its name to an entire New World nation. The mainland British colonies, despite their wide variations, constituted a rare meeting ground of political freedom and religious refuge.

New England counted over six hundred thousand people. In 1775, its settled area included most of Massachusetts, Connecticut, and Rhode Island, along with much of New Hampshire and the southerly portions of what are now Maine and Vermont. The former Puritan diaspora, rooted for a century and a half, had become a distinct new culture called "Yankee"—possibly from Jan Kaes or John Cheese, the name given to the New England settlers by the seventeenth-century Dutch. Over 80 percent of the New Englanders were white Protestants of English ancestry, making these provinces ethnically as well as religiously distinctive. The old-country parent region of Lincoln, Huntingdon, Cambridge, Norfolk, Suffolk, Essex, and Hertford, Cromwell's once-fierce Eastern Association, mustered twice the population in a smaller land area. Yet at war's outbreak, lower New England, with its countryside reminiscent of home, was America's most densely populated major section—and also the most belligerent.

The second center of revolutionary gravity, Greater Virginia, included that province plus the adjacent Chesapeake Bay area of Maryland, along with northeastern North Carolina, settled by Virginians in the mid-seventeenth century. Much more Cavalier than Puritan—the authorities in Jamestown had expelled local Puritans in the 1640s—Greater Virginia was also the heart of America's tobacco-growing plantation culture, the economics of which, as we have seen, was itself a war cause. The three colonies together had a population of over eight hundred thousand in 1775, about one-third of whom were free blacks and slaves.

Of the region's half million whites, roughly half were English Protestants. Germans, Ulster Irish, and Scots were also numerous; and the mixture of Germans, Celts, and Anglo-Saxons pouring down the western valleys from Pennsylvania was already creating a frontier culture at odds with the long-settled tidewater. However, the tidewater gentry, largely Low Church Anglicans, dominated each state, although less so in North Carolina, and their plantation culture provided the second major Revolutionary patriotic elite.

The southernmost colonies were less insurrectionist than New England or Virginia. Southeastern North Carolina was closer in spirit to semitropical South Carolina than to Virginia—visitors to the old rice plantations near Wilmington are usually surprised to see alligators half-hidden among the cypress knobs. Throughout much of the war, the Cape Fear Valley was a loyalist stronghold. South Carolina and Georgia combined had a population in 1775 of some 200,000, of whom about half were black slaves. This region had some early settlers from Barbados, Jamaica, and St. Kitts—and more than a hint of Caribbean racial tensions.

The pivotal and politically uncertain middle colonies included a relatively large population—200,000 in New York, 120,000 in New Jersey, 300,000 in Pennsylvania, and 37,000 in Delaware (established in 1704 from the "three lower counties" of Pennsylvania). What they did *not* constitute, singly or together, was a coherent cultural region or revolutionary force of the New England or Greater Virginia sort. White Protestants did number about 90 percent of the population, with Catholics perhaps 1 percent and blacks 7 percent. Their religious and cultural unity, however, was nonexistent. New York and New Jersey had large Dutch populations, many still Dutch-speaking, legacies from the years before 1664 when New York had been New Amsterdam. Pennsylvania, meanwhile, had America's most important concentration of Scotch-Irish—primarily Ulster Presbyterians of Scottish ancestry, who constituted America's third core of patriotic fervor.

Southern and eastern Pennsylvania also included the continent's largest German population. However, they divided into two distinctive cultural streams: *church* Germans (members of the Lutheran and German Reformed churches) and *pacifist* Germans (mostly Amish, Mennonites, Moravians, Dunkers, and Schwenkfelders). The pacifist Germans were akin to the Quakers in their refusal to fight in or support wars. Quakers themselves remained important in Pennsylvania and adjacent West Jersey, having earlier dominated politics on both sides of the Delaware River. Anglicans were a small minority, although influential. Each of these groups included a considerable admixture of loyalists and neutrals. Many of the Quakers, Peace Germans, and Dutch, in particular, distrusted the rebellion-minded Yankees, Scotch-Irish, and Virginians.

Our hypothetical political geographer could go on to suggest why the colonies beyond the thirteen would be less likely to join a rebellion led by New England, Ulster Pennsylvania, and Greater Virginia. Ethnic and sectarian differences, for one thing. The populations of Quebec, St. Jean (now Prince Edward Island), and Newfoundland, while sparse, were also largely French, Scottish, or Irish Catholics to whom the politics, culture, and religion of the rebellion were suspect. Countervailing political and military considerations would have to be strong.

The tropical sugar colonies, however annoyed by taxes and arrogant naval officers, would remain loyal for compelling reasons: strong ties to powerful British commercial interests, an influential supporting faction in Parliament, more favorable treatment for their sugar than Britain gave to Chesapeake tobacco, and considerable concessions to their trade interests (Jamaica and Dominica were allowed free ports). Possible slave uprisings would also be a caution. In Jamaica, where the mountainous "cockpit" of the island was controlled by runaway slaves called Maroons, 203,000 blacks vastly outnumbered 13,000 whites. The ratio in Barbados was 69,000 blacks to 19,000 whites. East and West Florida, as we have seen, were springboards for the British military, southern equivalents of Nova Scotia.

Leaders of the thirteen colonies had another reason for concern: these rival pieces of the empire were developing the better commercial relations with London. Britain's mid-century Whig Parliaments had seemed kindred in spirit to the Whig provinces, but the new House of Commons increasingly had favorites elsewhere: the East India Company, the Anglo-Irish landowners, the Society of West Indian Planters and Merchants, and even the Canada Committee. The northern mainland economies, being less rewarding to British oligarchs and aristocratic investors, had few spokesmen in London who were not simply paid agents. Benjamin

Franklin complained that "the West Indian planters by superior interest at home have procured the restraints to be laid on (our) commerce." John Dickinson, in his influential *Letters from a Farmer in Pennsylvania,* attacked the rival influence in Parliament not only of the East India Company, but of the Canadians, Nova Scotians, and Floridians.[2] These others, in short, had less cause to foresake the empire—and more encouragement to remain.

With these assumptions, the opening strategies in event of war could be more or less predicted: New Englanders and New Yorkers would lead an invasion of Canada. If that could be repulsed, Britain's reply must be to apply a tight naval blockade or to drive military and political wedges into the thousand-mile seaboard from Boston to Savannah. Advice to the King's ministers recommended three particular wedges: First, and most obvious, would be for Britain to seize New York's Champlain-Hudson Corridor. This offered the seaboard's only broad gap through the Appalachian mountain range, and much of its length was navigable for small to middling ships. British control would split seditious New England from the other colonies.

Thrusting into Pennsylvania was a second option. A mixed force of British and Indians could come down the Susquehanna Valley from Iroquois country in New York while the Royal Navy landed regular troops along the Delaware or in upper Chesapeake Bay to seize Baltimore or Philadelphia. The army also might strike for Philadelphia by marching through New Jersey. And the third approach would be to tear at Georgia and the Carolinas in order to split off the southern colonies.

The British ultimately tried all three approaches, but not as part of a well-coordinated plan. Map 4.2 shows the three major centers of rebellion—New England, Pennsylvania's American Ulster, and Greater Virginia—as context for possible invasion routes. Separating them was essential.

The avenue actually chosen, the Champlain-Hudson Corridor, will be discussed beginning on p. 148. Of the alternatives, a Chesapeake-Susquehanna invasion lacked the strategic attributes of the New York option. No broad lowland waterway cut through Pennsylvania's mountain barriers with the glacial directness that long-ago ice sheets had imposed on New York. Nor did any major

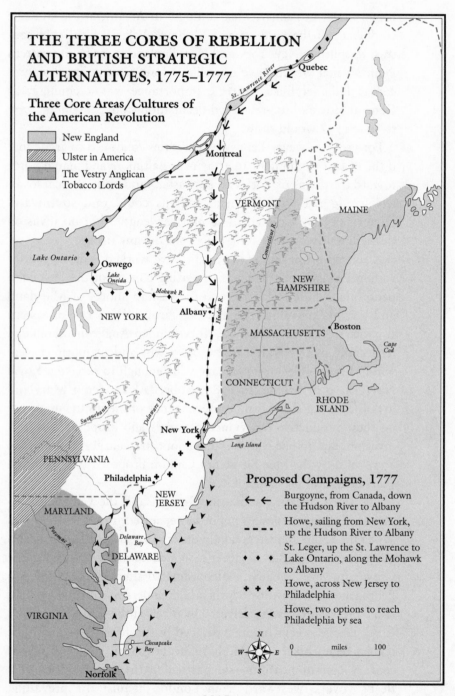

THE THREE CORES OF REBELLION AND BRITISH STRATEGIC ALTERNATIVES, 1775–1777

Three Core Areas/Cultures of the American Revolution

- New England
- Ulster in America
- The Vestry Anglican Tobacco Lords

Quebec

St. Lawrence River

Montreal

VERMONT

MAINE

Lake Ontario

Oswego

Lake Oneida

Mohawk R.

NEW HAMPSHIRE

Albany

Hudson R.

Connecticut R.

NEW YORK

MASSACHUSETTS

Boston

Cape Cod

CONNECTICUT

RHODE ISLAND

Susquehanna R.

Delaware R.

New York

Long Island

PENNSYLVANIA

Philadelphia

NEW JERSEY

MARYLAND

Potomac R.

Delaware Bay

DELAWARE

VIRGINIA

Chesapeake Bay

Norfolk

Proposed Campaigns, 1777

- ← ← Burgoyne, from Canada, down the Hudson River to Albany
- - - - Howe, sailing from New York, up the Hudson River to Albany
- ♦ ♦ ♦ St. Leger, up the St. Lawrence to Lake Ontario, along the Mohawk to Albany
- + + + Howe, across New Jersey to Philadelphia
- ◄ ◄ ◄ Howe, two options to reach Philadelphia by sea

N
W — E
S

0   miles   100

MAP 4.2

urban target in Pennsylvania compare to Albany, at the strategic confluence of the Hudson and Mohawk Valleys. Finally, in contrast to splitting New York and New England, a move into eastern Pennsylvania would have no reliable long-term political significance. Philadelphia's strategic importance was a chimera, as General Howe's little-rewarded occupation from September 1777 to June 1778 would show.

For years, however, Pennsylvania Tories continued to argue that if the British would land an army near Baltimore and march north toward the towns of York and Lancaster, thousands of local loyalists would rise to join them. Indians could raid southward. Historians have detailed these plots at length.[3] Yet no invasion through Baltimore ever took place, nor did any risings.

A related proposal, which might have worked, sidestepped invading Pennsylvania in favor of seizing control of the Delmarva peninsula, where Delaware and the eastern shores of Maryland and Virginia converge. The flat, rich farmland was one of eastern America's great breadbaskets, Tory-minded Anglicans abounded (especially in Delaware), and most towns and plantations were within fifteen miles of an estuary wide enough to receive a Royal Navy sloop or frigate. In 1780, Robert Alexander, a Maryland loyalist, set out the enormous dependency of the insurgent armies on these productive but vulnerable acres and proposed a British invasion. But no one was thinking about strategic grain supplies in 1776, and by the time Sir Henry Clinton proposed the operation years later, nothing came of it.

The third strategy, subduing Georgia and the Carolinas, assumed that these colonies might be separated from the other ten. When the King's ministers finally ordered a southern-focused campaign in 1779–1780, it scored some success. Unluckily for the Crown, however, the first, malcoordinated attempt was bungled in February 1776. Loyalist Scottish highlanders in North Carolina, rising prematurely, were defeated by rebels at the battle of Moore's Creek Bridge, weeks before a delayed British fleet arrived with the regular regiments that would have meant victory. Slow eighteenth-century communications—in particular, the uncertainties of a fleet's voyage westward from London against the prevailing winds—were crippling. Good timing was almost impossible.

However, by 1776, senior British planners, some with firsthand North American experience, had settled on a basic strategy still difficult to fault: to divide the New England colonies from the other nine by a three-pronged invasion to secure the Champlain-Hudson Corridor. But although achievable on paper, its execution in the field would be more difficult. The first complications came from Congress's own 1775 scheme to move the war far beyond the thirteen colonies. New England, under its Puritan "God of Warr," would strike first.

The American Attempts to Enlist Canada, Bermuda, and the Bahamas in the Revolution

The farthest reach of civil war in the English-speaking North Atlantic came quickly, in the first fifteen months while Britain was conciliatory and unprepared. Once the die of rebellion was cast on July 4, 1776, the British government mounted a strong financial, logistical, and military response under its new secretary of state for the American Department, Lord George Germain. The Earl of Dartmouth, in that same post through December 1775, had temporized in hopes of healing the breach. He took too long to grasp the colonists' willingness to enlarge it with attacks beyond their borders.

Consider: The Crown's own military power was at best weakly applied in 1775 after June's bloody setback at Bunker Hill. Nor was it on display in early 1776, especially in April, May, and June following General Howe's withdrawal from Boston to Halifax. Very few British troops were to be found in the thirteen colonies until July, when Howe's army and the Royal Navy, 32,000 men and 260 ships, descended on New York harbor from Halifax. The sight was awe-inspiring, overpowering. Residents of Tory-leaning Staten Island, in New York Harbor, watched from their hilltops in amazement. But few insurrections have been allowed to proceed so long with so little hindrance.

The American invasion of Canada was part of the British disarray. Many New England military figures, from Israel Putnam of Connecticut to John Stark of New Hampshire, had served in the colonial forces during the Hudson-Champlain campaigns of 1757–1760. The outbreak of hostilities at Lexington quickly returned their thoughts to the old, familiar battleground. A month later, expeditions from New England quickly overwhelmed the tiny caretaker garrisons of the four major English strongholds, now decrepit, left from the Great War: Fort Edward on the Hudson, Fort George on Lake George, and Forts Ticonderoga and Crown Point on Lake Champlain. By the end of May 1775, all four were in rebel hands, as was St. John at the Canadian end of the lake. The ordnance captured was pivotal in its own right. Most of Ticonderoga's eighty-six cannon would be hauled eastward by teams of oxen through early winter snows to bolster the siege of Boston. When these big guns were in position on the heights of Dorchester in March 1776, British departure was inevitable.

In passing the Coercive Acts, in early 1774, Parliament had *already* deemed Boston to be in a state of rebellion. This makes indefensible the slackness in not reinforcing either Canada or the upper New York forts. The British commander in Quebec, General Guy Carleton, had been a repeated voice for repairing and strengthening Ticonderoga. Yet, too confident of Canadians' loyalty and too unconcerned about possible war, Carleton had sent two of his regiments to Boston in mid-1774. When the New Englanders moved against the Hudson-Champlain forts, they found fewer than fifty soldiers at Ticonderoga, and mere handfuls at Edward and Crown Point. A single old soldier watched over what was left of Fort George. In the obvious battle area, just two regiments of British regulars, the 26th Infantry and the 7th Fusiliers, garrisoned Quebec, Montreal, the St. Lawrence Valley, and the two forts, Chambly and St. John's, that guarded the Richelieu River, Canada's equivalent of the Khyber Pass, as it descended from Lake Champlain to the St. Lawrence.

In August, when Whitehall was reeling from the news of Bunker Hill, American forces were already preparing to move against Montreal and Quebec before the winter snows. Brigadier Richard Montgomery, now a rebel but until 1772 an officer in the 17th Regiment of Foot, led the force of fifteen hundred men camped at Lake Champlain's northern end. Chambly and St. John's were his first objectives. Connecticut's Benedict Arnold was to lead a second force up the Kennebec River Valley.

That route led through northern Maine, alongside boiling whitewater and past chains of icy deserted lakes in what are still deep and lonely woods. From the Dead River, so called because of its lack of current and somber black quietude, the invaders crossed the Height-of-Land mountainous barrier to Canada, descending northward toward Quebec along the Chaudière River—*chaudière* being French for "cauldron." Forty-four days and two hundred miles from their start, Arnold's soldiers emerged on the southern shore of the St. Lawrence directly across from Quebec's old stone citadel.

Surprising, given this boldness, is that New England failed to mount a parallel naval expedition against the increasingly important British naval base and administrative center in Halifax, Nova Scotia. Local currents, tides, and sandbars were well known to Massachusetts mariners. Moreover, the half of Nova Scotia's population made up of recent emigrants from New England and Pennsylvania would have provided some support to an invasion that first year.

Had the New Englanders taken Halifax, weakly defended during that half-disbelieving summer and autumn of 1775, Nova Scotia—and perhaps all of Canada—could have wound up in rebel hands.[4] Without facilities at Halifax, the argument goes, the British fleet could not have maintained itself in winter Canadian waters waiting for late April and May when breaking ice in the St. Lawrence would finally permit access to Quebec, Montreal, and the Great Lakes. Later, many Canadian historians would insist that Quebec and Nova Scotia had little interest in the rebellion. But in 1775, curiosity was intense, especially along the Champlain corridor, through which the Continental Congress was pouring spies, pamphlets, emissaries, and official circulars, and also in the small Nova Scotian ports along the Bay of Fundy, with their close sea connections to New England. As the troops of Congress advanced in September and October, French-speaking *Canadiens* were friendly.

Hundreds joined the American armies as they marched down the Richelieu toward the St. Lawrence. As Montreal was occupied, support came from a wide range of sources: residents who hailed from the thirteen colonies, British merchants angry at the government's decision to reject local elections and to leave power with the French seigneurs, and ordinary French Quebeckers simply trying to pick a winner, to say nothing of the small minority of French anti-clericals and local admirers of Voltaire hopeful that a *Congressiste* Quebec could depose the priests, seigneurs, and their British protectors. At a large ironworks in Trois Rivières, hundreds more Canadians were casting mortars, bombshells, and weapons for rebel use.[5]

During that winter of uncertainty, French-Canadian popular opinion moved more or less with the tide of battle. The fall of Forts Chambly and St. John's in October and early November spurred attachment to Montgomery's invaders. So did Montreal's surrender, although there was a pause after the British captured Ethan Allen, leader of Vermont's famed Green Mountain Boys. Benedict Arnold, leading the second, smaller American force up the Kennebec, found the same welcome. When he reached French-speaking territory, seventy miles south of Quebec, the people of the upper Chaudière Valley sold food to the Americans, drove cattle to their camp—and some even signed up. Arnold, too, had enlisted a considerable number of French-Canadians by the time he reached Quebec in November.

Congress had gone so far as to authorize two Canadian regiments. One fell apart after fighting at Quebec; the second, under Colonel Moses Hazen, served through the war, finally demobilizing in 1783. Most of the recruits were French, enlisted in late 1775 and early 1776, and by April some 250 men were under arms. Yet as Hazen wrote to his superiors in New York, there were good reasons why the civil war in Canada was about to splutter out: the invasion's faltering at Quebec; the worthlessness of American paper money; Quebecker resentment of rebel troops taking goods and services at bayonet point; local disgust at being paid in badly depreciated paper money or unredeemable certificates; and, finally, the mounting evidence that the American cause lacked both solvency and the number of soldiers needed to maintain its headway in Canada.[6]

The collapse came quickly. After several failed attempts to capture Quebec City, the American commanders gave up in May as ice breaking on the St. Lawrence allowed the British fleet to relieve the city. Within days, the rebel forces were falling back to Montreal, then retreating along the Richelieu River, and, finally, streaming back to Lake Champlain in a nearly calamitous disarray, almost overtaken by the advancing British.

Congress did weigh plans for another Canadian invasion under the command of the Marquis de Lafayette in the winter of 1777–1778, following Burgoyne's defeat at Saratoga, and then again in the fall of 1778, in 1779, in 1780, and in 1781. No second invasion was ever mounted, but with France in the war, the British high command could not relax.[7]

The civil war context of 1775–1776 also extended to Nova Scotia, which at that time included the territory on both sides of the Bay of Fundy. Map 4.3 shows the battle areas of both Quebec and Nova Scotia. Of the twenty thousand Europeans on the eastern peninsula, some ten thousand were Yankees who had come from New England in the late 1750s and early 1760s. There was also an English contingent of three or four thousand in and around the military and government center of Halifax, as well as several thousand Scots and Scottish highlanders. On Fundy's western shore, in present-day New Brunswick, about half of the two thousand locals were emigrant New Englanders. Another third were French-speaking Acadians—brothers and cousins of those expelled by the British in the 1750s.

In 1775, most of Nova Scotia's emigrant New Englanders temporized. In what is now Passamaquoddy, New Brunswick, the local Committee of Safety applied to Congress for admission to the union. The members of the Nova Scotia Assembly for Annapolis and Granville remained away from the legislature because of their American sympathies. So did the three from Cumberland County. The latter weighed an appeal to George Washington to invade, but settled for an autumn 1775 petition to the Nova Scotia government to stop trying to force the transplanted New Englanders into the militia. This was granted. In March 1776, the pro-American Nova Scotians wrote to Washington that two to three hundred American troops could secure the region between the Chignecto Isthmus and Halifax. Investigating British officers agreed, reporting to Halifax that many ex–New England settlers would join or at least applaud an invasion. They just wouldn't start an uprising themselves.

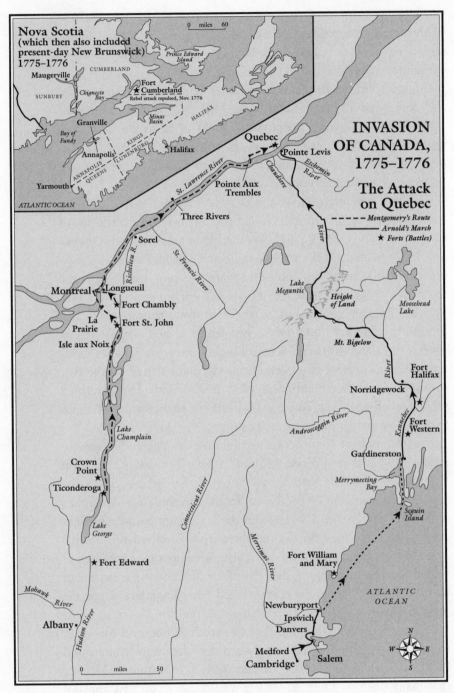

Nova Scotia
(which then also included
present-day New Brunswick)
1775–1776

CUMBERLAND

0   miles   60

Prince Edward Island

Maugerville

SUNBURY

Chignecto Bay

★ Fort
Cumberland
Rebel attack repulsed, Nov. 1776

Minas Basin

HALIFAX

Granville

Bay of Fundy

KINGS

Annapolis   Halifax

ANNAPOLIS   LUNENBURG
QUEENS

Yarmouth

ATLANTIC OCEAN

Quebec ★
Pointe Levis

Etchemin River

St. Lawrence River

Pointe Aux
Trembles

Chaudière

INVASION
OF CANADA,
1775–1776

The Attack
on Quebec

– – – – *Montgomery's Route*
———— *Arnold's March*
★ *Forts (Battles)*

River

Three Rivers

Sorel

St. Francis River

Lake
Megantic

Height
of Land

Moosehead
Lake

Richelieu R.

Montreal   Longueuil
              ★ Fort Chambly
La   ★ Fort St. John
Prairie
Isle aux Noix

▲ Mt. Bigelow

River

Fort
Halifax
★

Norridgewock ★

Lake
Champlain

Kennebec

Fort
Western ★

Crown
Point ★

Gardinerston

Ticonderoga ★

Merrymeeting Bay

Androscoggin River

Lake
George

Seguin
Island

★ Fort Edward

Mohawk River

Connecticut River

Merrimac River

Fort William
and Mary

ATLANTIC
OCEAN

Hudson River

Albany

Newburyport
Ipswich
Danvers

N
W   E
S

Medford
Cambridge   Salem

0   miles   50

MAP 4.3

But once the British army reached Halifax in April and word arrived of the disorderly American retreat from Quebec and Montreal, the point became moot. Halifax now teemed with British soldiers and sailors. Besides pumping gold into the local economy, their presence also reduced the need to threaten residents with militia service that could put them at sword's point with New England relatives.

What is now New Brunswick was a virtual no-man's-land in 1776—two hundred miles of barely settled coast. Besides Passamaquoddy on the border, population clustered in two places: the pro-American villages of French Acadians, still bitter at Britain, and the New England settlement at Maugerville on St. John's River. The Indian tribes of the area, the Penobscots of Maine and the Malacete of St. John's Valley, also had early leanings to the congressional side, especially after Malacete chiefs made a 1776 visit to Massachusetts. Had this area been strategic, a small American army could have held it.

What the Acadians and ex–New Englanders could *not* manage was an unaided invasion of Nova Scotia. And so the civil war in Nova Scotia petered out in the autumn of 1776 when rebel leaders, including an expelled member of the Nova Scotia Assembly, raised seventy-two men from the New England, Acadian, and Indian settlements of the St. John and went north to Chignecto to call for a rising against the British. Most of the local New Englanders and Acadians responded, as did other New Englanders from nearby Cobequid and Scotch-Irish Pennsylvanians from Pictou, for a total of two hundred. This was not enough to capture Fort Cumberland, which was eventually relieved from Halifax, and a considerable portion of Chignecto's former New Englanders and Acadians chose to leave for the new United States.

The bulk of Nova Scotia's former New Englanders, under the leadership of a Massachusetts-born cleric, Henry Alline, found a religious solution appropriate to a Chosen People: As British and American privateers brought a kind of seaborne civil war to the waters off Nova Scotia, Alline interpreted the evil conflict between two backsliding, English-speaking Protestant nations as jeopardizing the whole course of events since the Reformation. Remote, uncorrupted Nova Scotia would show the way and replace both Old England and New England as the City Upon a Hill.[8]

Canadians, in sum, were far from united in wanting to remain under the British flag. For a period in 1775–1776, the three biggest groups, French Catholic Quebeckers, Acadians, and Nova Scotia Yankees, showed a considerable interest in the American cause, but it waned after British troops arrived in force and Yankee tactics and practices had lost credibility.

Bermuda and the Bahamas also had enough American sympathizers to give pause to British authorities. At the outbreak of conflict, Silas Deane, one of Congress's agents, suggested that by keeping Bermuda supplied with food, the colonies might enlist the island as an excellent base from which light frigates and sloops could play havoc with Britain's traffic to and from the West Indies. The new American navy was too small for that. Even so, the mainland was Bermuda's principal source of provisions. In July 1775, local leaders sent a delegation to the Second Continental Congress. After expressing some sympathy with the American cause, the Bermudians reiterated a request for provisions, unofficially noting that Bermuda had one hundred barrels of the King's gunpowder to exchange. Shortly thereafter, the powder was quietly taken from the magazine and shipped to the mainland. The governor, indignant but powerless, reported to London that many members of the Assembly and even some councillors were involved. To keep food coming, during the war Bermudians provided the rebelling colonies with fast ships built of Bermuda cedar, and with salt, all-important for preserving meat. As late as 1780, George Washington was interested in a proposal for the United States taking over the island made by St. George Tucker, a Virginian with close family connections in Bermuda.[9]

Other colonies' stores of munitions were also great temptations to the new American authorities. The president of the governor's council of Barbados was impugned for selling powder to the rebels, and in 1775, General Gage, the British commander in Boston, wrote to the governor of the Bahamas that American ships were fitting out to attack New Providence and seize its military stores. In early 1776, a fleet made up of eight small warships captured Nassau, the seat of government, and occupied it for two weeks. But the cannon, mortars, shot, and some powder taken were then recaptured by the British navy. The reports sent home by Governor Montfort Browne from 1776 to 1780 make clear that many prominent Bahamians and officials colluded with the rebels just as Bermudians had, although the islands also supported many pro-British privateers who played havoc with American trade. A joint expedition of American naval frigates and Spanish troops from Cuba captured Nassau again in 1782, remaining in occupation until near the end of the war.

Even the sugar colonies gave the rebels some support. Besides the pro-American addresses sent to London by the Jamaica Assembly, kindred messages came from Tobago, from the Assembly of Grenada and the Grenadines, and from the Council of St. Vincent. The Assembly of Barbados established a fund for the people of Boston and dispatched a petition to the King critical of British policy. Governors in several of the islands noted a growth in planters' sentiment for republicanism and self-government, while local assemblies asserted new powers or claimed legislative coequality with the British House of Commons in a manner suggested by mainland leaders like Benjamin Franklin.[10] But racial ratios buoyed British rule. In Jamaica, support for the American rebels eroded in 1776 after an abortive local slave rebellion by house slaves who had become imbued with the spirit of liberty from hearing Whig planters discuss events in the mainland colonies.

Small fleets of American warships were not strong enough to cruise easily in the Caribbean, but several, including the *Oliver Cromwell*, flagship of the Connecticut state navy, raided Tobago between 1777 and 1779. An American vessel carried off gunpowder from Grenada, privateers besieged Dominica, and a mere eight-gun privateer, the *Johnson*, harassed coastal estates in Barbados.[11]

The Canadian invasion aside, none of this had much effect on the war. The preliminary American ambitions to gain control of Quebec, Nova Scotia, the Floridas, and possibly Bermuda and the Bahamas came to naught fairly quickly. East Floridians scoffed. Quebec and Nova Scotia might have been taken in 1775, but were not. Much of British North America had good reasons for remaining in the empire. The thirteen rebel colonies were all but unique. Yet partial collusion, along with some supporting constitutional interpretation, was more widespread than all but specialized histories suggest.

The Champlain-Hudson Corridor Strategy

Even in the beginning, not all of Britain's senior officials and military leaders were sanguine that *any* military strategy could put down an American revolution. The Earl of Dartmouth, the American secretary in 1775, preferred combining a naval blockade with efforts at conciliation; William Pitt told Parliament that force would not work. Viscount Barrington, the secretary at war, whose subcabinet job was mostly administrative, did not see any way by which Britain could hope to prevail. Friends knew he would have liked to resign.

But for others actually planning or charged with operations in America—King George himself, Lord North, Germain, General Guy Carleton as British commander in Canada, and John Burgoyne and William Howe as senior generals—the familiar corridor from Manhattan to Montreal emerged as the hub. Its strategic importance became so accepted that the British loss at Saratoga in October 1777 more than anything else brought France into the war. Defeat along the Hudson also forced a change in British strategy. Blocking American self-government through a military victory in the northern colonies was no longer likely. The troop transports headed south.

Back in late 1775, however, when rebel forces had already paraded through Montreal's Place D'Armes and were besieging Quebec, the corridor remained the expected key to the North. Its military centrality had become apparent in the 1670s, after English rule had replaced Dutch administration in New York, embroiling England and France as hostile, probing neighbors and fur trade rivals. By the mid-eighteenth century, they were rubbing shoulders and bayonets. England claimed and fortified the Hudson River watershed and King Louis's engineers that of the St. Lawrence. In fact, neither set of creeks and tributaries was easily defined, especially where they interlaced around the deep mountain lake that soon had two names—*Lac St. Sacrament* in French, Lake George in English.

Each generation saw British garrisons and fortifications edge north and west, while those of France spread farther south and west. The extent to which this rivalry was spreading into the Ohio and Mississippi Valleys sparked the Great War for Empire in 1754. But as we have seen, the Hudson-Champlain Corridor continued as the hemisphere's principal concentration of interior fortifications. Hence the assumption in 1775 that British generals, should they repulse an invasion of Canada, would logically pursue the retreating provincial columns down the St. Lawrence and Lake Champlain to occupy Albany and the Hudson Valley. The French had cherished their own Hudson Corridor hopes as far back as 1689, when an ambitious plan to invade New York was approved by King Louis XIV.

Burgoyne, choosing to establish himself as the new principal theorist of this approach in 1776, had already developed a commitment to New York's broader strategic importance. Following passage of the Coercive Acts in 1774, when the Ministry saw Massachusetts gain support up and down the seaboard, Major General Burgoyne, along with Generals Howe and Clinton, was sounded about a posting to America. Howe and Clinton, being senior, both had better claim to the top appointment, so Burgoyne injected a new idea: He could go in the independent capacity of military governor of New York, a post for which he had already been proposed several years earlier. Despite Burgoyne's taste for the dramatic, he was a reasonably serious strategist.* New York, he had concluded, was the focal point of the middle colonies. A military commander there, disposing three or four regiments, would be in position to help negotiate a peace or to help drive a wedge between Pennsylvania, New York, and New Jersey and the rebel Yankees to the north and east. But the Ministry rejected his request.

As a result, Burgoyne sailed for Boston in company with Howe and Clinton, the duties awaiting him unspecified and subordinate. But in May, as his ship neared shore, a passing vessel brought word about Lexington and the colonists besieging the British army in

---

*This topic will be discussed at greater length in chapter 7. His strategic talents were offset by his pomposity and overdramatization, but they were not insignificant.

Boston. As a Member of Parliament as well as a serving officer, Burgoyne perceived still another opportunity: He wrote to Lord North proposing that he leave the army and be commissioned as a peace negotiator to go to New York, Philadelphia, and other centers of the rebellion. The government had others in mind as negotiators, principally the more prominent Howe family, and after June's stunning British losses at Bunker Hill, His Majesty's junior major general in Boston reverted to military thoughts and advice. In a letter to Lord Rochford, secretary of state for the Southern Department, Burgoyne, now a career soldier again, proposed that foreign troops be hired to squeeze New York in a pincer movement. One force would go up the Hudson, the other move south from Canada.

This idea was not original. Still, it would be the ambitious Burgoyne, in late 1775 and early 1776, who put the strategic flesh on its conceptual bones. By the time he returned to England for the winter to politick and attend Parliament, reports had arrived about the fall of Forts St. John and Chambly on the approach to Montreal. With communications as slow as they were, even Quebec could have capitulated. Burgoyne, who had begun drafting his *Reflections upon the War in America* on shipboard, was reassuring: The Champlain-Hudson pincer approach would still work even if Quebec had fallen. The naval flotilla accompanying General Wolfe in 1759 had sailed past an enemy-held Quebec citadel. Ships could do so again.

The King and Germain both liked the plan. Burgoyne was named second in command in Canada, in place to take over should General Carleton, the embattled governor, turn out to be killed or captured. Germain's unusual orders to Carleton, whom he disliked, identified Burgoyne as "so fully instructed in every point" that further details from London would not be necessary.[12] Burgoyne sailed at the end of March, and on May 27, after entering the St. Lawrence, he found out that Quebec had not fallen, the Americans were in retreat, and Carleton was still in charge. Nevertheless, the next few weeks only confirmed their divergent temperaments: Burgoyne immediately proposed bold attempts, which he would lead, to cut off the rebel retreat. Carleton, as usual, acted cautiously, a godsend for the Americans, most of whom escaped to New York.

It was now June, the first reliable month in which British generals of prior wars had launched major expeditions in the north country. Burgoyne, with his flair as an amateur dramatist, wrote to his fellow general, Henry Clinton, that his favorite thought on retiring each night was a triumphant autumn union with Clinton and Howe on the Hudson. But Carleton, in no such hurry, took longer than expected to construct the flotilla of lake-craft he needed to overwhelm the rebel squadron being built on Lake Champlain. (The powerful British ships available on the St. Lawrence, unable to navigate the rapids of the Richelieu, might as well have been in Halifax.)

Burgoyne, impatient as precious weeks slipped away, proposed to lead an early diversion. He could take three battalions to Lake Ontario and then move down the Mohawk Valley toward Albany, forcing the rebels to shift troops away from Fort Ticonderoga (Carleton's own principal objective). Alternatively, he could move down the eastern shore of Lake Champlain, avoiding the rebel guns at Ticonderoga, and then divide his army, one force to seize the portage between Lake Champlain and Lake George and the second to destroy the shipyard at Skenesboro where the American fleet was under construction. Carleton considered the first idea, but ultimately rejected it. The second was impractical because no road went down Champlain's eastern side.

Yet Burgoyne's instinct for dash and action was not misplaced. The caution of the northern commander-in-chief was jeopardizing Burgoyne's all-important battle plan for 1776. Thirty thousand British and German mercenary troops had sailed into New York Harbor in July. Once New York was secured, which should not take long, a substantial movement northward up the Hudson was plausible. For troops moving south from Canada, Ticonderoga had to be captured by mid-autumn at best, for Albany to be reached before winter.

But months went by, with September producing its usual seasonal blaze of north-country maples, and Carleton's carpenters were still busy. Not until October 12 did his vessels finally engage the smaller rebel flotilla off Valcour Island just south of present-day Plattsburgh.

In immediate terms, Valcour Island was a decisive British victory—eleven out of seventeen American ships were lost and the rest withdrew. Strategically, however, it was a failure. By taking his extra month to build an additional eighteen-gun ship, the *Inflexible,* Carleton had made a poor exchange. At the sacrifice of September, the British fleet had more vessels and nearly twice the weight in cannon, in addition to the advantage of trained sailors and professionals drawn from the Royal Navy in the St. Lawrence.[13] Acceptance of higher British casualties and greater ship damage to achieve a harder-fought victory in September could have been decisive. Baron Riedesel, the German commander, said as much: "If we could have begun our last expedition four weeks earlier, I am satisfied that everything would have ended this year."[14]

Adverse winds and weather further slowed British movement, so that Crown Point was not occupied until October 18. The fleet did not begin landing troops near Fort Ticonderoga until October 28. Within a few days, on Carleton's orders, they were reembarked. Deciding that Ticonderoga looked too strong, and that November would be too late in the year to continue the campaign, the general from Quebec also abandoned Crown Point and returned to Canada. The war in the north country was over for 1776.

Many generations later, Winston Churchill would identify the battle of Valcour Island, in which General Benedict Arnold commanded the American forces, as one of the most important naval successes in U.S. history. The delay of Carleton, plus the abandonment of Crown Point, an advanced post that could have speeded next spring's invasion, helped to ruin British plans in both 1776 and 1777. No World War II aircraft carrier was ever named for Valcour Island to accompany those saluting related 1777 successes, the carriers *Saratoga, Oriskany,* and *Bennington.* Yet Arnold's holding action was more auspicious for the patriots than many technical victories.

At the end of October, the trees were almost bare on Sugarloaf Hill and Mount Independence, the principal heights surrounding Fort Ticonderoga. Had John Burgoyne and several of the artillerists accompanying Carleton landed to study the terrain, they might have seen, even more easily, what several of Burgoyne's officers quickly grasped when the British returned in July. Ticonderoga, erstwhile

Gibraltar of the North, could be captured by any army able to pack cannon to the top of Sugarloaf (soon to be renamed Mount Defiance) and fire at 1,400 yards into and over its walls. Had the invaders hauled cannon and howitzers up the goat terrain of Sugarloaf in October 1776, as Burgoyne's men did nine months later, the rebels would presumably have done what they, too, did nine months later: spike their guns and abandon the fort.

Carleton had also guessed wrongly about the winter weather, which proved unusually mild. The lakes remained navigable through much of December. The British commander *could* have used late November and early December to drive south to Albany and link up with forces that General Howe *could* have sent from New York. The latter had defeated George Washington at White Plains on October 28 (the same day British troops landed near Ticonderoga), and the last fort in Manhattan, cut off and isolated, fell three weeks later. Howe's conclusive victory in the lower Hudson region left him free—had circumstances so demanded—to move north to Albany instead of pursuing Washington through New Jersey.

Such was the importance of Valcour Island. Had Carleton not waited to overwhelm the rebel flotilla, instead of beating it earlier with less ease, the war might have been all but over before Washington, virtually at the end of his resources, could perform his near-magic feat on Christmas Day. This was when he crossed the icy Delaware from Pennsylvania, defeating the surprised Hessians at Trenton and revitalizing low American spirits with the moral equivalent of hot buttered rum. Had Carleton and Howe converged on Albany in November 1776, they would have drawn Washington north, and in November and December, the American general lacked the necessary strength.

There was a further irony in that autumn of 1776. The King and Lord George Germain had been aware that Howe might hesitate to link up with Carleton because the latter, outranking him, would assume overall command. To avoid this, they prodded Howe by installing Burgoyne, to whom Howe *would* be senior, as northern field commander, confining Carleton to his Canadian civil administrative role. Howe himself received the news on October 26, just before the battle of White Plains. However, the ship that carried

London's change-of-command instructions to Carleton and Burgoyne never got through, returning to England after three failed attempts to pass the icebound mouth of the St. Lawrence. *Burgoyne was to have been in charge by October*—and had he been, the fates of Crown Point, Ticonderoga, Albany, and even the new United States might have been different. Burgoyne almost certainly would have kept Crown Point as an advance post for an earlier and better-positioned invasion in 1777. He might have taken Ticonderoga. Moreover, had Burgoyne been this much further forward in late 1776 or early 1777, Howe would not have been able to back away from the Hudson strategy for another alternative.

This is not to overpraise Burgoyne, whose vainness, jealousies, pomposity, and weakness for theatrics all contributed to the final reckoning of Saratoga. But he had two considerable strengths: attention to strategy and boldness. Pressing on in October and November 1776 would have been in keeping with his entrepreneuring leadership of the 16th Light Dragoons in Portugal. It also would have matched his combative advice to senior officers both in Boston after Bunker Hill in June 1775 and on the St. Lawrence River eleven months later.

It must have been an irate Burgoyne, as well as an ill one, who took ship for England in November, and he soon found himself preparing a follow-up 1777 invasion plan increasingly at odds with Carleton's. The latter favored a redesigned two-pronged invasion from Canada—one force to descend to Oswego on Lake Ontario and move east down the Mohawk River, and the second to proceed down the Connecticut River into New England. Carleton now preferred to de-emphasize the Champlain-Hudson route, the locus of his miscalculation during the previous campaign. Burgoyne, however, restated the Champlain-Hudson argument persuasively, and the peeved King decided "to have the part of the Canadian army which must attempt to join General Howe led by a more enterprising commander."[15]

Whether that would be Burgoyne or Clinton remained undecided for several weeks. Germain leaned to Clinton, but the cabinet opted for Burgoyne, who, while spending part of the winter in Bath taking the warm waters, had completed a new and revised campaign plan entitled *Thoughts for Conducting the War on the Side of Canada*.

The ideas that would guide the decisive invasion of New York were now set forth in their greatest detail: The army to move south from Canada, Burgoyne argued, should include eight thousand regular troops, artillery, several thousand Canadians, and at least one thousand Indians. They would take Crown Point, then assault Ticonderoga. As a diversion, Colonel Barry St. Leger would take a mixed force of regulars, loyalists, and Indians to Oswego and then down the Mohawk River. Once Ticonderoga was captured, this final outline still left the force from Canada three options: effecting a junction with Howe at Albany; taking Albany alone in order to let Howe move south; or turning east down the Connecticut River to strike at New England. King George authorized only seven thousand regulars for Burgoyne, but indicated that Howe and Burgoyne should join in Albany.

Howe, who seems to have wanted either Burgoyne or his strategy to fail, had other plans. Several other plans, in fact. As even sympathetic historians have pointed out, between November 1776 and April 1777, he sent Germain three different proposals for the spring and summer campaign. The first, in November, outlined an attack on Boston from Rhode Island, while another large force moved up the Hudson. Then in December, he radically changed his advice. A double offensive against Philadelphia became the new centerpiece, with the main army proceeding across New Jersey and a second smaller force going by sea. Under this plan, Howe, presumably, would finish in Philadelphia in time to move north later in the year. Or so war planners in London still assumed. The early winter of 1776–1777 was close to the zenith of British optimism, although it cooled slightly after the bad news from Trenton.

Finally, in April, after assent to his second plan by the King and Germain had reached him from London, Howe shifted to a *third*: His army to capture Philadelphia would go by sea from New York. No mention was made of any move to join Burgoyne. Howe's sea trip eventually took over four weeks (July 23–August 25), a drawn-out voyage during which the British general's ability to restrain Washington's army was suspended and the odds for British success in the Champlain-Hudson Corridor worsened.

In London, Germain lacked the political strength in Parliament and at court to rein in Howe, a close relative of the King. But he could see when the general's final campaign outline arrived on May 18 that a golden opportunity was slipping away. The orders Germain sent back for Howe not to neglect Burgoyne arrived too late: Howe was already at sea.

Leaders on both sides were perplexed by Howe's actions. Even as the tide took the British fleet out of New York Harbor in July, George Washington and his staff were convinced that a deception was under way, that some British ships would turn back and head up the Hudson to join Burgoyne. Only days earlier, the Americans had found out that Burgoyne had taken Fort Ticonderoga on July 5. Why wouldn't Howe's force be moving in *that* direction?

In a later chapter, I will consider whether Howe, with his Whig and antiwar background, truly wanted a decisive military victory. He arguably threw away several chances: in his strategy at Bunker Hill, in the fighting around Manhattan in 1776, and then in 1777 by not supporting Burgoyne. Had Howe's army, rivergoing transports with even five to six thousand soldiers, pushed up the Hudson on July 23 instead of heading south, they would have needed only to break through forts Montgomery, Clinton, and Constitution guarding the Hudson highlands. Three months later, however, General Clinton would take all three in four days. Once through the highlands, a tricky passage where the Hudson narrows so that crosswinds can be as disabling for ships as cannon fire, Howe would have faced little rebel opposition.

How little is not always recognized. Massachusetts General John Glover, arriving with his own understrength brigade as a reinforcement in early August, found a "weak and shatter'd" American army of just three thousand camped nine miles north of Albany, trembling with every rumor and war whoop in the forest.[16] Only twenty-five miles farther north, Burgoyne himself had reached the banks of the Hudson on July 29 with his Indians and Hessians. Howe's redcoats forming up on Albany's quays would have made a joining of armies inevitable. Even without reinforcements, the way to Albany might still have been open for Burgoyne. Senior American officers would later agree that a strike force of five thousand soldiers moving quickly with only light baggage and artillery could well have taken the city.

Victory on the Hudson would not necessarily have won Britain the war. Independence for New England, at least, might have already become inevitable a year earlier after Bunker Hill. However, had British capture of Albany in late summer replaced Burgoyne's eventual capitulation to General Gates a few months later, a negotiated peace might have kept much of what became the United States loosely within the empire.

We will come back to Generals Gates and Burgoyne. But there is another point to consider. By August 1777, three and a half years had passed since an irate prime minister had asked Parliament to find Massachusetts in a state of rebellion. Nearly two and a half years had passed since the Revolution began at Lexington and Concord. Transatlantic logistics were difficult, but rarely has a government charged with tyranny (or even imperial ambition) taken so long to mount suppression of such mixed intensity. Too many senior generals began the war more anxious to negotiate than to fight. Several of the best known, as we will see, refused to serve in North America. As late as 1774, Howe had promised voters in his Parliamentary constituency that *he* would not serve. By the spring of 1777, his decision to invade Philadelphia by sea through Chesapeake Bay, whatever its motives, may have fatally compromised British chances for a military victory.

From March to July 1776, the British government, still hoping for conciliation, had only a handful of troops stationed in the thirteen openly rebellious colonies. Without overawing force, insurrection flourished. After the New York campaign of late 1776, General Howe's seeming unwillingness on several occasions to deliver a crushing blow to Washington's army had already produced bitter commentary and mocking verse among bewildered loyalists and critical staff officers.

In retrospect, a vital element of national commitment *was* lacking in the British war effort, a missing spark that had nothing to do with logistics, strategy, financial mobilization, or effective communications. Even the question has been ignored in most history books of the era—American, British, and Canadian. Yet one explanation flows all too easily enough from a reading of Anglo-American history.

The Unpopularity of an English Army Fighting English-Speaking Whig Protestants

Two hundred and forty years had passed between the English Reformation and the American Revolution. During virtually all of this time, English Protestants were too involved in proclaiming and believing themselves a Chosen People and Nation to fight others of their same religion, nationality, and tongue. The enemy was elsewhere. The English Civil War is a seeming exception. Or was it? When Royalists and Parliamentarians clashed, polar views of English culture and religion were barely beneath the surface. As we have seen, many Parliamentarians, Puritans especially, believed they were fighting the Stuarts to save England from Popish plots and Catholic monarchs.

Beyond the battlefields of 1640s, just one major confrontation pitted English Protestants against a mostly Protestant English army—and in retrospect, it was an embarrassment. This was Sedgemoor, in 1685, fought to unseat a Catholic king whose queen several years later would petition Pope Innocent for an alliance of Catholic princes to restore her husband's crown and the Catholic faith in England.[17]

Sedgemoor and the earlier Civil War battles aside, English armies spent the two centuries from the 1560s to the 1760s fighting French, Spanish, Irish, and Scottish Catholics, with interspersed (and less popular) combat with Dutch Protestants, Scottish Protestants, and German Protestants. Protestantism and nationalism were closely intertwined in most English wars. To send a late seventeenth- or eighteenth-century Protestant, Whig-inclined English army into the field to defeat an English-speaking Protestant and Whig-infused cause was something else. Sedgemoor and the infamous Bloody Assizes that followed left a bad taste. No *Protestant* king had ordered such a battle; no *Whig* ministry had ordered or tolerated such executions;

---

*In the words of historian Ray A. Billington, "This [anti-Catholic] feeling remained so strong through the early part of the Revolution that the president of Princeton University believed the common hatred of Popery caused by the Quebec Act the only thing which cemented the divergent religious groups in the colonies together sufficiently to allow them to make war, an opinion which was shared by English observers. . . ."

and a century later, when the dust of the American Revolution had settled, some critics suggested Britain's defeat was, in a sense, another warning not to fight fellow Protestants.[18]

This is not to suggest that the American Revolution was fought because of religion, although as we have seen, some think so.* What it clearly suggests, though, is that religion—dissenter denominations and politics, in particular—was at the root of responses throughout the empire, Britain included. As chapter 6 will detail, from Quebec to Ireland, Catholic bishops opposed the American rebels and urged their flocks to do likewise. Within England, dissenters were the most inclined to favor the Americans, Anglicans from Whig backgrounds were often in the middle, and High Church Anglicans the most anxious for coercion and a taste of the bayonet.

To many Englishmen of Whig background, there was an innate unpopularity in the idea of war with the Low Church Anglicans and Protestant dissenter groups who made up 90 percent of the white population of the thirteen colonies. The very confrontation reinforced old fears about growing Crown power. Victory over the American rebels would only strengthen the new imperial coalition in Britain and its views of politics and liberties. Use of force in Massachusetts and Virginia could be justified, however, to uphold the authority of Parliament and to keep the new empire together rather than let it break up. But the colonists had important perceptions on their side, too—not least, one imagines, that quite unlike any other enemy England might fight, the American colonials shared most of the political culture, religious beliefs, and even Chosen Nation assumptions of a Whiggery that had dominated England for several generations.

It would have been contrary to two and a half centuries of national history if psychologies like these did not help explain the reluctance with which important parts of Britain faced the possibility of war in 1774—and then the unpopular reality of it in 1775. However, before we look at these British internal divisions, we can usefully turn to the linchpin of diverging British and American political development: the civil war within the thirteen colonies, and who took which side and why.

5

THE MAKING OF A REVOLUTION

Patriots, Loyalists, and Neutrals

The nature of the Revolution (was) a religious and civil war on both sides of the Atlantic. Traditions of political thought and action were carried within and articulated by the mosaic of religious denominations which made up the British Isles and, still more, the American colonies . . . , Anglicans, Presbyterians, Congregationalists, Baptists, Quakers and a host of less numerous sects.

      —J. C. D. Clark, *The Language of Liberty*, 1994

Here [in South Carolina] the fierce civil war in progress between Patriots and Loyalists—or Whigs and Tories as they were locally called—was darkened by midnight raids, seizure of cattle, murderous ambushes, and atrocities such as we have known in our own day in Ireland. [General Nathaniel] Greene himself wrote: "The animosities between the Whigs and Tories of this state renders their situation truly deplorable. There is not a day passes but there are more or less who fall a sacrifice to their savage disposition. The Whigs seem determined to extirpate the Tories and the Tories the Whigs. Some thousands have fallen in this way in this quarter, and the evil rages with more violence than ever. If a stop cannot be put to these massacres the country will be depopulated in a few months more, and neither Whig nor Tory can live."

      —Winston S. Churchill, *The Age of Revolution*, 1951

> *Pennsylvania was not a nation at war with another nation, but a*
> *country in a state of civil war.*
>
> —Thomas McKean, Chief Justice of Pennsylvania,
> referring to the circumstances of 1776–1779

I N JUNE 1863, when Robert E. Lee's Confederate forces crossed the Mason-Dixon line into Pennsylvania, hoping to capture Harrisburg and Philadelphia to end the War Between the States, the American Revolution had been over for eighty years. Mythology had displaced reality. The brother-against-brother, cousin-against-cousin aspect of the earlier combat—the bitter viciousness to which General Greene, Pennsylvania Chief Justice McKean, and others referred—had been submerged in an uplifting national consensus.

In truth, the Revolution in South Carolina was a civil war in which 103 battles were fought with no one but South Carolinians on *both* sides.[1] And the acrimony in Pennsylvania had been enough to warrant an eighteenth-century civil war marker not far from those that would soon commemorate Gettysburg.[2] The Revolution, in reality, was not just one of America's civil wars; it may well have been the most bitter.

All of the cousins' fights were civil wars; indeed, *all* of them drew on a shared, and to an extent, identifying, cultural stream. Figure 5.1 suggests the threads and continuities involved which lesser conflicts than these three have lacked. As we will see, the alignments of 1775–1783 repeated some of the essential matchups of 1640–1649. Colonial dissenters and Low Church Anglicans, with large numbers of yeomen and artisans, and a flavoring of full-fledged radicals, became "Oliverian" by confronting High Church Anglicans, most of the aristocracy, and the staunchest adherents of monarchy. The continuity was obvious.

Indeed, the three major patriotic factions of 1775–1783 can be described in ways that hark back to the 1640s: the Puritans-turned–Yankee Congregationalists, the Low Church Anglican country party–turned–tidewater tobacco gentry, and the Scots Covenanters–turned–Ulster Presbyterians. The considerable resemblance of the Revolutionary alignment to the older one is no coincidence.

FIGURE 5.1   The Threads of the Cousins' Wars (I)

WAR	WINNERS	LOSERS
English Civil War (1640–1649)	Puritans and Nonconformists, Low Church Anglicans, Supporters of a Republic, Entrepreneurs, Small Industrialists, the Maritime Sector, Economic Nationalists, Backers of Westward Expansion	High Church Anglicans and the Established Church, Monarchy and Aristocracy, Royal Monopolists, Manorial Agriculture, Opponents of Westward Expansion
War for American Independence (1775–1783)	Yankees, Presbyterians, and Low Church Anglicans, Supporters of a Republic, Small Industrialists, the Maritime Sector, Economic Nationalists, Backers of Westward Expansion	High Church Anglicans and the Established Church, Monarchy and Aristocracy, Royal Placemen, Mercantilism, Coastal Residents Who Looked Backward Across the Atlantic to England
U.S. Civil War (1861–1865)	Yankees, Northern Presbyterians and Reformist Evangelicals, Supporters of a United Republic, Opponents of Slavery and the Plantation System, Entrepreneurs, Industrialists, Economic Nationalists, Backers of Westward Free-Soil Expansion	Liturgical Churches That Did Not Oppose Slavery, the Would-Be Southern Aristocracy, Slavery and the Plantation System, the South as a Region, Conservative Opponents of Democracy and Reform in the United States and Britain

NOTE: All of these capsules sacrifice precision for brevity. For example, it would be unfair to cite High Church Anglican or Episcopal religion as a major loser in the U.S. Civil War. But its conservative politics and positions were to an extent embarrassed on both sides of the Atlantic. As pp. 382–383 will note, a minority of New Englanders saw the 1861–1865 conflict as an extension of the previous wars to secure the Reformation.

It is also appropriate to think of the loyalties of 1775–1783 as having two faces: one that reflected a British past, the other that mirrored the American present. The past, reaching back into the England of Charles Stuart and Oliver Cromwell, helps to explain the prominence and persistence of seventeenth-century ethnic dislikes and sectarian animosities. The contemporaneous American visage had to do with stamp duties, Boston or Annapolis tea parties, tobacco debts, or the nuances of trans-Appalachian land speculation. This chapter will describe both loyalties and cleavages as they emerged and hardened from 1775 to 1777: the interaction of a *second* British civil war and a *first* American one.

Actual Loyalties in 1775–1783 and Their Divergence from the Abstract Origins of the American Revolution

Quarrels over the British Constitution, trampled rights, and unpopular taxes certainly helped to explain the colonies' drift to war. Such complaints, however, were not very predictive of who eventually fought on which side. Too many colonial leaders and legislators, men who had shared outrage over the Stamp Act in 1765 or exchanged doubts about Parliament's 1774 coercion of Massachusetts, went their different ways in 1776 when the question changed to one of independence, republicanism, and breaking ties with the mother country.

Economics, too, fails as an adequate litmus of wartime loyalty. True, merchants played an important early role in stirring up reaction against British duties and trade restrictions. Moreover, each of the three major centers of rebellion circa 1775 nurtured a regional economic grudge—New England's fury over British attempts to suppress smuggling; the indignation of Virginia tobacco planters over British prices and credit relationships; and the frustration of Pennsylvania's fledgling ironmakers at old-country restraints. Loyalism also had its economics. In cities like Boston, Newport, New York, and Charleston, the principal administrative, customs, and military centers had high ratios of Tories with vocational interests in continued British rule.

Yet, just as in the English Civil War, when swords came out of their scabbards, annoyance at government restraints on trade and entrepreneurialism, grudges over commercial matters, or anger at court favors or corrupt officials generally took second place to religion, culture, and ethnicity. New England smugglers reacted more as Yankee Congregationalists, and the most irate ironmasters of Pennsylvania and New Jersey were disproportionately Presbyterian. However varied and intertwined their overall motivations, covenants and Communion cups outranked crops and casting molds as denominators of loyalty. Up and down the Eastern Seaboard circa 1775, no other yardsticks mattered more.

In the 1640s, deep disagreement over religion was a *principal* cause of the fighting, and religious, sectarian, and ethnic differences were principal subsequent determinants of who fought with and for whom. By 1775–1776, religion was only one major spur among several. Still, religious, cultural, and ethnic divisions yielded the most important wartime tribalisms, even though yesteryear's intensity was easing.

As in the 1640s, the fighting of 1775–1783 also stirred many peppery local ingredients into the larger stew of national frustration. Prime examples include the enmities in North Carolina between the backcountry "Regulators" and the ruling tidewater planter elite, the violence in northern New Jersey between different factions of the Dutch Reformed Church, the hostility in Vermont between land claimants from New York and rivals waving grants from New England, and the bitterness in Pennsylvania between local settlers and the emigrants who claimed the Wyoming Valley for Connecticut. Hundreds of petty and family grudges helped to push longtime foes into hostile military camps.

This is a recurrent trait of civil wars. The English Civil War also had its parochialisms. Some historians have called it less an *English* civil war than a series of county-by-county confrontations, would-be neutralities and divisions that varied greatly, say, between Kent, famous for its insularity, or Wiltshire and Cheshire, to name some oft-cited examples. County-level variations were even more substantial in America, what with its ethnic and religious diversity and the unsettled status of so many boundaries and land claims. Pennsylvania is rarely singled out as a particular cockpit of acrimony, but one state historian has offered a vivid description of who took the loyalist side:

> Loyalists prove to be largely minority groups; their loyalism was in the main a reflection of their looking to Britain to maintain or restore an internal balance of power. They were the Pennsylvania settlers of the Wyoming country swamped by Connecticut invaders. They were the white men facing loyalist Indians on the outer frontier. They were the more devoted Anglicans, the Methodists, Quakers, Mennonites, Schwenkfelders and Moravians, and many others. Among the Lutherans and the German Reformed, where "scholastic" and anti-clerical tendencies were at work, they were the other side: the pietist element and many of the clergy. In every feud-ridden neighborhood they were one of the two local parties; for irrelevant disputes were generally not abandoned at the onset of war: instead they quickly took on, almost at random, the larger enmities of Whig and Tory.[3]

Nor can we forget how much wartime loyalty could pivot on another pressure: local military control and occupation. According to John S. Shy, the military historian: "Wherever the British and their allies were strong enough to penetrate in force—along the seacoast, in the Hudson, Mohawk, and lower Delaware valleys, in Georgia, the Carolinas, and the transappalachian West—there Toryism flourished." But in less accessible areas where the patriot side was strong, including most of New England, interior Pennsylvania, and inland Virginia, Tories were few and quiet.[4]

Yet despite the ebbs and flows, the critical die of wartime loyalty for most was cast in the early years. With several exceptions, this chapter's principal attention will be to who fought for what side or who inclined to neutralism or pacifism in the two and a half years from the war's opening to the critical turning point of October 1777. Once King Louis's forces were involved, British strategists gave up on winning the war in the northern colonies through large-scale troop commitment to achieve a decisive military victory. Staving off global French revanche for 1763 became more important. Within America, then, the King's ministers shifted their emphasis to: (1) the South, trying to pry that region away; (2) the frontier, where Indian raids, no longer restrained, were encouraged; and (3) American loyalist battalions and regiments whose service could release British regulars. This transformation brought the civil war aspect of the Revolution to its peak of viciousness in Georgia, the Carolinas, Chesapeake Bay, New Jersey, the Ohio Valley, and New York's Mohawk Valley during the years from 1778 to 1782.

For the most part, the basic loyalties of 1775–1777 remained in place, even though they could be frayed by massacres and by destruction that turned entire parishes and counties into wasteland. Initial allegiances could also be submerged by effective military occupation, as in South Carolina and New York. Or, as in Pennsylvania, they could be strained by the unfolding effects of a radical new constitution that alienated moderates and pushed neutrals toward Toryism.

Yet before dwelling on why people chose their side, it is useful to lay out the geography of a mistaken gamble—a bet on reconciliation, not suppression—made by a British government anxious to negotiate a peace and to keep the colonies in the empire without all-out war. This laxity increased Revolutionary prospects for success. From May 1775, when the events of Lexington and Concord became known, to November 1777, as the word of victory at Saratoga spread, the majority of the thirteen colonies were unoccupied for most of those thirty critical months. No significant British troops were present to interrupt rebel consolidation of political power. Hardly any were on hand to inhibit collection of local tax revenues, control of local militia, and procurement of food supplies, weapons, and munitions. Historically, this has not been the way to quell a revolution.

One colony, albeit not a strategic area, was untouched and unoccupied—New Hampshire. Aside from coastal incursions by the Royal Navy, three in the South were essentially allowed to sit: Georgia and both Carolinas. The citizenry of Delaware, Maryland, and Connecticut experienced the British military only on their peripheries. Rhode Island, in turn, was left alone until the King's forces occupied Newport in December 1776. Pennsylvania was essentially untouched from the spring of 1775 until the late summer of 1777 when General Howe's regiments marched from the upper Chesapeake to the Brandywine Valley and thence into Philadelphia. Patriot loyalties in these new states enjoyed important early grace periods.

Massachusetts, Virginia, New Jersey, and New York felt the sharpest early bayonet prick. British regiments garrisoned Boston until March 1776. After they left, however, Massachusetts was attacked only by sea—forays in 1778 and 1779 against New Bedford, Martha's Vineyard, and Cape Cod. The Norfolk and Williamsburg sections of southeast Virginia saw clashes in 1775 and early 1776, with Norfolk burning. Yet no British troops occupied Virginia from February 1776 through all of 1777. In New Jersey, a quiet year followed the gunfire at Lexington, but the new state became a major theater of war in the summer of 1776. So did New York, with Manhattan and its environs remaining occupied from mid-1776 through the end of the war in 1783.

Toryism quickly burgeoned in the garrisoned sections of New York and New Jersey. Elsewhere, lacking actual occupation, Britain's easygoing approach failed. Loyalism could not flourish where rebellion ran the courts, sheriff's offices, and sequestration processes. Popular support for the rebellion did not collapse, as the King and his ministers hoped. It did not succumb even after General Howe defeated American forces in four major battles in and around New York—on Long Island (August 27), in Manhattan (September 15), at White Plains (October 28), and in the capture of Forts Lee and Washington (November 16–20). Washington's military units might be stretched to the breaking point, but rebel governments in states like Pennsylvania and the Carolinas had made good use of 1775 and 1776 to put a political and civil infrastructure in place. Like their revolutionary forebears of the 1640s, they set niceties aside for the duration, ruling through extra-legal associations, fining, jailing, and even hanging Tory opponents, and imposing painful levels of taxation. Once Generals Howe and Burgoyne failed in 1777, the years that the rebels had been given to consolidate became unrecoverable British error.

Despite some regional nuances, rebellion had three particularly ardent cores: the New England Puritans who had become Yankee Congregationalists, the Greater Virginia tobacco lords, and the Presbyterian Scotch-Irish of Pennsylvania, America's transplanted

Ulster, who were also spreading south down the great valley into Maryland, Virginia, and the Carolinas. Another stalwart group was much smaller: the descendants of emigrant Scottish Presbyterian Covenanters, who were most numerous in New Jersey. Nor is it unreasonable to mention the Presbyterian and Congregationalist Church Indians of eastern New York and southern New England—the Mohegans, Stockbridge, Oneidas, and so-called Praying Indians of seven towns along Long Island Sound. There weren't many, but they mostly fought on the American side like their white neighbors and suffered even higher casualties than white New Englanders. The fierce commitment and pitiless determination that eventually won the war drew heavily on these three principal cultures of insurgency.

At the opposite pole, the highest ratio of Tories came among High Church Anglicans from New York, New Jersey, and New England; Crown placemen, officeholders, and retired British army officers; Scottish merchants from Chesapeake Bay south to Savannah; Scottish highland clansmen scattered from upper New York to North Carolina's Cape Fear Valley; and the Iroquois and Cherokee Indians closely tied to British Indian superintendents such as Sir John Johnson in New York and John Stuart in the Great Smoky Mountains. Other important numbers of loyalists also came from the ranks of divided communities like the Dutch, Germans, and French Huguenots.

Caught in the middle, the Pacifist sects opposed to war as a matter of belief—the Quakers and Peace Germans (Moravians, Amish, Mennonites, Dunkards, and others)—typically tried to be neutral. But to the American rebels, not a few seemed pro-British, Quakers especially, and some undoubtedly were. The principal concentration of sect members was in Pennsylvania, but prosperous enclaves of Quakers dotted the seacoast from Nantucket to North Carolina's Albemarle Sound. Peace Germans and Quakers were also a significant bloc in the North Carolina Piedmont.

More confusion attaches to the religious and ethnic groups that were divided among themselves—the marginal constituencies of their era. Their collectively weighty numbers will be our fourth focus. Most numerous were the Church Germans (Lutheran and Reformed), whose settlements mingled with the Scotch-Irish from

Pennsylvania southward. They tended to the patriot side, particularly the Calvinists, but some first-generation groups agonized about keeping their oath and loyalty to King George. The Dutch, important in New York and New Jersey, were also split. So were small but significant religious denominational groupings: Catholics, French Huguenots, Methodists, and Jews. Beyond the Church Indians, Native Americans were also split. The divisions of loyalty and side-choosing among blacks, both free and slave, can be summed up as follows: Southern slaves who sought their freedom mostly ran away to the British, while northern blacks, freemen in particular, were more likely to be in the rebel armies, especially New York and New England regiments.

Strategically, once the British let almost fifteen months pass after Lexington before their major reinvasion of the continent, the odds of American success grew. Even so, the thirteen colonies that renamed themselves the United States were a cultural, demographic, and religious crazy quilt, one that could have unraveled under the pressure of a British victory able to split the colonies. Even in 1781 and 1782, some worried that disunity would prevail. The intense sectarians so prominent early in the war—Congregationalists and Presbyterians—had almost as many enemies as friends.

The Sectaries and Vestries of Rebellion

These were the three core groups of the rebellion: two sets of dissenting Protestants, the Congregationalists and the Presbyterians, and the southern vestrymen, the Low Church Anglican gentry of the plantation states, whose vestries ruled their churches as they ruled their legislatures. The best place to start is with the Revolution's own starters.

Congregationalist New England

No region was less divided and more staunchly behind the Revolution than New England. The colonies' seventeenth-century Commonwealth and Oliverian legacy was an element. Indeed, it probably helped to spark the Boston Tea Party and the fighting at Lexington and Concord. Through eight years of war, New

England was also the rebellion's arsenal, livestock pen, and vital exchequer (because the region's considerable taxes were almost always being paid into patriot rather than royal coffers). Through these eight years, British cannon and infantry could never strike beyond the geographic fringes of Yankeedom: coastal Maine; the small Vermont towns within quick raiding distance of Lake Champlain; Boston, Cape Cod, and the Connecticut seaports; and the many fingers of Rhode Island's Narragansett Bay. In 1777, British troops landed at Westport on Long Island Sound and promptly marched twenty-five miles inland to Danbury, Connecticut, a military supply depot. Much of Danbury was burned, but as the militia gathered like the proverbial hornets, the British had to hasten to their boats. That attack was their deepest penetration of a well-settled area.

Part of New England's strength was its relative unity in culture and religion. Two-thirds of those inhabitants with religious affiliations were Congregationalists, the distant heirs of Cromwell's Puritans. Nearly the same ratio traced their families to the southeast of England or the famous Puritan towns of the West Country. Groups important in adjoining colonies—the Dutch of New York and New Jersey, the High Church Anglicans, and the Quakers—often disliked the Yankees with an edge that carried over to Revolutionary politics. Quakers remembered, all too well, how seventeenth-century Massachusetts had whipped, expelled, and even executed them. The Dutch knew the Yankees as quarrelsome and grabbing neighbors along their ethnic border from the upper Hudson Valley south to Westchester, Long Island, and northern New Jersey. The small but growing minority of High Church Anglicans in New York, New Jersey, and New England were bitter doctrinal foes of Congregationalism. In the middle colonies, these Quaker, Dutch, and Anglican suspicions complicated the patriot cause, but in New England itself, none were large enough to sway regional loyalty.

Despite the 134 years that had passed since Parliament delivered the Grand Remonstrance to Charles I, Congregationalism in New England was almost as potent an explanation for revolutionary politics and ensuing wartime loyalties as its ancestral Puritanism had been in East Anglia. Map 5.1 shows the respective ratio of church bodies in the New England colonies in 1775. Congre-

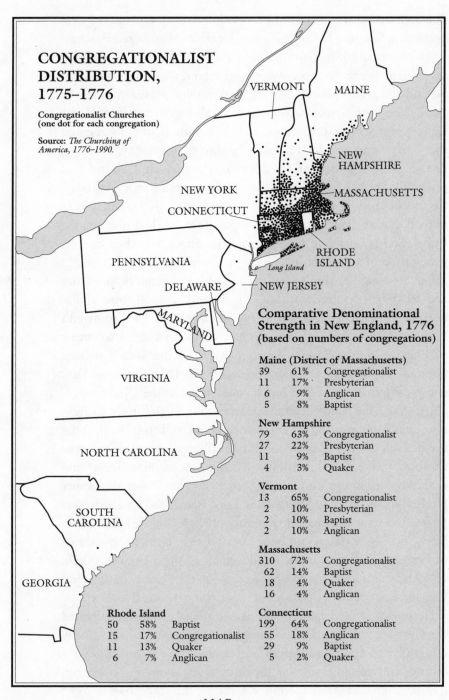

CONGREGATIONALIST DISTRIBUTION, 1775–1776

**Congregationalist Churches
(one dot for each congregation)**

Source: *The Churching of
America, 1776–1990.*

VERMONT

MAINE

NEW
HAMPSHIRE

NEW YORK

MASSACHUSETTS

CONNECTICUT

RHODE
ISLAND

PENNSYLVANIA

Long Island

DELAWARE

NEW JERSEY

MARYLAND

VIRGINIA

NORTH CAROLINA

SOUTH
CAROLINA

GEORGIA

Comparative Denominational Strength in New England, 1776
(based on numbers of congregations)

Maine (District of Massachusetts)

39	61%	Congregationalist
11	17%	Presbyterian
6	9%	Anglican
5	8%	Baptist

New Hampshire

79	63%	Congregationalist
27	22%	Presbyterian
11	9%	Baptist
4	3%	Quaker

Vermont

13	65%	Congregationalist
2	10%	Presbyterian
2	10%	Baptist
2	10%	Anglican

Massachusetts

310	72%	Congregationalist
62	14%	Baptist
18	4%	Quaker
16	4%	Anglican

Rhode Island

50	58%	Baptist
15	17%	Congregationalist
11	13%	Quaker
6	7%	Anglican

Connecticut

199	64%	Congregationalist
55	18%	Anglican
29	9%	Baptist
5	2%	Quaker

MAP 5.1

gationalism overwhelmed all other denominations in Massachusetts, Connecticut, and New Hampshire, the three colonies in which it was the established church. The exception was Rhode Island, where Baptists predominated, a legacy of founder Roger Williams. To the dismay of Congregational leaders, Baptist numbers were growing in northern New England, a frontier culture with less taste for hierarchy and authority. Even so, when war came, Baptists typically subordinated their complaints about the Congregationalist establishment and lined up on the patriotic side.

The mid-century's great schism within Congregationalism and Presbyterianism between Old Light traditionalists and New Light revivalists—a disagreement between scholarly rationalists and born-again enthusiasts—left little legacy in the wartime cleavage between rebels and Tories. The New Light Congregationalists would line up almost entirely on the patriotic side and the Old Lights scarcely less so, save for a small minority of conservatives close to the Anglicans. If the Great Awakening of the 1730s and 1740s helped promote divisions that would show in the Revolution, these lay in how a faction of conservative Congregationalists had been pushed toward the reassuring ritual of Anglicanism.

In 1720, New England had only a handful of Anglican churches. By 1750, there were forty-four Church of England congregations and by 1776, fully eighty-nine. The most fashionable, like King's Chapel and Christ Church in Boston, Trinity in Newport, and Queen's Chapel in Portsmouth, New Hampshire, counted royal officeholders and wealthy, favored merchants among their ranks. But not all Anglican parishes had prestigious congregations; there were important exceptions in coastal Maine and rural Connecticut.

Anglican politics in New England was thoroughly loyalist. Of the several dozen Anglican clergymen, as we will see, one, at most, failed to support the Crown. The bulk of their communicants also took the Tory side or tried to stay neutral. The line within New England between Congregationalists and Anglicans was also a critical Revolutionary divide.

Patriotism in New England was maximized, and Toryism reduced, by the extent to which the four states—save for Rhode

Island, where the British occupied Newport from 1776 to 1779—
remained under American control during the war. Yankee New
England avoided too much radicalism, remaining under the governance of broad-based factions, often the same groups that had
dominated prewar provincial assemblies. In the states where new
governments represented strong-willed revolutionary minorities
previously excluded from power—Pennsylvania in 1776–1779 under the Scotch-Irish Constitutional Party—moderates were pushed
toward Toryism. That was less of a problem in Congregationalist
New England.

New England's other centers of uncertain loyalty involved religious minorities on its geographic peripheries. The approximately
ten thousand Quakers in Massachusetts, concentrated in and
around Cape Cod, including a majority in seafaring Nantucket,
were its most conspicuous neutrals, and much the same could be
said for those in Rhode Island.[5]

Eclectic wartime politics was also common along the roof of
New England in Vermont, Maine, and northern New Hampshire.
Unlike the long-settled areas, much of this region was exposed to
invasions from Canada. Along the Maine coast, British naval
power posed an added threat. Degrees of collaboration or negotiation with the British were common. Staid Congregationalism, the
pillar of patriotic alignment in New England's older towns, also
had less appeal on the northern frontier, where itinerant preachers,
Baptists, deists, and freethinkers made inroads. Communities of
Scottish settlers on Vermont's Otter River and elsewhere provided
clumps of tartan-striped loyalism.[6]

This frontier within New England might be less conforming, religiously and politically, than the white-steepled Yankee heartlands
of the Charles, Merrimack, Housatonic, and Connecticut Valleys.
Yet there was a *second* frontier, this one beyond their region, in
which former New Englanders played a different and stalwart
pro-Revolutionary role. The most important emigrant settlements
were in New York, New Jersey, and Pennsylvania, where
Yankees—in these colonies, most joined the Presbyterian
Church—stiffened and sometimes led the forces of rebellion in the
middle colonies. Map 5.2 shows the areas involved.

THE YANKEE OUTLIERS:
New England Antecedents
in the Middle Colonies, 1775

NEW YORK

Springfield

Cherry
Valley

Harpersfield

Wilkes-Barre
(Claimed by
Connecticut)

Southold

PENNSYLVANIA

Long Island

Newark
Morristown
Middletown

NEW
JERSEY

Greenwich

Cape May

Areas of Yankee
Settlement

Note: Other Yankee settlements in 1775
could be found in St. John's Parish, Georgia,
and West Florida.

MAP 5.2

In New York, the Yankee outposts were in Suffolk County, on eastern Long Island, once part of Connecticut, and in the Connecticut-bred towns of eastern Westchester County. Spilled-over Yankees were also found on the eastern borders of Duchess and Albany Counties. West of the Hudson, Yankee emigrants were important in Ulster County and in frontier towns like Cherry Valley and Harpersfield. Such locales invariably favored independence.

In divided New Jersey, Yankee-populated areas were also among the staunchest rebel districts. Present-day Newark, in Essex County, was settled from Massachusetts and, like Suffolk County in New York, named for a Puritan parent shire in East Anglia. New Jersey maps no longer show the nearby town of Connecticut Farms, but in 1780, a vital, if little-known, engagement was fought there. Four understrength regiments of New Jersey Continentals slowed a British and Hessian force of six thousand, which sought to punch through the Hobart Gap and reach Washington's winter camp in Morristown beyond the Watchung mountains. They held until militia from the nearby Yankee-dominated counties of Morris, Essex, and Middlesex could arrive.

Yankee settlements and Presbyterian churches were the prime indicators of New Jersey wartime patriotism. Middlesex was another county where New Englanders and Long Islanders had made the original settlements—in Woodbridge, Elizabeth, Middletown, and Piscataway. Morris County was a more recent extension of Massachusetts and Connecticut, with a population influx right up to the war's beginning. Two other Yankee-seeded sections on the southern coast were also rebel strongholds: seafaring, whale-hunting Cape May, settled from New England and Long Island in the 1680s, and the tidal estuary ports of Cumberland County to the west.

Greenwich and nearby Fairfield were both named for parent towns in Connecticut. The Greenwich (New Jersey) Tea Party of late 1774, whose participants burned tea from the British brig *Greyhound*, was plotted almost entirely by members of the Greenwich Presbyterian Church.[7] The principal mover of the tea episode, Philip Vickers Fithian, who later wrote a book about plantation life in Virginia and served as chaplain to a battalion of New Jersey militia before dying in 1777, had the sort of heritage that made Tories gnash their teeth. A forebear, William Fithian, had been a Cromwellian officer, present at the execution of Charles I, who fled to Boston after being proscribed as a regicide.[8]

The Yankee impact on Pennsylvania was much less. Their only sizeable settlement was on the Susquehanna, near the present city of Wilkes-Barre, named by Connecticut settlers in 1769 for two pro-American members of the British Parliament, John Wilkes and Isaac Barre. Connecticut claimed this region, the Wyoming Valley, as being within the westward extension of the boundaries set out in its charter, exchanging blows with Pennsylvania in the so-called Pennamite Wars. When the Revolution began, the Yankee settlers were firm rebels. Just as New England–planted Cherry Valley, New York, was burned by a British and Indian raiding party in 1778, a similar raid by Tories and Mohawks under Chief Joseph Brant destroyed the Wyoming settlement. Arch-rebel New Englanders were always a favorite target.

But the importance of Yankee leadership in the Revolution, especially transplanted Yankee leadership, is most vividly and ironically conveyed by the rousing role of the southernmost Congregational church in the thirteen colonies: Midway, in St. John's Parish, Georgia, whose people had come from Connecticut. State historians agree that the St. John's New Englanders were in the forefront of local support for the Revolution, sending Georgia's first delegate to the Continental Congress.[9]

Ulster Presbyterians

The only Northerners to rival Yankees in their collective revolutionary intensity were the Scotch-Irish. With Pennsylvania as their great ethnic and religious base, they played an important role in most other colonies from New Jersey, Delaware, and Maryland south to Georgia and the Carolinas. Yet neither King George III, who called the Revolution a Presbyterian war, nor Horace Walpole, who joked about America running off with a Presbyterian parson, was quite correct. The loyalties involved were complicated.

In the middle colonies, the American war *was* a fight led by Scotch-Irish and Presbyterians. The Presbyterian role was decisive, politically and militarily. Descriptions of the rebel armies as being heavily Presbyterian or Irish—one British officer referred to Pennsylvania forces as the "line of Ireland"—all seem to have originated in this one region.[10] No other churches were torched so often by the British, although more smoke would have risen quickly enough from white Congregational steeples had the King's army ever been able to raid in force through populous sections of Connecticut and Massachusetts. In the South, however, both Scotch-Irish and Presbyterian politics were more confused.

Precise categorization is critical. Together, Scots, Irish, and Scotch-Irish almost certainly accounted for 20 to 25 percent of the white population of the thirteen colonies in 1775, next after persons of English ancestry. But it is inaccurate to talk loosely about the American rebellion being led by either the Scots *or* the Irish, properly defined. Among the Scottish merchants, officials, retired military officers, or highlanders resident in America, most favored the Crown. Those of Scottish descent born in America were the most likely to be rebels. Overall, colonists of Scottish birth or parentage were divided. In Scotland itself, as we shall see, prowar sentiment guided the established (Presbyterian) Church of Scotland and a virtually unanimous Scottish delegation to the British Parliament. Because of Thomas Jefferson's experience with Scots merchants in Virginia, a first draft of the Declaration of Independence actually criticized the Scots by name.

The greatest ethnic misdescription attended the "Irish." The term would be most accurate limited to describing Native Irish emigrants or their descendants, excluding the altogether different Ulster Presbyterians. But the Native Irish were not a large group in the thirteen colonies as they would become six decades later. Only between one-quarter and one-third of the too loosely defined "Irish" coming to America were non-Presbyterian and non–Scotch Irish, a residue which included Catholics and Anglicans alike. The Anglican "Irish" included a fair percentage of professionals—doctors, lawyers, clergymen, and administrators—with Tory inclinations. Many of lesser status, including most of the Native Irish of Catholic origins, would have been largely absorbed into the loose frontier Protestantism or non–church attendance of Appalachia or the South.[11] A large percentage came as indentured servants or transported criminals. These last categories of Irish—in particular, those who had arrived in the late 1760s or early 1770s—were those most likely to wind up as drifters or in British or loyalist regiments.

Which brings us to the Scotch-Irish. The 70 percent of those who left Ireland for America in the eighteenth century and fit that description had distinctive origins. Their ancestors were mostly Scots brought in during the seventeenth century to colonize the Northern Irish province of Ulster. Besides colonization, they were also to suppress the Native Irish. By the nineteenth century, being neither Irish nor still fully Scottish, they were sometimes identified in America as Scotch-Irish. Like the embattled English Puritans, the Scotch-Irish were suspicious folk, hostile to bishops and Stuart kings alike. Biblical intensity, political migration, and a sense of persecution made them think of themselves as a chosen people, quite unlike the stay-at-home Scots and the Native Irish.

Even the term "Scotch-Irish" does not fully convey their hybrid nature. The "Scotch" who moved into Ulster between 1610 and 1700 also included English Puritans and several thousand French Huguenots, while the lowland Scottish migrants themselves were atypical because they included a substantial ratio of Covenanters fleeing the so-called killing times of Stuart repression between 1660 and 1690.[12] By the time they started migrating to America in large numbers, the Scotch-Irish were already a toughened frontier breed, quite different from other Britons.

The melting pot of seventeenth-century Ulster also foreshadowed the feisty politics that Scotch-Irish stalwarts in America would bring to the Revolution. Independent-mindedness, because they had brought no lairds to tell them what to do; hardiness, imbued by two or three generations on a bloody and rugged frontier; and an intense Presbyterian religion and sense of persecution that made them hostile to the Crown and to established Anglicanism.[13]

To the strictest factions of Presbyterians, moreover, kings were God's mere vassals. When rulers exercised their authority improperly, resistance was justified. Thus, in the early eighteenth century, as the British Parliament began to withdraw religious privileges from Ulster Presbyterianism and impose economic restraints on a local agriculture and industry competing too successfully with England's, many residents resisted by leaving for America.[14]

No other pre-Revolutionary migration was so large. Between the end of war with France and Spain in 1713 and the American Revolution, roughly two hundred thousand people from Ulster came to America, principally in five waves—1717–1718, 1725–1729, 1740–1741, 1754–1755 and 1771– 1775—that demographers have likened to a fever chart of Ulster's economic health.[15] How much they and their descendants became pillars of the American Revolution reflected when they came to America, under what religious and political auspices, and where they took up residence. Much importance also attached to whether they were involved in an intensive transplanted Ulster Presbyterianism or wound up drifting loosely—and without Sunday sermons and brimstone—through the backwoods culture of the Appalachian South.

Pennsylvania, Maryland, and Virginia were the principal eighteenth-century Scotch-Irish destinations. A small minority did go to New England, but Massachusetts and Connecticut Congregationalists, like their English cousins in Essex and Suffolk, did not esteem the Presbyterianism, table manners, diction, or culture of the Irish and Scots. At a distance and in separate jurisdictions, they collaborated effectively; up close, they did not blend well.*

As to whether the Ulster emigrants regarded themselves as Irish, albeit Ulster Protestants, the place-names in the heart of Pennsylvania's transplanted Ulster indicate that they did. Map 5.3 (opposite) was prepared back in the 1960s to show how parts of the non-Yankee Northeast, in this case the old Scotch-Irish Andrew Jackson–James Buchanan Democrats, were behaving as the old U.S. Civil War political system broke up. The towns on the Pennsylvania map, all rebel strongholds in 1775–1776, were mostly named in the 1740s and 1750s for immediate memories of Ulster, not dim recollections of Scotland. These were places where Presbyterian ministers sent men off to war with invocations of Killicrankie, Londonderry, or earlier persecution by High Church kings. Local histories proudly recall that Colonel Bertram Galbraith of Derry Township, to take one example, was the great-great-grandson of

---

*In the 1740s, Scotch-Irish made up a fair percentage of those committed to Boston jails, and thirty years later, they provided some recruits for a local loyalist unit, the Loyal Irish Volunteers.

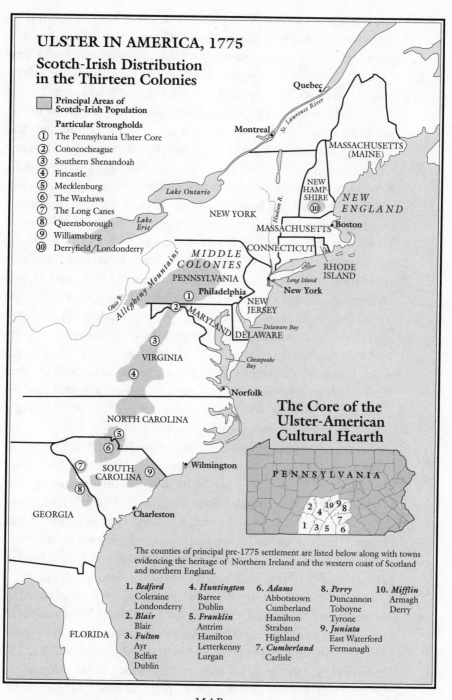

ULSTER IN AMERICA, 1775

Scotch-Irish Distribution in the Thirteen Colonies

Principal Areas of Scotch-Irish Population

Particular Strongholds

1. The Pennsylvania Ulster Core
2. Conococheague
3. Southern Shenandoah
4. Fincastle
5. Mecklenburg
6. The Waxhaws
7. The Long Canes
8. Queensborough
9. Williamsburg
10. Derryfield/Londonderry

Quebec

Montreal

St. Lawrence River

Lake Ontario

Lake Erie

MASSACHUSETTS (MAINE)

NEW HAMP-SHIRE

NEW ENGLAND

NEW YORK

MASSACHUSETTS • Boston

Hudson R.

CONNECTICUT

RHODE ISLAND

Long Island

MIDDLE COLONIES

Allegheny Mountains

Ohio R.

PENNSYLVANIA

Philadelphia

New York

NEW JERSEY

MARYLAND

DELAWARE

Delaware Bay

VIRGINIA

Chesapeake Bay

Norfolk

NORTH CAROLINA

SOUTH CAROLINA • Wilmington

GEORGIA • Charleston

FLORIDA

The Core of the Ulster-American Cultural Hearth

PENNSYLVANIA

The counties of principal pre-1775 settlement are listed below along with towns evidencing the heritage of Northern Ireland and the western coast of Scotland and northern England.

1. Bedford	**4. Huntington**	**6. Adams**
Coleraine	Barree	Abbotstown
Londonderry	Dublin	Cumberland
2. Blair	**5. Franklin**	Hamilton
Blair	Antrim	Straban
3. Fulton	Hamilton	Highland
Ayr	Letterkenny	**7. Cumberland**
Belfast	Lurgan	Carlisle
Dublin		

8. Perry	**10. Mifflin**
Duncannon	Armagh
Toboyne	Derry
Tyrone	
9. Juniata	
East Waterford	
Fermanagh	

MAP 5.3

the Reverend George Gillespie, whose tomb was ripped out of Kirkaldy Church and destroyed by Royalists in 1661, and the great-nephew of Covenanting minister Robert Gillespie, who died chained by the Stuarts in the dungeons of Bass Rock, the island prison surrounded by the cold waters of the Firth of Forth.[16]

Scotch-Irish politics in Pennsylvania paid little tribute to timidity. With roughly 30 to 35 percent of the total population, the Scotch-Irish seized far more power under the revolutionary Constitution of 1776 than they had ever managed in prewar politics. Two major mid-eighteenth-century factions, Quaker and Anglican, had all but imploded—the Quakers because of opposition to the war and the Anglicans because so many were Tories or Tory sympathizers. When Whigs swept the field about half of the members of the new legislature were Scotch-Irish, many of them fire-eaters from places named for Antrim, Down, and Derry. Historians disagree whether the Pennsylvania Constitution of 1776 was radical or merely a bold foreshadowing of later American democracy. However, Scotch-Irish militance in support of the Revolution carried a price. Many conservative Whigs, cautious "church" Germans, and Quaker, Mennonite, and Dunker pacifists shrank from it. Even American general Charles Lee, an Englishman born, joked about the dubious wisdom of replacing a monarchy with a Scotch-Irish "mac-ocracy."[17]

The Scotch-Irish of New York and New Jersey, less numerous, were also less of a political force. Both colonies had what amounted to Presbyterian parties in their assemblies, but in New York, voters of New England antecedents, not Scotch-Irish, were more important, as in the Patriot faction that emerged in the 1770s. The Scotch-Irish were numerous only in two west-of-the-Hudson counties appropriately named Orange and Ulster, the latter being one of New York's leading pro-Revolutionary counties.

The Presbyterian preeminence in New Jersey was unmistakable. According to historian Thomas Fleming: "At least half the citizens were active or hidden loyalists. Although economics played some part . . . religion was the primary factor in the choice of sides. The Presbyterians ran the Revolution in New Jersey, controlling all aspects of it, from the distribution of political jobs to the appointment of New Jersey officers in the Continental Army."[18] New

Jersey Presbyterianism, however, was not a "mac-ocracy," but a broader alliance of New Englanders, Scots Covenanters, and Scotch-Irish against Quakers, High Church Anglicans, and conservative Dutchmen.

In Delaware, where Yankees barely existed and Germans were few, the wartime pattern was modified Pennsylvanian: Scotch-Irish Presbyterians from the northern districts adjacent to Pennsylvania were at odds with the Anglicans of the lower counties. Quakers were neutral or shading toward Toryism in their distaste for the Presbyterian rebels. Because the state was closely divided, neither side was too provocative, avoiding internecine warfare.

To the south, Scotch-Irish activism blurs, although less so in Maryland and Virginia than in the Carolinas and Georgia. A minority of Scotch-Irish emigrants had always gone to southern ports—Alexandria, Charleston, and Savannah. Then, in the 1730s and 1740s, and especially in the 1750s, the Scotch-Irish immigration stream overflowed south-central Pennsylvania and poured southward down the Great Wagon Road into Maryland and Virginia, then into the Piedmont sections of North and South Carolina. The oldest settlements were the rebel strongholds. Maryland's Conococheague Valley and Augusta, Rockbridge, and Botetourt Counties in Virginia's fertile southern Shenandoah Valley were as outspokenly rebellious in 1775 as Pennsylvania's ethnic heartland. Rockbridge, with Ulster arrivals dating back to 1737, became one of the most strongly Presbyterian counties in America. In 1777, the county seat gave itself a new name: Lexington.

In Virginia and Maryland, however, Presbyterians were a minority who played second fiddle politically to the tidewater Low Church Anglicans who dominated patriotic councils in both states. Still, backcountry Presbyterians were usually allies who regarded the tidewater elites as tolerably fair in government and willing to give the backcountry legislative representation. Of the several Tory threats and disturbances in Maryland and Virginia, none involved the Scotch-Irish—with one exception, which can serve to introduce the greater Scotch-Irish unruliness in the Carolinas.

Because Tory activity in Virginia was limited, mostly involving a few High Church Anglican families and the Scottish merchants and tobacco factors of the tidewater, late twentieth-century scholars, seeking dissension in a patriotic bastion, have found some along the southwestern frontier. Montgomery and Bedford Counties, in the shadow of the Blue Ridge Mountains, were unlike the older, better-churched Scotch-Irish districts of the Shenandoah. Serious settlement in the southwest only followed the end of the Cherokee wars in 1762. The population flows of the 1760s were ethnically and culturally more diverse.[19] Drifters, malcontents, and Tories would have been mixed in.

Before turning to this raw frontier, which produced a different political coloration, it is appropriate to note the Carolinas' handful of old-settlement exceptions. By 1775, a few districts had a Pennsylvania-like mix of Presbyterian churches and organized Ulster culture. One such was the Williamsburg section of South Carolina. The second, better known, was the Waxhaw district, on the North Carolina frontier with South Carolina just below what is now the city of Charlotte. Within several years of the first cabin going up in 1748, the inhabitants organized the seven colonial Presbyterian congregations of Mecklenburg County. This region became famous—to the British, *notorious*—for radical religion and politics that were consummated in the Mecklenburg Resolves of May 1775, which declared the authority of George III annulled in language like Scottish Presbyterians had used against James II in 1689.[20]

Newer parts of the Carolinas, by contrast, had less-rooted populations. Travelers coming in the 1760s and 1770s were less likely to arrive in groups, to name their villages with familiar Ulster names, or to establish a congregation to which they would lure a covenanting Presbyterian minister. Lacking these Ulster milieus, they would be less solidly on the patriot side. This should be underscored. Great differences existed between the Scotch-Irish Presbyterian congregations and the very different culture of individual emigrants from Ireland arriving in the 1760s or 1770s (indentured servants, say, or English-speaking lapsed Catholics). The same applied to the differences between the churched Presbyterians and the Scotch-Irish or Irish who preferred the backcountry communities of loose hogs, lewd women, drunken lay-abouts, and corn-crib New Light Baptist chapels described so colorfully—unfairly caricatured, perhaps—by Charles Woodmason, the itinerant Anglican clergyman, in his journal, "The Carolina Backcountry on the Eve of the Revolution."

To call the older southern Presbyterian churches strong cultural forces is an understatement. In 1756, the congregation of the Timber Ridge Church in Staunton, Virginia, put up its first build-ing—still standing as the nave of a newer edifice—as a collective enterprise. The families donated to buy the materials, then the most able-bodied did the work: "The sand used for 'lyme' . . . was carried by the women on horseback from South River, a distance of five miles. The women rode under the protection of the men, who walked with long rifles at the ready" for Indians.[21] During the difficult years of the Revolution, this same congregation funded the nearby Liberty Hall School, which later became Washington and Lee University.

This fierce combination—of long rifle, kirk, and academy—had dozens of parallels elsewhere on the frontier. And where it pre-vailed, Scotch-Irish Presbyterians were, literally, the Minute Men of the Piedmont and foothills. Consider what happened in Rowan County, North Carolina, on a Sunday in January 1781 as Lord Cornwallis's troops were trying to overtake patriot forces. General William L. Davidson, for whom Presbyterian Davidson College was thereafter named, sent couriers to the Rowan Presbyterian churches, Fourth Creek, Centre, Thyatira, and Hopewell, asking for men. Three hundred came from the Centre Church area, ac-companied by their minister, and at Fourth Creek, the Reverend James Hall, in the midst of his sermon, stopped, read the message, enlisted much of his congregation, was elected captain, and joined Davidson on the Catawba River where the crossing British were to be stopped or slowed.[22] Where the Scotch-Irish were church-driven, they were pillars of the Revolution.

That was not everywhere. As the population of the thirteen colonies soared during the decade before the Revolution, no sec-tion grew faster than the Carolina backcountry. Part of the huge numerical increase represented a new demographic and vocational confluence: jail scrapings of the British Isles, runaway indentured servants, and the failures and ne'er-do-wells drifting west from the older settlements. The Ulster and Irish countryside of the 1760s and early 1770s, when rack-renting landlords drove tenants to despair of America, itself swarmed with peasant insurgencies. The participants, who called themselves Hearts of Oak, Hearts of Steel, and suchlike, were known more simply as Oakboys, Steelboys, and Whiteboys—the forerunners, in a sense, of the Good Ole Boys of the twentieth century. In contrast to the Presbyterian culture of learning, which seeded a dozen early American colleges, a second partly Scotch-Irish milieu was emerging by the 1760s. It was the southern backcountry culture—nurtured by transports that sailed every year after 1718 with the flotsam of English and Irish prisons—of what Americans would later call "crackers" or poor white trash.

The political relations between the backcountry and the seaboard, never too close, were also important to side-choosing in the Revolution. The backcountry and frontier districts in Maryland and Virginia had a political voice and were not at actual sword's point with the coastal gentry. Piedmont-based Virginia leaders like Patrick Henry, Thomas Jefferson, and James Madison, in particular, helped provide a bridge between the two camps.

Not so in fast-growing North Carolina, where a brazen tidewater political power structure treated the new counties being carved out of the wilderness as patronage and moneymaking opportunities. The backcountry response was a mass movement—the Regulators—with a substantial Scotch-Irish participation. Their principal demands were for reform of excessive taxes, abusive courts, and extortionate sheriff's fees and for fairer representation in the legislature.

South Carolina had a Regulator movement in a partly different mold, pairing demands to Charleston for political change with a vigilante-type crackdown on the lawlessness and anarchy of the colony's frontier, plagued by roving bandits and hunters. Even heavy-handed reestablishment of order earned some respect from the coastal gentry. Local courts were belatedly established in the backcountry, and the new Constitution of 1776 gave the backcountry some additional representation in the legislature. Most but not all of the former South Carolina Regulators who participated in the Revolution did so on the rebel side.

A bloody clash in North Carolina, where by the late 1760s, Regulators came to dominate six to eight backcountry counties, bred a more lasting resentment which affected wartime loyalties. After three years of petitions, protests, and sporadic violence gained nothing, frustration led to a military clash: the so-called Battle of Alamance of 1771, in which an imprecise number of Regulators died on the field or in nearby woods set afire by Governor Tryon. Six more Regulators were later hanged by provincial authorities. How many died on the battlefield and who they were remain undocumented. Folklore has it that mass graves were dug at a local Baptist church.

What would complicate Revolutionary politics in 1775 was that suppression of the Regulator movement four years earlier had been managed by the same seaboard plantation class now leading the fight for independence. By contrast, what official sympathy the Regulators had received came from Josiah Martin, who had replaced Tryon as the royal governor shortly after the battle. Martin's optimism about former Regulators flocking to the King's side in 1775 was never justified—not with the hated Tryon himself quickly donning the red coat and epaulets of a British major general—but rebel leaders took persisting backcountry resentment seriously enough. Outsidership and distaste for the coastal planters who crushed them at Alamance could have pushed some toward Toryism and more toward inactivity. In December 1775, the Continental Congress, worried about Regulator disaffection and hearing from the North Carolina delegation that "the educations of most of these men have been religious," turned to the Presbyterian clergy for assistance.[23] The latter duly evoked the sacred memories of Londonderry and Enniskillen.

Their success is unclear. Beyond Mecklenburg and Rowan Counties, the Scotch-Irish in North Carolina were less cohesive than elsewhere. So were Presbyterians. The sizeable population of Scottish highlanders, mostly Presbyterians, were largely recent immigrants who supported the Crown. Ulster Presbyterians were overwhelmingly rebels, but many Scotch-Irish were no longer Presbyterian in 1775, not simply for want of a local church or preacher, but because in the Carolinas, enthusiastic worship and the more lax Baptist lifestyle were gaining converts. Old Light Presbyterian ministers believed in lengthy, hectoring sermons. Small wonder young men preferred to spend a day at Sandy River or Deep River watching well-endowed young women in thin cotton shifts undergo adult baptism by immersion.

State historians believe that Baptists of one sect or another were already the leading denomination, and some have extended the effect into politics. Religious historian Sydney Ahlstrom has argued that the Regulator movement in North Carolina, like Shays' Rebellion in Massachusetts a decade and a half later, drew heavily on Baptists—revivalist Separate Baptists, in particular ("It is perhaps not coincidental that Baptists were numerous in both of these discontented areas").[24]

In Orange County, which included Alamance, a survey of the subsequent wartime allegiance of 883 persons who had earlier been Regulators found that 289 were rebels, 34 were Tories, and 560 avoided taking sides.[25] Many simply went west, over the mountains, into what would become Kentucky and Tennessee. On the other hand, two hundred former Regulators did join the loyalist forces at the battle of Moore's Creek Bridge in February 1776, although many left the field before the battle, and chronicles of wartime guerrilla units stress that those who rode with Tory leaders like David Fanning in North Carolina and Robert Cunningham in South Carolina represented a broad array of ethnic strains, Scotch-Irish included. Forceful personalities could often enlist their neighbors.

This close to the frontier, local Tories came from another source—westward flight on the part of individuals escaping servitude, militia duty, the war, or rebel communities in which they had become persona non grata. Still other backcountry men put on rebel or loyalist uniforms to pursue personal revenge, and the rootless, in particular, were inclined to switch units or sides when it suited them. Not a few of these drifters and vendetta-pursuers would have been Scotch-Irish, given their large share of the population.

Colonial historian Jack Greene, in his introduction to *An Uncivil War*, a particularly perceptive analysis of the Revolutionary War in the backcountry, has raised a related caveat: the insufficient attention chroniclers have paid to migration to the frontier by failures—not men simply looking for a new start but those who, rejecting their previous society, took up a hand-to-mouth existence as hunters, vagabonds, or plunderers. Concentrations of such malcontents, some active Tories, helped to give certain areas a reputation for disloyalty to the cause of independence.[26]

The final caveat to the Scotch-Irish being a pillar of American rebellion involves the different old-country psychologies of the last prewar wave of emigrants from Ulster in the early 1770s. For Presbyterians, the newness of their arrival would have mattered less in 1775 and 1776, when opinion back home was also pro-American. Irish Protestants not only sympathized with America's reasons for rebellion, but used the uprising across the Atlantic to pressure London for more self-determination. However, in 1778, after France entered the war on the American side, politics in Ulster changed. The British government had few troops to help defend against another possible French invasion like the brief occupation of Carrickfergus in 1760. So Irish leaders seized the opportunity to enlarge the local "Volunteers." Mostly but not entirely Protestant, they were half defense force and half political militia, ultimately reaching a strength of forty thousand. Fearful that Ireland, too, could explode, leaders in Westminster made major concessions in trade and self-government, as we will see. The Volunteers became semiofficial.

Which, in turn, helps explain the increased willingness come 1778 of some of the more recent Scotch-Irish and Irish emigrants to fight on the British side. Their loyalty to a United States they barely knew was minimal. After occupying Philadelphia, the British in late 1777 began organizing two regiments among Irish Catholics—the Roman Catholic Volunteers and the Volunteers of Ireland.[27] As we will see, by 1777, Irish Catholic recruits were already being avidly sought in the Old Country. When discipline in the first-named regiment collapsed, it was merged into the Volunteers of Ireland, whose red coats were faced, unusually, in a bold green. After a major infusion of Ulster emigrants, the Volunteers were formalized into the provincial army establishment in 1779.

But there is a revealing footnote. Because of its Ulster soldiery, the Volunteers were sent to South Carolina from 1779 to 1782, where they had some propaganda effect among the Scotch-Irish until the regimental commander, Lord Rawdon, posted a large detachment to the Waxhaws. The local Scotch-Irish, zealous revolutionaries, convinced many of the red-coated Ulstermen to desert. In short, while the American Revolution was not a Presbyterian war, it was a war in which most stalwart Ulster Presbyterians were also stalwart rebels.

The Chesapeake Tobacco Lords

George Washington, Thomas Jefferson, and Patrick Henry have ensured the historical resonance of Virginia's contribution to the patriotic side. Greater Virginia—tidewater Maryland and North Carolina's old-settled Albemarle Sound region, as well as Virginia itself—stands as the third core of the Revolution. Life in mid-eighteenth-century Virginia and Maryland centered on tobacco to an extent now scarcely imaginable. The calendar of its cultivation not only dictated Virginia's lifestyle, but, by some estimates, even explained the province's easygoing Anglicanism, virtually unchallenged by any other church as late as the 1740s. Yet by the 1760s and 1770s, the familiar world of the Chesapeake was in flux; tobacco's future was clouding—no less a planter than George Washington began switching cultivation to wheat. People of many new nationalities and religions were arriving, although most headed to the backcountry.

Tobacco aside, the term "Greater Virginia" must be used carefully. Maryland, founded by a Catholic proprietor, initially practiced religious tolerance and had a mixed population. North Carolina, for all that its early settlers came from Virginia and established Anglicanism in the province in 1702, was a particularly loose and disorganized colony. Church attendance was usually low, especially in the burgeoning backcountry. In 1725, the population of North Carolina had been only 30,000; by 1775, it was between 250,000 and 300,000. Because of the hugeness of the influx and the related Regulator troubles, the eastern plantation gentry had less of a hold on North Carolina than their peers did on Virginia and Maryland.

Virginia itself, the political linchpin and cultural center of the region, was the North American nursery of the Anglican church. In 1680, Virginia counted several score Anglican ministers to a relative handful for the rest of the mainland colonies. Yet its Low Church

Anglicanism displeased English High Churchmen. Local vestries had gained the power to hire and discharge clergymen. In 1690, the Bishop of London sent the Reverend James Blair, Scottish Presbyterian in family background, to Virginia as its Anglican commissary. Over four decades, as things turned out, he institutionalized the church's tint of Presbyterianism by accepting vestry control.

So tenacious was this locally directed Anglicanism that in 1775–1776, over half of its Virginia clergy would take the patriot side, a ratio exceeded only in South Carolina. Practical Virginia Anglicans were also ready to strike a political deal with the mushrooming Baptist population. This bargain, which brought Baptists into a wartime collaboration, helped to produce the Virginia Constitution of 1776, which proclaimed toleration. A decade later, the Virginia Statute for Religious Freedom set in motion the disestablishment of the Anglican church.

As of mid-century, the culture and economics of tobacco cultivation steered Virginia and Maryland, the two main producing colonies, to almost the same extent that sugar dominated the West Indies and that cotton would come to symbolize the pre–Civil War American South. Sociologists in Cuba and Brazil have described the local sugar or coffee "mentality," and an American historian's reconstruction of a similar tobacco mentality goes a long way to explain planters' angst in the 1770s.* Sugar was a crop for which the cultivator could do little; fate, not the planter, was in charge. Tobacco, by contrast, was a crop in which the cultivator's expertise, commitment, and good judgment were involved at virtually every stage, from a week or so after Christmas, when the seeds were planted, to their transplanting in late April, to cutting the ripe tobacco in September and then curing the leaves.

The better Virginia planters drew self-esteem akin to that of winemakers from the unique quality of their hogsheads of prime cured tobacco. Its cultivation, in which failure was taken to reflect dereliction, while success implied personal worth and integrity,

---

*Fuller exposition of this fascinating thesis can be found in T. H. Breen, *Tobacco Culture: The Mentality of the Great Tidewater Planters on the Eve of Revolution* (Princeton, 1985).

has even been used to explain the prevailing religion, "a calm, reasonable, low-church Anglicanism, a theology that did not challenge their rather inflated notions of human capabilities."[28] Congregationalism, with its town links, or Presbyterianism, committed to predestination, would not have served.

Seeds of personal and political frustration, however, were growing among the tobacco shoots. Virginia planters' extravagance had soared in the 1760s just as international tobacco economics was worsening. The credit Virginia growers enjoyed with British merchants soon deteriorated, and when, following the European credit crisis of 1772, these same merchants began calling in debts, even capable planters who prided themselves on success were forced to sell slaves and property. For many decades, Chesapeake tobacco cultivation had rested on largely self-sustaining plantations of thousands of acres, spread far apart, usually with several dozen or several hundred slaves. The relentless calendar of raising and marketing tobacco, in binding growers to their remote estates, left a lot of time for reading and study. Many of the isolated tidewater lords came to put a high premium not just on their manor's self-sufficiency, but on their own.

After the credit pressures of 1772, upholding personal economic independence and national political self-respect became simultaneous challenges. Even wealthy planters were drawn to take a radical Whig and threatened-liberties view of British policy and to perceive, in the words of Thomas Jefferson, a conspiracy by British factors and merchants "to give good prices and credit to the planter till they got him more immersed in debt than he could pay without selling his lands or slaves . . . so that the planters were a species of property annexed to certain mercantile houses in London."[29]

John Adams may well have gotten *his* conspiracy-minded view of the world from Puritan anti-popery, memory of the Stuarts, and anger at the suppression of New England manufactures and smuggling. The Virginia patriots seem to have derived much of theirs from tobacco economics. As we saw in chapter 3, Washington, like Jefferson, worried about Virginia being put in thralldom to Britain by debt, and both men were among the planters who had large obligations outstanding at the time of the Revolution. Two other aspects further isolate tobacco economics as a particular provocation: Of the Scottish tobacco factors and merchants who resided in Maryland and Virginia as agents for British firms, most fled in 1775 and 1776. Moreover, a comparison of the Revolutionary War loyalties of tobacco versus wheat-producing areas along Chesapeake Bay and in tidewater Virginia found loyalism greater in the wheat sections.[30]

Without the peril to tobacco, the political traditions of Greater Virginia might not have pointed so emphatically toward rebellion. Virginia, Maryland, and North Carolina all had early links to the Cavalier side during the English Civil War, in clear contrast to the Parliamentarian sympathy of New England. After Charles I was executed in 1649, both Virginia and Maryland declared for Charles II, and had to be visited by a Parliamentary naval expedition. Sir William Berkeley, governor for most of the years between 1640 and 1677, was a staunch Royalist who took a prominent role in expelling Virginia's Puritans during the 1640s. The Calvert proprietors of Maryland, Catholic until they turned Anglican in the early eighteenth century, were also allied to the Stuarts. North Carolina's own origins lay in a grant by Charles II to eight prominent Royalists in 1663.

But in addition to the Low Church character of its Anglicanism, Virginia did have several early Puritan architects, including Captain John Smith. Bacon's Rebellion in 1676 has also been singled out, especially by Virginia historians like Thomas Jefferson Wertenbaker, as a philosophic seedbed of the American Revolution. North Carolinians and Marylanders took up arms that year as well as Virginians, although in far fewer numbers and not at the same time. Wertenbaker is perhaps too definite, too enthusiastic, when he writes that "the flight of Berkeley to the Eastern Shore foreshadowed the (1776) flight of (Royal Governor) Dunmore to Norfolk and Gwynn's Island; the burning of Jamestown by the patriots in 1676 had its counterpart in the burning of Norfolk by the patriots of 1776; Bacon's Declaration of the People was the forerunner of the Declaration of Independence."[31] Yet staid Virginia did have a radical heritage, usually not emphasized, that set it apart from the other southern colonies. Kinship with more militant northern cultural streams came more easily than might have been expected.

Not that Greater Virginia was *entirely* in the patriotic camp, although as we have seen, the same caveat could be attached to New England and Pennsylvania. The region's most important Tory blocs were High Church Anglicans (more in Maryland); Scottish tobacco merchants (thickest in Norfolk but of considerable importance along the Potomac and in Maryland's Chesapeake Bay seaports); residents in the exposed Eastern Shore sections of both provinces; and indentured servants, runaways, and drifters along the frontier. Fence-sitters also recognized that wide, tidal waterways like the James, Rappahannock, and York Rivers allowed British navy–transported raiding parties to penetrate fifty to sixty miles inland—sometimes with no warning.

Coastal South Carolina, the Anglican plantation culture around Charleston and the Low Country, was like Virginia in dating back to the seventeenth century and being Low Church and vestry-driven. But it was more Barbadian, subtropical, and easygoing. When the British, turning south in 1780, invaded and reconquered most of the state, some local patriots raised the possibility of South Carolina becoming neutral. Britain had done better by Carolina rice and indigo than by Chesapeake tobacco. Nevertheless, it is hard to imagine the leaders of Virginia proposing a similar abstention.

These were the three cultural streams that most drove the American cause: Yankee, Scotch-Irish, and Virginian. However, before moving along to the groups that sought to be neutral and then to the communities that were deeply split, it makes sense to look next at the *opposite* cultural, religious, and ideological pole. These were the vanguardsmen—High Church Anglicans and Scottish merchants and highlanders—of transatlantic loyalism to the British Crown. As with the core rebel groups, the lineage from the century-earlier fight between the Puritans and the Stuarts is unmistakable.

Trinities, Tartans, and Tomahawks

If the coat worn by Joseph in the Bible had many colors, so did the Toryism of the American Revolution. Some particularly conspicuous hues were *vocational*: for example, the high ratios of loyalism among senior royal officials and judges, customs officers, superintendents of Indian Affairs, their subordinates, and white traders who lived in the Indian villages. This category also included merchants prospering from military contracts and planters who thrived furnishing Britain with subsidized commodities like indigo or naval stores. Other loyalists could be described as *circumstantial:* refugees who fled to the frontier, one side in a bitter local feud (especially in provinces like New York and Pennsylvania where non-Yankees were angry at Yankees), residents of British-occupied areas where loyalism was safe and profitable, ex–indentured servants embittered at the patriot gentry, and others who simply took whatever side seemed opportune. Loyalists of another sort were numerous among groups that divided in their wartime loyalties: Church Germans, Dutch, Irish Catholics, and Methodists, to name just a few.

These earlier pages, however, are about the two groups of Tories who gave the fighting of 1775–1783 its principal poles of loyalism and most conspicuous continuity with opponents of previous British revolutions: High Church Anglicans and Scottish placemen and highlanders. No other major ethnic and religious groups in America had such strong links with King and Empire.

The Church of England's Crown

The importance of the Anglican population, by actual church membership less than 100,000 in 1775 out of a white population of roughly two million, varied enormously from province to province. Anglican congregations were the most numerous only in two colonies, Virginia and Maryland. Elsewhere, some other denomination led, even where Anglicanism was the established church (as in North Carolina, South Carolina, and Georgia).

We have seen that in the five southern jurisdictions where Anglicanism was legally, if loosely, established, it was hardly a nursery of Toryism. On the contrary. The vestry-controlled rural plantation parishes of Maryland, Virginia, and the Carolinas bred the Low Church Anglican gentry who led the patriot cause across much of the South. Virginian contributions are too obvious to belabor, but consider the case of Edenton, North Carolina, where St. Paul's Church, built in 1736, had a vestry forty years later that included Joseph Hewes, signer of the Declaration of Independence; James Iredell, associate justice of the first Supreme Court; Samuel Johnston, Continental congressman and first U.S. senator from North Carolina; and Hugh Williamson, surgeon general of the North Carolina militia and signer of the federal Constitution.

Christ Church in Savannah, Georgia, also had a notable body of rebel leaders, and when the loyalist rector refused to proclaim July 20, 1775, a fast day as ordered by Congress, he was declared un-friendly to America, forbidden to preach in Savannah, and re-placed by a layman.[32] In South Carolina, the British burned the vestry-run Anglican churches, like Prince William's, or stabled horses in them, as with Prince George's Church, Winyah. Low Church Anglican gentry had been equally prominent as allies of the Puritans against the Crown in the early 1640s.

The relationship of church and rebellion were different in the middle and New England colonies. A new missionary-minded, eighteenth-century Anglicanism—High Church in its beliefs, sup-portive of the monarchy, often allied with royal governors, and a bitter rival of more numerous Presbyterians and Congregation-alists—was very much the nursery of loyalism that angry patriots claimed. As a result, from Maine to New Jersey, Anglicanism and loyalism, while not synonymous, had a very substantial overlap. To continue the English Civil War analogy, these would have been the adherents of Archbishop William Laud.

The distinctive regional evolutions of colonial Anglicanism are the key. In 1680, when Virginia had 107 Anglican clergy, the northern colonies had none. New York had been under Dutch control until sixteen years earlier. West Jersey was Quaker. New England was a dissenter stronghold, with three of its four provinces having a Congregationalist established church. It was in precisely these milieus, however, that a more aggressive eigh-teenth-century Anglicanism began to make major strides. At the outbreak of the Revolution, fewer than 7 percent of the congrega-tions in New Hampshire, Massachusetts, and Rhode Island were Anglican. However, 12 percent were in New Jersey, 16 percent in New York, and 18 percent in Connecticut.[33]

The Anglicanism in these provinces was a far cry from the lo-cally dominated, Low Church, "country party" faith predominant across the plantation South. Save around New York City, where Anglicanism had a partial establishment in four counties, its status was more that of a church-militant, colluding with royal governors and drawing its clergy (and often their salaries) from the London-based Society for the Propagation of the Gospel. An aroused Thomas Jefferson called the ministers of the SPG "Anglican Jesuits."[34] In New Hampshire, Massachusetts, and New York, the first Anglican church was established by a royal governor, and politicians and prelates alike regarded its credos (and its prominent prayers for the King) as a bulwark of political support for the Crown. In West Jersey, the early eighteenth-century beginnings of local Anglicanism were owed to the SPG. By the 1760s, these provinces, and not those in the South, were those in which a zealous Anglican clergy was petitioning London for an American bishop and a more aggressive form of church organization.

In Virginia, South Carolina, and Georgia, vestry Anglicans did not want bishops any more than the dissenters did. One prominent South Carolina Anglican advised that it wouldn't be safe for a bishop to set foot in Charleston. The demand for episcopacy came, very lopsidedly, from New York, New Jersey, and New England. Even there, not all of the Anglican clergy agreed. These petitions and letters for an American bishop, however, reliably forecast the colonies where virtually all of the Anglican clergy would take the loyalist side in the war. In these northern provinces, rank-and-file Anglicans were likely to be Tories, not patriots.

Carl Bridenbaugh, the colonial historian, bluntly said of the northern provinces between 1766 and 1776 that "one thing above all is clear. The colonial clergy (of the Church of England) formed the core of the American Tories."[35] In New England, Anglican communicants, although a relatively small group, were particularly important to rank-and-file loyalism. In New Hampshire, where loyalists were few, royal governor John Wentworth was overthrown in 1775 by Congregationalists who transferred the government away from Portsmouth, seat of the Anglican merchant and political elite, to Congregationalist Exeter. Massachusetts was the province obliged to sort out its internal divisions most quickly, and of the 928 Bostonians who accompanied the departing British troops to Halifax in March 1776, half were part of the Bay Colony's small prewar Anglican minority which, at most, had represented 3 percent of churchgoers.

In Connecticut, where a half-century of Anglican inroads under-lay bitter relations with Congregationalists, most of the loyalists were Anglicans. Their concentrations, beyond urban upper-class parishes, were in the southwestern Fairfield County towns of Newtown, Redding, Ridgefield, Stratford, Stamford, and Norwalk, extending as far north as Woodbury, Litchfield, and Waterbury and as far east as New Haven. Connecticut Anglicanism was strongest in Fairfield County, nearest to New York, where it was the church of one adult out of three.[36]

Anglican-Presbyterian relations in New York were likewise sour. While not established in the province as a whole, the Anglican church was tax-supported in four principal counties around the City of New York: New York, Staten Island, Queens, and Westchester. Wartime loyalties in the New York environs were fur-ther complicated, as we shall see, by the views of Dutch Reformed and Quaker worshippers. But Anglicans were the preeminent loy-alists. New York Anglican ministers Samuel Seabury and Charles Inglis, for example, have been called the foremost Tory propagan-dists of 1775–1783. Before the war, the New York Assembly was described as divided into Presbyterian and Anglican parties, and the fight over episcopacy—an Anglican bishop for the colonies—was a pivotal issue in the Assembly elections of 1769.[37] When war broke out, these same cleavages appear to have furnished the most intense dividing lines.

New York was clearly an important source of loyalists. That might not have been true absent the huge British armada of 1776 bringing some thirty thousand royal troops to New York, but the long British wartime occupation of six counties—New York, Kings, Queens, Suffolk, Richmond, and part of Westchester—cre-ated its own political culture. Moreover, even those who insist, plausibly, that New York never had an actual plurality of loyalists agree with the centrality of religious divisions. Kings County, largely Dutch, was an exception, but in Queens, Westchester, Dutchess, Ulster, and Albany Counties, basic divisions matched Anglicans against Presbyterians and Independents.

Tory strength followed the contours of Anglicanism—from parishes in Schenectady and Albany down the Hudson to Newburgh, Poughkeepsie, and Philipse and Van Cortlandt manors. Westchester County was about one-third Anglican, and these communities formed the principal core of loyalism. On Long Island, the centers of Toryism in Queens County were also the centers of Anglicanism: Hempstead, Oyster Bay, and Jamaica.[38] Loyalism in Manhattan itself ballooned as refugees, many of them Anglican, sought British protection. As the city filled up with refugees in 1776 and 1777, the existing Anglican churches were inadequate and the governor made "the great court-room in the City Hall" available for services.[39]

New Jersey Anglicans were also a loyalist mainstay. According to the New Jersey Historical Society, "the Anglican clergy, with only one exception, refused to give its allegiance to the new state, and for much of the war period the churches were closed unless they were in an area occupied by the British forces. . . . In general, adherents of the Church of England were hostile to the Revolution."[40] In Delaware, the principal analysis of Toryism comes to the conclusion that loyalists may have outnumbered patriots. The latter's strength was in New Castle County, on the Pennsylvania border, which was two-thirds Presbyterian. Kent and Sussex Counties to the south were more than half Anglican, and local ministers preached loyalism, castigating the Revolution as a Presbyterian movement.[41]

The lines in Pennsylvania are more complex. The local proprietors, the Penn family, returned from Quakerism to Anglicanism in the early eighteenth century. When the Revolution came, the Anglican clergy split. Those outside Philadelphia, all funded from London, supported the Crown. In Philadelphia's vestry-controlled churches, however, half of the clergy supported Congress (at least before Presbyterians took over the state government in 1776–1778). In Lancaster and York, Pennsylvania's second and third cities, prominent rebel leaders were Anglicans. Edward Hand, adjutant general of the Continental Army, was a parishioner of St. James's Anglican Church in York. Presbyterian-Anglican hostility was probably less intense in a province where both groups had also been at loggerheads with Quakers, who had dominated the province right up to 1775. Indeed, Anglicans and Presbyterians *co-operated* against Quaker government in 1764. Hostility didn't fully bloom until the Presbyterians were in power, so that loyalist reaction in Pennsylvania was greatest in 1777–1779.

Episcopal church historians have offered their own capsule of the divisions. In *A History of the American Episcopal Church*, W. W. Manross concluded that "where the Church expanded in sections which were generally hostile to it (as in New England), its adherents were likely to stand out as loyal to the Crown, because whether they were new arrivals or converts, they would be out of sympathy with the prevailing sentiment of the colony and would naturally look across the water for encouragement."[42] Circumstances were quite different in the Anglican plantation colonies. William Warren Sweet, another scholar, has more or less agreed: Colonial Anglicans were most likely to be loyalists in the provinces where they were weak.[43]

The caution is that even in the South, the High Church portion of Anglicans were especially likely to have Tory leanings. They were also most likely to consider uprisings against rebel authorities or to serve in loyalist regiments.[44]

The wartime tilt of Anglicanism was also influenced, as we have seen, by agricultural tobacco economics and by whether churches were controlled by local vestries or from London. In the northern colonies, where Anglicanism largely appealed to a High Church minority, it was *the* principal denominator of loyalism, although there was an overlapping vocational caste of royal officials, retired military officers, judges, lawyers, doctors, and well-connected merchants who clustered in the fashionable Anglican parishes of towns like Portsmouth, Boston, Newport, and New York. This convergence made northern Anglicans the principal core group of American Toryism.

The loyalists who left the new republic in 1783 were not all Anglicans; indeed, under half were. However, the effect on the American branch of the Church of England was devastating. A majority of even Virginia's one hundred parishes were defunct by the end of the war, with the ranks of active Anglican clergymen shrinking from ninety-one to twenty-eight Pennsylvania, North Carolina, and Georgia each had only one active Anglican priest in

1783.[45] Anglican churches that survived the war often bore physical scars akin to those picked up by English churches in the 1640s and 1650s: pews taken for firewood, altars stripped, and steeples and weathervanes pockmarked by musketballs. In the North, hostile Yankee and Presbyterian militia were often responsible—a measure of the perceived regional identification between Anglicanism and loyalism.

Jacobites, Tobacco Factors, and Highlanders

In the southern colonies where Low Church Anglicans captained the patriotic cause—Maryland, Virginia, and the two Carolinas—British soldiers were often those applying the torch to parish churches. In these jurisdictions, a *second* cultural stream came to the fore as loyalists: *Scots,* as distinguished from the usually quite different Scotch-Irish. Toryism in these provinces also had its economic linkage: Indigo planters enjoyed British subsidies, as did producers of naval stores. But more prominence attached to Scots as an ethnic group, with loyal vocations ranging from Indian agents, colonial administrators, and military officers to frontier traders and tobacco merchants. All reflected the new role being played by Scots in the post-Jacobite British Empire.

Scots were hardly confined to the South. Upper New York had thousands. Scores of military officers from the Great French War retired to baronial land grants in the Adirondacks, with their lakes, moors, and crags so like the highlands. Ordinary soldiers joined them on tracts like the "Scottish Grant" in Hebron Township. Hundreds of kilted Catholic MacDonnell clansmen brought from Invernesshire stood guard over Johnson Hall, the New World feudal seat of Sir John Johnson. Serving British officers were well aware of this concentration, and at least one suggested that armed Scots could provide the soldiery of a northern loyalist stronghold.[46] In Massachusetts, British garrison orders for October 1775 noted that Scottish merchants, having offered their services, would be formed into a company called "The Royal North British Volunteers," and would wear a blue bonnet with a St. Andrew's Cross. The larger Scottish role, however, began in Chesapeake Bay and ran all the way to East and West Florida. Map 5.4 is a portrait of Scottish America at the onset of the Revolution.

With respect to the entirety of the thirteen colonies, Scottish support of the American Revolution has been overstated in two ways: first, by an excessive focus on New Jersey and Pennsylvania, where well-known Scots were prominent on the patriot side; and second, by the difficulty of fully separating the Scots and the Scotch-Irish. In New Jersey, the purely Scots contribution to the patriotic side does leap out—the Scottish ancestry of the famous family of William Livingston, the state's Revolutionary war governor; the fierce evangelical Presbyterianism of the descendants of the seventeenth-century Covenanter emigrants who settled several districts of East Jersey; the contributions of theologian John Witherspoon, who left Scotland in 1768 to become president of what would become Princeton University, emerging as a principal theorist of independence and then serving in the Continental Congress; and the Revolutionary battlefield prominence of two other Scots, General William Alexander, claimant to the Scottish earldom of Stirling, and General Hugh Mercer, killed at Princeton, whose memorial tablet at Fort Mercer shows him in a highland bonnet.

But from Chesapeake Bay south, as in the northern New York of MacDonnell clansmen and retired highland soldiery, the weight of the Scots in America favored the same politics that their cousins chose in Edinburgh and in the Parliament at Westminster: the side of George III and his ministers. They were also quicker than the English to commit, having a better nose for intended rebellion, as well as a greater scent of the new imperial opportunities.

In Virginia, the royal governor, the Scottish fourth Earl of Dunmore, took the events at Lexington as a call to arms. His mother traced descent from the royal Stuart line, and as a boy during the Forty Five, he had been a page to Prince Charles Edward Stuart at Holyrood. Already an experienced Indian fighter by 1775, he quickly organized a military force around the Tory element of the Anglican population, together with the large group of Scottish merchants and traders based in the Virginia tidewater. Norfolk-area loyalists became known as "the Scotch Party," echoing the occasional prewar political division between Scots, who wore orange badges, and English, who wore blue.[47] Autumn saw Dunmore de-

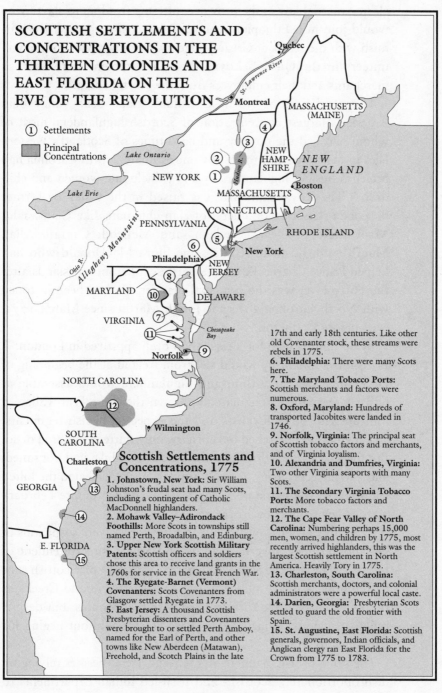

SCOTTISH SETTLEMENTS AND CONCENTRATIONS IN THE THIRTEEN COLONIES AND EAST FLORIDA ON THE EVE OF THE REVOLUTION

① Settlements

▨ Principal Concentrations

Quebec

St. Lawrence River

Montreal

Lake Ontario

Lake Erie

Ohio R.

Allegheny Mountains

NEW YORK ①

②

③

④

Hudson R.

MASSACHUSETTS (MAINE)

NEW HAMP-SHIRE

NEW ENGLAND

Boston

MASSACHUSETTS

CONNECTICUT

RHODE ISLAND

PENNSYLVANIA

⑥ ⑤

Philadelphia

New York

NEW JERSEY

⑧

MARYLAND ⑩

DELAWARE

VIRGINIA ⑦

⑪

Chesapeake Bay

Norfolk ⑨

NORTH CAROLINA

⑫

Wilmington

SOUTH CAROLINA

Charleston ⑬

GEORGIA

⑭

E. FLORIDA

⑮

Scottish Settlements and Concentrations, 1775

1. Johnstown, New York: Sir William Johnston's feudal seat had many Scots, including a contingent of Catholic MacDonnell highlanders.
2. Mohawk Valley–Adirondack Foothills: More Scots in townships still named Perth, Broadalbin, and Edinburg.
3. Upper New York Scottish Military Patents: Scottish officers and soldiers chose this area to receive land grants in the 1760s for service in the Great French War.
4. The Ryegate-Barnet (Vermont) Covenanters: Scots Covenanters from Glasgow settled Ryegate in 1773.
5. East Jersey: A thousand Scottish Presbyterian dissenters and Covenanters were brought to or settled Perth Amboy, named for the Earl of Perth, and other towns like New Aberdeen (Matawan), Freehold, and Scotch Plains in the late

17th and early 18th centuries. Like other old Covenanter stock, these streams were rebels in 1775.
6. Philadelphia: There were many Scots here.
7. The Maryland Tobacco Ports: Scottish merchants and factors were numerous.
8. Oxford, Maryland: Hundreds of transported Jacobites were landed in 1746.
9. Norfolk, Virginia: The principal seat of Scottish tobacco factors and merchants, and of Virginia loyalism.
10. Alexandria and Dumfries, Virginia: Two other Virginia seaports with many Scots.
11. The Secondary Virginia Tobacco Ports: More tobacco factors and merchants.
12. The Cape Fear Valley of North Carolina: Numbering perhaps 15,000 men, women, and children by 1775, most recently arrived highlanders, this was the largest Scottish settlement in North America. Heavily Tory in 1775.
13. Charleston, South Carolina: Scottish merchants, doctors, and colonial administrators were a powerful local caste.
14. Darien, Georgia: Presbyterian Scots settled to guard the old frontier with Spain.
15. St. Augustine, East Florida: Scottish generals, governors, Indian officials, and Anglican clergy ran East Florida for the Crown from 1775 to 1783.

MAP 5.4

claring martial law in the province, offering freedom to slaves who would join his "Ethiopian regiment" but losing the decisive skirmish with the rebels at Great Bridge in December. Most of the volunteers in the Queen's Loyal Virginia Regiment were Scottish merchants and their employees from the Norfolk area.[48]

The sand hills of North Carolina's Cape Fear Valley held America's largest concentration of Scottish highlanders, most of whom had fled the poverty and hard times of Scotland's Western Isles in the 1760s and 1770s. By one estimate, North Carolina had fifteen thousand highlanders by 1775, including women and children.[49] The Royal Standard was raised in the valley by former tacksmen (lesser landholders) of clan chieftains like Clanranald, MacDonald of Sleat, Maclean, and McLeod. Captain Allan MacDonald, husband to the same Flora MacDonald who had helped Prince Charles Edward Stuart escape from the islands after the Forty Five, was the principal planner. He had been in touch with North Carolina governor Josiah Martin since March 1775, even before Lexington.

By autumn, a plan for a rising had been approved in London: A British fleet and army would sail from Ireland at the beginning of December, and three thousand highlanders would assemble at Cross Creek, thereafter marching down the Cape Fear Valley to join up with other loyalists and the expected British regiments. The highlanders marched in February, only thirteen hundred or so. But the British fleet, three months behind schedule, had not sailed, and a Whig rebel army, roughly similar in size, defeated the kilted clansmen at the battle of Moore's Creek Bridge in late February 1776. They would never rise again.

In South Carolina, meanwhile, patriot forces were suspicious of yet another Scot, Inverness-born John Stuart, superintendent of Indian Affairs for the Southern District, who with his Scottish staff had almost as much influence with the Cherokees and Creeks as the Johnsons of New York enjoyed with the Iroquois. But despite rebel suspicions, Stuart fled to East Florida without urging his tribesmen to attack.

The same British planners of 1774 and 1775, besides relying on disproportionately Scottish- and Irish-led Indian departments to control the American frontier and counting on the local highlanders to rise in eastern North Carolina, had even broader plans: to raise highland regiments in America, not just in Scotland's own Highlands. Three American-based Scottish retired officers were the organizers, two MacDonalds and a Maclean, and it was the latter—Colonel Allan Maclean, a scarcely veiled Jacobite given to wearing a Stuart white cockade—who obtained command of the Royal Highland Emigrant Regiment. Its two battalions were to be recruited in large measure from Nova Scotia, New York, and North Carolina.

The Scottish Highlanders had already become an unusual British wartime resource during the Great French War. That would be even truer in the American Revolution. By contrast, no knowledgeable officer in the British army would have dreamed of enlisting regiments of Royal East Anglian Emigrants or Royal West Country Emigrants. In 1775–1776, recruits for the British army in America could barely be had in these parts of England, to say nothing of among their progeny on the other side of the Atlantic.

The unusual distribution of the Scottish population in British America had a further relevance. Beyond the thirteen rebellious colonies, Scots also played a considerable role in the five adjacent provinces: Quebec, Ile St. Jean (the future Prince Edward Island), Nova Scotia, East Florida, and West Florida. Nova Scotia Scots were mainstays, alongside the military, of the loyalism that kept the province British in 1775–1776 despite the ambivalence of French Acadians and ex–New Englanders. In East and West Florida, British only since 1763, Scots were the cutting edge of empire. Several of the governors were Scots; so were many senior military officers; the merchants were largely Scottish; and the Indian agents were named McDonald, McGillivray, Cameron, and Stuart. Even the Anglican clergy in the Floridas were usually graduates of Edinburgh and Aberdeen universities. In West Florida, Fort Bute, near Manchac, with its Scottish-owned plantations, was named for Lord Bute, their patron in London. "With a little imagination," wrote the principal historian of the American Revolution in the Floridas, "one could almost see a highland horde charging through Florida's saw palmettos, angrily waving claymores."[50] Both of the Floridas had small prewar populations of only three thousand or so Europeans, but an influx of southern loyalist refugees, not a few Scottish, soon doubled or trebled their populations, and loyalist sentiment only intensified. Even in 1776, the local reply to rebel invitations to send delegates to the Continental Congress was to organize Tory military units named the East Florida Rangers and the West Florida Royal Foresters.

Patriot leaders from the Chesapeake and the Carolinas were only too aware of the Scottish complexion of southern loyalism. Thomas Jefferson, furious at Virginia's Scottish tobacco factors, penned a first draft of the Declaration of Independence that included a line attacking the King for sending "not only soldiers of our common blood but Scotch and foreign mercenaries to invade and destroy us."[51] This singling-out of one particular ethnic group was unacceptable—and eliminated from the final version.

The Scottish-born tobacco factors and merchants of tidewater Virginia, scattered from Norfolk to Alexandria, while probably fewer than a thousand in number, were overwhelmingly loyalist, even most who had been in the province for twenty or thirty years. By 1776, the better part of these were returning to Britain, joining a loyalist regiment in New York, or making their way to East Florida. North Carolina, too, had its small group of Scottish tobacco representatives in the Albemarle Sound ports. Chesapeake Bay, Maryland, besides its Scottish tobacco merchants, had also received several boatloads of exiled Scottish Jacobites after the Forty Five.

The Scottish presence in South Carolina rivaled that in Virginia. Several prominent Scottish loyalists were indigo planters, a profitable crop which enjoyed British subsidies. Many more, however, were merchants, tradesmen, or artisans in the Low Country around Charleston, as well as members of the learned professions, government officials, and persons dealing with the Indians. In 1775, many of the substantial Scottish population of Charleston were recent immigrants and almost all of the adults were Scottish-born, and they kept in close touch through the St. Andrews Society. Dislike of them was fierce enough, in the words of one biographer, to produce an "anti-Scottish party" on the Whig side.[52] In 1778, many declined to take the new state's loyalty oath and took ship for Britain, the Bahamas, and elsewhere. Some went to East Florida, where South Carolina and Georgia residents of

Scottish extraction such as Thomas Brown and Evan McLaurin had already taken prominent roles in organizing the East Florida Rangers.

The Scots in Georgia were at once less numerous and more divided in their politics. Merchants and Indian traders were the principal loyalists.[53] However, Georgia, in contrast to South Carolina, also had an older Scottish settlement. These Scots, brought in 1735 to help defend Georgia against Spain, were Macintoshes from Inverness, who had been accompanied by a feisty Presbyterian dominie, and in 1775, their declarations on the patriotic side reached back into Scottish history in the manner of the early-settled Ulster strongholds to the north.[54] Parenthetically, one of the oldest highlander districts in North Carolina was settled from Argyll in 1739 and also took the rebel side. But among highlanders, such loyalties were more the exception than the rule.

So bitter were memories that in several states Scots were not welcome for years after the war. In 1783, Georgia passed a statute forbidding entry to natives of Scotland unless they had fought for American independence.[55] The principal analysis of loyalism in South Carolina notes that members of the prewar Scottish community were usually not allowed, or did not wish, to take up residence again.[56]

While some of the Scots in Virginia, the Carolinas, and Georgia were Catholics or Anglicans, the great majority would have been Presbyterian, and so the Revolution in the South simply cannot be called a Presbyterian war. The ethnic, cultural, and religious divisions throughout the South, as should be apparent by now, were more complicated than those in New England and even New York and New Jersey. The alignments of the 1775–1783 fighting show that the Revolution was still in many ways a British war, rooted in beliefs and tribalisms that the American frontier was only modifying and dispersing, not yet replacing or eliminating. This was even true on the frontier itself.

The Tomahawk and the Cross

The prominent role played by Scots in managing British relations with the various Indian tribes leads into the last core group of loyalists: a few of the most committed Indian tribes, as well as the Europeans who lived and fought with them as what the settlers called renegades or white Indians. Despite contrary folklore, the tribes did not fight almost entirely on the British side. Many tried to stay neutral and a few allied with the American rebels.

Location made the Six Nations of the Iroquois Confederation, based in New York, especially important to both sides. The individual tribe most tightly tied to the British, over several generations, was the Mohawks of the valley named for them. British allies against the French since the late seventeenth century, a number of their chiefs had been taken to London on visits. The foremost, Joseph Brant, held a commission in the British army and had been feted in London in 1774, including sitting for portraitist George Romney. Part of the Mohawk tie was to Sir William Johnson, the Irish Catholic-turned-Anglican, who ran the Indian Department for the northern colonies. Brant's sister, Molly, became Johnson's common-law wife on the death of his first wife, a Palatine German. The granddaughter of a famous Mohawk chief, Molly Brant was a far cry from the popular image of a "squaw." In 1777, she fled from the Mohawk Valley after helping to bring about the successful British ambush of the valley militia at Oriskany. The rebel Committee of Safety official and Oneida warriors who pillaged her home in Canojoharie found "sixty half Johannesses, two Quarts full of silver, several Gold Rings, eight pair of Silver Buckels, a large quantity of Silver Broaches. Together with several silk gowns."[57]

Her brother Joseph, educated at the Mohawk Valley Anglican mission, later worshipped in the Anglican church at Fort Hunter and from time to time with the Johnson family at St. John's in Johnstown or at St. George's in Schenectady. He was a High Church Anglican, like many other Mohawks. They appreciated not only the church's ceremony but its lack of moral piousness (not least willingness to baptize infants, including the illegitimate plentitude sired by Johnson, without asking Presbyterian-type questions about the behavior of their parents). Brant was sufficiently involved to translate some of the gospels into the Mohawk language; and he referred to the Oneidas, who took the rebel side, as damned Presbyterian Indians.[58]

Religion was only one factor. Tribes taking the rebel side usually lived close to or within white-settled areas. Southern New England's coastal Pequots and Narragansetts of Connecticut, Rhode Island, and Cape Cod served on state and U.S. naval vessels and privateers as well as in army units. So did the Church Indians of eastern Long Island. Mohicans were found in several places, most notably Stockbridge, Massachusetts. Even as late as 1775, the Stockbridge Indians, an amalgam of Mohicans, Housatonics, Schaghticokes, and Wappingers, chose several selectmen and shared the town government of Stockbridge with white officials, although that would not last. A company of Stockbridge Indians served with General Washington's army and was cut to pieces in a fight with British dragoons in what is now Van Cortlandt Park in New York City. So lopsided was this support that the Mohicans, the Stockbridge Wappingers, the Pequots—half of the Pequots serving in Connecticut regiments never came home—as well as New York's Oneida could well have been mentioned with Congregationalist New England, being as much on the rebel side as the Mohawks were in the British camp.

The best proof of religion's prominence lay in how the New York and New England Indians supporting the rebel side usually had a dissenting Protestant religious education or connection. Typically, that meant Congregationalist or Presbyterian, although some had attended the Reverend Eleazer Wheelock's school for Indians at what became Dartmouth College. Sir William Johnson, before he died in 1774, had expressed growing concern over the influence within the Iroquois Confederation of three dissenting ministers—Samuel Kirkland with the Oneida, Aaron Crosby at the mixed Mohawk-Oneida-Tuscarora town of Oquaga, and John Sargent at Stockbridge. The Oneidas and Mohawks both lived close to the white settlements; the Oneida, however, came under the influence of Presbyterian minister Kirkland, taking up that faith and allying themselves with the rebels as war came. Oneidas served with the American forces in New York, New Jersey, and Pennsylvania campaigns, and one of their principal chiefs was killed fighting alongside Mohawk Valley settlers at the battle of Oriskany in 1777.

Also found along the frontier were the bands of whites and mixed-race persons closely allied to the traders and Indian Department officers. Many were hunters, banditti, or renegades who couldn't go back to the settlements, and they often served as Tory irregulars. Joseph Brant had his own white auxiliaries: Brant's Volunteers, with a hundred or so members. The officers of the Indian Department and the provincial Tory units like the Queens Rangers and the Royal Greens were typically Scots or Irishmen, and rarely English.[59] For Scots and Irish to wear warpaint—which in these frontier roles they often did—was no extraordinary cultural transformation. Ancestors on both sides of the Irish Sea had painted for battle well into the Middle Ages; moreover, both the Scots and the Irish came from societies of clans and chiefs, and in their sword-swinging battle charges, both could match any Seneca or Wyandot clan for blood-chilling screams (these, of course, lived on as the famous "rebel yell" of the American Civil War).

This frontier Toryism was most important on the long and open New York, Pennsylvania, Carolina, and Georgia borders from the Mohawk Valley, Oswego, and Niagara to western Pennsylvania, south through the Cherokee and Creek towns into the British-held territory of West and East Florida. The prewar banditti of the southern backcountry furnished many recruits to loyalist militia units and to the feared East Florida Rangers.

The last section in this chapter will come back to the substantial Tory minorities, as well as to the even larger rebel contingents, produced by divided communities and cultural streams from the Church Germans to the Dutch Reformed and French Huguenots. For the moment, however, let us leave the frontier, with its renegades, Indians, and Scottish traders and proconsuls, and move east toward the settlements of the pacifist sects. Their otherworldliness, their refusal to take up arms, and their desire to be left alone during the Revolution had been shaped in abattoirs of seventeenth-century Europe. The Quakers were a product of the civil and religious wars that brutalized the British Isles, while the German Mennonites, Moravians, and others were the product of the far more ruthless and repetitive fighting that ravaged southern and western Germany.

The Would-Be Neutrals:
Quakers and Peace Germans

Every civil war has neutrals or would-be neutrals. Some seek to avoid military involvement because of religion or belief. Some seek neutral status because they are on the periphery of the fight or separate from the peoples involved. Others find themselves in what has become a neutral zone. Occasionally, the inhabitants of an area crisscrossed by troops mobilize against further incursions by either army. Still others are allowed a de facto neutralism because a principal belligerent finds that status convenient.

The fighting from 1775 to 1783 produced many examples. Pennsylvania's Anabaptist Ephrata Brethren sought neutral status in 1776 not because of pacifism but on the unusual grounds that, being under a higher magistrate, they were "consequently emancipated from the civil government."[60] As we have seen, several New England–settled towns in Nova Scotia petitioned the royal authorities in 1775 to be allowed to be neutral rather than fight their relatives, and an unofficial neutrality was allowed in some cases. Parts of South Carolina and New York's Westchester County emerged as de facto neutral zones. Vermont's claims to independence and dickering with the British in 1781–1782 established a vague neutrality.

These pages, however, are about the most important would-be neutrals of the American Revolution: the religious pacifists. Among the dozens of such groups were the influential Quakers and the very kindred Peace Germans—Amish, Dunkers, Mennonites, and Moravians. The Mennonites, in particular, were sometimes called German Quakers because their doctrines were similar, and William Penn, the Quaker founder of Pennsylvania, had encouraged their migration to his colony.

Among most settlers of English, Welsh, Scotch-Irish, or even Scottish antecedents, those whose families had been in the thirteen colonies the longest were also those most likely to have developed community roots and North American outlooks inclining them toward the pro-independence rebels. Not so the Quakers. Many of the third and fourth generation, rooted and prosperous, were among the staunchest objectors to the Revolution; and a significant minority were virtual (if rarely aggressive) Tories.

Beyond religious pacificism, there were good reasons, both socioeconomic and political, for the Quakers to stand apart from the
Revolution and to prefer continued English rule. By 1775, they
were disproportionately men of commerce, the professions, and
moderate-to-substantial farm holdings rather than workers, mechanics, porters, servants, and suchlike. In maritime trade and
whaling, a network of Quaker-influenced or -dominated ports ran
from Nantucket to Newport, Rhode Island, several towns on
Long Island, Cape May, New Jersey, and Albemarle Sound, North
Carolina.

Politically, however, the Quakers were what sociologists have
called "declining elites"—onetime hegemons losing their earlier
local power. This was true in each of the seven provinces where
they still represented over 10 percent of the religious congregations circa 1775: Delaware (19.4 percent), North Carolina (18.2
percent), New Jersey (15.5 percent), Pennsylvania (15.3 percent),
Rhode Island (12.6 percent), Maryland (10.9 percent), and New
York (10.9 percent).[61] Their concern was reinforced by their particularly low numbers and weak influence in the home provinces
of the war's principal protagonists, New England (especially
Connecticut) and the plantation Low Church Anglican centers of
Virginia and South Carolina. The third major rebel culture, the
Scotch-Irish, stirred even greater Quaker apprehension. The Ulster
Presbyterians were their principal opponents within Pennsylvania,
and the two loathed each other. When the Scotch-Irish Paxton
Boys marched on Philadelphia in an angry 1763 demonstration,
Quakers flocked to the militia and even took up muskets. Several
historians suggest that the chance to take a righteous shot at an
Ulster Presbyterian overrode their pacifism.[62]

At the war's outbreak, the five colonies with the highest ratio of
Quaker congregations—Delaware, North Carolina, New Jersey,
Pennsylvania, and Rhode Island—were those where three or four
generations earlier, Quakerism had been influential enough to control the provincial government or, at least, to have elected several
early governors.[63] The pattern that was in place by 1775 was the
breakdown of one of the least appreciated dimensions of the early
colonial period: Quaker eminence. Founded only in 1647, amid
the English Civil War, the Quakers—named for how their leaders

trembled while they preached—were probably the least liked sect to emerge from it, both in Puritan New England and in the Restoration England of Charles II. Unpopular practices of those years included attending and interrupting the services of other denominations, going naked for a sign (in 1666, two young Quaker girls walked into a Puritan service in Duxbury, Massachusetts, "dressed only in Eve's first costume to testify to the nakedness of the land"), calling others by the terms "thee" and "thou," hitherto used for social inferiors, and refusing to pay tithes to support the established church. During the reign of Charles II alone, 13,562 Quakers were imprisoned, 198 were exiled, and 338 died in prison or from wounds received in assaults on their meetings.[64]

Small wonder that substantial numbers, especially those with wealth who wanted to avoid tithes, taxes, confiscations, and fines, took ship for the half dozen American colonies where they were welcomed or accepted. Their substantial settlements in Rhode Island began in 1657, and those in North Carolina and in West Jersey, as we have seen, in the early 1670s. But the major Quaker exodus from England and imprint on the New World in 1681 came from William Penn's success in obtaining a charter and the proprietorship of Pennsylvania from Charles II and the King's brother, the future James II.

Pennsylvania, well favored in its location, soil, and climate, and kept peaceful for three generations by Quaker policy toward the Indians, drew several thousand Quaker settlers within the first few years. It had a population of about six to eight thousand by 1686, when persecution of Quakers in England ended. This did not slow emigration much, because the largest group of settlers for the first two decades were Welsh, predominantly but not exclusively Quakers, who wished to establish a Welsh-speaking territory in the New World. Penn gave them forty thousand acres—the Welsh Barony—in the high ridge along the future main line of the Pennsylvania Railroad with its still omnipresent Welsh names: Wynwood, Haverford, Merion, Bryn Mawr, Radnor, St. David's, Berwyn, and Duffrin Mawr, the "Great Valley" just west of Chester.

James II, seeking to advance the position of Catholics within England by promoting a larger religious toleration, decided in 1686 to free thirteen hundred Quakers from English jails, generally ending their oppression. Both Stuarts, Charles and James, had owed William Penn's father, Admiral William Penn, the sum of £16,000, huge at the time, for services in the early years of the Restoration. It was to pay this old debt in 1681 that the House of Stuart had deeded over the roughly fifty-five thousand square miles that included present-day Pennsylvania and more. However, the relationship between the Stuarts and the Penns would soon become more controversial. Penn himself returned to England in 1684, staying on after James's accession in 1685 and becoming the King's close advisor. Quakers themselves were critical, believing that the new King was using Quakers, admittedly to their short-term advantage, as part of a plot to restore Catholicism. After James was dethroned, Penn had to hide to escape arrest, and his reputation never recovered.

This episode is relevant in weighing Quaker vulnerability in the American Revolution a century later. At first blush, the backing for James II was an anomaly, a situation personal to Penn. But the founder's descendants were Anglicans again by the early eighteenth century, and other wealthy Quakers followed their migration into the pews of Philadelphia's own Christ Church.

Even more to the point, Pennsylvania's prosperous Quaker and Quaker-turned-Anglican establishment of the eighteenth century had understandably favorable memories of the monarchy. By the 1770s, they also sensed that Quakers had done far better under loose rule from London than they would fare under rule by the King-hating rebels. This would especially include the Scotch-Irish, the Quakers' provincial foes, but also the Yankees (Massachusetts had expelled and executed Quakers, and rapacious Connecticut was trying to grab part of the Susquehanna Valley). Nor did the vestry Anglicans of Virginia care for Quakers or Moravians, and Virginians were contesting Pennsylvania's claim to the area around Pittsburgh.

By mid-century, Quakers found themselves all but opposed to the overall westward thrust of British North America. It would disturb peace with the Indians, compel the unwanted militarization of Pennsylvania, and fill up the western part of the province with political foes. Expansionists would wrest control from the Quakers, just as Quakers had already watched their early domination of Rhode Island, New Jersey, and North Carolina vanish in the first years of the eighteenth century.

Wars were also a threat. The French danger of the 1740s and 1750s had forced Pennsylvania's Quaker government to fund a military defense. In 1775, as another war appeared on the horizon, one of Philadelphia's two militia companies was Quaker, even though many of the participants were figuratively drummed out of their Quaker meetings. The news from Lexington brought a *rage militaire* to even Philadelphia, and when the Quaker Blues marched in the August Grand Review, the somberly dressed Quakers in their broad-brimmed hats who lined the parade route must have had deep premonitions. A century of province-building was at risk.

If most Quakers did not want to go to war, many also did not want a politics that would end ties to the Crown. John Pemberton, a Quaker leader, had contended in a January 1775 pamphlet that because Quakers, especially those in America, had received general clemency from the King and his royal forebears since the 1680s, they should stay out of any war that could cause bloodshed and even loss of religious liberty by its challenge to kingly authority.[65] A Quaker meeting convened in New York in mid-1776 took a similar approach. The delegates agreed that "the benefits, advantages and favors we have experienced by our dependence on and connection with the king and government . . . appear to demand from us the greatest circumspection, care and constant endeavors to guard against every attempt to alter, or subvert, that dependence and connection."[66]

Quaker insistence that they favored neither side, and that their refusal to pay taxes or to serve in either army was evenhanded, was undercut by several other circumstances. Collaboration was common when the British occupied an area with a major Quaker population—Philadelphia and environs (from September 1777 to May 1778); parts of New Jersey at different times; Westchester and Long Island in New York (from August 1776 until the end of the war); Newport, Rhode Island, and its environs (1777 to 1779); and Nantucket and Cape Cod (the off-and-on landings of British warships). Critics also saw barely repressed loyalism in how, during the war, over four hundred Quakers were read out of meeting and disowned for participating in the fighting on the American side while just six were read out for assisting the British.[67]

Counties and districts with substantial Quaker populations inevitably showed up as centers of disaffection when inhabitants' willingness to take loyalty oaths to the new state governments was a criterion. Because they disbelieved in oath-taking, Quakers would not do so. However, this unwillingness, like their refusal to cheer the news of Saratoga or even Yorktown, was not simply a matter of religious obligation blocking personal sentiment. Many probably would not have wanted to cheer; independence itself— even obtained without bloodshed—was a development quite a few would not have welcomed.

They paid a high price. Next to Anglicanism, Quakerism was the American denomination most weakened by the Revolution. While few Quakers left the country, many left their Friends meetings. This trend had begun before the war, but it accelerated. Some who had fought in the Revolution tried to maintain themselves thereafter as Fighting Quakers, but these efforts were not successful.

By the early nineteenth century, Quaker influence, although no longer dominant, survived best in the core region around Philadelphia—the three eastern counties of Pennsylvania (Philadelphia, Chester, and Bucks), adjacent western New Jersey, and northern Delaware. In peripheries like Massachusetts and North Carolina, many Quakers converted to other faiths and a surprising minority headed to the frontier.[68]

The war-shunning majority of Quakers in the thirteen colonies cannot be called Tories. However, as a declining elite whose interests were threatened by both separation from Britain and the rising influence of the core groups pressing rebellion, neither were they very strictly neutral. Genuine neutrality was not a Quaker heritage. During their formative years in the mid-seventeenth century, Quakers had soldiered for Parliament in the English Civil War. Less than a century after the War of Independence, while most Quakers refused to bear arms in the American Civil War, those in the North largely supported it, embraced the Republican Party that managed and fought it, cheered Lincoln's proclamations, paid taxes to support the North's blue battalions, and made more than a little money out of burgeoning war industries. The Tory-flavored insistence on neutralism of Quakers in the American Revolution was an anomaly.

Genuine, unstinted neutrality was more common among the German pacifist sects. The devastation of Germany by seventeenth- and early eighteenth-century wars exceeded anything in civil war England. The German sects were more otherworldly than the rich and entrepreneurial Quakers. And the Amish, Mennonites, and Moravians, in contrast to the Quakers, were not lamenting lost hegemony or influence in five provinces. Whereas by 1775, Quaker mansions and gardens were among the finest in the Delaware Valley—many are still showplaces—no visitor to towns like Ephrata, Nazareth, and Bethlehem in Pennsylvania, as well as Salem in North Carolina, could doubt the German religious refugees' desire for seclusion and simplicity far from the European wars they had hated so much.

Pacifist German settlements could be found in New Jersey, Maryland, and North Carolina as well as Pennsylvania. Even so, the southeastern section of the Penns' province was their heartland—and not by accident, because the Quaker proprietor had encouraged Mennonites and Moravians to come there. At the start of the Revolution, the Peace German population of Pennsylvania numbered ten to fifteen thousand, or 3 to 5 percent of Pennsylvania's total. No other province would have had more than a thousand or two.

During 1777–1778, a number of their Pennsylvania towns that were safely out of the paths of the armies—the Moravian villages of Bethlehem, Nazareth, Gnadenhall, and Lititz, the Ephrata cloister of the German Baptist Brethren, with its still-extraordinary medieval German timbered buildings—turned their brethren's houses, sisters' houses, outbuildings, and barns into hospitals for the American sick and wounded from the battles of Trenton, Princeton, Brandywine, and Germantown. Besides the hundreds of soldiers who died, so did scores of the German volunteer doctors, helpers, and ministers and their families as smallpox, typhus, and camp fever swept through the facilities. Foodstuffs of every kind were requisitioned. Paper itself was so needed for cartridges that

the unbound leaves of the "Martyr Book," the *fraktur* or illuminated calligraphy published by the community at Ephrata, were
carried off in two wagons guarded by six troopers.[69]

Compared to the Quakers, the German pacifist sects were more
deliberately helpful to the rebels, in nonmilitary and noncash
ways. But there were caveats. Being good farmers on rich lands,
they were more than a little resentful of the Americans' incessant
requisitions, fines, and demands. Local histories in Pennsylvania
and North Carolina have details that German-American chronicles omit. The Moravians, in their North Carolina settlement of
Wachovia, always gave the Whig soldiers the foodstuffs and supplies they requested, taking near-worthless paper money in return.
The Mennonites and Dunkers, however, were more inclined to
collaborate with the British. In 1780, reeling under the pressure of
inflation, impressments, requisitions, fines, and taxes, four
Pennsylvania Mennonite and Dunker ministers drew up a petition
to the King, to be sent through Sir Henry Clinton in New York.
Expressing a desire to aid the British cause—even suggesting that
they could help to stifle the rebellion by refusing to plant their
crops!—the sects asked for instructions.[70]

Clinton never replied. However, between 1780 and 1783, some
of the indignant Plain People turned their words into activism in
discouraging enlistments in the American army, in providing
refuge for American deserters, and in helping British prisoners escape from guarded stockades at Lancaster and near York. Late in
1782, U.S. military authorities discovered that these escapes had
been incited and arranged by German sectarians, with the fugitives
harbored and conducted to the Delaware River and the border
with New Jersey by an "underground railroad" of Plain People
and Quakers, and as a result, forty men and four women were
prosecuted by Pennsylvania authorities.[71]

If many Quakers, living in prosperous coastal areas, and conducting substantial businesses, were tempted to collude with
British occupying or visiting forces, the Peace Germans were in a
different dilemma. They lived inland, in farm areas under
American control, and suffered abusive treatment, relentless requisitions, and punitive fines and taxation. Yet reactions like those
above were uncommon.

The behavior of the two major groups of would-be neutrals is not central to the broad architecture of loyalties, church or ethnic, in the years after 1775. Quaker circumstances were unique. The German sectarians were relatively few. More importance attaches to blacks and Indians, and to seven other European groups, ethnic and religious, whose communities, deeply divided during those years, accounted for at least one-fifth of the population of British North America: Church Germans, the Dutch of New York and New Jersey, the French Huguenot Protestants, Jews, Irish Catholics, Baptists, and Methodists. Here, too, religion is confirmed as a central factor in wartime loyalties.

The Divided Ethnic and Religious Cultures

Many among the German, Dutch, and French communities of English-speaking North America found it difficult to choose between two sides in a British Protestant civil war. The late seventeenth- and early eighteenth-century wars in the Rhineland, Ireland, and the Low Countries were simpler for the Protestant Dutch and for the French Huguenots. They usually fought with the British army, on the continent or in the British Isles against the Stuarts. Protestant Germans had also been on the British side, especially since 1714 and the accession of Hanoverian kings of Britain with strong ties to Hanover, Brunswick, Lunenburg, and Mecklenburg. Henry Melchior Muhlenberg, the Pennsylvania Lutheran leader, had actually grown up in Hanover.

Perhaps not surprisingly, when the German, Dutch, and French Protestants in North America did divide over the Revolution, there was a degree of denominational logic. As we will see, members of Calvinist and Reform churches tended to be on the rebel side, plausible enough given the heavily Calvinist origins and leadership of the Revolutionary forces in New England and the middle colonies. Tory sentiment was greater among the French Huguenot elites, many already largely Anglican, and among the Dutch and German congregations that were High Church in worship or tied to Europe through the Hanoverians, the Church of England, or the Classis of Amsterdam. Nonreligious ties to the House of

Hanover—land grants, settler assistance—also influenced German colonists to feel an obligation to the Crown.

French Catholics, ironically, seem to have been as divided as French Huguenots. A sizable minority of those in Quebec had shown some early interest in the *Congressiste* cause, but the Catholic hierarchy kept most of them on the British side. Two other French groups had a much higher ratio of collaboration with the rebels: the five thousand or so remaining Acadians of Nova Scotia, left behind when their fathers, sisters, and cousins had been expelled by the British in 1756, and the thousand or so French woodsmen, traders, and settlers of the Ohio Valley. Several hundred helped George Rogers Clark capture Kaskaskia and Vincennes in what are now Illinois and Indiana. Doubtless most recognized that the Ohio Valley, if not the St. Lawrence, would become *Congressiste*.

But before turning to the Irish and German Catholics and the German, Dutch, and French Protestants, who represented at least 30–40 percent of the white population in New York, New Jersey, and Pennsylvania, and perhaps 10 percent in the Carolinas, and whose internal alignments further amplify the theses of this book, it is important to note two other groups, also divided by the fighting, to whom a widespread British civil war was something new: the Indians and blacks.

The former, as we have seen, far from being monolithically pro-British, were indeed divided. Besides the Oneidas, Mohegans, Pequots, and other Church Indians, the Catawba of the Carolinas fought mostly on the side of the colonists. The Caugnawaga or St. Francis Indians of the Quebec-Vermont border showed a partiality to the rebel side, acknowledged in British correspondence, because most of their chiefs had New England ancestry—having been taken captive by raiders in their boyhoods, having attended Ebenezer Wheelock's school, or both. Members of the Scaticook tribe enlisted in various New Hampshire regiments. A dozen Pigwackets from the Maine district petitioned Massachusetts to be able to sign up.

The wartime divisions among blacks, however, command a greater attention because of their importance for the future: the way in which the American Revolution and the Constitution of 1787 set the scene for the U.S. Civil War, just as the English Civil

War had for the American Revolution. This is principally discussed in chapter 8, yet the way in which blacks chose sides in the Revolution, and the reaction that produced at the time and then later, can appropriately be discussed at this point.

British officials, almost from the first, had perceived the large, vulnerable slave populations from Chesapeake Bay south as a rebel Achilles heel. Slaves owned by rebel planters could be convinced to run away, to work for the British, or, in some cases, to enlist with British units. The governor of Virginia, Lord Dunmore, organized a black unit in 1775, the Ethiopian Regiment, and by promising freedom to slaves who could reach British lines, he enlisted hundreds and tantalized thousands. Runaways set out to join the British from as far away as New Jersey and New York.[72] But loyalist slave owners protested, and few other royal officials followed suit.

Then, in 1779, as the principal theater of war shifted to the South, Sir Henry Clinton issued his own proclamation: Blacks who deserted from an enemy master would have full security to follow any occupation they wished while inside British lines.[73] Also, during the next three years, British army and naval expeditions often carried off rebel-owned slaves by the hundreds. They could be put to work for the British forces or easily sold. One especially active slave-taker was Colonel Banastre Tarleton of the British Legion, the infamous "Green Dragoon" of South Carolina memory, whose own father was a pillar of the still-legal English slave trade. In 1781, the British army in South Carolina briefly deployed a black mounted unit. For the most part, however, blacks were used in supporting roles—as teamsters, workers, and orderlies.

Large numbers of slaves were lost, especially in areas of heavy British military presence. Eleven pillaged counties in tidewater Virginia lost about 12,000 slaves. Over the entire state, Thomas Jefferson estimated the wartime loss at 30,000 slaves out of a total of about 200,000.[74] The comparable figure in South Carolina has been set at 25,000 out of a slave population of 104,000.[75] Some 5,000 to 10,000 blacks left Charleston with the British evacuation in 1783.[76] Most were ex-slaves. Another 4,000 left with the British from Savannah. To reach England or Nova Scotia meant freedom.

The plantation South verged on panic. In Maryland, the Dorchester County Committee of Inspection reported that "the insolence of the Negroes in this country is coming to such a height that we are under a necessity of disarming them. We took about eight guns, some bayonets, swords, etc." Slave uprisings were a constant fear along lower Chesapeake Bay, and in 1781, a boatload of mostly black raiders came ashore and plundered Upper Marlboro.[77]

Virginia also had its Chesapeake raiders. However, the chance of a large-scale slave uprising ended in December 1775, when Dunmore and his Ethiopian Regiment were beaten at the battle of Great Bridge. As a partial offset among whites to slave enlistment with the British, as many as five hundred free Virginian blacks served in the rebel military during the 1775–1783 period, and the blacks in Virginia's own state naval forces included some slaves.[78]

In North Carolina, slaves were not even one-third of the population. Nevertheless, whites worried because the British commander of Fort Johnston and the royal governor, Josiah Martin, were both believed to be encouraging slaves to revolt, while Dunmore, just across the Virginia border, was openly doing so. A small uprising did occur in eastern North Carolina in the summer of 1775; and in late autumn, when North Carolina troops marched north to oppose Dunmore's mixed-race army near Norfolk, their route was chosen to prevent slaves in a half dozen far northeastern counties from fleeing to the British.[79] A small number of North Carolina blacks, mostly freemen, served in the rebel armies, but historians have characterized a much larger percentage as pro-British or ready to revolt. So much so that in 1778, apprehensive sheriffs began rounding up free blacks (most of them manumitted by Quakers) and selling them back into slavery. Exceptions were made only for those who had enlisted by 1777 in Continental or North Carolina state forces.[80]

The underlying fear of insurrection was highest in South Carolina and Georgia—unsurprisingly, the states also most unwilling to let slaves or even free blacks take up arms. The South Carolina state navy was the only service to enlist blacks, who were a familiar part of Low Country maritime life. For army units, Georgia and South Carolina—and Virginia, too—awarded slaves as bounties to encourage *white* enlistment. All three also set a death penalty for slaves who joined British land or naval forces. No real parallel existed in the plantation South to the white panic that would envelop Saint-Domingue (Haiti) after a black revolution broke out there in 1791, but white insecurity persisted.

The opposite was true in the North. New Jersey aside, slave rebellions were no threat, and the military and civilian role played by blacks was lopsidedly on the patriot side. In the early stages of the war that followed Lexington, Concord, and Bunker Hill, black soldiers were numerous enough in New England militia companies—often several men out of fifty or seventy-five—to provoke a racial debate within the Continental Congress. Southerners succeeded in having black enlistment curbed. Even so, by August 1778, 755 black soldiers served in the fourteen brigades of the Continental Army. The largest number in one brigade was 148, most of them from Connecticut. Five blacks were among the three dozen marines on the Connecticut state navy frigate *Oliver Cromwell*.

Next door, the First Rhode Island Regiment, by itself, had nearly two hundred blacks in 1780, and was widely known for its black and Indian soldiers.[81] The principal aide-de-camp to General Rochambeau, the commander of the French army in America, observed at Yorktown that when the Continental Army passed in review, "three quarters of the Rhode Island regiment consists of Negroes, and that regiment is the most neatly dressed, the best under arms, and the most precise in its maneuvers."[82]

In some New York regiments, blacks represented about 10 percent of those enlisted. The Hudson Valley had one of the North's largest slave populations. Hundreds were freed to do military service in place of their masters. In 1781, New York added a further statutory temptation: that a master who delivered a suitable slave to a recruiting officer would receive a land bounty of five hundred acres.[83]

New Jersey, where blacks exceeded 10 percent of the population in several counties, was the principal exception to the rule that northern blacks generally served in the rebel armies. Hundreds ran off to join the British, and by 1777, black and partly black units began appearing in engagements on the British side: the Black Pioneers and Guides at the battle of Navesink, and irregulars under "Colonel Tye," a former slave named Titus, in raids up and down Monmouth County.[84]

The ratio of blacks in the Continental Army climbed highest in the last years of the war. Baron Von Closen of the French army, who visited the American camp at White Plains on July 4, 1781, estimated that blacks were a quarter of its force.[85] In the army's last months at Newburgh, New York, in 1783, they might have reached one-third. Northerners paired this service with the Revolution's commitment to liberty in a way that encouraged them to end slavery. The experience of white Southerners was otherwise. The divisions of the nineteenth century were taking shape by the eighth decade of the eighteenth century.

The divided groups of European ancestry faced a different set of considerations, ones that usually involved the pulls of religious denomination or faction, as well as disinclination to revolt against Crown or community. The largest were the "Church Germans," the 200,000 to 250,000 persons of German descent in the thirteen colonies of 1775 who belonged to the Lutheran, Reformed, or Evangelical churches rather than the pacifist sects. Lutherans were slightly more numerous, although they and the Reformed were well matched in Pennsylvania, where German population was about one-third of the total. In Maryland, it was perhaps one-fifth. Map 5.5 shows the principal German-settled areas of 1775.

The Germans in the oldest settlements—the Palatines who came to New York and Pennsylvania a half century before Lexington and Concord—largely took the patriot side. But in New York's Mohawk Valley, particularly, parochial counterforces buoyed loyalists. Sir William Johnson, the British seigneur of the valley, had married a Palatine girl, and an influential minority of the Palatines owed jobs and contracts to the Johnson family. The result was a local Palatine civil war, with many of the Palatine Tories moving to Canada during and after the hostilities.

Denominational differences counted heavily. Studies of coalitions within the Pennsylvania legislature of the 1770s and 1780s have found that German Calvinists from the Reformed Church were enthusiastic political allies of the rebellion-minded Scotch-Irish, while the Lutherans, although split, tended to group with the

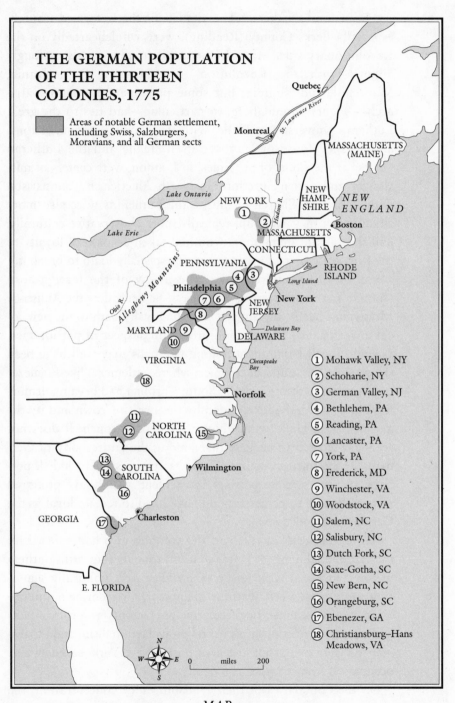

THE GERMAN POPULATION
OF THE THIRTEEN
COLONIES, 1775

Areas of notable German settlement,
including Swiss, Salzburgers,
Moravians, and all German sects

Quebec

St. Lawrence River

Montreal

MASSACHUSETTS
(MAINE)

Lake Ontario

NEW YORK
①

NEW
HAMP-
SHIRE

NEW
ENGLAND

Lake Erie

②

Hudson R.

MASSACHUSETTS

Boston

CONNECTICUT

Allegheny Mountains

PENNSYLVANIA

④ ③

RHODE
ISLAND

Philadelphia

⑤

Long Island

Ohio R.

⑦ ⑥

NEW
JERSEY

New York

⑧

MARYLAND

⑨

Delaware Bay

⑩

DELAWARE

VIRGINIA

Chesapeake
Bay

⑱

Norfolk

① Mohawk Valley, NY

② Schoharie, NY

⑪

③ German Valley, NJ

⑫

NORTH
CAROLINA

⑮

④ Bethlehem, PA

⑤ Reading, PA

⑬

⑥ Lancaster, PA

⑭

SOUTH
CAROLINA

Wilmington

⑦ York, PA

⑯

⑧ Frederick, MD

GEORGIA

⑰

Charleston

⑨ Winchester, VA

⑩ Woodstock, VA

⑪ Salem, NC

⑫ Salisbury, NC

E. FLORIDA

⑬ Dutch Fork, SC

⑭ Saxe-Gotha, SC

⑮ New Bern, NC

⑯ Orangeburg, SC

N
W E
S

0   miles   200

⑰ Ebenezer, GA

⑱ Christiansburg–Hans
Meadows, VA

MAP 5.5

Anglicans and Quakers.[86] The citadels of the Reformed Church, especially Berks County (Reading), were wholeheartedly on the Revolutionary side. Many Lutheran districts were also strongly aligned with the Revolution, especially in Pennsylvania, Maryland, and Virginia, but some prominent Lutheran patriarchs—Henry Muhlenberg, in particular—had ties to the great Lutheran University of Halle, with its Hanoverian connections, and to the House of Hanover itself. Halle and the Lutheran Chapel at the Court of St. James, in London, were centers of missionary and settlement efforts in North America. By comparison with Reformed Church members, the Lutherans were also more ritualistic in their worship, typically more conservative culturally, and their recent immigrants who had taken an oath of loyalty to the King on arriving in America were especially loath to break it.

For these several reasons, quite a few of the foreign-born German Lutherans were as anxious to be neutral as the Amish or Moravians. Many, refusing to take the loyalty oath to the new local governments, became nonjurors and suspect in patriot eyes. Overall, loyalist sentiment among Germans may well have been strongest in the southern colonies, where settlements like Ebenezer in Georgia and Saxe-Gotha in South Carolina had been made during the 1730s and 1740s, aided by the British Crown and by the authorities in Halle with whom they kept in touch. It does not seem far-fetched to suggest that among the entire body of Germans in the thirteen colonies in 1775, peace sects included, perhaps 40 percent were patriots, 40 percent would have preferred neutrality, and 20 percent would have liked to remain loyal to the German-descended King.

At the outbreak of the war, the colonies also had some sixty thousand inhabitants of Dutch descent, roughly four-fifths of them in New York and New Jersey, where they were politically significant minorities. Their wartime alignment, far from being monolithic, was determined by three principal factors: (1) local conflicts and economic relationships; (2) religious factionalism; and (3) residence inside or outside the area under New York–based British occupation from 1776 to 1783.

On the boundaries of their Hudson Valley concentration, the eighteenth-century Dutch rubbed up against other ethnic groups with whom they quickly developed disagreements over land titles, commerce, and politics. Along the borders of Massachusetts and what would become Vermont, their squabbles with the expanding Yankee population often made them loyalists or Tory-leaners during the campaigns of 1775–1777. But in Schenectady, west of Albany, the commercial rivalry of Dutch merchants and traders with Sir William Johnson's Mohawk Valley adherents put them overwhelmingly on the rebel side.

Dutch loyalties were also considerably affected by the British wartime occupation of Manhattan and its environs, which put at least half of the New York–New Jersey Dutch community within British lines and the nearby neutral zones. The prosperous Dutch farmers of Kings County (Brooklyn), nearby Queens County, Staten Island (across New York harbor), and Hudson River-fronting New Jersey made tidy sums in good British gold selling their produce to support an occupation which lasted from the summer of 1776 to the autumn of 1783.

On the ragged peripheries of the British occupation, in northern New Jersey and New York's lower Hudson Valley, civil warfare was persistent—and as bloody as it would be in the Mohawk Valley, the Carolinas, and Georgia. The principal split within the Dutch community, fierce enough to put them to sabering one another, was between factionalists of Dutch Reformed religion. The *Conferentie* looked overseas to the episcopal-minded Classis of Amsterdam and were on good terms with the Anglican Church (to which an affluent element of the New York Dutch population had already migrated). The *Coetus* faction, less fashionable, were more revivalist, determined to run their own congregations without Amsterdam hierarchs, and closer to the Presbyterians in practice and politics.[87] So bitter was this disagreement that in the decade before 1775, there had been fears that the *Conferentie* might shift to the Church of England and the *Coetus* go over to the Presbyterians.[88]

The principal battleground of this local civil war, although by no means the only one, was the pipe-smoking, stolid Dutch valley of the Hackensack River from Haverstraw, New York, to Newark Bay, only a few miles west of the lower tip of Manhattan. Much of this area, centered on Bergen County, New Jersey, is now—from

Saddle River south to Ridgewood—the sleek suburbia of corporate parks, upscale malls, and BMW dealerships. But let us take just one revealing paragraph from historian Adrian Leiby's chronicle, *The Revolutionary War in the Hackensack Valley: The Jersey Dutch and the Neutral Ground:*

> The patriot militiaman farmed during the day and did sentinel duty at night, never knowing when Van Buskirk's Greencoats would raid his farm and carry him and his sons off to Sugar House Prison, never knowing whose home and barns had been next marked for the torch. British spies and Highland gang leaders used the Dutch countryside as a highroad to the thin American lines; American scouting parties and raiders occupied the Dutch villages in their turn. British foraging expeditions of thousands of men too often reaped the harvests that Bergen County farmers had sown, for the American forces in the Hudson Highlands were seldom able to help their friends between the lines. Indeed, more than once, the Americans were forced to strip Bergen County farms for their own existence, and many a Jersey Dutchman who had risked his life for years in the patriot militia found that to a foraging Continental, he was just another damned Tory.[89]

Two other groups with particular concentrations in New York and other major commercial centers who experienced British occupations of considerable length (New York, Charleston, Savannah, and Newport) or lesser duration (Philadelphia and Boston) were also divided: French Huguenots, who numbered about thirty-five thousand in the thirteen colonies, and Jews, perhaps six or eight thousand in number. The two refugee elements, to whom England had been one of Europe's best havens, had in common disproportionate ratios of merchants, artisans, doctors, and other professional men.

The prevailing wartime images of both—disproportionate involvement on the patriot side—come partly from symbolic portraiture: Haym Salomon's role, with Robert Morris, as a principal financier of the American Revolution; Huguenot silversmith Paul Revere's famous ride; and the Faneuil family's much visited Boston hall. The Faneuils, in fact, were mostly Tories, as were the Olivers and Delanceys, along with many other wealthy Huguenots, some of whom had turned Anglican. Both groups, Huguenots and Jews, would have been split in their loyalties by the effects of British occupation and their own vocations.

But there was one vital difference, which would become all-important as Jewish emigration teetered between the Old World and the New World in the nineteenth century. The dissenting Protestant groups that dominated the Revolutionary camp in the United States were marked by a propensity for Bible-reading, evangelism, concern about "Israel," and belief that they, too, were a Chosen People that was uncommon in Europe and out of sorts with state-church Anglicanism, Lutheranism, or Catholicism. At various points in the seventeenth and eighteenth centuries, it was a wry joke among British officials and officers that the Puritans, Scots Covenanters, and Ulster Presbyterians all knew more about the geography of Palestine than about the geography of the British Isles.

This did not necessarily make the New England Yankees or backcountry Presbyterians—or later Southern Baptists or Methodists—culturally close to Jewish immigrants, but it made them accepting of the Nation of Israel while the very diversity of dissenting Protestantism in the new American republic made tolerance necessary and a state church implausible. Over a century earlier, Oliver Cromwell and the first English republic had also been sympathetic to Jewish refugees, and in 1655, Jews were readmitted to England—so that in 1899, the tricentenary of Cromwell's birth, when a statue of him was put up in Parliament Square, leaders of Britain's Jewish community were prominent at the dedication.

Catholics in general were divided. We have seen this in the case of the French *Canadiens*. It was also true of the Irish Catholics and the broader category of Irish of Native Irish and Catholic ancestry who had lapsed in religion. To describe the numbers involved as vague and inaccurate is probably an understatement. The number of practicing Catholics in the colonies circa 1775 was about ten thousand, and most of them were in Pennsylvania and Maryland.

By one estimate, the six Catholic congregations in Pennsylvania at the war's outbreak were principally German in makeup.[90] Reliable information is thin, but a considerable percentage may have been would-be neutrals or Tories. Descriptions of plans for a Tory uprising in south-central Pennsylvania to coincide with a British invasion in 1779 indicate that a Hanover resident named Scherrop had organized a loyalist regiment of six hundred, mostly Catholics, who were a significant minority in that area.[91]

The Maryland-Pennsylvania border country in the area now bounded by Gettysburg, York, and Frederick had a considerable number of Native Irish lapsed or nonpracticing Catholics for another reason: Many had been transported to the colonies, principally Pennsylvania, Maryland, and Virginia, as prisoners or indentured servants. They served their time or ran away, and the border country was a favored destination. During the 1777–1779 period, British sympathizers and Anglican clergy like Maryland's Jonathan Boucher, emphasizing the harsh treatment many of the felons and servants had received from their colonial owners, suggested their amenability to British recruitment.[92] Presumably some found a home in the British army's Volunteers of Ireland.

On the other side of the coin, the small Irish Catholic upper-middle class in and around Philadelphia produced a number of senior military officers on the rebel side: Commodore Joshua Barney and Generals Thomas Fitzsimons, Stephen Moylan, James Mease, and George Meade. But Irish historian David N. Doyle has noted an anomaly: Such were the cultural pressures that within several generations, most members of these families had turned Protestant.[93] In Maryland, by contrast, Catholicism was an established, if in the eighteenth century covert, upper-class tradition reaching back to the days of Lord Baltimore. The scions of the English Catholic Maryland tobacco gentry, like their Protestant peers, fought in the famous First Maryland Regiment, which suffered murderous casualties in 1776 protecting Washington's retreat in the battle of Brooklyn.

The last two groups to be profiled, Baptists and Methodists, are generally described as at some odds with the established Anglican and Congregational Churches and thus divided politically, although more on the patriot than British side. At the time of the Revolution, the founder of Methodism, John Wesley, took the King's side and indeed, the Methodists and Wesley himself were still counted as Anglicans, despite their theological differences.

They did not have anywhere near the numerical strength they would command in the nineteenth century, and were significant only in Maryland, where their small population concentration on the state's Eastern Shore had a reputation for some Toryism.

The Baptists were a much larger force, frowned upon up until the 1770s by New England Congregationalists and Virginia Anglicans alike. Reliable statistics are few and far between. However, Baptists may have been the largest single denomination in Rhode Island—the Congregationalist Church was not established there and the colony's Baptist roots went back to the era of Roger Williams. Quite conceivably, by 1775 they had become a plurality in North Carolina, where the population explosion in the backcountry during the previous decade had been all but uncountable. Baptists were also a sizeable minority in Virginia, where they made an arrangement to support the tidewater Anglican patriotic leadership in return for religious tolerance and ultimate disestablishment of the Anglican Church. In Massachusetts, where Baptists were numerous in the western Massachusetts backcountry and in the Maine district, they were also mostly on the rebel side, but with quibbles. Isaac Backus, the leader of the Baptists in the Bay State, several times embarrassed the Revolution's New England Congregationalist leadership by criticizing their home-state discriminatory religious attitudes and practices before congressmen in Philadelphia.

The result has been a persisting undercurrent of doubt about Baptist commitment to the Revolution in the Yankee and southern backcountry. The Baptist districts of the New England frontier were more at risk to the British and less committed to the Congregationalist power structure. Baptists may well have dominated parts of the Carolina and Virginia frontier, including sections where the prewar Regulators were strong, the tidewater Whig elites unpopular, and Revolutionary commitment ambivalent. Several historians have commented on noninvolvement or even disinterest in the fighting in some of these districts. One chronicle of New Hampshire's formative years notes that although Baptists were often linked to Toryism, they were usually no more than neutral and often more caught up in the religious revival and proliferation of Baptist churches going on than attentive to the war.[94] No doubt some of this skepticism is whetted by the unmistakeable cleavages of the early and mid-nineteenth century in which backcountry Baptist politics was often a polar opposite of northern Congregationalist establishment politics or southern Episcopal leadership.

———

But not all of the American War took place in what would become the United States. We have seen the fighting elsewhere in the Atlantic. The confrontations, Parliamentary maneuvers, and petitions within the British Isles, to which the next chapter turns, drew on many of the same ethnic and religious cleavages just described. Absent these powerful inhibitions, the British government probably could have applied the military power needed for some degree of victory. Hindered by this internal dissension, as well as by weak generalship, Britain's seven-year war effort ended in failure.

6

SUPPORT FOR THE AMERICAN REVOLUTION WITHIN THE BRITISH ISLES

The American Revolution was doubly a civil war in that it tended to divide social groups in Britain as well as America: few ranks, professions or denominations even approached unanimity. . . . [Opinion] among dissenters was nearly as virulently disaffected as that in America.
—J. C. D. Clark, *The Language of Liberty, 1660–1833*, 1994

What chiefly compromised enthusiasm for the war at its start was quite simply that it was a civil war, not just in the sense that both sides had so much in common, but also in that each side was split within itself. . . . Opinion within Great Britain was just as seriously fractured. And this needs stressing, because so many historians have chosen to concentrate either on radical opposition to the war or on conservative support for it, whereas what mattered most at the time was that responses were neither overwhelmingly pro-war nor uncompromisingly anti-war, but instead profoundly mixed.
—Linda Colley, *Britons*, 1992

By denying to the king and Lord North's administration the national unanimity that they sought in the face of colonial rebellion, the pro-Americans [of London] justified their own assertion that the American War of Independence was in fact a civil war.
—John Sainsbury, *Disaffected Patriots: London Supporters of Revolutionary America 1769–1782*, 1987

Only now [because of new studies of popular petitions] is it possible to say that the people of England were divided concerning the use of force against their American brethren. For many Englishmen, the American Revolution was not an unnatural rebellion, but a tragic, unnecessary, and unnatural civil war.

—James E. Bradley, *Popular Politics and the*
American Revolution in England, 1986

WHILE THERE WERE NO ATTEMPTS at the time to measure what ordinary Britons thought about the war in North America, a number of indicators point to the fact that, at least in the early stages and in various ways throughout the conflict, war with the colonists was unappealing and divisive. And although the political landscape had changed considerably in the century and a half since the 1640s, kindred wartime geographic, religious, and cultural fault lines were still important.

Such perceptions on the part of the King and his ministers may help explain why they took the rebellion very seriously, especially in 1775 when the chance that it might spread to Ireland, Canada, and the Caribbean put the empire itself at risk. Fifteen months after Lexington and Concord, when the thirteen colonies produced their Declaration of Independence, the threat had more or less narrowed to those thirteen alone. This was true although the global danger to Britain would widen again—and internal opinion take a new turn toward king-and-country patriotism—when France joined the fighting in 1778.

This chapter, though, is mostly a consideration of how the "political nation" of Britain—the Crown, the aristocracy, the House of Commons, the Parliamentary electorate, and those who could only sign petitions and protest—reacted to the war against cousins and fellow countrymen in its earlier stages: the two and a half years between the war's outbreak in April 1775 and Burgoyne's defeat at Saratoga in October 1777.

When the political battle was joined in Parliament in 1774 and 1775, Lord North was able to marshal two-to-one and frequently three-to-one majorities in favor of suppressing rather than placating the wayward colonies. When the struggle ended in early 1782, following the final British defeat at Yorktown, the prime minister could not even maintain a simple majority in support of a failed war effort. The evolution of such changed sentiment in Parliament and where it came from is our first focus. The second will be on the battle of popular petitions waged in 1775–1776 in a number of counties and boroughs over the question of *coercing* or *conciliating* the Americans. A third vital relationship involved religion: the cleavage between the pro-American views of many Protestant dissenters—Congregationalists, Presbyterians, Baptists, and Quakers—and the pro-ministerial views of High Church Anglicans.

Even the Royal Navy and army divided over the American issue, with a surprising number of officers declining to serve against the colonists. And the difficulty that the British army had finding recruits in England meant that soldiers had to come from elsewhere—the cash-hungry petty princes of Germany, of course, but also Ireland and Scotland. On the other hand, the old Jacobites and high Tories who had sympathized with the attempts to restore the Stuarts in 1715 and 1745 were mostly, by 1775, enthusiastic supporters of George III against the American colonials and their noxious Whig slogans. In other words, the internal British division over the American war, as we shall see in some detail, will follow a familiar geography.

The contention that ordinary people in Britain, Europe's most politically aware nation, simply deferred to upper-class leaders was as implausible in the mid-1770s as it had been in the early 1640s. Indeed, opposition to the Crown's treatment of the colonies centered in the same groups most vocal against the Stuarts: artisans, shopkeepers, religious dissenters, and republicans. This was true not only in London and its environs, but in other large towns like Bristol, Norwich, and Newcastle. Regional sympathy for the colonists was greatest where Puritan and Covenanter support had been highest: in East Anglia and the urban East Midlands, in the old Puritan West Country, in the ports and the clothing towns, and in Ulster and the populist Presbyterian districts of the southwest of Scotland.

Not that popular grumbling necessarily mattered when it opposed the Crown's or Parliament's wishes. Despite its advanced representative government compared to continental Europe, the Britain of 1775 was far from democratic (or representative) in the modern sense. Five hundred fifty-eight Members of Parliament sat for constituencies that ranged from large counties and freeman boroughs with several thousand voters to one hundred and fifty or so corporation-boroughs and other "pocket" boroughs controlled by a few officials or patrons. In the national elections of the period, usually only a small minority of seats were contested— ninety-eight in 1774, fewer still in 1780. Academicians can hardly be blamed for insisting that public opinion mattered little next to local issues and patronage considerations.

The electorate itself was small. Of the two to three hundred thousand English adult males eligible to vote in 1774 out of a total of some two million, under one hundred thousand actually did so. Many constituencies represented more sheep or abandoned cottages than voters, and were at the disposal of the government or powerful families and interests. Even so, the several score of constituencies with sizeable electorates *and* contested elections gave some inkling of what the lesser gentry, yeomanry, lawyers, ministers, merchants, and better-off artisans and tradesmen were thinking.

Nor were elections the only avenue of political expression. Petitions to Parliament or the King, in which a majority of signatures often came from those not qualified as voters, had established themselves in the 1640s, resurged in the 1670s, and flared again in the 1760s over issues such as the Stamp Act and insistence that a radical, John Wilkes, be allowed to take his seat in Parliament. That petitions soon followed on how to deal with the American rebels signified serious popular interest.

Even as the American colonies were becoming alienated from the Crown in the late 1760s and early 1770s, the groups drifting into opposition during those years in Britain's own Parliament— the London radicals, the Rockingham, Chatham, and Shelburne groups—also had distinctive and somewhat parallel origins. They had considerable roots in seventeenth-century London support for the Commonwealth, in anti-royal prerogative politics, in dissenting Protestantism, and among the groups most sympathetic to Whiggish cultures in Ireland and America, as well as those most suspicious of Jacobitism, Catholicism, and Scots. These factions and their electorates were also shaping a loose, new politics,

Whig-like in its greater fear of what seemed to be a new Toryism than of independence for the colonies.

Parliament and Support for the American Cause

During the American Revolutionary era, just one adult male out of six might qualify to vote in the United Kingdom, and as we have seen, only a small minority of seats were contested. Elections did not have a great effect on either the makeup or mind-set of the House of Commons. Only a fraction of the Parliament that sat from 1774 to 1780 reflected even the modest British middle class, whose support would have mattered most to some forty or fifty Members of Parliament in counties and boroughs like Southwark, Bristol, Norwich, Middlesex, Westminster, Norfolk, Gloucester, and Coventry.* Many other ancient towns were corporation boroughs, in which officials of the municipal corporation picked the MPs. In fashionable Bath, where Palladian architecture and omnipresent sedan chairs already thickly encircled Britain's only hot springs, the mayor, ten aldermen, and twenty-four councilmen alone chose the Member.

Parliament's rule was in collaboration with the King. The House of Commons chosen in 1774 was controllable by the first treasury lord or prime minister, Lord North, because he had support from the monarch, as well as from several major factions, sinecure holders, and members from controlled boroughs. Admiral Lord Howe, whose peerage was Irish, not English, sat for the Royal Navy–dominated constituency at Dartmouth. Parliamentarians of middling importance were kept loyal by government salaries as Clerk of the Green Cloth or Deputy Ranger of Whittlebury. Others had contracts to provide rum for the navy or boots for the army. Favors and emoluments were known for accomplishing a change of heart overnight. Lord Lyttleton had spoken in Parliament on behalf of the Americans in the autumn of 1775 shortly before he was appointed warden and chief justice in Eyre of His

---

*Most of the emerging industrial centers—Manchester and Birmingham, for example—played no role because they still lacked Parliamentary representation.

Majesty's parks, chases, and warrens beyond the River Trent. A few days later, he was on his feet defending ministerial policy.[1]

The potential vulnerability of any government rested with the several hundred "country gentlemen," members of considerable independence and sensitivity to government expenditures and tax rates. They typically sat for constituencies to which they had some residential, family, or landholding connection. When enough of them became disenchanted, as in the winter of 1781–1782, the North Ministry fell. Its difficulties in the small minority of seats that were contested in the national elections of 1780 did not matter much. The collapse of confidence among the gentry after Lord Cornwallis's surrender did.

To most Members of Parliament, "public opinion" with respect to the American war was neither knowable nor important. The poorest half of the population had almost no political role, and what counted most of all were the viewpoints of some three, four, or five thousand noblemen and landowners, Anglican churchmen, senior military officers, rich bankers and merchants, and MPs and other government officeholders. In 1775, several hundred of them, perhaps a thousand, regarded the attempted coercion of the thirteen insurgent American colonies as wrong, foolish, or unlikely to succeed. Four dukes and a half dozen earls were included.[2] Most of the rest would have been supportive of the government, especially after the Declaration of Independence was thrown in both the King's face and Parliament's.

The picture that Parliamentary elections can paint of constituency sentiment is limited. In England and Wales, most adult males lacked the franchise and only sixty or so constituencies were usually contested. Participation in Scotland was even narrower—an electorate of only three thousand voters. Given these constraints, the best electoral reading of the British "political nation" below the ruling elite must be sought in the English counties and boroughs with a relatively high rate of political participation: London and its immediate environs; a territorial swath in the east from Maidstone and Canterbury in Kent north through Hertfordshire, Northamptonshire, Cambridgeshire, and East Anglia to Leicester, Nottingham, Lincoln, and Hull; and a ladder in the west climbing from Taunton, Bridgwater, Bristol, and Gloucester into

Warwickshire and Coventry and north into the Lancashire clothing towns and the West Riding of Yorkshire. Constituency opinion mattered much less in the rest of England, especially the southwest, with its overrepresentation of controlled boroughs.

The detailed local research permitted by computerization of parish and town records has undercut many old interpretations. No longer can it be assumed of Parliamentary selection that local issues and factions dominated, with national themes scarce. Voters in the larger urban centers were reading a fast-growing array of opinionated newspapers, mobilizing behind outspoken Parliamentary candidates, and petitioning the Crown on issues that ranged from taxation to constitutional rights. Rural England might be caught in the haymows and hedgerows of an agrarian yesteryear, but London and the two urbanizing corridors were quickening politically as well as commercially.

Of the MPs who cast "pro-American" votes during the 1775-1782 period, a small minority did sit for pocket boroughs or other constituencies at the disposal of the great Whig magnates, especially Lord Rockingham in Yorkshire.* But the great majority of the venal seats were represented by government supporters. The bulk of pro-American votes, in turn, came from the English sections mentioned, with their history of economic innovation, religious dissent, and political assertiveness. Greater London was the same cockpit of reformist and anti-court sentiment that it had been in the days of Pym, Hampden, and Cromwell. Still, radical London MPs like John Wilkes, Frederick Bull, George Hayley, and John Sawbridge were sympathetic not because their hearts were in Rhode Island or Virginia but because they feared the inroads on *British* rights that would follow from American defeat.

In the House of Commons, what began as sympathy for America in 1774 and 1775 and then, by 1778, became war-based disillusionment, principally centered in London and the two urban corridors.

---

*The pro-American Earl of Shelburne, who became prime minister in 1782 in time to help favor America in the peace negotiations, paid £97,000 for a Gloucestershire borough, Calne, with three seats that he doled out to followers. One was Colonel Isaac Barre, also a pro-American, whose name is commemorated in the names of Wilkes-Barre, Pennsylvania, and Barre, Vermont. Rotten boroughs could send pro-rebel as well as pro-establishment legislators to London.

Members from the populous counties were especially pro-American (as defined by key votes) during the Parliament that sat from 1774 to 1780.[3] Several dozen of the large borough seats also had substantial electorates and a high ratio of pro-American MPs.[4]

Even so, the MPs who supported the American colonies on early Parliamentary divisions were an embattled minority. The Massachusetts Regulating Act of 1774, one of the Coercive Acts, passed the House of Commons by 239 to 64. Edmund Burke's resolution of 1775, which tacitly abandoned Parliamentary supremacy and gave in to the Continental Congress on taxation, lost by 270 votes to 78. A kindred conciliatory bill offered by Burke in December was defeated by 210 to 105. The historian Edward Gibbon observed that the typical division on the American issue was about 250 to 80 or 90.[5]

Lord North would later claim what even many twentieth-century British historians still believe: that the fight with America was a war of the British people, a combat they widely supported. However, the pro-American MPs, with their weight in populous constituencies, conceivably represented a majority or close to a majority of the Englishmen who had cast Parliamentary ballots in 1774. This was not a majority of *all* Englishmen, because the rural poor would not have been much involved—or might indeed have deferred to the gentry. On the other hand, it seems plausible to say that the war lacked the support of a reliable majority of the middle class and lower-middle class, petition-signing, newspaper-reading "political nation" of England, some four hundred thousand strong.

Openness to the American case among middle-class voters and petitioners eroded somewhat after the Declaration of Independence in 1776 clarified that the thirteen colonies were insisting on separation. However, sentiment in these circles regrouped again following Burgoyne's defeat at Saratoga. By early 1778, the Rockingham and Shelburne opposition factions had united around a logical common argument: that war against the colonists should be concluded so that Britain could concentrate on beating the real enemy, France. Parliament declined to agree, defeating such a motion by three to two. By this point, the pro-American MPs—defined as those voting to end the war—almost certainly *did* represent a majority of the popular ballots cast at the previous general election. In early 1782, after word had come of Cornwallis's surrender at Yorktown, Sir James Lowther's motion in the House that no more force should be used in America fell short by only 220 to 178. A month later, when a similar motion was offered by General Conway, the government's majority shrank to one. To call all of the pro-withdrawal MPs pro-American is somewhat misleading; some were—but many were simple realists, men who knew that the war was no longer winnable.

At the same time, many Britons did not expect much from Parliament, with its well-known limitations and venality. Other avenues of protest were readily seized. The ministry, concerned in mid-1775 about divided public opinion, had encouraged loyal municipal corporations to send to the King addresses in support of his policy toward the colonies. This stirred American sympathizers to reply with signed petitions for conciliation. Elsewhere in the British Isles, voters had little political voice in Scotland while the Irish Parliament was in London's jingling pocket, so Scottish dissidents looked to Presbyterian church assemblies while restive Irish Protestants anxious to pressure the Crown organized and paraded the equivalent of a political militia.

Popular Petitions for and Against the Coercion of the American Colonies

Petitions to Parliament and the Crown were the most revealing measurement of popular opinion, or at least that of the middle and lower-middle class. Half of the Englishmen who signed petitions had no other way of being heard. In five major freeman boroughs, Coventry, Nottingham, Bristol, Liverpool, and Newcastle, one researcher found that an average of 51.8 percent of the signers were not voters in Parliamentary elections.[6] In some constituencies, dissenting ministers ineligible to vote found their voice circulating pro-American petitions.

The Crown, however, enjoyed an important procedural edge. When loyal addresses from Lancashire or Manchester reached the King, most were published in *The London Gazette*, a government organ. Supportive localities were duly publicized. By contrast, the

King soon declined to formally accept petitions *against* coercing America. Few of these, as a result, were published or noted in the press. Lost, miscatalogued, and buried in the Public Record Office, they slipped from history's view—until the late 1970s when an American professor of religion, James Bradley, began research that exhumed them.[7] His work has shaped a new perspective.

These petitions and addresses, once examined, recast perceptions of what Britons thought of the American war. While they do not substantiate the view that ordinary persons in 1775 favored the Americans, they do leave several impressions: first, that the Crown, in seeking popular approval of coercion, knew that it had to offset a serious opposition; and second, that a relatively conservative eighteenth-century government, instead of disparaging public opinion, sought to rally and claim it. Wars with English-speaking cousins had to be explained—in newspapers and coffee-houses as well as in Parliament.

The first petitions for conciliation had come to Parliament in early 1775 from trade-sensitive merchants and manufacturers in London, Bristol, the Midlands, Yorkshire, and Lancashire. The House of Commons, however, declined to accept or to discuss them. The American unrest was categorized as politics—a matter of colonial subordination to Parliament, not an issue of trade.

With Parliament unresponsive, pro-Americans and conciliators redirected their petitions to the King. Between April and July 1775, the London Common Council and the city's liverymen in Common Hall submitted three that urged conciliation and repeal of the Coercive Acts. Ministerial strategists, heartened by the first loyal addresses from Manchester and Lancashire, which were unsolicited, quickly determined to solicit others and by September, the battle for signatures had been joined.

Between 1775 and 1778, some two hundred addresses and petitions were sent to the Crown regarding America.[8] About half came from official bodies, being drafted and voted by them instead of circulated among the public for signatures. For Scottish officialdom, this was the norm. Of the thirty Scottish county and forty-one Scottish burgh addresses to the Crown in support of coercing the Americans, only four were signed. To Professor Bradley, this adherence by so many lord mayors, baillies, and councillors lent "some support to the claim of the radicals that the government of George III was associated with Scotland and Stuart despotism."[9]

Across the Irish Sea, the cities of Dublin and Cork and the County of Dublin sent loyal addresses with public signatures to the throne in support of coercion. But they were outscored three-to-one by the conciliatory petitions. Dublin was pro-American by 2,986 to 1,055 and Cork by 500 to 160.[10] These petitions reflect Protestant Whig sympathies because Catholics were disenfranchised. Even so, participation was greater in Dublin alone than in all of Scotland.

The most revealing data come from England, with its larger middle class and more open politics. From 1775 to 1778, more than one hundred addresses, petitions, and appeals were delivered. Two dozen were coercive accolades from borough and town corporations that included no public signatures. Two from universities were unsigned and five more came from justices of the peace and militia units. These, by and large, mirrored the patronage and political influence of the government.[11] The remaining eighty or so, however, document how divisions over the war and treatment of the colonies cut right through the heart of England. Signed addresses to the King in favor of coercion outnumbered signed petitions in favor of conciliation by about 3 to 2, but the pro-American messages had more signatures by 19,854 to 18,521.[12] Lancashire aside, the populous sections of England were the most likely to lean toward conciliation.

Upper-middle- and middle-class England were closely divided over the war. Anglican churchmen and parishioners, most members of the local "corporations" that ran the boroughs, the bulk of the lawyers, and virtually all of the merchants with contracts or ties to the government were on the King's side. Coercion, they felt, was not only proper but necessary. Conciliatory views were strongest among dissenting congregations and their ministers, the yeomen smallholders, the shopkeepers, the artisans, and a fair number of manufacturers. Some who framed coercive addresses sought to chill local pro-Americans by accusing them of abetting rebellion. In the two dozen boroughs and counties in which political competition, at its most heated, generated both loyal addresses *and* conciliatory petitions, the conciliatory petitions carried many more names.[13] Nothing else so closely approached an English middle-class referendum.

The geographic divisions will be detailed later in this chapter. But in general, the pro-American viewpoint was greatest where it might have been expected: in London and its environs, in East Anglia, and in a few other locales like Newcastle-on-Tyne and the clothing districts of Yorkshire. Bradley also emphasizes that support for the Crown was greatest in Lancashire, where residents sought to erase suspicions of local loyalty left from 1745, and in the West Midlands, the latter being "a traditional Tory stronghold and a prominent center of the Forty Five."[14] But before turning to the regions, it's useful to set out a principal underpinning of pro-Americanism: the politics of England's Protestant dissenters.

Dissent in Religion: British Nonconformist Support for the Americans

In 1775, the share of England's population made up by Protestant dissenters—Congregationalists in the east, Presbyterians in the west and near the Scottish border, Quakers, and Baptists—was somewhere between 5 and 10 percent.[15] It had been higher in 1640, yet despite this low overall percentage, nonconformists were an important force in many of the larger boroughs. They even dominated the municipal corporations of Nottingham and Coventry. By contrast, in the American mainland colonies under arms, as we have seen, the share of church membership enjoyed by the above four denominations approached 60 percent. In Bermuda and Nova Scotia, dissenters may have been 20 to 40 percent of churchgoers. Suffice it to say that on both sides of the ocean, there was no greater yardstick of revolutionary readiness or sympathy.

George III had been quick to label the Revolution as a Presbyterian war. Many Americans saw a mirror image: coercion as a particularly favored cause of old foes like High Churchmen, Jacobites, Tories, and Scots.[16] Edmund Burke, to whom dissenters were the core of the Whig Party and of the middle class, agreed that the prominence of High Church Anglicanism, in condemning the colonies, bespoke a resurgence of Toryism. Equally to the point, analyses of the coercive addresses to the Crown versus petitions for conciliation have identified alignments otherwise obscured by narrower Parliamentary electorates and the scarcity of contested seats.

The coercive addresses, some brought to London from counties, but most procured from pro-Ministry boroughs, were endorsed by four particularly conspicuous groups: Anglican churchmen (vicars, rectors, prebendaries, deans, canons); contractors, pensioners, and placemen in the revenue and customs service; lawyers, doctors, esquires, and gentry; and members of borough (municipal) corporations (mayors, aldermen, sheriffs, and common councillors).[17]

Those who circulated and subscribed to conciliatory petitions also fell into four loose categories: dissenting clergy and laymen; artisans, shopkeepers, and skilled craftsmen; tavern keepers and coffeehouse owners; and a more radical minority of the gentlemen, lawyers, and printers. The comparisons are especially useful in the boroughs that produced both loyal addresses and pro-American petitions.[18]

Both in Parliament and in the signature wars, the variation on a division between Anglicans and dissenters was that an important body of Low Church Anglicans—occasional conformists, in particular—had been closely allied with the dissenters in the old Whig Party and remained collaborative in the 1770s. This is the cleavage of British politics set out by historians from Commonwealth theorists to George M. Trevelyan: that of loyalty to the Church of England versus the protection and promotion of dissenters' rights.[19] Because the conflict with America touched these sensitive divisions in Britain, it also touched old chords of civil war.

Unhappiness in the British Military: Refusal to Enlist or to Serve Against America

By the middle of 1775, the King and his ministers had another qualm: The war was not popular enough for many Englishmen to take the King's shilling and enlist. Recruiting efforts in the south of England were especially unsuccessful; naval press gangs and army recruiters sometimes fought over the same slim pickings. The municipal authorities in London, opposed to coercion, declined to cooperate. The wounded soldiers, widows, and orphans of the Revolution for whom Londoners first collected funds were *American colonials*.[20]

The officer corps had its own share of reluctance. The King's first choice to command in North America, Lord Amherst, who had led the expulsion of the French from New York in 1759–1760, refused the appointment because of unwillingness to serve against the Americans.* General Sir Henry Conway, who had been secretary of state for the colonies in 1766, opposed the coercion of Massachusetts in 1774, and then refused to serve in America. The Earl of Effingham resigned rather than take an American appointment.

Admiral Augustus Keppel, a cousin of the pro-American Duke of Richmond, declined an American naval command, but accepted one in European waters. When Keppel was court-martialed in 1778 for allegedly avoiding an encounter with the French, the London mob, hostile to ministerial politics, celebrated his acquittal with a riot. The townhouses of Lord North and Lord George Germain were among those damaged.

Two prominent officers who had earlier opposed an American war took commands there along with simultaneous appointments as peace commissioners—Admiral Lord Howe and General William Howe. And as chapter 4 has noted, General Burgoyne proposed a peace negotiator's role for himself in 1775.

Popular hostility to military enlistment was not confined to London. In Kent, the *Kentish Gazette* rejoiced in resistance to recruiting for the American service and in the refusal of prominent officers to serve. Agents reported to London that in Nottingham, the municipal corporation itself, dissenter-led, hindered army recruiting.[21] Conciliation supporters in Hampshire joked about so many Anglican clerics (thirty) signing the coercive address because the Church was planning to organize its own company of grenadiers.[22]

Many of the soldiers needed had to be hired abroad. Although the Empress Catherine turned down a British request in 1775 to

---

*Amherst has been better memorialized in America than in Britain. A college is named for him in Massachusetts, a county in Virginia, and towns in Massachusetts, New York, and elsewhere.

hire twenty thousand Russian troops, essentially that number were secured from the German states of Hesse-Cassel, Brunswick, and others. Hanover, the King's own German domain, assumed the burden of protecting Gibraltar and Minorca, freeing the Ministry to transfer those garrisons to America. And in 1776, when the Irish Parliament voted to condemn the Americans' resort to force, the government in London felt able to withdraw four thousand men and send them across the Atlantic.

Which leads to the revealing crux: that the Ministry found itself looking for soldiers along the same British peripheries to which the Stuart kings and pretenders had repeatedly turned in their own fights with Puritans and Whigs—Scotland, especially the Highlands, and Catholic Ireland. To begin with the Highlanders, they had been brought into the army during the Great French War, playing a particularly effective role in North America. Many would be sent there again in the 1770s. From 1776 through the end of the war, the Black Watch fought from New York and New Jersey to Charleston, South Carolina, and Portsmouth, Virginia. Of the thirteen British regiments brought into service between 1775 and the winter of 1778, fully *ten* were Scottish—seven from the Highlands (the Fraser, Macleod, Argyll, MacDonnell, Athol, Seaforth, and Aberdeen Highlanders) and volunteer units raised by local Ministry supporters in Lanarkshire, Glasgow, and Edinburgh.

This was anything but a coincidence. Beginning in the summer of 1775, former Jacobite lairds and chieftains in the Great Glen that bisects the Highlands from Fort William to Inverness competed, literally, to raise regiments to fight the Americans. The Fraser, Argyll, and MacDonnell Regiments were especially speedily formed and embarked. The goal was to prove Scotland's new loyalty and that of the clan chieftains. Four additional loyalist regiments were raised among Scots and Scots Highlanders living in the North American colonies: the Royal Highland Emigrants, the North Carolina Highlanders, the Caledonian Volunteers (eventually merged into the British Legion), and the Royal North Carolina Regiment.

Roughly one-fourth of the British officers serving in America were Scots. Moreover, Scottish troops accounted for almost as high a percentage of the British troops in the field, which explained the bitterness voiced against the kilted clansmen in heavily English Whig areas like New England, parts of New Jersey, and Virginia. The occasional Scottish Highlanders to march into England under Stuart orders—into Cumberland, Lancashire, Worcestershire, and Derbyshire between 1648 and 1745—had never penetrated to the south of England. In America, however, they were ordered through counties named Essex, Middlesex, Gloucester, and Monmouth to name jurisdictions in New Jersey alone. Highlanders became as unpopular as Hessians.

The considerable minority of Highlanders who were Catholics, moreover, were at least nominally prohibited from serving in the British army—which was one reason why London proposed in 1778 to relieve Catholics, both Scottish and Irish, of some of their civil disabilities. To Whitehall's surprise, this produced such an outcry in Scotland that the suggestion was shelved for Britain. The Popular Party of the Church of Scotland, with already well-established American sympathies, led the fight. Catholic soldiers, they said, should not be used in America against the party's "co-religionists."[23]

Catholic Ireland itself was a bulwark of support for the British war effort. Like the mostly Protestant Scots, the small Catholic middle class of Ireland had given up Jacobite inclinations during the Great French War. Their new intention was to establish a record of loyalty to the Crown. As war broke out in 1775, a group of influential Catholics memorialized the authorities in Dublin, stating their abhorrence of the rebellion and offering to encourage recruiting, even though Catholic enlistment was barred.[24] Acceptance of this offer quickly brought the regiments stationed in Ireland up to strength. This made Irish *Protestants*, already sympathetic to the Americans, even more so. Enlistment in the armies bound across the Atlantic was further encouraged by the bounties offered to recruits by Catholic peers and gentry. The Catholics of Limerick, for example, put up half a guinea per volunteer for the first two hundred to enlist with Major Boyle Roche. Recruits also responded to exaggerated talk that they could expect forfeited estates and cultivated lands in the colonies when the rebellion was beaten.[25]

In Ireland, unlike Scotland, proposals for Catholic relief *were* successfully enacted in 1778. Local merchants, not least among the expanding Catholic middle class, were prospering from providing food, supplies, and transportation for the British army. One pro-American politician complained that Ireland, with its strategic location, was "being converted into a magazine to support the unnatural war with the colonies."[26] The two Celtic peripheries, quite simply, saw major opportunities in the war that their old Whig foes in England opposed.

At the same time, the opposition to coercion within England, particularly within the Rockingham, Shelburne, and Chatham factions of yesteryear's Whigs, had initially prompted the King and his ministers to give the principal American commands to political generals whose involvement would enlist those factions. Some, like the Howe brothers, were inclined to temporize, as chapter 7 will pursue in more detail. Their elder brother, Brigadier George Augustus Howe, killed near Lake George in 1758, had been so admired by the colonists that the Massachusetts House voted money to put a memorial tablet to him in Westminster Abbey, a rare sentiment.

Such backgrounds mattered. General William Howe, soon to be greatly disliked by American Tories in 1776–1777, seems from papers and memoirs to have voiced more respect for the Whigs in arms against the Crown than for the loyalists he disliked to deal with in New York. General Sir Henry Clinton, whose father had been governor of New York, also put little reliance on loyalists. And General Burgoyne, who had been a young army officer during the Jacobite rebellion and then a Whig MP in a Lancashire constituency (Preston) in which he was opposed by Catholics, disliked Jacobites and wound up in 1783 as a pro-American.[27]

Whatever the abstract strategic opportunities, Britain was fighting a war that much of England did not want. Across Protestant England, it was no asset that yesteryear's Jacobites were among the greatest enthusiasts. These internal British politics, with senior commanders who exemplified their memory, may have been as much of a barrier to ultimate success as the vastness of the territory to be reconquered.

Internal British Division
over the American War:
A Familiar Seventeenth-Century Geography

To insist that the American Revolution reawakened the internal political cleavages and battle lines of the seventeenth-century British Isles is overly simple. Too much had changed during the 130 years since the English Civil War and the 90 since the Glorious Revolution.

Relations between Scotland and England had a new setting from the Act of Union in 1707, further rearranged by the suppression of the Highlands after 1746. A beaten, broken Ireland had been tied more closely to British rule. Wales was no longer remote—or an easy military recruiting ground. Just as important, the colonies, in turn, were *English*-settled. Their fate would embroil psychologies and affinities in England in ways less felt elsewhere.

Nevertheless, reactions did follow essentially familiar alignments. On the more or less pro-American side, London was the usual hub of radical opposition to a monarch with High Church tendencies, a taste for power and imperial glory, and a swollen retinue of officials and placemen. The old Puritan centers of East Anglia and the West Country were quieter venues of related sentiments. Then there was the partiality across England of Low Church Anglican "country" Whigs easily aroused over royal power or expensive wars. In Scotland and Ireland, they were joined by small but important Presbyterian Covenanter streams. The overlap is not precise, but much of the internal geography of opposition to Charles I and James II reemerged as collection boxes of a less-focused discontent circa 1775 over issues like American rights, the venality of British government, the aggrandizement of the Crown, and alleged promotion of Catholicism.

Supporters of the King against the Americans also echoed the old confrontations. Still another willful ruler was finding his greatest support in England among High Churchmen, placemen and contractors, and deep-dyed Tories of the Lancashire and West Midlands variety whose Jacobite feelings had half tempted them to rise in 1715. While no Stuart, George III did try to heed the famous injunction attributed to Princess Augusta, his mother:

"George, be King." Thus did he begin to reverse the old constituency base of George I and George II, who were applauded by dissenters, but were the butt of jokes by many High Churchmen. With the third George, it was the other way around. "There was no doubt," wrote one English historian, "where the inclination of the Anglican clergy lay, and they made no secret of their desire to stoke the fires of anti-Americanism. In many parts of the country, the pulpit reinforced a national political campaign for the first time in many years."[28]

The turnabout was completed when George III and his ministers looked to the neighbors to whom the Stuarts had turned: Ireland and Scotland. Freedom from England might be a cherished battle cry in each, but internal freedom was not. Neither objected to having a king with autocratic leanings so long as he would aid their interests, and this George III did. Conclusive Irish and Scottish loyalty in the Great War of 1754–1763—each declined to flirt with the French, recognizing that Jacobitism had died in 1745— put both Celtic elites in a position to start spreading their thin oatcakes with the butter and gooseberry jam of the new empire. That opportunity included furnishing troops that the Cabinet knew would never be raised in Middlesex, Suffolk, or Berkshire to fight cousins in Massachusetts. But it had already extended much farther.

By the mid-1760s, English radicals of the Wilkes stripe, like their ideological kinsmen in America, were reviling George III for giving too many positions and commercial opportunities to Scottish friends of arbitrary government. By 1774, many of the same English critics, ever vigilant against an ever-less-relevant Stuart resurgence, were concerned about indulgence of Catholicism in the Quebec Act, as well as a disturbing High Anglicanism in the King's worship and his private support for episcopacy in America. The Scots and Irish, of course, had more practical reasons to see religious, civil, and political gains in the King's service.

Clear as the important alignments are in retrospect, they were only dimly perceived at the time. Washington, Adams, and Jefferson presumably knew that they had a civil war on their hands in North America. But once the loose hopes of 1775 for a sympathetic eruption in Britain failed, what few Americans (or their sympathizers) recognized from late 1775 to mid-1776 were the quieter but important opportunities with elements of English opinion. Lord Rockingham's disinclination to generate popular petitions for conciliation was one missed chance. But Benjamin Franklin and John Adams also had little to say. The King, North, Germain, and the other leading ministers were shrewder. Obtaining supportive loyal addresses became a priority. Where the Ministry, in turn, mishandled the war lay in its haphazard North American grand strategy and in its self-hobbling political criteria of selecting top commanders. Too many of the admirals and generals appointed had part-time careers as members of parliament and arrived in America thinking as much about peace negotiations as military and occupation tactics.

These mistakes tend to be forgotten. Given the failures and misperceptions on both sides, after peace came in 1783 it behooved Philadelphia and Whitehall alike to suppress the civil war aspects and misplaced opportunities. Better to nurture the myth of a simpler war fought by two relatively united peoples and nations. No such war existed—in America or in Britain.

Middle-Class and Radical London

London's role as a canker of opposition to George III has already been touched upon. The earlier seventeenth-century city had been a center of opposition to Charles I, a pillar of support for Parliament in the English Civil War, and a nursery of efforts to exclude the Catholic James II from the succession. The mob also had its Royalist moments, but London's small merchants and artisans were a radical vanguard again in 1775.

Support for the Americans had begun to seep into this reemergent radicalism during the 1760s debates over the Stamp Act and the Crown's alleged abuses of power. On the outbreak of the American war, the Common Council, London's municipal governing body, and the London liverymen in Common Hall were quick to criticize the Crown, although they withheld the open embrace some colonists had hoped for. Nine of the twelve MPs from Greater London were radicals and pro-Americans, however, and the liverymen instructed the London MPs to move in Parliament to find out who were "the (king's) advisers of those fatal measures which have planted Popery and arbitrary power in America, have plunged us into a most unnatural civil war, to the subversion of the fundamental principles of English liberty."[29] The Common Council, more cautious, merely petitioned the King to suspend hostilities and adopt such "conciliatory measures as may restore union, confidence and peace to the whole empire."[30]

Londoners were particularly inclined to an ethnic suspicion: When tyranny was simmering, Scots were in the kitchen. In less than a decade after James I arrived from Scotland in 1603, Parliament began withholding money because of his prodigal outlays on Scottish favorites. The next three Stuarts, Charles I, Charles II, and James II, had all turned to the Scots for help when England's own doors or treasuries were closed. Thus the London radicals were infuriated in 1762, when George III appointed as first minister his Scottish boyhood adviser, John Stuart, the third Earl of Bute. Scots, many former Tories and Jacobites, had started obtaining civil and military preferment during the Great French War. Now George III and Bute, the fear went, would indulge both Scotland and autocracy. Wilkes, the radical and pro-American, was also England's most vituperative critic of the Scots. He saw their plaids and ambitions lurking behind every bush. So, of course, did Thomas Jefferson and, to a lesser extent, John Adams. London's radicalism and America's had a surprising overlap.

The effusive language of pro-American Londoners has been captured by British historian John Sainsbury in a book entitled *Disaffected Patriots: London Supporters of Revolutionary America, 1769–1782*. Meetings of electors in London, Middlesex, and elsewhere around the capital in 1775 could generate daring toasts to "General Putnam, and all those American heroes, who like men nobly prefer death to slavery and chains" and the like.[31] This early bombast slackened after the Declaration of Independence, when London's pro-Americans found it harder to pretend that transatlantic disaffection was all the fault of the King, corrupt ministers, and placemen in Parliament. Patriotism now buoyed the government, which in late 1776 and much of 1777 started to regain the upper hand psychologically, even in cynical London. General Howe's successes in reclaiming New York added to pro-ministerial support, although Burgoyne's surrender a year later broke the bubble. North and his ministry looked to be failing, after all.

For radical London, the rebel triumph at Saratoga was a godsend which allowed the Shelburne and Rockingham factions of the opposition finally to unite behind a viable political proposition: the unconditional withdrawal of British troops from North America and the recognition of American independence. French entry into the war in February 1778 increased the pressure. Now the London radicals, who had urged the King to offer peace terms to the Americans, partly to keep them from a French alliance, no longer stood alone, although North's government would take four more years to fall.

From early 1775 to early 1778, a once-hawkish London, whose apprentices and trained band militia had been so essential in protecting Parliament and the city in the 1640s, opposed or equivocated with respect to the military mobilization directed against America. The Radical Whig municipal administration of London in 1775 openly withheld assistance from the war effort. In January 1778, after Saratoga, the radicals, although in opposition, were still able to defeat a motion in the London Common Council to pay bounties to help recruit soldiers and sailors. One opposition project that winter, aided by Rockingham and Shelburne, was to raise £5,000 to ameliorate the conditions of the 924 American prisoners in English jails. John Wilkes, MP for Middlesex but always testing the limits of constituency patriotism, had gone so far as to salute the news from Saratoga by saying, "I am sorry that 800 valiant English and Germans were killed in a bad cause, in fighting against the best constitution on earth."[32]

Old Puritan England

Skepticism about the war was also widespread next door in East Anglia and, more broadly, in Oliver Cromwell's onetime military confederation, the Eastern Association of Essex, Hertfordshire, Cambridgeshire, Huntingdonshire, Suffolk, Norfolk, and Lincolnshire. The rural parts of Old Puritan England were less aggressive than London in their displeasure, but local support for the war was thin. Recruiting for the army was difficult. New regiments could not be formed for service in North America. In the words of one historian, "early links with America, kept alive in local memory by way of folk histories, by records in family bibles, and by transatlantic correspondence, seem to have made many East Anglians deeply antipathetic to the war, not least because it was in the New England colonies that the first blood was spilt."

By this view, East Anglia was one of the "three parts of Great Britain where public responses to the outbreak of the war were more or less monolithic."[33] No records exist, but one can only wonder what the people of the Stour Valley, on the Essex-Suffolk border, where the towns are named Harwich, Dedham, Newton, Sudbury, and Haverhill, must have thought in the spring of 1775 when the word came that their cousins, the militia of far-off towns with the same names, in Massachusetts counties with the same names, had risen and encircled four regiments of British soldiers in Boston. The English counties of Lincoln, Cambridge, Hertford, and Huntingdon, to the west of Essex, Suffolk, and Norfolk, were scarcely more supportive of the war. None of the seven shires and only five local boroughs—Colchester, Great Yarmouth, Cambridge, Sudbury, and Huntingdon—produced popularly signed loyal addresses to the Crown in favor of coercing the American colonies. The last two, moreover, were corrupt or venal boroughs.[34]

Messages from the old Cromwellian strongholds in favor of conciliating the colonies were not spontaneous or volunteered. However, in Colchester, Great Yarmouth, and Cambridge, petitions were quickly obtained in the autumn and winter of 1775 to reply to the coercive addresses procured in those towns. Conciliation drew a collective 1,015 signatures, overwhelming the 439 obtained in support of the government.

No other petitions were launched until 1778, after Saratoga, when populous Norfolk weighed in with a huge petition for conciliation bearing over five thousand signatures. In the eastern counties, gathering names was hardly necessary to establish the popular mood. Local Parliamentarians provided ample evidence. Eight of Norfolk's twelve MPs were pro-American, with a particular base in the major towns—Norwich, Thetford, and King's Lynn.[35] Under urging from Charles James Fox, the pro-American

255

faction in Norwich, then England's third largest city, used buff and blue—the uniform of the American Continental Line—as local colors.[36] Other regional seats like Hertford, Cambridge, Colchester, and Maldon in Essex and Ipswich and Bury St. Edmunds in Suffolk either elected pro-American MPs or saw serious campaigns in which American policy was a major issue.

As discussed earlier, the best framework for looking at England emphasizes the two corridors of relative political activism: the eastern one running from Kent north to Lincoln, Nottingham, and Leicester in the east midlands, the other ascending from Exeter, Dorchester, Taunton, and Bristol in the West Country through Gloucester to Warwickshire, Coventry, and the cloth towns of Lancashire and West Riding of Yorkshire. Along with Greater London and its southward commercial and naval extension into Berkshire and Hampshire,* these were the heartlands of the "political nation" of England. They were the concentrations of voters, newspapers, political clubs, dissenting churches, and intensifying commerce that produced support during the 1760s and 1770s for Stamp Act repeal, Wilkes, and then for fairer treatment (and, ultimately, independence) for the American colonies.

Beyond East Anglia, the eastern corridor extended north into other boroughs with high political-participation characteristics: Northampton, Leicester, and Nottingham. Puritan and Parliamentarian strongholds during the English Civil War, their dissenter-versus-Anglican political rivalries produced pro-American activities in the 1770s. Nottingham was General William Howe's own Parliamentary constituency and a reformist and pro-American stronghold. During the 1774 election, Howe had come out against the Coercive Acts aimed at Massachusetts, promising to support their repeal and to refuse service should war in America

---

*Berkshire and Hampshire tend to get short shrift from studies of the parts of England most closely tied to America. However, they gave overwhelming support to Parliament and Puritanism in the 1640s, sent their share of emigrants to Virginia and New England (Massachusetts has both Berkshire and Hampshire Counties, while New Hampshire is the only New England state to be named for a British county), and petitioned lopsidedly for conciliation of America in 1775. Berkshire petitioners for conciliation outnumbered loyal addressers for war by 853 to 302. The Hampshire numbers were nothing less than stunning: 2,500 for conciliation and 201 for coercion.

break out. In October 1775, after he had gone to serve with the army in Boston, 230 residents of Nottingham addressed the King in support of coercion in America. In less than two weeks, however, 328 others had signed a counterpetition for conciliation.

The principal dissenting minister of Nottingham, George Walker, in whose High Pavement Presbyterian Church the mayor and many town leaders worshiped, was a bitter critic of what he called "a detested and ill-omened war." He excoriated the "wicked great men" in the ministry who brought it about.[37] Besides Howe, no other British general of the American war sat in Parliament for a leading antiwar locale. His views were bound to have been affected.

Nottingham, being a center of hosiery production, should also be used to make a further point: Clothing workers and small manufacturers were generally for the dissenter-backed cause as they had been in the 1640s. In 1775, the woollen textile towns of Halifax and Leeds in West Yorkshire, under the home-county influence of Lord Rockingham, rebutted coercive petitions totaling 924 signatures with conciliatory petitions having 2,459. Coventry, in Warwickshire, another manufacturing center with a large dissenter population, turned in a conciliatory petition with 406 signatures in October three weeks after pro-coercion forces had gathered 159.

Lancashire, always a divided county, in this instance was still smarting from its hint of disloyalty thirty years earlier. Loyal addresses quickly came from Preston, from Manchester, and from slave-trading and shipbuilding Liverpool. Another six thousand signatures came from the entire county. Conciliatory petitions gained four thousand signatures countrywide, many in the cotton textile towns of Manchester and Rochdale.

Practical economics and sentiment were sometimes at odds. Like the naval and maritime centers that were solidly for Parliament back in the 1640s but unable to side with the colonists in 1775, the clothing towns had economic relationships to the war effort. Whereas Parliament, not the King, had controlled the shipyards and army clothing contracts of the English Civil War, thereby uniting religion, ideology, and commercial opportunity on the same side of the ledger, circumstances were different in the American war. The North Ministry was effective in using its control of military purchasing.

The West Country was quieter than might have been expected. Taunton, in Somerset, was one of the clothing towns influenced by military contracts in 1775 and 1776. Its dissenters' academy, to say nothing of its seventeenth-century political heritage, made it an obvious potential center of pro-Americanism.[38] But close oversight from London—Lord North also held a local sinecure as Recorder of Taunton—made it one of the rare English towns where a coercive address slightly outdrew a conciliatory petition.

Even after ninety years, Monmouth's Rebellion may also have had a chilling effect. Taunton was one of the half dozen west-of-England towns visited in 1685 by the Bloody Assize of George Jeffreys, the "Hanging Judge," who executed 333 men and women, many innocent, for complicity in that year's rebellion against James II. One historian, examining the Somerset and Gloucester petitions of the 1760s in favor of John Wilkes, said that he discerned the familiar names of seventeenth-century West Country Puritanism.[39] Elsewhere in England, that same continuity led to pro-Americanism. But the West Country would have found it hard—especially in 1775 when the British government had just declared the Americans rebels and proclaimed supporting them potentially treasonous—to rise above its uniquely sanguinary memories. Indeed, Dorchester, Taunton, and Exeter, the principal venues of the Assize, had little to say in 1775 and 1776, although many towns in New England were named for them. They had paid too heavily in 1685.

Wales

Wales is enigmatic. In the 1770s, friends of John Wilkes drew support there and hardly any in Scotland, which led them to speak of the Welsh as lovers of liberty while the Scots were not.[40] British historian Linda Colley, herself of Welsh background, suggests that Welsh support for the colonies had three focal points. The first was the radical movement centered on Richard Price, the nonconformist minister who in 1776 authored *Observations on the Nature of Civil Liberty, the Principles of Government, and the Justice and Policy of the War With America*. Second were considerable ranks of Baptists whose denomination had gotten much of its start in Wales. Third were the Welsh Quakers, many of whom had relatives settled in Pennsylvania. On the other hand, Wales, especially the still-Catholic part, had been a Royalist stronghold in the 1640s, and even in 1745, many had expected the Stuart army to march from Lancashire into Wales and a friendly local reception.[41] Just three Welsh constituencies responded to the American issue in the 1775 petition drives—Haverfordwest, Carmarthen brough and the county of Carmarthen—and all three addressed the throne in support of coercion. They were old English market towns, to be sure, not the wild uplands of Owen Glendower. Yet Wales was obviously divided, and its sentiments have stirred little research.

Ireland

The Ulster of 1775, not surprisingly, was a hotbed of sympathy for the thirteen colonies because it was Ireland's most Protestant and Presbyterian section—and half of Ulster had cousins in Pennsylvania. But ethnic and religious descriptions must be set out carefully. Discussing Ireland as a whole, one Irish MP from Dublin pronounced in 1775 that "here we sympathize more or less with the Americans, we are in water color what they are in fresco." A more accurate Irish politico was also more specific, indicating that "we are all Americans here except such as are attached securely to the castle or are Papists."[42] Catholics tended to support the Crown, while most of those attached to the castle—Dublin Castle, the seat of viceregal government—were allies of the Ministry and probably Anglicans or Church of Ireland members.[43]

Late twentieth-century Irish historians have generally concluded, as one of them, Owen Dudley Edwards, put it on the occasion of the American bicentennial in 1976, that "our independent investigations had all moved to the same conclusion of Irish Catholic hostility to the American Revolution."[44] But he also contended that this new consensus would take time to undo "the vigor of the myth of Irish Catholic support" for the Revolution.

The Presbyterians, based in Ulster, together with the Low Church Anglicans, were the source of considerable support for the

Americans, at least until 1778. Two hundred fifty of the principal Protestant inhabitants of Belfast—essentially, the entire Presbyterian power structure—called on the King to dismiss his ministers and sheath his sword. Later in 1775, a meeting of the principal Dublin merchants' guild and then a second including Dublin's Parliamentary electors both gave support to the Americans. Parallel opposition was expressed to the Quebec Act, which established "Popery" in Canada, and to any related legislation which might increase Catholic power in Ireland.[45] The lopsidedly pro-American petitions from Dublin and Cork have already been noted on p. 243 in this text. Shared Protestant sensitivities were a bond between the American colonies and Ireland. The Irish Protestants, still having a near-complete monopoly of voting and political power, were attentive to its maintenance on *both* sides of the Atlantic.

In the late eighteenth century, as before and after, most Irish loyalties had religious underpinnings.[46] The Irish most likely to be in agreement with American insurgency were those Protestants who shared transatlantic concern about the effects of royal power and its abuses, including taxation without representation, and those who believed that George III was a High Churchman like the Stuarts and might be just as inclined to favor and mobilize Catholics in Ireland as Charles I and James II. Suspicion of Catholicism and support for America often went together. On the other hand, a second strain of Irish Protestantism sympathetic to America circa 1775 would take a more ecumenical direction during subsequent decades, guided by further revolutionary credos, and wind up linking Presbyterians and Catholics as United Irishmen in the rebellion of 1798.

But to return to the beginning of the American wars, although Lord North and his ministers confronted crisis in Ireland with deep concern, they enjoyed considerable resources. During the summer of 1776, the Irish Parliament—more controllable even than its British counterpart because fully half the seats were for sale (and because one recent parliament, under George II, had sat for fully thirty-two years)—was persuaded to vote by ninety-nine to forty-nine to condemn the Americans' actions. This backing was acknowledged to have carried a steep price: "Creation of twenty-two new Irish peerages and eight steps upward for those already in the peerage. And a follow-up program of £11,000 a year in new pensions for forty well-placed persons designed to insure a proper majority" in the new Parliament scheduled to be elected later that year.[47]

High as the cost might be, so was the importance of keeping Ireland in line. The island had become a major cog in Britain's North American war effort, and as early as 1776 this status brought with it several trade concessions, including the right to export directly the clothing and equipment needed by troops overseas, along with the eligibility of Irish ships for certain bounties. In 1778, Ireland was further authorized to export a large array of goods directly to overseas British colonies. The Irish economic grievances that paralleled the prewar trade complaints of the rebellious Americans were being whittled down, although hardly eliminated.

King Louis's declaration of war further cooled Protestant Ireland's ardor for the American cause while renewing its old fear of a French invasion. *Both* Irelands, Catholic and Protestant, were courted by a nervous ministry in London. The Catholics got two relief acts. The first, in 1778, conceded the right to enter into leases and to inherit or bequeath property. The second, in 1782, gave them the same rights as Protestants to purchase, lend, possess, and draw wills, as well as to bear arms and to give their children educational instruction. Protestant Ireland, in turn, got the chance to organize their Volunteers, a peacock assemblage eventually forty thousand strong, which could have taken over Ireland with barely a shot.

Ireland's own revolution was avoided, at least until 1798. After a series of concessions that culminated in 1782 with the sole empowerment of the Irish Parliament to make national laws, the British government had conciliated the "Protestant nation" of Ireland in a manner earlier denied to the American colonies. By this point of course, Charles, Earl of Cornwallis, had surrendered his army, and Frederick, Lord North, had surrendered his government. The new, albeit short-lived, British government under Prime Minister Charles Watson-Wentworth, Marquess of Rockingham, was a friend to both old Whig political cultures—Protestant American and Protestant Irish. But the Americans alone had a new framework that would last.

Scotland

The last portion of Britain sympathetic to the American cause was the southwest of Scotland, a dozen miles across the Irish Sea from Ulster and closely connected to it in religion and culture. The bulk of the Scottish settlers in Ulster had come from these nearby counties—Ayr, Wigtown, Renfrew, Argyll, Lanark, Kirkcudbright, and Dumfries. Here, not surprisingly, was the part of Scotland that had bred William Wallace and Robert Bruce and had taken up arms against the Stuarts during the 1640s and then again during the 1670s at Drumclog and Bothwell Brig. If Edinburgh, Inverness, Perth, and Aberdeen have been the Scotland of kings and authority, the Scotland that even Edmund Burke deplored as "tinctured with notions of despotism," the southwest has been the Scotland of *insurgency*—in religion as in politics.[48] As we have seen, three of the old Covenanter counties in the southwest were the only ones in 1745 to send loyal addresses to George II opposing the Stuart invasion.

This part of Scotland, in the years leading up to the American Revolution, had the strongest second- or third-generation ties across the Atlantic—from the emigration and forced deportation of Covenanters; from mutual ties to Ulster; from a common network of preachers, evangelism, and revivalism; and from the importance of western Scottish ports like Dumfries, Ayr, Greenock, and Glasgow to surging transatlantic trade and commerce. The merchants who traded in tobacco with Virginia may have been on the loyalist side when war came in 1775, but the opposite was true of the lowland preachers who exchanged theology with Congregationalist New England and the Presbyterian sections of the middle colonies. Together with the Ulstermen, they shared values in Great Awakenings, evangelical revivals, jeremiads against monarchical and governmental corruption, and concern about the future of the various New Israels (English, Scottish, Ulster, Pennsylvania Ulster, and New England).

Representative government itself had no great vitality in eighteenth-century Scotland. Members of Parliament were chosen by an electorate of about three thousand that was minuscule, lairdly, and oligarchic. However, as an alternative forum, a larger, looser, and Calvinist "political Scotland" poured considerable attention into the Presbyerian Church and its assemblies, quarrels, secessions, and offshoots. In the seventeenth century, the regional synods and National Assembly of the Church of Scotland occupied a place in national life not much lower than the Scottish Parliament, and this increased when the Edinburgh Parliament was dissolved in the Union of 1707. Debates within the Kirk were serious events. For those who followed such things, the formation of the Secession Church in 1733 reflected not only evangelical and covenanting dissent. It also foreshadowed mid-eighteenth century resentment of how the official and "moderate" faction of the Church of Scotland was coming under the control of lay patrons, landowners, and even the Crown.[49] However, the bulk of the evangelism and radicalism remained within the Church of Scotland as a faction called the Popular Party, described less kindly in the more fashionable new Georgian squares and crescents of Edinburgh as "the wilds."

In politics, the Popular Party also overlapped with the ideas of the American rebels. One party leader was John Witherspoon, who, after two decades preaching in Ayr and Renfrewshire, left in 1766 to become president of the (Presbyterian) College of New Jersey, later Princeton, and to help write the Declaration of Independence. Another was John Erskine of the Greyfriars Church in Edinburgh, famous for his pamphlet *Shall I Go to War with My American Brethren?* James Boswell, the companion of Samuel Johnson, was another well-known Popular Party supporter, who stopped attending a moderate-faction church because its preacher supported the war.

Future leaders of the American Revolution admired the Popular Party. Ezra Stiles, later president of Yale, in 1761 proposed an evangelical alliance that would include the Congregationalists, Presbyterians, Scots Popular Party, and the English dissenters.[50] With Witherspoon's role at the future Princeton, the Popular Party had a unique connection with what would become the American Ivy League. Before the eighteenth century concluded, the Popular Party, saluted by the president of Yale, also raised funds for both Princeton and Dartmouth.[51] But more important, when other sympathetic voices in Scotland faded after the Declaration of Independence, the leaders of the Popular faction continued to speak out.

Little was achieved at the annual general assembly in either 1776 or 1777. But after Burgoyne's surrender, Popular leaders in the Synod of Dumfries framed a peace overture for debate by the general assembly, which then modified its 1778 address to the Crown. After Cornwallis' surrender in 1781, Popular factionalists in the Synod of Galloway (Wigtown and Kirkcudbright) passed an address congratulating the King on ending the war.[52] The Synod of Glasgow and Ayr was a third convocation (out of fifteen) with substantial Popular faction and American sympathy. In the larger arena of Glasgow politics, indeed, pro-Americans had earlier been strong enough to beat back a proposed loyal address to the Crown in support of coercion. The south and southwest of Scotland were also the region where "country party" thinking and American sympathy had support from several noblemen: the Earls of Selkirk and Lauderdale.

Despite this glaring regionalism, discussion of Scottish opposition to the American war has usually emphasized Edinburgh's best-known philosophers. David Hume did, in fact, think that the colonies should be allowed to go their own way, while political economist Adam Smith insisted as the war began that the colonies and Britain would have to arrange a fairer, more equitable union. The Popular Party, by contrast, has suffered from seeming too primitive and reactionary to take seriously, because of its intense opposition to recruiting Catholic Highlanders for the British army and its indirect role in stirring what became fierce anti-Catholic riots in Scotland in 1778. The truth is that similar views prevailed in Ulster, among many radicals and reformers in London, as well as among Congregationalists, Presbyterians, and Low Church Anglicans in the emerging United States. English-speaking popular politics of that era, including those with a Scottish burr, were often an odd mix, blending democracy and intolerance, reaction and progressivism.

The Auld Jacobites and High Churchmen

The Crown's core English constituencies for coercion, of course, were High Church Anglicans and old-line Tories from traditional bailiwicks like rural Lancashire and the West Midlands. The Anglican clergy were particularly supportive of coercion, but study after study has also shown a sharp polarization among voters and petition-signers of the 1770s between dissenters and Anglican parishioners.[53] Professor Namier, despite concluding that Tory-versus-Whig divisions were a thing of the past in the 1760s, acknowledged the persistence of the Midlands Tory type—"genuine reactionaries, heirs to the Counter-Reformation, to the authoritarian High Church and the Jacobites."[54] Other remnants were also identified. The minority of the House of Commons who voted against repeal of the Stamp Act in 1766 was found to include a roll call of the old Tory families: Bagot, Curzon, Grosvenor, Harley, Knightley, Mordaunt, and Bamfylde. To one historian, Paul Langford, they were the "very backbone of the Tory squirearchy. A decade or so later, the same men or their successors were solidly behind North, supporting him steadily in the Commons and, no less importantly, whipping up a country campaign in favor of his policy."[55]

Some Americans had reached much the same conclusion as soon as lines began hardening in 1774–1775. Arthur Lee, the representative of Congress in London, said that the principal proponents of coercion were "the Tories, the Jacobites, the Scotch . . . they see it is the old cause, though we cannot."[56] Certainly, churchmen were prominent, as we have observed, both in lauding the King and royal authority and in promoting coercive addresses.

If few of the Jacobites in the Midlands had come out or even shown their hand in the Forty Five, most in Scotland and a few in Cumbria and Lancashire had. These were strong recruits to the coercive coalition, hastening in 1775 to provide the King and the government with two particular evidences of their loyalty and support—coercive addresses to the throne and badly needed (Highland) regiments to serve against the Americans.

Enthusiasm for coercion of the Americans, like commitment to the King against Parliament in 1642, was high among the government's pensioners, contractors, customs men, municipal corporation officials, and other placemen. Analyses (and dismissals) of the various coercive addresses are full of their participation—ten from the customhouse at Cowes on one petition, more than half of the subscribers in Lymington being "placemen in the Salts, Customhouse, Excise offices, Etc."[57]

Besides these specific groups, the strongest support for the King and coercion was on Britain's peripheries—Scots (outside those in the old Covenanter southwest) and Irish Catholics. This was a particularly vivid example of how the 1770s drew on the old cleavages. A well-known, mid-seventeenth-century portrait of Charles II had shown that monarch, too, being prepared for the battle of Worcester against the Puritans by an allegory of Scotland presenting a pistol and Ireland adjusting his armor.[58]

Part of the continuity, just as in the 1640s, was that neither late eighteenth-century Ireland nor late eighteenth-century Scotland shared the culture of Parliamentary representation, constitutional debate, and restraint of kings so important in England and the English-bred colonies. In 1780, when a war-wearying Parliament narrowly passed John Dunning's motion that "the influence of the Crown has increased, is increasing and ought to be diminished," it did so thanks to the English MPs. Of the Scottish members, forty-five in number, only seven supported it, while twenty-three were opposed and fifteen were not on hand.[59]

Moreover, when the first shots echoed at Lexington, Scotland and Ireland were at this point already embarked on several generations of profiting from the expanding British Empire in terms of commerce, food and textile production, imperial patronage, and, by the Napoleonic Wars, the chance to provide roughly half of the empire's soldiers (although fewer of its sailors). The greatest benefit went to the Scottish doctors, ship captains, merchants, administrators, and many officers who went off to India, Jamaica, and Canada. But Ireland also gained. Almost a third of the British army was Irish, and the ranks of Catholic middle-class merchants were growing. By 1829, when emancipation gave otherwise qualified Catholics the vote, the empire seemed to be making a place even for the Irish.

As we have now seen, the notion that Britain was united in confronting the American Revolution is clearly a myth. Just as the previous chapter displayed how the thirteen colonies themselves were caught up in a civil war, not just a war for independence, this one demonstrates the kindred aspects of the British side of the conflict. However, it remains wise to close by repeating an earlier caution. In 1778, after Britain found itself at war with France, as well as the Americans, national opinion underwent a significant transformation. Many of those who were the strongest pro-Americans in 1775 and 1776 were extremely hostile to Catholic France, the old enemy—the Ulster Presbyterians were one example, the London radicals another. What had been pro-American sympathy now often metamorphosed into patriotic practicality: Fighting a losing war in America is especially foolish now, the argument went, when *France* is the important foe.

More and more of the somewhat independent "country gentlemen" who could swing Parliament found themselves thinking the same thing. Some had come to that conclusion after Saratoga, others did so later as taxes rose and a Franco-Spanish fleet cruised off England's south coast with the Royal Navy too weak to attack. Once Cornwallis surrendered, this support among the country gentlemen all but collapsed. Few were as coercion-minded in 1775 as the High Church Anglican prelates, and in 1782, they voted for a short-lived pro-American ministry. But their empathy should not be overstated.

British opinion toward the American Revolution seems to have gone through four major stages. At first, from 1774 to mid-1776, a fair portion of the so-called political nation sympathized with many of the colonists' complaints and even with their armed resistance. Then, after the Declaration of Independence and British military success in retaking New York in the summer of 1776, patriotic support for the Crown and the war effort increased, narrowing pro-American opinion to its hard-core centers in London, towns with dissenter strength, and the Presbyterian citadels of Ireland and southwest Scotland. But then Burgoyne's defeat and French intervention brought a third stage: a patriotic rallying against the French even by pro-American Whigs, combined with a growing sense that it was best to let the thirteen colonies go and concentrate on the French challenge. Some historians have also identified a fourth stage, in the years between 1780 and 1784, in which disillusionment, radicalism, and the Gordon riots added up to a revolution narrowly avoided in Britain herself.[60] Be this latter as it may, "pro-American" is not a particularly useful term in describing the evolution of British thinking.

Yet for all that the civil war in British North America did not lead to open fighting in Britain itself, the middle-class "political nation" of Britain—and even the aristocracy—divided over the war too substantially either to fight it well or to sustain it when developments became adverse. British Whig ideals not only infused America's demand for independence, but in a sense, they crippled the British internal response and thereby helped the Revolution succeed.

Once again, though, we are ahead of ourselves. Having looked at the American war within a divided Britain, we must now turn back to New York in the spring of 1777. General John Burgoyne is getting ready to push south from Canada without the help of the Royal Highland Emigrants, a loyalist regiment he has rejected because its colonel is a Scottish Jacobite. And General William Howe, the embattled Whig MP for an antiwar constituency where he promised never to fight the Americans, may, in his own way, be trying to keep to the spirit of that pledge. He and his brother, the British admiral commanding in American waters, both of them simultaneously peace commissioners, are preparing to take the British army to sea instead of linking up with Burgoyne in Albany.

7

TRAUMA AND TRIUMPH

Saratoga and the Revitalization of the British Empire

If British commanders had waged war on the colonists as remorselessly as Grant and Sherman did on the Confederates, or if Washington's army had been as decisively defeated in 1776 or 1777 as Lee's army was in 1865, patriot morale in all probability would have been shattered as completely as the final campaigns of the Civil War demoralized the South.

—Maldwyn Jones, in *Sir William Howe: Conventional Strategist*, 1969

When the King and Germain persisted in the struggle (after Saratoga) against mounting difficulties, they believed that victory was still possible . . . and there were very good grounds for their hopes. . . . Whether the victory would have proved worth winning in the long run is a question which the historian of the war is not obliged to face: it is enough that it could have been won.

—Piers Mackesy, *The War for America, 1775–1783*, 1964

The impact of the American Revolution on Britain proved to be one of the great turning points in its history. . . . the loss of America and the resultant end of the Anglo-French rivalry in the Atlantic certainly helped to make India the fulcrum of empire, with consequences that were immense.

—J. H. Plumb, *The Impact of the American Revolution on Great Britain*, 1975

F EW MYTHS OF BRITISH HISTORY have been more misleading than the notion of the American Revolution as causing only
a minor ripple or two in the stately mirror pond of the empire. Indeed, there were periods of real fear. In the summer of 1779, the circumstances of the overall war were precarious enough that a
French-Spanish invasion fleet cruised, virtually unattackable, off
Plymouth; its garbage floated ashore from Hampshire to Devon. In
retrospect, what minimized the negative effects of 1775–1783 was
the war's even larger benefit: British military and imperial overconfi-
dence received a badly needed and timely jolt.

Loss of thirteen of the oldest colonies in North America
prompted reform elsewhere—in Canada, Ireland, and India—and
spurred modernization of a still-archaic British financial system
and war machine. Beyond the casualties of battle and disease,
there were few lasting downsides, and imperial Britain went on to
greater glory in the Levant, India, and the Orient.

For British politics and government, then, the late war years and
the postwar decade were, in succession, a trauma and then a triumph—a renewal around a crisis-hardened Tory coalition that
proved able to hold power for most years through 1832. The
United States, even independent, remained Britain's closest commercial partner. Transatlantic trade was not lost to France or Holland. The grain that Wellington needed for his armies fighting
Napoleon in Spain came from the fields of New York, Pennsylvania, Maryland, and Virginia.

Yet in 1776 there had been nothing small about British military
commitment to the war in North America, or about British war-
related financial commitment and the national debt, which almost
doubled, or, for that matter, about the fears of King George III and
many others in 1775–1776 that the whole empire, from Ireland to
the Caribbean, would unravel if the thirteen colonies were permitted to secede. Fear and effort went together.

The British fleet and army that sailed into New York Harbor in
the early summer of 1776 were awesome, however slowly gathered. It was, at that point, the largest military expedition ever to
cross the Atlantic: over four hundred ships and a total of thirty-

two thousand soldiers. The people of Sandy Hook, New Jersey, and Staten Island, New York, must have marveled at the temerity of the delegates assembled in Philadelphia about to declare American independence. These same residents boggled, almost literally, at the naval might collecting in New York Harbor. Years later, one Staten Islander recalled that he had climbed the tallest tree on his father's farm to see the anchored fleet. The bay, full of ships with bare masts and furled sails, resembled a vast cedar swamp.[1] Colonial America had never seen anything like it.

But the mobilization was on behalf of an unpopular and possibly unwinnable war. Famous generals either declined to serve or served badly, as will be detailed later in this chapter. British manufacturing towns petitioned for conciliation, as we have seen. In Quebec, Nova Scotia, Bermuda, and the Bahamas, important elements flirted with the rebels. German mercenaries had to be hired in Brunswick, Hessen, and Saxony because Englishmen could not be recruited in Bedford, Hampshire, and Sussex.

When the North Ministry finally collapsed in 1782, war disillusionment within Britain—military, political, and governmental—was pervasive. Two large British armies at Saratoga and Yorktown had been surrendered. The global exhilaration of 1763 had been reversed. Bourbon France had its revanche. Memoirs and diaries kept by the upper classes abound with expressions of contempt for the corruption of national political life and the incompetence of the Ministry. The King himself even considered abdicating. But he decided to remain on the throne, allowing opponents of the war to take over the government and make peace.

The trauma, in short, was vaguely akin to what defeat in Vietnam was for twentieth-century Americans. In both aftermaths, voters and opinion-makers shared a poignant awareness of muddled leadership. But the 1782–1783 period had sent an added message. For a people nurtured on the chosen-nation anthems of the earlier Hanoverians, a successful war of separation led by the English populations of New England and Virginia must have involved an unusual cultural dislocation.

The brief-ripples-in-the-pond interpretation of the impact of the American Revolution is to contend that it was minor *because* Britain picked itself up and carried on. Yes, Britain did. But this chapter will suggest that the intensive dislocations, which could have led to the unraveling the King feared, instead produced a complicated and fortunate catharsis in the country. This mood forced a badly needed political transformation, administrative reform, military reorganization, ethnic broadening, and imperial reorientation. Thus did Saratoga and Yorktown help lead to Trafalgar and Waterloo.

The aftermath of the Revolution in the United States, which had its inglorious as well as stereotypically grand aspects, was a different story. But that is for chapter 8 and the framing of the 1861–1865 Civil War. In the meantime, let us return to June 1777. The American War for Independence is still unfolding—and the outcome is still unclear.

The Hudson: Hinge of Fortune

Had Sir William Howe sailed up the Hudson that summer instead of heading south toward Philadelphia, there might have been no United States. Britain might not have made the internal changes and reforms that improved her odds of prevailing against Napoleon. The poor and oppressed of nineteenth-century Europe, especially Catholic Europe, might thereafter have emigrated in far higher ratios to Spanish- and Portuguese-speaking lands. Their Argentine, Brazilian, and Chilean sons and grandsons might never have spoken English to New Jersey, Illinois, or Montana drill sergeants in 1917 and 1941 or gathered curiously on deck for a first look at England, as their troop ships steamed into Southampton, Portsmouth, and Plymouth.

All of this was still at issue in the late spring of 1777. Better British management of the Champlain Corridor campaign of 1776, as we have seen, could have left Howe no choice in 1777 but to sail north, presumably to victory. Fort Ticonderoga could have been in British hands—seized in late October 1776 by the army briefly disembarked near its walls—had General Carleton insisted on serious reconnaissance and initiative. The American troops might have fled as quickly as they did in the following July, when Burgoyne's artillerists put cannon and howitzers on nearby Mount Sugarloaf. That would have ensured very different strategic thinking around the dinner tables of Philadelphia, New York, Montreal, and London during the winter of 1776–1777.

With success glimmering on the northern horizon, Howe, as British commander in New York, would have lost the option of refocusing his 1777 campaign elsewhere. Springtime's priorities would have been well discussed and bluntly conveyed: Burgoyne to move south from Ticonderoga to Albany; Howe to move north up the Hudson to join him and assume overall command.

For the rebels, George Washington, back in New Jersey after his last forts in upper Manhattan capitulated in late November, would have been at wit's end. Even without Ticonderoga's loss, he confessed in December that "with a little enterprise and industry," the British would have been able "to dissipate the remaining force which still kept alive our expiring opposition."[2] After being driven out of New York, the American army was melting away. Further weakening was inevitable after thousands of enlistments expired on December 31. Large numbers of disheartened New Jerseyans were taking British oaths on terms that Howe had made easy. What gave Washington his tactical opportunity was Howe's self-indulgent freedom to refocus on Philadelphia, rather than stay fixed on the north.

The real-world effect of autumn's British failure on Lake Champlain was to leave the negotiation-minded Sir William—success in New York had brought him a knighthood—able to point his forces southward. With his Philadelphia intentions as an emerging backdrop, he had decided to push New Jersey posts farther west than was entirely safe—to Trenton, on the shore of the Delaware River. The Hessian troops that Washington surprised on the morning after Christmas arguably should not have been there. To protect West Jersey's numerous loyalists, and unworried about an American counterattack, Howe and Cornwallis had extended their lines a post too far.[3]

Thus did fortune smile on Americans. Had a captured Ticonderoga been tugging British thoughts northward by November, a well-entrenched New Brunswick would have been a logical, and safe, westernmost post. Such blockage of his revitalizing victory at Trenton would have left Washington stymied. He might have lacked the new enlistments necessary to *survive*, never mind to send reinforcements north. Yet the need to block Burgoyne would have been even greater.

The Howe brothers, credentialed as military commanders yet also peace commissioners, would have toasted 1777 for its increasingly favorable prospect: a single, overwhelming military stroke, launched simultaneously from the lower Hudson and Ticonderoga, potentially able to end the war without the excess of bloodshed that would bar reconciliation. While the navy helped to move six or eight thousand troops up the Hudson in early summer to meet Burgoyne's army arriving in Albany, other ships and men could have raided up and down the New England coast or even thrust from Rhode Island toward Hartford or Boston. Either tactic would have inhibited New England leaders from sparing militia for the showdown along the upper Hudson. The colonials might have been too weak to fight. With Ticonderoga as a forward base, Burgoyne and Howe could have joined forces in Albany by July 4, chilling the first anniversary of the Declaration of Independence.

Could the Revolution have then collapsed? Conceivably. Without a success like Trenton and Princeton, the melting of patriotic support so apparent in late 1776 would have continued. Loyalists in the middle colonies would have been in high spirits. The Howes, no strangers to good living, would have spent the winter wining, dining, and planning their grand expedition against the Hudson highland forts and great iron chain that blocked the river fifty miles above Manhattan at what is now West Point.

A victorious British convergence in Albany might indeed have come in early July. Burgoyne, sensitive to cold, would not have spent an American winter even in a British-held Ticonderoga. He probably would have paused at that fortress in June for a few days to add or leave artillery before leading his army for the last seventy miles. The best route was a short zigzag overland to Lake George, down that lake by bateaux to Fort George at its southern end, then by road to Fort Edward at the head of navigation on the Hudson, and then a last forty-five miles to the quays of Albany. St. Leger, charged with sweeping down the Mohawk Valley, would have had to leave Canada in early June. Map 7.1 illustrates the terrain.

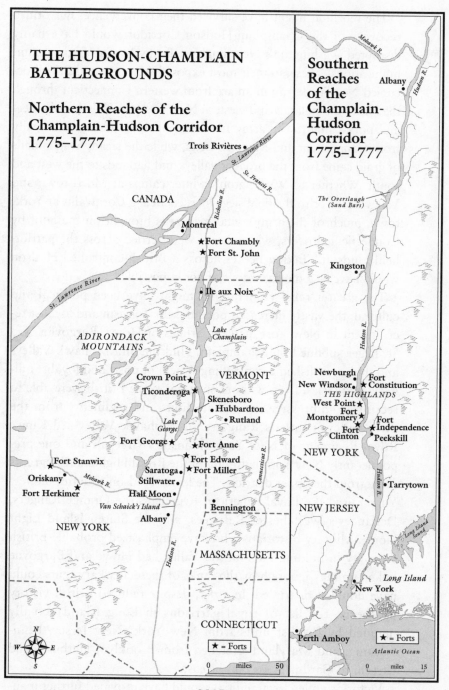

THE HUDSON-CHAMPLAIN BATTLEGROUNDS

Northern Reaches of the Champlain-Hudson Corridor 1775–1777

Trois Rivières

CANADA

Montreal

★ Fort Chambly
★ Fort St. John

Ile aux Noix

Richelieu R.
St. Lawrence River
St. Francis R.

ADIRONDACK MOUNTAINS

Lake Champlain

Crown Point ★
Ticonderoga ★

VERMONT

Skenesboro
• Hubbardton
• Rutland

Lake George

Fort George ★

★ Fort Anne
★ Fort Edward
★ Fort Miller

Fort Stanwix ★

Oriskany
Fort Herkimer

Mohawk R.

Saratoga •
Stillwater •
Half Moon •

Van Schaick's Island

Albany •

Connecticut R.

Bennington •

NEW YORK

Hudson R.

MASSACHUSETTS

CONNECTICUT

★ = Forts

0   miles   50

N W E S

Southern Reaches of the Champlain-Hudson Corridor 1775–1777

Mohawk R.

Albany •

Hudson R.

The Overslaugh (Sand Bars)

Kingston •

Hudson R.

Newburgh •   Fort
New Windsor • ★ Constitution
THE HIGHLANDS
West Point ★
Fort
Montgomery ★   ★ Fort
          Independence
Fort • Peekskill
Clinton ★

NEW YORK

Hudson R.

• Tarrytown

NEW JERSEY

Long Island Sound

Long Island

New York •

Perth Amboy •

★ = Forts

Atlantic Ocean

0   miles   15

MAP 7.1

The rebellion might have survived their convergence. But British recovery of the Champlain-Hudson Corridor would have badly disrupted Washington's New England–Pennsylvania–Virginia communications. These, in their most exposed sector around British-occupied New York, ran in an arc from western Connecticut through the Hudson highlands and western New Jersey to Philadelphia. Beef and pork came to the army from east of the Hudson, principally from Connecticut and Massachusetts, while the steady wagonloads of grain came from the broader valleys and flatlands to the west and south. Whether to Washington's winter camps at Morristown and Valley Forge or to the final siege lines encircling Cornwallis at Yorktown, much of the army's vital meat was brought on the hoof by Connecticut drovers, whose herds were ferried across the patriot-held Hudson.[4] Taking beeves across a British-controlled Hudson would have become hazardous, if not impossible.

The greater rebel vulnerability might have been political and cultural: the vastly increased potential for Toryism and loyalist recruitment in New York had the armies of Howe, Burgoyne, and St. Leger subdued the Champlain, Hudson, and Mohawk Valleys and then established a controlling system of posts and loyalist military auxiliaries. Even without such posts, the British were able to recruit an impressive list of battalions and regiments from the three valleys. Butler's Rangers, the Mohawk Valley–led King's Royal Regiment of New York (Johnson's Greens), and one preponderantly New York battalion of the Royal Highland Emigrants came from the upper districts. The lower Hudson counties of New York raised the Loyal American Regiment, the Orange Rangers, DeLancey's Westchester Refugees, and the Staten Island Light Horse. Military historians who have emphasized probable British difficulty in holding the Hudson Valley had Howe and Burgoyne linked up may ignore how the ranks of these auxiliary units could have doubled or tripled. In 1781, despite reduced British victory prospects, the list of royal garrisons in Long Island actually manned by loyalist units from New York, New Jersey, Pennsylvania, and Maryland stretched from Brooklyn, Flatbush, and Utrecht to Gardiner's Bay in the east.[5]

Victory-swollen loyal militias would have provided further manpower. During the occupation of Manhattan and its environs, the

British were able to build a militia network of thirty-five hundred men which helped to keep order.[6] The Loyal Queens County Militia were a particular example. Full control of the Hudson below Albany would have extended this opportunity, probably subduing the bitter civil war in Westchester County, described in James Fenimore Cooper's famous novel *The Spy.* That combat might have moved into adjacent Connecticut, where Fairfield's Anglican Tories would have been emboldened. The negotiations that Vermonters carried on with the British during the 1780–1782 period would have been more serious. Green Mountain neutrality could have become a fact. Hamstrung by this new political geography, Connecticut, Massachusetts, and New Hampshire troops might not have been able to contest the Champlain-Hudson Corridor again.

The near inevitability of victory by the revolutionaries would not, under these circumstances, have been inevitable at all. The civil war within the Atlantic empire, resolved in 1778 without the embitterments of 1780–1782, could have produced much less upheaval. The New England provinces alone might have become independent; the rest might have won some new status within the empire. The imperial exuberance of 1763 described by Horace Walpole could have more or less continued. The United Kingdom could well have reached the year 1793 with the same medieval accounting system, inadequate debt management, corrupt navy yards, inhibited enlistment of Irish and Scottish troops, and second-echelon national political leadership on hand in 1775. Disaster at Saratoga changed everything.

The Road to Saratoga

What *did* happen after Burgoyne led his army down Lake Champlain is almost anticlimactic. For the British, the loss of what could have been won verged on Shakespearean tragedy—especially for the general himself, serious dramatist and friend of David Garrick, the century's leading Shakespearean actor and impresario. Garrick, in fact, had just brought out John Burgoyne's own satire, *Maid of the Oaks,* at Drury Lane in 1775.[7] By September of 1777, one can only imagine the fateful parallels to *Hamlet, Julius Caesar, and Richard III* shadowing the playwright general's mind. For the rebels, what could have been a disaster in late 1776 was close to being a triumph plucked from thorns. However, even in these reduced springtime strategic circumstances, with the ill-fated Burgoyne having to begin anew before Ticonderoga in 1777, the die was not cast.

British information gatherers had been ineffective in late 1776 under Carleton. Burgoyne was justifiably critical of the Canadian commander's lack of advance scouting. British preparations for the 1777 campaign, in turn, would have profited greatly from an April and May in Ticonderoga, hearing reports from friendly Tory and Iroquois scouts. Instead, both Burgoyne, heading south on June 12, and Barry St. Leger, bound for Oswego, left Canada unwisely advised and equipped.

Burgoyne had only half of the wagons and carts he had hoped for, one-third of the horses, and too few woodsmen. Much of the difficulty came from his insistence on an oversized train of 138 cannon, many of them heavy guns, and five hundred artillerymen. The intention was to batter Ticonderoga into submission, to break up smaller ad hoc rebel entrenchments and to make a captured Albany bristle with impressive ordinance.

Although Burgoyne's successes during the French War had been principally as a cavalryman, he had also been a protégé of Count Wilhelm La Lippe, commander of the British-Portuguese troops in Spain. Praise from La Lippe, Europe's top artillerist, gave Colonel Burgoyne not just his own dragoon regiment but a commitment to artillery which he continued in the American war. Piers Mackesy, the definitive British military historian of the war for America, contends that against an "ill-equipped enemy and in a situation where mobility was everything," Burgoyne's heavy guns were his undoing.[8] Had Ticonderoga fallen the year before, artillery would have been less of a priority in 1777—and much less of a physical and tactical albatross for the army from Canada.

The artillery itself turned out to be largely unnecessary. The "Gibraltar of the North" fell to a handful of midsized guns hauled up to an overlook the Americans had ignored. In a double irony, the reverse was true for St. Leger. Based on poor intelligence, he had left behind the heavier ordnance he would truly need. Fort Stanwix, the key to the western Mohawk Valley, had been repaired and strengthened by Colonel Peter Gansevoort and his New Yorkers in June, leaving the British six-pounder cannon and small mortars inadequate to force its surrender before American reinforcements arrived.[9]

During the previous autumn of 1776, Burgoyne had concurred with Carleton's decision not to attack Ticonderoga only because he assumed that nearby Crown Point would be held. So he was livid when Carleton also withdrew from Crown Point. He conveyed his dismay to General Clinton, saying in a November letter that "I think this step puts us in danger . . . of losing the fruits of our summer's labor and autumn victory."[10] Burgoyne, when his turn came in 1777, put much more of a premium on scouting and intelligence, at least at first. Most of all, he said he had heeded a comment attributed to the Marquis de Montcalm, who commanded at Carillon (Ticonderoga) twenty years earlier, that for defenders, the fort without the accompanying possession of Sugar Loaf was only "a doorway to disgrace for a gentleman."[11] Within a few days of their late June arrival, Burgoyne's engineers and artillerists perceived that artillery hauled to the summit of Sugarloaf, now renamed Mount Defiance, would force its surrender. That had been the unrealized opportunity of the previous year. When the Americans abandoned the fort on July 5, the British general's exuberance is all too easy to imagine.

The last Briton to capture Ticonderoga, Jeffrey Amherst, succeeded in 1759 after Abercrombie's failure—and found laurel wreaths waiting. He became commander-in-chief in North America and eventually Lord Amherst. Alongside James Wolfe, the martyred captor of Quebec, Amherst became the hero of the war. When the fortress fell a second time, Burgoyne's reveries would have been of Amherst's peerage or even of Henry V in his St. Crispin's Day speech before Agincourt, not of some unlucky Shakespearean. Whereas the Burgoyne of 1775 and 1776 had been respectful of the American soldiery after the bloody scarlet-and-gold litter on the slopes of Bunker Hill, by the summer of 1777 he had become cocky, he later admitted, when the rebels' panic at Ticonderoga was followed by flight at Skenesborough (July 6), abandonment of old rundown Fort Anne (July 7), and retreat at Hubbardton (July 7). Victory had seemed to be there for the taking.

Pursuit of the beaten rebels at Skenesborough, two dozen miles south of Ticonderoga, had an unanticipated consequence: It pulled Burgoyne's forces away from what was probably the better route to Albany, the one going south down Lake George. The lesser road from Skenesborough ran through swampy terrain which had been transformed into muddy corduroy by the endless trees felled by retreating Americans. Burgoyne decided not to go back to Lake George, though, partly because of "the general impressions which a retrograde movement is apt to make upon the minds of enemies and friends."[12] So delayed, he did not complete the thirty miles to Fort Edward, at the Hudson River head of navigation, until July 29. On Lake George, meanwhile, the small and vulnerable American force had chosen to evacuate. Reaching Fort Edward by that route might have been four or five days faster.

Yet with no fight for Ticonderoga, Burgoyne was not really behind schedule. He had been obliged to reduce his force by the size of a Ticonderoga garrison, because Carleton in Quebec refused to provide one. But Albany was just forty-five miles away from Fort Edward. Boats could take some of his baggage and supplies, and there would be a good road. Burgoyne did not know until August 3 that Howe had just sailed south, but reinforcements did not yet appear vital. On August 6, Burgoyne, still optimistic, wrote to General Clinton about reaching Albany late in the month.[13]

What Burgoyne did *not* know in early August told a different story—about St. Leger halted before the walls of Fort Stanwix, about fifteen hundred New Hampshire troops joining the Green Mountain Boys in Vermont, and about the area twenty to thirty miles east of his invasion route, largely unpopulated even at the end of the Great War, starting to swarm with New England militia. Adversity was preparing to narrow his autumn options.

Howe's Philadelphia strategy was a glaring error, absent unusual, personal, and political motivations to which we will return shortly. To instruct Howe to ensure the success of the upper New York invasion by meeting Burgoyne in Albany was so vital that Germain, in London, was to blame for not making that priority unmistakable. Sir William's belief that capturing Philadelphia, the new national capital, would bring the rebels to terms was an illusion. Even full control of the New York–Philadelphia axis, which the British enjoyed from October 1777 to May 1778, was outweighed by the Champlain-Hudson debacle, at least in the eyes of every party that mattered: the American rebels, the French government, and the British Parliament.

A related mistake made matters worse. Howe's decision to move to Philadelphia by sea, rather than by land, took the sharp bayonet of New Jersey–based British infantry from Washington's back, letting it rust during a humid, monthlong midsummer sea voyage. That trip wound up depositing Howe's bedraggled troops and dying cavalry mounts at a landing place—Head of Elk, Maryland— little closer to Philadelphia (forty miles) than his army had been at its embarkation in New Jersey (sixty miles)! For Howe to have simply marched his men across New Jersey would have required a major battle. From the British standpoint, however, such an earlier confrontation would have accelerated pressure on Washington to withdraw soldiers from the northern army marshaling against Burgoyne.

Instead, the Americans made use of August. At the beginning of the month, Massachusetts general Glover, arriving near Albany, saw a small, bedraggled force of three thousand men. Two weeks earlier, units fleeing from Ticonderoga to Fort Edward swelled that garrison to forty-five hundred troops in mid-July. But with no more aid in sight, and the fort scarcely defensible, the American commander, General Philip Schuyler, moved his forces five miles closer to Albany.

As Indian raids intensified, two Massachusetts militia regiments sent as replacements decamped for home. Desertions also increased. Schuyler's force was soon depleted to fewer than three thousand men, and he ordered further retreats: first to Fort Miller at the mouth of the Battenkill, then to what is now Schuylerville, then down to Stillwater, and ultimately to Van Schaick's Island where the Mohawk River emptied into the Hudson, just nine miles from Albany itself.[14] Map 7.1, on p. 275 shows the extent of the retreat to Van Schaick's Island, where Glover's Massachusetts regiments found them in early August. During this period, the British had a much greater opportunity than they realized.

The only reinforcement Washington could send in July had been a contingent of six hundred Continental regulars detached from Peekskill under Brigadier General John Nixon. Two New England generals, Benedict Arnold and Benjamin Lincoln, also arrived under Washington's instructions to begin rallying New England enlistments. Concerned about facing Howe in Pennsylvania, Washington allowed only one more unit to head north—General Daniel Morgan's famous brigade of Virginia and Pennsylvania sharpshooters. Otherwise, he sent only a message: "Now let all New England turn out and crush Burgoyne."[15]

The New England delegates to Congress, in the meantime, had lost faith in General Schuyler, a New Yorker, because of his misjudgments at Ticonderoga. They further reasoned that if Massachusetts, Connecticut, New Hampshire, and Rhode Island were to provide the men to stop Burgoyne, they should insist on naming their own northern commander—Major General Horatio Gates. Duly elected by Congress in early August, Gates arrived in Albany on the nineteenth. He was lucky; fortune was *already* turning.

St. Leger, seventy miles west on the Mohawk, had been stalled. Part of his fifteen hundred–man army of British regulars, Tories, and Indians had defeated Brigadier General Nicholas Herkimer and a relief force of Tryon County militia at the battle of Oriskany on August 6. Weeks earlier, however, the British commander had accepted bad advice that rebel-held Fort Stanwix could be taken with light artillery and coehorn mortars. Even upon learning otherwise, he had pushed on, declining to wait and send back to Canada for heavier ordnance.[16]

This mistake was pivotal. Gansevoort, the American commander, subsequently admitted that if the British had brought a few eighteen- and twelve-pounder cannon, the fort would have fallen. Instead, St. Leger sat. Nor did his misjudgment end there. When Mohawk chief Joseph Brant and the Tory leaders, Colonels Claus and Johnson, argued for overtaking the retreating Herkimer and dealing the shattered militia a finishing blow, St. Leger refused. He did not want to divide his force. Yet, weighing the fears expressed by senior American officers has led at least one chronicler to conclude that St. Leger "missed an opportunity to strike the Americans just when they were the weakest and most demoralized.

Pursuit would almost certainly have meant a further battering of the retreating militia and would have dealt a near-fatal blow to the American defense of the Mohawk Valley. It also would have given incalculable encouragement to the Tories of that region."[17]

Schuyler, in one of his last moves as northern commander, had detached Benedict Arnold with twelve hundred men to relieve Stanwix. Arnold's inspiration was to send ahead of his force a half-witted Tory named Han Yost Schuyler, whose mother and brother were held hostage for the success of his bullet-ripped clothing and his concocted story that Arnold was coming with a large force. His simpleton's tale disturbed the British and panicked the Indians into leaving. At this point, on August 22, St. Leger and his soldiers had little choice but to retire themselves.

Had St. Leger brought the right artillery, Stanwix would have fallen quickly. His Tories and Indians would have poured down the Mohawk Valley in early August when patriot fears were already high and militia musters low. A smudged western horizon of blazing cabins and burning wheatfields would have spread panic to Schenectady and Albany. New York regiments would have been pulled from the camp at Van Schaick's Island to protect the western frontier. The late August and September buildup against Burgoyne would have been undercut. Instead, on September 4, the unlucky general found out that St. Leger had retreated.

Burgoyne had already learned about Howe sailing south. Some in New York had given up Burgoyne's chances the moment they watched Howe's fleet turn its broad canvas backs on the Hudson campaign. Colonel Charles Stuart, who would become a general during the Napoleonic Wars and capture Minorca in 1798, could scarcely credit the fleet's direction, writing that "I tremble for the consequences."[18] Sir Henry Clinton, left in charge in New York, had argued with Howe for weeks that Philadelphia was a futile objective and that it was necessary to sail north to join Burgoyne. Clinton's papers show that as late as July 18 he believed that Howe would "deceive us all, and when the southerly wind blows this afternoon with the flood you will go up the N(orth) River to the highlands. You can mean nothing else."[19] Like Stuart and hundreds of bitter New York Tories, Clinton simply could not believe Howe's neglect of the obvious.

In August, the buildup against Burgoyne around Albany, while growing, remained vulnerable. By the seventeenth, the entire patriot force still totaled only 5,888. Gates arrived on August 19 after soliciting various state authorities for help, and within two weeks his numbers had swelled. New units included the Ulster County regiment of the New York Line, Morgan's finally arriving corps of 578 riflemen, and Arnold's brigade back from their relief of Fort Stanwix. On September 7, Gates had 7,548 Continentals, with Morgan's riflemen and various militia adding enough to put the total strength at over 10,000 men.[20]

As harvests were gathered, the militia flooded in, further encouraged by British defeats to the east and west. On August 10, twelve days before St. Leger began his retreat from the Mohawk, Burgoyne had detached a mixed force of not quite a thousand Germans, loyalists, Indians, Canadians, and British commanded by Colonel Friedrich Baum to raid next door into southern Vermont for cattle, grain, wagons, and horses. Unless major opposition gathered, they were ordered to forage widely, recross the Hudson, and rejoin the main army near Albany in two weeks. It was not necessarily a blunder. If serious opposition did develop, Baum was told to hold back, and to contact Burgoyne for further orders.

Weeks earlier, though, amid the shock waves of Ticonderoga's fall to Burgoyne, the New Hampshire Assembly had voted to send a force to Vermont to cooperate with the local Green Mountain Boys. Brigadier General John Stark, well respected from his service in Rogers' Rangers during the Great War, enlisted 1,492 volunteers in six days, including a group that the minister of the Concord Congregational Church gave leave to depart in the midst of Sunday service.[21]

By August 14, the two small armies, Baum's and Stark's, were converging on Bennington, Vermont. Moreover, each had reinforcements coming. Stark's boldness could have failed had Baum followed his orders to be cautious and had the German reinforcements under Breymann come up at a normal pace instead of sluggishly. Neither occurred, so the American victory on the sixteenth was substantial—nine hundred of the King's German auxiliaries killed or captured. News of the victory at Bennington spread like wildfire in western New England.

Two days later, moreover, the same heavy rains that had several times interrupted the mountainside fighting west of Bennington produced a flood on the Hudson near Saratoga. This ill luck for Burgoyne washed away a bridge of rafts over which the British were preparing to cross to attack the rebels' northern army at Stillwater. With only six thousand men still under Schuyler, the American force remained small enough to be beaten.

A British attack on the northern army on the eighteenth would have had the additional advantage of striking amid the confusion of a change of command: Schuyler on the eighteenth, Gates on the nineteenth. However, by August 26, when the British had built a new bridge at a better location, the rebel ranks were ballooning and Gates was moving the army north toward terrain better suited for a fight. Midsummer's opportunity was dissipating, and Burgoyne knew it. His letter of August 20 to Lord George Germain lacked his post-Ticonderoga cockiness. Instead, Howe's failure to cooperate is bewailed, the likelihood of serious help from loyalists dismissed, and the New England militia taken very seriously indeed: "The New Hampshire grants in particular, a country unpeopled and almost unknown in the last war, now abounds in the most active and most rebellious race in the continent and hangs like a gathering storm on my left."[22]

The common observation that the British fatally overestimated loyalist support, however, is not altogether true. What Burgoyne and his generals lacked was up-to-date knowledge. The Champlain-Hudson invasion route led through a relatively loyalist section of the King's North American domain—upper New York. The Mohawk Valley, upper Hudson, and Lake Champlain regions had already furnished several regiments of loyalists. The area northeast of Albany had particularly close ties to the Scottish Highlands through former officers and men of the Highland regiments.[23] The Hampshire grants to the east, however, were a much more confused place, claimed by New York, New Hampshire, and the independent government of what already styled itself Vermont.

Within this area, residents of the grants who claimed title under New York jurisdiction—Scots, English, and Dutch—were more likely to be Tories. But the much larger influx was of the New Englanders who justified Burgoyne's description of them as "the most active and most rebellious race on the continent."

New York's Hudson Valley border country east and north of Albany, containing perhaps ten thousand people in 1775, did include a fair ratio of Tories. This was Burgoyne's route. Besides the hundreds of men from these districts who had earlier joined the famous loyalist regiments, he did get new recruits in 1777. Even on the Bennington raid, the 150 local Tories were increased by 90 more before the battle, and one Yankee rebel from the border country noted that "we took four or five of our neighbors—two Sniders and two Hornbecks. The bigger part of Dutch Hoosick was in the battle against us."[24] One recent chronicler attentive to local detail has suggested that several hundred Tories fought at Bennington, and that many were executed by the rebels after the battle.[25] Until then, British army recruitment in northern New York arguably had been at least as productive as that in much of southern England.

The loyalties of the residents of the actual Saratoga battlefield further illustrate the division: Jotham Bemis, the tavern keeper whose name lives on in the Bemis Heights battle site, was a Tory; so was Isaac Leggett, the Quaker tiller of Freeman's Farm, the scene of another day's intense local combat. Freeman himself had run off to serve in a loyalist unit. What hurt was that this population was minor compared with the post-1763 Yankee flood into western New England. The towns being settled and enlarged had hundreds of militia companies only three to four days' hard marching from Stillwater and two to three days from Bennington. Their numbers dwarfed the Tories of the Champlain-Hudson invasion corridor.

As September began, Burgoyne still had the strength to withdraw to Ticonderoga or Canada. But by the time the rebel northern army's ranks exceeded ten thousand on September 7, the British probably no longer had the capacity to fight through to Albany unaided. If so, this made the great Saratoga battles of September 19 (Freeman's Farm) and October 7 (Bemis Heights) more about whether Burgoyne could *escape* back to Canada than whether he could *win*. In the meantime, though, a second line of British activity—the long-awaited invasion up the Hudson—finally developed in early October, without the person of Sir William Howe, but with a surprise and success that provided the last great "what if?" of the 1777 campaign.

The four weeks between the fighting at Freeman's Farm and Burgoyne's ultimate surrender of his remaining 5,895 men on October 17 stand as the military watershed of American independence. In the words of one participating general, on September 19, "both armies seemed determine to conquer or die," and when the American soldiers, most of them in homespun, inflicted many more casualties on professional British and German troops than they received, the psychological impact was enormous. This, John Burgoyne later admitted, was when he realized that he had underestimated his foe, and several younger British officers set down a hard truth in their diaries: They would never see Albany; the army was now too weak.

The American tactics, in their own way, were as brutal as European bayonet work. Many of the rebels' part-time soldiers were good shots, especially the riflemen, and at Saratoga they concentrated their fire on the officers, with their splendid uniforms and silver gorgets, and the artillerymen manning the cannon and howitzers. September 19 was one such day—thirty-five officers died; October 7, when Burgoyne's army was finally wrecked, was another. Rare is the volume about Saratoga that does not remind how Tim Murphy, the most famous marksman among Morgan's Riflemen, sat in a tree and, with his third bullet, brought down Brigadier Simon Fraser, commander of the British right wing.

But in another sense, even the Saratoga battlefield cannot tell the full story of these climactic weeks. In the days after the British army was halted at Freeman's Farm, other American units were striking to the north, recapturing Fort George, capturing supply ships on Lake Champlain, and starting to arrange themselves to block any British attempt to retreat back up the Hudson to Fort Edward, Ticonderoga, and Canada.

Sir Henry Clinton, in Manhattan, moved to help Burgoyne, who now seemed poised to surrender an entire army. With some seven thousand troops, half British and half provincial, Clinton had understood in September that Burgoyne was in danger, probably still thirty to forty miles from Albany, and embattled in part because of

General Howe's abandonment. So he had written to Burgoyne on September 12 to say that he would try to send a force up the Hudson later in the month. Shortly thereafter, Washington withdrew half of the rebel troops in the Hudson Highlands to enlarge his army facing Howe in Pennsylvania, improving the odds for a successful British thrust. Then, in early October, when Clinton received seventeen hundred reinforcements from Europe, he made a swift decision: to send a naval force under Commodore Sir James Wallace upriver with three thousand British infantrymen to attack the Hudson Highland forts and make a diversion, if not something more, on behalf of Burgoyne.

Success rewarded surprise. Guided by loyalist Colonel Beverley Robinson, who had grown up nearby, swiftly traveling British columns of regulars, Hessian chasseurs, and Tories from Robinson's own Loyal American Regiment snuck up on and captured Forts Montgomery and Clinton from their exposed and uncompleted land side—around the back of the Dunderberg and other hills that gave the highlands their name. Once the forts fell, the small American flotilla was burned by its own commanders. The British dismantled the iron chain across the Hudson, and Commodore Wallace's fleet sailed through. Only four days were needed. The untakable had been taken, just as at Ticonderoga.

Word reached General Gates near Saratoga on October 8: The British had broken through the highland defenses. In several days more, troop transports were sailing north toward Kingston, the temporary capital of New York, halfway between the highlands and Albany. The reports and rumors caused both sides to revise their preliminary discussions of possible capitulation: Burgoyne because he had a glimmer of military salvation, Gates because generous terms could secure a quick British surrender before any possible reinforcement confused the matter.

The change of fortune did not last. Pilots refused to take the fleet closer to Albany than forty-five miles, near the six-mile "overslough," where the sandbars became tricky and rebels were gathering on both riverbanks. Sloops might pass, but not the ship-rigged British vessels. The flotilla burned Kingston and sailed downstream. Burgoyne's surrender had become inevitable, because six miles to the north, where markers along the Hudson still identify Stark's Knob, the New Hampshire general had already positioned artillery to block a British retreat. Yet Clinton's sortie had proved a point. The highland forts had indeed been taken; a major diversion had been made on Burgoyne's behalf. Had the latter been able to reach Albany, he could have been supplied.

If Clinton could not relieve Burgoyne, his actions impugned Howe's judgment. Taking and holding the mid-Hudson forts could have made a follow-up invasion feasible in 1778 had the army from Canada survived. Their capture showed that the basic strategy had been workable. The next question, alas, for those involved, would be more embarrassing: *Who failed?* Since July, Burgoyne himself, in his hubris and taste for drama, had become a major contributor to the unfolding debacle. He should have returned to Canada in late August, but as he later admitted, Ticonderoga's fall had nurtured a disdain for the rebels not cured until their victory at Freeman's Farm. By that point, neither retreat nor British victory was plausible, and the tragedy of John Burgoyne was about to become a major, if less than Shakespearean, historical drama. Howe and Germain, however, have generally been identified as the greater culprits.

General Howe, indeed, added to his embarrassment in the eyes of history by ordering Clinton in October to give up the captured highland forts, Montgomery and Clinton. The soldiers who manned them were needed in Philadelphia, he insisted, where the last rebel river bastions on the Delaware still remained to be taken. Some historians have echoed the fundamental criticism Sir Henry chose to make in subsequent years: that the forts were too important to yield, because they gave the Royal Navy control of the Hudson. Even the loss of Burgoyne's army, Clinton would argue later, could have been a justifiable sacrifice to possess the forts and be able to mount another advance on Albany. George Washington made a similar observation.[26] In theory, perhaps, this view is correct, but it ignores the political and propaganda damage that Saratoga did to the British cause.

The intersection of Burgoyne's bad luck and Howe's hard-to-explain actions was the turning point of the war. France decided to intervene because the surrender of a major army showed the British Crown in danger of losing a civil war, already two and a half years old. Intervention by the forces of His Most Christian Majesty could ensure revanche for 1763.

French assistance in 1778 was almost certainly decisive. By 1780 and 1781, the rebels were worn down again, so that some fortunate British stratagem—a successful betrayal of West Point by Benedict Arnold, for example—might have brought the war to a compromised conclusion. The caveat is *political*: After four additional years, support in Parliament for the war's continuation had also eroded. Back in 1777, the north Ministry had two-to-one and three-to-one majorities that would have rallied on a Burgoyne victory (with its presumed discouragement of France). Parliament certainly would have provided a year or two more of large-scale funding for the successful conclusion of coercion in North America.

Four years later, not just France but also Spain and Holland were opposing Britain. This vulnerability was a greater concern in Parliament than gambling on American colonies that already seemed lost. Wartime outlays had enlarged the British national debt to a point in 1781 that nobody would have imagined in 1777. Fiscal and political circumstances, as well as the mood of Parliament, were simply not the same. Saratoga was indeed the pivot.

But the outcome was not inevitable—not at all. Had things gone differently—had Carleton been more forceful in 1776, had Howe sailed north to join Burgoyne in 1777—Britain and the colonies might have patched up their relations for a few more decades. That, paradoxically, could have put the English-speaking future at risk.

Whig Generals and the Politics of Defeat in America

The unusual late eighteenth-century involvement of military officers in politics and as sitting Members of Parliament was a British Achilles heel of 1775–1783. It is not enough for historians to raise doubts about the tactics or wholehearted commitment of individual generals and admirals—broadly, or in particular battles and campaigns. The question of what could have gone differently in 1775–1783 requires another kind of examination. These next pages will pursue it by looking at ten admirals and generals of

Whig or Whig-leaning background whose views or commands made them especially important. From the behavior of these men, we can say that few great powers have approached a rebellion in the way that Britain did in 1775.

Of the ten men, including a former government minister and a former North American commander-in-chief, three flatly declined to serve in America. The generals were Lord Amherst and Sir Henry Conway; the admiral was the Honorable Augustus Keppel. The other seven were commanders whose records during 1775–1777 raised questions of American sympathy or preference for a negotiated settlement: Generals Thomas Gage, Guy Carleton, and William Howe, and even John Burgoyne and Henry Clinton, as well as Admirals Thomas Graves and Richard Viscount Howe. Had they favored prompt and tenacious coercion of the colonies in 1775, history could have been rewritten on a grand scale.

All were Englishmen, save for Carleton with his Ulster background, although several of the English had the odd Dutch or German ancestor. What was striking was their political involvement, even for the eighteenth century when serving officers commonly sat in Parliament. Half were members of the House of Commons (both Howes, Burgoyne, Conway, and Clinton) or the House of Lords (Amherst). Viscount Howe, parenthetically, could belong to the British House of Commons because his family's title was in the peerage of Ireland. Others included a former Cabinet member (Conway), cousins, in-laws, and siblings of dukes and earls (Burgoyne, Clinton, Keppel) or members of families that controlled at least one Parliamentary borough (Gage). Virtually all, in short, were part-time politicians or close relatives of those who were. The two professions were closely intertwined.

Politically, most of the ten had Whig antecedents—which, of course, was the point. Half of them—Amherst, Conway, Gage, Carleton, and William Howe—had served in North America during the Great French War. Amherst and Gage were married to Americans. Clinton had spent his boyhood in New York as the son of a royal governor. According to scattered references by historical specialists, most had ties to the pro-American Whig cliques and factions headed by William Pitt (Earl of Chatham), the Duke of Grafton, Lord Rockingham, Lord Shelburne, the Keppels, and

Charles James Fox. In personal terms, Carleton was close to the Keppels. Burgoyne looked to Pitt, was a friend of Fox, followed Grafton in favoring religious dissenters, and had been proposed for military governor of New York by Shelburne. The Howes also looked to Pitt and had ties to Grafton.

Carleton and Gage were already military commanders in America as the war took shape. Neither was a hard-line advocate of coercion. Carleton's wife was the daughter of the Earl of Effingham, who resigned his commission rather than fight in America. Three episodes are most commonly cited to indicate Carleton's sympathy for conciliation: his refusal to unleash Sir John Johnson and his Indians against the American frontier in 1775, his decision in June 1776 to let Benedict Arnold and the fleeing survivors of the American invasion of Canada escape, and his freeing of the American prisoners captured at the naval battle of Valcour Island in October 1776.[27] When the Whigs came back to power under Rockingham in 1782, Carleton, anxious to negotiate a reconciliation with the colonies, was initially pleased to be appointed a peace commissioner. Coercion had not been his forte.

Gage, too, was relatively well liked in America. When he had left New York in 1773, the mayor and council conferred on him the freedom of the city. Bostonians, in turn, later appreciated that as local commander he had kept a tight rein on British troops.[28] Meanwhile, Gage's urgings, by late 1774, that the Coercive Acts should be suspended and all troops withdrawn in favor of a blockade made him unpopular in London. After Lexington and Concord, while he still commanded in Boston, Gage refused to declare martial law or to fortify the Charlestown and Dorchester peninsulas. He was unwilling to begin offensive operations before political remedies were exhausted. One of his biographers, military historian John Shy, suggests that "perhaps, as has been said about other British leaders in the Revolutionary War, he had no heart for the fight against fellow Englishmen."[29]

Sir Henry Clinton loosely cooperated with the Opposition when he came back to Britain in 1782. Admiral Thomas Graves, who commanded British naval forces in North America in 1775 while Gage held sway on land, was likewise criticized for his early unwillingness to take offensive actions while political remedies remained possible. Back home in 1779, Graves joined with the Opposition in criticizing the Ministry's political court-martial of Admiral Keppel. Not that Keppel was any kind of martyr. He was one of the most political flag officers of the eighteenth-century Royal Navy.[30]

The commanders whose behavior would be most pivotal, Burgoyne and the Howes, were on record in 1774 and early 1775 preferring conciliation to coercion. All three had sought peacemakers' roles, the Howes with greater success. Indeed, by 1780 and 1781, when Cornwallis's surrender at Yorktown began to support the criticisms of the Parliamentary Opposition, the Howes, Burgoyne, and Carleton were all more or less back on that side. The initial selection of such men to cope with the American rebellion itself has to be seen as a political calculation. Their appointments held out the velvet glove, not the mailed fist. These selections were an appeal to supporters of Pitt, Rockingham, Shelburne, and Fox, not to the Ministry's High Church stalwarts of coercion. To a small extent, such choices also mollified swing constituencies and petition-signers in Sussex, Northamptonshire, and Yorkshire, not faithful burgage-holders in Cornish pocket boroughs. And as we have seen in chapter 6, these issues engaged a considerable minority of British constituencies in 1775.

John Burgoyne's political personality, which may initially seem out of place on this list, was far more interesting (and much more radical) than the usual profile of Gentleman Johnny, gambler, poseur, and bon vivant. His early interest in negotiation and conciliation may not have been a fluke. Within a few years after Saratoga, he was outspokenly on the American side.

As a son-in-law of the Earl of Derby, he sat for the family borough of Preston, Lancashire, which, as we have seen, was a major way station on the old Stuart invasion trail from Scotland. He had been a young army lieutenant stationed near London during the Forty Five, and those old controversies were still very much alive in the Preston elections of the 1760s and 1770s. By 1768, Burgoyne had a Presbyterian ticket mate, Sir Henry Hoghton, in the two-man constituency. Their opposition had a Jacobite flavor, enjoying Catholic support at the polls (even though Catholics were not supposed to be able to vote).[31] So hotly contested was that election that it went for decision to the House of Commons itself, and through his public career, Burgoyne remained a dedicated foe of the Jacobites. In 1771, he led a Parliamentary investigation of Scottish-tinged corruption in the East India Company, and in 1777 he refused to accept into his invasion force the Royal Highland Emigrants Regiment commanded by Colonel Allan Maclean, a Jacobite who enjoyed provoking English Whigs by wearing a Stuart white cockade in his bonnet.[32]

Besides taking his cue in imperial affairs from Pitt and Shelburne, on matters of importance to Protestant dissenters Burgoyne sometimes followed the Duke of Grafton, one of their principal defenders.[33] Shortly before the American war, Burgoyne admitted subscribing to the old Whig view, pursued against Charles I and James II, that if a ruler was unjust, insurrection was in order.[34] He simply denied that this had any relevance to George III, although he took pains to prefer conciliation to coercion. Against this backdrop, the playwright general's swashbuckling approach to the American war over the next few years was probably driven more by ambition than by latter-day Toryism. Even amid his theatrics as a general newly arrived in Boston, he suggested a surprising conciliatory gesture: freeing the Americans taken prisoner after Bunker Hill.[35]

After his surrender at Saratoga, Burgoyne demanded a Parliamentary inquiry into the conduct of the campaign, which was denied, presumably because of the potential embarrassment to Germain and the ministry. In 1779, he took his seat with the Opposition and his old friend Charles James Fox. By 1781, after Cornwallis's rout at Yorktown, he went so far as to charge in Parliament that "the American war was but part of a general design leveled against the constitution of this country and the general rights of mankind."[36] John Wilkes and Samuel Adams would not have exaggerated much more.

The Howe brothers were especially prominent pre-1775 Whigs. The debate over whether they wanted the colonies to remain just strong enough to oblige reconciliation, rather than be sweepingly defeated and embittered, is an old one, oft revisited. Thomas Paine suggested, wryly, that Americans ought to erect a monument to Sir William Howe. Horace Walpole recalled a Whig who was the general's close friend saying that "I have no apprehension from General Howe taking the command; he is one of us and will do the

Americans no harm."[37] Loyalists in New York and New Jersey, for their part, muttered that was exactly the problem: Howe was not on their side. A popular historian of the 1930s, John Hyde Preston, went so far as to speculate that "there may have been—there seems to have been—some mysterious motive behind his actions. Perhaps one day some roving historian will discover the true secret of Howe's heart. It is not impossible that he was a better friend to America than she ever knew he was."[38]

It is not impossible at all. Since that observation, three generations of historians, American and British, have poured through official documents, family papers, public records, local poll books, and ancient election returns to greatly increase the body of available knowledge regarding British generals, war strategy, political factions, elections, and petitions during the 1770s and 1780s. Unfortunately, the Howe family papers are not among them, having been destroyed early in the nineteenth century in a fire at the family estate in Ireland.* Even so, the brothers can be fitted, beyond dispute, into the conciliatory wing of a British ruling class seriously divided over the American war. Theirs was a society in which even a surprising number of generals and Parliamentarians found it difficult to fight fellow Englishmen or to suppress an emerging Whig political culture with which they had considerable sympathy.

The questions about Sir William's military intentions began in 1775 in Boston, a city to which he hoped not to be sent because of his family's sympathies. George Washington himself could never understand why the British—General William Howe commanding—did not attack his provincial forces besieging Boston in December when enlistments were expiring: "Search the vast volumes of history through, and I must question whether a case similar to ours is to be found; to wit, to maintain a post against the flower of the British troops for six months together . . . and at the end of them to have one army disbanded and another to raise within the same distance of a reinforced enemy."[39] Howe himself had been open enough about his doubts of military success to advise Lord Dartmouth in early 1776 that without large reinforcements it might be "better pol-

---

*General Carleton's biographers also note that at his request, his widow burned the entire collection of his personal papers after his death in 1808.

icy to withdraw entirely from the delinquent provinces and leave the colonists to war with each other for sovereignty."[40]

The next major puzzlement has to do with his excessive caution and restraint in chasing Washington out of New York City in 1776 without delivering a coup de grace. He later acknowledged that political considerations were a factor. The third set of skepticisms and cynicisms, of course, has to do with Howe's faulty choices in opting for Philadelphia over the Hudson in 1777.

British scholars may concede that Howe's failure to capitalize on early numerical advantages unavailable to later commanders "allowed the rebellion precious time to take root (and) was probably the decisive factor in the outcome of the struggle."[41] Most, however, explain his sloth not by politics but by his adherence to the military conventions of the era. Like other European generals, Howe rarely chose to campaign in the winter and regarded a large army as an expensive national asset hard to replace and not lightly to be risked. His maneuvers in 1776–1777 were also traditional in seeking to occupy a wide area with a major show of force, cowing the rebels into submission and convincing them of the futility of further resistance.[42] Another view, derogatory but nonpolitical, was that Howe, good enough as a battalion or regimental commander, was overwhelmed by the larger task that confronted him as commander-in-chief.

The political and tactical explanations are not necessarily incompatible. Professor Ira Gruber, the principal biographer of the Howe brothers, has suggested that they made their earlier comments about America more warlike in order to be selected for senior commands, but that they always had in mind a *dual* role. They would be military leaders, yes, but also peace commissioners—and with ultimate reconciliation, not embittering battlefield suppression, as the larger goal.[43] The elder brother, Richard, Lord Howe, vice-admiral of the White and naval commander-in-chief in North America, was the head of the family and the dominant influence, and Gruber has summarized his mind-set as follows:

> Howe assumed command in July, 1776, determined to promote a negotiated settlement of the American rebellion. He may well have persuaded his brother, who commanded the British army, to forego chances for a decisive battle at New York. He clearly did

delay imposing a naval blockade, made repeated overtures to Congress and urged the captains of his ships to "cultivate all amicable correspondence" with the colonists. These measures not only failed to produce a negotiated peace but helped the rebellion to survive and gain strength.[44]

To merely note that the brothers favored conciliation of the colonies and pursued hopes for peace in a way that colored their military tactics is to sidestep the true uniqueness of the Howes' role: their relationship and connections as a family. Their maternal grandmother, Baroness Kielmansegge, had been the mistress of George I while he was Elector of Hanover. Their mother, Mary Sophia, being more or less acknowledged as the old King's illegitimate daughter, cut a considerable figure in Hanoverian London even in the 1770s. She received a pension from the Crown, and her children were regarded as relatives. William Howe was close enough to George III for the King to have cried on his shoulder over the desertion rate of British soldiers disappearing into the Massachusetts countryside, and Richard Howe received only a minor admonition from his royal cousin after he had been reported criticizing the King in public over his policies toward America.[45]

The second Viscount Howe, whom Mary Sophia married, was governor of Barbados, but not a major figure in early Hanoverian England. Their eldest son, George Augustus Howe, who became the third viscount, was the one expected to do great things. Brigadier in the army and second-in-command (to General James Abercrombie) of the British forces attacking French-held Ticonderoga in 1758, Lord Howe was killed in a skirmish there before he could fulfill the family's hopes.

He may, however, be one of the most unrecognized figures of Anglo-American history. During his several years in America, Howe—colonel, then brigadier, and nephew of King George II— became the colonists' favorite British officer. He fraternized with them, shed his glittering uniform to go on missions with the provincial Rangers, yet enjoyed enough military reputation to be chosen as the operational commander, under the lackluster Abercrombie, of the first British attempt to capture Fort Ticonderoga. When Howe was killed, the army and the colonials mourned.

Abercrombie then bungled the attack that the nephew of George II would have led, and the British were repulsed. The Massachusetts General Court (legislature) voted £250 for a commemorative monument to Lord Howe in Westminister Abbey. It was a unique memorial to a unique officer.

The two older Howe children, George Augustus and his sister Caroline, appear to have been the leaders among the siblings. Caroline Howe herself emerges briefly in the London annals of late 1774 and early 1775 arranging private political discussions, albeit approved by the government, between her brother the admiral and Benjamin Franklin.[46] When George Augustus was killed in 1758, Richard Howe, then a naval captain, inherited his title and the responsibility of burnishing his memory. Biographer Gruber, convinced that these sentiments remained powerful two decades later, notes that the new Lord Howe personally supervised work on the Massachusetts-funded monument, which was unveiled in July 1762. Howe, for some years, intended to erect an obelisk as a reciprocal gesture to Massachusetts, expressing not only "his love and Veneration for his brother's virtues, but his Gratitude and Respect for that Public and Patriot Voice, whose generous applause has adorn'd their memory."[47]

William, the younger brother, besides taking the Parliamentary seat in Nottingham which had been held by his dead brother, also tried to walk in his footsteps on North American military matters by developing a similar skill in light infantry tactics and leading the detachment that scaled the Heights of Abraham to make possible the capture of Quebec in 1759. Two years later, he declined the military governorship of Belle-Isle, a fortress on the French coast, to return to America. But his self-confidence was modest; he never spoke in Parliament, usually voting with his brother Richard. Indeed, in 1758, on his eldest brother's death, he implored Richard, also a risk-taker, "to live and be a Comfort to us all—Remember how much our dependence is on you. If we lose your only support left to us, we shall fall never to rise again."[48]

Presumably, those memories exercised a strong pull. George Augustus Howe, had he lived, would almost certainly have been offered the American commander-in-chief's role in 1775. This he almost certainly would have turned down as Amherst did (absent sweeping powers as a peace negotiator).

When William Howe agreed to go to America in 1775, he had hoped it would be to New York, not to the Boston that had lauded his brother. That psychology might have been a partial explanation for the military inactivity in Boston that so astounded Washington. From time to time, Howe's pro-American views came through. In January 1776, he had advised Lord Dartmouth that the American army "had all or most of the young men of spirit in the country," whereas he never had much good to say about the loyalists.[49] Contemporary statements by both his wife and his very politically minded sister Caroline also indicate that his principal objective in America was much as the loyalists suspected: *peace and reconciliation.*[50]

We can ask ourselves: If General Howe would not attack Washington after taking command in Boston in the autumn of 1775, what would have made him want to go north in 1777, when the rebels seemed sure to fight, and when his bayonets might have killed New Englanders and destroyed their cause in the very same settings—the Mohawk Valley, Ticonderoga, Lake George, Fort Edward, and Albany—where his eldest brother had become the future rebels' hero two decades earlier?

By 1778 and 1779, when a Parliamentary investigation briefly confronted these possibilities, it chose to sidle away. The generals most under a cloud, Howe and Burgoyne, were themselves Members of Parliament from well-connected families. Support for the American war was already ebbing as the French challenge took priority. And when the surrender of Cornwallis brought Rockingham, Shelburne, and the Whigs to power in 1782, it was a measure of the reversal of affairs that the conciliatory generals and admirals reemerged in a brief Indian summer of eighteenth-century Whigdom: Sir Henry Conway, who had refused to serve in America, became army commander-in-chief. Sir William Howe became lieutenant general of the ordnance. John Burgoyne took over as commander-in-chief, Ireland. Sir Guy Carleton became commander-in-chief, North America. For the Royal Navy, Lord Howe hoisted his flag over the Channel fleet, leading it to the relief of Gibraltar. Admiral Augustus Keppel, who had refused to serve in America, became first lord of the admiralty.

The ancien régime Whigs, by being correct about America, had ensured that the English-speaking world would have two pillars.

In return, the new, more democratic one across the Atlantic, criss-crossed with counties and towns named Pitt, Chatham, Rocking-ham, Camden, and Amherst, would enshrine eighteenth-century Whiggism in a way that Britain itself never would. The new state of Georgia went so far as to name a half dozen of its counties for British friends of the American cause—the Earl of Chatham, John Wilkes, the Earl of Camden, the Earl of Effingham, Edmund Burke, and the Duke of Richmond.

But for Britons and Americans, although in different ways, much of what seemed to be emerging in 1782—British disarray, American independence as a powerful example, and Whig princi-ples also triumphant in England and Ireland—was an illusion. The new United States was much weaker than it had seemed in the echoes of Yorktown's Franco-American trumpets and kettle drums. The Whig resurgence in Britain, in turn, could not have been more transient. Whiggism, sadly, had all but played itself out in giving the new United States favorable boundaries and proud memories. One important but unexpected legacy of the American Revolution, so deeply imbued with suspicion of government power, was that *both* nations would spend the remainder of the 1780s and much of the 1790s building stronger central govern-ments and developing a more conservative and tougher-minded politics to survive in a world of turmoil.

The changes that Britain required, as we will see, would not have been possible without the American Revolution and the crisis it pro-duced for *both* British ideologies: a tired neo-Whiggery that needed a half century out of power and a court-party neo-Toryism that needed to move beyond legacies like Royal Prerogative and episco-pacy. But although the upcoming transformation was unknowable in 1783 and 1784, the jolt of embarrassment over losing America was already producing an impressive leader and forcing a corrupt and, in places, archaic system to tighten its fiscal and military cinches.

The Far-Reaching Effect of the American Revolution on Britain

The American War for Independence and its aftershocks rocked the empire from Quebec to Calcutta and from Ireland to the

Caribbean. Ministerial needs for support in Parliament, provisioning, and military recruitment forced greater attention to the Celtic peripheries. The war and its inglorious finale also produced a broad new coalition in Parliament, a modernized, reconstituted Toryism with some military and fiscal reformist instincts led by a prime minister with Whig roots and a famous name: William Pitt the Younger. Much of the change that helped to beat Napoleon in Europe was seeded by frustration over defeat in North America.

Too many assessments of the impact of the Revolution beyond America's shores are anecdotal and unfocused: how Ho Chi Minh of North Vietnam was inspired by the Declaration of Independence 170 years later, or how French officers aiding America brought home ideas that they added to the pre-Revolutionary ferment of the 1780s. We are told, also, that Meyer Rothschild, who went on to found Europe's most famous banking house, got his start with the Landgrave of Hesse, advising that notable on renting troops to the British government and investing the proceeds,[51] and that because France's outlays connected with the American war doubled her national debt, the additional tax burdens this imposed on merchants in Lyon or peasants in Orleans helped to bring on the French Revolution.

Perhaps they did. But Britain, too, nearly doubled her own national debt in the course of the 1775–1783 war, yet the 1780s brought fiscal reform, not revolution. Which brings us to the most important international aftershocks of the American war, felt, appropriately, in the two polities most closely bound up with the American colonies, their history, and their people: *the British and Dutch empires.*

Holland's ties to America were as old as any country's. By 1783, the Dutch had drifted into a deepening popular insurgency of their own, the Patriots' Revolt, which not coincidentally mirrored the divisions that the American Revolution had provoked: the Netherlands' aristocracy and the House of Orange taking the pro-British side while the more Calvinist, reformist "Patriot" faction cheered the Americans and reprinted their new state constitutions in newspapers from Friesland to Leiden.[52] Indeed, some historians believe that the Dutch Patriot movement began when the city of Amsterdam recognized the insurgent colonials against the wishes of the ruling stadtholder.[53]

In the Netherlands, however, the revolt failed. Power politics prevailed. Britain (and Prussia) intervened in 1786 to shore up the Orangists, suppressing the Patriot faction in Holland a good deal more effectively than the British and German armies had been able to deal with the Hudson Valley patroons, Schenectady merchants, and Reformed Church dominies only a few years earlier.

Policy-makers in Britain were already displaying a lesson they had learned from America: the need to be tougher, with the nation's future so much at risk. A second lesson related to sophistication and management: the parallel need to be shrewder and more anticipatory in global strategy and better organized to deal with economic and military challenges.

Ripple effects from the American war, direct and indirect, affected Britain's own politics, government, culture, and imperial demeanor. Insistence that the effects were only minor usually reflects too confined a measurement: a not very great change in colonial policy alone, for example, or the (minimal) disruption of British trade with North America after the war. Many policies and attitudes, however, changed profoundly.

Part of what did not last was the Whig reformist mode of 1782–1783. The Marquess of Rockingham died in July 1782, only three months after becoming prime minister. His successor, the Earl of Shelburne, held office only another nine months. Shelburne gave the Americans a favorable peace treaty and generous boundaries, but his plan for knitting together Britain and the United States commercially was naive—or at least premature. The so-called American Intercourse bill, defeated in Parliament in 1783, did not square with the conservative reaction already setting in.

The House of Commons chosen in the 1780 elections returned easily enough to an imperial course. The new Parliament elected in 1784 was at least as conservative. Radicals—or what would later be called progressives—constituted only a small minority. The Rockingham and Shelburne interludes, in short, were a political fluke occasioned by the collapse of the North Ministry's American policy. This is what underpins the analysis, entirely justifiable, that Britain took few *affirmative* examples from American ideology or the lost war. The most important impacts involved *negative* perceptions: of unwise softness and outdated governmental mechanisms.

While the Whigs had indeed been percipient on the American war, it was for reasons rooted in the bygone values of the early and mid-eighteenth century. As a credo for the imminent and imperial nineteenth century, revived Whiggery was in many ways out-of-date. A particular Whig empathy catered to home rule for kindred Whig communities beyond England—those other political cultures, principally in America and Protestant Ireland, that read the tracts of Locke, Sidney, Milton, and Harrington. The two principal figures of 1782–1783, Lords Rockingham and Shelburne, both had Irish estates and connections in addition to their pro-American biases.

The independent and unsubordinated Irish Parliament they arranged in 1782 turned out, under succeeding Tory governments, to be less of a breakthrough than reformers had hoped. British officials in London, working through the lord-lieutenant in Dublin, usually ran the show. The serious electoral reforms discussed during the Whig zenith, ranging from a redistribution of seats and a wider franchise to annual parliaments and exclusion of placemen from the Irish Commons, were never enacted. By 1785, the bubble of reformism had popped in *both* capitals—Dublin and London.

In 1798, renewed war between Britain and France led the French to encourage a serious Irish revolt, in which some Protestants and Catholics made common cause. As a result, officials in London insisted on full-fledged Irish union with Britain in 1800. The Dublin Parliament was abolished, and Irish Protestants—but not yet Irish *Catholics*—gained representation in the British Parliament. Practically speaking, this amounted to submergence. Ireland came completely under ministerial control. The Whig experiment was over.

The lessons of the American war were part of what made the younger Pitt and his New Tory coalition better attuned to the new imperium. The perception that spread in ruling circles was not the wisdom of embracing American ideology, but the sense that more firmness might have squashed or confined it. Given the European challenges that Britain soon faced, electoral reform was less important than strength and realpolitik. After 1783, the Whigs would be unable to hold serious national power again, save for the wartime coalition government of 1806–1807, until the watershed election following the Reform Act of 1832.

Thus, although Parliamentary and electoral reform in Britain became a major cause in the late 1770s and early 1780s in part through American stimulus, the impetus was short-lived. Ties to transatlantic revolution were not a useful mid-decade imprimatur. Even the British electoral reforms of 1782 were small stuff: one enactment to disenfranchise government revenue officers, another to bar government contractors from the House of Commons, and a third to abolish a number of government and court appointments. It is doubtful that they merited Charles Fox's description of a "good stout blow to the influence of the Crown."[54]

The younger Pitt's own ideological migration is symptomatic. He began his long years as prime minister (1783–1801, 1804–1806) by carrying on his family's Whig and reformist heritage. However, historians conclude that he gave up after his third sweeping constitutional reform bill, which would have extinguished some venal boroughs and shifted seats to counties and metropolitan areas, was defeated in the House of Commons in April 1785 by 248 to 174.[55] Other national demands were more pressing.

In the subsequent language of political scientists, Britain had swung to the right in reaction to the American Revolution. Much the same thing had happened after the English Civil War. The Restoration Parliament had wiped away Cromwell's electoral reforms and barred further democratization. That conservative countertide, like the one in the 1780s, had been incompatible with increasing the political representation of urban areas or the middle classes. Yet the 1780s did not follow the repressive 1660s in the matter of religious dissent. Whereas the Restorationists had used the Clarendon Codes to suppress Puritanism, late eighteenth-century imperial strategists had different, ecumenical objectives.

Catholics in Scotland and Ireland, having helped to fight the Americans, gained legal relief. For Scottish Catholics, assistance came in the nationwide Catholic relief legislation of 1793. For Ireland, the principal Catholic Relief Bills had cleared the Dublin and London Parliaments between 1778 and 1782. Further enactments in 1792, together with the sweeping act of 1793, freed Catholics from other educational, marital, and professional disabilities. They also won the vote in Irish local elections, the right to hold municipal and borough posts (but not to sit in Parliament), and the right to hold officer's rank up to colonel in Irish forces. The legal status of dissenting or nonconformist Protestants improved even more quickly. Full Catholic emancipation was still four decades away, but the independent Irish Parliament of the 1790s, too venturesome for London, began even that bruising debate.

The failure in America also spurred the British ruling elite to reaffirm both its governance and its competence. When opportunity next presented itself in the 1790s, attention was paid to glorifying the empire, the success of British arms, and the achievements of aristocratic leadership. Protecting and enlarging British commerce was a more immediate critical focus in the 1780s. With the Americans gone, securing the primacy of the British navy and the huge numbers of seamen it required was even more vital. The embarrassments of 1775–1783 also led to overdue modernization of British fiscal management and military procurement. The timing was all-important. Because the ignominy of Saratoga and Yorktown provoked Britain to grapple with these challenges almost immediately, she had an all-important decade in which to replace ineffective imperial postures and wartime procedures before the great confrontation with France began in 1793.

However, a survey of the reorientations of the 1780s should begin with a more sweeping vista: *The very geography of British imperialism changed as the First British Empire, oriented toward North America, gave way to the Second British Empire, which looked east to India and more authority-minded political cultures.* The First Empire, Whig-built, English in ethnic origin, Low Church Protestant in religion, with a westward and American bias, had kept British governments pointed in just these directions. Transatlantic kinships had tugged on old bonds and shared history, and in the process produced tactical and imperial uncertainty in Whitehall.

The Second British Empire, by contrast, was a religious, geographic, and ethnic amalgam toward which imperialism came much more easily among ordinary Britons. It bred proconsuls, not

Massachusetts yeomen, Virginia squires, or ambiguous Whig generals. Hauteur, itself, was less mismatched in dealing with French Quebeckers, Hoogly merchants, and Malacca Straits rajahs than it had been with the descendants of Cromwellian captains, Lincolnshire poachers, and Ulster borderers.

The 1780s proved that George III and many others had been wrong to worry that if the American colonies broke away, so might Ireland, Canada, and the West Indies. Instead of collapsing, the empire flourished, albeit with an increasingly Eastern bias. Yet there had been some close-run events, and by 1783, many Britons could reasonably conclude—the elite certainly did—that their global interests demanded stronger, more centralized government and a calculating aloofness. The Scots and the Irish contributed, not simply by providing soldiers, engineers, and administrators, but by infusing the empire with the hunger of those who had only recently won a place at the high table—and whose national preoccupations with representative government and the rights of Englishmen were minimal.

Within the British Isles, England was still the unquestioned center. Regionally, however, influence continued to shift from East Anglia, home to the powerful in Tudor times when the country's population and commerce had looked east across the North Sea, to the midland and northern industrial districts, the Celtic peripheries, and the southern and western seaports from which the frigates and East Indiamen sailed for faraway continents. The First Empire had really been English. Even in 1775, a narrow majority of the two million white colonials in the thirteen provinces were of English extraction.

No one in Sussex or Shropshire would make that mistake about the Second Empire. Irish and Highlanders might garrison it, Scots might manage its banks or design its bridges, but the imperial subject population was largely non-British—and colorfully non-English. In Canada, French Catholics were a majority; in the West Indies, black slaves; in Ireland, Catholics; in India, Hindus and Muslims; in Gibraltar, Spanish Catholics; and in Australia, which had only been charted by Captain James Cook in 1771, aborigines. The small populations of British Protestants were mostly loyalist and overlords. Empire, not rebellion, was the watchword.

Thus, for example, in India, to avoid provocation or the slim risk of a new Virginia or Massachusetts, ordinary British settlers were kept out.

Although not yet the jewel in the British Crown, the subcontinent was at least a golden glow on the Oriental horizon. The fortunes being made there encouraged Parliament to inquire into East India Company corruption as early as 1771. By the 1780s, Britons were arriving to rule as well as trade, taking over sugar, indigo, and jute plantations. The loss of the American colonies was a further encouragement. J. H. Plumb, in a bicentennial commentary on what the Revolution meant for Britain, concluded that the loss of America and the transfer of Anglo-French rivalry from the North Atlantic to the Mediterranean, the Levant, and Indian Ocean "certainly helped to make India the fulcrum of empire, with consequences that were immense."[56]

The rising tropical British empire in the East also detracted from the commercial importance of the West Indies. Barbados and Jamaica had been seventeenth-century England's most important plantations—in 1675, they held a larger combined population than Massachusetts and Virginia. However, the sugar islands enjoyed their heyday in the 1760s, and "by 1822, the West Indies were of far less value to Britain than they had been a half century earlier. Nor can there be any doubt that even in the eighteenth century, Barbados and the Leeward Islands had become economically stagnant."[57] The war of 1775–1783 constricted the West Indies' access to cheap American foodstuffs and goods, which increased the region's own local production costs. The East India Company began marketing competing sugar from Bengal in 1791. By the time the American Civil War broke out in 1861, India had even become an alternative, if limited, British source of cotton hitherto largely supplied by the American South.

The new Canada was a product of the post-Revolutionary settlement. American editorialists and politicians of the early 1800s periodically boasted about U.S. ability to invade their next-door neighbor, a braggadocio that was punctured as neatly in the War of 1812 as the cockiness of British frigate captains who ran from Brother Jonathan. Yet Britain did face a unique post-1783 challenge in governing the northern half of North America. Together with the various Irish bills and the India Act of 1784, a more imperially reattuned Parliament also produced the Canada Act of 1791. Besides dividing the region into two provinces, English Upper Canada and French Lower Canada, the act was a pointed, though belated, Tory reply to American independence. As a counterpoint to government in the United States, both Canadas, although having elected assemblies, were also each given an appointed executive council to imitate the role of the House of Lords and to advise an appointed governor general. Charles Inglis, a refugee loyalist cleric who had been rector of New York's Trinity Church, was chosen as the first Anglican bishop.[58] In Canada, brimming with displaced Anglicans, Crown and miter would stand together.

The Second Empire also provided a grand new banner to replace what, as late as the 1730s and 1740s, had still been English and Protestant nationalism. That old definition had weakened during the early reign of George III, with his much-lampooned Scottish chief adviser. It slipped further in the 1770s, as much of southern England, especially avid Protestant nonconformist sections, shrank from a war that was particularly aimed at the oldest and most English colonies of New England and Virginia. As the role of the Scots, Irish, and Welsh, not least the anxiously sought military recruits, became more important, the proud imagery of the *British* empire—it obviously was *British*, not just English—became a unifying force.

Historian Linda Colley, a principal expositor of this theme in her book *Britons*, had pointed out that the new imperialism also rested on glorifying British military victories and the country's essentially aristocratic leadership. However ineffective on Bunker Hill or the upper Hudson, that leadership had managed to prevail against Napoleonic arrivistes and virtually the whole of Europe: "The British elite's ability in the aftermath of the American war to associate itself with patriotism and with the nation in a new and self-conscious fashion proved invaluable to its continuing authority and confidence."[59] J. H. Plumb has identified another boon to the aristocracy: "The acquisition of India and the loss of America both helped to strengthen the class system in Britain: the former made status more numinous; the latter made middle-class radicalism unpatriotic."[60] New paving stones were being set into the separate cultural paths of the two English-speaking nations.

Bourgeois commerce itself became better administered. Where Grenville and Townshend had hemmed and hawed, started and stopped, in the decade after 1763, Parliament and the Ministry of Pitt the Younger became entirely serious about the Navigation Acts and customs reform. The hard line that Parliament took in 1783 on American trade turned out well enough. Besides recapturing the West Indies trade, British ships boasted extraordinary shares of the foreign tonnage entering the United States—for the 1787–1789 period, 80 percent of what came into Philadelphia and 98 percent of what arrived in New York was British.[61] Fully half of America's trade was still with the mother country, and a quarter of Britain's was with the United States. Each nation was the other's best customer. And the British Merchant Marine, the Royal Navy's all-important maritime nursery of trained seamen, remained strong.

Aspects of America's growing commerce were a sore point. With Britain and most of Europe at war for twenty years after 1793, blockading Royal Navy cruisers suppressed the trade of France and her continental allies. Ships under the neutral American flag sailed into the breach, with U.S. exports leaping from under $30 million a year before the war in 1790 to $108 million in 1807. Members of Parliament and the leading London newspapers periodically fulminated: U.S. ships were taking advantage of British control of the seas to bring goods to the Crown's enemies.

A few Britons saw a second, brighter side. The expanding, lucrative market in the United States, by consuming a full third of British wartime manufactures, helped to finance Britain's industrial expansion and thus, indirectly, to underwrite the war with France. Historian Plumb has embraced that interpretation: "The growth of the American economy made for the vastly increased profit of Britain and enabled her to sustain a long and expensive war against France and Napoleon."[62] Moreover, an embattled Britain was ever more dependent on American wheat, and even as the War of 1812 approached, most of the grain that supported the future Duke of Wellington's army in Spain, the vital battleground against Napoleon, came from the Middle Atlantic states.[63]

Luckily for Wellington, the misadventure of 1775–1783 had also led to a sweeping overhaul in the management of public finance. The ballooning of the British national debt during the Great French War virtually repeated itself during the American fiasco, almost doubling from £131 million to £245 million. This time, however, the fiscal strain drove home the need for modernization, with criticism of the existing system rising as the war moved toward humiliating defeat.[64] Professor Ian Christie notes that when Pitt took office in 1783, "the officials' best guide to the system of the exchequer was still the 12th century *Dialogus de Scaccario*" and "wooden tally sticks were still used in public accounting as in Angevin times." From 1783 to 1787, the Pitt Ministry undertook dozens of reforms that ranged from putting government contracts out to public tender, modernizing the revenue services, and obliging the navy to keep its balances in the Bank of England, to the enactment of Pitt's famous Sinking Fund Act of 1786. In Christie's words, these changes represented "the watershed between medieval and modern financial administration. . . . As so often, war was the stimulus to administrative improvement."[65]

On the military front, the subordination of the position of secretary at war had not worked well during the American campaigns. Thus, when war came again in 1793, the attentions of those who remembered quickly upgraded the position to secretary of state for war, who was fully empowered to direct the army's operations and to present its case in the Cabinet and in Parliament.[66] The dockyards of the Royal Navy, also a scandal, had been run by officers who filled them with relatives and dependents, often sustaining this patronage by arranging and approving improper expenses. In 1786, Pitt began a series of far-reaching reforms under Sir Charles Middleton, the comptroller. These expanded the dockyards, repaired and enlarged the fleet, systematized supply, and prepared the navy for its turn-of-the-century glories under Nelson, St. Vincent, and Hood.[67]

Few historians dwell on the connection, but the lessons of American independence directly supported the changes that stood Britain in such good stead later. Even in 1780, failure had pressed enough that Lord North created a statutory commission to examine the public accounts. Over the next seven years, the commission produced fifteen reports that underpinned many of Pitt's reforms. "The losing struggle" of 1775–1783, wrote military historian Piers Mackesy, "had tested the system and exposed its weaknesses":

> Was it right that the administration of the army should be at the mercy of an haphazard and occasional organization implemented at the King's pleasure? That the public purse should support a large system of sinecures and patronage? That public indignation could be ignored in the House of Commons? That knowledge of finance in a public servant should be a matter for derision?[68]

Last, but not least, the war in America, especially the tactics applied in the plantation states and the promise of freedom to slaves, helped to push Britain into one of its most important early nineteenth-century roles: leadership of the worldwide drive to end slavery. These inhibitions, as much as anything else, constrained the Palmerston government from recognizing the independence of the cotton-rich Confederacy in 1862 and early 1863.

Part of the spur to antislavery activism and politicking in the United Kingdom of the 1780s was philosophic: the influence of the Enlightenment and the intensifying worldwide dialogue over freedom and liberty. Religion was a second ingredient, particularly the prominent role of Quakers and other nonconformist sects, as well as the suasion of the small "saints" faction in Parliament led by William Wilberforce. British leadership in the antislavery crusade, they insisted, was a matter of moral atonement.

But besides philosophy and morality, no small part of the impetus was political and pragmatic. It is easy to imagine a post 1783 calculation by some Britons to recapture their historic role of fighting for freedom, while at the same time exposing slave-owning Americans' hypocrisy about liberty, prying apart the shaky Spanish empire, and extending the stop-and-search authority of the Royal Navy. To Britain's ruling class, the antislavery position also offered a low-cost appeal to the increasingly important religious evangelicals and to the urban industrial electorates so well represented in antislavery petitioning. There was even a smidgeon of nationalism. The British Empire in some ways—religious emancipation (1829), Parliamentary reform (1832), and slave emancipation (1834)—prided itself on having become a *reformist* empire.

A kindred blend of philosophy, religion, and self-interest stood out in the northern United States, particularly New England. One has to be struck by the interaction and common chronology: In 1780, Pennsylvania adopted a gradual emancipation law; in 1783, Quakers on both sides of the Atlantic petitioned both Parliament *and* Congress to end the slave trade; in 1783, the case of *Commonwealth v. Jennison* in Massachusetts was interpreted as removing judicial sanction for slavery (akin to Britain's ambiguous *Somerset* decision of 1772); in 1784, Connecticut and Rhode Island enacted gradual emancipation laws; in 1788, the London Society helped to organize a nationwide petition campaign against the slave trade; in 1792, the House of Commons voted to terminate the slave trade in 1796, but the House of Lords disagreed; in 1793, Upper Canada enacted a gradual emancipation law; in 1794, the U.S. Congress prohibited Americans from engaging in the slave trade with foreign countries; and so on.

A new triangular trade of sorts was developing in ideas. New England Federalists even developed a political rhetoric akin to that Britons indulged in during the War for Independence. Yankee critics delighted in embarrassing the egalitarian Jeffersonian faction by emphasizing a particular aspect of liberty, opposition to slavery, in which the southern Jacobins were conspicuously backward.

On the other hand, the cynicism often advanced about Anglo-Saxon morality frequently going hand in hand with political and economic self-interest can be applied to the slavery issue in both Englands, Old and New. If dislike of slavery was a convenient credo for the American North in 1850, especially for industrially pioneering New England, it had been just as timely for the late eighteenth-century Britain of Manchester and Sheffield, of Priestley and Watt—the seedbed of the Industrial Revolution and the new wage economy. The political economics of emerging industrial capitalism was a long way from selfless.

As we have seen, the West Indies sugar colonies, the empire's principal centers of black slavery, were close to their peak or already declining by the end of the eighteenth century. The emergence of India as an alternative tropical producer with a cheap labor supply conveniently rested on a different foundation: custom and religious caste. Even the West Indies plantations, it turned out, could be tended economically by contract laborers from West Africa, China, India, and Java, who worked under penal sanction, lived little differently from black slaves, and were recruited and transported in much the same manner.[69] What mattered was that they were part of the *ascending* economic culture: wage labor.

Besides, although the slave trade was still profitable for the United Kingdom in the early 1800s, the handwriting of emancipation already was on the red-brick wall of the Industrial Revolution. Wage-capitalism was replacing chattel-ownership. By leaping into the vanguard of world activism against the slave trade, British policy-makers used morality to establish the Royal Navy as the policeman of the sea lanes around Africa and Asia, precisely where the commerce of the new empire was growing the most.

The American Revolution, then, while hardly *creating* the slavery issue that would figure so prominently over the next nine decades, obviously framed it with a vastly more important moral intensity and political prominence in both Britain and the United States, the two countries that would be most involved. Just as the first cousins' war in the 1640s furnished a surprising continuity for the second cousins' war in 1775–1783, so that second clash helped lay down a considerable framework for the third, as chapter 8 will examine in detail.

Perhaps the War for America did not have to happen. Certainly it did not have to conclude with its same result. Still, it is hard to avoid a feeling that both sets of cousins were again fortunate. Had Sir William Howe ended the American war in 1776 or 1777, but in a way that produced only an artificial, transient reconciliation, we can fairly wonder: Would a stagnant, unreformed Britain have been prepared for the wars of the 1790s? Finally, could Britain have won against France and her allies had the late 1790s also produced a simultaneous second revolution against the Crown—probably unstoppable, inevitably disruptive—in a still-colonial Massachusetts, Pennsylvania, and Virginia? Such a war could have been the one that justified the King's fears of 1775 about upheaval in America also leading to disaster in Ireland, India, and the Caribbean.

By the late 1780s, George III himself may have realized that things had not gone entirely awry. Perhaps he, too, ultimately perceived what Richard Rush, the American minister to Britain, discussed in 1820, following the old King's death after sixty years on the throne, in musing on the results of his extraordinary reign:

> Britain and the United States are destined to become . . . the predominating nations of Christendom. . . . Each an encumbrance to the other when together, their severance seems to have been the signal for unequaled progress, and boundless prospects to each.[70]

But more strains were ahead. When the United States had become a recognized, independent nation in 1783, it had also become a nation divided—by the unequal economic despoliation of the war, by religious and sectional differences, and, most of all, by slavery and its still-to-come, nineteenth-century zenith. The two major English-speaking nations had to face these rising sectional, economic, racial, and religious issues and divisions, which again straddled the Atlantic, in one more great civil war, the most destructive of the three.

PART THREE

The Final
Cousins' War

8

SECTIONALISM, SLAVERY, AND RELIGION

The Continuity of the Second and Third Cousins' Wars

The American Revolution freed Southern slaveholders from various imperial restraints, opening the way for Indian removal and for a westward expansion of slavery that met no serious opposition until the rise of the Republican Party in response to the Kansas-Nebraska Act of 1854. The United States Constitution gave slaveholders privileges and powers that exceeded the wildest dreams of the beleaguered West Indian whites.

—David Brion Davis, *American Slavery and the Revolution*, 1983

The American Revolution produced an ambiguous legacy. It created the illusion of a young nation united on the principles of liberty and equality, when in fact from the very inception there were invidious divisions along geographical, demographic, and ideological lines. Building upon the revolutionary ideal of political freedom, the "commercial" states of the North moved towards the gradual extinction of slavery. Driven by a different set of imperatives, the "plantation" states of the South entrenched and extended slavery, the very antithesis of freedom. The federal Constitution, which banned the slave trade after 1808 but implicitly recognized the existence of slavery, preserved the moral con-

traditions present in the situation and passed on to another gen-
eration the problem of creating the "more perfect union."
—Sylvia Frey, "Slavery and Anti-Slavery," in the
Encyclopedia of the American Revolution, 1991

The great danger to our general government is the great southern
and northern interests of the continent being opposed to each
other ... the states were divided into different interests not by
their difference of size but by other circumstances; the most ma-
terial of which resulted partly from climate but principally from
their having or not having slaves.
—James Madison, 1787

D ESPITE THE TREATY BETWEEN Britain and the United
States, effective in 1783, that ended the war and recognized the
new republic, some of the new nation's leaders remained apprehensive, not about the reasonable terms, but about the former colonies'
continuing disarray. A disturbing number of the gloomy predictions
that critical loyalists had voiced back in 1775–1776 seemed to be
coming true. Without the constraint of British rule, the thirteen
states, loosely bound under the Articles of Confederation agreed to
in 1777 (and ratified in 1781), sometimes verged on anarchy.

Jefferson and Hamilton, from their different perspectives, had
sensed this danger several years earlier. A strongman might
emerge; one or more European powers might intervene. By late
1782, Barbe de Marbois, the French envoy to the United States,
was advising Paris that chaos was possible. Sir Guy Carleton,
commanding the British evacuation in 1783, predicted that Congress would be overthrown by the Americans themselves.[1]

Independence—*successful independence*—remained insecure.
The jeopardy after 1783 came from the limited authority of the
government created by the Articles of Confederation. Americans
and Britons alike commonly measured the new nation's perils
against those faced by the only previous English-speaking republic. During its existence from 1649 to 1660, the Commonwealth
and Protectorate administered by Oliver Cromwell and then by his
son, Richard, called Tumbledown Dick, had been threatened and
finally toppled by anarchy, inept leadership, and resurgent demand
for the assurance of a monarchy.

By the summer of 1786, similar forces were thought to be bubbling in the United States. Washington himself wrote that "prominent citizens had begun to discuss a monarchical form of government without horror." James Madison, early the next year, acknowledged that the shortcomings of Confederation had "tainted the faith of the most orthodox republicans."[2] The civil-war aspect of the eight-year struggle had left scars visible from Maine to Georgia and deep sectional divisions were already opening up around the slavery question.

But the fledgling United States was more tired and strained than radical. The analogy to the English Commonwealth turned out not to apply. Even in New York and Philadelphia, radicalism was minor compared to earlier republican London. Cultural sectionalism itself was probably no worse in the new United States than in the mid-seventeenth-century British Isles.

What *was* uniquely divisive in the new republic, having been focused by the ideals of the Revolution, agitated by British war stratagems to incite black upheaval, and then institutionalized by the controversial racial settlement of the U.S. Constitution, was the slavery-related rivalry of two sharply different cultures. The "Saxon" North and the "Cavalier" South were about to face off over the great English-speaking issue of the early and mid-nineteenth century. On this emerging battlefield—this sectional geography of "irrepressible conflict"—the outlines of the third cousins' war leap right out of the political and legal settlements of the second.

The new United States could hardly have faced a friendlier English prime minister in late 1782. Lord Shelburne took care that the new boundaries stretched from the Atlantic west to the Mississippi, and from the Great Lakes south to the northern border of Florida, which Britain was returning to Spain. Gone was the earlier British hope of splitting part of the South away from the provinces given independence. The Earl's territorial generosity rested in part on naivete: He hoped to maintain much of the old colonial connection through a loose Anglo-American federation conceived around economic and defense coordination.

His vision, submitted to Parliament as the American Intercourse Bill, at first enjoyed substantial support, especially from mercantile constituencies that had been pro-American during the war. The mayor, aldermen, and commons of London announced their "firm Persuasion that the great Commercial Interests of this Country and of North America are inseparably united."[3] But when Shelburne's Ministry fell in March 1783, his commercial dream collapsed like so many other hoped-for Whig reforms.

Critics charged that to let the ex-colonists carry goods to the West Indies and the rest of the empire in their own vessels, as of yore, would simply permit Brother Jonathan to poach British imperial markets, seamen, and shipbuilding opportunities. But while that argument doomed the bill, many in Britain were also reaching another and not especially disagreeable conclusion: that the former colonies might not succeed for long on their own. Half of the thirteen states were coming off painful internal civil wars. The South, in particular, had born the brunt during the 1779–1782 period, when Britain had emphasized arming loyalists so that American would fight American. A second part of the British plan—to stir up slave disaffection—was of little importance in the northern states, save for New Jersey. But its effects were devastating below the Mason-Dixon line.

North Carolina historian Don Higginbotham, a military affairs specialist, is one who has concluded that the lower South was "ravaged by the war as no other section." He summed up its governmental processes as "collapsed" and its society as disintegrated to the point of approaching John Locke's state of nature. The patriot commander in the South, General Nathaniel Greene, set out such conclusions in his personal papers and official communications. In Higginbotham's words, Greene "repeatedly expressed alarm over these developments, which he felt could do lasting harm to the country and its republican institutions."[4]

In later years, General William Moultrie, another South Carolinian, would recollect the horrors of returning home after the war: the countryside desolate, with little to be seen but evidence of ruin and exploitation, like turkey buzzards here and there picking at the carcasses of the unburied dead.[5] Plantations were devastated, crops destroyed. Guerrilla bands, some of them black, kept operating even after the war. On the Georgia border, three hundred ex-slaves, who had borne arms for the British, continued to style themselves "the King of England's soldiers."

They plundered by day and hid by night until their fortified encampment was burned in 1786 by Georgia and South Carolina militia.[6]

Rebuilding local government—after first resolving who had been patriotic enough to vote and hold office—also weighed most heavily on the South because of the drawn-out, divisive British occupation. Georgia sometimes had three governments: one British and Tory-run in Savannah, two Whig regimes elsewhere.[7] For a while in 1780 and 1781, Georgia had *no* patriot government. Divided wartime authority also left a bitter legacy in the Carolinas. The British had occupied coastal commercial centers like Wilmington, Georgetown, and Charleston while rebels controlled the hinterland. Not surprisingly, the patriot winners held postwar grudges against the former collaborators. Although sour memories were nationwide in 1783, the southern states, along with the occupied area centered on New York City, carried the deepest scars.

The victorious American Whigs, of course, were in a position to take revenge on their beaten foes. And they did, just as the English Royalists had in the 1660s. Important provisions of the U.S.-British peace treaty, carefully negotiated, had given loyalists amnesty; protection against further confiscations, persecutions, or arrests; and a right of temporary readmission to the United States to settle their affairs. But citizens and politicians mocked these provisions and ignored them.

In Virginia and South Carolina, the intensity of feelings against returning loyalists stirred riots, mob violence, and tar-and-featherings.[8] In New York, where opinion was curdled by a seven-year British occupation of Manhattan and Long Island, the governor and legislature passed a test act—mocking the terms of the peace treaty—that disenfranchised all who would not swear that they had never abetted the enemy. The state's trespass act, even more radical, allowed citizens who had abandoned homes and premises in New York City and its environs in the face of the British advance to sue and recover damages and accrued rents from the occupiers. Defendants were expressly barred from citing a British civil or military order as justification.[9] These punitive statutes were not repealed until 1788.

The depth of hostility to the Tories, northern and southern, produced an emigré outpouring far exceeding that from Revolutionary France a decade later. The roughly 100,000 loyalists who left the United States between 1775 and 1784 constituted some 4 percent of the total population. France, by contrast, lost 30,000 out of 15 million, well under 1 percent of the entire nation. Some 70,000 of the Americans who left were Anglicans.[10]

Economics aggravated postwar unrest. Debt and tax pressures lay heavily. The rural western parts of Massachusetts and Pennsylvania, already pinched, were drifting toward violence. The South, however, had carried an added burden in the ruin of much of its economic structure: Plantations had been burned; foreign markets for tobacco, rice, and indigo had been reduced or lost; slaves had run off or had been stolen, lured into the British army, or swallowed up in the war. This was the so-called Southern Strategy embraced by the British Ministry after 1778. By occupying key towns and large swaths of territory, mobilizing loyalists against Whig rebels, and disrupting the slave economy, Britain sought in part to split the plantation states from the others, perhaps even keeping them in the empire after the war.[11] The Carolinas and Georgia were seen as particularly detachable.

The slave states, more than the free states, thus finished the war in severe straits. Virginia suffered from "a post-war depression and a money shortage which injured everyone but most of all the debtors and the less well-to-do farmers"; North Carolina, with the same problems, had greater difficulty in collecting taxes adequate to meet the government's obligations.[12] Whole swaths of coastal and interior South Carolina were in ruins, and ire over the weight of tax payments and debts brought legal processes to a halt in some areas. In the Camden district, a crowd of one thousand surrounding the Court of Common Pleas in 1785 verged on insurrection.[13] In Georgia, "with half of its property destroyed and the institution of slavery disorganized, the state's poverty was appalling. Taxes could not be collected, repeated new issues of paper money were rendering valueless the currency already in circulation, and slaves, land, livestock and personal belongings were all accepted as mediums of exchange."[14]

The Unacknowledged Legacy of 1775–1783: Slavery and a Divided United States

However much the years from 1775 to 1783 may have uplifted political theory, they also led to a greater racial problem in the new nation. Philosophically and rhetorically, Revolutionary egalitarianism pulled opinion in a liberty-minded direction. The day-to-day reality of southern economic disarray and racial fears worked the other way. During the 1780s, these would make protecting slavery a high priority of Carolinians and Georgians both in Congress and the Constitutional Convention.

The overall legacy of the Revolution was stressful from the start, the dichotomy between rhetorical commitment to liberty and the actual persistence, during the next ninety years, of *legal* slavery in six of the original states that signed the Declaration of Independence: Delaware, Maryland, Virginia, the Carolinas, and Georgia. There was no way to square the two, and the southern retreat from the antislavery pronouncements of leaders like Jefferson and St. George Tucker, as well as the contrast with the human rights promise of the Declaration, added to the embarrassment.

Pressures to rebuild the plantation system tightened southern attitudes. Servitude in many of these states had been looser in the early and mid-eighteenth century. South Carolina had let blacks enroll in the militia, and several hundred fought alongside white soldiers in the Yemassee War of 1718.[15] Black slaves appear to have accounted for about 10 percent of the Virginians in arms against Governor Berkeley during Bacon's Rebellion in 1676.[16] But as the plantation economy grew in the second half of the century, especially after 1785, so did the slave populations of Virginia, the Carolinas, and Georgia. The slave insurrections and raids of 1775–1783, as we have seen, intensified white concerns. By the 1790s, the laws of the southern states were tightening with respect to slave manumission, bearing arms, and the rights of free blacks.

Americans have come to understand that the War for Independence was a major event in slave quarters as well as plantation houses. What historians debate is whether more of the effect was negative than positive.[17] In the South, that seems to have been the case.

The "South," of course, should not be described too sweepingly. Maryland and Delaware were already border states. Virginia was culturally as well as topographically divided by the high ridges of the Appalachians. North Carolina—much of it poor and backward enough to be nicknamed "the Ireland of North America"—displayed plantation economics only near the coast.[18] Views of slavery and race were hardly uniform.

In the border states, as in the North, the initial philosophic impetus of the Revolution was egalitarian. In Delaware and the northern sections of Maryland, manumission of slaves swelled the free percentage of the black population. Delaware's rose from under 10 percent in 1776 to about one-third in 1810 and over 90 percent by 1860. Free blacks in Maryland, just 4 percent of the black population in 1776, were 20 percent in 1810 and almost half by 1860.[19] Northern Maryland had most of the free blacks. The lower part of the state was more like Virginia, where the rhetoric of the Revolution seems to have faded quickly.

This initial post-Revolutionary ambiguity toward blacks had even extended to elections. Of the states that did not exclude them from voting in 1787, three, surprisingly, were border or piedmont southern—Delaware, Maryland, and North Carolina. Thomas Brown, a free black horse doctor, actually ran for the Maryland legislature in 1792, although his vote was small enough not to have been recorded.[20]

Such had been the immediate flush of liberty. But in the border states, it was short-lived. As the nineteenth-century plantation-mentality countertide began to flood, Maryland (1810), Missouri (1821), and North Carolina (1835) passed laws disenfranchising free blacks. Delaware had done so in 1792 and Kentucky in 1799. Criteria of race, not status, came to the fore. Slaves became nonpersons. Southern free blacks became nonvoters. In New England and New York, by contrast, free blacks received political attention from the early nineteenth-century Federalists.

The late eighteenth-century divergence of northern (especially Yankee) and southern approaches to black military enlistment and service, and thereafter to free black status and enfranchisement, were harbingers. By the turn of the century, while some northern states were prohibiting slavery or emancipating slaves, albeit typically at some date fifteen or twenty-five years distant, the plantation South was working to *strengthen* its local slave system for a cotton and plantation zenith still to come. Circumstances justify those who have called the Revolutionary era as much of a watershed in black life as the later Civil War and then civil rights periods.[21]

A few have gone further. To David Brion Davis, the Revolution freed U.S. policy-makers from British imperial restraints that would have limited Indian removal and the expansion of slavery. Then, still more significantly, the terms of the Constitution guaranteed southern slave owners "state autonomy within a federal system" in which they could count on "disproportionate national power as a result of slave representation, federal assistance in the recovery of fugitive slaves or the suppression of insurrections, and non-interference in matters relating to race and labor."[22] He contends, in short, that the political settlement of the 1780s itself became a basis of the mid-nineteenth-century slavery crisis.

A university lecturer in American history at Oxford, Duncan Macleod, greeted the U.S. bicentennial with a more biting contention: that independence served to midwife a new political sociology, even theology, of racism. The looser colonial slave codes of the mid-eighteenth century were "discriminatory, but not sacred. Developments during the Revolutionary era changed all this and produced a coherent racist doctrine that became a sacred, significant totem in American society."[23] In light of American rhetoric about men being free and equal, the lesser status of blacks could only be justified by their being innately different: *dangerous, savage, inferior.* Free blacks, Macleod concluded, also had to be put in the same lesser category. Exceptions were not workable; sweeping racial generalizations were necessary.

The emergence in the 1790s of a doctrine of black inferiority, overpowering revolutionary egalitarianism, found voice through legislators and politicians who sought to convince voters, southern and northern, of the legitimacy of the South's constitutional insistence and bargain. As a theory of conscious, planned malice, Macleod's analysis seems overstated. Such things are rarely plotted. But as a stumbled-into postwar attitude, developed to deal with the large new numbers of freed blacks, who could not be dismissed as slaves, it has plausibility.

The divergent economic effects of the Revolution on the three major regions of the new nation—New England, the Middle Atlantic, and the South—have not been widely examined by historians or economists. Data are too sparse. But it would be fair to say that widespread British destruction of agriculture in the South (burning of crops and plantations and alienation of slaves) transparently helped to end that region's colonial-era preeminence in American wealth and exports. In the 1780s, this hegemony passed to the Middle Atlantic region, which firmed its lead through population growth, agricultural expansion, and the rise of industry.[24] Even King Cotton, a half century later, could not reclaim a regional wealth advantage.

Wartime damage helped to push the southern states toward a new economic agenda that ranged from debt postponement and paper money to compensation for slaves taken by the British. Suspicion of northern financial and commercial interests and intentions also mounted. And virtually every economic issue—from tariff and inflation to debt relief—also touched slavery.

Slavery itself became the central circumstance over which the plantation states needed to reach agreement with the North. The constitutional stipulation finally negotiated in 1787 was a concession to the South: that for purposes of choosing representatives in Congress and electors for president and for sharing fiscal assessments, three-fifth of slaves would be counted in state populations, along with all of the nonslaves.

This mathematical arrangement gave the slave states almost as large a voice in the House of Representatives—in 1790, 45 percent of its membership—as the northern states with their much larger white populations. New England was unhappy, but Georgia and South Carolina seem to have regarded the three-fifths provision, along with another clause securing the slave trade through 1808, as a virtual condition of union. Even one North Carolina delegate to the Constitutional Convention, William R. Davie, said as much.

The Articles of Confederation had covered some of the same ground, in debates over whether slaves should be taxed, but the deliberations over the Constitution made slavery-related sectionalism a recognized fact of political life. James Madison of Virginia called it "pretty well understood" that the "institution of slavery and its consequences formed the line of discrimination" between the states at the convention.[25] Charles Cotesworth Pinckney of South Carolina observed that there were "two great divisions of Northern and Southern Interests."[26] This bolsters the case for the American Revolution as a pivot: *Besides aggravating racial tensions, it quickly led to a new federal governmental system in which slavery could and did flourish under political and constitutional protections unavailable in the British Empire.*

Moreover, Southerners now had an argument that they had made a constitutional compact with the North. Pinckney came back to South Carolina to say: "By this settlement, we have secured an unlimited importation of Negroes for twenty years. Nor is it declared when that importation shall be stopped; it may be continued. We have a right to recover our slaves in whatever part of America they may take refuge. In short, considering all the circumstances, we have made the best terms for the security of this species of property it was in our power to make."[27] Many Northerners also acknowledged a bargain. Roger Sherman of Connecticut said it had been better to allow the Southern states to go on importing slaves than to have them leave the Union.[28] Belief in a bargain was something Southerners never yielded.

Such was the unplanned legacy of Cornwallis, Tarleton, Rawdon, and the other British commanders. Their depredations that failed to stymie independence did help sow the seeds of another civil war. The worse a state's guerrilla warfare and slave losses, the greater the postwar political and economic disarray. Georgia, the Carolinas, and Virginia all bore witness. With less devastation, these postwar preoccupations would have been less intense. Protecting slavery might not have seemed so vital. The implications for future sectionalism and civil war might not have been so ominous.

U.S. Politics After the Revolution:
Rightward Reaction and the
Brief Reempowering of the Old Colonial Elite

The war democratized many aspects of the politics of the new nation. Monarchism collapsed and, initially at least, many loyalists

327

emigrated. Political power and representation followed the Conestoga wagons and canal boats into the more egalitarian backcountry. However, in contrast to the throes and convulsions of the English Revolution during the late 1640s, neither religious sects nor political radicals got out of hand. No disarray akin to that which brought back Charles Stuart in 1660 ever threatened to restore monarchy in the United States. In fact, what developed in Britain in the 1780s also emerged three thousand miles to the west: *a postwar conservative countertide on behalf of order and stability.*

The radicalism of the American Revolution—its stark rejection of the patronage, corruption, and aristocratic system of the Crown and even of the monarchy itself—was genuine only within an eighteenth-century dimension. Its mainsprings were a Whiggism drawn principally from three cultures that had already shown conservative as well as revolutionary streaks on both sides of the Atlantic: New England Congregationalism, Covenanter Presbyterianism, and Virginia Low Church "country party" Anglicanism. These groups' mid-seventeenth-century forebears in East Anglia, Scotland, and the Thames Valley had mostly questioned or shrunk from the extremes of Ranters, Diggers, Fifth Kingdom men, and Levellers. Many of those forebears doubted Cromwell's Rump Parliament itself in the late 1640s when England went from political confusion to regicide and a mild form of military dictatorship. Such wartime advocates of constrained, limited radicalism could—and, after 1783, did—easily transform themselves into proponents of stability and conservatism.

High Church Anglicans on both sides of the Atlantic, expectant that the republican experiment of the American "Oliverians" would fail like its old-country predecessor, were misled by ignoring this lineage. The American rebels, they pointed out, were as willing as Cromwell and his allies had been to imprison Royalists, strip them of office, confiscate their estates, and even execute them. Such tactics and abuses of power did mock the libertarian pretenses of 1776 just as the practices of the late 1640s and 1650s mocked the reformist goals laid out by Parliament in 1640 and 1641.

Harsh use of power, however, is not the same thing as counterproductive radicalism. Pride's Purge, the barring of a hundred members of the House of Commons in 1648 by army colonel Thomas Pride and his musketeers, never repeated itself in Congress. Counties in New England, unlike those of Old England, were never ruled by major generals appointed for Lancashire or Cheshire. Congress, unlike the Puritan Parliament, never abolished Christmas. Indeed, Puritan Massachusetts Bay leaders themselves had been unnerved by the nearness of anarchy in the England of the late 1640s, and the province's own seventeenth-century historians put subsequent emphasis on Massachusetts's underlying distrust of the sectaries and religious radicals.[29]

In about half of the thirteen states, post-1783 politics was not very different from the prewar variety. The power structure stayed much the same: moderately conservative. Three of the New England jurisdictions—Connecticut, Rhode Island, and New Hampshire—retained their familiar political elites, as did Delaware, Maryland, Virginia, and South Carolina.[30] Somewhat greater transformations occurred in states like Pennsylvania, New York, North Carolina, and Massachusetts where major conservative, loyalist, and Anglican factions were eliminated by the outbreak of war or where egalitarian state constitutions were put in place. Pennsylvania, through its Constitution of 1776, which established an all-powerful people's legislature with no governor, was the one state to even flirt with the provocative politics of the Levellers circa 1646.

Less political importance now attached to religious differences. Before the war, they had been the only significant cultural factor in legislative alignments.[31] Particularly in the Middle Atlantic, religious labels like Anglican, Church, Presbyterian, or Quaker party had been appropriate to describe the political alignments and matters of disagreement. They also helped to set the scene for wartime loyalties.

That changed with independence. The parties or factions that reflected Quakerism and Anglicanism essentially collapsed. Postwar politics quickly rearranged itself around new subject matter. Religion was collateral (except in Pennsylvania and in New England, where legal establishment of the Congregational Church remained at issue). Controversy was forming along a new critical divide: Would the United States keep a loose federal framework to

329

suit an independent-minded agrarian yeomanry or would it establish a moderately strong central government with well-paid judges, national banks to promote commerce, a navy to protect shipping, and an innate bias toward the rich and powerful—in other words, a government somewhat akin to the British regime against which so many Americans had just fought? This debate served to reunite much of the prewar colonial elite behind what became the federal Constitution and the Federalist Party. It would also, by 1812, help lead to another war with Britain.

Colonial historian Jackson Turner Main, in his survey of "Political Parties Before the Constitution," divided members of the state legislatures of the years between 1783 and 1787 into two camps. The first, in favor of a relatively strong central government and its concomitants, wound up supporting ratification of the proposed U.S. Constitution, and many of its members became Federalists. The other side, typically with lower incomes and less fashionable domiciles, feared too much government—especially when it was allied to banks, lawyers, and speculators. Such men supported easier money and debt extension, opposed giving loyalists back property or voting rights, and criticized the coastal and mercantile elites as all too ready to ally with former Tory foes. Many would oppose ratification; most became anti-Federalists and, later, Jeffersonians.[32]

Wherever they lived, Anglicans (now Episcopalians) and Quakers, the two major religious groups least committed to the Revolution, were lopsidedly in the camp of hard money and property, well-empowered government, readmission of former loyalists, ratification of the Constitution, and the politics of incipient Federalism. That at least suggested religion as a factor.[33]

Other wartime religious political alignments were also transformed. Presbyterians, especially on the Scotch-Irish frontier, generally opposed the cosmopolitan, pro-ratification, and Federalist side, which included their old commander-in-chief, George Washington. The principal exception came in New Jersey, where many of the Federalist-leaning Presbyterians were transplanted Yankees with Congregationalist antecedents. Congregationalists themselves, generally cohesive during the war, split during the 1780s along caste and class lines. The poor, rural, and anti-Tory became anti-

Federalists, while the coastal and commercial cosmopolitans of New England, over the next generation, became the single most important national support base of the Federalist Party.

This regrouping of elites around a partial counterrevolution stood 1775–1776 relationships on their heads. Even though one hundred thousand Tories and loyalists had left the United States, two or three hundred thousand would have remained, plus at least as many neutrals. Within a few years of independence, conservative factionalists in some states were openly recruiting them or, in the case of emigrés, enlisting their return. In loyalist districts of southern Delaware and eastern Maryland, few had ever moved.

Bitterness suffused the debate. Just months after the peace treaty of 1783, the town of New Haven, Connecticut, extended an invitation to former loyalists to return, prompting President Ezra Stiles of Yale—labeled by loyalists as a "seminary of rebellion"—to complain about efforts "silently to bring the Tories into an Equality and Supremacy among the Whigs."[34] In South Carolina, low country conservatives of the Charleston area led the fight against angry upcountry opposition to restore the property and political rights of loyalists and British merchants. In New Jersey, several years after the war ended, Governor William Livingston, a staunch rebel, lamented that "I have seen Tories members of Congress, judges upon tribunals, Tories representatives in our legislative councils, Tories members of our Assemblies. . . . I have seen self-interest predominating and patriotism languishing."[35] Returned and reenfranchised Tories in these and other states also became controversial again a few years later for their involvement in promoting ratification of the new U.S. Constitution.

Without the new governmental framework brought about by ratification, the nineteenth-century commercial and diplomatic emergence of the United States might have been at risk. The financial classes of Charleston, Philadelphia, New York, and Boston certainly thought as much. Both nations, Britain as well as the new republic, found it necessary to follow up the war by centralizing power and tightening the administrative rigging of the ship of state. Nevertheless, pro-British pejoratives stuck easily to a partly counterrevolutionary politics, especially one that enlisted the returning Anglican loyalists (and those who never departed) and the neutral Quakers alongside the wealthy conservative elites who had been on the patriot side. Backcountry opposition to what looked like British-type government ultimately grew into the Massachusetts and Pennsylvania upheavals of 1786–1799—Shays' Rebellion, the Whiskey Insurrection, and Fries' Uprising—all of them agrarian insurrections against the pro-creditor and hard-money policies of state and national Federalist administrations.

Controversial constituencies and policies made Federalism a relatively short-lived national regime, although not as transient as the British Whigs of that same era. In 1788 and 1792, with George Washington as their presidential nominee, the Federalists swept all before them. By 1796, as Federalism began to weaken and emaciate, its corpus increasingly displayed a backbone of the old colonial elites and bulging veins of wartime loyalism: Charleston and the South Carolina low country, the Scottish-settled upper Cape Fear Valley and commercial towns and ports of eastern North Carolina, the mercantile centers of tidewater Virginia (Wiilliamsburg, Alexandria, Petersburg, and Richmond), eastern Maryland, Delaware, greater Philadelphia, New Jersey, the lower Hudson Valley, the Connecticut Valley, and coastal New England. John Adams, a narrow winner in 1796, proved to be the last Federalist president.

Politically as well as religiously, the three elite religious denominations of the colonial period, Anglicanism, Quakerism, and Congregationalism, were weakening. Within a few generations, they all wound up as clear losers from the 1775–1783 war and the subsequent democratization of the nineteenth century. The former Church of England was disestablished everywhere in the South and border states by the 1790s. Much reduced in status, it became the Protestant Episcopal Church in the United States. The decades surrounding the Revolution, although less tumultuous than the era of the English Civil War, also hosted a surge of revivalism, enthusiasm, and new sects. The church pews of the new century—in raw power and popular outpouring, at least—would belong to the Baptists.[36] Quakers lost their great influence in Pennsylvania, just as they had many years earlier in Rhode Island, North Carolina, Delaware, and New Jersey. And one by one, the New England states disestablished Puritan Congregationalism: Connecticut acted in 1818, New Hampshire in 1819, and Massachusetts in 1833.

Federalism, as America's only colonial-sprung national party, was good for little beyond orchestrating the transition of the 1780s and 1790s to more effective government. Its capacity to be a window on the philosophic future was negligible. The War for American Independence had been too much a British civil war fought around old-country constitutional, religious, and cultural cleavages, however modified, to produce a new postcolonial polity and culture overnight. Other slow transitions were visible alongside the persisting English conservative Whig attributes and seaboard orientation of late eighteenth-century Federalist politics. British currency was accepted in the United States for decades to come. British merchants—Scots, in particular—returned to the Carolinas. For another generation, courts in many states used the English common law that had been in effect in 1776. Even in the 1820s and 1830s, Scottish Gaelic speech brought overland from the late eighteenth-century Carolinas could be heard in rural Alabama and Mississippi. (Even some *slaves* in post-Revolutionary North Carolina spoke Gaelic.) Welsh cadences persisted in Duffrin Mawr, the Great Valley west of Philadelphia, for almost as long.

The chaotic American frontier of the 1760s and 1770s, symbol of the new continent, had itself been less an unprecedented New World melting pot than a backwoods stew pot of the same Protestant religious and ethnic groups—Scots, English, Scotch-Irish, Huguenots, and some Germans and Dutch—that had, in smaller measure, already met and mingled along Ulster's own rugged seventeenth-century border. Ulster's mix, in turn, had been prefigured on the battlefields of seventeenth- and eighteenth-century Europe where different Protestant nationalities marched together. The Protestant army that came ashore with William of Orange in 1688 was, as we have seen, not just English, but also Dutch, Swedish, and French Huguenot. Not coincidentally, the Protestant alliance included *all* the major seventeenth- and eighteenth-century settler groups visible in the thirteen colonies. Ethnically as well as culturally, America took more than a generation to become clearly *post-colonial*.

The new United States, however, needed a myth, and one soon took shape around the idea of an independent, liberated America as an altogether new kind of country: liberty's refuge, freedom's shining beacon, a nation destined to spread across the continent and perhaps even to redeem the world. True in some measure, the irony is that these very boasts had British antecedents and British qualities—Huguenots, Palatine Germans, and before them Flemings and Dutch refugees had regarded England as such a beacon. The refugee leader of the short-lived Corsican Republic, Pasquale Paoli, spent most of the 1776–1783 period not in Boston or Philadelphia, but in the London of the tyrant George III. Manifest destiny was as implicit in the New World endeavors of Sir Walter Raleigh and the coronation anthems of George Frederick Handel as it was explicit in the U.S. political oratory of 1850. Parading themselves as a unique chosen people was an exaggeration that Americans carried in their Tudor, Covenanter, and Hanoverian genes. Under Jefferson and then Jackson, however, the American frontier political culture, understandably enough, ignored the inheritance to trumpet the newness.

Yesteryear's characteristics fell away more easily after the second war with Britain ended in 1815 with the United States on the threshold of another great expansion and transformation: the peopling of the trans-Appalachian region and the emergence of Jacksonian Democracy. The colonial imprint might persist along the seaboard, be it Sir William Pepperell's mansion on Maine's Kittery Point or the royal coats of arms on Carolina Anglican church chancels, but west of the Appalachians an unmistakably new nation was taking shape.

The War of 1812 and the Political Death Agonies of Federalism

But if westward expansion shed the characteristics of colonialism, the sectionalism established in the East, whether or not we trace it to the British Isles, was none so easily lost. Presidential elections themselves became a mirror. Once George Washington's two terms had ended, geographic divisions became institutionalized in the contests of 1796 and 1800. New England voted Federalist. The

South—Virginia, the Carolinas, Georgia, Kentucky, and Tennessee—supported the Republicans of Thomas Jefferson, and with the usual support of the border states and Pennsylvania, this became the winning coalition. The divided middle states were the critical battleground and would remain that way through the Civil War.

Federalism withered, but had a party based in New England managed to dominate the national politics of the early nineteenth century, America's westward expansion would have been slowed. Many Federalists, New Englanders in particular, had opposed the admission of Kentucky and Tennessee in the 1790s and then the Louisiana Purchase during the next decade. Yankees able to exercise far-reaching authority in Washington would have accelerated the slavery debate. But when John Adams's single term ended in March 1801, he was not simply the last Federalist president. Over the next two decades, the Federalist Party and the stalwarts of New England sectionalism virtually died in each other's political arms.

Election results chiseled the epitaph. After a milestone of slippage in 1800 and then another following the War of 1812, the outcome of 1818 shrank Federalist strength in Congress to just 7 of 42 U.S. senators and 27 of 183 members of the House of Representatives.[37] The resultant control of Washington by expansion-minded southern presidents and allied Congresses came close to writing its own successful midcentury *finale*: the submergence of New England within a Caribbean-facing, southern-led nation in which slavery might have lasted until 1875 or 1890.

Why, then, did Federalism shrivel? In part, certainly, because of unsuitability to the new and more democratic politics of the nineteenth century.[38] The party's reunification of old colonial elites across Revolutionary War divisions, its backing from ex-Tories, and its pro-British sympathies and connections reinforce such a conclusion. The pro-English tendency—Thomas Jefferson's derisive caricature of the Federalists as "Anglomen"—became particularly crippling after the War of 1812, especially outside of New England. Accusations that Federalists in New London, Connecticut, had hung out blue lanterns to signal British warships that Stephen Decatur's fleet was about to sail especially stung: "Blue-lantern" Federalist became to the lexicon of political recrimination in 1815 what "Copperhead" would be to the name-calling of 1864–1865.

The War of 1812 was what ultimately brought the vulnerability of the Federalist Party and its home region to a head. New England, commercially and culturally tied to Britain, raised plausible criticisms of the weak defense preparations and frequently ineffective foreign policy of Presidents Jefferson and Madison. But when war was declared, most maritime Yankees were opposed. The cost would be too high. The "War Hawks" tended to be from the South and West, from states like Kentucky, Tennessee, Georgia, and South Carolina.

Part of the reason why war with England was so unpopular in the coastal North was the degree of commercial intermingling that still continued. Sorting out American ships and seamen from their transatlantic cousins was not easy. If British naval officers provided the arrogance, maritime America, in turn, provided no small part of the confusion "with a great subterranean network of smuggling, collusion, clandestine partnerships and other practices."[39] In the decades after the peace treaty of 1783, where money was to be made, American vessels and crews were all too anxious to sail under British colors, with false registers and a suitable sprinkling of Cornish or East Anglian accents. This is the reverse side of the valid American complaint about Royal Navy officers impressing seamen whose speech patterns actually evidenced a home in Gloucester, Massachusetts, not King's Lynn, Norfolk. Huge numbers of American seamen were indeed British-born or recent runaways from British service.

No other U.S. war, let it be said, has been begun against so much division and sectional objection. The Declaration of War in 1812 passed by only seventy-nine to forty-nine in the House and nineteen to thirteen in the Senate. Federalists, even the relative handful from the South, were unanimous in their opposition. Sectionally, New England senators and congressmen were the most hostile. Parts of the Federalist case were valid. However, the region's covert trade with Canada and dealings with the British navy, coupled with the refusals by Massachusetts, Connecticut, and other states to let their militia serve beyond their boundaries, created an overall image of dubious patriotism, even near-treason. The sole Federalist member of the House Foreign Affairs Committee, encircled by War Hawks, was Philip Barton Key of Maryland. He happened to have been a loyalist who had fought for the British in the Revolution.[40] These, in the end, would be the sort of national memories that prevailed.

Utter political disaster struck in January 1815. Several weeks earlier, as the war had seemed to drag out to British advantage— only a few months had passed since the King's soldiers had invaded Maine and burned Washington—New England Federalists had gathered in Hartford, Connecticut, to discuss possible courses of action. Hints of secession had been in the air. Instead, the Hartford Convention, as it became known, sidestepped such inflammation to consider practical if unrealistic political and constitutional efforts to reduce the ability of the South and West to undertake any future war so at odds with the interests of New England and the Middle Atlantic states.

Steered by Massachusetts and Connecticut, the assembled delegates voted on January 5 in favor of a far-reaching group of constitutional amendments that would have required: (1) a two-thirds vote for Congress to declare war, interdict trade with a foreign nation, or admit new states to the union; (2) a sixty-day limitation on embargoes; (3) an end to counting three-fifths of slaves in apportioning representation in Congress; and (4) a limitation of presidents to one term, along with a bar on electing a president from the same state twice in a row. The last two objectives, in particular, aimed directly at southern power in Congress and the Virginia dynasty in the White House.[41]

Bad timing turned the Hartford Convention into a disaster for New England Federalism instead of a powerful indictment of a shaky government. The Treaty of Ghent, which ended the war on reasonable terms for the United States, had already been finalized on December 24, although word did not arrive in New York until early February. News came more quickly of Andrew Jackson's stunning early January victory over the British at the Battle of New Orleans. With almost no loss, his Tennessee dirtyshirts, Mississippi dragoons, Baratarian pirates, Choctaw Indians, and French Creole militia had routed veterans of the Napoleonic Wars from famous British regiments.

The popular press went wild. Enthusiastic descriptions of how Jackson had defeated "Wellington's invincibles," thereby making himself "the conqueror of the conquerors of Europe," created a new mythology. The United States, instead of having been on the brink of defeat and fiscal collapse, had won the war and laid down the Treaty of Ghent. The Second War for American Independence became a second glorious victory. The Hartford Convention, in turn, became a near betrayal.

Thus the politics. Commerce-minded Federalism, in its splendid Cape Ann mansions, Philadelphia banks, and Piscataqua shipyards, became tarred with disloyalty as well as Toryism. If the aristocratic-led British victory over Napoleon at Waterloo made postwar Britain safe for privilege, which it did, the populist, frontier-style American victory at New Orleans over the Duke of Wellington's brother-in-law made the postwar United States equally secure for Jacksonian Democracy. The Federalist Party, impugned with unpatriotism and anti-expansionism, in addition to unpopular economics, would prove as much a victim as the slain British general, Sir Edward Pakenham, whose body was brought home in a cask of wine. Jackson himself later said that if he had been stationed in New England, he would have court-martialed the "monarchists and traitors" who had organized the Hartford Convention.[42]

In carrying America west, this new, exuberant expansionism of backcountry Pennsylvanians, southern planters, Baptist church deacons, and Tennessee Indian fighters also carried slavery west. The weak Federalists of 1812 and 1820 and the proper Whigs of the 1830s and 1840s too often would seem to oppose the frontier, westward expansion, and war, a collectively unappealing platform. Slaveholders, by contrast, made the frontier an ally. In Britain, expansionism was imperial, Tory, and aristocratic-led. In the United States, the embrace of manifest destiny was republican, egalitarian, and Democratic-led in its politics. It was also anti-British, because for several generations after 1783, expansion was blocked or inhibited by periodic British involvement with Wyandot, Shawnee, and Chippewa raiding parties of the Great Lakes or warring Creeks and Chickasaws of the Alabama frontier, off-and-on boundary warfare in Maine's Aroostook Valley, ambitions in

Oregon, and schemes to make an independent Texas Republic into a buffer zone.

During the early decades of the nineteenth century, the Democratic Party, usually southern-led, was Indian-fighting, anti-British, and strongly favorable to U.S. expansion. This put it in tune with popular opinion—and slavery hitched a thirty-year ride. Meanwhile, the stalwarts of antislavery politics—Pennsylvania Quakers and New England Congregationalists—were trapped in a slowly dying, seaboard-tilted party, disdainful of "Andy" Jackson or "Davy" Crockett and given to speaking in the nearest U.S. equivalent to an English accent. This party system of 1800–1828 shepherded by Jefferson and the successor alignment forged by Jackson, in both of which Yankees were sidelined, successfully advanced southern sectionalism and slavery entirely within the original constitutional compact of 1787.

The extent to which sectional antagonism and the shadow of yet another civil war had emerged during the American Revolution and been consolidated in its aftermath bolsters the idea of an 1861–1865 war long in the making. Each of the cousins' wars, rhetorically and contextually, has seeded and encouraged the next. As the nineteenth century unfolds, then, we can usefully see the relationship as a framework: Irrepressible sectionalism and irrepressible conflict were marching together.

In the century and a half since William H. Seward, Lincoln's future secretary of state, described the imminent U.S. Civil War as an "irrepressible conflict," a significant minority of historians have set out essentially the opposite thesis: that the social, economic, and political differences between North and South were indeed compromisable, and only irresponsible agitators and second-rate politicians on both sides inflamed them into open conflict.[43] Kindred arguments have been made for the flukish or unnecessary character of the English Civil War and the War for American Independence.

Once, quite possibly. Twice, conceivably. But not *three* times. Wars with the continuity of these are not accidents, needless eruptions, or the product of a misled and gullible public. Their origins go deeper. The God of English-speaking Protestants was, as we have seen, "a God of Warr." The English-speaking peoples had used armed conflict to achieve external success from Crécy and Agincourt to the defeat of the Spanish Armada. Small wonder that three times during the seventeenth, eighteenth, and nineteenth centuries, that same resort to arms would be accepted—after long debate, and when no other course remained—to resolve profound *internal* differences.

The parallels between the English Civil War and the American Civil War, which the following three chapters will elaborate, support the continuity and irrepressibility interpretations. In many respects, the southeast of England circa 1640, with its commercial, maritime, and Puritan coloration, stood to the semifeudal west and north of England much as the Yankee North of 1800 or 1860 stood to the Cavalier South—cultures apart. And as chapter 5 has suggested, recurrent "threads" connect the *three* conflicts: alignments of wartime loyalty that at least partly repeated themselves, together with the effect of each outcome in chastening aristocracy, monarchy, or High Church religion and in spurring economic modernization and westward or commercial expansion.

Because the English-speaking peoples have operated in relatively free political cultures, the cousins' wars have been awash in ideology and acrimony. Meandering creeks of sectional, class, denominational, and cultural self-interest have become cresting floodwaters of political insistence and demands for upholding imperiled liberties. By 1860, the sectional and antislavery controversy in the United States, as we have seen, harked back at least eight decades to the end of the War for Independence. The American Civil War became the bloodiest of the English-speaking internal wars only after its prelude became the most drawn-out and bitter.

Moreover, the continuity has been further enlarged by another factor: the extent to which interpretation and counterinterpretation of the two earlier cousins' wars became interwoven in the acrimony leading up to the third. The conspiracies, slogans, and confrontations of the previous wars found further relevance. Some new abuse invariably demanded comparison with the previous great tyrants, Charles I, Cromwell, Parliament, or King George III. To an extraordinary extent, rough underlying divisions returned in the new sectionalisms: Low Church versus episcopacy, Puritans versus Cavaliers, even Normans versus Saxons, for all that this was more posture than fact. In the nineteenth-century once again, a new war would gather around old divisions.

The South and the Frustration of Tropical Manifest Destiny

Amid the heady cotton boom of the 1840s and 1850s, the South, with its bursting warehouses, growing millions of slaves, and porticoed romanticism, overlooked warnings for the landed gentry that both previous conflicts, carefully pondered, should have raised. Commerce and liberty had the history of winning. In the 1640s, after all, the manor-based Cavaliers had *lost* the war to the town-based parvenus. Then the American Revolution, aggravated by the ferocity of 1779–1782 warfare in the plantation colonies, had depleted the wealth of the agricultural South below that of the mercantile North.

A few Southerners of the 1840s and 1850s even toyed with a dismaying but perceptive conclusion: that their region, in a way, had actually *lost* the War for Independence.[44] The political economics were clear: Commerce, not agriculture, had been the gainer in each cousins' war—and it would be again in 1861–1865.

The gap between South and North in industry, population, and wealth kept widening in the nineteenth century, even just prior to the Civil War when the slave economy enjoyed unprecedented cotton prosperity. The South, in practical terms, was becoming increasingly defined by plantation states growing the great bottomland crops of long-staple cotton, sometimes nine to twelve feet high and yielding twenty-five hundred to three thousand pounds per acre: South Carolina, Georgia, Alabama, Mississippi, Louisiana, and Texas. In 1860, these six produced three million of the country's four million bales. As the cotton crop became both the mainstay of slavery *and* America's largest and most profitable export, the shift in Dixie's agricultural geography carried over into temperament. The genteel South, essentially Virginia, increasingly gave way to a South that was hot-tempered as well as *nouveau riche*. The Cotton Belt had most of Dixie's small infusion of seventeenth- and eighteenth-century white emigrants from the tropics— planters from Barbados and Jamaica, onetime indentured Irish

341

from St. Kitts, and the other Leeward Islands. It also held the two most notable French communities: the Huguenots of low-country South Carolina and the Creoles of Louisiana. Such a culture would be just as likely to expand south to the Gulf of Mexico as west.

By 1860, when Cotton States secessionists—the "fire-eaters" of contemporary parlance—weighed Lincoln's election, they had good reason to think that Deep Southern interests might profit from secession, independence, and reliance on "cotton diplomacy." Textiles, Europe's biggest industry, needed the South's long-staple fibers. An England cut off from southern cotton, contended Senator James H. Hammond of South Carolina, "would topple headlong and carry the whole civilized world with her, save the South. No, you dare not make war on cotton. No power on earth dares make war on it. Cotton is King."[45] Surely such might could make and uphold an independent Confederacy.

Southern planters, almost born on horseback, had equal faith in physical prowess. If secession did lead to trial by combat, well-bred southern Galahads would prevail. In the two recent wars fought by the United States, with Britain from 1812 to 1815 and with Mexico from 1846 to 1847, the slave states had produced both the "war hawks" and the triumphant generals: Andrew Jackson of Tennessee, Zachary Taylor of Louisiana, and Winfield Scott of Virginia. Both times, New Englanders had been embarrassed as weak, defeatist, and unpatriotic.

James McPherson, perhaps America's preeminent Civil War historian, chose to begin his epic *Battle Cry of Freedom* on a great plateau of that second military triumph—Chapultepec, Mexico, in 1847. He depicts weary but victorious American troops, sent by a pro-slavery Democratic president dedicated to expanding U.S. territory, standing to attention as Old Glory rose over the ancient capital of the Aztecs.[46] And in several ways, Mexico did first bring together the principles and the principals of the Civil War: territorial ambitions, slavery, and most of the future's famous generals.

Politically though, Mexico was the first major pre-1861 battle ending in southern defeat. Had the American flag remained flying over Chapultepec, or had it unfurled again a decade later when President James Buchanan urged, unsuccessfully, a U.S. protectorate over Mexico, an alternative chronicle of southern triumph might have begun. A new Caribbean empire, with a half dozen tropical states, could have ensured southern political domination in Washington and perpetuated slavery. What Mexico turned out to be instead was a chimera, a geopolitical illusion.

Not that Southerners of 1847, who wished to remain Americans, had much choice. Expansion of the United States into Mexico, the Caribbean, and Central America offered the South's only remaining geographic route to the necessary new slave states. Nothing less could maintain the implicit North-South compact struck in 1787. This backdrop was vital: As U.S. troops left a beaten, vulnerable Mexico in 1848, politics in the United States was divided at fifteen free states versus fifteen slave states.

National governance itself was chafing under an extraordinary and lengthy partial stalemate. The balance of power loosely agreed to in 1787 had been kept—and kept. The election of 1800 had taken place among eight free states and eight slave states. The presidential contest of 1820 was held amid a twelve-twelve division. A dozen were still on each side of the fence in 1832. By 1840, the split was thirteen versus thirteen (see Map 8.1).

Expansion-minded southern presidents stand as the essential architects of the closeness: George Washington thought first and foremost of Virginia, but Thomas Jefferson and his successors were more sectionally minded. Even in 1783, Jefferson had observed that "if a state be first laid off on the (Great) Lakes, it will add a vote to the Northern scale. If on the Ohio, it will add one to the Southern."[47] Southerners in Congress fought through the 1780s to block the admission of Vermont as a state until another could be brought in from the trans-Appalachian southwest—Kentucky, as it turned out.[48] The battle was already under way.

Hopeful Southerners of the 1790s assumed that the new Southwest—from Kentucky, Tennessee, and Alabama west to the Mississippi—would fill up faster than the Old Northwest, thereby tipping the national balance toward the slave interest. In addition, Jefferson's Louisiana Purchase of 1803 had, by 1848, yielded four new states. Three of them—Louisiana, Arkansas, and Missouri—allowed slavery. Just one, Iowa, prohibited it. Another acquisition, Florida, pacified by Andrew Jackson and purchased from Spain in

THE PRECARIOUS BALANCE:
Free States and Slave States,
1788–1848

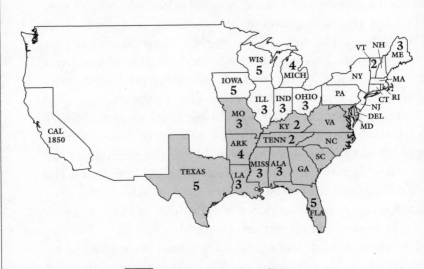

	1788, Free States (Original)
2	Free States Admitted, 1789–1800
3	Free States Admitted, 1801–1820
4	Free States Admitted, 1821–1840
5	Free States Admitted, 1841–1848

	1788, Slave States (Original)
2	Slave States Admitted, 1789–1800
3	Slave States Admitted, 1801–1820
4	Slave States Admitted, 1821–1840
5	Slave States Admitted, 1841–1848

MAP 8.1

1819 by James Monroe of Virginia, entered the Union in 1845 as a slave state. That same year saw President James K. Polk, a Tennessean, annex slave-owning Texas, the biggest of them all. Its entry into the Union had even produced a rare concession: Texas could divide into as many as five states with ten U.S. senators (although it was never seriously pursued). However, although these admissions kept the sectional balance in the Senate, rapid population growth in states like New York and Pennsylvania gave the North a growing edge in the House of Representatives.

Happy to go to war with Mexico in 1846 on thin pretense, Polk won a military triumph lopsided enough for the United States to buy for just $15 million two Mexican jurisdictions that could become states, California and New Mexico. Their square miles, added to those of Oregon and Texas, made Polk the president to have most enlarged U.S. territory. He would like to have added more: *all of Mexico*. However, opponents in Congress, including most Whigs and a minority of northern Democrats, were in a position to block any such move and its obvious objective: the admission of new slave states. Texas, in fact, would turn out to be the last. The House of Representatives had already framed the famous Wilmot Proviso, which insisted on barring slavery in any territory acquired from the Republic of Mexico.

For southern leaders looking due west from Charleston or Montgomery, the horizon was almost bare. California, despite a considerable southern population and sympathy, entered the Union as a free state in 1850. New Mexico, which adopted a slave code in 1859, was kept in territorial status until 1912. Mormon Utah, where pre-civil war slavery was uncommon but legal, stayed a territory until 1896. Pro-slavery forces lost Kansas in 1858. After California, the only new admissions of the 1850s were two other free states: Minnesota in 1858 and Oregon in 1859. Even Indiana, Illinois, and Iowa, free states but southern in their early settlement, tipped toward a more antislavery politics in the 1850s as Yankee settlers flooded west through the new railroad and canal systems.

Northern strategists, in turn, with transcontinental victory in sight, saw shutting the South's door to Mexico as mandatory. After California, Minnesota, and Oregon, only a few more territories were ripening for statehood: Kansas (finally admitted in 1861) and

345

Nebraska (1867). Colorado would not move up the ladder until 1876.

In short, the political mathematics worked out the same way on either side of the Mason-Dixon line. Should the South add Cuba and six to eight Mexican states to the slaveholding side, the North would be hard put to match them. *Without* Cuba and Mexico, though, the South was blocked—not simply checked, but *checkmated*. Thus, by 1859 and 1860, Southerners, not surprisingly, were also talking about pursuing Caribbean acquisitions as an independent nation. The Charleston *Mercury* assumed that "we shall have all of the Gulf Country once we have shaken ourselves free of the puritans."[49] This could have been true. A Confederacy allowed to secede in peace almost certainly would have added new tropical states.

As for Mexico, despite its abolition of slavery in 1829, the geography and climate were suitable. Some two hundred thousand black slaves had been brought into Mexico in the sixteenth and early seventeenth centuries, principally to work in the silver mines. Most were absorbed into the huge Indian population, for whom the end of slavery only produced a new, serflike status called peonage that continued well into the twentieth century.[50] The same plantation crops—sugar, cotton, cacao, and indigo—that required peons could have supported a slave economy, as Texans, Floridians, and Louisianians knew full well.

Following the peace treaty of Guadalupe-Hidalgo in 1848, the most obvious further U.S. acquisitions or purchases were along the border: five Mexican states that stretched from sparsely populated Baja (Lower) California in the west through Sonora, Chihuahua, and Nuevo Leon to the tropical lowlands of Tamaulipas in the east, across the Rio Grande from the Texas port of Brownsville. An American filibustering expedition led by William Walker briefly captured the Baja California capital of La Paz in 1853, but had to flee from a stronger military force in next-door Sonora. Yet Baja was a plausible objective. Seven years later, the Mexican political faction led by Benito Juarez would propose to trade Lower California for American recognition.[51]

Sonora and Chihuahua, across the Rio Grande from present-day Arizona, New Mexico, and West Texas, also seemed ripe to fall.

Small American filibustering expeditions into Sonora were commonplace in the 1850s, and President Buchanan himself, in two formal addresses (1857 and 1858), called for U.S. supremacy in the Gulf of Mexico and a U.S. protectorate over northern Mexico. Diplomats pursued the purchase of Lower California and the northern sections of Sonora and Chihuahua.[52] James Longstreet, the future Confederate general, was part of a plot to get Chihuahua to enter the Union as a slave state.[53]

To the east, the governor of Nuevo Leon, Santiago Vidaurri, not only negotiated with the Texans but in 1863 proposed that the Confederacy annex northern Mexico.[54] Cross-border plots were routine. Merchants and planters in Texas had provided backing a decade earlier for Mexican insurgents to create a new country, the Republic of Sierra Madre, in the hinterland of the state of Tamaulipas.[55] U.S. Senator Albert Gallatin Brown of Mississippi summed up his region's ambition: "I want Cuba, and I know that sooner or later we must have it. . . . I want Tamaulipas, Potosi and one or two other Mexican states; and I want them all for the same purpose—for the planting or spreading of slavery."[56]

Yucatan, the tropical southeastern Mexican peninsula that points toward New Orleans due north across the Gulf, was another target. Much of its commerce was with the Crescent City, and Polk at one point had asked Congress for authority to send U.S. troops into Yucatan.[57] This, too, was a purchase he had sought in 1848. Louisianans eyed Yucatan as Floridians did Cuba, their own Spanish-speaking neighbor. In Mississippi, Senator Jefferson Davis, calling the Gulf of Mexico a basin of water that belonged to the United States, declared himself in favor of taking Yucatan *and* Cuba.[58]

Cuba itself was the nineteenth-century St. Domingue, the last and greatest of the nouveau-riche sugar islands. Keeping it out of the hands of France or Britain had been a U.S. strategic imperative for half a century. Now Cuba's occupation also made increasing sense to guard the sea-lanes to any new U.S. canal across the Central American isthmus. But the slavery controversy was crippling. By 1859, Republicans in Congress were drawing two geopolitical lines in the sand: one against the acquisition of Cuba and the second against any U.S. protectorate over northern Mexico. Congressman Justin Morrill of Vermont spoke for many others in his party when he dismissed the protectorate plan as a device for increasing the number of slave-state senators.[59]

Fascination with Central America itself was short-lived and peripheral. William Walker, the filibustering Tennessean who had briefly captured Baja California, made an even bigger splash when he took over Nicaragua in 1855–1856. Immigrants from the United States were invited, and Walker boldly reestablished slavery. He was forced out of Nicaragua in 1857, but before that he became a southern hero, inspiring the expansionist Central American plank adopted by the Democratic National Convention of 1856.[60] Not that anything ever came of it.

Professor Robert E. May, in his book *The Southern Dream of a Caribbean Empire,* emphasizes these episodes' critical prewar timing.[61] It is hard not to agree: Mexico, Cuba, and the Caribbean, more vitally than Kansas and Nebraska, were the late 1850s battlegrounds on which Southerners would either secure new slave states or lose their national political leverage. Southern cynicism was warranted. Growing elements in the North were simply waiting to overturn the existing political and legal chessboard.

Looking back a century and a half later, the territories coveted by southern expansionists circa 1855—the deserts of Sonora, the steaming parrot-jungles of Yucatan, the cane fields and sixteenth-century *fortalezas* of Cuba—may seem too alien for Anglo-Saxon absorption. At the time, however, the U.S. frontier of two generations had been marching across what was once Spanish America, from the Castillo de San Marcos in St. Augustine to the former Spanish Pensacola, Spanish New Orleans, and Spanish St. Louis. Farther west, Texas, New Mexico, and California had been Spanish and then Mexican well into the nineteenth century. Even Colorado, when it became a state after the Civil War, included a considerable Spanish-speaking population. These were mostly in the valleys of the Conejos River, Rio Chama, and Morenos Creek, the northernmost tributaries of the Rio Grande, and in the great river's own headwaters, near present-day Alamosa. Spanish-speaking portions of the South's hoped-for Caribbean empire, still sparsely settled, could easily have been reacculturated. James Buchanan said as much while serving as secretary of state under

THE GOLDEN CIRCLE:
Southern Territorial Ambitions in Mexico, the Caribbean, and Central and South America, 1846–1860

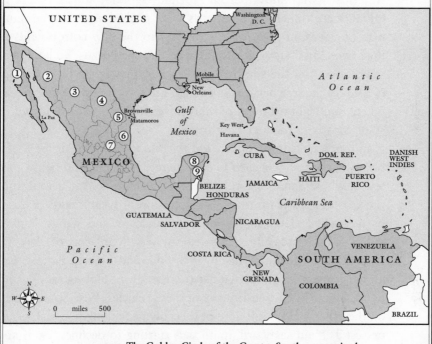

The Golden Circle of the Greater South as conceived by the Knights of the Golden Circle, 1855

The Mexican States proposed for purchase or annexation by U.S. politicians, 1845–1860

① Baja California
② Sonora
③ Chihuahua
④ Coahuila
⑤ Nuevo Leon
⑥ Tamaulipas
⑦ San Luis Potosí
⑧ Yucatan
⑨ Quintana Roo

MAP 8.2

Polk. If we annexed Cuba, "it would speedily be Americanized, as Louisiana had been."[62]

From 1801 to 1850, eight men southern-born and-raised occupied the presidency for forty-two years. The two Northerners—John Quincy Adams and Martin Van Buren—served a total of just eight years. Democratic presidents could and did turn expansionism into almost a religion. To clear a pathway westward, Native Americans were moved from Florida, Georgia, and Alabama to Oklahoma. Vulnerable Spaniards were pushed aside. Large numbers of slaves, in turn, were sent west to the new cotton fields of the lower Mississippi, the Red River, and the Brazos. So large was migration from the south Atlantic states that by 1850, about 40 percent of the free persons born in South Carolina were living elsewhere and eighty-three thousand slaves had also been sold out of state, mostly to the new Southwest.[63]

Chronology is important: *Until the disappointments of the Mexican War, the South seemed to be winning.* New England politicians, few of whose names we still remember, watched and criticized from the second-class platforms of a succession of weak major political parties—the Federalists, National Republicans, and Whigs. Yankee voters of the 1830s and 1840s also toyed with an array of ideological splinters: the Anti-Mason, Free Soil, and Liberty Parties. Regional leaders' protests against the rise of a "Slaveocracy" were handicapped by the inadequacy of these vehicles. Wise Southerners, on the other hand, took note of their own emerging political weaknesses: The old seaboard South was starting to decline; few if any new slave states were feasible within U.S. boundaries; and the last three presidents of the 1850s, Fillmore, Pierce, and Buchanan, were Northerners, albeit reasonably friendly ones.

Worries like these helped launch Dixie's figurative great expedition to the Gulf and Caribbean. By this time, manifest destiny—a term coined in 1850—was developing a tandem mythology below the Mason-Dixon line: the aristocratic South as the standard-bearer of racial expansion in the manner of the medieval Normans and seventeenth-century cavaliers. Southern spokesmen and writers, exaggerating both Virginia's tincture of seventeenth-century cavalier ancestry and South Carolina's partial shaping by Royalist emigrés from Barbados, wove a glorious tapestry. This depiction of a Royalist and cavalier past was grossly overstated, an American version of the romantic nationalism widespread in the nineteenth-century Europe of Wagner, Garibaldi, and Louis Napoleon. But like the European myths, it resonated, and by June 1860, on the threshold of war, the *Southern Literary Messenger* would proclaim that "the Southern people come of that race recognized as cavaliers ... directly descended from the Norman barons of William the Conqueror, a race distinguished in its early history for its warlike and fearless character, a race in all times since renowned for its gallantry, chivalry, honor, gentleness and intellect."[64] Such portraiture evoked a sense of glorious invincibility.

The true ancestry of the South, while distinctive from that of New England, had little to do with a quasi-Norman heritage borrowed from *Ivanhoe*. Even in Virginia, with its genuine strain of aristocratic emigrés, old families, and plantation culture reaching back to the reign of Charles I, the cavalier impress was relatively minor. Jeb Stuart, the Confederate cavalry general, wore golden spurs to burnish his image as *beau-sabreur* and knight-errant, but his particular Stuart ancestry was Presbyterian Scotch-Irish by way of Pennsylvania.[65] A part of Virginia's population was also descended from indentured servants and transported criminals. The principal research work on "White Servitude and Convict Labor in America, 1607–1776" notes that convicts were sent to Virginia and Maryland in such numbers that the two were described as practically penal colonies.[66] Even in Virginia, pedigree was a two-edged sword.

Still another interpretation of southern martial ethnicity, more plausible, emphasizes the region's ratios of Celtic Irish, Scotch-Irish, and Scots, along with English from the less sedate northern and western uplands. Yet if matching a Norman South against a Saxon North is genetically absurd, it is also an exaggeration to call the Civil War a conflict between a largely Celtic South and an Anglo-Saxon and Teutonic North, as have several twentieth-century historians.[67] In this framework, the southern infantry, with their wild Celtic yells, become the heirs of broadsword-swinging Highland clansmen and Irish woodkerns and gallowglasses, while the southern cavalry of Stuart, Mosby, and Forrest reincarnate the moss-troopers who pounded the moors and gorse on both sides of the Scottish border. Not quite.

Less romanticized and more easily documented is the greater imprint put on the South by frontiersmen and frontier military-mindedness—not just by Kentucky riflemen or the spirit of the Alamo but by more distant old-country antecedents. Dixie's British-sprung population included a higher ratio of forebears from the old English western and northern frontiers—the warfare-oriented "marches" or former counties Palatine—as well as from the eighteenth-century Celtic borderlands and mountain redoubts. We can think of these streams as the fighting Britons, in contrast to the urban, commercial, and seafaring English who dominated the eastern or Puritan states. The two regions' ethnicity was some-what different, and as accumulating folklore fed their mutual hostility, the psychological cleavage widened even further.

Whatever Virginia's claim to gentility, the lower Mississippi Valley was new and raw. The *Southern Literary Journal* acknowledged back in 1836 that "in the West (the South-Central states), money is everything. Its pursuit, accompanied as it is by baneful speculation, lawlessness, gambling, Sabbath-breaking, brawls and violence, prevents moral attainment and mental cultivation."[68] When first-generation cotton planters of the southern backcountry of the 1830s and 1840s imbibed the cavalier themes of Walter Scott or southern historical novelists, the nationalism that emerged was intense but shallow. Dixie's red clay gentry confused a William Walker in Nicaragua with a Norman baron or a Stuart cavalier.

In this imagined scheme of things, the South was not designing a territorial framework for the perpetuation of slavery, but beginning a great new Anglo-Saxon empire. Historian William R. Taylor, in his chronicle of the rival myths of *Cavalier and Yankee*, explains the driving impulse: "No explanation for the decline of the seaboard South had greater and more sustained appeal than the idea of a dynamic, expanding South, racially and culturally homogenous, spreading across the mountains and out toward the fertile Mississippi Delta and extending itself onto Mexico and even down into the tropics. . . . Nowhere were Americans so willing to fight, live and die for the idea than in the Southern states."[69]

In 1841, William Caruthers, a prime mythmaker, published a novel, *The Knights of the Horseshoe,* about a southern organization devoted to westward expansion that adopted a golden horse-shoe as its emblem. A decade later, George Bickley, a Virginia-born magazine editor, brought the idea to life as the Knights of the Golden Circle. His "golden circle" centered on Cuba, and included most of the border states, the South, Mexico, Central America, the West Indies, and part of South America. Bickley called his Texas chapters "castles" and his Maryland-based newspaper *The American Cavalier.*[70] This southern taste for plumed cavaliers and knights lived on even after the collapse of Appomattox; the hooded riders who sought to rescue the post–Civil War South from the political clutches of freed slaves and Yankee scalawags also styled themselves Knights—of the Ku Klux Klan.

In the 1850s, Yankees and slavery advocates, moving closer to war, each drew on their British revolutionary heritage for much more than Norman-Saxon analogies and Cavalier-Roundhead caricatures. Each side, in its own sectional cause, cited the cavalcade of English-speaking defenses of liberty that reached from the 1640s to Bunker Hill and Cowpens. Each side also pictured its most important concepts of liberty as foully endangered. Tyrants were at work—elected ones, to be sure, rather than hereditary. Pym, Hampden, and Cromwell had feared conspiracies between the King and the Irish or the Pope. Washington, Adams, and Jefferson had seen them among London tyrants, royal ministers, bishops, and tobacco merchants.

Yankees and Southerners of the decade leading to the Civil War, however, identified the hostile plotting and the threat to the republic with especially familiar conspirators: *each other.* By 1860, there were no geographic escape hatches left, just political and military ones.

Puritan New England and Its Slowly Reawakening "God of Warr"

Southerners, in fact, were not the new republic's first secessionists. Those first threats and murmurings—in 1804, 1808, and 1814— came from Yankees who stole half a century's rhetorical march on Jefferson Davis. In 1804, under the leadership of Massachusetts senator Timothy Pickering, they considered establishing a northern Confederacy to include the New England states, New York, and New Jersey. Daniel Webster, in later years, would be embarrassed by the possible secession and civil war he had discussed as an eager young New England Federalist.

Souring New England politics and deteriorating prospects were to blame. The nineteenth century had opened with the nation's capital moving below the Mason-Dixon, population spreading over the mountains, and the presidency passing to Jefferson's hands. All three made Yankees testy. New Englanders found themselves confronting loss of control over the national government, not just for a few years but for the foreseeable future. Their post-1783 political vehicle, Federalism, had broken down. The archconservative "High Federalists" of Massachusetts, the famous Essex Junto, retreated into a shrill regional politics with strong elitist, pro-British, antifrontier, and anti-southern overtones.[71] If the new western states didn't leave to form their own republic, as some Yankee plotters surmised, and if southern overrepresentation in Washington couldn't be trimmed, then New England might have to form its own federation. John Adams and his associates had also thought that might be necessary for a while back in early 1776.

So open was this regional pique in 1810 that Lord Liverpool, the British foreign secretary, predicted that if no material change occurred in the U.S. government, "the result will probably be, the Separation of the Eastern from the Southern states."[72] Jefferson in 1813 wrote to Adams about his fear that the rivalry between Massachusetts and Virginia had the makings of "a civil war, a La Vendée."[73] Even in 1820, President James Monroe believed that Senator Rufus King of New York, one of the last Federalists, aspired to lead a confederation of that state and New England.[74]

The slavery-related sectionalism visible during the Revolution and in drafting the Articles of Confederation was only a prelude to what followed the 1787 implantation of the three-fifths clause in the Constitution, which counted that portion of the slaves in determining southern representation in Congress. Independence itself, as we have seen, was what gave sectionalism its vituperative federal framework. The plantation colonies of 1765 or 1770 had no need to worry about London banning slavery. The plantation states of 1787, however, had good reason to worry about the politics of the nonslave states. New Englanders and New Yorkers, for their part, feared that the southern states would block the new federal powers needed to uphold maritime and commercial interests. Each section could squeeze the other in ways impossible when they had been fellow British colonials.

New England politicians were content in the 1790s because the North had won the early financial and commercial battles. Congressional support for Alexander Hamilton's debt program of 1791 divided along regional lines. On the issue of the federal government assuming state Revolutionary War debts, northern members of the House voted yes by twenty-four to nine while their southern colleagues voted no by eighteen to ten. On the related question of a national bank, northern members favored it by thirty-three to one and those from the South were opposed by nineteen to six.[75] The regional bias of subsequent payments justified the politics. Of the $1.2 million laid out by the government in 1795, almost two-fifths went to the four New England states; Massachusetts alone received more than all of the states south of the Potomac.[76] Support for the controversial Jay Treaty of 1794 with Britain, principally on trade, debt, and boundary matters, followed the same Federalist geography.

Jefferson's defeat of Adams in 1800 turned the tide in favor of southern and western economics. The national debt reduction of 1802 was one signal, followed by the counterproductive Embargo Act of 1807, which crippled New England commerce by confining American vessels to port in a fatuous protest against English and French abuses of U.S. shipping. The Jeffersonians again shook the pillars of northern finance in 1811 by refusing to extend Hamilton's First Bank of the United States.

The "North" of the 1780s was a fuzzy entity. The four New England colonies of Massachusetts, Connecticut, New Hampshire, and Rhode Island had been called "Eastern" because of their Atlantic-thrusting location. "Eastern States" they remained until well into the nineteenth century. But under whatever name, this was the arch-sectional counterforce to the South: New England or what it would become by the 1850s—*Greater New England.*

These were the districts and townships settled by people from Massachusetts, Connecticut, Vermont, New Hampshire, and Maine that spread across New York and the northern tier of Pennsylvania into the Great Lakes region. Back in 1775, "Little New Englands" in New York, New Jersey, and even Georgia had been the most stalwart pro-independence districts in their respective states. The pre-Civil War period, in turn, would produce a similar display: Little New Englands from New York to Minnesota emerging as the strongest antislavery, free-soil, and then pro-Republican districts.

But to return to the early part of the nineteenth century, once the twelve years of Federalist rule under Washington and Adams came to an end, New England, with its commercial and antislavery biases, lost its national power. The surge of Puritan and neo-Puritan political potency that had characterized the years leading up to the 1640s and 1770s was nowhere to be seen—and with great significance.

Not that Federalism gasped an immediate last breath. Faithful to New England in 1814 and 1815, the party received considerable local loyalty in return. In New Jersey, Federalism was alive enough in 1819 to hold what was probably the first meeting held in the nation to oppose the extension of slavery into Missouri. Several dozen congressmen and senators held on in the 1820s amid the disarray of the national party system. The nineteenth Congress that served from 1825 to 1827 still included five House members with Federalist labels and five Federalist senators—two from Massachusetts, two from Tory Delaware, and Rufus King from New York. The last Federalists from Rhode Island, Connecticut, and Vermont, however, had retired from the Senate in 1821. The last from New Hampshire had left in 1817. Despite a famous senator, Daniel Webster, and two single-term presidents of the United States, John Quincy Adams (1825–1829) and Franklin Pierce (1853–1857), New England took thirty years to find a new strong political voice in the Republican Party.

In virtually every other field, the New England of the 1820s, 1830s, and 1840s witnessed a social and religious mobilization or, in art and literature, what Van Wyck Brooks called a regional flowering. But not in politics. Besides Federalism's cultural and constituency failings, its narrow countinghouse conservatism, by embracing theories of states' rights, nullification and interposition, and possible secession up through 1815, diminished Yankee credentials to rebut the kindred southern threats and arguments voiced after 1828. With the Whigs sectionally divided, no suitable national political vehicle would arrive for another generation. By that time, however, yet another great religious awakening had provided a party agenda. New England's intertwined religious and civic ambitions—Yankees believed that government's principal purpose was moral—would help to shape not just the Republican Party but the coming of war.

Can it be an accident, a coincidence, that each of these three wars has followed a Protestant religious revival powerful enough to pump fervor into gathering ideological abstractions? Probably not. The rise of Puritanism in the late sixteenth and seventeenth centuries did much to set the scene for the English Civil War. The First Great Awakening in the mid-eighteenth century helped to stir the American Revolution from hundreds of pulpits. The Second Great Awakening of the nineteenth century helped to seed the American Civil War. None of these conflicts developed overnight. Each time, three or four decades of rising religious excitement and political contention were necessary to beat plowshares and candlesticks back into swords.

The first two surges drew their greatest response in Puritan and Presbyterian areas. The Second Great Awakening, which one New England historian has usefully called the Third Puritanism, arguably concentrated its greatest political and mobilization effects in New England during the first third of the nineteenth century.[77] Far more attuned than the First Great Awakening to social reform and moral perfection, the Second became, in the words of Vernon Parrington, "quite as much the golden age of the New England conscience as of the New England mind."[78] The perfectibility-of-man creed of the 1830s—father of a dozen "isms" from utopianism to abolitionism—traced back to "the old millennial spirits, the Diggers and Levellers of Commonweath times."[79]

While southern pamphleteers and novelists called up the memory of Norman barons and ostrich-plumed Cavaliers, a bemused Ralph Waldo Emerson catalogued Boston's Chardon Street Convention of 1840, an activists' gathering, as follows: "Madmen, madwomen, men with beards, Dunkards, Muggletonians, Comeouters, Groaners, Agrarians, Seventh-Day Baptists, Quakers, Abolitionists, Calvinists, Unitarians, Philosophers—all came successively to the top, and seized their moment, if not their hour . . ."[80]

It was all too familiar. For a seventeenth-century forerunner, one need only consult the chronicles of the 1640s with their own descriptions of Adamites, Anabaptists, Diggers, Familists, Grindletonians, Levellers, Muggletonians, Quakers, and Ranters.[81] But the analogy is not complete. The New England of the 1830s and 1840s, after two centuries of de facto and then de jure self-government, was a culture of proven achievement, a polity in the process of putting its stamp on much of the northern half of the United States. And so, as the Yankee exodus of the two pre–Civil War decades moved into northern Illinois, Michigan, Iowa, Wisconsin, and Minnesota, its message was of achievable, if still provocative, social reform. Notwithstanding southern innuendo, cranks were rarely in charge.

In contrast to the First Great Awakening of the mid-eighteenth century, sternly focused on the First Commandment, the mood of the Second in the Yankee states and regions has been described as Second Commandment Christianity, concerned with loving (or *improving*) thy neighbor. Between 1805 and 1845, many of the most famous colleges of New England—Yale, Dartmouth, Amherst, and Williams—set aside turn-of-the-century Jacobinism and atheism for religious revivals, albeit reasonably sedate ones. Yale alone had fifteen.[82] The new Puritanism soon took itself beyond missionary societies and Bible distribution into social causes. The United States, like the England of Charles I, was to be made over in God's image.

Education was a prominent emphasis, from expanding public elementary schools to founding scores of new colleges. Drunkenness and alcohol became targets. The Massachusetts Society for the Suppression of Intemperance began in 1813; the American Society for the Promotion of Temperance followed in 1826 and the American Temperance Union in 1836. In those early years, antislavery drew less attention than strict keeping of the Sabbath. And temperance applied to food as well as drink. Larger towns even had a "Female Retrenchment Society" to defend women against the temptations of "tea, coffee, rich cake, pastry, preserves, snuff and tobacco, as well as wine and cordials."[83] Women's rights cohered as an issue in the 1830s, then swelled in the 1840s under the leadership of activists born in New England or upstate New York like Lucy Stone, Susan B. Anthony, Lucretia Mott, and Elizabeth Cady Stanton.

Utopianism was yet another Yankee predilection. Some of it had a philosophical component—Brook Farm, for example, and the Oneida Community founded by perfectionist John Humphrey Noyes. Some was almost comic, including the "Pilgrims," three hundred strong, who gathered in Woodstock, Vermont, wore long beards and bearskin girdles, fasted in sackcloth and ashes, foreswore bathing, practiced free love, and assumed divine inspiration for everyone.[84] Southern "cavaliers" reacted as contemptuously to the Third Puritanism as the Cavaliers of the 1640s had to the First. The diocesan publications of the Catholic Church were just as scoffing.

Even Yankee disapproval of the War of 1812 was institutionalized by the founding of the Massachusetts Peace Society in 1815. This sought to replace fear of lost markets and captured ships with a larger philosophy of rejecting war because man was made for loftier purposes. New England's flourishing peace movement encouraged it to become the center of opposition to a *second* conflict: the war with Mexico in 1846–1847.

Few causes or reforms went unpursued. Committed Yankee radicals tended to be involved not just in one or two but three or four. From Maine to Minnesota, temperance, Sabbatarianism, women's rights, and antislavery themes all spread with the Yankee population, taking root. Then, by the late 1840s, these themes began to burst from pulpits, colleges, and town meetings into local elections, state legislatures, and national party platforms. By the early 1850s, antislavery, in particular, would help to destroy a Democratic-Whig party system which, it turned out, no longer enjoyed public confidence. Something new, something bolder, was in order.

Religion and morality also shaded into paranoia, another old inheritance. Fear of the southern "Slaveocracy" was just the beginning. The ethnic homogeneity of the New England states, whetted by their Puritan legacy of fearing conspiratorial elites, put them in the forefront of nineteenth-century agitation against secret orders like the Bavarian Illuminati and Masons and the threat posed by foreign immigrants and the Pope, Protestantism's ever-present

"Romish Cabal" against freedom and liberty. Thus, in the three decades between the final collapse of Federalism in the mid–1820s and the organization of the Republican Party, New England led the nation in support of *two* kinds of single-issue politics. The first, more goal-oriented, was exemplified by the temperance movement and the Liberty and Free Soil Parties. The second, more anticonspiratorial, included the Anti-Mason, Native American, and American (Know-Nothing) Parties. Figure 8.1 illustrates the Yankee proclivity to support splinter parties. From 1840 to 1852, New England was usually the region strongest for Whig presidential candidates, given their support of creditor economics, religion, education, and civic virtue. However, the simultaneous Whig focus on the upper south, especially Kentucky and Tennessee, and the extent to which the mercantile bias of Whiggery straddled the "ism" issues gave minor parties opportunity after opportunity in New England, reducing Whig percentages.

The politics of commerce and the politics of moral righteousness eventually fused, in tried and true Puritan style, with the emergence of the Republican Party. Between 1854 and 1856, it cobbled together a coalition of all the politically potent Yankee "isms"—anti-Masonism, temperance, anti-Catholicism, muted nativism, and free-soil sentiment mixed with abolitionism. As we will see, some of these attracted voters. Others repelled the electorate and were hushed. On the presidential level, what stands out is how the 33 percent of the national vote compiled in 1856 by the new party's first nominee, John C. Frémont, followed the map of greater New England from Machias and Cape Cod west to Wisconsin and Iowa, maximizing along a trail of townships and counties named for Vermont birthplaces, Connecticut politicians, and dead Massachusetts Revolutionary War generals.

The six additional percentage points of more moderate backing that Abraham Lincoln managed to add in 1860, mostly from non-Yankees, gave him essential victories in Illinois, Indiana, and Pennsylvania—and the election. However, Southerners were not wrong in assuming that the new national politics in motion was essentially the vehicle of their old New England foe. Constituencies named Middlesex, Hartford, Suffolk, Norfolk, and Essex were again on the march. The point is this: The cultural divisions and

FIGURE 8.1 New England as the Center of Splinter Party Support in U.S. Presidential Elections (1828–1852) and New England Importance to the National Republicans in 1828 and the Whigs in 1840–1852

1828	Top 5 states supporting John Quincy Adams (National Republican) in a two-way presidential reace	R.I.—77%, Mass.—76% Vt.—74%, Ct.—71%, Me.—60%
1832	Top 5 states supporting William Wirt, Anti-Masonic candidate for president, in a three-way race	Pa.—42%, Vt.—41%, Mass.—22%, R.I.—14%, Conn.—10%
1840	Top 5 states supporting James Birney, Liberty Party nominee for president, in a three-way race	N.H.—1.5%, Mass.—1.3%, Vt.—0.6%, N.Y.—0.6%, Ohio—0.3%
1844	Top 5 states supporting James Birney, Liberty Party nominee for president, in a three-way race	N.H.—8.5%, Mass.—8.2%, Vt—8.1%, Mich.—6.6%, Me.—5.7%
1848	Top 5 states supporting Martin Van Buren, Free Soil nominee for president, in a three-way race	Vt.—29%, Mass.—29%, Wis.—26%, N.Y.—26%, Mich.—16%
1852	Top 5 states supporting John Hale, Free Soil nominee for president, in a three-way race	Mass.—22%, Vt.—20%, Wis.—14%, N.H.—13%, Me.—10%

Source: *Congressional Quarterly, Guide to U.S. elections*

Overall, New England's strongly regional politics behind Adams in 1824 and 1828 suggested a desire for a New England-dominated party, but the transient National Republican party did not survive. And the Whig Party was not New England-dominated. The presidential nominees between 1836 and 1852 were born and raised in slave states. As the data below show, New England usually provided the best Whig states between 1840 and 1852. However, the heaviest-in-the nation splinter party support shown above reduced the region's Whig presidential backing.

1840–1852: Top Five States Ranked by Margin of Victory

1840	1844	1848	1852
Vermont—28 points	R. Island—20 points	R. Island—28 points	Vermont—21 points
Kentucky—28 points	Vermont—18 points	Vermont—25 points	Mass.—6 points
R. Island—23 points	Mass.—11 points	New York—23 points	Kentucky—3 points
Louisiana—19 points	Kentucky—8 points	Mass.—19 points	Tenn.—1 point
Mass.—16 points	Conn.—5 points	Kentucky—15 points	Delaware—0 points

sectionalism that dominated the American Civil War, already in place by the War for American Independence and intensified by the events of 1775–1783 and the Constitution of 1787, were now about to come to a boil within the new framework that independence had created.

Even more significantly, by 1860 and 1861, the South—in its cotton-chivalric reincarnation of Norman barons and Stuart cavaliers—confronted a Greater New England that had pushed aside the peace-mindedness of 1815 and 1846. Politicians and preachers alike were rediscovering the Lord of Hosts who had guided and blessed their Puritan forebears at Naseby, Bunker Hill, and Saratoga. In Massachusetts, Walt Whitman wrote of drums beating and warlike America rising. Charles Eliot Norton called the cause "a religious war. . . . a man must carry with him the assurance that he is acting in the immediate presence and as the commissioned soldier of God." Oliver Wendell Holmes penned the "Army Hymn," described as "a fervent appeal to the Puritan God of battles," and even Quaker poet John Greenleaf Whittier penned a new version of *"Ein feste Burg ist unser Gott."*[85]

Opposition to slavery was only part of a larger fervor and mobilization. Broader national destinies were also buckling on old, familiar sword belts. Where Federalists had sulked and commercial Whigs had cowered, the new Republican Party shipped cases of "Beecher's Bibles." In place of blue lights for frigates of the Royal Navy, Massachusetts Peace Association agendas, and drawing-room grumbles over the invasion of Mexico, New England had found another "God of Warr."

9

THE FINAL
COUSINS' FIGHT
Causes and Origins of the
American Civil War

*The situation of England in 1642 is curiously paralleled by that of the
United States at the opening of the Civil War. The American North, like
the English Parliament, had behind it the more populous regions and
by far the greatest wealth. It had the fleet and could command the seas.
It had the largest cities and the chief industries. The South had a
smaller population, but it had a society of country dwellers who could
ride and shoot, and were consequently better adapted at the start for
the business of war. It was a trial of physical strength, a submission of
two irreconcilable faiths to ordeal by battle.*

—John Buchan, *Oliver Cromwell*, 1934

*Those who think that (the coming collision) is accidental, unnecessary,
the work of interested or fanatical agitators, and therefore ephemeral,
mistake the case altogether. It is an irrepressible conflict, between opposing and enduring forces, and it means that the United States must
and will, sooner or later, become either entirely a slave-holding nation
or entirely a free-labor nation.*

—William H. Seward, 1858

THE EXTRAORDINARY PARALLELS between the English and
American Civil Wars, which deepen with examination, illuminate
the importance of both conflicts among the great shaping forces of
Anglo-American history. The Puritan and moral banners, the clash of
irreconcilable faiths, the inevitable auxiliaries of commerce and English-

speaking destiny, all were related. Over three centuries, much the same battle, for separate but kindred national futures, had to be fought *twice*.

On one side, in each war, were the constituencies of commerce, industry, the maritime sector, the centers of immigration, the principal cities, reformist evangelical religion, and the proselytizing middle class. On the other side was landed agriculture, with its feudal remnants and servitude, its hierarchical and liturgical religion, and its greater ratios of horsemen, soldiers, and cavaliers. At a certain point in each nation's history, it was a necessity—perhaps it was also destiny—for the former to push aside the latter.

The outbreak of each war, however, was confused by unexpected clashes, proposals for compromise, and the would-be neutralism of important regions and communities. In 1860 and 1861, this uncertainty and reluctance was especially strong along *both* sides of the Mason-Dixon line and its de facto extension, the Ohio River. Residents along this border area distrusted the sectional and ideological extremes at work in New England and the Cotton South, much like Englishmen in the earlier "border" of the 1640s that had run through Berkshire, Wiltshire, and Dorset had distrusted the extremes of Puritan East Anglia and the Cavalier North and West.

Far from spoiling for a sectional clash in 1860–1861, much of southern and eastern Pennsylvania, the bulk of New Jersey, and New York's lower Hudson Valley were skeptical of abolitionists, the emerging Republican Party, and Abraham Lincoln. Coercing the South was initially unpopular. Similiar doubts pervaded the lower sections of Ohio, Indiana, and Illinois.

Below the Mason-Dixon line, the Upper South and Border, with their lesser slave ratios, opposed joining the cotton confederation even in early 1861. Four of these states—Virginia, North Carolina, Tennessee, and Arkansas—left the Union only in late spring after Lincoln called the North to arms. Four more (Delaware, Maryland, Kentucky, and Missouri) never did exit. Together, the Lower North, Upper South, and Border counted off half of the U.S. states and two-thirds of the population—a true Middle America. Consciousness of this "in-between" status even generated brief talk of the middle and border states forming a separate confederation of their own.

FIGURE 9.1 The Threads of the Cousins' Wars (II): The Parallels Between the English and U.S. Civil Wars

Beyond the larger threads of the three cousins' wars set out in chapter 5, the English and U.S. Civil Wars show surprising parallels—and not just in the Cavalier versus Roundhead caricatures that began in the first and were often repeated in the second. Here is a capsule of the points already made and those that chapter 9 develops.

	English Civil War	U.S. Civil War
National Evolutionary Role	Transition from agriculture to commerce and industry and away from semifeudal monarchy toward nation-state	Transition from agriculture to commerce and industry and away from loose confederation toward nation-state
Core Regions	Cavaliers with Celtic allies versus Puritan England centered in the East and East Anglia	Cavaliers with southern Celtic stock allies and, in the North, Irish sympathizers versus Yankee Greater New England
Religious Divisions	High Church liturgical and confessional religions with bishops against antibishop Low-Church Anglicans, Independents (Congregationalists), Presbyterians, and Sectaries	Southern Episcopal elites from old Anglican states (like South Carolina and Virginia) and antireform Baptist followers versus Greater New England Congregationalists, Presbyterians, and Unitarians, with liturgical churches not opposed to slavery (Catholic and some Lutheran) ambivalent
Commercial and Economic Divisions	Manor agriculture and royal monopolies versus entrepreneurs, cottage industry, small industrialists, and most financiers	Plantation agriculture and its regional economic allies versus northern yeoman farmers, small industrialists, and emerging capitalists, with ambivalence among established manufacturers and merchants (from cotton textiles to carriages) selling to southern markets.
Maritime and Naval Divisions	Most ship-owners favored the side of Parliament and the Puritans, and most of the navy was in their hands.	Seaborne commerce and the navy were lopsidedly on the Federal side.
Social Divisions	The King had two-thirds of the nobility and gentry, many of their tenants, and the rootless poor ready to enlist in the army; Parliament had majorities among the townspeople, artisans, the middling sort, and the small landholders. The caricature was of gentlemen versus clerks, Cavaliers versus Roundheads.	The plantation-owning southern aristocracy and would-be aristocracy was at the heart of Confederate support when the war began; the middling sort—the yeomen, artisans, and small businessmen—were the stalwarts of Lincoln support in the North. The southern gentry made jokes not unlike those of the Cavaliers two centuries earlier.

These, then, are the suspicions, reluctance, and dissent that identify the cross-pressured and therefore pivotal loyalties of 1861–1865. Although politically and militarily, the Lower North and Upper South were the principal battlegrounds, the deeper antecedents of the war, as we have seen, lay in the northern and southern polar regions. For three generations, New England and the Deep South had been contesting over slavery, finance, and commerce, demeaning each other's culture, sending huge migrations westward, and plotting territorial expansions to give their side more new states, more representation in Washington, and thus greater national power. Yankees, although opposed to wars to extend slavery southward and westward, were missionary in their own westward settlement, and in 1863, one evangelical journal, looking back, called the 1830–1860 competition a second Thirty Years War.[1]

The poles of this clash between the Second Cavaliers and the Third Puritans have just been set out. This chapter will pursue its nature—the seeming "irrepressibility" of a cultural and political rivalry with older and deeper roots than mere North American sectionalism.

South Carolina, to begin with, was not just a single state but the cultural hearth and political fount of the Deep South, with Caribbean-influenced origins. By the firing on Fort Sumter, its role in U.S. history dated back two centuries. It was no coincidence that the newer cotton states, from Alabama and Mississippi west through Louisiana and Texas, were an agricultural and psychological extension of the lowland Carolinas and Georgia. Six years before Eli Whitney's invention of the cotton gin, delegates to the Constitutional Convention in 1787 had been struck by the three states' expansionary mood and confidence: "It has been said," noted Gouverneur Morris of New York, "that N.C., S.C. and Georgia only will in a little time have a majority of the people in America."[2]

New England's own ambitions, infused as we have seen by the God of the Puritans, went back to the seventeenth century. Massachusetts Bay was scarcely planted before it confederated with Plymouth, extended jurisdiction over the Maine district, and eyed New Hampshire. Connecticut, after peopling eastern Long Island and part of East Jersey in the 1600s, was busy settling northeast

Pennsylvania, Vermont, and even the banks of the Mississippi by the Revolution. The Yankee tide that later rolled through New York and westward was also an old and proselytizing one, called to duty seven generations earlier from now-distant English pulpits.

Map 9.1 divides the political nation of 1860 two ways. The sectional portrait in the first is state-based and simple: the North, the Cotton Belt, and the Border and Upper South. These are the frameworks used for this chapter's analyses of political loyalty and wartime choice. But because cultural divisions follow roads, rivers, and canals, not state lines, and because the southern portions of Illinois, Indiana, and Ohio were border-state in character, the map also jumps political boundaries for a different four-way dissection: Greater New England, the Lower North, the Upper South and Border, and the Cotton Belt. This chapter draws upon both terminologies.

The "in-between" Civil War politics in the Lower North and Upper South mirrors what were also "in-between" settlement patterns and origins. Chapter 5 has described how in the three decades before the American Revolution, Pennsylvania Scotch-Irish and Germans had poured down the Great Valley into Virginia and the Carolinas. Other, later generations of Middle Atlantic stock, including the New York and New Jersey Dutch, departed directly from Pennsylvania, New Jersey, and lower (non-Yankee) New York and migrated into the midsections of Ohio, Indiana, Illinois, and beyond. When their sons and daughters reached Iowa and the northern tier of Missouri in the 1840s and 1850s, they often gave Ohio or Indiana as their state of origin. But many could be described appropriately enough as Greater Pennsylvanians, given the state's late eighteenth-century centrality to so much of Presbyterian, Quaker, Amish, Mennonite, and German Lutheran and Reformed religion and culture. Map 10.6, in the next chapter, illustrates this somewhat confusing cultural hearth role of Pennsylvania.

Meanwhile, many southern descendants of those early Pennsylvania emigrants joined fellow Virginians and Carolinians in the early nineteenth-century trans-Appalachian movement that filled in much of Tennessee, Kentucky, Arkansas, and Missouri. Parts of these states, like sections of the southern piedmont, took on a "Greater Pennsylvania" feel. Neither of the major Pennsylvania-linked cul-

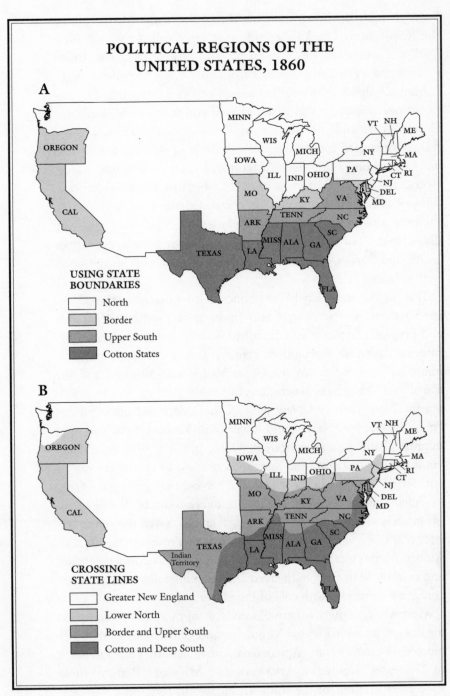

POLITICAL REGIONS OF THE
UNITED STATES, 1860

A

MINN
WIS
IOWA
MICH
ILL   IND   OHIO
MO   KY
ARK   TENN
MISS   ALA
TEXAS   LA
OREGON
CAL
VT   NH
ME
NY
MA
PA
CT   RI
NJ
DEL
MD
VA
NC
SC
GA
FLA

**USING STATE
BOUNDARIES**

- ☐ North
- ☐ Border
- ☐ Upper South
- ☐ Cotton States

B

MINN
WIS
IOWA
MICH
ILL   IND   OHIO
MO   KY
ARK   TENN
MISS   ALA
TEXAS   LA
Indian
Territory
OREGON
CAL
VT   NH
ME
NY
MA
PA
RI
CT
NJ
DEL
MD
VA
NC
SC
GA
FLA

**CROSSING
STATE LINES**

- ☐ Greater New England
- ☐ Lower North
- ☐ Border and Upper South
- ☐ Cotton and Deep South

MAP 9.1

tural streams, Middle Atlantic or Appalachian, was in the forefront of either pro-slavery or antislavery agitation. In general, settlers from this background added to the mixed views and hesitation of the Lower North and Upper South.

The cultural streams of the estate-country and tidewater eastern section of Virginia—as opposed to those of upcountry or Appalachian antecedents—were surprisingly unimportant elsewhere beyond Virginia in the events of 1860–1861. This is because the two most conspicuous cultural transplants, the Virginian-settled horse country of the Kentucky bluegrass and Missouri's northeastern "Little Dixie," each led the secessionist cause in their respective border states and each failed because the two states were too divided. Kentucky and Missouri remained in the Union.

As early as the seventeen-nineties, James Madison had cannily predicted that Pennsylvania's eventual choice between the sections would be critical.[3] After being solidly Democratic in 1856, and trying to maintain good relations with the South through 1859, Pennsylvania wound up endorsing Lincoln by a wide margin in 1860. In contrast, Virginians, all but ignoring the Republican nominee in 1860, had opposed secession at their state convention in early April 1861. Yet on April 17, two days after Lincoln's call for troops, a second Virginia convention, irate, voted to go with the rest of the South. Scotch-Irish Rockbridge County, in the Shenandoah Valley, seat of Virginia Military Academy, had opposed earlier secession calls. In May's statewide popular vote to ratify secession, Rockbridge voters blew a bold bugle: 1,728 favored secession, 1 opposed.[4]

The line between Virginia and Pennsylvania was finally being drawn, figuratively and politically. To ink it culturally and geographically would have been more difficult. Western Virginia was as mountainous as Pennsylvania. The Blue Ridge of the former became the Blue Mountains of the latter with barely a gap. Virginia, not Pennsylvania, was the state that as late as 1784 laid claim to Ohio, Indiana, Illinois, Michigan, and Wisconsin and during the Revolution had sent George Rogers Clark west to Vincennes and Kaskaskia to drive out the British. Together, Virginia and Pennsylvania had parented a half dozen nearby states, with some claim to more. The Old Dominion, by itself, had almost as much industry as the cotton states combined.

Yet at Virginia's heart, where English settlement began in 1607, was North America's oldest plantation and manor culture—the showplace of James River Valley English Renaissance architecture, Georgian brickwork, and boxwood maze-gardens that stretches fifty miles from Carter's Grove to Shirley Plantation, still trim and southern to the core. Above the Mason-Dixon line, by contrast, Pennsylvania was becoming the nation's Workshop of Vulcan—the Western Hemisphere counterpart to the coal and iron districts of the British midlands.

For Pennsylvania in 1861 to wind up allied with New England and at war with next-door Virginia was a historic milestone. Many old Pennsylvania Democrats, allies of southern presidents and politicians—and almost as many Philadelphia merchants and manufacturers—were appalled. Only in January, U.S. Senator William Bigler, a close ally of James Buchanan, the southern-allied Democrat about to leave the White House, had declared in a Senate speech urging compromise that "Pennsylvania will never become the enemy of Virginia. Pennsylvania will never draw its sword on Virginia."[5] What happened was somewhat like the process, two centuries earlier, whereby metalworking Birmingham and mine-tunneled Derbyshire joined distant but commercial neo-Puritan East Anglia, winding up at war with the nearby Royalist manor lords of a still late-medieval Cheshire, Shropshire, and Worcestershire. The coupling of steel and railroads with far-off neo-Puritan countinghouses and New England maritime interests was just as new to nineteenth-century U.S. politics. From 1800 through 1856, Pennsylvania and Virginia had voted for the same party in each presidential election save two. That relationship would not exist again. Like the earlier English alignment of sword-makers, weavers, and Puritan sea captains, the Pennsylvania–New England alliance presaged a different national future.

Even among Pennsylvanians, few today can name the state's own fine eighteenth-century colonial mansions—Pennsbury Manor, Graeme Park, Hope Lodge, and others. The sooty caricature of Pennsylvania still prevalent is the one created by the war boom of the 1860s: the world's first successful oil well in Venango County, the endless seams of hard black anthracite, the open hearth furnaces around Pittsburgh, and the crowded railroad yards of Reading and Altoona. To the adolescent United States, the war of 1861 to 1865 was what the first cousins' war was to a still-immature seventeenth-century England—the beginning of a major reshaping of old political and economic relationships into the more mature arrangements of an emerging world power.

Toward this end, the four years of warfare between April 1861 and April 1865—the events from Fort Sumter and the First Bull Run through the carnage at Antietam in 1862, the decisive Union triumphs at Vicksburg and Gettysburg in 1863, and then the final northern victories in the South that led to Robert E. Lee's unconditional surrender on that spring day at Appomattox—served much the same historical purpose for the American republic that had been served in England by the four years from the battle of Edgehill in 1642 to the final collapse of Royalist support with the surrender of Oxford to Parliament in the summer of 1646.

Yankees and Southerners: An Irrepressible Conflict?

The Lower North had enough doubters to come close to giving up early in 1863, and then to pause again in the uncertain summer of 1864. But in looking for the war's origins—in measuring irrepressibility and the intensity of wartime and political alignments—Greater New England and the cotton states remain the cockpits.

As we have seen, several scholars have tried to take the underlying sectional polarizations of 1861 back to the cultural and ethnic divisions of the seventeenth-century British Isles. C. Vann Woodward, in a similar pursuit, has added his voice to Max Weber's on how "the early history of the North American colonies is dominated by the sharp contrast of the adventurers, who wanted to set up plantations with the labour of indentured servants, and live as feudal lords, and the specifically middle-class outlook of the Puritans."[6]

This contrast already mattered in 1774 and 1775. During the Continental Congresses of those years, Southerners suspected the New England delegates of being prematurely committed republicans. Yankees charged the southern gentry with undue fear of independence. Southern legislators and military officers were particularly appalled by New England's wartime egalitarianism:

companies *electing* their officers, to say nothing of militia captains who were barbers or cobblers sometimes shaving or mending shoes for the men they commanded.

Distinctive cultures were emerging—if, indeed, they were not *reemerging*. Roots in the Puritan, Commonwealth, and republican side of the English Civil War gave Yankeedom a bias toward merchants, yeomen, and the "middling sort." The South, although claiming North America's small portion of aristocratic lineage—Massachusetts Bay had openly *discouraged* titled emigration—also included the later generations of the three jurisdictions used as penal colonies (Maryland, Virginia, and Georgia). This was not a mix that appealed to Northerners. In 1861 and 1862, Yankee troops writing home from the southern battlefields found themselves appalled by the stratification. The gap they saw between manor houses and hovels was a far cry from Lebanon, Pennsylvania, or Niles, Michigan. Some English observers, in turn, thought that southern independence made sense in part because the North and the South were close to being two different countries.[7]

Puritans scorned fox-hunting, horse-racing and the gentleman's duelling code. Southerners embraced them—one Texas newspaper wanted to make the Code Duello into state law—and mocked Yankee Sunday-closing laws. Yankee townships emphasized public education; most southern communities gave it a low priority. The South built private academies for the children of the gentry, but in 1860 counted only 30 of the nation's 321 public high schools. Dixie, in the words of one famous historian, "was for the most part a land without free public schools—a land where the poor man's son was likely to go untaught, and the workingman or small farmer to be ignorant if not illiterate."[8]

The status of women was another barometer. Those in New England were more likely to be activists, religious leaders, writers, or even doctors than those below the Mason-Dixon line, where the upper classes, at least, put women on cultural pedestals. This, too, mirrored a seventeenth-century difference between Puritan East Anglia and the more manorial sections of England.[9]

Peddling, inventing, trading, and sea captaining were disproportionate Yankee vocations. A small minority of Southerners, in turn, were the only Americans connected to the patriarchal world of plantations and private chapels—the transatlantic partial equivalent of England's manor culture.

Slavery was a decisive ingredient, underpinning both the South's aristocratic self-image and the huge gap between the plantation aristocracy and poor whites. Indeed, attitudes toward servitude had revealed southern, middle-colony, and New England divergences from the start. South of New England, more than half of all persons who came to the colonies were servants. In New England, servants were few and the number entering after 1645 was negligible.[10] The early plantation colonies had indentured servants, but by the late eighteenth century, the emphasis had turned to slavery. The middle colonies had a moderate number of slaves, but wound up emphasizing indentured labor. The president of the Council of Pennsylvania stated in 1756 that "every kind of business here . . . is chiefly carried on and supported by the Labour of indented Servants."[11] The New England colonies had a small number of slaves, but also the lowest ratio of indentured servants. Indenturing was not popular there and ships bringing English or Irish servants were often made to take them back.

Religion was another of the deep differences that widened the cultural fissure. The southern elites were substantially Methodist Episcopal or Episcopalian—two of the handful of U.S. denominations that boasted bishops. One Confederate general, Leonidas Polk, was also the Episcopal bishop of Louisiana. He fought, he insisted, for southern altars as well as southern hearthstones and constitutional liberties.[12] Besides comforting an aristocratic worldview, southern Episcopalianism easily accepted slavery. In his acclaimed *Religious History of the American People,* Sydney Ahlstrom notes that "even its own historians have found the church's extraordinary passivity difficult to understand, but the explanation probably lies in the fact that Episcopalians were generally conservative and for good reason well satisfied with the status quo."[13]

New England's Congregational Church, by contrast, was anti-aristocratic and as critical of slavery in 1860 as it had been of the monarchy in 1775. Greater New England politicians and ministers, in attacking the South as a "slaveocracy," also cast it as an aberrant aristocracy—a natural Puritan foe. The South's notion of itself as a second Norman aristocracy, however far-fetched, also fit a familiar divide. New England—at its heart, the old Massachusetts Bay, with counties named for the East Saxons (Essex) and Middle Saxons (Middlesex)—had already wrapped itself in an Old World heritage of free Saxons against George III. John Adams and James Otis had taken these pre-Norman bloodlines back to English folkmoots and seventh-century German forests.

In the days of Pym and Cromwell, Puritan radicals had condemned what they characterized as the "Norman Yoke." This ethnolegal concept included such burdens as the oppressive role of statutes and lawyers, the manorial system which sat heavily upon the land, and the mandate of inheritance by primogeniture. Better, disgruntled Puritans said, to reestablish the laws of the free Anglo-Saxons.[14] The abolitionists and Republicans of the Third Puritanism, decrying the pretensions of the South and the burden of its 1850s dominance of Washington and the U.S. Supreme Court, all but framed a New World version of the Norman Yoke. Stalwarts like William H. Seward spoke of forsaking the statutes and unelected judiciars of the "slaveocracy" for natural or "higher law."

In the churches of the South's lower-caste whites, nineteenth-century revivalism was much more emotional and exuberant during the Second Great Awakening than was the middle-class evangelical response of New England Congregationalists and Presbyterians. New England's redemption-minded social concern made its mark in marshalling temperance crusaders, foreign missionaries, self-improvement societies, women's rights activists, and, most of all, movements to abolish slavery. The major denominations below the Mason-Dixon line, both Baptist and Methodist, took a very different tack. Most southern churches suppressed only routine or biblical sin: the obvious, day-to-day devil's work. Indeed, lower-caste southern groups like the Primitive and Predestinarian Baptists were overtly "antimission"—opposed to the middle-class morality and causes of the Yankee revival. The elites southern denominations, as their principal work of the 1840s and 1850s, transformed themselves into vocal defenders of slavery and a slave society.[15] Northern and southern religion had a lot to disagree over.

Awakenings themselves took different forms in New England and the South, somewhat akin to the contrast between the somber, book-and-learning oriented Puritans of the seventeenth-century English towns and southern counties and the more emotional sects of the northern shires. In the eighteenth century, the Great Awakening in the Presbyterian and Congregationalist North, while enthusiastic and emotional, had more bias to reform and politics, while the Baptist revivals in the New England backcountry and the Appalachian frontier involved the sort of emotion preoccupied with religion and its experience and often disinterested in the Revolution going on not far away. In the nineteenth-century, the Second Great Awakening in the South, while powerful, lacked the reformist side so visible in New England.

Nineteenth-century newspaper editorials, letters, and diaries make clear how often Yankee settlers in eastern Ohio or northern Illinois scoffed at the crude huts, illiteracy, and bare feet of the transplanted southern poor whites in the lower Ohio River counties. Frederick Law Olmsted's reports deplored worse in the South itself—a majority of the Tennessee peasantry going barefoot through the winter, while half of white Mississippi clothed itself in homespun. Connecticut preachers with Yale divinity degrees and book-lined studies, in turn, dismissed southern total-immersion mass baptisms and open-air prayer meetings as thinly disguised saturnalias—equal-parts mixtures of repentance, liquor, and fornication.[16]

Close precedents can be found in seventeenth-century Puritan disdain for "the dark corners of the land" in the north and west of England. Olmsted himself might have been an East Anglian clergyman or Hampshire squire describing a visit to Stuart-era Cumbria or Westmorland. Post-Reformation Catholicism, after lingering in districts like these, gave way in part to seventeenth-century enthusiasts and doubters of Old Testament moral law like the Diggers, Ranters, and Anabaptists and then, in later centuries, to other emotional Protestant sects. These northern and western English hills and dales, the clothing towns aside, never produced the more severe university-bred and commercial Puritanism of the better-developed southern counties. This suggests that there is some truth to late twentieth-century attempts to explain the culture and religion of the American South by alleging its seventeenth- and eighteenth-century ancestry in northern and western England and the Celtic portions of the British Isles.[17] Clashes with Puritanism would have been instinctive.

Indeed, the origins of the First and Third Puritanisms were partly parallel. The early English Puritans, far from being mindless fanatics, were responding to circumstances also seen two centuries later. The worsening drunkenness and collapsing morals visible in early seventeenth-century May fairs and taverns, which so excited the preachers, had roots in the corrosive inflation of the so-called European Price Revolution. Historians of early Stuart England routinely note how bawdy houses and alehouses proliferated together with clipped coins and diminishing real wages. The West Riding of Yorkshire alone contained about two thousand alehouse keepers in 1638 and five hundred more who brewed without permits, and every few years a new act would be passed to curb "the odious and loathsome synne of Drunkenness . . . late growen into common usage."[18] Harmless high-spiritedness it was not. In 1632, the justices of the peace in Somerset regretted that many women had been indicted "for murdering bastard children begotten at wakes and revels."[19]

The Puritans who arrived in Massachusetts between 1629 and 1640 were a product of this much-too-merry England. Their descendants in early nineteeth-century Greater New England confronted some of the same provocations. Europe's revolutionary and wartime years from 1790 to 1815, engines of another inflation, had produced related if less extreme price increases, moral loosening, alcoholism, and urban chaos.

In the United States, early nineteenth-century drunkenness was so widespread—in North and South alike, and this *before* large-scale Irish and German immigration—that annual per capita adult consumption of liquor had climbed to the extraordinary equivalent of seven gallons of 200-proof alcohol. Once temperance efforts finally led to Prohibition laws beginning in Maine and Vermont, then spreading widely during the 1850s, per capita consumption declined to less than two gallons.[20] Temperance advocates were not gratuitous bluenoses.

Like their Puritan forebears, however, Greater New Englanders leavened their moralism with incorrigible commerciality. Successful joint-stock companies were their spiritual Michaelmas feasts; miles of fat white pine logs rafting down the Saginaw, Muskegon, and Au Sable were their harvest homes. Sabbatarians couldn't resist starting all-but-Sunday stagecoach lines. Abolitionists opened up free-grown produce groceries. New Englanders were also, in Hamilton's apt description, "navigating," while southern fire-eaters, like the Cavaliers of the 1640s, rarely knew a foremast from a forecastle. Here again one must be struck by the parallel between the English and American pre–Civil War polarizations.

Which brings us to the question of irrepressibility: *Why was another such fight necessary in 1861? The underlying divisions—sectional, economic, religious, and cultural—were important, obviously, and they will be detailed in the next chapter. But the time frame was also critical.* By the 1850s, sectionalism and political infighting between Yankees and Southerners had stalled commercial progress and economic expansion. Democratic presidents like James Buchanan vetoed river and harbor improvement legislation important to the North and opposed a homestead law that would encourage western settlement. Neither side would support a transcontinental railroad route that did not follow its own sectional route. Northerners saw the Fugitive Slave Law, the repeal of the Missouri Compromise, and the *Dred Scott* ruling expressing a flagrant southern power over the federal government that previously had been muted. Southerners, meanwhile, found their own hopes for expansion in Kansas, Mexico, and the Caribbean frustrated by the North even as King Cotton made Dixie richer than ever. Northern population and power were starting to pull ahead.

The moral debate became harder to sidestep. Widened by the Kansas-Nebraska Act of 1854 and by the Supreme Court's 1857 *Dred Scott* decision, which cosseted slavery, the divergent constitutional interpretations of the two regions grew more embittered. And by 1853–1854, the breakdown of the shaky Jacksonian-Whig party structure, shaken and pummeled by a broad range of issues, including the decade's record levels of Irish and German immigration, was creating a new political system that would not only recognize sectionalism but mobilize it.

Chapter 12 will return to the parallels between the cousins' wars, including their extraordinary repetition of themes and terminology. For the moment, however, it is useful to view particular causes and origins of the American Civil War through the same lenses applied to the English Civil War in chapter 2 and to the American Revolution in chapter 3. Once again, the causations center around the economy, religion, and culture; disagreement over constitutional rights and tyrannies; and the rival sections' alternative strategies for westward expansion and manifest destiny.

At first blush, economic causation seems to loom high. Determinists who have located commercial and preindustrial taproots of the English Civil War can more easily point to a grand U.S. confrontation between rival sectors (agricultural and industrial), opposite commercial philosophies (manorial and entrepreurial), and hostile labor systems (free and slave). In addition to which, the South and North had been at great economic loggerheads since the beginning of the republic—over tariffs that protected northern industry at the expense of southern agriculture, over northern favoritism to maritime interests, and over banking and currency arrangements that divided the debtor-oriented South from the creditor-minded North.[21] These issues also tapped basic divisions.

Moreover, practical economics would have made Abraham Lincoln and his advisors as unwilling to let the South secede as King George III and his Ministry had been to accept American independence. Back in 1775, because the thirteen provinces took about a third of British manufactured goods, they seemed indispensable to ongoing British prosperity. Much the same could be said in 1861 of the seceding South.

While much of the pre–Civil War South's cotton went to Britain, it traveled in northern cargo holds to Yankees ship-owners' great profit. The plantation states were also a huge, almost captive market for northern products. The catch, however, was that most northern goods were cheaper in Mobile or Chattanooga only because of high U.S. tariffs on rival foreign manufactures. These tariffs, which financed 85 to 90 percent of the operations of the federal government, directly and indirectly fell most heavily on agricultural districts, principally in the South and West. Economists have a phrase for this: internal colonialism.

Upon becoming independent in early 1861, the Confederacy speedily announced a schedule of tariffs much lower than those in the next-door United States. Were the new nation to survive, this new low-tariff arrangement would pose several threats. By attracting cheaper foreign manufactures directly to southern ports, it would undercut northern industry. Westerners of the Mississippi Valley would be tempted to set up a new Confederacy of their own and get foreign goods more cheaply through low-tariff New Orleans rather than through high-tariff New York. Finally, Washington would lose the very considerable portion of federal revenues collected from tariffs on goods and manufactures ordered by the South—and perhaps by the West.

Concerned Northerners quickly began to speculate about the sort of domino effect that British ministers had feared eighty-five years earlier. Vital markets and revenues would be lost. Foreign rivals—most of the concern revolved around British ship-owners and manufacturers—would grab away commerce and the carriage of goods. The Mississippi Valley West might follow the South out of the Union. Manifest destiny could crumble.

During the tense weeks after Lincoln's inauguration, the Philadelphia Press predicted that the federal government "to prevent the serious diminution of its revenues will be compelled to blockade the Southern ports . . . and prevent the importation of foreign goods into them."[22] The Boston Transcript, fearful that commercial realignment was the real goal of secession, called for the president to take action:

> The difference is so great between the tariff of the Union and that of the Confederated States that the entire Northwest must find it to their advantage to purchase their imported goods at New Orleans rather than New York. In addition to this, the manufacturing interests of the country will suffer from the increased importations resulting from low duties . . . the (government) would be false to all its obligations, if this state of things were not provided against.[23]

Still another economic parallel to the American Revolution deserves note. The seceding states promptly repudiated debts owed by southern traders to the North, totalling over $100 million, just as 1774 and 1775 had seen Virginians and other southern commodity producers race into local courts to stay their existing debts to Britain. The effects of 1861 Confederate debt cancellation or postponement, like those of 1775, were to give important groups a stake in the new regime.[24]

It was all very worrisome for six or eight weeks. Republicans who spoke about saving the Glorious Union undoubtedly had many philosophic, historical, and sentimental reasons. But practical economics must have played a part. Abraham Lincoln was sworn in as president on March 4. In mid-April, he called for seventy-five thousand troops to defend the Union; and in the patriotic fervor that followed, he got these and many more. The first blockading federal warships were on station within weeks.

What must limit the importance of economics in bringing about war in 1861 is what also undercut economic explanations of the 1640–1649 and 1775–1783 conflicts. Both times, as we have seen, the most reliable overlaps of allegiance have been with *religion or ethnicity*, economics being more coincidental. In the English Civil War, for example, the sympathy of workers and entrepreneurs in the emerging clothing industry was overwhelmingly Parliamentarian while holders of monopolies from the King—in soap, wine, tin mining, or whatever—largely stuck with the Crown. However, the cloth-makers were also overwhelmingly Puritan while the favored commercial monopolists were court Anglicans with a Catholic admixture.

The War for American Independence had similiar dualities. The onetime New England smugglers lopsidedly on the rebel side were also mostly Congregationalists. Their commitment came more from Scripture than from cargo manifests. Quakers from places like Newport, Falmouth, and Nantucket, whatever they, too, might have smuggled in 1774, were more likely to be neutral or pro-British when war came. Tobacco merchants and factors in Chesapeake Bay or the Carolinas were more divided by whether they were Scottish or not than by anything else.

The *grand* division of 1861–1865 does seem clear: industrial North versus agrarian South. In retrospect, the polarization jumps out. But the caveats of 1860 and early 1861 are many: The richest Whig planters and slaveowners in Louisiana and Mississippi were skeptical of secession, not ardent. The famous "Cotton Whigs" of Massachusetts, whose profitable factories produced textiles from long-staple southern cotton fibers, tried to avoid the slavery issue until the late 1840s. And many shunned Lincoln through 1860. Philadelphia's Whig oligarchs, with commercial ties to the South, remained leery of the Republican Party, abolitionism, and the threat of civil war even after the shooting began. Industrial New Jersey was torn, the argument went, because the South walked on Newark shoe leather.[25] Much of it also rode on Connecticut carriage wheels. Commercial priorities like these resembled the peace-mindedness eighty-five years earlier of London merchants, Warwickshire iron manufacturers, and Nottingham hosiery-makers who sold half of their goods in North America.

The free laborers to whom the Republicans appealed were also divided. The best guides to how northern factory workers and artisans would align politically were not industry or income but ethnicity, religion, and culture: Were they native-born or immigrant, Catholic or Protestant (with some caveat for Lutherans and Baptists), southern-born or Yankee? In the burgeoning Pittsburgh area, religion and ethnicity were the principal factors in local political alignments during the 1848–1860 period.[26] The same pattern leaps out in lesser industrial sections of Pennsylvania, in New York, in Michigan, and in New England.[27] The overall "immigrant vote" in 1860 and 1864, as we will see, divided less by class or vocation than by ethnicity and religion.

However, if strictly economic causations appear inadequate, a variation can be offered: that Puritanism, Presbyterianism, or Congregationalism in eighteenth- and nineteenth-century America, as in seventeenth-century England, resembled the continental Calvinism of the Reformation in providing quasi-economic belief systems for emerging capitalism. Theology and commerce, in short, became close allies in seeking to replace aristocratic and church hierarchies associated with old regimes; to clear away feudal, mercantilist, or guild-system rules that blocked entrepreneurialism; and to advance wage labor and enterprise rather than manorial relationships or slave labor. Puritanism was virtually an adjunct of economic development in encouraging temperance, neatness, education, and hard work.

The perceived meddlesomeness of this Yankee ethic and culture—its pious interference with Sundays, beer gardens, racecourses, and strong language—was offensive to agrarian Southerners, Ohio Valley Butternuts (the poor whites of southern Ohio, Indiana, and Illinois), and northern Catholic immigrants, especially the Irish.

Moralizing repelled many of them even more than the dangers, work hours, and inequalities of industrial capitalism. Besides which, not a few leading stalwarts of temperance, Sunday closings, and abolition—Sabbatarian leader Lewis Tappan for example, or abolitionist stalwart Thaddeus Stevens—were wealthy businessmen who found no problem with the wages and conditions of capitalism. Slavery had all of the flaws and capitalism none. What mattered—*all that mattered,* it often seemed—was the freedom of owning one's own labor. Pay levels and employment safety were not moral issues. Not surprisingly, some leaders of the fledgling labor movement worried that abolitionism was at least partly a diversion.

In Yankee areas, Calvinist Protestantism and the early Industrial Revolution were so intertwined that it was hard to tell just which force was shaping or provoking whom. If the line was almost impossible to draw in 1640, it was little easier two hundred years later in Connecticut, Pennsylvania, and Michigan. Perhaps the answer is that the line between Puritan religion and economics should not be overemphasized.

The agrarian South, in turn, had very little of the Industrial Revolution–nurturing sort of Calvinism. Its preindustrial elites were largely Episcopalian or Methodist Episcopal, its rural masses predominantly Baptist—and often of a primitive sort. With no industrial culture to placate, southern spokesmen and planters could blister northern capitalism and wage slavery perceptively enough to strike a chord among some workers in Britain and the North, particularly Catholic immigrants who had little liking for their northern Protestant Republican employers.

Here again, there are ties between the rival philosophies of the English Civil War and those of America's midcentury strife. One southern advocate, George Fitzhugh, eccentric scion of an old but threadbare Virginia family, challenged the Puritan and Lockean North with no less than the ideas of Sir Robert Filmer, a seventeenth-century Royalist. Filmer had criticized the emergence of Parliament and the Revolution of 1688 for increasing the power of the moneyed interest at the expense of the Crown, church, and nobility, "the natural friends, allies and guardians of the laboring class."[28] In the years leading up to the American Revolution, Filmer's ideas were disliked as much by New England's John Adams and James

Otis as they had been by English Whigs in the years of Charles II and James II. To Fitzhugh, in turn, the North reincarnated John Locke's progressive, egalitarian Whigs, while the South reassembled Filmer's patriarchal Tories. His parallel has been supported by at least one English historian who has called the aristocratic cousin-ships of the English County of Kent and Virginia's James River Valley the two best mid-seventeenth-century examples of their kind.[29]

Like many other Southerners, Fitzhugh enjoyed mocking "bloomer's and Women's rights men, and strong-minded women, and Mormons, and anti-renters, Millerites, and Spiritual Rappers, and Shakers, and Widow Wakemanites, and Agrarians, and Grahamites and a thousand other superstitions and infidel Isms of the North."[30] Primitive or Antimission Baptists and other low-income southern sectarians shared the High Episcopal disdain from a different perspective—and those in southern Ohio were mocking foes of Western Reserve Republicans.

Fitzhugh, defender of episcopacy, even wrote in 1863, before Gettysburg, that "we attempt to roll back the reformation in its political phases, for we saw everywhere in Europe and the North reformation running to excess . . . a profane attempt to pull down what God and nature had built up and to erect ephemeral Utopia in its place."[31] Yankee abolitionists like Lyman Beecher, Theodore Parker, and Joshua Giddings saw the relationship in reverse—the evangelical movement and the unfolding nineteenth-century combat as the great climax of a worldwide revolutionary process launched by the Protestant Reformation and upheld in the revolutions of 1642, 1688, and 1776.[32] Historians focused on slavery, such as David Brion Davis, have concurred: "We have not sufficiently appreciated that for many protestants, the reformation, even more than the Revolution, was the model of a timeless, archetypal experience that had to be re-enacted, in almost ritualistic fashion, if freedom was to be preserved. . . . Repeatedly, the opponents of slave power likened their stand to that of protestant reformers from Luther to Wesley, and thought of their crusade as a re-enactment of sacred struggles against the Kingdom of Darkness."[33] The Anglican-Puritan hostility is another continuity.

Of the Calvinist churches, closest heirs to the Reformation, the Congregationalists were almost nonexistent below the Mason-Dixon line, the Dutch Reformed and German Reformed few and far between. The Presbyterian Church had divided, in several stages beginning in 1837, into a southern-centered "Old School" denomination and a northern "New School." The latter was close to Congregationalism in Pennsylvania and the Great Lakes, overtly antislavery by the war's outbreak, and a favorite church of Yankee businessmen. The official regional separation came only as the war began. Upon retiring back to Pennsylvania in 1861, ex-President James Buchanan, an old Presbyterian, refused to join the New School church.[34]

Church separatism was sectional politics by another name. The Southern Baptists, too, broke away in 1845 to become a separate, pro-slavery church. The Southern Methodists had done so in 1844. The Southern Presbyterians not only defended slavery but worked up a biblical theology on its behalf. As late as 1864, they formally avowed that "it is the peculiar mission of the Southern Church to conserve the institution of slavery and to make it a blessing both to master and slave."[35]

No industrializing nation could have produced such theology, but that was part of what the South lacked: factories. In 1860, Dixie had just 16 percent of U.S. manufacturing capacity, 35 percent of the railroad mileage, a small sliver of the bank deposits, and under one-third of the nation's white population. Northern states had manufactured 97 percent of the country's firearms and 93 percent of its pig iron.[36] City dwellers constituted 36 percent of the 1860 population in the North, but only 9.6 percent in the South.

Slavery and its corollary, impoverished white ruralism, also gave Dixie aspects of a separate polity. North-South tensions were writ large in the Federalist-Jeffersonian rivalry, as we have seen, and then in the unstable Whig-Democratic party system. The Civil War Republican-Democratic party system, still forming, was explicitly sectional from the start. Of the fifteen slave states—the future Confederacy plus nonseceding Delaware, Maryland, Kentucky, and Missouri—Abraham Lincoln had ballot position in 1860 as the Republican presidential nominee in only five. His statewide totals ranged from low to laughable: Delaware (23.7 percent), Maryland (2.5 percent), Kentucky (0.9 percent), Virginia (1.1 percent), and Missouri (10.3 percent).[37] In Virginia, Maryland, and Delaware, virtually all of the Lincoln support could be found within thirty miles of the Pennsylvania border. Competition in the true South of palmettos, live oaks, and Spanish moss would have been pointless.

Pre-Civil War politics in the South itself had narrowed to a Democratic Party that endorsed a hard line and embraced secession versus local Unionist coalitions that stood against secession until the die was cast. The contests of the late 1850s had included economic disagreements over tariff, internal improvement, and local questions. By 1860, however, these mattered little. South of Pennsylvania and the Ohio River, the only two serious contenders were John C. Breckinridge of Kentucky, the southern or states rights Democrat, and John Bell of Tennessee, the Whig-bred, compromise-oriented Constitutional Union nominee. On Election Day, Breckinridge won all the cotton states, where slavery was most vital. Bell did best in the compromise-oriented Upper South and Border, running well in the old southern Whig sections, carrying Virginia, Tennessee, and Kentucky and losing by only narrow margins in Maryland, North Carolina, and Missouri.

In the Upper South and Border, concerns about keeping the Union intact yet upholding southern honor against Yankee double-dealing gave politics its ambivalence until Lincoln's April 1861 mobilization. The local importance of slavery, however, was usually the pivot. Where slaveholding was greatest, even Border-state politics resembled the Deep South—impatient and pro-Confederate. For example, three counties in southern Maryland with especially high slave-population ratios—Charles, St. Mary's, and Prince Georges—gave Breckinridge his biggest state margins over Bell. Six months later, when war broke out, this very part of non-seceding Maryland sent the most men to enlist in the southern armies.[38]

The cotton states themselves included several dozen mountainous counties, especially in northern Georgia and Alabama, where cotton was usually uneconomic and slaveholding negligible. In many, majorities opposed secession and local enlistment in the *Union* Army would be considerable.

Slavery, in other words, was central. Further proof can be found in the anti-abolition and anti-Lincoln sentiment of the old Dutch counties in New Jersey and New York, which had the North's largest slave populations in the early nineteenth century. (Note: These will be further discussed on pp. 426–428). Pro-slavery Democrats in Bergen County, New Jersey, called for recognition of the South in 1861 and urged citizens to resist the tyranny of the Lincoln administration. As late as September, when all was still quiet along the future Potomac battlefields, sympathizers raised a secession flag in the still-Dutch Hackensack Valley.[39]

But if slave-ownership and attitudes toward slavery were principal yardsticks in a number of secession situations, they were less precise denominators of wartime loyalty and acceptance of military service. Regional pride and disdain for Yankees could motivate non-slave-owners, too. Still, in posing the question of whether slavery was an economic interest, a moral and religious bone of contention, or a sidebar of debate over liberty, freedom, constitutional rights, and tyranny, this chapter will conclude that it was all three. Like the line between religion and economics, the nature of the slavery issue is not easily defined.

Each of the cousins' wars, moreover, has pointedly involved heartfelt belief and intense disagreement over the complex of issues just summed up: *liberty, freedom, constitutional rights, and tyranny*. In 1861, as in 1642 or 1775, feelings like these might overlap with religious sectarianism or economic self-interest. However, they were not necessarily submerged in it. They had a compelling force of their own.

During the lead-in to the English Civil War, Parliamentarians and Puritans believed they were fighting for liberties and constitutional rights against Stuart tyranny. The rebels of the 1770s complained about the tyranny of George III and the Crown's violation of the rights of Englishmen. The other side, each time, replied to political and constitutional abuses with its own slices of English history.

Eight decades later, a whole new litany of threatened liberties, suppressed rights, violated constitutions, and nefarious conspiracies blazoned its way across the 1850s. To Northerners, slavery was an obvious denial of liberty. The rule of the Slaveocracy, in turn, was tyranny. Wartime Republicans denied that individual states had a right to secede and leave the Union. Southerners, for their part, saw the bargain of 1787 as having accepted slavery and given it constitutional status. Yankee attempts to rescind the compact were nothing less than attempts to deny the South equality, respect, and honor. Such denial was tyranny. The literature and debates of the previous fights, in 1642 and 1775, were as much arsenals for the combat of 1861 as the buildings at Harper's Ferry or Springfield.

In 1850, John C. Calhoun of South Carolina had pointedly linked southern anger to "the fact that the equilibrium between the two sections, in the Government as it stood when the Constitution was ratified and the Government put in action, has been destroyed." During this last speech he made in the Senate, Calhoun went on to cite the cumulating abuses of northern politicians in trying to abolish slavery in the District of Columbia, prohibit the slave trade between the states, abrogate the clause of the Constitution that called for the delivering-up of fugitive slaves, prohibit slavery in the territories, and prevent the admission of any state which did not prohibit slavery in its constitution.[40] When South Carolina left the Union in 1860, its "Declaration of the Cause of Secession" picked up where Calhoun had left off: "We assert that fourteen of the states have deliberately refused for years past to fulfill their constitutional obligations. . . . Thus the constitutional compact has been deliberately broken and disregarded by the non-slaveholding states; and the consequence follows that South Carolina is released from her obligation."[41]

Northern lawyers and judges wriggled on the constitutional hooks. Slavery was manifestly lawful. The right of secession was unclear. Abolitionists and sympathetic churchmen, however, sought recourse to a "higher law." Harriet Beecher Stowe, in explaining the New England beliefs that underlay her book *Uncle Tom's Cabin*, argued that Puritan emphasis on a higher law dated back to the overthrow of Charles I. To pull down temporal authority, the Puritan Parliamentarians had called on a divine sovereignty.[42] In 1776, the General Court of Massachusetts, justifying resistance to the King, had said that God's power flowed only to the people. Turning to that higher law or power has been a pivot in all three English-speaking civil wars—a critical theological stage of mobilization. Mere statutes, courts, or royal pronouncements could not be allowed to prevail.

Yankees themselves had been insistent on the right of a state to leave the Union as late as 1815, which kept them relatively mute on the subect during the 1820s and 1830s. By the 1850s, a new crop of Greater New England leaders too young to remember the

Hartford Convention entertained no doubt: *States could not be allowed to leave*. The hypocrisy was widely noted below the Mason-Dixon line.

In *moral* terms, the South might be making a last argument for an unworthy cause—human slavery—on the verge of being extinguished. Purely within the narrower context of U.S. law and the Constitution, Southerners had a point. And as a culture committed to its own aristocratic self-image, the honor of the South did demand that the constitutional bargain be maintained. William Drayton, chief justice of the South Carolina Supreme Court, had observed even in 1778, under the Articles of Confederation, that "the honour, interest and sovereignty of the South are in effect delivered up to the care of the North."[43] The more formalized political and constitutional compact of 1787 only added to that sensitivity.

If honor helped bring on the war, so did conspiracy-mindedness. Within the two polar regions, enough leaders and citizens were distrustful enough of the institutions, values, and culture of the other section not to want to live under a national government that their foes controlled. And as heirs of seventeenth- and eighteenth-century, English-speaking political paranoia, both sides saw plots everywhere—by Puritans and Black Republicans; by "secesh," the Slaveocracy, and the Slave Power. To a fair number of northern Protestants during the 1850s, moreover, the Democratic Party represented the Pope as well as the Slaveocracy. Preoccupation with conspiracy was another tradition common to the 1640s, 1770s, and early 1860s. By 1859 and 1860, it had become part of the irrepressibility. Appendix 2, on pages 615–617 details the conspiracy-chain aspect of the three wars.

The end of the 1850s gave the debate a final-hour intensity by adding armed confrontation—not just "Bleeding Kansas" but John Brown's raid on the federal arsenal at Harper's Ferry in 1859. A less obvious signal was the South's deepening intellectual immersion in justifying slavery and even finding merit in it. This fixation had begun in the 1830s. By the 1850s, it pervaded the mentality of the cotton states.

The increasing hostility of world opinion was probably a spur. Force might be able to secure what arguments no longer could. The British Empire had ended slavery in the 1830s; France did so in 1848. Beyond the United States, slavery as of 1860 remained legal in only two major nations: Brazil and the Spanish Empire, most notably Cuba.

Changing economics was part of what made slavery a trap. Providing the raw material to the world's biggest and most profitable manufacturing industry, British cotton textiles, had made the South rich—on paper. Soaring cotton prices, besides fetching more British gold, added to the value of the region's black slaves. These numbered nearly four million, up from six hundred thousand at the close of the American Revolution.

By 1860, they also accounted for a dangerously high ratio of the South's capital. On paper, white male Southerners had twice the per capita wealth of white male Northerners. But most of it was invested in slaves, vulnerable to abolition or to the collapse of cotton prices, both subjects of intense speculation by then. When the British government had abolished slavery in 1834, it paid slaveholders about £20 million ($US 100 million) for somewhat over five hundred thousand slaves.[44] That would make the nearly four million slaves in the United States thirty years later worth at least $US 1 billion, and discussions in 1860–1861 put the figure two or three times higher. Buying their collective freedom was not a plausible option, fiscally or politically. The nonabolitionist majority of white Americans, especially in the Ohio and Upper Mississippi Valleys, would never have supported such an outlay. The collapse of slavery, on the other hand, would devastate the South economically. No solution was apparent.

From the perspective of the cotton states in 1860, secession made more sense. It might have worked if the South had acted six to eight years earlier. Once Lincoln was elected, time was awasting. With the Republicans in office, the South could not count on leaving the Union unopposed. But until the Republicans *were* in office, hopeful Southerners had found reasons to procrastinate.

However, we must now step back from economic interests, shaky cotton prices, sectional culture, and cavalier honor. The "higher law" starting to appear in northern rhetoric, together with the Cromwell-like stanzas of great martial hymns, are again mobilizing a nation. Religion, the vital context of the previous cousins' wars, is still near to the center of English-speaking politics.

Mine Eyes Have Seen the Glory: Religion and Politics in Mid-Nineteenth-Century America and Britain

Religious denominationalism, as much as economics or ideology, drove the great transatlantic political currents that ultimately ended slavery, maintained the United States as one nation, and inhibited the British government, despite its huge textile industry, from aiding the embattled cotton states. That British reluctance, in turn, ensured northern victory and with it the success of representative democracy in *both* nations during the last third of the nineteenth-century.

Those great currents, the two nations' Protestant belief systems, were surprisingly similar. In the United States, especially in Greater New England, the Second Great Awakening bred an evangelical politics of social and moral intervention that coalesced into the Republican Party and underpinned the election of Abraham Lincoln, for all that he wisely softened the neo-Puritan message. Fast-growing British nonconformist Protestantism and evangelicalism shaped a related Whig and Liberal Party politics of reform and moral regeneration. In both nations, nineteenth-century electoral politics still strongly reflected religion and denominationalism.

This imprint on the parties was only the beginning. Religion was important enough that the dissolution of three major U.S. denominations—Baptists, Methodists, and Presbyterians—into separate northern and southern churches did not simply hint at a clash; the religious hostility intensified by the division itself fed the sectionalism. A third effect came after the war began: The armies on both sides periodically countered the horrors of war with the faith of religious revivals. Most famous of all was the 1863 "revival on the Rapidan" which uplifted the southern army on its way home from the carnage and disillusionment of Gettysburg.[45]

Why religious denominationalism does not get its due in early nineteenth-century U.S. electoral alignments and politics probably reflects the transience of the parties: Most were not around for long. The slow Federalist demise after the War of 1812 led into the confusion of the election of 1824, won by John Quincy Adams and a faction called the National Republicans. Their short welcome, in turn, led to the rise of the Democrats of Andrew Jackson, who held the White House from 1829 to 1837. By then the Whigs had arisen in opposition. During what is overstated as the full-fledged party system including the terms from 1828 to 1856, the Democrats won six times and the Whigs just twice.

The Democratic-Whig system, like the earlier Federalist-Jeffersonian structure on which it rested, was more feeble, more short-winded, than this nominal span. Its momentum came from Jackson—the anti-aristocratic, bank-baiting, Scotch-Irish back-countryman who still carried British sabre scars for his pro-revolutionary outspokenness as a fourteen-year-old. The Whig Party gathered around values that were the antithesis of Old Hickory's: countinghouse and mercantile, often coastal, sober, and hierarchical, churchgoing, neighborhood-improving, unwarlike, and socially concerned, albeit principally in the North, about the treatment of Native Americans and slaves.

The majority of Americans, however, were Jacksonians.* Most Southerners cheered as the Democrats of the 1830s and 1840s not only lambasted Philadelphia bankers and Boston financiers, but relocated the defeated Cherokee, Choctaw, and Seminole Indians from lands needed for cotton expansion. Backcountry poor whites also disliked middle-class Whigdom as missionaries, Indian-lovers, abolitionists, and anti-expansionists. Frontier politics found its ultimate expression in the Democratic vice-president inaugurated in 1837: Senator Richard Mentor Johnson of Kentucky, leader of the fight to keep Sunday mail delivery, who ridiculed Sabbatarian leaders as Puritans and bluenoses. At the Battle of the Thames in 1813, when Johnson had been the professed killer of Tecumseh, his mounted riflemen claimed they had cut razor strops out of the dead chief's skin.[46]

The minority Whigs were likened by Ralph Waldo Emerson to overprotective physicians who prescribed "pills and herb tea."[47] Their infrequent power, like Federalism's prior short tenure, weak-

---

*This chapter's analysis of Jacksonian democracy emphasizes the cultural side. My analysis of the economic side of Jacksonian politics, more in keeping with Arthur Schlesinger's emphasis, is in *The Politics of Rich and Poor* (Random House, 1990).

ened New England's potential political voice. Of the major U.S. political parties, Whiggery alone never had an "era."

What it had was *brevity*. The Whigs did not exist in the first election Jackson won: the brouhaha of 1828. They were grouping, but still categorized as National Republicans, in Jackson's *second* election: the landslide of 1832. The name "Whig" as a formal designation came in 1834.[48] The Whig organization was still haphazard in 1836 when three different Whigs ran for president and divided the vote. By the time the first Whig president, William Henry Harrison, was elected in 1840, a forerunner of the *next* system was already dividing the Whig vote—the antislavery Liberty Party. Figure 9.2 shows the various presidential candidacies and their levels of success, as well as the reshaping of the party system, between 1840 and 1860.

The Whigs of 1844 lost, partly because of growing support for the Liberty Party. In 1848, the Whigs won again, with Zachary Taylor, also a war hero in the Harrison mold. However, the Free Soil Party, replacing the Liberty Party, took 10 percent of the national vote, finishing second in New York and Massachusetts.

The presidential election of 1852 then turned out to be the last one the Whigs contested—once more with a popular general, Winfield Scott; he was defeated, however. He was alleged to have Catholic sympathies—his daughters had been educated in convent schools.[49] More telling was yet another Free Soil candidacy to divert Yankee support, as well as sharp Whig declines in the cotton states. Even Zachary Taylor, the last elected Whig president, during his short 1849–1850 incumbency, had begun to talk about replacing the Whig Party with something else.[50]

These institutional shortcomings made Whiggery a seedbed of deeper conflict, not a suppressor. The ongoing sectional changes and religious realignments in the United States of the 1820s, 1830s, and 1840s may have been powerful enough to make *any* party system unstable and transient. One historian divided the Whig and Democratic constituencies as follows: "Most of the 'devotionalist' Protestant groups—the Unitarians, Finneyites, 'perfectionists' and New School Calvinists, as well as Quakers, Free Will Baptists and others—found a place in . . . the Whig Party. Opposing this alliance were the 'confessional' bodies in the Democratic Party, an even more incongruous assemblage of Roman Catholics, German

FIGURE 9.2 The Democratic-Whig Party System and Its Breakup, 1840–1860

	Whig Framework	Democratic Framework	Greater New England, Anti-slavery Framework	Slavery and Secession Framework	Percentage of Presidential Vote Outside Whig-Democratic Framework*
1840	Whig presidential vote—52.9% Winner: William Henry Harrison	Democratic presidential vote—46.8% Martin Van Buren	Liberty Party presidential vote—0.3% James Birney		0.3%
1844	Whig presidential vote—48.1% Henry Clay	Democratic presidential vote—49.5% Winner: James K. Polk	Liberty Party presidential vote—2.3% James Birney		2.3%
1848	Whig presidential vote—47.3% Winner: Zachary Taylor	Democratic presidential vote—42.5% Lewis Cass	Free Soil Party presidential vote—10.1% Martin Van Buren		10.1%
1852	Whig presidential vote—43.9% Winfield Scott	Democratic presidential vote—50.8% Winner: Franklin Pierce	Free Soil Party presidential vote—4.9% John Hale		4.9%
1856	Whig-American Party presidential vote—21.5% Millard Fillmore	Democratic presidential vote—45.3% Winner: James Buchanan	Republican Party presidential vote—33.1% John C. Frémont		33.1%
1860	Constitutional Union presidential vote—12.6% John Bell	Democratic presidential vote—29.5% Stephen A. Douglas	Republican Party presidential vote—39.8% Winner: Abraham Lincoln	Southern Democratic presidential vote—18.1% John C. Breckinridge	57.8%

*Excludes other minor parties, candidates, and scattered votes.

Source: *Congressional Quarterly Guide to U.S. Elections.*

Lutherans, Dutch 'True' Calvinists, Old School Presbyterians and antimission Baptists."[51]

The Republican-Democratic system beginning the mid-1850s turned out to be the lasting one, in part because it provided the long-awaited vehicle through which New England theology and evangelicalism could reassert itself in the revolutionary style of the seventeenth and eighteenth centuries.* The Whig Party, despite its national inadequacy, did serve as early-stage assembly line of later local Republican coalitions. Across much of Greater New England, Whig organizations fitted together many of the components that the replacement Republicans would build into a powerful engine—evangelical Yankee Protestantism, antislavery sentiment, suspicion of Catholicism, and some other "isms" to boot.

Some of these themes were more religious than others. But all had at least *some* roots in the Second Great Awakening. Evangelicalism grew across most of the United States during the first half of the nineteenth century, in the South as well as New England. Yet most historians agree that its most powerful expression came in Yankee social consciousness and the fusion of politics and morality in the decades before the Civil War. Elaborations and acknowledgments of this impact can be found in the writings of both religious and Civil War historians ranging from Vernon Parrington and Sydney Ahlstrom to James McPherson and Eric Foner.[52]

Nativism and anti-Catholicism both have obvious religious antecedents. Nineteenth-century New England nativism and Anglo-centrism hark back to seventeenth-century Puritan pride and the

---

*Civil War history being so popular, some readers may have begun with this section instead of with the foreword and the early chapters on the English Civil War and the American Revolution. Thus I want to repeat here a paragraph from of the foreword relative to the framework of the seventeenth, eighteenth, and even nineteenth centuries: "The importance of religion surprised me, as it probably will many readers. After three years of study and writing (to do this book), the triangle of religion, politics, and war is unmistakable during the three centuries. I would not have thought so when I began, so hopefully readers will bear with me as the evidence unfolds, war after war." Because those starting with Part III, the U.S. Civil War section, will not have followed that evidentiary development, these chapters, absent that backdrop, may seem over-attentive to religion and excessively disposed to find seventeenth- and eighteenth-century parallels. Portions may seem at odds with historical portraiture that involves only the U.S. Civil War as a stand-alone phenomenon. However, the force of religion, while declining by the mid-nineteenth century relative to the previous eras, is still powerful.

Anglophilia of High Federalism. Still ethnically homogeneous, New England perceived itself as keeper of both the Reformation and the sacred fire of Anglo-Saxon liberty. "God had sifted a whole Nation," one early New Englander had written, "that he might send choice Grain over into this wilderness."[53] With its Chosen People psychology, Puritan Massachusetts had rarely welcomed outsiders—not Quakers in the seventeenth century, not Baptists or Scotch-Irish Presbyterians in the eighteenth. Even the Louisiana Purchase of 1803 struck a sour note. New England Federalists and Congregationalists did not welcome the French and Spanish Catholics who came with the new territory.

The Catholic Irish flood of the 1840s and 1850s was even less welcome, coinciding with two deepening sensitivities. The nearly three million immigrants arriving in America between 1846 and 1854, a number equal to 14.5 percent of the *entire* U.S. population in 1846, constituted the largest proportionate addition of immigrants ever received.[54] The cities of the North, inundated, appeared to spawn slums, crime, drunkenness, and pauperism. The new arrivals expanded the power of big-city political bosses, mostly Democratic (and often corrupt), some of whom, such as New York's Tammany Hall, practiced fraudulent naturalization. Many state constitutions of the 1830s and 1840s allowed aliens to vote before they became citizens or laid out minimal residency requirements as befit an era of large-scale internal immigration. Reformers had reasons for concern.

Sensitivity number two went right to the heart of American Protestantism: From half to two-thirds of the new arrivals were Catholics, making the hierarchy of the Catholic Church in the United States far more important and aggressive than it had ever been before—and in an era when Catholicism, pressed by the European revolutions of 1830 and 1848, was in a counterrevolutionary mood. Protestants in the North were annoyed by the insistence in 1853 and 1854 on ecclesiastical ownership of church property—a transfer of Catholic churches and real estate from lay trustees to the clergy. More broadly provocative to Protestants were pressures by the clergy and their political allies to stop Bible reading in public schools and to secure public financial assistance for parochial schools. But Daniel Walker Howe, in his sweeping study *The Political Culture of the American Whigs,* offers a further-reaching analysis:

> The ethnic and religious hostilities of the nineteenth century need to be taken seriously. In view of the magnitude and suddenness of the Irish influx (1.2 million people in a decade), the wonder is that social conflict was not even greater. Since the Whigs identified political freedom with a cultural matrix of which Protestantism was an important part, they found the growth of Catholicism disturbing. Concern that the Church of Rome was less than enthusiastic about free institutions cannot be dismissed as irrational Protestant bigotry; Gregory XVI and Pius IX were not John XXIII. American Whig criticisms of the papacy, though placed on the *Index,* were welcomed by Italian nationalist revolutionaries. And Beecher's charges that Catholic educational and proselytizing activities in the United States were being financed by Metternich's Austria, far-fetched as they sound, have been partially substantiated. Catholic immigrants sided overwhelmingly with the proslavery wing of the Democratic party. Their political impact was felt quickly as a result of the Democratic policy, implemented in many states, of enfranchising resident aliens.[55]

One can shrug off the alleged role of the Austrian secret police and still come to an obvious conclusion. New Englanders, given their Puritan heritage, would be in the vanguard of the brief midcentury surge of native (or nativist) American and anti-Catholic politics.

Prohibiting liquor sales was another evangelical priority. Temperance activists even capitalized Rum—as in Demon Rum. From first enactments in Maine (1851) and Vermont (1852), Prohibition laws spread across Greater New England in the 1850s, quickly gathering a serious constituency. Preachers led the charge. To Connecticut's Lyman Beecher, the hostile state Democratic Party included "nearly all the minor sects, besides the rum-selling, tippling folk, infidels and ruff-scuff generally." He might have mentioned hard-drinking volunteer fire companies, one of which refused to fight the flames as Beecher's church burned down.[56]

Protestant Prohibitionists prevailed in New England, where they didn't care about offending the ever-thirsty Irish Catholics. But in states like Ohio, Illinois, Wisconsin, and Iowa, politically undismissable Germans cherished their beer gardens and wineries and rallied on this issue as on no other. Chicago's famous "lager beer" riots of April 1855, occurring as a law prohibiting Sunday beer sales took effect, forced the army to bring in field guns to cover the approaches to city hall. Breweries were even more important in Wisconsin. There were scores in Milwaukee alone—a city where Schlitz also became a park, and Pabst a theatre. Even when the Wisconsin legislature's Maine Law of 1855 exempted beer, cider, and wine to appease the Germans, the Democratic governor profited by vetoing it.[57]

Protestant Germans swung the critical weight. Charles Reemelin of Cincinnati, their Ohio leader, was also a wine producer. When he broke with the Democrats over Kansas-Nebraska and slavery (as well as the "intrigues of papal agents"), the German Protestants' partial shift to the Republicans included conditions relating to Prohibition and immigrant naturalization.[58] By late 1856, Ohio Republican state legislators deliberately split on Prohibition legislation to keep it from becoming a party issue.[59]

Sunday blue laws were another church-fanned controversy. Connecticut forbad children to whistle or enjoy themselves on Sunday, and the circus was declared a public nuisance in 1839. Ohio, partly settled from Connecticut, forbad work or pleasure on Sunday and fined any who might "profanely curse, damn or swear by the name of God," gamble, duel, or "fight or box at fisticuffs."[60] Such laws could make Democrats out of Episcopal squires as well as Catholic immigrants.

In New England proper, party politics were also colored by the religious combats of disestablishing Congregational churches in Connecticut, New Hampshire, and Massachusetts during the years beween 1817 and 1833. Overthrow in Connecticut came after a Democratic governor, Oliver Wolcott, won in 1817 on a disestablishment platform aided by a coalition of Baptists, Episcopalians, Methodists, and political Jeffersonians.[61] By the 1830s and 1840s, Congregationalists were the mainstay of New England Whiggery, while Baptists, Episcopalians, and the lesser Protestant sects were largely Democrats.[62] Divisions like these carried over into the Civil War Democratic-Republican rivalry, as we will see.

New England support for Yankee causes was something of a seamless web. "Government," said one well-known Yankee, "is the expression of morality."[63] Charles Finney, prominent as both an abolitionist and evangelist, put it another way: "Politics," he said, "was an indispensable part of religion."[64]

Not that all moral and religious issues were equal. Evangelical northern Protestants were especially caught up in suspicion of Rome and in the slavery and free-soil issues. These last two also had an immediate religious twist. As the war approached, abolitionists found their anti-Catholicism reinforced by the pro-slavery, anti-Negro politics of the Irish. "The Catholic press upholds the slave power," charged the Boston Commonwealth, a Free Soil organ. "These two malign powers have a natural affinity for each other."[65] Emancipation supporters in New York also complained about Archbishop John Hughes' insistence that while the local Irish would fight for the Union, they would not fight to free blacks.[66]

New Englanders, although the strongest Whigs north of the Mason-Dixon line, had been driven toward third parties by the slavery-related straddling tendencies of Whig presidential candidates. The Liberty Party itself was a display case of the religious genesis of abolitionist politics. The party's first address, denouncing slavery as a crime against man and God, demanded its immediate destruction. The Bible was its political textbook, and according to historian Eric Foner, "Liberty party tickets were often prefaced with quotations from Scripture, and a number of Liberty party conventions adopted lengthy resolutions on the Biblical reasons for abolishing slavery. As one Western Liberty leader wrote, 'the truth is that most of our leaders and political speakers have been and are ministers—not statesmen or politicians.'"[67]

New England's several Puritan drumbeats increased during the early 1850s. As abolitionism was gathering force, immigration into the United States soared, so that the new Know-Nothing Party did much better than minor nativist splinter parties had in the 1840s. By 1854, local Democratic parties in the North bore the burden of seeming too pro-Catholic as well as too pro-southern and proslavery. Know-Nothings defeated them in state after state.

But the Know-Nothings, in turn, found it impossible to straddle the slavery debate. Despite their huge, sudden successes of 1854 and

1855, in which they ran ahead of the new Republicans in states like Massachusetts, Pennsylvania, and New York, no party of undiluted nativism unwilling to take a stand on slavery could become the northern political alternative to the Democrats. By 1856, as the dust settled, the North had opted for another new party, at the state level variously calling itself Fusion, Independent, or Republican. One key to its opportunity was timing—emerging and consolidating as the other parties lost voter confidence. However, the Republican Party also pulled together virtually all of the cultural and ideological strands of Second Great Awakening Yankee Protestantism.

To be sure, several of those evangelical strands—Prohibition, blue laws, and nativism—had worn out their earlier success. Yet all were woven, at least in safe, small ways, into the cultural cloth of the new party. Voters who cared deeply about antiforeign and Sabbatarian themes had mostly become Republicans. The new party's quieter displays—its leaders' past involvement in several of the fading causes, the balance of nominations between factions, the distribution of patronage, the familiar names of clubs (the 1860 Wide-Awakes, for example, borrowed a Know-Nothing name), evocative slogans and loaded phrases—were as important as the carefully phrased statements and calculated omissions of biennial platforms.

Northern Republicanism was essentially Protestant, with little Catholic support. But the party did have widespread *immigrant* backing—the great bulk of the British Protestants, most of the Scandinavians, and growing numbers of Dutch and German Protestants. After the temperance and Know-Nothing fights, Republican leaders in the western states with the highest foreign-born ratios of 1860—Wisconsin (36 percent), Minnesota (34 percent), Illinois (19 percent), Iowa (16 percent), and Ohio (14 percent)—understood that nativism was coalitional poison. Not only were immigrants essential to peopling the new free states that were starting to tip the political balance in Washington, but most of the British, Scandinavian, Dutch, and German Protestants shared two important attitudes with Yankees: opposition to slavery and suspicion of Catholicism. To offend *these* immigrants with delayed citzenship or voting constraints or inability to qualify for homesteads would be foolish. According to one activist in Illinois, a strong antinativist position would attract "the Germans, English, Protestant Irish, Scotch and Scandinavian vote . . . more than double the Know-Nothing strength."[68]

What the new party did not have, or expect in any quantity, was support from *Catholic* immigrants. Even in Wisconsin and Illinois, states with particularly large immigrant populations, Protestant-Catholic divisions were assumed and electorally acceptable. Well-known anti-Catholic Whig and Know-Nothing politicians were prominent in Republican ranks: Nathaniel Banks and Henry Wilson of Massachusetts, Simon Cameron and Thaddeus Stevens of Pennsylvania, Schuyler Colfax of Indiana, and Shelby Cullom of Illinois.

However, being so Yankee in its origins, the new party in its first years was much less appealing to the non-Yankee, native-born Protestant voters of the Lower North. This cultural split had important denominational overlaps: New England–sprung Congregationalists and Unitarians were overwhelmingly Republican; Presbyterians were not far behind.

Methodists and Baptists, two fast-growing major denominations that had already split into separate northern and southern churches, were more affected by geography. They leaned Republican if they were of Yankee stock in the orbit of Greater New England. In the border zones of the Lower North, however, a much larger ratio voted Democratic. Southern Baptists in the Ohio Valley sections of Ohio, Indiana, and Illinois were mostly Democrats.

Republican strategists had to be careful which issues they emphasized (or downplayed) and where. Nativism was minimized in the states with large blocs of German immigrants. On the other hand, it was indulged through state-level coalitions and shared nominations in conservative, heavily Protestant, but largely non-Yankee states like Indiana and Pennsylvania. By 1860, opposition to slavery, while the single most important issue in the North as a whole, was also de-emphasized in many of the states amenable to nativism—New Jersey, as well as Pennsylvania and Indiana.

Greater New Englanders had been more or less enlisted by 1856. When the 1860 election returns were tabulated in New England proper, Ohio, Michigan, and Wisconsin, Abraham Lincoln received essentially the same share of the vote already taken by John C. Frémont, the 1856 nominee. Lincoln's acceptance of the revised but obvious Republican strategy of 1860—to add the critical support needed for victory in New Jersey, Pennsylvania, Indiana, and Illinois while retaining closely won New York—called for moderating the Third Puritanism. The party needed to harness more ex–Know-Nothing support and to enlist more voters whose opposition to slavery owed little to evangelicalism or abolitionism and a good deal more to economic sensitivity—and even to Negrophobia.

The new tactics worked. Lincoln ran 24.2 points ahead of Frémont in Pennsylvania, 19.6 points in New Jersey, 10–11 in Illinois and Indiana, and 7.4 in New York. Each of these states had pro-abolition sections, usually New England–settled, but a larger part of the electorate couched their opposition to slavery in a different context: *supporting free white labor and its wages by prohibiting the immigration of free blacks as well as the institution of slavery.* By 1860, Illinois, Indiana, Iowa, and Oregon had all prohibited Negroes from entering their boundaries. Congressman David Wilmot, the Pennsylvanian, whose name lives on with the Wilmot Proviso to bar slavery in any territories taken from Mexico, made no bones about white-supremacist motivations: Far from any "squeamish sensitiveness on the subject of slavery, (or) morbid sympathy . . . I plead the cause of the free white man." He urged that the West be reserved for whites because "the negro race already occupy enough of this fair continent."[69]

Neither religion nor moral fervor underpinned this aspect of the Republican Party's free-soil strategy. Stalwart abolitionist ministers were disappointed. Other Third Puritan themes like Prohibition, Sunday blue laws, and ethnic exclusivity were also downplayed in the final late-1850s stages of Republican coalition-building. Yet the political role of the churches can hardly be exaggerated. The breaking-up of the Baptists, Methodists, and Presbyterians radicalized preachers in both sections. William W. Sweet, the church historian, has gone so far as to say that "there are good arguments to support the claim that the split in the churches was not only the first break between the sections but the chief cause of the final break."[70] Henry Clay, on the eve of his death in 1852, had shown the same concern: "I tell you, this sundering of the religious ties which have bound our people together I consider the greatest source of danger to our country."[71]

Because of their desire for self-justification, the sectional churches did indeed fan the fervor. "In this hardening of attitudes," concluded religious historian Ahlstrom, "the churches were a powerful factor. . . . They gave moral grandeur to the antislavery cause and divine justification for slavery. In the North, the churches did much to hold the party of Lincoln on its antislavery course."[72]

British Protestantism also had a major role in the American war. But relative to the United States, early nineteenth-century British politics remained even more firmly in the grip of eighteenth-century religious memories and tensions. The British general election of May 1807, for example, although fought in the gloomiest trough of the Napoleonic Wars, has been described as one in which "the popular constituencies turned largely on the Catholic issue (Catholic relief) and reflected popular prejudices dating back to Elizabeth I and to 1689."[73] Indeed, the "Catholic issue"—at its core, political and religious rights for Catholics in Ireland—gripped Britain until Catholic Emancipation in 1829 gave them the same civic and legal status as Protestant dissenters and opened virtually all public positions in England and Scotland.

Meanwhile, two-party politics in nineteenth-century Britain routinely continued to reflect differences and schisms within Protestantism. From Thomas Macauley to George Trevelyan, a school of British historians have characterized the sometimes vague alignment between Whigs and Tories (and then between Liberals and Conservatives) as principally arising out of the division between the Church of England and the body of dissenting Protestants. In Trevelyan's words, "the dualism of the English religious world and the disabilities imposed on dissenters form a larger part of the explanation of the peculiarly English phenomenon of two continuous political parties in every shire and town of the land, surviving even when obvious political issues seemed asleep or settled."[74]

The hostility between the Puritans and the High Church Anglicans of Charles I and Archbishop Laud was a chapter in this chronicle of tension. So, too, for the polarity of 1775 in which High Church Anglicans opposed Presbyterian, Congregational, Baptist, and other dissenters in England as well as in the American colonies. The period leading up to the American Civil War, in turn, was kept on the old track by another surge of nonconformist religion and politics in Britain. This one was the most powerful since Cromwell—and, fittingly, it was an era in which favorable views of Cromwell, Pym, and other English Civil War leaders made their first, albeit small, modern English comeback in working-class, nonconformist, and radical circles.[75]

The early nineteenth-century nonconformist emergence was akin to what Americans described as the Great Awakening across the Atlantic. Between 1800 and 1840, powerful currents of evangelicalism exploded the numbers of Methodists, Congregationalists, and Baptists in Britain by 300–400 percent. By another measure, the six decades from 1760 to 1820 saw the proportion of nonconformists in the population increase almost tenfold to 30 percent. In any event, the 1851 census found that fully 40 percent of churchgoers in England and 75 percent in Wales attended nonconformist chapels.[76]

Nonconformists were the "life of the agitation" for the Reform Bill of 1832. Then its passage further increased their influence. As the electorate grew by about 50 percent, the inevitable Whig and Tory concentration on political organization and individual registration (on the National Register of Voters) depended heavily on religious denominations and church organizations.[77] Whigs sought out nonconformists because they were Whig or Liberal in politics by a ratio of between 8 and 12 to 1, according to one calculation. Anglicans were Tory or Conservative by a ratio of between 2.5 to 1 and 4 to 1. The 1832 and 1867 Reform Acts further confirmed religion as the primary yardstick of party.[78]

This expansion also increased British political responsiveness to two religious propositions: the beliefs that moral conduct was the test of the good Christian and that it was within man's capacity, under God's guidance, to work toward a state of social and spiritual harmony on earth. Despite broad national support, by midcentury this viewpoint was particularly associated with the Whig Party and its successor, the Liberal Party. Both had similar coalitions: A large majority of nonconformist voters joined with an important minority of Liberal Anglicans.

As a result, British Whig and Liberal politics, usually dominant in Parliament from 1832 to the 1880s, had a dual emphasis that would not have been out of place in Michigan or Ohio. On one hand, political, economic, and social reform. On the other, a religious policy bent that combined dissenter rights, disestablishment of state churches and state religious education, overtones of anticlericalism in foreign policy, and some lingering anti-Catholicism. Its grand reformism produced the most famous legislation: Catholic Emancipation (1829), the electoral Reform Act (1832), and abolition of slavery in the British Empire (1834). But along with this trio came advances in penal reform, education, public health, and treatment of the insane, as well as movements for Bible study, self-help, temperance, and better urban conditions. The parallel to aspects of U.S. Whig politics in the 1830s and 1840s and then to the more sedate wing of the Republican Party is unmistakeable.

However, mid-nineteenth-century relationships within England, Ireland, Scotland, and Wales involved a quilt of state churches and church-related educational systems—and with them church-state questions and a raison d'être of Liberal politics that had largely faded in the United States after Massachusetts ended (Congregational) church establishment in 1833. In Britain, disestablishment issues added to the religious backdrop to national affairs. A well-received study published in 1986 by Dr. J. H. Parry, fellow of Peterhouse College, Cambridge, concluded that "politics, in the 1860s and 1870s, cannot be understood if it is treated merely as a secular activity. . . . For most politicians, politics had a religious dimension; for vast numbers of voters, it was conceived as an activity of significance mainly because religious issues were so prominent."[79]

Many of the issues involved—the Irish Church Act, university admissions, religious tests for officeholding, government appointment of Anglican bishops, and the like—are collateral to this book's subject matter and can be left aside. During the period of the American Civil War, however, religious questions can fairly be called central to British politics. Moreover, the fastest-expanding nonconformist denominations—Presbyterians, Congregationalists, Methodists, and Baptists—shared ties to progressive politics, antislavery activism, and a view of government moral responsibility reasonably akin to that of the American North. Evangelists, missionaries, and lecturers moved easily between nonconformist Britain and the United States, and further views were exchanged at large meetings like the Anglo-American evangelical conference in London in 1846.

Between 1851 and 1861, moreover, nearly a half million Protestant emigrants from England, Scotland, Wales, and Ireland, largely nonconformist and mostly working-class and lower-middle-class, left for the United States, some arriving through Canada. Ninety-five percent went to the North, principally Yankee or industrial areas where they quickly blended into the comparable culture and denominationalism: Welsh and English to the Ohio potteries; Scots, English, and northern Irish to greater Pittsburgh and the New England mills and machine shops; Welsh to the Ohio and Pennsylvania collieries; Cornish "Cousin Jacks" to the Wisconsin lead mines and the Lake Superior copper pits; and Scots and Welsh to the Vermont quarries.

What made this so important, as the United States of 1860 and 1861 moved toward a civil war, was that Britain itself was about to become a major battleground—not in the cavalry-trodden manner of Northamptonshire or Leicestershire in the 1640s, but once again, as in the 1770s, in the ebb and flow of opinion-molding. This struggle would take place on the floor of the House of Commons, in the chapels of Nottingham and Bristol, in the workmen's clubs of London, in Manchester's Free-Trade Hall, and in newspaper typesetting rooms from Plymouth to Paisley. Once more, the nature of British armed intervention and involvement across the Atlantic would be swayed by the winds of British politics, nonconformism, and public opinion. To call this nonconformist resurgence a Second Cromwellism has no real basis, but there is nothing excessive about suggesting—as chapter 11 will—that without these countertrends, upper-class Britain would have been more likely to intervene on behalf of the Confederacy.

As before, however, this is getting ahead of our story. The British government under Lord Palmerston has not yet reached its 1862–1863 crisis points. No depression has shut the Lancashire cotton mills. No Cabinet meetings have debated whether to recognize the independence of the cotton-growing South or to risk war with the North. In the United States, it is late spring 1861. The Republican Party, coalesced by Greater New England and the Second Great Awakening, has elected and just inaugurated a president,

Abraham Lincoln, whose Electoral College majority came from a low 39.8 percent of the popular vote in a four-way race. The southern response on April 12, to bombard Fort Sumter, in the harbor of Charleston, South Carolina, has rallied the North, whose citizens are oversubscribing to Lincoln's call for soldiers. That has prompted the four uncertain Upper Southern states—Virginia, North Carolina, Tennessee, and Arkansas—to join the cotton South. The full Confederacy is now in place.

The three churches that divided over slavery and sectionalism are sending chaplains by the hundreds to their respective armies. The Southern Baptist and Southern Methodist churches will support the Confederacy as vehemently as the Congregationalist, Unitarian, and Scandinavian Lutheran churches of Greater New England back the Union. But the most important role of religion in the American Civil War has already been played: shaping the political vehicles, infusing the morality, and furnishing the banners and battle hymns.

In wartime politics and alignments, denominationalism will be an important underpinning, but not an immediate or driving force. The distinction is critical. The fighting of 1861–1865 is to be a war of morality, nationalism, and sectional animosity, not a panorama of religious battlefields as in the 1640s or a landscape of burned and gutted churches as was sometimes the case in the 1770s. It is these loyalties, in more detail, to which we will now turn.

10

THE U.S. CIVIL WAR

Loyalties, Alignments, and Partisanships, 1861–1865

The issue of slavery lay at the heart of what many on both sides thought they were fighting for. But it was not a simple or clear-cut issue, and for one side (the North) it threatened for a time to divide more than to unite them.

—James M. McPherson, *What They Fought For,* 1994

The intense individualism of the abolitionists, historians are agreed, derived from the great revivals of the Second Great Awakening.

—Eric Foner, *Politics and Ideology in the Age of the Civil War,* 1980

In the early 1850s an intensified anti-Catholicism emerged simultaneously with a hostility to politicians and an impatience with established parties.

—Michael F. Holt, *The Politics of Impatience,* 1978

THE THREE COUSINS' WARS are not just a ladder of British and American national emergence. Taken together, their internal loyalties and alignments are another ladder, this one of social and cultural evolution—each rung or war with many continuities, but each more complicated than the one before. Which, of course, is altogether logical. The kinships and animosities, ethnic and denominational mistrusts, and local feuds and calculations that spanned the British North Atlantic of 1775–1783 included many more threads and textures than the fabric of what had been a clash principally within the British Isles during the 1640s.

The U.S. Civil War, in turn, involved even more sectional and ethnic nuances, with the further complication of millions of recent immigrants in the United States. Their political and religious self-perceptions, although in transition, nevertheless still added a new set of old-country loyalties and denominational factionalisms. The British political and popular involvement of 1861–1865 in still another North American war—tactical, moral, and rhetorical, to be sure, not military (although that may have been a close call)—also had many strands. However, as in looking at the Revolution, the British alignments are dealt with separately in chapter 11.

This chapter, in beginning with Civil War party politics and wartime loyalty in the North, starts with the same group that led off the discussion of the patriot side in the Revolution: Yankee New England. Sentiment was more divided in the Lower North— the Middle Atlantic states and the Ohio Valley—principally because these regions had either stretches settled from the South or districts where slaveholding had been substantial through the end of the eighteenth century. Religion itself was almost as important in 1860, through issues like temperance, sabbath-keeping, and Catholic-Protestant distrust, as well as the debate over slavery, as it had been in 1775. The important new ingredients in northern alignments were the huge numbers of Irish immigrants and the extent to which these helped to precipitate a new wave of anti-Catholicism, along with the comparable importance of a massive influx of German immigration, which also dwarfed any of the eighteenth-century movements. The Germans, as we will see, played an important role in the U.S. wartime politics of 1861–1865, and to fathom their alignments, the reader will need a new small set of tools—a map of a Germany still not quite united in the eighteen-sixties (see page 439) and a willingness to entertain why Lutherans from Pomerania might have arrived in the 1830s or 1840s with a different set of views from Bavarian Catholics or the anticlerical "Forty-Eighters" who fled after the abortive German revolutions of that year.

As in the description of Revolutionary alignments in chapter 5, the examination of northern loyalties of 1861–1865 in these pages is followed by a juxtaposition with the core of the other side: the slave-owning Cotton South, epitomized by the first seven states to secede in 1860–1861 and form the Confederacy. The last subsection, appropriately enough, will look at the divided regions in between: the eight states of the Upper South and Border. Four of them, after some reluctance, went with the cotton states. The other four, with reluctance of their own, stayed in the Union.

Civil War Party Politics and Wartime Loyalty in the North

Seventy-one years and seven months after Robert E. Lee surrendered to Ulysses S. Grant at Appomattox, the state of Vermont, which gave Abraham Lincoln his highest statewide share (76 percent) of the presidential vote in 1860, provided the same salutation for Alfred M. Landon, the Republican nominee in 1936. Vermont was just one of two states that year to stick with the party of Lincoln. And the top Democratic states? The same seven that seceded to set up the Confederacy in the months following Lincoln's election. Or almost: By 1936, Arkansas was a shade more Democratic than Florida, already a northern retirement center, which dropped to eighth place. The two states still the most Democratic in that presidential election—South Carolina (98.6 percent) and Mississippi (97 percent)—had been the first two to leave the Union back in that angry winter of 1860–1861.

The party politics and wartime loyalties of the American Civil War, in short, were commitments to take seriously. Four years of war and a bitter peace were an awesome forge. Fidelities were not necessarily the same in 1861 and in 1860—nor, for that matter, were they the same in the afterglow of Fort Sumter's bombardment as they had been earlier that April. Indeed, there was a significant change in the North by November 1864 relative to the gloomier days of November 1862. The caution about the English Civil War quoted on page 40—that it changed alignments and issues as it progressed—is still worth heeding two hundred years later.

Having said this, a revealing look at the alignments within the North can be found in the map drawn by the election of Lincoln in

November 1860. Its portrait of cultural and sectional frustration and de facto willingness to support war speaks volumes—and the best place to start is in the Green Mountains, with the characteristics of the most Republican state of them all.

Patent Medicines, Water Witches, and Graham Crackers

Vermont did have its mansions and archetypal white Congregational churches—in particular, Bennington's famous "Old First," which might as well be in Connecticut. But for the most part, Vermont was a newer, less rooted place. Migrants flooded in after 1783, and large numbers left again after 1815 to settle upstate New York, Michigan, Wisconsin, and Minnesota.

Itinerants, inventors, and radicals were almost the norm. Causes were everywhere. Stewart Holbrook, whose book *The Yankee Exodus* elaborates New Englanders' westward trek, described northeast Vermont's quirky nineteenth-century population: "The Dorrellites, the Perfectionists, the Christians (from nearby Lyndon); and so to the Anti-Masons, the anti-nicotine forces, the Temperance shouters, the hydrotherapists, the anti-calomel men, the hosts of assorted Sabbatarians, the sellers of lightning rods. So also, the Friends of Liberia, the vegetarians, the Grahamites, the Thomsonians, the homeopaths."[1]

Native son Holbrook wryly recalled how in hard times, Yankees made gadgets to sell to each other like tin calf weaners, patent water witches, and soapstone stoves. And how as Vermonters adopted statewide Prohibition—they were second, after Maine— the Green Mountain Seths, Jethros, and Calebs were careful to stock up with patent medicines and elixirs, from Dr. Herrick's Liver & Blood Invigorator to Green's August Flower. Large quantities of "preservative" alcohol, rarely mentioned on the labels, had been included to help warm cold New England winters. Indeed, Holbrook's description leaves out some of the most interesting Vermont offspring—the polygamist Mormons (founder Joseph Smith came from Whitingham, Vermont), the nonbathing Pilgrims, the free-love Oneida Community, and the Vegetarian Emigration Company, organized in 1855 to help settle Kansas by a disciple of Sylvester Graham, the culinary Puritan who invented graham crackers.

The little New Englands to the west were similar. Frederick Jackson Turner described the Yankee emigrant stronghold in western New York, called the "burned-over district" for its fiery crusades, as the breeding-ground of the Anti-Mason movement and "the home of isms and reform movements."[2] A Whig state legislator from Ohio's Western Reserve in later years recalled it, too, as

> the home of the various *isms*, the vagaries, *mental ailments* many called them, of a people noted throughout the land for this distinctive feature, so that whoever had a hobby elsewhere rejected, rode it straightway to the Reserve, where it was quite certain of hospitable pasturage and shelter.[3]

Such was the Yankee Republican quintessence. Anyone weighing mid-nineteenth-century Vermont (or the burned-over district or the Reserve) against the backdrop of the wars of 1642 and 1775 must wonder: Did these sections have some unusual ancestry in the zealots of the English Civil War—the "agitators" or political officers of the New Model Army, the wilder chaplains and Puritan lecturers, the Fifth Kingdom men, Anabaptists, and familists? No more, apparently, than other New Englanders. Yet it bears repetition that Vermont and similar rural and small-town areas of Greater New England—and definitely not fashionable Boston, Newport, New Haven, or the small Episcopalian towns of southwest Connecticut—were the seedbeds and strongholds of the Republican Party.

Farmers, artisans, and small businessmen from Maine to Minnesota were its electoral paladins. Below Vermont, the next highest eight states of 1860 Republican presidential allegiance march across that same cultural North Country geography of hemlocks, birches, causes, and contraptions: Minnesota (63.4 percent), Massachusetts (62.8 percent), Maine (62.2 percent), Rhode Island (61.4 percent), Connecticut (58.1 percent), Michigan (57.2 percent), New Hampshire (56.9 percent), and Wisconsin (56.6 percent). Here, too, had been the hotbeds of abolitionism. Maps 10.1a and 10.1b show how the core areas of support for the antislavery Free Soil ticket in the 1848 election were, in general, the future peaks of the Republican Party in the presidential elections of 1860 and 1864. The counties shaded for Free Soil fidelity in 1848 almost all fell within Greater New England. Those in the 1860–1864 portrait are still Yankee-centered, but with additions in greater Pittsburgh, lower Ohio, and parts of northern Illinois and Wisconsin settled by Germans, Swedes, and Norwegians.

However well the Republicans fared in the nouveau-riche sections of Pittsburgh, Cleveland, and Chicago, their taint of radicalism hurt in the older establishment precincts of the urban East—Philadelphia, New York, and even Yankee Boston. So much "Cotton" Whig sentiment lingered in the halls of Boston's fashionable Somerset Club that in early 1863, Republican stalwarts withdrew down Beacon Street to form their own group, the Union Club. A colleague in the new party pointedly—and correctly—observed to William H. Seward in 1856 that "our greatest obstacle is the respectable, fashionable well to do class."[4]

Few of the Yankee Republicans who attacked southern aristocrats thought of themselves as speaking for that same class in the North. Their professed commitments were to the small entrepreneur, the storekeeper, and the yeoman farmer as exemplars of "free labor" and social mobility that made today's hired laborer tomorrow's capitalist. Republicans who talked of labor rarely meant an urban proletariat. They meant, in Abraham Lincoln's words, people who worked in shops and on farms, "taking the whole product for themselves and asking no favors of capital on the one hand, nor of hirelings and slaves on the other."[5] This structure, widespread across Greater New England, was as incompatible with southern slavery as the small-scale Puritan entrepreneurship of England's cloth districts, cheese towns, lead-mining hillsides, and cutlery centers of the 1640s had been with the late-feudal manor agriculture and royally bestowed wine, soap, and coal monopolies of Stuart England.

Yankee domination within Greater New England was such that statewide or regional support for the Republican Party of 1860 was in the 60–75 percent range. Of the Yankee Congregationalists and Presbyterians, probably 80–90 percent voted Republican. Their militant small towns, the Oberlins, Elyrias, Coldwaters, and Vermontvilles, stood out on early maps of Free Soil support like

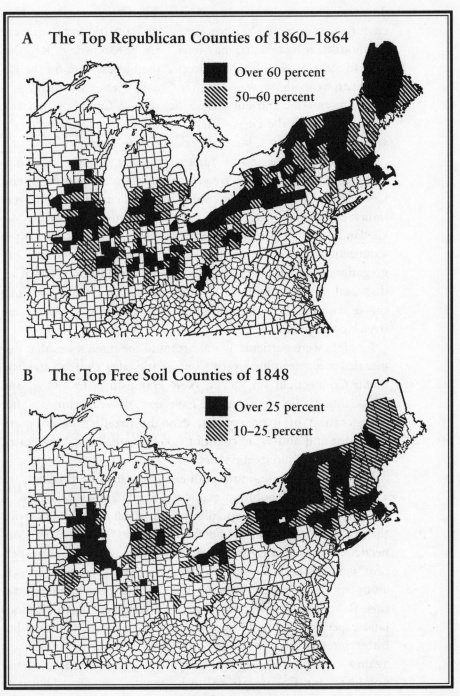

MAPS *10.1a & b*

Tawney's Puritan clothing towns rising like Genevas from the Lancashire countryside. Yankee Free-Will Baptists and Northern Methodists, less stalwart, may have been 70–80 percent Republican. In most of New England proper, the biggest drag on the Republican vote share was another Stuart-era reenactment—the nearly monolithic anti-Puritan politics of Irish Catholics, this time close at hand in the cities. They cast some 10–15 percent of the vote in Massachusetts, but less in the other five states.

Even so, the cohesion of Yankee Protestantism was not complete. Explanations of the frequently close elections in Protestant Connecticut and New Hampshire—Republican strategists were unnerved in 1864 as Democratic presidential nominee George McClellan drew 47.4 percent in New Hampshire and 48.6 percent in Connecticut—pivot on the tensions between establishment Congregationalism and other denominations. Lyman Beecher's earlier dismissal of the "minor sects" in the Democratic Party was long out of date by 1860. Methodists and Baptists were important all over New England.

Grudges were particularly important in the three states that dismantled a nineteenth-century Congregationalist church establishment: Connecticut (in 1818), New Hampshire (in 1819), and Massachusetts (in 1833). As we have seen, disestablishment, after a generation of maneuvering, brought together potent anti-Federalist and anti-Whig coalitions of Episcopalians, Methodists, Baptists, deists, and freethinkers.

In New Hampshire, more than elsewhere in New England, the 1860 and 1864 Republican presidential vote still correlated with the earlier Whig-Democratic division in which Democrats carried the poorer, heavily Baptist northern counties.[6] In southern Connecticut, a powerful Episcopalian vote, perhaps as high as 30 percent, made Fairfield County go Democratic for president in 1852, along with two eastern counties with high Baptist-Methodist ratios. Revolutionary War history also affected the local religious landscape. Fairfield had been the scene of Connecticut's small but bitter internal civil war—for the most part pitting Anglicans against Congregationalists. Episcopalian support for Democratic nominees, anti-Congregational in its genesis, remained high during the Yankee Republican crisis of 1860–1864.[7] These legacies were less divisive among New England–sprung Protestants in the Great Lakes, who had newer animosities to think about. But where bad blood went back a century or two, old divisions held on.

Butternuts and Knickerbockers: The Lower North as a Pivot

Map 10.2 divides the northern states of 1860 into Greater New England, the southern-settled "Butternut" portions of the Ohio and Upper Mississippi Valleys, Old Pennsylvania, Old New Jersey, and the Lower Hudson Valley of Old New York, together with the extensions of these regions into the Midwest. The Old Pennsylvania, Old New Jersey, and Old New York sections of this Lower North essentially correspond to the sections settled in the seventeenth- and eighteenth-century colonial era by non-Yankees. Only a half dozen counties in these sections have New England origins. Relations between New England and the Yorkers, Pennsylvanians and New Jerseymen, had been strained from the start.

In 1861 political terms, one can think of this non-Yankee countryside—the Delaware, Susquehanna, and Lower Hudson Valleys—as the eastern equivalent of the Ohio Valley. Both sections enjoyed pivotal leverage on the governorships and electoral votes of crucial states. Disenchantment with the war and even southern sympathy came close to undercutting the Lincoln administration at the ballot box in 1862, and provided a lesser scare in the pre-election summer of 1864.

No equivalent of the Mason-Dixon line provides a neat surveyor's contour. But Map 10.2 begins the approximate border of the non-Yankee Northeast in the middle of New York's Long Island, near Oyster Bay, where the eastern margin of Dutch burgherdom edged into Connecticut-settled countryside. Crossing Long Island Sound, our vague and imprecise demarcation moves north near the New York–Connecticut and New York–Massachusetts boundaries to the petering-out of the old colonial Dutch settlement east of Albany. Thereafter, the line goes west through the Dutch and German settlements of the Mohawk Valley and then south through James Fenimore Cooper's "Leatherstocking Country"

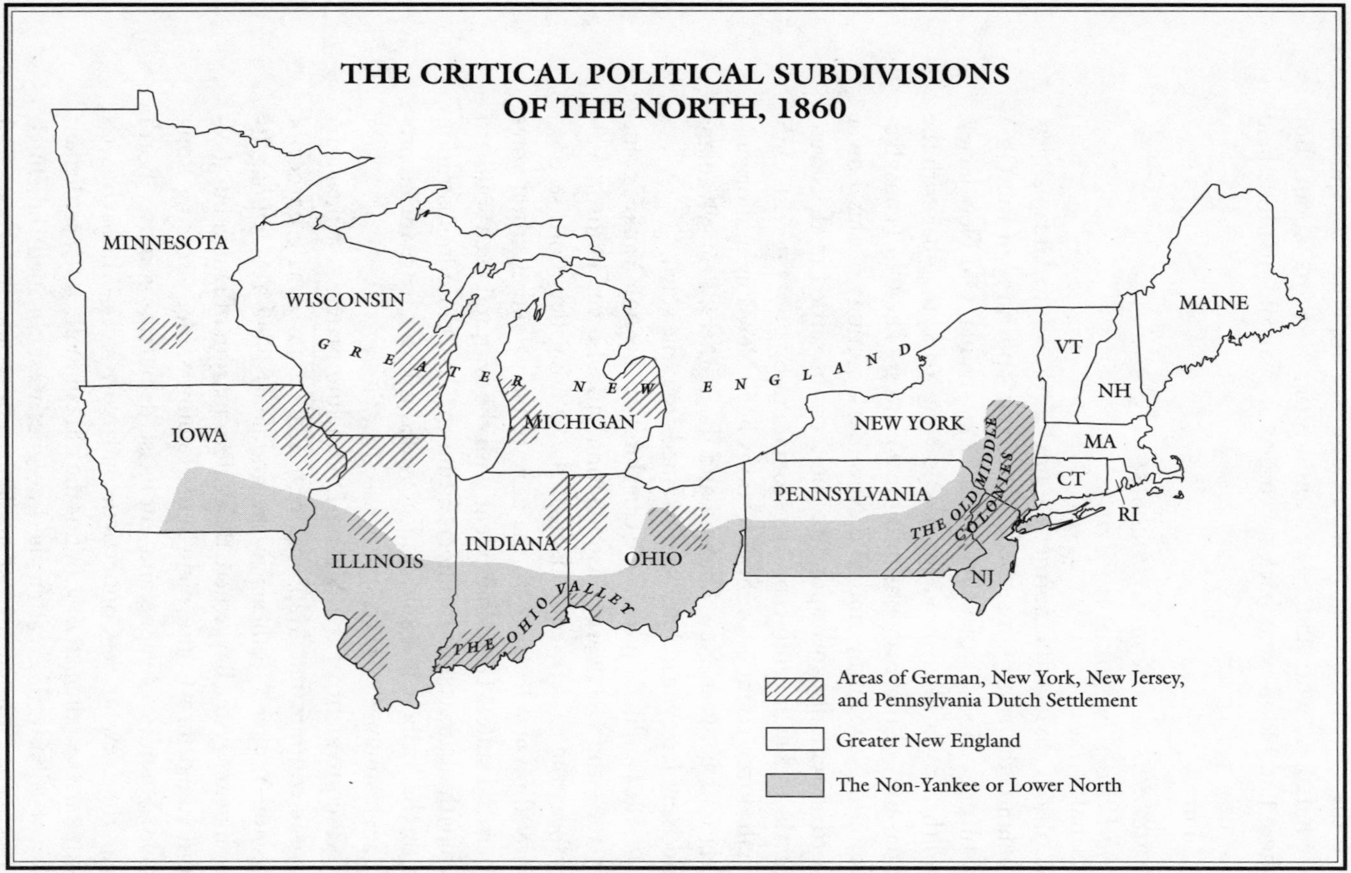

THE CRITICAL POLITICAL SUBDIVISIONS
OF THE NORTH, 1860

MAINE

NH

VT

MA

CT

RI

NEW YORK

NJ

THE OLD MIDDLE COLONIES

PENNSYLVANIA

OHIO

THE OHIO VALLEY

INDIANA

ILLINOIS

GREATER NEW ENGLAND

MICHIGAN

WISCONSIN

MINNESOTA

IOWA

Areas of German, New York, New Jersey,
and Pennsylvania Dutch Settlement

Greater New England

The Non-Yankee or Lower North

MAP 10.2

into the eastern watershed of the Susquehanna, past Elmira and Binghamton, New York, to Scranton and Wilkes-Barre, Pennsylvania. From there, the cultural transition zone goes west following the curve of the Susquehanna and then the line of the Blue Mountains more or less to Altoona. Turning there, it goes west to Pittsburgh and then to Ohio.

In 1860, the sections of New York, New Jersey, and Pennsylvania marked off by this vague line were Yankee-distrusting and politically inclined to the Democrats. Their Dutch, English Anglican, German Palatine, Pennsylvania Dutch (German), and Quaker populations hadn't liked the New Englanders much in the eighteenth century, and nineteenth-century developments had kept these sensitivities alive. Pennsylvania had its own not-always-popular little New England along its northern tier and in the Connecticut-settled Wyoming Valley. As for New York, by the 1830s, Yankee emigrants had so overrun its northern sections—over half the delegates to the New York Constitutional Convention of 1821 were said to have New England origins—that Old Yorkers, or Knickerbockers, Dutch and English alike, were culturally defensive and politically watchful. To keep the old Knickerbocker New York City of the Van Cortlandts, Philipses, and Schuylers from being overwhelmed by pushy Grinnells, Morgans, and Greeleys, the old elite even organized clubs to counter New England influence.[8]

John Adams and Benjamin Franklin, both Boston-born, had on occasion made slights themselves—Franklin's famous 1751 remark about Pennsylvania being in danger of turning German and Adams's later disparagement of both Dutch and German torpidity.[9] But the tensions had deeper roots. The New Englanders were as grabby commercially as they were geographically. The Dutch of New York and New Jersey, moreover, were also the northeastern population group who kept slaves the longest and remained the most supportive of slavery up to the Civil War era.

Nevertheless, the older sections of New York, New Jersey, and Pennsylvania were political pivots. As the old system broke up in the 1850s, the new Republican Party's necessary but risky northern sectional strategy required winning four or five of the six states of the Lower North—New York, New Jersey, and Pennsylvania in the East and Ohio, Indiana, and Illinois in the West. Only two,

New York and Ohio, had supported Republican nominee Frémont in 1856. Moreover, the Yankees in these states were not the key, having been largely enlisted for Frémont by 1856. Three "swing" groups, marginal Democrats or former Whig voters who had not yet become Republicans, were identifiable in all six states.

In no particular order, the first contingent—probably the least auspicious Republican prospects—were Protestant voters of southern origins, pro-slavery sentiment, or commercial ties to the South. Next came the ex-Whigs and 1856 supporters of third-party nominee Fillmore, some of them Yankees, to whom economic issues, anti-Catholicism, or nativism was more important and to whom abolitionism was a low priority or distasteful. This was the most important available pool. The third group included Germans and Dutch. In the East, most of these were Old Dutch, "church Germans" whose forebears came in the eighteenth century, and so-called Pennsylvania Dutch. Those in the Midwest were mostly nineteenth-century German, Dutch, Swiss, and Bohemian immigrants, but with an admixture of transplanted "Yorkers" and Pennsylvania Dutch in Ohio, Indiana, and Michigan.

The bulk of these swing voters were conservatives. This was true of the rural Dutch and Germans, and the 1856 American Party vote for Fillmore was substantially a "no change" vote. Many read newspapers that blamed New England for everything from free love to John Brown's raid on Harper's Ferry. Whatever the origins or elevated intentions that Yankees might proclaim for civil war in Massachusetts pulpits or Michigan town meetings, a prospective Lincoln presidency had to be shaded very differently for voters in Schoharie, New York, Bedford, Pennsylvania, or Evansville, Indiana. That recasting was accomplished, but it helps to explain how the causes and purposes of the American Civil War became confused for several years.

Old Whigs who had voted for the third-party American candidate in 1856 and cross-pressured Germans ultimately provided Lincoln's biggest 1860 gains over Frémont's showing. However, it makes sense to begin an examination of swing voters with the obvious soft underbelly: the southern-leaning sections of the Lower North. These ran the gamut from barely literate Primitive Baptist congregations in southern Indiana to Whiggish Virginia-settled valleys in Ohio and two-century-old Dutch farm districts in New Jersey, places where favorable memories of slavery still influenced local politics. Areas where economic circumstances were the pro-southern influence included midwestern states with banks heavily invested in southern bonds; farm districts dependent on shipping through New Orleans; manufacturers located in Philadelphia, Newark, New Haven, or Boston whose markets were in the South; and New York City, where banks and commerce also had southern connections and where important Democratic politicians were convinced that the nation's greatest port should also secede and became a free-trade entrepôt.

The Ohio Valley: Soft Underbelly of the Union

West of the Appalachians, southern sympathy was mostly a matter of territory and ancestry. The prime examples were counties adjacent to Missouri, Kentucky, or Virginia (now West Virginia) or settled from southern or Border states. Dixie-born voters in Illinois dominated below an extended Mason-Dixon line in sections due west of Virginia and Kentucky. This hypothetical extension is less useful in Indiana, though, where river valleys running north-south complicated migration patterns, and still less in Ohio, where post–Revolutionary War land grants to Virginians and other settlers further scrambled latitudinal logic.

There is some irony in how Indiana, Illinois, and Iowa came into the Union as free states between 1818 and 1846. Their early population was mostly drawn from the Upper South and concentrated along the Ohio and Mississippi Rivers near Kentucky and Missouri. By 1860, these "Butternuts," who were nicknamed for the bark-made coloring with which they dyed their cheap homespun, were outnumbered by later-arriving Northerners, but they still represented 30 to 40 percent of each state's population. Abraham Lincoln, who grew up in Butternut country, used a famous simile to describe the local Baptists' un-Yankee-like taste for camp meetings and "ministers who preached as though they were fighting bumblebees."[10] Ohio, Indiana, and Illinois, it should be said, had the only large, concentrated, southern-sprung population within the political boundaries of the North.

With the exception of a small group of prosperous Virginians taking up lands in central Ohio, the emigrants from upcountry Virginia, Kentucky, Tennessee, and North Carolina, when they crossed to the north side of the Ohio River, favored nearby hilly, forested areas with wild game, timber for log cabins, utensils, and fuel, as well as navigable waterways for communications. On these lands, with their poor soil and familiar topography, the Butternuts sustained much the same lifestyle they had been used to south of the river. Few from "Kaintuck" or the Holston were drawn farther north to the less forested prairie, rewarding as these lands were for neat Yankee farms and towns. The resulting poor white milieu was one at which the New Englanders of northern Ohio, Indiana, and Illinois could and did sneer.

As war clouds gathered in the winter of 1860–1861, a few of these jurisdictions, including Perry County, Ohio, and Pope County, Illinois, considered joining the southern Confederacy. Many more voters were interested in the idea of joining a western Confederacy that would trade southward down the Mississippi while politically escaping the "Puritans" of New England—the word recurs time and again as a bitter epithet—with their tariffs, middle-class churches, and temperance movements.[11]

Not that the Butternut Midwest was favorable to slavery. Few counties gave more than a small vote to Breckinridge, the southern Democratic presidential candidate of 1860, even though he was a Kentucky neighbor. Most would probably have voted to simultaneously bar plantation owners with their wage-lowering black slaves *and* Yankee abolitionists. Indiana, Illinois, and Iowa, while prohibiting slavery, were three of the four northern states, along with Oregon, to decide in the 1850s to prohibit blacks from coming within their boundaries. Until 1849, Ohio had also had "black laws," which forced Negroes to post $500 bonds signed by freeholders, barred their testimony in court, and excluded them from public schools. As late as 1860, efforts to establish a prohibition on black entry fell only a few votes short in the Ohio House of Representatives.[12] "Free Soil" politics might stand for "freedom and rights for Negroes" in the Western Reserve; two hundred miles south along the Ohio River, however, it meant "no slavery— and no blacks—wanted here."

The Republicans of 1860 did succeed in raising their share of presidential vote in Illinois from 40.2 percent to 50.7 percent and in Indiana from 40.1 percent to 51.1 percent. Abolitionism and even slavery were downplayed. The party made major gains in the southern half of both states, winding up with 30–45 percent of the vote in most counties. In southern Indiana, for example, where Frémont had won only eighteen thousand votes in 1856, Lincoln drew over fifty-four thousand four years later.[13] Most of these were old Whigs who had gone for Fillmore, the American Party nominee, in 1856.

Lincoln himself was a vital catalyst. His Illinois-bred politics was more centrist than abolitionist. He also touched each of the region's three major cultural bases—Yankee, Butternut, and German—with a sureness that would have been envied by twentieth-century New York City politicians seeking similar rapport with electorates tied to Ireland, Israel, and Italy. The first Lincoln in America had been an English Puritan who came to Massachusetts, and before the 1860 election the Boston newspapers, unaware of this fact, credited the Republican nominee with the physiognomy of a Yankee.[14] Yet Lincoln and his parents came to Illinois by flatboat from Kentucky, an eminently Butternut arrival. Finally, as part of an effort to build ties to the Illinois German community, Lincoln in 1859 privately bought control of the state capital's German-language newspaper, the Springfield *Staats-Anziger*.[15]

Even in the Ohio Valley, a patriotic response to the attack on Fort Sumter cooled postelection disaffection, as did the northern troops quickly on the scene. But then in 1862 and early 1863, as northern generals suffered defeat after defeat, parts of southern Illinois and southern Indiana experienced riots as well as banditry that verged on pro-Confederate guerrilla activity. In late autumn, the nervous Republican governor of Illinois asked the federal War Department for permission to raise four regiments to deal with internal disturbances. In Indiana, the feisty Republican wartime chief executive, Oliver P. Morton, advised Secretary of War Stanton that Democratic politicians in Ohio, Indiana, and Illinois, beginning to assume that the South was about to secure its independence, had also begun to think about the ramifications: What would that mean for the Ohio Valley, with its all-important

Mississippi Basin links to the South? Morton concluded with a blunt apprehension:

> I give it here, as my deliberate judgment, that should the misfortune of arms or other causes, compel us to the abandonment of this war and the concession of the independence of the Rebel states, that Ohio, Indiana and Illinois can only be prevented, if at all, from a new act of secession and annexation to those states, by a bloody and desolating Civil War.[16]

The October and November elections in the Midwest had followed a series of negative developments for the Republicans. Military embarrassments included the excruciating casualty lists of Antietam and the cockiness of the successful southern cavalry raid on Chambersburg, Pennsylvania. Lincoln's preliminary announcement, on September 22, of the Emancipation Proclamation that would free the slaves in the South had also been unpopular. Hard times also plagued the Upper Mississippi. Once river traffic was shut down by the war in 1861, commodity prices weakened, many banks failed, and railroads kept raising their freight charges. Economics was an important part of the disillusionment—at least until the Mississippi was open again in 1863.[17] No comparable burden attached to Republicans in other sections.

The party's losses in the 1862 elections in the Northeast were minor to middling, but voters in Ohio, Indiana, and Illinois tilted decisively to the Democrats, giving them fourteen of nineteen U.S. House seats from Ohio, seven of eleven from Indiana, and nine of fourteen from Illinois. The southern-settled areas produced Democratic landslides, and the Democrats took control of the Illinois and Indiana legislatures. Luckily for the Republicans, however, the governors of both states had been elected to four-year terms in 1860, while Ohio's statehouse had been filled in 1861.[18] None of the three were at risk in the nervous autumn of 1862. Lincoln himself was concerned enough in January 1863 to tell Senator Charles Sumner of Massachusetts that he feared "fire in the rear"—Democratic politics and potential rebellion in Ohio, Indiana, and Illinois—more than purely military defeat.[19]

The blaze that might have been is not hard to imagine. Had autumn gubernatorial elections chosen Democrats for the three statehouses, their inaugurations in early 1863 might have ended support for the war months before the all-important northern victories at Vicksburg and Gettysburg. Professor Wood Gray, whose book *The Hidden Civil War* tells of these shadowy events, described the lack of 1862 gubernatorial elections as "these fortuitous circumstances [that] deserve recognition among the decisive factors in the outcome of the Civil War."[20]

By 1862, then, with the Yankee Republicans of these states temporarily abandoned by swing voters, federal strength in the Ohio Valley hung on Fortune's smile. Which underscores how chancy it had been, amid the bitter politics of the late 1850s, to create enough Republican support in southern Indiana and southern Illinois to enable Lincoln to win both states' vital electoral votes. Unalloyed Yankeeism would have failed.

Slavery, Commerce, and Cotton: Three Ties to the Confederacy

To the east, the Lower Northern states of Pennsylvania, New Jersey, and New York had minor southern-born populations. The closest approximation was Greene County, a Virginia-settled Democratic stronghold in the far southwest of Pennsylvania. War doubts usually hung on two other ties: commercial relationships with the South or a mixture of past slave-ownership and sympathy with slavery or cultural hostilities to Yankees.

Economic considerations bulked especially large in the mercantile and manufacturing centers along the East Coast. Had the Confederacy been able to secede, history books would have told how commercial and financial pressures had outweighed religious and moral fervor. Gold coin would have counted more than black Republican abolitionism. So, too, if the war had gone badly for the North and then been terminated by British intervention, a decisive Democratic victory in the 1862 elections, or both. The Third Puritanism was weak enough in the Lower North that commercial considerations, white voter hostility to blacks, and the war dislocations of 1861–1862 could have produced a different result.

The potential economic cost of any war had been a major fear in 1860. In Greater Boston, many "Cotton Whig" textile magnates,

423

who bought cotton fiber from the South and sold clothing back, were unreconciled to the Republican Party. Their ballots and contributions went to John Bell, the ex-Tennessee Whig nominee of the compromise-minded Constitutional Union Party. His running mate was Massachusetts's own Edward Everett, an old Cotton Whig. The Bay State gave the Bell-Everett ticket a stunning 13.2 percent of the vote, whereas no other above the Mason-Dixon line gave it even 5 percent.[21] Boston gave Bell and Everett a full quarter of its vote.[22] In next-door Connecticut, Bridgeport and New Haven had dozens of manufacturers who made carriages for the South. These vocations, along with the large Episcopalian population in Fairfield County, produced some unusual local strength for Bell, the compromiser, and Breckinridge, the southern Democratic presidential candidate—a combined 37 percent in Fairfield County and 30 percent in New Haven County.[23]

New York City, in turn, was full of banks holding southern bonds and preoccupied with possible debt default. Over a third of the city's seaborne commerce was with the South. Its politics were Democratic and city voters had opposed Lincoln. Sympathy with slavery was commonplace. The American Tract Society and the Society for the Diffusion of Political Knowledge, two local learned groups, openly defended it. To some extent, so did the Roman Catholic archbishop, John Hughes, whose first job had been as a slave overseer in Maryland. Numerous illegal slave-traders or "blackbirders" operated out of the city, one brazenly sailing under the burgee of the New York Yacht Club. Blackbirders, in general, enjoyed the minimal concern of the Democratic U.S. attorney, James Roosevelt, who said he assumed that anyone convicted would simply be pardoned by President Buchanan.[24] Early in 1860, William Cullen Bryant's *Evening Post* had opined, quite plausibly, that "the City of New York belongs almost as much to the South as to the North."[25]

The wish of many New Yorkers, after Lincoln's election, was that the Confederate states be allowed to depart in peace. James Gordon Bennett, publisher of the *New York Herald,* who saw no problem with southern secession, also had a further idea: The Union could be reorganized with a Southern Constitution that would exclude New England.[26] August Belmont, a Democratic politician who also represented the Rothschild interests, made a kindred suggestion. Should the Union dissolve, New York City ought to "cut loose from the Puritanical East and her protective tariff. . . . she would open her magnificent port to the commerce of the world" and become the new Venice. In early January, Mayor Fernando Wood, a defender of slavery, proposed the same thing to the City Council: that when the Union broke up, New York City would itself secede and become a free port. Upstate New York had been imbued with "the fanatical spirit" of New England, but city residents sympathized with their "aggrieved brethren" in the slave states.[27]

While New York City never seceded, some of its sympathy remained with the South, and the nation's worst draft riots occurred there in July 1863. Mostly Irish mobs rioted for a week, partly against the draft, partly against blacks, dozens of whom were killed. Only a month earlier, in the Republican dark hours before Gettysburg, *Tribune* editor Bennett had predicted that in 1864, Mayor Wood himself might ride the swelling national peace movement into the White House. Then there would be an armistice.[28]

Across the Hudson River, the leather industry concentrated in the "swamp" district of Newark, New Jersey, produced a meaningful percentage of the South's shoes, and furnished another anti-Lincoln example in 1860—New Jersey being the only northern state to deny him a majority.[29] Philadelphia was more of the same: a fat mercantile and Whig stronghold in the 1850s. To call its movement toward the Republican Party reluctant and glacial is an understatement. Philadelphians gave Frémont only 11 percent in the 1856 presidential race while 34 percent backed Millard Fillmore, the American Party nominee. Even in 1857, only 19 percent of the ballots in the City of Brotherly Love were cast for Republican gubernatorial candidate David Wilmot, an antislavery activist. He finished third after Hazlehurst, the American (Party) nominee, who had been a prominent national nativist leader.[30] Selling its manufactures south was a pillar of Philadelphia prosperity, and Republican editorialists blamed the "Market Street Cottonocracy." One early party historian has described how, as the Whigs collapsed, the Democrats made inroads among conservative businessmen, especially the "Cottonocracy" of old-line Whig families.[31] Even after the war began, support for Lincoln was so lukewarm in the established Philadelphia clubs that Republican activists had to form the Union League Club.

Economic qualms, in short, inhibited early war support. Midwestern farmers might like Republican homesteading proposals, but they sat uneasily in any alliance with New England financiers, eastern railroad magnates, and Pennsylvania ironmongers, especially while the closure of the Mississippi kept warehouses glutted and corn, pork, and flour prices depressed. Manufacturers who sold to southern markets, far from acting like pillars of an Industrial North desperate to crush the Agrarian South, were an early drag on the Republican radicals. One of them, Senator Zachariah Chandler of Michigan, complained before hostilities began that "some of the manufacturing states think that a fight would be awful." He added that "from the days of Carthage to those of James Buchanan, the great mercantile centers have been peaceable—ever ready to buy immunity but not to fight for it."[32] Enthusiasm came only when tariff benefits gained magnitude and war contracts started flowing.

Parts of the old colonial sections of New York, New Jersey, and Pennsylvania had another psychological tie to the South: remembrance of their own early nineteenth-century local reliance on slavery and a persisting distaste for abolition. The blackbirders who sat around Sweet's restaurant on Fulton Street, arranging their bribes and false ships' papers, were no geographic fluke. Two generations earlier, New York City, in the words of one scholar, was "the center of the heaviest slaveholding region north of the Mason-Dixon Line."[33]

Census reports for 1790 showed districts where at least one-fifth of the families owned slaves running along the Hudson River like a sleeve—a baggy Dutch sleeve, with its biggest concentrations in Albany; Hudson Valley towns like Kingston, Saugerties, and Poughkeepsie; and especially Manhattan and its neighboring counties. In farm-rich Kings, Queens, and Richmond, 39.5 percent of white households owned slaves, higher than the statewide ratios in Maryland (36.5 percent), South Carolina (34.0 percent), and North Carolina (30.7 percent).[34] In the fattest Dutch farming sections of Kings County (Brooklyn), the towns of Flatbush and New

Utrecht, two out of every three families owned slaves, and blacks were 41 percent of the population.[35]

Slave numbers peaked in 1800, and manumission was complete by 1827. However, the rural Dutch, who used their slaves as agricultural workers, retained both their sympathy for slavery as an institution and their view of blacks. They leaned Democratic in 1860 (Douglas carried counties like Albany, Schoharie, Greene, and Westchester by substantial margins), besides which, these Hudson Valley counties also cast huge majorities against a statewide ballot proposal for black suffrage. The Irish, who feared low-wage job competition, were the other major New York group well known as hostile to Lincoln, abolition, and blacks.

Slave-ownership in northern New Jersey was part of the Dutch culture that circled New York City, with its highest ratios in what are now three wealthy suburban counties—Bergen, Somerset, and Monmouth. But with abolitionist sentiment weak in New Jersey, slavery held on longer than in New York. In 1830, Monmouth County had 224 slaves. By 1840, the number had dropped to 85, yet there were still 75 in 1850.[36]

New Jersey's reaction to the election of 1860 was a lot like New York City's. There was even talk of secession, with ex-Governor Rodman Price and other Democrats openly saying that the state should go with the South.[37] In addition to being the only northern state to deny Lincoln a majority, New Jersey, through its legislature, elected a pro-southern Democrat, James Wall, to the U.S. Senate in 1863. That same year, Democratic governor Joel Parker deplored the Emancipation Proclamation as an improper trespass on states' rights and the Democratic Assembly passed a bill barring Negroes from the state. The legislature elected in 1864 also refused to ratify the thirteenth Amendment to the U.S. Constitution ending slavery.[38]

Pennsylvania's abolitionist movement was more substantial. Yet its old settled eastern and south-central sections had counties that were passive on the slavery question or even somewhat pro-southern. The Pennsylvania Germans, standoffish toward abolition, were lopsidedly behind the Democratic Party in national elections through 1856. The state's eastern German strongholds gave anti-slavery Republican nominees their worst beatings of 1856–1857.[39] The other two areas of Republican weakness in 1856–1857 were around Philadelphia and in the old Scotch-Irish districts from the Susquehanna Valley west to the Blue Mountains, where Fillmore, the Know-Nothing, had run ahead of Frémont in 1856. Only sixty-four slaves still remained in Pennsylvania in 1840, but from 1790 until then, this section, along with Philadelphia, had the highest slave ratios.[40]

Philadelphia had the state's biggest slaveholdings, though, and views there were more pointed. William Dusinberre, in his book *Civil War Issues in Philadelphia, 1856–1865,* links the city's social conservatism to racial views. In sharp contrast to the 1850s Whig politics of Vermont or the Western Reserve, Philadelphia's Whiggery was more southern-tinged and hostile to abolitionists and rights for blacks. In December 1859, fifteen thousand Philadelphians assembled—despite a hailstorm—for a pro-southern rally under bunting that proclaimed "Pennsylvania Greets Her Sister State, Virginia."[41]

Historian Thomas Fleming has posited the existence in 1860 of a "white supremacy belt" that included the lower two-thirds of Illinois, Indiana, and Ohio, most of Pennsylvania, New Jersey, and the lower half of New York.[42] This stretch had the North's heaviest concentration of blacks—and its lowest numbers of Yankees. Incautious as Fleming's term may be, it has the merit of fairly encapsulating the region's views—and the role of the Lower North as a conservative counterpoint to Greater New England.

Rum, Romanism, and Rebellion: Competing Political Phobias

The second broad group of swing votes targeted by the Republicans in 1860 were the northern Whigs who had voted in 1856 for Millard Fillmore, the former Whig president running on the American Party ballot line, rather than support Frémont. This targeting of the Lower North succeeded because whereas Fillmore had gathered 340,000 votes north of the Mason-Dixon line, John Bell, the ex-Whig on the 1860 ballot, was held to only 80,000. The debate among historians is not over *whether* Lincoln got most of those Fillmore votes, but *how*—in response to what appeal?

The American Party had a Know-Nothing and nativist tinge, but in a number of states, the Republican Party itself had evolved during the mid-1850s through fusions and joint tickets with the Americans and nativists. Some scholars contend that these relationships—backstopped by party promises of careful naturalization and veiled rhetoric about foreign criminals—helped Lincoln to attract many of the Fillmore backers. Others argue that although many ex–Know Nothings wound up on Lincoln's side, the Republicans made few concessions to get them.

The key lies in understanding the wellsprings of the 1856 Fillmore vote, which represented just over 20 percent of the national total. In the South and Border, it was the old Whig vote—anti-Democratic, mostly pro-Union, by and large unhappy with the new immigration, but also opposed to Republican Yankee sectionalism and abolitionism. The Fillmore electorate was strongest in the Border, which included four of the American Party's five best states: Maryland (55 percent), Kentucky (48 percent), Tennessee (48 percent), and Missouri (46 percent). The vote of victorious Democrat Buchanan, by comparison, was highest in the core South—South Carolina, Texas, Arkansas, and Alabama. Republican Frémont's five top states clustered at the opposite pole—Vermont, Maine, Massachusetts, Rhode Island, and Michigan. Yankeedom was also the part of the country where Fillmore was weakest. Brattleboro, Coldwater, and Vermontville had no interest in equivocating.

Nationally, the conclusion leaps out: Supporting Millard Fillmore was the electoral equivalent of rejecting cotton state fire-eaters and Yankee abolitionists alike while hoping, somehow, for a return to the old Union and Constitution. Other voters would have been just as anxious to recapture the old Whig economics of Henry Clay—tariff protection and river, canal, and harbor improvements.

By this analysis, backing for Fillmore in the North should have maximized, not among the suspicious Protestant neighbors of bulging Irish tenements and raucous German breweries, but in the districts most "in between" on sectionalism, slavery, and the "irrepressible conflict." Which is just what happened. Wisconsin, with the nation's largest foreign-born population, was Fillmore's *worst* state. The eleven northern states where he did best fell into the three areas just examined: the old middle colonies (New Jersey, New York, Pennsylvania), the non-Yankee parts of the Ohio and Upper Mississippi Valleys (Iowa, Illinois, Indiana, and Ohio), and the "Cotton Whig" manufacturing belt of lower New England (Massachusetts and Rhode Island). The fourth cluster was along the Pacific, where the new state of California (and Oregon, not admitted until 1859) blended northern and southern voting streams.[43] More details and data on the American Party electorate appear in the endnotes.

Within these northern contours, the Fillmore vote of 1856 came where it should have: in places where skepticism of Yankees and abolitionists undercut northern Whig willingness to back Frémont. Its peaks were in the old Whig sections of New Jersey and in southeastern Pennsylvania along or near the Mason-Dixon line border with Maryland. In the Midwest, it concentrated in the southern sections of Ohio, Indiana, and Illinois.[44] Support for Fillmore in Massachusetts and Rhode Island was highest where cotton textiles counted most—in commercial Boston and in the mill canyons of the Merrimack and Blackstone Valleys, where taunting abolitionists charged "the lords of the loom" with abetting "the lords of the lash." The rest of Greater New England had little interest in Fillmore—the six northern states where he drew 3 percent or less were Wisconsin, New Hampshire, Vermont, Michigan, Maine, and Connecticut.

But before nativist politics can be put aside, the anti–major party movement during the peak years of immigration between 1851 and 1854 should be understood as not quite as simplistic as it seems. In addition to its anti-Catholic and antiforeign themes, the Know-Nothing cause took some major reformist positions—rotation in office, returning power from the party machines to the electorate, and a commitment to antiparty or fusion politics.[45] Secondly, the Know-Nothing surge of 1853–1855, following the desultory presidential contest between Franklin Pierce and Winfield Scott, was vital in turning that Democratic-Whig party system into the shambles that forced a new alignment. In important northern states like Massachusetts, New York, and Pennsylvania, and aided by their outsider, antiparty rhetoric, Know-Nothings scuttled the Whigs and ran ahead of the new Republicans in defeating the Democrats.

Beyond these collateral assets, nativism simply did not have the makings of a central issue in the 1850s any more than in the 1750s when German Lutherans and Scotch-Irish Presbyterians were the transient targets. The critical cleavage—the one that had so often driven English-speaking politics over three centuries—involved *Catholicism*, not Lutheranism or Presbyterianism. In England, too, nativism had never been a more than intermittent patter against Dutch emigrants, French Huguenots, German Palatines, or even Scots. Animosity toward *Catholic* French, Scots, Germans, or Irish was what burned with such historical intensity.

A pivotal effect of the Know-Nothing excesses, then, lay in helping to break up the Democratic-Whig system and creating a new alignment, over most of the North, in which the Republicans became the party of a more respectable and commercial Protestantism. This powerful new politics cost the Democrats their former majority. They became the party of Catholics, as well as of a mixed bag of confessional and unfashionable Protestants, and many of the irreligious. By the late 1850s, Catholics in the United States were numerous enough—several million Irish, in particular—to support the first open and aggressive Catholic hierarchy in an English-speaking country since the brief English Counter-Reformation under Queen Mary in the 1550s. The large portion of American Protestants who still looked back to the themes of the Reformation reacted by enlisting around an increasingly alarmed Protestant versus Catholic polarization, one that would not have been plausible before the 1850s. The Democratic Party, especially in such urbanizing states as Massachusetts, Pennsylvania, and New York, became increasingly Catholic-dominated. It added voters on one hand, but offended the established Protestant citizenry on the other.

To put a larger perspective on the upheaval of the mid-nineteenth century, the cumulating social, economic, technical, and cultural ferment was enormous—from the impact of the telegraph and escalating railroad development to the expanding pressure of immigration, big-city crime, and squalor, all of these interacting with the fervor of abolitionism, evangelism, and secessionism. The agitation of the U.S. electorate was high. This would have been especially true of the "in between" districts of the Border and Lower

North, which—beyond their sectional ambivalence—counted most of the big U.S. cities save Boston and New Orleans, much of the industry, and about three-quarters of the recently arrived immigrants.

The trampling of a shallowly rooted party system like the Democratic-Whig division in such turbulent times seems inevitable. The two principal credos that routed it—the unacceptability of slavery and fear of Catholicism—both flowed from 250 years of Anglo-American concepts of freedom. Given Anglo-American history, it would have been hard for these questions *not* to have become central.

Nativism itself, however, was almost innately counterproductive. The three great ethnic migrations into the United States of the 1830s, 1840s, and 1850s were not religiously uniform but divided: between Irish who were mostly Catholics, Germans who were slightly more Protestant than Catholic, and British from England, Wales, Scotland, and Ulster who were almost entirely Protestant. So comfortable, indeed, were these New British arrivals—dissenting Presbyterians, Methodists, Congregationalists, and Baptists whose politics at home had also been labeled Whig— that they could quickly change from being Pope-baiting Whig Methodists in South Wales or Rome-fearing Presbyterians in Paisley to being the same thing in Ohio or Pittsburgh. The publications of Catholic dioceses frequently attacked the role of British emigrants in the supposedly "nativist" and "anti-foreign" Know-Nothing movement, even though the New British were nominally foreign and would have shared qualms about delayed enfranchisement or about limited homestead eligibility.

The huge German influx, as we have seen, was what doomed *nativism*, while leaving untouched the underlying party polarization in the North between Catholics as Democrats and Third Puritans and northern Evangelicals as Republicans. The number of Americans born in Germany jumped from 584,720 in 1850 to 1,301,136 in 1860. Teutons might stand together, Catholic with Protestant, against the Sunday closing laws or liquor prohibitions. But in larger milieus like New York, Pittsburgh, Cincinnati, or Chicago, the new arrivals would also remember their likes and dislikes of *other* Germans: Prussians, Wurttemburgers, Catholics,

Protestants, Methodists, obscure sects, prelates, or anticlerical Forty-Eighters.

By the early 1850s, as Cincinnati teutonized to the point of having six German-language newspapers and resident consular officials from virtually every German kingdom, principality, or free city, including Lubeck, the overwhelmingly Democratic German community was dividing: Most Catholics backed the regular or Miami leadership, while much of the German Protestant community became anti-Miamis. Within a few more years, the anti-Miamis, concerned about papal plots as well as the abuses of the southern Slaveocracy, were on their way into a Republican Party that—at least in the Midwest—had discovered that it no longer favored anti-immigrant rhetoric, voting-rights obstructions, or restraints on beer gardens. The "nativists" in Pittsburgh likewise had immigrant allies: the Ulster Irish "Protestant Associations" and the "Muscovies" of German Protestants.[46] The boats from Bremen, Liverpool, and Cork disembarked Old World religious tensions, as well as immigrants.

Beer Gardens and Brandenburgers

Which brings us to the Germans as the third swing voter group. This electorate did move substantially to the Republicans between 1856 and 1860, a behavior that also included the old eighteenth-century German settlements in New York, northwest New Jersey, and Pennsylvania, many of the latter still German-speaking, as well as their transplants in Ohio. Pro-Republican German opinion-molders like Carl Schurz were also sent to these areas in 1860, with Schurz even writing to his wife that "these old 'Pennsylvania Dutch' follow me like little children"—a considerable exaggeration of the election returns.[47]

The contention about Germans providing the critical votes to elect Lincoln in 1860, widespread after the Civil War, was overstated, save in Illinois. What *can* be said is twofold: that German voters were important, though not decisive, in the 1856–1860 Republican trend, and that religious differences carried over into politics. Catholics, more than other Germans, were both Democrats and war resisters.

433

With the Republican share of the vote usually exceeding 60 percent across Greater New England, from Maine to Minnesota, Lincoln's 1860 margins were big enough not to need German ballots. Yankee Protestants were strongly Republican, despite lesser backing among Baptists, Episcopalians, smaller sects, and freethinkers. Catholics were the only large northern group that was overwhelmingly Democratic. In New England, they were mostly Irish. In New York, Pennsylvania, and New Jersey, although the Irish were again the most important Catholic group, the German admixture was larger than in New England. These were the states where the new Republican Party indulged nativism in the late 1850s to the discomfort of midwestern colleagues. The Irish Catholics, 95 percent Democratic, were unlikely backers and often more useful as foils.

West of Philadelphia, however, Germans were usually more numerous than Irish. Immigrant support became more pivotal—and internal cleavages and hostilities within the German community became the stuff on which candidacies and causes rose or fell.

To observe that the politics of emigrants from the land of Martin Luther, the Holy Roman Empire and its Counter-Reformation, Ulrich Zwingli, John Huss, the Anabaptists of Munster, the Moravians, Jacob Amman of the Amish, and former priest Menno Simons of the Mennonites might divide along religious lines is to state the obvious. The Germans wrote the books—or at least published the *Ninety Five Theses*, the *Address to the Christian Nobility of the German Nation,* and the *Edict of Worms*—that threw central Europe of the sixteenth century into generations of bitter religious warfare. The denominational complexity they brought with them to the United States was almost as intricate, and by 1860, the 20 million people of the North included about 4 million who were German-born or of German descent. Fathoming their political reactions to the new circumstances in the United States all but requires a religious denominational guide, as well as a gazetteer of a fragmented German nation still a decade from unification.

After all, within the English-speaking United States circa 1860, political and wartime divisions still related to the seventeenth-century British Isles. Would-be Norman cavaliers lined up against Saxon Roundheads. Irish peasants in Boston and New York slums became partial allies of distant Episcopal cavaliers because they had the same Psalm-singing, commerce-driven Puritan enemies. Mid-nineteenth-century Germans in the United States brought their own tensions and legacies.

For readers presented with raw, glaring statistics, the denominational cleavage of German-American electoral loyalties circa 1860 and 1861 can seem improbable. This is true despite cataloguing by a half dozen historians.[48] Eric Foner, a respected chronicler of Republican Party emergence during the 1850s, criticized such slicings of the midwest electorate by religion and ethnicity for replacing the one-dimensional "economic man" of the progressives with "an equally one-dimensional 'religious man.'"[49]

Most of the data-based ethnoreligious portraits have omitted relevant history, both in North America and Europe, that would have breathed greater life into their regressions and coefficients. That being said, the profiles are very revealing, with respect both to German-American politics and, most of all, to the role of religion in the upheavals of the 1850s.

As we have seen, the German immigrant vote was not big enough to have been decisive in Lincoln's large statewide margins in Ohio (10 points), Michigan (15 points), Wisconsin (14 points), Iowa (11 points), or Minnesota (29 points). Even more to the point, though, a majority of German voters in these states seem to have backed the *Democrats*. The exception was Minnesota, new enough in the Union that the Republicans did not have to overcome a mid-1850s legacy of nativism and Know-Nothingism, where perhaps one-third of *Catholic Germans* appear to have voted for Lincoln. In Indiana, German immigrants were too few to explain even Lincoln's fairly narrow margin, although they, too, leaned Democratic.

In Illinois, where Lincoln edged out fellow resident Stephen A. Douglas by just twelve thousand votes, the German-born male electorate was large enough (about thirty-five thousand) and Republican enough—perhaps 60 percent to 65 percent in 1860—to have made the difference. Illinois may also have been the exception that proved the rule. The local German population had more than tripled between 1850 and 1860, the fastest increase in the Midwest. Republican politicians, not least Lincoln himself, were especially attuned to its importance.

Ironically, Douglas was weaker among Germans in his home state than elsewhere. They had been aroused in 1854 by his masterminding of the Kansas-Nebraska Act, which they did not like because it opened both territories to slavery. Douglas, however, also suffered from his home state's close attention to the act's legislative provisions. Southern members of Congress, hostile to the idea of popular sovereignty, made speeches about thousands of dumb antislavery Germans in the Great Lakes states just waiting to hitch up their wagons and ride in. Dixie legislators also succeeded in adding nativist amendments that would have restricted immigrant voting and officeholding in Kansas and Nebraska. These, although eventually dropped, fed Illinois Germans' sense of betrayal. As a result, they swung heavily against Douglasite congressional candidates in the 1854 elections.[50] Six years later, Douglas took his lumps again, being weaker among Germans at home than in next-door Indiana, Iowa, and Wisconsin.

Most calculations of the German impact, however, omitted the Protestant eighteenth-century immigrants, many of whose descendants were still German-speaking four generations later. With old-wave Germans in Pennsylvania accounting for 20 to 25 percent of the state electorate, the shrinkage of their huge two-to-one margin for Buchanan in 1856 could have produced half of Lincoln's statewide edge. Outside the Mennonite areas, the Pennsylvania Germans were cool to abolitionism, which helped Lincoln to do better than the more radical Frémont.[51] Pennsylvania Germans were also a major factor in the population of next-door Ohio, especially in the area around New Philadelphia, and of some consequence in Indiana. Including these voters increases the potential for Germans to have affected the Ohio and Indiana outcomes.[52]

The alignments of the German electorate reinforce the centrality of religion and denominationalism among Anglo-Saxons, Celts, and Teutons alike. Economics circa 1860 only modified essentially religious electoral patterns. It did not shape them.

The most stalwart German Republicans of 1860 were the so-called Forty-Eighters, the largely Protestant, freethinking, and usually anticlerical refugees from the Germany of the unsuccessful revolutions of 1848. Many had been journalists, academicians, army officers, and even members of parliament. Their major concentrations were in St. Louis and Hermann, Missouri; Belleville and Chicago, Illinois; Davenport, Iowa; New Ulm, Minnesota; and Cincinnati, Ohio. Before the war, Forty-Eighter leaders like Carl Schurz, Franz Sigel, and Friedrich Hecker had served as Republican speech-makers, newspaper editors, and officeholders. When the fighting began, dozens became regimental, brigade, and division commanders. To midwestern Catholic newspapers, however, the Forty-Eighters were Red Revolutionaries and godless German Jacobins.[53]

Adverse reaction to a Republican Party led not just by "Red" Forty-Eighters but by Yankee abolitionist fanatics and ex-Whig Know-Nothings made most German Catholics strong Democrats—almost as committed as the Irish. Tabulations in states like Michigan, Ohio, Iowa, and Wisconsin showed homogeneous rural German Catholic townships with 85 percent, 92 percent, or even 98 percent Democratic support levels in the 1860 presidential election.[54] Religion, more than German ethnicity, was the key. In Wisconsin, where the most complete records survive, Catholics of Belgian, Dutch, and Luxembourger antecedents were just as Democratic.

Between the anticlerical Forty-Eighters on the Republican side and the transplanted Catholic European villages, German political fidelities in the United States reflected a broad spectrum of German regional origins and denominational commitments. Old-style devotional Lutherans from northern Germany—Pomerania, Mecklenburg, and Brandenburg—where princes changing religions centuries earlier had kept much Catholic ritual, were the most likely to be Democrats at odds with the politics of Yankees, Forty-Eighters, and Protestant Evangelicals. This was especially true of the so-called Old Lutherans, ritualists who emigrated to the United States after the decision in 1817 of Prussian King William IV to unify the Lutheran and Reformed Churches.[55] Lutherans from southern German districts like Wurttemburg and the Palatine, where rival Catholics were majorities or large minorities, were less likely to be ritualistic and somewhat more inclined to anti-Catholic politics (and to Republicanism in the United States). Map 10.3 shows the states and regions of Germany in the eighteen-sixties.

437

Sects and denominations were also crucial, according to those who have combed the electoral decision-making of German immigrants. The most ritualistic Lutherans—those of the Wisconsin and Romanized Buffalo Synods—were the most Democratic. Members of the Missouri Synod, less ritualistic, were more divided.[56] The capsuled explanation is that the ritualistic churches emphasized doctrine and liturgy instead of the individualism, pursuit of redemption, and reform so characteristic of pro-Republican U.S. Protestant denominations. Neither the Catholic Church nor the major German Lutheran synods in the U.S. had taken issue with slavery by 1860.

Members of the German Reformed Church, in turn, were more evenly divided between Republicans and Democrats. German Evangelicals and Methodists—more pietistic and concerned about personal redemption, social reform, and eradication of sin—were the most Republican, resembling the Yankees and Protestant evangelicals in their commitment to temperance, sabbath-keeping, and distaste for slavery.[57] In township after township, these identifications, more than any others, explain loyalties to causes and parties.

As for the other major Lutheran and Reformed Church immigrants, Scandinavian and Dutch, somewhat comparable divisions prevailed. The split among Netherlanders involved schisms in the Dutch Reformed Church. In New Jersey, where there was some southern sympathy, the principal anti-abolitionist, anti-Republican sentiment concentrated in the True Reformed Dutch Church, based in Bergen and Passaic Counties.[58] But in the Middle West, antislavery sentiment made Republicans out of most Dutch Protestant emigrants arriving in the 1850s and 1860s.

The Scandinavians, meanwhile, were more Republican—and lopsidedly antislavery in their politics and Civil War alignment.[59] This was true of Norwegians and Swedes alike, but Norwegian emigration was the larger, much of it bound for Illinois, Iowa, Wisconsin, and Minnesota. The principal exception lay among the High Church, ritualistic minority of Norwegian Synod Lutheranism, whose preachers were sometimes accused of being proslavery because they found no biblical basis for being critical.

THE STATES AND REGIONS OF GERMANY, 1860S

SWEDEN

DENMARK

NORTH
SEA

BALTIC
SEA

SCHLESWIG

HOLSTEIN
Lübeck

Hamburg

MECKLENBURG

Danzig

EAST PRUSSIA

POMERANIA

WEST PRUSSIA

Oder R.

Vistula R.

POSEN

Posen

RUSSIAN
EMPIRE

OLDENBURG

HANNOVER
Hanover

BRUNSWICK

NETHERLANDS

Weser R.

Elbe R.

BRANDENBURG
Brandenburg

ANHALT

Elbe R.

SILESIA

WESTPHALIA

Düsseldorf

BELGIUM

Rhine R.

RHENISH
PRUSSIA

HESSE

THURINGIAN
STATES

SAXONY

Dresden

AUSTRIAN
EMPIRE

Meuse R.

Frankfurt

Main R.

RHENISH
BAVARIA

Lorraine

Stuttgart

Danube R.

Nuremberg

BAVARIA

FRANCE

Alsace

Rhine R.

WÜRTTEMBURG

HOHEN-
ZOLLERN

BADEN

Munich

Lake
Constance

SWITZERLAND

N
W E
S

0   miles   100

Prussia by 1867

Independent German States,
1867–1871

MAP 10.3

Political, religious, and cultural cleavages within the North during 1862–1864 came close to jeopardizing a federal victory. Just how close no one will ever be able to say. However, in contrast to the short-lived U.S. political alignments created by the earlier divisions between Federalists and Jeffersonians and Democrats and Whigs, those produced by the Civil War era were deep and lasting. For a century, they lived on in a politics that could be described as an extension of war by other means. However, it is now time to leave the North and turn to the opposite ideologized pole of 1860: the cotton states and the core of the new Confederacy.

Boll Weevils, Ballots, and Bullets

What drove secession in the winter of 1860–1861 is beyond debate. The seven original Confederate states even left the Union in nearly the order of their slave ratios. South Carolina, where 48.7 percent of the white families owned slaves, was first in December 1860. Mississippi (48.0 percent) followed in January. Then came Florida (36 percent), Alabama (35.1 percent), Georgia (38 percent), Louisiana (32.2 percent), and Texas (28.5 percent).[60] Even more striking is how virtually the same order still prevailed in highest support for the Democratic presidential nominee in 1936.

The essential bonds were between secession, slavery, and cotton production (see Map. 10.4). On the state level, of course, a precise relationship was weakened by Cotton Belt extensions into west Tennessee and southeastern Arkansas. In general, long-staple–producing bottomlands, slave concentrations, and ultimate secession commitment went hand in hand. Some of the 1861 secession conventions and referenda, however, can disguise the relationship with slavery, and for several reasons. At the secession conventions held in the Deep South during the winter of 1860–1861, spring's war fever had still to gather, while a considerable minority of secession opponents stood out among the old Whig plantation-owners and men of commerce who had a lingering distrust of the Democratic politicians leading the secession movement. By April and May, these ex-Whigs had mostly been swept up in post-Sumter war fever, as had many nonslave-owners. However, studies have made it clear that the relatively few *wartime* antisecession counties in the seven states of the original Confederacy were upcountry, piney-woods, plains, or bayou areas with few slaves.

The Plantation South held the fire-eaters and drumbeaters. South Carolina and Mississippi seceded with very little internal dissent. Fifteen years later, once Reconstruction ended, memories were so powerful that all but a few whites supported the Democratic Party until the civil rights upheavals that followed World War II. Not a single South Carolina county had any significant mountain Republicanism; nor was there enough wartime pro-Union sentiment to form even one South Carolina military unit in the federal service. Mississippi, perhaps surprisingly, produced several military units in the federal service—the First Mississippi Mounted Rifles and the Tippah and Mississippi Rangers.[61] The men of Jones County, in the Gulf Coast pineywoods, sour in 1861 over secession and the unwelcome prospect of a "planters' war," declared their county the "Free State of Jones." From hideouts in the Leaf River swamps, they raided Confederate troops and supplies and managed to keep state troops at bay through war's end.[62]

In Florida, Texas, and Louisiana, support for the federal side was principally confined to ethnic minorities and fringe populations. Louisiana's wartime federal military enlistments and later white votes for Republican presidents came mostly from the French Cajun and German populations in New Orleans and the adjacent bayou parishes. Five white Louisiana regiments of cavalry and three of infantry wore Yankee blue, and the end of hostilities left a 15 to 25 percent white Republican vote in southwestern Louisiana. In Florida, the sway of the state government and Confederate cause was weak in coastal areas reachable by federal naval power. White Floridians manned two Union cavalry regiments and a federal ranger company in the Florida Keys.[63]

Texas support for the Union was likewise strongest on the periphery—in the German hill counties near San Antonio, the Mexican-American border districts between San Antonio and the Rio Grande, and along the Indian frontier in North Texas. Enough Mexican-Americans and German-Americans were killed in engagements with Texas Rangers or Confederate troops to implant that dissent in later politics. Even in 1936, two dozen counties in southern Texas gave the Republican presidential candidate 20 to

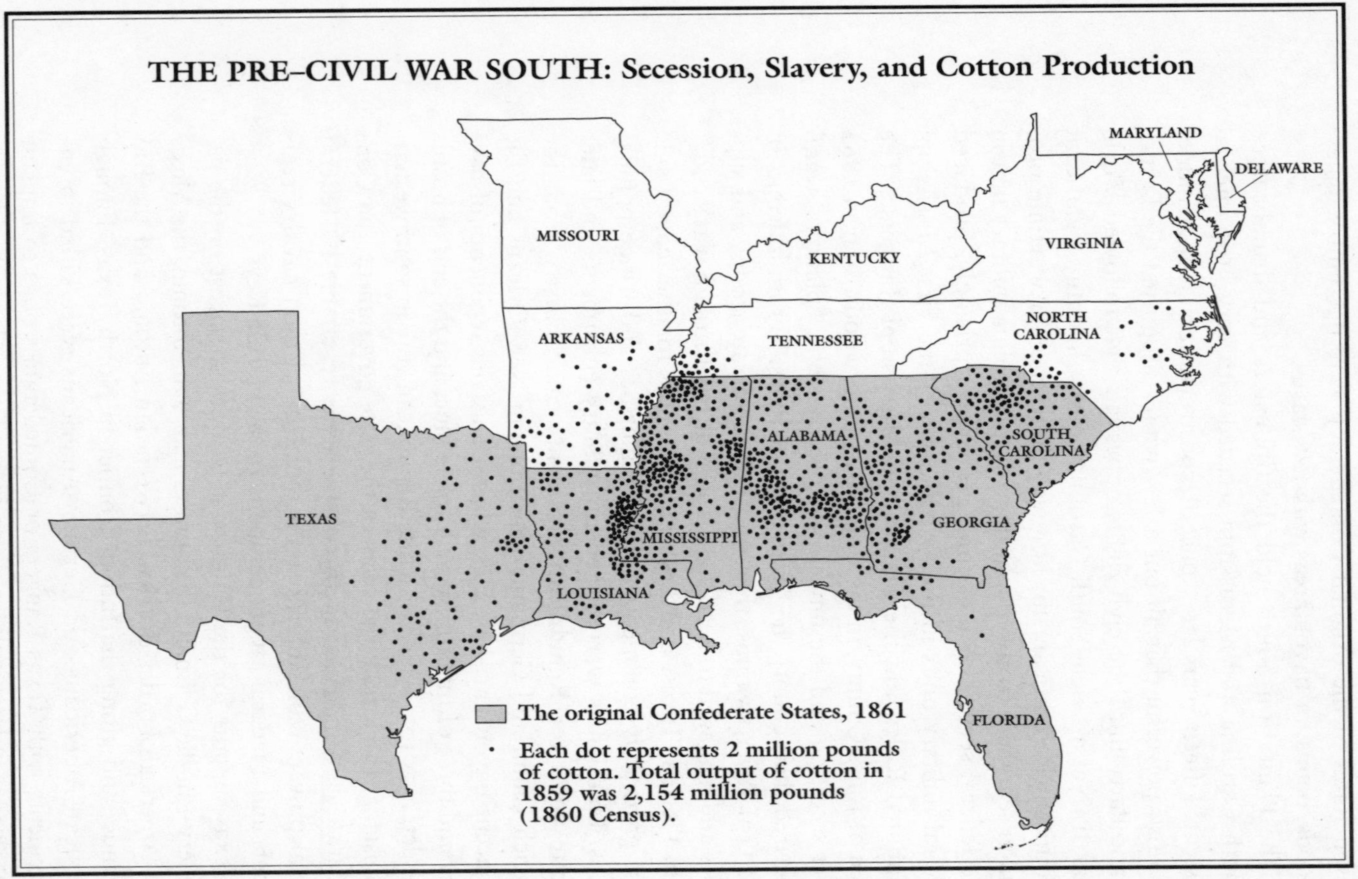

THE PRE–CIVIL WAR SOUTH: Secession, Slavery, and Cotton Production

DELAWARE

MARYLAND

VIRGINIA

NORTH CAROLINA

KENTUCKY

TENNESSEE

MISSOURI

ARKANSAS

SOUTH CAROLINA

GEORGIA

FLORIDA

ALABAMA

MISSISSIPPI

LOUISIANA

TEXAS

The original Confederate States, 1861

Each dot represents 2 million pounds of cotton. Total output of cotton in 1859 was 2,154 million pounds (1860 Census).

MAP 10.4

40 percent. Several German-American strongholds—Gillespie and Kendall Counties—actually turned in GOP majorities.

The small minority of federal sympathizers in the last two states of the Confederacy's original seven—Alabama and Georgia— lived mostly in some thirty upcountry or mountain counties more akin to nearby Tennessee than to the fertile plantation-district bottomlands. Had the federal government been able to establish East Tennessee as a separate state in the manner of West Virginia, small chunks of adjacent Appalachian Georgia and Alabama might have been included. Indeed, after Alabama decided to se- cede, several of its pro-Union Appalachian counties considered trying to become a separate state called Nickajack.[64] The citadel of opposition to secession, Winston County—now as then thinly set- tled and mostly forest—was pro-federal during the 1861–1865 fighting and thereafter became the state's only regularly Republi- can county. Other nearby mountain counties, however, also con- tributed troops to the Union armies, especially to the famous First Alabama Cavalry, U.S.A. This unit, a thousand strong, won com- mendations from General William Tecumseh Sherman for its role in scouting and foraging for his blue-coated army on its march from Atlanta to Savannah and the sea and then north through South Carolina.

Northern Georgia was also Appalachian. Nearly a score of mountain counties along or near the Tennessee border provided several thousand soldiers for the federal armies, although no indi- vidual unit of any stature emerged. Even in bad years like 1936, Republican presidential candidates drew 20 to 55 percent of the vote locally. Map 10.5 shows these pro-Union peripheries.

Further embroidery would be misleading. Save for Texas, much of which was still frontier, the cotton states lined up behind the Confederacy with as much or more unanimity than Greater New England backed the Lincoln administration. Two of the state capi- tals were not taken until the war's end: Austin and Tallahassee. Of the other five, Baton Rouge, Louisiana, and Jackson, Mississippi, fell or were briefly taken early. But Atlanta did not surrender until 1864, and Columbia and Montgomery until 1865.

Even when the war ended, the cotton states, not surprisingly, be- came the drillfield of postwar Reconstruction. The first three states

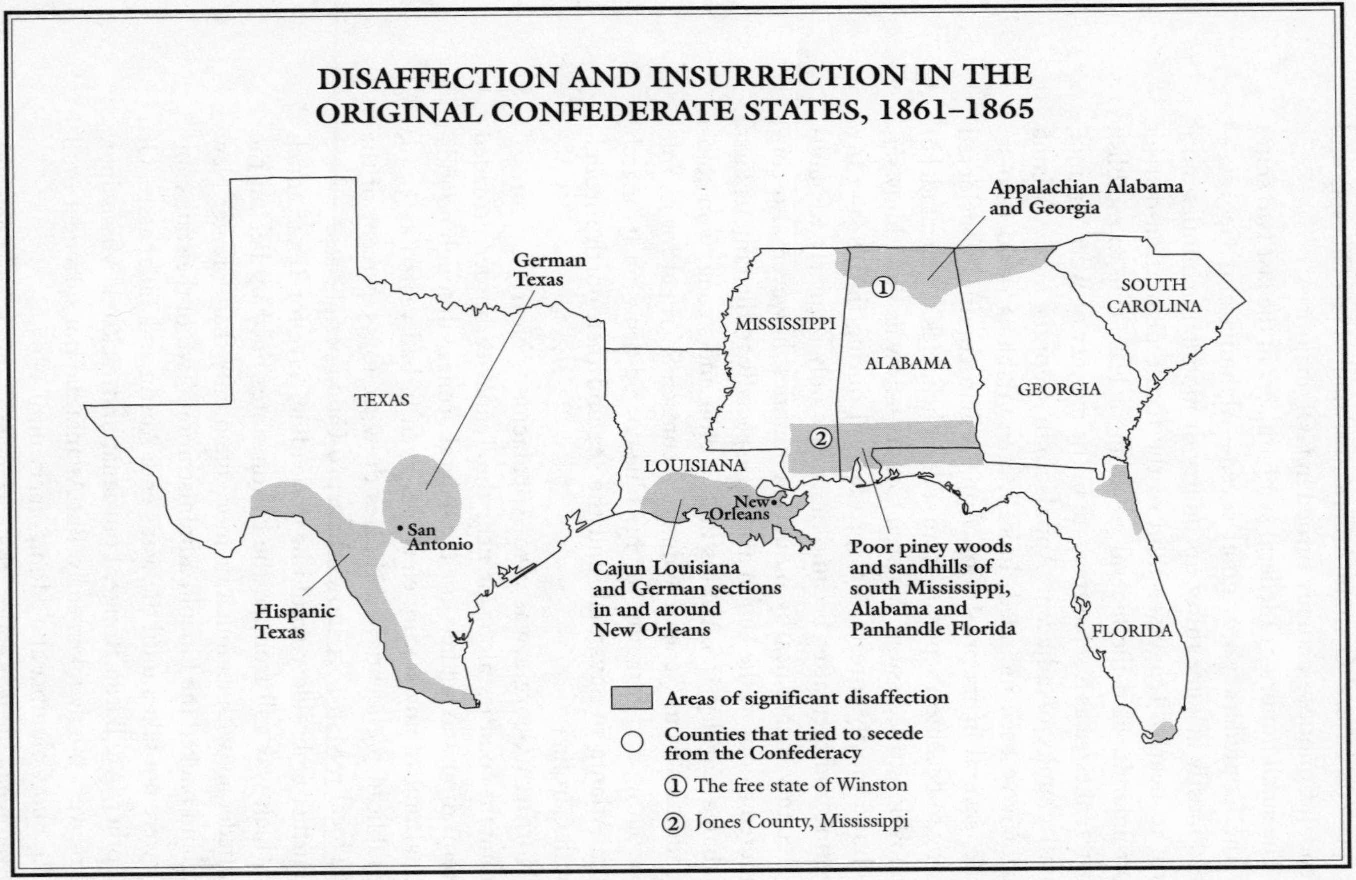

DISAFFECTION AND INSURRECTION IN THE
ORIGINAL CONFEDERATE STATES, 1861–1865

SOUTH CAROLINA

GEORGIA

FLORIDA

ALABAMA

MISSISSIPPI

LOUISIANA

New Orleans

TEXAS

San Antonio

Appalachian Alabama
and Georgia

Poor piney woods
and sandhills of
south Mississippi,
Alabama and
Panhandle Florida

Cajun Louisiana
and German sections
in and around
New Orleans

German
Texas

Hispanic
Texas

Areas of significant disaffection

Counties that tried to secede
from the Confederacy

① The free state of Winston

② Jones County, Mississippi

MAP 10.5

to enter the Confederacy—South Carolina, Mississippi, and Florida—were also the last three to escape military occupation. Federal troops only exited in 1877 after the sectional bargain struck to resolve the Hayes-Tilden election.

But the cotton states were also a more complex and interesting society than the propaganda of New Englanders made out. The principal Indian tribes themselves had slaves—the Cherokees, Creeks, and Choctaws sent west to Oklahoma in the 1830s took their blacks with them and generally fought on the Confederate side during the war. Slave risings and rebellions were few and far between in 1861–1865, and in 1861, the free mulattos of New Orleans had proposed to organize a regiment for *Confederate* service. During the last year of the fighting, the Confederate Congress and government finally considered proposals to put black regiments into the field wearing Confederate grey. The earliest discussions, begun by General Patrick Cleburne of the Army of Tennessee in 1864, were squelched by Jefferson Davis. However, by the time Davis and his Cabinet got serious—encouraged by the governors of Virginia and Louisiana and by commanding general Robert E. Lee—it was February 1865 and too late.[65]

The outcome of the war in the cotton states produced a sequence devastating to blacks and, less directly, to poor whites: military occupation, the rise of the Ku Klux Klan, the substantial failure of Reconstruction, the North's eventual abandonment of freed southern blacks, and the stagnation of the Deep South and its quasi-colonial agricultural economy until World War II. One can fairly wonder: Had the Confederacy opted, in late 1862 or in the spring of 1863, for a policy of phasing out slavery over ten to fifteen years, beginning with the manumission of blacks for three years of Confederate military service, would that have secured British intervention on the side of King Cotton, changed northern opinion, or provided an added manpower sufficient to change the military outcome at Vicksburg or Gettysburg?

Conceivably. But for the leaders of the cotton states to have been that sage, that compromise-minded in early 1863, the architects of secession would have to have been very different in 1860—conciliators rather than the fire-eaters who put so much emphasis on slavery and its legitimacy.

The Upper South and the Border States:
Ambivalent Loyalties and Cultural Defeat

For several months in 1861, the Upper South and Border held the balance of power and the fate of the United States in their hands. But it was an ephemeral importance. These states fared better than the Cotton States. However, both groups—even the Border states that avoided Reconstruction—wound up more as vanquished than victors.

Daniel Boone's own wanderlust traced the Border and Border South as well as anyone. Fifteen years after he was born in Berks County, Pennsylvania, in 1734, his Quaker family took the Great Wagon Road south into the Yadkin Valley along the Virginia–North Carolina frontier. Boone himself trailblazed much of the Cumberland Gap region near where Virginia, Tennessee, and Kentucky came together. When the Revolution came, some of the Boones and Bryans, his wife's family, inclined to neutralism or Toryism and found it easier to move west to what became new settlements in Kentucky—Boonesborough and Bryan Station.[66] In 1799, the ever-restless Boone left Kentucky, moving on to a new frontier: the valley of the Missouri River, just west of what is now St. Louis. He died there in 1820, the preeminent symbol not just of the border moving west, but (as Map 10.6 shows) of the eighteenth-century Pennsylvania origins of a large percentage, probably a majority, of the population streams that settled the Border and piedmont and mountain sections of the Upper South. In 1790, for example, 15 percent of the people of Kentucky were born in Pennsylvania, while another 25–35 percent came from North Carolina and Virginia stock of Pennsylvania background.

This is the caveat to Pennsylvania's status as a northern state, not a Border one. Pennsylvania was the northern "parent"—and Virginia the southern one—that together nurtured much of the Border. Delaware began as the lower three counties of Pennsylvania. Western Maryland was settled from Pennsylvania. So was much of western Virginia and the North Carolina piedmont, both on the Great Philadelphia Wagon Road. Like Daniel Boone, some of these settlers and their progeny then pushed west into Tennessee and Kentucky. Even Ozark Arkansas and Missouri were an exten-

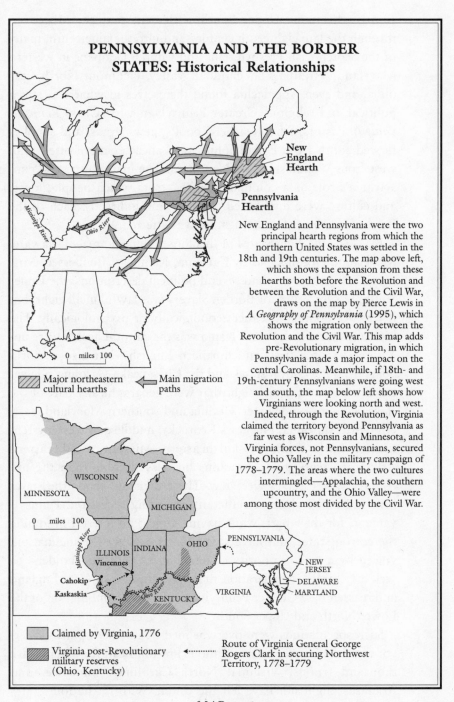

PENNSYLVANIA AND THE BORDER STATES: Historical Relationships

New England Hearth

Pennsylvania Hearth

New England and Pennsylvania were the two principal hearth regions from which the northern United States was settled in the 18th and 19th centuries. The map above left, which shows the expansion from these hearths both before the Revolution and between the Revolution and the Civil War, draws on the map by Pierce Lewis in *A Geography of Pennsylvania* (1995), which shows the migration only between the Revolution and the Civil War. This map adds pre-Revolutionary migration, in which Pennsylvania made a major impact on the central Carolinas. Meanwhile, if 18th- and 19th-century Pennsylvanians were going west and south, the map below left shows how Virginians were looking north and west. Indeed, through the Revolution, Virginia claimed the territory beyond Pennsylvania as far west as Wisconsin and Minnesota, and Virginia forces, not Pennsylvanians, secured the Ohio Valley in the military campaign of 1778–1779. The areas where the two cultures intermingled—Appalachia, the southern upcountry, and the Ohio Valley—were among those most divided by the Civil War.

Mississippi River

Ohio River

0 miles 100

Major northeastern cultural hearths

Main migration paths

WISCONSIN

MINNESOTA

MICHIGAN

0 miles 100

Mississippi River

PENNSYLVANIA

ILLINOIS INDIANA OHIO

Vincennes

NEW JERSEY

Cahokip

DELAWARE

Kaskaskia

Ohio River

VIRGINIA

MARYLAND

KENTUCKY

Claimed by Virginia, 1776

Virginia post-Revolutionary military reserves (Ohio, Kentucky)

Route of Virginia General George Rogers Clark in securing Northwest Territory, 1778–1779

MAP 10.6

sion of this same Upper South settlement pattern. Moreover, through the late eighteenth century and into the nineteenth, many of the Scotch-Irish Presbyterians and Church Germans in western Maryland, Virginia's Shenandoah Valley, Piedmont North Carolina, and even Appalachia found themselves in what was still a political and religious Greater Pennsylvania (or *Gross Pennsylvanien*). Pastors, schoolteachers, books, newspapers, and supplies flowed south from Philadelphia and Lancaster more often than west from Williamsburg or New Bern. The map illustrates Pennsylvania's role as a colonial "hearth" from which people, ideas, and culture were distributed. Directly and indirectly, each of the Border and Upper Southern states was affected.

By 1860, the eight states of this loosely linked area—Delaware, Maryland, Virginia, North Carolina, Kentucky, Tennessee, Missouri, and Arkansas—had several political descriptions: the Upper South, Border South, or Border. Slavery was lawful in all eight, but it was not dominant, either economically or psychologically. The highlands for which Pennsylvania was the cultural hearth were un-Yankee—Scotch-Irish and northern English—but also a world apart from the cotton states and the Chesapeake-Carolina tidewater. The portions of the eight that were geographically part of the slave economy—tidewater Virginia and southern Maryland, eastern North Carolina, bluegrass Kentucky, middle and western Tennessee, Little Dixie in northeastern Missouri, and eastern Arkansas—were more populous but less sizeable than the up-country where slaves were few. These divisions made the states involved ambivalent or reluctant regarding secession. Pennsylvanians, for their part, while having almost no interest in joining the cotton states, did have some winter 1860–1861 inclination, voiced by a small minority of newspapers and officeholders, to seek a Central Confederation that shed any ties to New England and reassembled Greater Pennsylvania or some combination of the Lower North and Upper South.

Such speculations were overwhelmed by northern patriotic fervor after the Sumter crisis. Without Lincoln's call for seventy-five thousand troops, Virginia, North Carolina, Tennessee, and Arkansas might not have left the Union. With it, the four states did secede. But even as they did, the North itself, including Pennsylvania, was at least temporarily unified by its own patriotic surge. The new Republican administration's attention quickly swung to the Border—Delaware, Maryland, Kentucky, Missouri, and the fair prospect that the western part of Virginia might be pried away from the already-departed remainder.

Despite the Pennsylvania ancestry of portions of Maryland, Appalachian Virginia, North Carolina, and Tennessee, there was little of Pennsylvania's bandwagon Republicanism in their 1860 presidential voting. These four states gave their support almost equally to Breckinridge and Bell, the Southern Democratic and Constitutional Union candidates. As Map 10.7 shows, the Border and Upper South were the compromise-oriented Bell's best region. Lincoln did little better in Delaware, Maryland, Kentucky, and Missouri. Even there, his support was confined to peripheries—in Delaware, industrial Wilmington, just a few miles from Pennsylvania; in Maryland, a thousand votes in Baltimore (many German) and 25 to 30 percent in a few Allegheny County mining areas on the Pennsylvania line; and in Missouri, a plurality in St. Louis and adjacent German areas, especially Forty-Eighter–shaped Gasconade County. The notion, held by more than a few officials in Washington of March 1861, that the Border teemed with northern sympathizers was as miscast as some of the British views of 1775 and 1776 that colony after colony abounded with loyalists.

What did abound in the Upper South and Border, at least in the first four to five months after the 1860 election, were Unionists who scoffed at cotton state "secesh." Virginia, Tennessee, and North Carolina all turned back secession drives in February 1861. Many of the counties with high slave-owning ratios, though not all, were ready to secede; sections with low ratios were cool. They preferred to remain in the Union, although they opposed coercing the Confederacy. It was felt that the seven states, if allowed to depart, would probably come back, assuming that no others joined them.

After Sumter and Lincoln's call for troops, Union sentiment over much of the region shrank like April's last hillside snow patches. The principal exceptions were in the mountains—eastern Tennessee, western Virginia, western North Carolina, and the Ozark rim of northwestern Arkansas. Many of the leading conservative

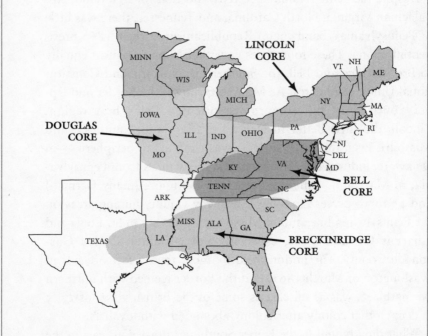

CULTURAL REGIONALISM IN THE 1860 ELECTION

Top 5 Douglas Democratic States
- Illinois (47.22%)
- Iowa (43.2%)
- Wisconsin (42.7%)
- Indiana (42.4%)
- Ohio (42.3%)

Top 5 Lincoln Republican States
- Vermont (75.7%)
- Minnesota (63.4%)
- Massachusetts (62.8%)
- Maine (62.2%)
- Connecticut (58.1%)

Top 5 Bell Constitutional Union States
- Tennessee (47.7%)
- North Carolina (46.7%)
- Virginia (45.6%)
- Kentucky (45.2%)
- Maryland (45.12%)

Top 5 Breckinridge Southern Democratic States
- South Carolina (100%)
- Texas (73.5%)
- Florida (62.2%)
- Mississippi (59.0%)
- Alabama (54.0%)

Note: The figures in parentheses represent that nominee's percentage of the total statewide vote for president. Also, these calculations exclude the three states (New York, New Jersey, and Rhode Island) where Breckinridge and Bell did not appear on the ballot with Lincoln and Douglas.

MAP 10.7

Unionists from lowland Whig backgrounds, feeling betrayed by Washington, served either in local government, the Confederate Congress, or in their home-state regiments. In areas where the federal army or navy established its control, Unionists often began to reemerge as loyalists—a pattern the British had also found in 1775–1782. However, the federal authorities had mixed results in trying to reestablish local government (also like the British in Philadelphia and the South).[67]

The enlarged Confederacy's additional challenge, once the four Upper Southern states had been recruited, was difficult verging on impossible. First, to hold its new boundaries by blocking any federal attempt to dismember the western part of Virginia or to separate the other large pro-Union section of a seceded state, eastern Tennessee (which even in June had voted aganst secession by 32,323 to 15,782). Second, to grab the Union arsenals at St. Louis and at Harper's Ferry in what would soon become West Virginia. Third, to switch Border Kentucky from self-proclaimed neutrality to membership in the Confederacy. And fourth, to pursue any opportunity in Maryland and Missouri, where substantial but outnumbered secessionist movements might be helped to fruition.

Federal strategists faced less daunting obstacles, even though the disputed areas were all slave-owning states where "damnyankee" was one word. Northern military power, however, was much closer at hand. Within ten weeks of the attack on Sumter, federal forces had taken over much of Maryland, especially key railroad lines. They had expelled southern troops from the pro-Union northwestern section of Virginia, agreed at least temporarily to the Kentucky legislature's declaration of neutrality, and outmaneuvered pro-southern officials in Missouri, driving them from St. Louis and Jefferson City, the state capital, to Neosho near the Arkansas state line. By September, when Kentucky neutrality collapsed in favor of active alignment with the North, the Confederacy had effectively lost the Border states.

These individual small battles and maneuvers were pivotal— General George McClellan's victory at Philippi in West Virginia on June 3; General Nathaniel Lyon's crushing successes in St. Louis, Jefferson City, and Boonville; and General Benjamin Butler's effective use of water transport down Chesapeake Bay in late April to bypass Baltimore, reinforce embattled Washington, and establish federal control of secession-minded southern Maryland. Collectively, these were more important than the prominent northern defeat at Bull Run just outside Washington in July.

The Maryland legislature probably favored secession. However, the Unionist governor—elected as a Know-Nothing—refused to call the legislature into session until federal military forces were in control. The Military Department of Annapolis was established on April 27 and Baltimore was occupied on May 13.[68] Missouri's governor and much of the legislature also supported secession, but were chased around the state by federal forces and then replaced by a "convention" that governed Missouri until 1865. On November 28, the Confederate government admitted Missouri as the twelfth Confederate state, after a shadow government and legislature in Neosho had voted to secede, but the pretense verged on farce. So did the admission of Kentucky as the thirteenth. It, too, had a Confederate shadow government in Russellville near the Tennessee border. Delaware, of course, had never really been free to consider secession, despite widespread sympathy in Sussex, its southernmost county.

Probably there was never much chance that even Kentucky, Missouri, or Maryland would manage to secede. The latter, hamstrung as long as Virginia remained in the Union, was only free to choose in April. Had Virginia seceded in February, say, Maryland might have joined the Confederacy before Lincoln could take office. The outgoing Buchanan administration might have done nothing. However, the importance to a just-inaugurated President Lincoln—and to the Union—of blocking Maryland secession in April, May, or July (after Bull Run created a second wave of interest) was enormous. Thus the importance of General Butler's quick action. The Bluegrass State was almost as vital. Lincoln himself said that it would be nice to have God on his side, but that it was imperative to have Kentucky.[69] As for Missouri, which could have been reconquered from adjacent Illinois, Iowa, and Kansas, effective secession was probably impossible. But the inspired action of Connecticut-born Nathaniel Lyon, who during the twelve weeks before he was killed at the battle of Wilson's Creek went from captain commanding the federal troops at the St. Louis Arsenal to brigadier general commanding the federal troops in Missouri—including four regiments quickly raised among St. Louis Germans—nipped Confederate hopes in the bud.

Compared with the weak or lackadaisical approach of the British Crown in putting down rebellion in 1642 and 1775, the Republican government of the United States was fast off the mark in 1861—and just as fast to suspend democratic procedures. Although Delaware, Maryland, Kentucky, and Missouri never seceded and thereby avoided the official Reconstruction imposed on the Upper South as well as the cotton states, their politics were, in a sense, crushed and rebuilt by federal troops as early as 1861.

There was a common pattern. In Maryland, which had to choose a governor and a legislature in November 1861, federal troops were used to prohibit voting by anyone who sympathized with the South. With only about half the normal ballots cast, Unionists won overwhelmingly. In Kentucky, the franchise was restricted and martial law declared in 1863. In Missouri, the test act of 1861 disenfranchised many Confederate sympathizers who would have been Democratic voters, and the turnout in the presidential election of 1864 was fifty-two thousand lower than that four years earlier. In Delaware, the Democrats usually won, but in 1863, nearly all of them boycotted a special congressional election to protest the presence of federal troops at polling places and the required oaths of allegiance.[70]

The stakes were huge. Maryland's secession would have isolated the capital in Washington. Pennsylvania, which came within fifteen thousand votes of electing a prior Confederate sympathizer, Judge George Woodward, as governor in 1863, would have become the southern edge of the Union. As such, it might have been a shakier reed than it was. Kentucky's departure, in turn, could easily have shifted what became the drawn-out war in Tennessee north to the Ohio Valley, with the potential for a massive rebellion in the areas of lower Illinois and Indiana that were, in any event, so restive in late 1862. Had a Confederate Kentucky marshalled large Confederate forces just across the Ohio River, the Civil War could have been all the more easily lost in the elections of 1862 and 1863.

Small wonder, then, that federal military power was applied so quickly in the Border—and because of McClellan, Lyon, and Butler, so effectively. On the other hand, the Border states, for their part, did not come out of the 1861–1865 fighting with any great affection for the national Republican Party. Each had put more soldiers in blue uniforms than in gray—overwhelmingly in Delaware, almost two-to-one in Maryland, perhaps a little less in Kentucky, and three-to-one in Missouri. Yet, when these states got to vote for president in the relatively bayonet-free atmosphere of 1868, three were among General Ulysses S. Grant's five worst: Kentucky went 74.6 percent Democratic, Maryland 67.2 percent, and Delaware 59.0 percent. Only Missouri backed Grant because it alone of these still had a test act. Between 1876 and 1892, all four went Democratic in each and every presidential election.

A brief digression is in order to note that the last two "border" states of 1860 were western: California and Oregon, both of which Lincoln carried by only hairbreadth pluralities, with a sizeable minority of voters opting for the southern Democratic nominee, John Breckinridge (28 percent in California, 34 percent in Oregon). On the eve of war, the western states and territories, like those in the Ohio Valley, were places where large southern and northern populations mingled.

In California, San Francisco and the north coast were Union-dominated, and along with other local units even forming a "California battalion" to serve in the 2nd Massachusetts Cavalry.[71] In late 1860 and early 1861, however, some neutral observers had expected California to support the Confederacy or opt for the independent Pacific Confederacy so many local Democratic office-holders were talking about. Of the state's 380,000 people, almost 40 percent were from slave states, and only seven of fifty-three newspapers had supported Lincoln. Confederate flags were flown in San Jose, Visalia, Stockton, and a number of mining towns, and pro-southern sentiment was so strong in Los Angeles and San Bernardino that northern California infantry and cavalry units had to be moved into the area to guard against any Confederate force coming from Texas and New Mexico (Tucson, for example, sent a delegate to the Confederate Congress). Tennessee-born U.S. Senator William Gwin left California for the Confederacy in early 1861. Unionist sentiment grew after South Carolina fired on Fort Sumter, and Copperhead activity slackened after the Confederate invasion of New Mexico was turned back at Glorieta Pass in March 1862.

Circumstances were similar in the other western state, Oregon, which had a population of fifty-two thousand in 1860. The southern-born were numerous, especially in the mining camps, and one of them, U.S. Senator Joseph Lane, had been Breckinridge's running mate in 1860. This explains the ticket's unusually high support. By December and January, pro-Confederate views were widespread, as was interest in joining California in an independent western confederation. Yankees and Iowans kept the state in the northern column, but in 1863 and 1864, some twenty-five to thirty thousand Missourians, many of them ex-Confederate soldiers and their families, fled home-state military occupation and guerrilla warfare by taking the Platte River road west to Oregon. Miners gave their camps names like Confederate Gulch and Fort Sumter, and in northeastern Oregon in 1864, loyalist Iowans were barely able to outvote emigré Missourians to give their county its new name: Union.[72] Oregon cannot fairly be called an extension of Missouri, but it *was* an extension of the Border—and these settlement striations lived on in its voting alignments for another century and more.

The Republicans, of course, were much better off in the true Border back east between 1868 and 1892 than they had been in 1856 and 1860. With the 1861–1865 fighting as the forge, they put together Border state coalitions for the late nineteenth century that were compatible with their national electorates—Germans in St. Louis and environs, Kentucky's Ohio River cities, and Baltimore; mountaineers from the Cumberlands and Appalachians to the Ozarks; upper-income groups (commercial elements of the old Whigs), blacks, and some others. These were substantial minorities, and from time to time, they prevailed. And, of course, from 1896 to 1932 the Republican electorate was reinvigorated into a new industrial-era majority coalition that updated the Civil War framework of U.S. politics. The Border became more or less competitive.

On the other hand, that was not critical. A new divide between Pennsylvania and the adjacent states below the Mason-Dixon line had been drawn and underscored by the war. Pennsylvania had gotten fat on war contracts, emerged as one of the world's foremost industrial regions, and become increasingly Republican in its politics. With Greater New England, it became a seat of the Republican Party and its national leadership of a capitalist, industrialist United States. Yesteryear's ties to the Border lost importance.

In looking at the Upper South and Border and what the war meant for these regions, it is hard to avoid a sweeping assessment: that the U.S. Civil War was another great watershed in which victory went to a zealous, skilled, and destiny-minded minority—the principal cadre of which just happened to be descended from the intense and grasping Puritan and Yankee minority that had also been the largest single force in the two previous cousins' wars. The defeat of southern culture, agriculture, and politics did not end at the borders of the former Confederacy.

Each cousins' war, as we have seen, was fought amid a geography that made this aggressive minority's home territory—East Anglia, New England, Greater New England—the stronghold, relatively little touched by combat, of the winning side. So it was again in 1861–1865. Each war validated, if only for a while, this elite's view of commerce, middle-class republicanism, and Anglo-Saxon expansion. The Civil War certainly did. Within the still-whole United States, this elite, with its religious nonconformism and Anglocentricity, was also edging closer to the late nineteenth-century hour when the two major English-speaking nations would begin the great rapprochement that would dominate the twentieth century. The industrial and imperial momentum of the U.S. Civil War foreshadowed that, too, although almost a decade would pass before the subsidence of northern anger over the covert assistance the British ruling class was thought to have rendered to the Confederacy.

11

THE U.S. CIVIL WAR
AND THE
FRAMEWORK OF
ANGLO-AMERICA

If the election had been held in August 1864 instead of November, Lincoln would have lost. He would thus have gone down in history as an also-ran, a loser unequal to the challenge of the greatest crisis in the American experience. And Jefferson Davis might have gone down in history as the great leader of a war of independence, the architect of a new nation, the George Washington of the Southern Confederacy.
        —James M. McPherson, 1991

In late 1862, the government of Great Britain debated the possibility of masterminding a European intervention in the American Civil War . . . The Lincoln Administration's greatest fear in foreign affairs was that England would extend diplomatic recognition to the Confederacy. If the British announced recognition, the Union's minister in England was to suspend his functions as a diplomat, thereby setting the two Atlantic nations on a path that could lead to war.
        —Howard Jones, Union in Peril, 1992

WINSTON CHURCHILL SET OUT his own speculations in a 1932 essay. Had Robert E. Lee won at Gettysburg in 1863, the South, gaining Britain as an ally, would have gone on to conquer Mexico and beat the North. The British, Churchill said, would have avoided the First World War, watershed of the country's subsequent twentieth-century decline.[1] Without World War I, ironically, there would have been no rise of Nazi Germany to make Churchill prime minister in 1940.

The Library of Congress has a catalogue of "imaginary histories" among which are possible alternative fates of Anglo-America ranging from good weather for the Spanish Armada to ill fortune for Parliament on the battlefields of 1643–1645 or greater success for Sir William Howe in coordinating with Burgoyne in 1777. Were this chapter to offer an alternative scenario for 1861–1865, which it will not, the pivot would be different election calendars for 1862 and 1864. Yet, it is also true that a southern victory at Gettysburg could easily have led to Confederate capture of the Pennsylvania capital of Harrisburg, a threat to nervous Philadelphia, and even worse riots in New York City, along with insurrections in New Jersey and lower Illinois, Indiana, and Ohio. Northern leaders could have been forced to inquire about an armistice.

The common threads of the three wars make taking alternative outcomes seriously more difficult. A flow of great events was under way. On the other hand, perhaps that essential framework itself would never have been in place without a Puritan and Parliamentary victory in the 1640s as Professor Trevelyan has suggested (see p. 35).

In our real world, though, the capitulation at Appomattox means that the progression that began in 1642, erupted again in 1775, and then reemerged in 1861 is drawing to a close. The English-speaking peoples would not have another major civil war. The party system built around the American Civil War would be the last U.S. internal political alignment steeped in sectionalism and religion and then forged on domestic battlefields.

Notwithstanding the devastation of the South, the huge casualties, and the embitterment of transatlantic relations by British flirtation with the Confederacy, the future of Anglo-America during the rest of the nineteenth and twentieth centuries would turn out to be extraordinary. The three wars had made it possible; the necessary political circumstances, the demographic and economic momentum, were in place.

In this chapter, we will look at the U.S. Civil War's big winners: capitalism, industry, the Republican Party, and the citadels of this new regime, Greater New England and Pennsylvania. There were also obvious losers: agrarianism and the cavalier manor lords: But at this point it is also appropriate to look at the three peoples—the Irish, the blacks, and Native Americans—who can be called the collateral losers from the entire three-century sweep of the cousins' wars. The British, in turn, were not open belligerents in the fighting of 1861–1865, but they were closely involved—and as we will see, greatly interested, politically divided between North and South, and then powerfully affected by the egalitarian implications of the northern victory. The bad blood left in the North by British flirtation with the Confederacy in 1862–1863 lingered for a decade or two, but then faded in the 1890s as the United States, accelerated by the Civil War into world industrial primacy, discovered that it was also an empire of sorts. The result, as the last section of this chapter details, was the rapprochement between Britain and the United States that led to the alliance of the twentieth century.

The 1861–1865 War and the Political and Economic Rise of the U.S. Nation-State

The loose, possibly unraveling U.S. Confederation of early 1861 and the emerging nation-state of late 1865 were almost different countries. Memoirs of the postwar period describe a sea change. And the massive transformation that would last through the 1890s was just beginning.

In 1861 and 1862, much of upper-class Britain, offended by the idea of an English-speaking republic rooted in unfashionable Protestant nonconformism, had wondered, as in 1783 and 1810, whether the United States might still come apart. That was the weight of previous evidence; most other republics had. After a year of war, the U.S. federal system still seemed very much at risk. Its latter-day Roundhead troops of Norwich clerks, Manchester clothing workers, Bristol merchants, and Cambridge tutors, for all their first-rate Puritan battle hymns, were hobbled by second-rate generals. The cadences of "John Brown's Body" were no substitute for strategy and tactics. From the surprise at Bull Run to the stone wall at Fredericksburg, federal armies were losing battle after battle to the latter-day southern cavaliers whom the landed gentry of the United Kingdom regarded as the nearest New World approximation of English gentlemen.

Were Britain to become involved, Her Majesty's government had a military plan of sorts. One draftsman of the 1861–1862 memos on the strategies from Canada had a familiar name—General Sir John Fox Burgoyne, British inspector-general of fortifications and seventy-nine-year-old illegitimate son of the playwriting Burgoyne defeated at Saratoga. The state of Maine, which was believed amenable to union with Canada, would be invaded by seaborne troops. The Royal Navy would blockade major ports, including New York City.[2] Should California and Oregon form a separate Western Confederacy, that might be a chance for British influence to seep south from Puget Sound.[3] There was a chance that the United States itself might split into three or four separate pieces.

By the spring of 1865, circumstances had turned 180 degrees. The victorious North had one million men under arms, seasoned veterans of the first large-scale nineteenth-century war to be fought with railroads, steamships, and telegraphs able to move and coordinate great armies. Great arsenals, smelters, engineering works, packing plants, and power looms had grown up to equip, feed, and clothe them. Europe's earlier military inventions—the shell gun, the rifled breechloader gun, and the minie ball, which extended infantry fire to an effective range of eight hundred yards—had been extended in the U.S. by the first serious wartime production of ironclads, torpedoes, rotating turrets, and Gatling guns. Industry and technology surged. By Lee's surrender, the loose North American confederation, which might have been consensually dissolved as late as 1861, had made itself over into a nation-state and incipient world power.

In the North America of 1865, the reach of the United States was supreme. Federal troops could have taken and garrisoned the border cities of Upper and Lower Canada in two weeks. Fifty thousand battle-hardened veterans moved to the Mexican border did force France to withdraw support from a puppet Hapsburg prince, Maximilian, that Paris had set up as Emperor of Mexico in 1863. The U.S. Atlantic seaboard, meanwhile, had become a coastline that even the Royal Navy was not strong enough to blockade. The U.S. Navy had expanded sixfold, from slightly over 100 ships in early 1861 to 671 at war's end. Of these, 237 were steam-powered craft built in northern shipyards between 1861 and 1865. More than 40 were also ironclads. Washington retired these unneeded vessels quickly after Lee's surrender, but in mid-1865, at least, the wooden battleships with which the British could have encircled New York City four years earlier would have provided little more than coastal target practice for the steel-plated U.S. flotillas.[4]

For British conservatives or aristocrats of the vintage of Lord Palmerston, the prime minister, who had begun in the War Office during the Napoleonic era and had whetted a low regard for the ex-colonials during the Brother Jonathan years, the more subtle embarrassment of northern victory was domestic. By 1863, the threat of British military involvement on the side of the South and slavery had stirred working-class and middle-class Britons, many of whom had cousins or closer relatives in the northern states. When federal forces finally prevailed, instead of democracy flying apart in North America, its precepts became contagious even in relatively deferential Britain—and a second electoral reform loomed as a follow-up to 1832.

War effects in the United States followed the threads of the two previous conflicts. A setback for aristocracy brought, as usual, a temporary surge of democratization. Latter-day Puritanism—perhaps by this time more accurately described as commercially minded Yankee Protestantism—increased its sway. Prewar political constraints on economic and industrial growth were reduced or eliminated. Commerce expanded and naval power advanced. Westward migration and global expansion triumphed. And then, as always, came counterrevolution, the conservative reaction against wartime dislocations and the seeming excesses of democracy that had been unleashed.

The defeat of monarchy or aristocracy, at least on the battlefields, is a vital continuity. We have seen how Charles I lost his head and George III was disavowed in British North America and rebuked at home by Dunning's resolution in Parliament. The U.S. Civil War, following suit, unseated a manorial gentry that likened itself to Norman barons and Stuart Cavaliers, led by a Confederate executive branch with initial dreams, at least, of a milieu akin to a European court.[5]

This gentry was beaten, in late 1864 and 1865, by what was almost a second New Model Army, the product of the North's greater weight of industry and practicality. The veteran forces of Generals Sherman and Sheridan marched through Georgia, South Carolina, and the Shenandoah with a power, logistics, and destructiveness that would have impressed a Cromwellian or Williamite general teaching a similar lesson to seventeenth-century Ireland (or, for that matter, to Royalist Cheshire or Lancashire circa 1645). Hollywood has made a staple of Civil War movies in which some southern belle, watching her family plantation burn, curses the "nameless, fatherless Yankee scum" of a northern cavalry troop about to ride off. British audiences have watched similar dramas of a Wiltshire castle or a Gloucestershire manor house being occupied or torched by Ironsides cavalrymen named Hosea, Hiram, and Hezekiah whose manners match their East Midlands accents.

The North's anti-aristocratic impulse was threefold, but cautious. The plantation South was belabored as a landed gentry upholding an outdated agrarian economy and blocking commercial and industrial expansion. Slave-owners were condemned as an elite whose practices demeaned not just black slaves but free white labor. Perhaps most tellingly, the Cotton South was attacked as a "Slaveocracy" that controlled the Democratic Party, Washington, and the Supreme Court. Shrewd northern politicians like Seward had understood how the bogeyman of a Slave Power could mesh older abolitionist and religious arguments with practical opposition to a rival national governing elite *and* slavery's threat to free white labor. This rhetorical fusion tapped the egalitarian currents so important in American society and recently intensified by Jacksonian Democracy. Yet its simultaneous political opposition to southern usurpation also took on aspects of northern power politics and sectional self-interest.[6]

Lee's surrender collapsed what were already fading memories. The planter aristocracy never regained its antebellum glories. Once slavery was abolished, most plantations were broken up by market forces. The national political dominance of Southerners, in turn, ended in 1861 and never recovered until the 1930s. Between

1789 and 1861, slave-owners from a future Confederate state had occupied the presidency for forty-nine years out of seventy-two. But a century would pass after 1865 before a resident of an ex-Confederate state could win the office again. So, too, with the Supreme Court, the House Speakership, and the Presidency Pro Tem of the Senate. Half to two-thirds of the justices, speakers, and Senate presidents before 1861 had come from the South. For the next fifty years, not one speaker or Senate president would come from the former Confederacy and just five of the twenty-six Supreme Court justices.[7] Northerners ruled. Each Republican president in the sixty years from U.S. Grant to Calvin Coolidge had partial or predominantly Yankee antecedents.

During the U.S. Civil War, the anti-aristocratic tenor of confrontation, with its emphasis on liberty and its attacks on abusive elites, once again stirred an ancillary debate. In the late 1640s, while Parliament discussed the fate of Charles I, it also weighed how far England should level its internal gradations of rank and privilege and expand religious freedom. The new United States of the 1780s, in historian Carl Becker's words, pursued "who would rule at home" once George III was pushed aside. Neither the Levellers of the 1640s nor the radicals of the 1770s succeeded for long. The comparable struggles of the 1860s—and retreats of the 1870s—are more complex, however, because they involved black as well as white political participation.

Cromwell's citizen soldiers had argued throughout the 1640s that those who fought ought to be able to vote in Parliamentary elections. The Instrument of Government in 1654 eliminated many rotten boroughs and increased representation, but these changes were wiped out in the Restoration.[8] The Pennsylvania Constitution of 1776, in turn, gave the vote to every freeman who had resided in the state for one year and paid taxes. More broadly, as we have seen, the franchise at war's end was liberal enough in five of the new states to allow blacks to vote. Women may have as well in a few jurisdictions.[9] None lasted more than a decade or two. The Thirteenth, Fourteenth, and Fifteenth Amendments to the U.S. Constitution, ratified from 1865 to 1870, not only ended slavery, but gave blacks the equal protection of the laws and the vote.[10] Another countertide would not be far behind.

Black enfranchisement was controversial from the start. Even in Greater New England, many went to war in 1861 to keep the Union intact in order to achieve America's larger national destiny, not just abolition. Even in a preserved Union, though, the Republicans had to counter the possibility that the South, if readmitted to the Union without constraints, might recapture national power with the help of the Border states, New York, New Jersey, Ohio, Indiana, and Illinois.

Greater New England itself was the national Republican bulwark. The top eight Republican states in the 1876 presidential election were Vermont, Nebraska, Kansas, Rhode Island, Minnesota, Iowa, Massachusetts, and Maine. Yet Yankee control of national politics was precarious enough to need further backstops: black control of part of the South, internal migration, or both. If Kansas and Nebraska had been secured in the late 1850s, the Far West was still being filled in. Parts of northern California, Oregon, and Washington were already taking on an unmistakable New England stamp. Hawaii and the South Pacific drew New England missionaries, and Maui became a virtual colony of Connecticut. Secretary of State Seward, an undisguised imperialist, wanted to expand U.S. boundaries in virtually every direction, including Canada and the Caribbean, although he is best remembered for the 1869 purchase of Alaska, called "Seward's Folly," which it clearly was not. Less success, however, attended internal plans, especially those for Yankee resettlement in the South.

Early expectations had been considerable. In April 1862, Massachusetts's Edward Everett Hale had predicted that a northern victory would launch a colonization by Yankee veterans who would bring the inevitable benefits of church and schoolhouse, forge and factory.[11] In contrast to the large-scale confiscations of the 1640s and the 1775–1783 period, however, the lands of Confederate rebels were never seized for distribution to either ex-slaves or Yankee soldiers. After the election of 1868, Horace Greeley, concerned about the electoral future, suggested that three thousand northern colonists in Florida; five thousand each in Arkansas, Alabama, Louisiana, and Mississippi; and a thousand each in Virginia, North Carolina, and Texas would make the South Republican and politics safe for commerce and industry.[12]

Part of why this never happened was cultural hesitation. But wartime reality also had already subverted some of the earlier crusading spirit of the Second Great Awakening. As the North took over the federal government, securing authority became more appealing than revolution. Few Yankees favored Irish draft riots and Butternut guerrilla warfare in the Ohio Valley. The theory of rebellion itself became disconcerting. This was much the same discovery Cromwell had made in the late 1640s and New England's Congregationalist and Federalist Establishment had made confronting Shays' Rebellion in the 1780s. By 1864, New England Congregationalist leaders like Henry Bellows and Horace Bushnell had begun praising the "divine right" of rulers and the sovereignty of magistrates.[13] The zealotry that had sent emigrants and rifles to Kansas a decade earlier was gone.

There were signs of caste outpacing conscience. Francis Parkman, the historian, took pleasure in how many Massachusetts regiments were commanded by gentlemen whose exploits upheld aristocratic values and rebutted the notion of cavaliers as being exclusively plantation-born. James Russell Lowell told the Harvard Commemoration of July 1865 that the martial valor of the fallen alumni had disproved the assertions of southern "Cavaliers" about the plebeian origins of Yankee "Roundheads."[14]

The most salutary effect of the war, Lowell thought, was its certification to Americans of their new power and confidence and its announcement to the world of "a new imperial race." To Herman Melville, in whose books American whalers sailed the seven seas and overcame cannibals in the South Pacific, the postwar United States faced the future with "empire in her eyes." Empire was a theme that preoccupied Melville in his mid-1865 collection *Battle Pieces*.[15] Walt Whitman had predicted it in 1860, chanting "a new empire grander than any before . . . my sail-ships and steam-ships threading the archipelagoes, my stars and stripes fluttering in the wind."[16] Yankee "republican imperialism," so visible in the rhetoric of the 1770s, was being reborn.

Northern victory in the Civil War provided the essential outcome through which a still-intact Union could resume a major transcontinental expansion. Success for the South would almost certainly have meant rapid Confederate enlargement in Mexico and possibly the Caribbean, but the former United States would have been split—and who is to say that western boundary issues would not have generated a fourth cousins' war? Federal triumph, on the other hand, ensured united, undivided westward expansion, although postwar convergences in Colorado, Oregon, Montana, and other western states gave ranchers, miners, and loggers with Yankee antecedents plenty of opportunity for political bickering with ex-Confederate refugees from Texas, Missouri, and Georgia.

The framework of renewed expansion had been quickly put in place in 1861–1862, amid the war, when the new northern-run Congress broke the logjam of the 1850s by passing homestead legislation, establishing land-grant colleges, and deciding on a transcontinental railroad route. Between 1860 and 1880, the population of Michigan, Iowa, and California doubled. That of Oregon tripled, while Minnesota's quadrupled, and Colorado's quintupled. Expansion in Kansas was ninefold.

Commercial and industrial growth in the North bespoke an even larger transformation: the Civil War as economic revolution. The first part involved eliminating archaic economic systems and political inhibitions on growth. Parliament had done this in the 1640s by curbing the King's power over nonparliamentary taxation and monopolies, while Cromwell's Navigation Acts built an effective colonial trade framework. The War for American Independence, in turn, ended the economic subordination of the North American colonies under British laws that restrained manufactures, shipping, and currency. The U.S. Civil War, even more sweepingly, ended slavery, empowered industrial capitalism, and, as we shall see, redistributed capital within the United States on a grand scale.

The second expansive force came from war's own demands for increased production, which also had precedents. In the seventeenth century, Parliament's success in providing large amounts of clothing, shoes, food, weaponry, cannon, and gunpowder for its soldiers, financed by relatively high taxes, may well have been an unappreciated factor in English industrial expansion.[17] In both Britain and the U.S., the 1775–1783 war nurtured some of the same early industries, notably metallurgy and clothing.[18] One compendium of the Revolution's effects in the United States has noted that the increased promotion of muskets, cannon, cannon balls, shot, iron chains, and the day-to-day hardware of army camps "pointed the way to the phenomenal interaction of war and industry that marked the next two centuries." For example, fourteen-year-old Eli Whitney, converting his father's tool shed into a nail factory, began a career that subsequently included the first large-scale attempt at mass production in America in the manufacture of muskets.[19] Besides the creation of federal departments of foreign affairs, finance, and war in 1781, the later years of the war also saw the formation of the Bank of North America in Philadelphia by citizens wanting to assist the army.[20] Historians have acknowledged insufficient attention to the economic effects of both earlier wars.

During the American Civil War, economic growth was magnified beyond any uncertainty by the new technology of war and by the enormity of the fiscal and military mobilization.[21] Charles Beard and other economic determinists correctly looked back to see a mighty industrial economy pushing a lesser agrarian one out of the way, although they underestimated the simultaneous moral and religious impulses. The transformation that Republican politicians—and behind them, many northern capitalists—pushed through the congresses of 1861–1865 was nothing less than a neo-Hamiltonian revolution, one that would have been impossible without the southern absence from Washington and the demands of an all-out war.

In addition to westward expansion tools like the Homestead Act and a northern transcontinental railroad route, the Republican agenda, in retrospect, rested on four major pillars: (1) a vast increase of $2.5 billion in national debt to pay for the war and related economic expansion; (2) a wide new range of internal taxes—income, inheritance, and excise—to help meet war costs; (3) an expansion of the protective tariff to record heights to raise revenue and shelter fledgling northern manufacturing interests; and (4) the creation of a national banking system to bring banking under one roof and to displace state banknotes with uniform federal paper. Taken together, these represented an extraordinary upheaval.

These measures almost certainly helped the North to prevail in a war that became increasingly dependent on resources and logistics. But they also represented the national economic overhaul sought by three generations of mostly northern conservatives. The new policy, moreover, took hold on an especially grand scale because of its interaction with a gargantuan war effort that would put a million federal soldiers in the field and balloon the federal budget to $1.2 billion in 1865 from a mere $63 million in 1860. Not even the mobilization for World War II eighty years later involved such staggering rates of increase.

As with the Parliamentary side in the much smaller England of the seventeenth century, the federal government became by far the country's largest single purchaser. Particularly rapid growth followed in industries such as iron, textiles, shoes, and meatpacking. Pig-iron production expanded by a third. Shoe production doubled. Woollen mills in the North, facing less competition from cotton, increased their output by nearly two-thirds. The massiveness of the investment involved comes through even in a single city: Philadelphia industrialists alone built fifty-eight additional factories in 1862, fifty-seven more in 1863, and then another sixty-five in 1864.[22] The northeastern and Great Lakes states were also great beneficiaries of industrialization.

Even an early "industrial policy" of sorts came into being as federal authorities built arms factories and pharmaceutical laboratories, chartered the Union Pacific and Central Pacific Railroads, and established the Bureau of Internal Revenue (to collect nontariff revenues), the Bureau of Immigration, the Department of Agriculture (to increase farm productivity), and the National Academy of Sciences (to help harness science for the war effort).[23] Taxes at the federal and (northern) state level were considerably higher during the decades after the Civil War than they had been before—between 1860 and 1870, they tripled in five northern states, increased fivefold in Michigan, and sixfold in New Jersey.[24] In the words of one major study, *War and the Rise of the State*, "Appomattox thus represented not only the defeat of the South but the defeat of the whole Southern economic and political system, and the triumph of a state-fostered industrial and financial complex in the North."[25]

The "Great Barbecue," as cynics called it, depended on the favors of activist government. Many of the great American fortunes of the Gilded Age got their start in the greenback deluge of 1863 to 1865: John D. Rockefeller in the gushing Pennsylvania oil fields, J. P. Morgan in the financial district of New York, and Andrew Carnegie in the steel mills and railroad yards of Pittsburgh. Wartime ethics were as crude as the Oil Creek petroleum. Wits even joked that Standard Oil could do anything with the Pennsylvania legislature but refine it.

The stimulus of federal purchases was matched by that of a rapidly expanding money supply. Economist Milton Friedman, analyzing the money stock in the hands of the U.S. public of 1867, found that about three-quarters was of Civil War origin, a "type of money that had not existed only six or seven years earlier." He linked this money-supply growth to the enormous expansion of the U.S. national income and manufactures during the 1860s.[26]

Railroads were another prominent component. Whereas the iron and textile industries had ballooned during the war, railroad building had slowed. With peace, it resumed at a faster pace than ever, crossing the deserts and bridging the wide rivers: the Ohio at Cincinnati in 1867, the Mississippi at St. Louis in 1874. From twenty-nine thousand miles of track in 1860, U.S. railroad mileage grew to forty-nine thousand in 1870. Despite its vastness, the United States built an adequate national railway system almost as quickly as the compact industrial nations of western Europe. This demand for iron and coal had another, smaller cousin more specifically born in the war. Andrew Carnegie had seen the future: burnt-down wooden bridges should be rebuilt with steel.

Other gains were comparable. Between the end of the Civil War and the beginning of the Spanish-American War in 1898, American agricultural production soared—wheat by 256 percent, corn by 222 percent, and refined sugar by 440 percent. Coal output jumped by 800 percent; oil—new in the mid-nineteenth century—by 1800 percent. Production of steel rails was up by 523 percent, with the miles of railway track increasing by 567 percent.[27] The data in Figure 11.1 identify the Civil War as the great accelerator of the U.S. share of world manufacturing output.

In 1851, the British manufacturers attending the giant Crystal Palace Exhibit in London had been impressed by American technology. War spurred further innovation. However, the politics of sus-

FIGURE 11.1   Relative National Shares of World
Manufacturing Output

	1800	1830	1860	1880	1900
Britain	4.3%	9.5%	19.9%	22.9%	18.5%
U.S.	0.8	2.4	7.2	14.7	23.6
Germany	3.5	3.5	4.9	8.5	13.2

Source: Paul Kennedy, *The Rise and Fall of the Great Powers*, p. 202.

taining Republican and capitalist rule once the war ended looked difficult, in part because of the very flood of money and corruption the war had unleashed. Small entrepreneurs, farmers, and reformers, important to the national Republican Party, were put off by the new capitalists, railroad kings, and industrial buccaneers. This suspicion became part of the new postwar political milieu. Once the war had been won, the slaves freed, and the South chastened, the growing excesses of industry and capitalism, overlooked when victory hung in the balance, would themselves move to center stage.

Even the Republican Party would be torn. In the dark days of the summer of 1864, when even many party strategists thought he would lose, Abraham Lincoln had picked as his running mate on the Union ticket a War Democrat from the South. This U.S. senator, Andrew Johnson of Tennessee, a spokesman for the poorer eastern section, had already anticipated the Greenbacker and Granger agrarian radical movements of the 1870s in his prewar attacks on the economic aristocracy—"parasites," he called them.[28] On becoming president following Lincoln's assassination in April 1865, Johnson was quickly at loggerheads with the Radical Republicans who advocated punitive policies toward the defeated South and were on close terms with the nouveau-riche war multimillionaires. By 1866, he was warning in speeches that "an aristocracy based on nearly two billion and a half of national securities has arisen in the Northern states to assume that political control which the consolidation of great financial and political interests formerly gave to the slave oligarchy. The war of finance is the next war we have to fight."[29] Prophetic as this would be by 1872, it was also before its time. Moreover, Johnson's desire to readmit the southern states to the Union with relatively mild restraints was poorly conceived and unacceptable in the still-angry North of 1866. Indeed, he barely survived impeachment in 1867.

Yet many other wartime Republicans and Unionists also found themselves alienated by how the new capitalist class had displaced the yeomanry and artisans of prewar Republican theory. Abolitionist Wendell Phillips left the Republicans in 1870 to run for governor of Massachusetts as the candidate of the Labor Reform Party, advocating legislation to improve the conditions of labor and control the behavior of corporations.[30] On election day, though, he polled only 12 percent. Other so-called Liberal Republicans—from Charles Sumner and Charles Francis Adams of Massachusetts to Carl Schurz of Missouri and Lyman Trumbull of Illinois—abandoned the party in 1872 to support ex-Republican Horace Greeley as the Democratic–Liberal Republican fusion presidential nominee. Many Democrats, however, found Greeley unacceptable and the fusion was a failure. Once launched in the 1860s, the rise of the American capitalist nation-state was not going to be stymied. Indeed, for another generation, it would scarcely be regulated.

The two previous English-speaking civil wars, as we have seen, displayed another recurring behavior: punishment and revenge by the winners against the losers. Sometimes these overlapped with reactions against the excesses uncorked during the war and its aftermath. With Parliament in the 1640s having indulged its revenge by executing the King and confiscating estates, the restored Royalists of 1660 followed with their own executions of regicides and repression of Puritans. Cromwell himself had curbed radical excesses during his Protectorate in the 1650s. A second variation came in the rhythm of politics and revenge after the American War for Independence. The predictable post-1783 drive to confiscate Tory property and to deny loyalists the right to return or to vote was led by the wartime patriots of a more radical or egalitarian stripe. The wealthier patriot faction, which dominated by the late 1780s, preferred recruiting the loyalists for conservative government.

The uncertainties after the U.S. Civil War more resembled those following the War for Independence. The moderate faction of the victorious Unionist coalition, led by Andrew Johnson, the southern-born accidental president, favored minimal revenge and coercion. The Radicals, however, demanded a far-reaching program of treating the southern states as conquered provinces and readmitting them only after they had been reconstructed around northern principles and the enfranchisement of ex-slaves. This position was upheld in 1866 when Radicals swept to two-thirds majorities in both houses of Congress.

From an abolitionist or Republican political perspective, radical Reconstruction was not merely logical; it was imperative. Even the northern branches of the churches that divided before the war were militant, trying to gobble up southern denominations. The case for aggressiveness in politics was particularly compelling because the Civil War Republican majority was artificial, a product of southern secession combined with wartime federal military influence over voting in the Border states. Unfettered readmission of the southern states would doom the Republicans in Congress and the Electoral College alike. To calculating party leaders, whereas it had been necessary in 1863–1864 to save the Union by freeing the slaves and then arming them—some two hundred thousand served in northern armies—the new necessity of 1865–1867 was to use the blacks to "reconstruct" the South and Border politically. Majorities of whites in most ex-Confederate states were opposed. New statewide governing coalitions would have to be built around ex-slaves and Unionist whites. Protection by federal troops would be necessary, certainly in the beginning.

Between 1866 and 1875, dozens of reconstruction statutes were passed—the basic Reconstruction Act of 1867, implementing legislation, authorization for a Freedmen's Bureau, and various civil rights bills and enforcement acts. Their relatively short-lived effect can be seen in the list of southern and Border states voting Republican in 1868 and 1872 elections, followed by the shriveling of 1876 and the implosion of 1880.

In 1868, only five ex-Confederate states had been readmitted, but with ex-Confederates disenfranchised and ex-slaves voting, all went Republican. The full eleven were back in the Union in 1872, but most were still under military occupation. The result was a lopsided electoral victory for Republican President Ulysses S. Grant. By 1876, however, support for the Republican nominee had shrunk back to Greater New England plus the three southern states still at bayonet point. These electoral votes from Florida, Louisiana, and South Carolina, hotly disputed, were all that enabled the Republicans to hold the White House. And in March

FIGURE 11.2   The Post-Reconstruction Collapse of Southern Republicanism

1868	1872	1876	1880
Alabama	Alabama	Florida	None
Arkansas	Arkansas	Louisiana	
Missouri	Delaware	South Carolina	
North Carolina	Florida		
South Carolina	Louisiana		
Tennessee	Mississippi		
West Virginia	North Carolina		
	South Carolina		
	Virginia		
	West Virginia		

1877, to avoid what some feared could be another civil war, a bargain was struck between Republican leaders and Southerners: The three states' electoral votes would be cast for just this last Republican president and then federal troops would be withdrawn.

To say that the Republican presidential vote had shrunk back to Greater New England in November 1876 is an understatement. Unpopular black equality and neo-Cromwellian rule by major generals below the Mason-Dixon line were coming on top of the railroad monopolies and the scandals of the Grant administration. In all but a few northern states, presidential nominee Rutherford Hayes—ironically, a reform governor of Ohio—drew a *lower* share of the presidential vote than Lincoln had in the four-way race of 1860. California, Iowa, and Oregon were the three exceptions. Between 1876 and 1892, moreover, not a single Republican presidential candidate ever got a *majority* of the national popular vote. Their shares ranged from a low of 42.96 percent to a high of 48.25 percent, and they trailed the Democratic nominee four times out of five. Even in Greater New England, five states were Democratic or close at least once: Connecticut, New Hampshire, Maine, Wisconsin, and Michigan. Even with the bargain of 1877, the politics of industrial capitalism barely survived.

If the rise of the U.S. share of world manufacturing output confirmed the Civil War's importance to America's industrial future, the voting statistics of 1860–1876 should underscore how vital even a short-lived Reconstruction was to sustaining vulnerable Civil War

473

political alignments and to implanting neo-Hamiltonian economics. Republicans remembered how they had lost ground in the election of 1862 and then feared losing the presidency during the summer months of 1864. No such gamble was taken between 1866 and 1872. In the minds of hard-boiled power brokers, Reconstruction may have been less a long-term commitment to blacks—the Lower North itself was rejecting racial equality in legislature after legislature—than a six- to eight-year partisan necessity. Federal troops kept ex-slaves enfranchised, and ex-Confederates disenfranchised, across the South long enough for the Republican Party to consolidate much of its economic, commercial, and industrial revolution and a necessary minimum of its political revolution.

The economic downturn of 1873 had cost the Republicans control of Congress in 1874. Grant's leverage in occupying the White House through March 1877 was what enabled the great North-South bargain to be struck over the Hayes-Tilden election: Northern troops would be withdrawn and the cause of black voting rights substantially abandoned. What *would* be upheld were the interests of manufacturers, bankers, and capitalists.

Much the same thing, of course, had taken place during the decade after the American Revolution. As a prelude to C. Vann Woodward's *Reunion and Reaction*—the title of which so effectively describes the North-South arrangement of 1877—the compact of 1787 can be described as *Constitutional Union and Reaction*. The North recognized slavery and agreed to the three-fifths rule in return for southern acceptance of the Constitution and its provisions for a federal role in commerce. Five years later, Alexander Hamilton, on behalf of the financial interests of the North, had struck a further bargain: His party and allies would accept the relocation of the U.S. capital below the Mason-Dixon line into slave territory. Southerners, in return, would provide enough support in Congress to enact Hamilton's bank- and creditor-oriented financial program even though those arrangements basically favored the North.

The similar arrangement of 1877 did not offend northern opinion. On the contrary, in some respects, the arrangement mirrored it. As we have seen, much of the Lower North had been suspicious of abolitionism and opposed to fighting a war to emancipate slaves who might then compete with white labor. These racial attitudes continued after the war. In 1867, even as Northerners in Congress pressed the enfranchisement of blacks on the South through Reconstruction, only seven of the twenty northern states and none of the four Border states allowed it within their own boundaries.[31] Black voting rights were principally found in Greater New England. In 1860, New Yorkers defeated black enfranchisement in a statewide referendum, and between 1865 and 1870, when the Fifteenth Amendment secured black voting rights, a total of seven northern states *rejected* what northern representatives in Washington were trying to impose below the Mason-Dixon line.[32] In 1867 alone, four northern states—Kansas, Michigan, Minnesota, and Ohio—turned down popular referenda submitting constitutional amendments to enfranchise blacks.[33]

Moreover, between 1865 and 1870, five states in the Lower North opposed one or more of the Thirteenth, Fourteenth, and Fifteenth Amendments to the Constitution framed to end slavery and secure black rights. New Jersey at first rejected both the Thirteenth Amendment (in 1865) and the Fifteenth (in 1870) and withdrew its support for the Fourteenth in 1868; Ohio tried to withdraw its support for the Fourteenth (in 1868) and then at first voted to reject the Fifteenth (in 1869); New York sought to withdraw its support for the Fifteenth (in 1870); Oregon tried to withdraw its support for the Fourteenth (in 1868) and did not ratify the Fifteenth until 1962; and California did not ratify the Fifteenth until 1959.[34] In these states, one can argue that support in Congress for Reconstruction represented politics, hypocrisy—or both.

Yankeedom, as we have seen, had lost some of its own commitment. Few New Englanders had supported the efforts of Wendell Phillips and other abolitionists in 1864 to supplant Lincoln with John C. Frémont as the Republican presidential nominee or to promote confiscation of rebel property in the South for distribution to freed slaves.[35] Property rights were too sacred. Talk about revolution itself had lost its prewar cachet, and Ralph Waldo Emerson suggested in 1865 that the nation had simply exhausted its political energy on the war.

Others suggested that four years of fratricide had squelched the early and mid-nineteenth-century utopianism so visible from Vermont to the Western Reserve. This is plausible because much the same thing happened after the English Civil War. The utopianism and many forms of radicalism visible in the 1640s faded in the 1650s and became a subject of mockery in the 1660s.

The rise of scientific and philosophic Darwinism in the 1860s also helped to cool reformism and humanitarianism. If everything was a function of evolution, then words like "right," "truth," and "morality" were relative. Failed farmers and laborers, as well as minimally evolved races, should not be rescued. Evolution meant progress—and survival of the fittest was a key discipline of evolution. As theories of evolution and survival of the fittest undercut concern about ex-slaves and gave more support to industrial capitalism, it is tempting to suggest that New England, as in the Federalist period, shifted its commitment from meetinghouse to countinghouse. Self-interest and practicality abandoned radicalism and idealism.

The reestablishment of North-South commerce also promoted conservatism over reformism. As soon as the Confederate surrender reestablished the cotton trade, brokers and manufacturers from Boston to Philadelphia—the postwar equivalent of the prewar Cottonocracy—emphasized restoring friendly relations with the South and maximizing labor force efficiency to keep raw cotton prices down.[36] Maintaining too many troops in the South would be expensive as well as provocative. For that and other reasons, the number stationed there for Reconstruction purposes dropped from fifteen thousand in 1867 to six thousand in 1872 and three thousand by 1876.[37]

The economic bargain was certainly no blessing for the entire white South. The Compromise of 1877 that left ex-slaves out on a weak political and economic limb did the same for the poorer two-thirds to three-quarters of white Southerners. The Southerners who accepted Hayes's election as president in return for a new political and commercial relationship with the North were, for the most part, former Whigs, now conservative Democrats, who shared the Republican bias toward pro-business government. Although not all of the Compromise of 1877 was implemented, Professor Woodward has described the quid pro quo for ensuring the white southern power structure of nonintervention in race policy and promising them a share in the new economic order:

In return, the South became, in effect, a satellite of the dominant region. So long as the Conservative redeemers held control, they scotched any tendency of the South to combine forces with the internal enemies of the new economy—laborites, western agrarians, reformers.[38]

Talk about a New South, while mutually convenient, was exaggerated. If the North no longer occupied the South after 1876, Dixie was kept tributary in an economic sense. Whatever the southern justification for complaining about the unequal effects of federal policy before the war, it was greater afterward. While southern representatives in Congress were missing during the war, high tariffs were enacted to favor northern industry. And a transcontinental railroad, heavily subsidized, was ordered to run from the Pacific to terminate in the Upper Mississippi Valley. If tariff protection distorted manufacturing development to favor the North, the politics of railroad construction put a similar twist on the U.S. transportation system.

In the wake of wartime devastation, moreover, southern taxpayers had to help pay the interest and principal on the $2.5 billion federal debt taken on by the North to beat the South, although nearly all of the bond payments went to Northerners. Taxpayers below the Mason-Dixon line also had to help support the huge cost of pensions to federal veterans and their widows and dependents, though no such pensions were paid to Confederate veterans. Such disbursements, obviously, were spent in the North. In these various ways, according to economic historian Robert Russel, Southerners paid approximately $1.2 billion to the rest of the Union over a period of half a century—more than the indemnity Prussia levied on France after the Franco-Prussian War of 1870–1871.[39]

Besides, most of the South's *capital* was destroyed in the war—or freed by the Emancipation Proclamation and the Thirteenth Amendment. This has often been ignored in economic computations. The abolition of slavery wiped out at least $2 billion of capital and reduced the value of real estate by at least that amount.[40] Two-fifths of southern livestock had been killed in the war, and half of the farm machinery wrecked. Thousands of miles of railroad had been ruined.[41] Professor Albert Moore of the University of Alabama also added the property rights lost by postwar repudiation of Confederate currency, the Confederate bonded debt, and the war debts of the eleven Confederate states. His estimate of $3 billion lost is too high because of severe wartime inflation and the extent to which part of the Confederate bonds were held overseas, not least in Britain.[42] On the other hand, free-spending Reconstruction governments added several hundred million dollars to the debt levels of southern states during the late 1860s and early 1870s. Some of the outlay was legitimate, but part represented waste and graft. Public credit was badly damaged in the region that obviously needed it the most.

Because public expenditures rose so sharply, taxes across the South increased by 400 to 1,600 percent, further reducing property values that had been driven down by the war. In 1870, tax valuation in the former Confederate states was about half of what it was in 1860, despite inflation, while taxes were four times as large.[43]

The loss in human resources—the 250,000 Confederates who died of wounds or disease—was as large in relation to the southern white male population as the losses by major European participants in the twentieth-century wars. One historian has calculated that if the North had suffered the same proportionate losses, the region would have lost over a million men rather than 360,000. The World War II losses of the United States would have been over 6 million men instead of somewhat over 300,000. Militarily and regionally, "the Confederacy rendered the heaviest sacrifice in lives . . . ever made by Americans."[44]

In his 1942 presidential address to the Southern Historical Association, Albert Moore contended that "in some respects conditions in the South at the end of the radical regime remind one of the plight of the Germans at the end of the Thirty Years War."[45] According to C. Vann Woodward, by 1880 the per capita wealth of the southern states ($376) was in the same ratio to that of the Northeast ($1,353) as Germany's was to backward Russia's.[46] The Yankee economic victory was no more in doubt than the military one.

James McPherson, in Battle Cry of Freedom, has assembled data that parallel Moore's radical-seeming conclusion. Two-thirds of southern assessed wealth vanished during the war in what amounted to a massive regional redistribution. Prewar northern and southern per capita output had been about the same, and the average per capita income of Southerners, including the slave population, was about two-thirds of the northern average (for southern whites alone, it would have been about the same). However, by 1870, the North's lead was overwhelming—and the re-arrangement of capital availability ensured that it would continue. According to census data, southern agricultural and manufacturing capital declined by 16 percent between 1860 and 1870, while northern capital increased by 50 percent. The South had contained 30 percent of the national wealth in 1860; ten years later that had dropped to 12 percent.[47] Appomattox surrendered more than the southern past and present. Three to four future generations also paid the price.

The North's success—aided by this extraordinary capital transfer—is a matter of history. Even the post–Civil War Republican political system, while shaken from the 1870s to the 1890s, was not toppled until the 1930s. The United States that gained the industrial leadership of the world was really the Civil War winner—the industrial North. Eight decades after the end of Reconstruction, the National Emergency Council created to examine the Depression of the 1930s reported its findings to President Franklin D. Roosevelt: The South, it said, had been reduced to the status of a colony.[48] While this is an exaggeration, because other rural areas also suffered, it is not a great distortion.

Without the enormous impact of the war, could America—these two separate Americas on each side of the Mason-Dixon line—have reached these same positions? Of course not. Gettysburg and the march through Georgia, like England's own seventeenth-century sortings-out, were vital. Fifty years later, Stephen Vincent Benet distilled the relationship in verse:

> *Out of John Brown's strong sinews the tall skyscrapers grow*
> *Out of his heart the chanting buildings rise*
> *Rivet and girder, motor and dynamo,*
> *Pillar of smoke by day and fire by night*
> *The street-faced cities reaching to the skies.*[49]

So they did. It took just one generation beyond 1865 for the United States to become the world's leading industrial power.

The Losers of the Cousins' Wars: The Irish, Blacks, and Native Americans

If the cavaliers, Stuart and southern alike, were repetitious losers, they were not alone. For three cultures involved in these wars, the rights and liberties of Englishmen or Americans were an irrelevant, ironic travesty. As generation after generation would experience, such rights simply did not apply to Irish, black slaves (or ex-slaves), and Native Americans. And in turning these ethnic and racial minorities into repetitious losers, the three wars also helped to shape or worsen some of the most demanding British and U.S. internal problems of the nineteenth and twentieth centuries.

These are not pleasant tales. The rise of Anglo-America and the downfall of the Irish began together under the Tudors and early Stuarts in the peak years of Europe's religious wars between Catholic and Protestant. Slavery, in turn, was the simultaneous sixteenth-, seventeenth-, and eighteenth-century fate of millions in Africa and Arabia (and even thousands of European galley slaves on Spanish or Barbary ships). Native Americans, for their part, were overwhelmed or exterminated from New England to the Caribbean.

The impact on Ireland came first. After absorption into Britain, the Cornish, Welsh, and Scots largely became Protestants. In Ireland, interminable Catholic-Protestant enmity was most of what made the English conquest of the 1500s and 1600s a much more brutal affair. Although the English presence dated back to the twelfth century, the suppression by Elizabeth I of the "Revolt of the Earls" that began in the 1590s sounded "the death knell for the medieval societies of Gaelic and Gaelicized Ireland."[50] The native Irish chieftains were dispossessed, the bards banned, the warriors forced to abandon traditional dress, the earls exiled, feudal agriculture commercialized, and the landholding and inheritance laws redrawn in the English direction. The English made few attempts to conciliate, convert, or integrate the Irish masses, who were dismissed as savages.[51]

The gore of the 1640s and 1690s was worse. The Irish uprising of 1641, in which several thousand Protestants were killed by Catholics who claimed to be allied with Charles I, helped to precipitate the English Civil War and, ultimately, Parliamentary retribution. After Cromwell's victories over the Catholic and Royalist forces at the Battles of Drogheda and Wexford in 1649, Catholics were forcibly resettled in the west of Ireland—"to hell or Connaught"—and their lands given to Cromwellian soldiers.

Cromwell's brutality was not simply gratuitous. In January 1649, the Earl of Ormonde, the King's lieutenant in Ireland, had reached an arrangement with the Confederated Catholics of Ulster, who were to provide the men for an invasion of England under naval cover to be provided by Prince Rupert. This threat, reinforcing the view Cromwell shared with so many other Englishmen—of the "mere Irish" as barbarians—prompted the Irish campaign that lingers as the principal stain on his own military record.

Sir William Petty, the political economist, calculated that out of an early seventeenth century population of a million and a half in Ireland, some six hundred thousand, five-sixths of them Irish, perished by war, famine, or pestilence.[52] Thousands more were deported to the West Indies—one-fifth of the population of Barbados and a third of that of the Leeward Islands, especially St. Kitts, were Irish by the 1670s.[53] Some thirty to forty thousand Irish also left to enlist in the Catholic armies of Europe. Prior to 1641, according to Petty, Catholics held about two-thirds of the good land in Ireland. By 1660, two-thirds had passed into the hands of Protestants.

In 1689, when William of Orange landed in England to challenge James II, the Ulster Protestants of Londonderry, Enniskillen, and Coleraine, fearing another massacre like 1641, closed the gates of their towns to James's Catholic troops. Londonderry and Enniskillen held out and entered Protestant legend. William defeated James's army at the Battle of the Boyne in 1690. Then his Dutch lieutenant general, Godert de Ginkel, on the field at Aughrim in County Galway in 1691, won the last decisive battle ever fought in Ireland. The subjugation of the seventeenth century was almost complete. In the words of one Irish historian, "Aughrim was more fatal to the old aristocracy of Ireland than Flodden had been to the knighthood of Scotland, or Agincourt to the chivalry of France. After it, the Catholic aristocracy disappeared from the Irish scene."[54]

The fabric of Native Irish politics and culture was pulled apart. Once again, the Irish were pushed west to poorer land, an exodus that prefigured the disposition of the American Indians over the next two centuries. What was left of the Catholic military leadership forfeited its estates but was allowed to leave the country. These were the famous "Wild Geese" who fought under the banners of Spain, France, and Austria.

Within Ireland, ethnic and religious capitulation was virtually complete. During the first quarter of the eighteenth century, Catholic bishops were banned and priests required to register. Catholics lost their right to vote, hold office, own a gun or a horse worth more than £5, or live in towns without paying special fees. Nor could they purchase land or lease it for more than thirty-one years. Although Catholic landholdings were deliberately broken up, the eldest son could inherit everything by converting to Anglicanism. Catholic landholding plummeted again. By 1700, just 14 percent of Irish land was in their hands. By 1750, that had fallen to 5 percent.[55]

In the American colonies by 1775, there may have been one hundred thousand persons of Native Irish ethnicity and some degree of Catholic antecedents. Very few remained practicing Catholics; as a people in colonial America, they did not cohere. What these pages seek to convey is more the opposite: the Native Irish as a broken and dispersed culture, nation, and fighting force. They were the first internal British casualty of Protestant nationalism, the early cousins' wars, and the rise of Anglo-America.

The war of 1775–1783 simply confirmed the problem. "The Irish" had no truly Irish role. A half dozen Irish Catholics, mostly from a small upper-middle-class element in Philadelphia, served as senior officers on the patriot side. Within a few generations, though, most of these families had turned Protestant.[56] America's Ulster Presbyterians of largely Scottish origin were the prominent rebels. Poor Native Irish Catholics, whether they enlisted in Philadelphia, Cork, or Leinster, served predominantly in British or loyalist regiments. In America or at home, Irish Catholics had been beaten down by the seventeenth and early eighteenth centuries. When Ireland's impoverished masses flooded into the mid-nineteenth-century United States, they became, on arrival, its principal white underclass and immediate urban problem.

The Catholic Irish who arrived in the late 1840s and 1850s—over a million of them—were mostly rural peasants fleeing the Great Famine caused by blighted potato crops. Even the first Irish immigrants from Protestant Ulster had been unpopular in the Boston of the 1720s. The huge midcentury Catholic wave, however, stirred Protestant fury at a population that seemed to equal squalor, drunkenness, crime, and unthinking support for big-city political machines. Irish Catholic immigrants, for their part, quickly came to understand that Anglo-Saxon Republican Methodists in New York or Ohio were a lot like English Whig grocers or factory-owners in Manchester or Bristol. Ironically, the potato famine, the callous English response to its effects, and the surge of Irish departures for America were an important catalyst for the Know-Nothing movement that helped to shatter the old Democratic-Whig system and bring on the Civil War. Beyond that, the emigration from sod huts and blackened potato fields was a factor in crystallizing a Darwinian late nineteenth-century U.S. politics in which Irish Catholics were urban bogeymen.

The Irish role in the American Civil War has also been hotly debated. However, despite the stalwartness of the federal army's Irish Brigade and other units in battles like Fredericksburg, some historians have made the argument—to be examined in chapter 12—that Irish Catholic immigrants were not much more enthusiastic about military service between 1861 and 1865 than they were in the War for Independence. Recruiting officers in Confederate prison camps, like British officers nine decades earlier, made it a point to look for Irish-born Catholic immigrants whose short time in North America made it easy to change sides.

By the 1870s, three centuries of suppression, discrimination, and rejection had made Irish Catholics the principal white underclass of the English-speaking societies on both sides of the Atlantic—in Glasgow or Liverpool, Boston or New York. Regius professors of history at Cambridge and U.S. political cartoonists found it socially acceptable to draw similar unflattering portraits: the Irish as simians. The only large group that had even greater basis for complaint were the four and a half million blacks, mostly ex-slaves, who made up about one-seventh of the U.S. population in 1865. Although they and the Irish competed for jobs, black circumstances were considerably worse.

Seventeenth-century slavery has been called less individually and culturally debilitating than later versions because human chattel status was then *multiracial*. In 1547, the English Parliament passed an act providing that persistent vagabonds should be enslaved and branded with a large S. It was repealed as unworkable, but not on moral grounds. In the seventeenth century, captured Englishmen rowed as galley slaves for the Barbary pirates and Spanish alike. Indians, too, were slaves, especially in Mexico and South America. English, Scots, and Scotch-Irish indentured servants were common, and in Caribbean colonies like Barbados and St. Kitts, the Irish convicts, bound servants, and laborers frequently made cause with black slaves to the point of brewing insurrections together.[57] According to one description: "Before 1720 slavery was but one of a number of subordinate statuses in colonial America. Blacks worked alongside white indentured servants, transported criminals and apprentices, and all were subject to the discipline and whims of their masters and mistresses."[58] But the more large-scale plantation agriculture grew, especially the production of cotton for the mills of Massachusetts and Lancashire, the more uniquely slavery became black—and the more racialism, as opposed to chattel-owning, grew as a psychology.

The effects of two unusual centuries and two shattering civil wars may help explain the stronger cultures that twentieth-century sociologists have attributed to New York City blacks with British West Indian antecedents in contrast to blacks with six or eight generations of U.S. domicile. Although the West Indies sugar colonies became brutal, black-majority slave cultures generations before those on the American mainland, they also peaked much earlier. Before the end of the eighteenth century, in a sign of somewhat more relaxed circumstances, free blacks in the Caribbean were enlisted in local militia and military units. Slavery itself was banned by 1834. True, several sugar-producing centers—Barbados, Jamaica, and Demerara—experienced substantial black rebellions in the two decades before slavery ended.

The Framework of Anglo-America

However, these uprisings, along with the periodic capture of some islands by the French, were minor compared with the trauma of the U.S. wars of 1775–1783 and 1861–1865. Wartime effects, in turn, were further aggravated by the legal and political reversals and disillusionment that blacks faced in both aftermaths.

The Reconstruction of the South from 1865 to 1877, at which point northern protection of freed blacks was relaxed, hardly stands alone. The American Revolution also put hints of freedom in the air for slaves below the Mason-Dixon line. Then, as we have seen, within a decade or two of the arrival of peace in 1783, most southern and Border states began tightening their laws relating to slavery and free black status, and by the early decades of the nineteenth century, many northern states were also passing "Black Codes." These not only denied free blacks the vote, but forbade their testimony in courts and excluded them from juries and public schools. Between 1790 and 1830, as the number of slaves in the U.S. soared from 600,000 to 1.8 million, the legal and political climate in the areas with the largest black population may have chilled almost as much as it did in the four decades from 1870 to 1910.

Even the War of 1812 provided its own small addendum. The British returned to their earlier tactics of liberating or promising freedom to slaves. Six hundred carried off from raids in Virginia in 1813 were given the option of enlisting or settling in the West Indies. The Chesapeake campaign of 1814 produced even more runaways. The departing British fleet carried off two thousand, most of whom wound up living in Canada's maritime provinces.[59]

By 1860, the South had roughly four million slaves, more than double its 1830 total. Within the North and South, racial tensions were almost certainly greater than they had been back in 1775. Yet, whereas five thousand blacks had served in the patriot forces between 1775 and 1783, between 1861 and 1865 some two hundred thousand did. Black expectations after Appomattox would have been much greater than those following Yorktown. Once again, however, the racial experiment succeeded only in New England, where blacks were few, and largely failed everywhere else. One could argue that the North withdrew its protection in 1877

485

as it had in 1787, again trading racial autonomy to the South for that region's support of northern economic policy objectives.

Both wars were devastating for blacks, but they raised hopes. Both peacetimes were devastating because, after a while, they smashed hopes. No other major industrial nation has any comparable pattern. No large black population elsewhere has been burdened by a similar psychological whipsawing. The impact on the United States in the later years of its national trajectory remains to be seen. However, if Britain's Irish problem sometimes seems intractable, there are parallels in America's racial difficulties.

The third ethnic group beaten down in the three civil wars—the tribes of Native Americans—came into the twentieth century counting for much less numerically. Yet the pattern of being swept aside in the name of expansion, despite service in two wars, is notable.

Even the English Civil War had an indirect impact on the American Indian. The most expansion-minded settlers were the future core groups of revolution: the aggressive New England Puritans, English Virginians, and Ulster Scotch-Irish. Cromwellian emigrés were especially belligerent. War was part of their theology. Nathaniel Bacon drew attention leading Virginians against the Occaneechee Indians in 1676, before his name became immortalized in Bacon's Rebellion. John Leverett, a former cavalry captain under Cromwell, was the governor of Massachusetts who finally won King Philip's War, crushing the Pequots and Narragansetts after they tomahawked and scorched the Massachusetts frontier back to within twenty-five miles of Boston.

The Scotch-Irish, who did not arrive until the early eighteenth century, brought skills honed on the most brutal battlefield in the British Isles: the Ulster frontier, plagued by its intermittent religious massacres and Catholic Irish guerrilla bands for whom the epithet "Torie" was first coined. James Logan, the provincial secretary of Pennsylvania and an Ulster-born Quaker, explained in 1720 why two years earlier he had recruited Scotch-Irish to settle what became Donegal Township in Lancaster County: "We were apprehensive from the Northern Indians. . . . I therefore thought it might be provident to plant a settlement of such men as those who had formerly so bravely defended Londonderry and Enniskillen as a frontier against any disturbance."[60] Massachusetts authorities had similar motives in sending newly arrived Scotch-Irish to an arc of frontier danger points that stretched from Bangor, in what is now Maine, to Coleraine, Massachusetts.[61]

As hard times and unpopular laws drove more Scotch-Irish from Ulster, a high percentage turned to America, especially the border-lands from Pennsylvania to the Carolina upcountry. Their fortified homes in the Blue Mountains resembled the strongholds and cattle bawns of Ulster in spirit if not in architecture. If they missed the sudden raids and Celtic battle cries of the descendants of the old Irish redshanks and woodkerns, the screeches and war whoops of vermilion-striped Seneca, Shawnee, and Cherokee were a fair North American substitute.

The result was essentially the same. Like the Catholic Irish, the natives of eastern North America in the eighteenth century were beaten and pushed west. Disease was as deadly as famine was in Ireland. By the 1830s and 1840s, Oklahoma, the Indian Territory, became a hotter, dustier transatlantic Connaught. The Creek, Choctaw, and Cherokee had been moved west to clear Georgia and Alabama lands for new cotton fields. Other tribes had been drifting west since the Revolution.

Part of what guided Indian loyalty during the American Revolution in upstate New York, as we saw in chapter 5, was religious Europeanization. The Anglican Mohawks sided with the Crown, and the Presbyterian Oneida chose the rebels in what became a full-fledged civil war in the Iroquois Confederation. So advanced was the Iroquois political system, moreover, that one British lieutenant governor likened it to that of the Romans.[62] Their villages were also impressive. Colonel William Butler of the 4th Pennsylvania, who burned Oquaga in 1778, acknowledged it "the finest Indian town I ever saw. On both sides of the river, there was about forty good houses. Square logs, Shingles and stone Chimneys, good Floors, glass windows."[63] When the Oneida, allies of the colonists, wound up as refugees, they petitioned Congress to compensate them for lost and destroyed property that included frame houses, wagons, livestock, farm equipment, kitchen utensils, rugs, teacups and saucers, punch bowls, and looking glasses.[64]

Wartime service made little difference. Professor Colin Callaway, in *The American Revolution in Indian Country*, contends

487

that revisionist interpretations of the Revolution have bypassed Indians, leaving intact a mistaken impression that they not only chose the wrong side and lost but did so with recurring savagery.[65] In fact, the colonists enlisted them—or tried to—as quickly as the King's representatives. Ethan Allen of Vermont sought Abenaki help in invading Canada in the autumn of 1775. And British officers took earliest umbrage, at the killing of sentries and pickets by the Stockbridge Indians who had joined the American army encircling Boston that summer.

The Iroquois Confederation was the most prominent victim of civil war within the Indian community—Oneida against Mohawk, even Tuscarora against Tuscarora. When expansion pressures at war's end elevated acquisition of Indian lands into national policy, tribes that had fought with the rebels, the Oneida and Stockbridge, fared little better than the others. They wound up on reservations in Wisconsin.

Much the same thing happened in the Civil War. The Indians were divided. A Seneca, Eli Parker, became a Union general. A Cherokee, Stand Watie, commanded a Confederate cavalry brigade that saw action in Kansas and Missouri as well as the Indian Territory, often opposing northern forces—the Kansas Indian Home Guard—that included Delaware and Potawatomi units. Some of the Civil War divisions within the tribes were haphazard, the stuff of grudges. But just as the more informative Native American loyalties of 1775–1783 involved religion—the rivalry of Anglican Mohawk and Presbyterian Oneida—there were definite examples between 1861 and 1865 of tribal (or factional) attitudes toward slavery being important.

This was certainly true in the Indian territory, where the Five Nations—Cherokee, Creek, Choctaw, Chickasaw, and Seminole—had about four thousand slaves and free blacks. The Cherokee, in particular, divided between a pro-Confederate majority, which included the Cherokee slaveholding elite and associated secret societies and lodges involved in capturing and punishing abolitionists who interfered with slavery in the Cherokee Nation.[66] The pro-Union minority, in turn, pivoted on the Keetowah Society, five thousand strong, which advocated the abolition of slavery and good relations with the United States. Even to the east, in Virginia and the Carolinas, the tribes most supportive of the Confederacy in the war were those that had a long history of collaborating with white authorities or of helping to capture runaway slaves.

The eastern band of Cherokee, some of whom had helped North Carolina officials during the earlier Indian removals, played an important role as Confederate rangers in the wartime Smoky Mountains. The Catawba, who had served white South Carolinians in the eighteenth-century wars with the French and Cherokee and then thrived as trackers of runaway slaves, were quick to join South Carolina volunteer regiments in 1861, and the nineteen who served are commemorated by a monument in Fort Hill, South Carolina.[67] Lumbee and Pamunkey Indians in Virginia and North Carolina, unhappy with their white neighbors, tended to aid Union forces.

Native American involvement in the Civil War on the Confederate side is often glamorized by listing some of the units: the Cherokee Mounted Rifles, the Creek and Seminole Battalion, the Januluska Zouaves (Eastern Cherokee), and the First Choctaw Battalion of the Mississippi Cavalry. On the federal side, among the Delaware tribe's 201 males of age, by 1862, 170 had volunteered, mostly in the Kansas Indian Home Guard.[68]

In the end, wartime service availed little for most tribes. The story repeated that of the American Revolution. Westward expansion still required a one-sided myth—not of Seneca brigadiers, Kansas Indian Home Guards, or a Cherokee Nation as much divided as wartime Kentucky, but of Comanches terrorizing the exposed Texas frontier and of blood-crazed Santee Sioux burning and killing settlers in Minnesota. At war's end, the wagons rolled again—and the Indians were overwhelmed.

The Impact of the U.S. Civil War on Britain

History, in its twentieth-century retrospect, generally agrees that Britain's global manufacturing leadership peaked by the 1870s even though its riches and world influence continued to mount through 1914. Small wonder, then, that some British leaders reacted to the outbreak of civil war in the United States with an intermittent hope that the emerging transatlantic colossus might be divided and its democratic example weakened. Had the 1860s become a decade in which the United States split into two or more regional confederacies while Bismarck's Prussia mishandled the final years of its bid to unite the long-divided German states, the subsequent emergence of Britain's two principal economic and industrial rivals might have stalled or reversed.

The British prime minister privately hoped so from time to time. However, even among English-speakers, far fewer people remember *his* name—Henry John Temple, third Viscount Palmerston—than remember the era's more famous unifiers: Abraham Lincoln and Otto von Bismarck. Yet, as 1861 opened, all the world would have counted Palmerston the more important. At age seventy-six he had more or less come of age with the century: secretary at war (the old styling) in Tory regimes from 1809 to 1828; British foreign secretary under the Whigs for most of the two decades between 1830 and 1850; and then, intermittently after 1855, prime minister.

Disdain for Americans was a Palmerston hallmark. After the War of 1812, the former colonists kept a sour memory of British admirals Alexander Cochrane and George Cockburn, who raided the Chesapeake and burned Washington and whose bombships off Baltimore had illuminated the Star-Spangled Banner that so inspired Francis Scott Key. But "Young Pam" in the War Office—Palmerston was just thirty in 1814—would have had much to do with the orders. Fifty years later, as one of the United Kingdom's oldest prime ministers, he had left a record of describing Americans as dishonest men, disagreeable fellows, rogues, and vulgar bullies.

Equally to the point, his record in the War Office and Foreign Office included a half dozen minor to middling altercations with the United States: the British attempts in the late 1830s to keep Texas independent of the U.S.; the "Aroostook War" of 1839 along the Maine–New Brunswick border; the U.S. arrest and trial of a British subject, Alexander McLeod, which prompted Palmerston to consider war measures; the mid-1840s Oregon border dispute; and the 1854 affair when a U.S. warship, the sloop *Cyane*, bombarded a Central American port in the Mosquito Coast territory claimed by Britain, prompting Palmerston to splutter about retaliation that would "burn (U.S.) seacoast towns."[69] Nor did this particular Eminent Victorian shrink from private analyses of how it would be better for Britain to slow the growth of the United States.[70]

The British had equal reason for jaundice about the new Republican secretary of state chosen in 1861, William H. Seward. His unflinching abolitionism and distaste for aristocrats were conjoined with an overt Anglophobia and a willingness to discuss war with Britain—at one point as a device to reunite North and South against a common foe. Prior to taking office as secretary of state, he had actually told one British diplomat that if he reached power, he expected to insult Britain.[71] The brusque views of both men, Palmerston and Seward, complicated what was already inflammatory: how *both* nations would manage a relationship that had now become trilateral with the South's belligerency.

Immediately after the 1860 election, British opinion leaned to the North on the assumption that slavery was the dominant issue. This changed in 1861 as the South seemed well on its way to independence while both the federal and Confederate governments insisted that the war was about secession, not slavery. Lincoln himself said as much. This freed upper-class Britons, or so the argument goes, to think about their own political and commercial advantage and the merit of an end to the bloodshed. Politically, a cleavage of the United States between the North and the South would diminish an emerging rival, reopen the Western Hemisphere to a more active British influence, and undercut the enthusiasm in parts of Britain and Europe for democracy and America's nearly universal white male suffrage. Commercially, an independent South would mean an open, low-tariff southern market, with a concomitant blow to northern manufacturing industries.

The Confederates' own insistences of fighting for independence, not slavery, would not have diverted a British Cabinet meeting beyond a comment or two. However, the simultaneous assertion by Lincoln that slavery was not the pivot—so contrary to U.S. interest in antislavery Britain—had influence. Either the Lincoln administration truly was preoccupied with secession rather than slavery per se, or it was dissembling politically because of the white supremacy viewpoints of much of the North. Whichever the explanation, British elites were skeptical and the British government was free to turn to self-interest.

To say that the British Cabinet and people were confused over the Lincoln administration's early positions on slavery, while undoubtedly true, is unfair. The Republican Party itself was confused and so were U.S. voters. As discussed in chapter 9, a firm and clear position by Lincoln could have *supported* the institution of slavery by confining the Republican Party to the losing Frémont constituency of 1856. That would have cost it the 1860 election. Even in mid-1861, after April's federal mobilization had pushed the Upper South to secede, the new president was jockeying—and to an extent, *dissembling*—to keep the Border states of Maryland, Kentucky, and Missouri in the Union. The electorate of the Lower North had been ambiguous before the attack on Fort Sumter, and the onetime "Cotton Whig" textile manufacturers and merchants of Massachusetts and Rhode Island, who opposed Lincoln in 1860, were as profit-focused and opportunistic as their compatriots in the British cotton industry, who largely favored the South. British opinion—capital and labor alike—was not much more confused in the autumn of 1861 than the manufacturing and financial leadership of eastern Massachusetts and adjacent Rhode Island had been a year earlier.

Britain's national self-interest was not so easily defined. The extent to which Lancashire and the Merseyside, in the spring of 1861, had warehouses bulging with an excess of cotton and textiles left from 1860 reduced the South's export leverage, at least for a while. As for Britain's interest in ensuring the breakup of the United States by recognizing the Confederacy, that made sense only when southern independence was almost a fait accompli. Premature or misjudged British recognition could backfire. Southern reliance on slavery inhibited British collaboration with the Confederacy, but probably not as much as sheer *macht politik*—whether Dixie could win militarily.

Moreover, nineteenth-century British antislavery commitment had typically been opportune and strategic—an asset in establishing commercial sway in South America, pressuring Brazil, or giving the Royal Navy an additional license to prowl the sea-lanes. Should the commitment cease to be opportune, as in cotton supply, it could be pushed aside. By the summer of 1862, when the Confederacy had won victories from the Shenandoah and the

Seven Days' battleground to the Second Manassas, while lack of cotton shut down much of Lancashire and three-quarters of the half million cotton mill workers were unemployed or on half-time, such a reconsideration seemed to be under way. Pro-Confederate Britons even let themselves think that an independent South, guided by Britain, would itself do away with slavery.

In mid-1862, Palmerston and his Cabinet leaned to the South, but cautiously. In July, when the House of Commons appeared about to pass a resolution calling for mediation between North and South, the prime minister forced its withdrawal. Southern success on the battlefield was not quite decisive enough. Ultimately, the autumn 1862 stalemate at Antietam—the North had higher casualties, but Robert E. Lee gave up his invasion of Maryland and returned below the Potomac—gave the British further pause, as did Lincoln's announcement that the Emancipation Proclamation would be issued on January 1, 1863. Elements of the British press took Lincoln's advisory as desperation or opportunism. Still others, given fresh British memories of the 1857 Sepoy Rebellion in India, in which many British civilians were killed, worried about racial violence. However, antislavery opinion was strong enough in Britain that when the Proclamation was actually issued, the northern cause gained important support overall.

Pro-southern elements in Parliament tried to help the Confederacy again in 1863 and 1864, but the chance of British involvement faded after Vicksburg and Gettysburg in the summer of 1863. That was fortunate on both sides of the Atlantic. Howard Jones, in his book *Union in Peril: The Crisis over British Intervention in the Civil War,* concludes that given the other midcentury tensions between Britain and the United States, "British intervention would almost certainly have led to a third war between the Atlantic nations with repercussions reaching well into the twentieth century."[72] The great British-American rapprochement of the 1890s would have been delayed—or made impossible.

Many volumes have detailed the diplomacy, Cabinet maneuvers, and Parliamentary politics involved.[73] The different emphasis of this subchapter is that British opinion on the war divided along important and familiar lines, helping ensure a northern success that was also a victory for British democracy and the Anglo-

American future. A number of late twentieth-century studies have posed insinuations to the contrary: that the aristocracy was not lopsidedly pro-southern, that working-class British opinion didn't count because such Britons hadn't been enfranchised in the Reform Act of 1832, and that even if laborers' opinions *did* count, those in Britain were divided rather than behind the North. The foreign secretary, Lord John Russell, had observed, in his 1859 biography of Charles James Fox, that there was no way to know what the views of the British common people were in 1775.[74] It was scarcely easier to know in 1861.

The evidence of the three cousins' wars, however, is that artisans, craftsmen, and what we now call middle- or lower-middle-class Britons—not, however, the agricultural peasantry or farm laborers—were surprisingly aware and involved each time. Each of the three periods was marked by expanded political communications from newspapers and broadsides to public petitions. (The pattern during the years leading up to the English Civil War is described on pp. 47–48, and the parallel during the 1770s is set out on pp. 233–239.)

Indeed, the continuing disfranchisement of most of the working class and part of the lower-middle class was a major element of what ordinary citizens saw at stake in America: If the North won the war, the steel puddlers of Birmingham and the weavers of Bradford and Bolton could expect to win the right to vote from a concession-minded Parliament. But were the gray cavaliers of South Carolina and Virginia to prevail, victory at Westminister would go to the antireform forces, not least Tory MPs bearing many of the same names that rode with Charles I. The democratic experiment that had failed on U.S. battlefields would be pushed aside in Britain. Industrial areas would remain underrepresented, the electorate relatively small. A narrow elite would keep control. Even in 1865, half the House of Commons either belonged to the peerage or the baronetage or were connected to it by marriage or descent, while eleven of the fifteen Cabinet posts in Palmerston's second government were filled by members of the great families.[75] The reforms of 1832 had lost force.

Assessments from many points on the spectrum support the extent to which aristocratic and upper-class opinion favored the South in 1861. The only question is one of degree. Charles Francis Adams, Lincoln's ambassador to London, observed in 1862 that "the great body of the aristocracy and the commercial classes are anxious to see the United States go to pieces while "the middle and lower class sympathize with us" because they see the convulsion as involving the rights of labor and their own future. W. S. Gladstone, still some years from being prime minister, thought most members of Parliament were friendly to the South, and Richard Cobden believed that three-fourths of the House of Commons would be glad to find an excuse to vote for the dismemberment of the U.S. republic.[76] As the British labor movement began to rally to the side of the North in late 1862 and 1863, speakers made frequent references to the aristocracy and "West End clubs" being for the Confederacy while those who worked supported the North.[77]

The Times of London made no bones that "excepting a few gentlemen of republican tendencies, we all expect, we nearly all wish, success to the Confederate cause." The *New York Times* agreed that in what had once fondly been called the mother country, there was no support for the U.S. among the rulers, aristocracy, or governing classes, who saw nothing but "vulgar democrats," while "our friends, and there could be no grander tribute paid to the genius of the Republic—are the dumb masses."[78] In fact, even middle-class and professional opinion split, and along familiar lines. Many of the more affluent Britons supporting the North were nonconformist Protestants as opposed to Anglicans.

To a certain extent, the divisions visible in 1861 and 1862 had been prefigured in the opinion journals and middlebrow British literature of the 1850s. Authors like Anthony Trollope, William Makepeace Thackeray, Charles Kingsley, and Louise de la Ramée (who wrote as "Ouida") popularized the notion of the South as the region of dash and daring, another aristocratic and genteel England. Conservative thinkers implied that the South had never been at one with the democratic North, and that a separation would be appropriate. Thackeray suggested that southern aristocrats were several cuts above the "Dutch traders of New York and the money-getting Roundheads of Pennsylvania and New England."[79]

Within this culture, strong pro-federal opinions were voiced by only a few peers like the Duke of Argyll. One can even suggest that a larger and more conspicuous group of dukes had been open in support of the American rebels in 1775–1776! True, the leadership of the Conservative Party, which included most of the landed wealth, held back from the conspicuous pro-southern sentiment of many of its backbench MPs. That would have been as much pragmatism as federal sympathy. Lord Derby, the Tory leader, had been in and out of government as prime minister and foreign secretary for a decade. Party policy had evolved a "hands off" approach to the internal affairs of other nations, at odds with Palmerston's well-known penchant for interventionism.[80] Tory leaders with a foreign policy brief, such as Benjamin Disraeli and the Earls of Malmesbury and Clarendon, were usually cautious, although others, including a future prime minister, Lord Salisbury, were overtly pro-Confederate. This hardly rebuts the southern inclination of most of the gentry.

British industrialists were divided over the American Civil War in 1861. However, this says nothing not already said about manufacturing and mercantile centers from Philadelphia to Boston, which included the principal textile production districts. Furthermore, as southern markets and cotton supplies shut down in the winter of 1860–1861, the northern cotton industry felt a lesser version of the pain felt in Lancashire. In Philadelphia, like Liverpool an entrepôt of commerce with the South, textile manufacturers anticipated a crisis, business bankruptcies spread, and for manufacturing of all kinds, one estimate put 40 percent of operatives unemployed or on part-time by January.[81] Throughout the U.S. textile industry as a whole, cotton production slumped during the war years by 30 percent. Wool goods surged. From Philadelphia to Boston, as we have seen, anti-Lincoln sentiment remained so high in the best clubs that staunch Unionists decamped to new ones that were pro-Republican. Not until 1864, at the flood crest of war contracts and profits, did northern industrialists substantially unite behind the politics of the Lincoln administration.

Northern labor leaders and activists had doubts of their own. Wartime inflation rose faster than wages, causing a decline in workers' real earnings. Capital, obviously, stood poised to do better. The Republican Party, with its ties to northern industry, was no friend to labor organizers; and within the fledgling U.S. labor movement, some of the greatest skeptics were old Chartists who had emigrated from England after that cause's failure in 1849.

Against this backdrop, the divisions of 1861–1862 over the U.S. Civil War found within the ranks of British labor and industry make sense. Indeed, it would have been extraordinary had they not existed. The war's ultimate usefulness and probable outcome were in doubt on both sides of the Atlantic. Perceived or actual self-interest was dominant.

In Britain, pro-northern, working-class views in general and cotton-worker opinion in particular seem to have consolidated in the winter of 1862–1863, thanks to several overlapping factors. Cotton-related unemployment in Lancashire peaked in December and started down as new supplies of cotton came in from India, Egypt, China, and Brazil. Also, favorable changes in the leadership of the labor movement and the labor press occurred and several pro-Confederate officials were replaced. In addition, the preannouncement of Lincoln's Emancipation Proclamation in September 1862 and then the actuality of it on January 1, 1863, removed most doubts as to the centrality of slavery as a war issue, which thereupon mobilized the British antislavery movement, working-class organizations, and nonconformist churches on the northern side. Fourth, British opinion warmed following the arrival in Liverpool in February 1863 of the *George Griswold*, the first of several ships from the North carrying foodstuffs for the relief of Lancashire. And lastly, the growing European doubt about a Confederacy victory seems to have been persuasive by 1863, despite flurries of activity and interest in June 1863 and then again in the summer of 1864.

Readers may find themselves wondering: Doesn't this assume an unlikely degree of involvement by British workingmen in a war being fought three thousand miles away? In fact, such popular engagement, which numerous accounts confirm, is a central part of the story. In the Birmingham smelters, Welsh collieries, Cornish copper mines, and Lancashire cotton mills alike, the attention reflected a mix of politics, religion, and family ties.

The memoirs of English-born Samuel Fielden, one of the Haymarket Martyrs executed in connection with the Chicago bombing of 1886, recalled the "intense interest" among the people of Lancashire. They came together in church halls, libraries, and institutes, and during the summer "every night of the week there would be seen groups of men collected in the streets and at the prominent corners, discussing the latest news and forecasting the next."[82] In the West Riding of Yorkshire, "maps of America and detailed plans of the battle areas sold like hotcakes in Bradford bookshops."[83] Professor R. J. M. Blackett, an expert on British working-class reactions to the war, sums up as follows:

> News of the war was eagerly awaited throughout Great Britain. Battle reports were read and maps consulted to pinpoint the locations of the war's contests. The diary of John Ward, a weaver from Low Moor, contains many entries about his regular hikes to Clitheroe to read newspaper accounts of the war and political developments in America. At Stalybridge, telegrams from the United States were posted at the Mechanics Institute and attracted large crowds . . .
> An estimated ten thousand people attended an open-air meeting in the marketplace at Ashton to hear opposing sides debate the British positions on the war. British interest in the war was intense.[84]

The influence of family relationships—the huge numbers of working-class and lower-middle-class Britons who had relatives or friends in the industrial districts of the United States—has commanded much less analysis. The largeness of the early to mid-nineteenth-century emigration is acknowledged, although precise numbers are unavailable. Roughly half a million persons born in England, Wales, Scotland, and Ulster had emigrated to the United States during the previous fifteen years, and for all that U.S. tabulations of the foreign-born are inadequate, the U.S. population in 1860 of British-born persons who were not Irish Catholics was probably in the seven hundred thousand range.[85] Almost all of them—over 90 percent—had chosen to go to the North, where they were the third largest group of foreign-born after the Germans and Irish.

Their politics, however, was different from these other groups.' From the textile mills and machine shops of New England to the Pittsburgh ironworks, Ohio collieries, and Lake Superior copper pits, they were almost entirely nonconformist Protestants, lopsidedly against slavery, overwhelmingly Republican, overwhelmingly pro-Lincoln, and overwhelmingly pro-Union. Even postwar analyses of coalfields, logging camps, and copper mines have confirmed the pattern: Scots, Welsh, or Englishmen would be 75 percent or 80 percent Republican; the Catholic Irish, Slavs, and Croatians next door or a neighborhood away would be Democratic.[86] Detailed analyses by historians and political scientists like Paul Kleppner, Ronald Formisano, and Lee Benson have described the "New British" voters of the mid-nineteenth-century United States as 90–95 percent Whig and then similarly Republican, with the principal exceptions being freethinkers and radical ex-Chartists distrustful of the Whig and Republican bias to capital and industry. The Welsh even had a name for the Republicans: *Plaid Werinol*, party of the folk.[87]

Most numerous in the industrial sections of New England, New York, Pennsylvania, Ohio, Michigan, and the Upper Midwest—in short, within Greater New England, where they quickly blended in—the New British and their letters back to parents, grandparents, and siblings in Glamorgan, Antrim, Lanarkshire, or Lancashire must have been a powerful pro-Union reinforcement by the winter of 1862–1863 as public opinion in the North crystallized and hardened. Aging Welsh miners walking to the town library to look at posted headlines or youngsters racing down Lancashire hills to a Clitheroe or a Colne would not have been looking for news of the 20th Alabama or even the 3rd Virginia. They would have wanted word of Ohio regiments from Jackson and Gallia counties ("The Cardiganshire of America") with grandsons they had never seen or of favorite uncles in units like the Cornish "Miners' Guard" company of the 2nd Wisconsin Volunteer Infantry, which marched off after Lincoln's first call in April 1861.

But not all industrial areas would have been affected this way, which helps explain why revisionist historians have modified the case for lopsided British laboring-class and Lancashire worker backing for the North. In 1861 and 1862, that support, far from being lopsided, was divided. By 1863 and 1864, working-class commitment to the North was firming both nationally and in Lancashire. Specific discussions of mid-nineteenth-century Lancashire, however, are complicated by its large population and its considerable internal variations. On the one hand, it was most famous as the center of the British cotton textile industry, based in Manchester, Oldham, Stalybridge, Blackburn, Ashton, and elsewhere. On the other hand, Lancashire also included the huge seaport of Liverpool, as well as the largest Irish immigrant population in England (deck passage across the Irish Sea was just ten pence at the time). There was also a considerable rural agricultural population in the hills and dales of its northern section adjoining Cumberland and the Lake District. This had been the most Catholic section of rural England during the Stuart era (witness the volunteers of 1715 and 1745), and elements of that conservative political culture lingered.

Back in the English Civil War, the loyalties of Lancashire had been complex, although loosely describable as clothing towns versus countryside. In the War for American Independence, Liverpool was a center of British military transshipment and West Indian trade, which encouraged support for coercion. As we have seen, the once-Catholic countryside, seeking to live down a Jacobite reputation, also rallied around the Crown. Although the clothing towns leaned toward conciliation, businessmen were influenced by war contracts as in the southern counties. More grandly, Lancashire's address of 1775 to the Crown in favor of coercion, the first by any county, had a unique political motivation: to replace memories of Lancashire's Stuart connections of 1745 with an impression of militant loyalty to George III thirty years later. Lancashire's signatures of 1775 divided this way: 6,273 on the loyal address, 4,014 on the conciliatory petition quickly produced over the next ten days. Many of the conciliatory signatures came from the clothing centers of Manchester and Rochdale, and perhaps even more to the point, according to a twentieth-century analysis, support for conciliation was most concentrated among lower socioeconomic groups, including clothing workers.[88]

The county's side-taking of 1863 and 1864 was no less complex. The squirearchy, though probably unaware that Virginia's cavalry was led by a Stuart, would have instinctively leaned to the Confederacy. So, too, for a majority of cotton mill–owners. According to one examination, while owners of large mills who were political Liberals were divided, no Conservative mill-owners have been identified as supporting the Union.[89] Liverpool, a former seat of the slave trade and center of prewar commerce with the Cotton South, leaned in the Confederate direction. Next-door Birkenhead, a shipbuilding center, was the home of Laird & Company, shipbuilders, in whose Merseyside yards was built the famous Confederate raider *Alabama,* which played havoc with northern shipping and became a bone of bitter contention between Washington and London. John Laird, the owner, was the arch-Tory, pro-Confederate Member of Parliament for Birkenhead.

Hardly any of the area's large Irish population would have been able to vote for Parliament or any local office. But some of those employed on the docks or in the shipyards, navvy gangs and cotton mills, would have attended the area's political meetings, especially because sentiment in Ireland at that time was both aroused and pro-Confederate. The reasons have been summarized as follows by historian Kirby Miller in *Emigrants and Exiles: Ireland and the Irish Exodus to North America:*

> Irish public opinion—at least as expressed by newspapers, politicians and clergymen of nearly all persuasions—sympathized with the Confederacy and condemned wartime emigration, especially after December, 1862, when New York's Irish-American brigade suffered virtual annihilation at Fredericksburg: "driven to mere slaughter," said the Irish press, by incompetent generals and nativist politicians. Anti-American sentiment only intensified as emigrants sent home accounts of having been tricked or coerced into the Union army and afterward grossly mistreated.[90]

With the popular Irish ballads of the period cursing "Yankees" and "savage blacks" in whose cause Irish blood ran in rivers, these sentiments were probably in evidence at Lancashire meetings.[91] But although substantial segments of Lancashire would have been pro-Confederate, the working-class rallies in the principal cotton towns between late 1862 and 1864 were overwhelmingly pro-northern. Examples from the autumn of 1862 came in Blackburn, Stalybridge, and then, on December 31, the giant rally of six thousand, mostly textile workers, in the Free-Trade Hall in Manchester, who unanimously voted sympathy with the North in an address to President Lincoln. The pro-Confederate Oldham *Standard* lamented how a conclusion must spread that "Manchester, the center of the populous cotton manufacturing districts, has made common cause with the Republicans of the northern States and expressed its ardent hope that the aristocratic South may be speedily crushed."[92]

By the end of 1863, similar rallies had been held in London, Edinburgh, and many smaller cities. In Lancashire itself, pro-Confederate meetings held under the auspices of the Southern Independence Association and the Society to Promote the Cessation of Hostilities in America were common through 1864, but they were principally meetings of other groups and vocations, not workers.[93]

Once emancipation clarified the question of which side favored liberty in North America, working-class Britons quickly pressed on to its all-important corollary: Would the North win strongly enough in North America to carry an expansion of voting rights in Britain, too? Pro-northern reformers began to make the connection so bluntly that some U.S. diplomats worried that aristocratic Britain could still be driven into helping the South. In one particularly emotion-charged speech, John Bright, a radical MP and supporter of the North, told a giant London meeting that "privilege thinks it has a great interest in it [the contest in America] and every morning with blatant voice it comes into our street and curses the American Republic. Privilege has beheld an afflicting spectacle for many years. It has beheld thirty millions of men happy and prosperous, without emperor, without king, without the surrounding of a court . . . and privilege has shuddered at what might happen to old Europe if this great experiment should succeed."[94]

Historians generally agree that the U.S. Civil War made electoral reform almost inevitable. As the North moved toward victory on the battlefield, working-class Britons pointed to how they had been correct, how *they* had stood with the North when most in Parliament, aristocracy, and the fashionable press had favored the South. By beating the cause of the aristocracy, the northern republic, led by a former rail-splitter, had proven its critics wrong and further burnished its example. In his book *Great Britain and the United States*, English historian H. C. Allen concluded:

Feeling for the North and joy at Northern triumphs became more and more associated with the movement for parliamentary reform in Britain, and its future became closely bound up with the outcome of the Civil War. There is no doubt that the Northern victory greatly facilitated the passage of the reform bill of 1867.[95]

It would be an exaggeration to say that the fight for a democratic franchise in late nineteenth-century Britain, ultimately fulfilled in the reforms of 1867 and 1884, was won on the battlefields of Virginia, Georgia, and the Carolinas. However, the U.S. Civil War did see an extraordinary and still-unsung transformation. Instead of Americans circa 1775 seeking the rights and liberties of Englishmen, the interaction had come full circle: Englishmen were looking to the cousins' wars to secure them the rights and liberties of Americans.

The Anglo-American Rapprochement of the 1890s

Victory by the North in the American Civil War was absolutely essential to the future emergence of an Anglo-American alliance. Confederate success would have turned a fragmented North America into a cockpit of renewed European rivalry. No rapprochement between the United States and the United Kingdom could occur, however, until the 1890s and the early 1900s, by which time the United States had filled in its frontier—U.S.-British relations had no greater sticking point—and begun to assert a shared value: an emerging *American* imperialism.

Several revisionist historians have made the case for an intermittent collaborative effort in British policy toward the new republic between 1783 and 1860. The case for British goodwill usually begins with Lord Shelburne's favorable boundaries and proposed American Intercourse Act of 1783. It goes on to include the attempt by Pitt the Younger and his foreign secretary, Lord Grenville, to achieve some of the same thing in the Jay Treaty of 1794, which led to the so-called rapprochement of 1795–1805. Then came Lord Liverpool's West Indian trade concessions of the 1820s, the settlement of the Maine and Oregon boundary disputes in the 1840s, and the partial agreements of the late 1850s over U.S. hopes for a canal across the Isthmus of Panama.[96] If anything, British policy-makers were more likely than Americans to recognize the intermingled economies and futures of the two nations. During the Napoleonic Wars, Members of Parliament and editorialists frequently contended that the Royal Navy, in practical terms, protected America's seaborne commerce as well as Britain's. This had elements of truth, although that result was a side effect, not a motivation.

What economic and diplomatic histories rarely capture, however, are the pride and prickliness of the frontier, as well as the bitter memories left in the United States after the wars of 1812–1815 and 1861–1865. The Treaty of Ghent in 1815 effectively ended British-incited Indian raids, but unresolved boundary disputes crowded the map, along the Maine–New Brunswick border and the northwest frontier between the Rockies and the Pacific, in the Oregon Country and "the north westernmost head of the Connecticut River."[97] Points of irritation were everywhere. Five years after the end of the War of 1812, the U.S. War Department ordered two expeditions into Minnesota and the south shore of Lake Superior to remove British flags and establish American influence.[98] During the 1820s, several British and American maps improperly claimed Spanish and then Mexican San Francisco—the great prize of the Pacific—as within each country's territory.[99]

The so-called Aroostook War took place along Maine's vague boundary in 1839 until firm lines were finally locked in by the Webster-Ashburton Treaty of 1842. Far away in Texas, British officials schemed to keep that new republic independent as a buffer between the U.S. and Mexico. Disagreement in Oregon gave American warhawks the slogan "Fifty-Four Forty or Fight," although compromise prevailed over cannon. The brief and bloodless "Pig War" in the San Juan Islands of Puget Sound came in 1859. Frictions in Minnesota's Red River Valley were deferred by the Civil War.

The Civil War ended with many Americans still bitter at British assistance to the Confederacy, particularly the construction of commerce-raiders like the CSS *Alabama*. Prominent Washington officials, including Secretary of State Seward, again discussed annexing Canada. Seward talked of damages owed to the U.S. because of British actions in prolonging the war (by building the *Alabama* and other raiders) that were so large that they could be paid only by a Canadian cession. However, this issue was resolved, in practical politics, by the Canadian Confederation of 1867, that nation's modern unification, and then by international arbitration in 1871, which pegged British liability for the *Alabama* at just $15 million.

The postwar U.S. flirtation with annexations in Canada and the Caribbean receded during the 1870s. Washington was constrained by cooling Republican braggadocio, the inhibitions of divided government, and a national preoccupation with industrial growth and the completion of westward expansion. Seven states were admitted to the Union between 1884 and 1894. Serious quarrels with the British were few and far between until the Venezuelan boundary dispute of 1894. In this test of wills, unimportant in its details, the British ultimately gave way, acceding to U.S. arbitration and thereby all but accepting the interpretation of the Monroe Doctrine that proclaimed U.S. authority supreme in the hemisphere.

Richard Van Alstyne, whose book *The Rising American Empire* identifies New Englanders and Virginians as expansionists—imperialists in waiting—from the time they came ashore as colonists, puts great emphasis on the cohesion secured by the North's victory:

> The long-range effects of this war were incalculable. Success for the South would have meant the rise of a new but weak and backward nation. If the Southern states did not get their supply of capital from the North, they would have to borrow it from Europe. A tendency to Balkanize North America would have been the result, which in turn would have exerted a profound influence on the state system of Western Europe. The problems of dealing with two separate and mutually hostile American nations while supporting the Dominion of Canada would have strained the resources of British foreign policy to the breaking point and smoothed the road for Imperial Germany.[100]

Historian Allan Nevins has offered still another variation. Had Britain intervened to help the South, the results might have included French retention of Mexico, a northern conquest of Canada, and the probability that the Anglo-American coalition in World Wars I and II would have been impossible.[101]

A divided North America, in which the economic and military weight of the Untied States was much reduced, would have created an altogether different great-power playing field. Britain, for one, would have accelerated its maneuvers, not ended them. Instead, the North's victory in 1865 established its indisputable continental hegemony, and along the northern U.S. border, once Canadian Confederation was a fact, Britain in 1871 withdrew its remaining troops. By the 1890s, the increasingly imperialist objectives of the United States, thrown into bold relief by the Spanish-American War, left little doubt of U.S. ambition—or that the two English-speaking powers were converging in philosophy, interests, geopolitics, and the logic of collaboration.

New England, which had been unable to sustain affection for France for even a decade after 1783, had returned to its ancestral bias with the Jay Treaty of 1794 and the vehement hostility of Congregationalist New England to the Jacobins and antireligious sloganry of the French Revolution.[102] By the early 1800s, Yankee children were taught to sing "Rule, New England" to the tune "Rule Britannia," and ultra-Federalists like Fisher Ames of Massachusetts boasted that the New England states were "the most respectable and prosperous . . . more unlike and more superior to other people (the English excepted)."[103]

But for the nation as a whole, historian Michael Kammen has traced the evolution of U.S. attitudes toward Britain by using a clever measurement: how Americans discussed Britain and the War for Independence. By this yardstick, not just the aftermath of the War of 1812 but the period from 1821 to 1846 was a time of bitterness and acrimony. Attitudes in the United States softened in the 1850s, when relations were improving. Then Civil War tensions brought a sourness in the 1860s, even in New England. The 1871 agreement over the *Alabama* damages produced another thaw, even resulting in the first British observances of the Fourth of July. In 1875, when the poet John Greenleaf Whittier wrote a commemorative "Lexington, 1775," he told a friend that he had added two verses, "mainly for the sake of bringing the British lion and the Yankee eagle together."[104]

The next two decades saw a further warming, save in the Middle West where hard-pressed farmers resented the British role in deflationary U.S. monetary policy and the Gold Standard. Then, between the settlement of the Venezuelan boundary issue and the outbreak of the Spanish war in 1898, Kammen's examination finds characterizations of the Revolution beginning to approach their measured twentieth-century posture.

The war with Spain in 1898 was a major watershed. Her Majesty's government, mindful of needing friendly powers, was coming to think of the United States—kindred, and with its military power and ambition centered in the Americas and increasingly the Pacific—as by far and away the most logical choice. The collaboration in 1898, while short of an actual alliance, was in retrospect a prelude to one. In the Pacific, from Samoa to the Philippines, Anglo-American cooperation tended to maximize when the Germans or Spanish were on hand. The first was an emerging enemy; the second an old one.

With the German threat on the horizon, the British were happy to have the crumbling Spanish empire, the old *fortalezas* and treasure-galleon anchorages of Manila, Cuba, and Puerto Rico, pass under the sway of another English-speaking power. In early 1898, when the U.S. fleet, having coaled to capacity in Hong Kong, sailed for the Philippines to do battle, sailors in the British warships were ordered not to cheer. But no one had so told the soldiers and sailors on a hospital hulk, so cheer they did.[105] In 1761, one of the last British-colonial joint ventures was an expedition to Cuba that captured Havana, even though the 1763 treaty restored it to Spain. What Royal Navy captain or Massachusetts militia colonel on hand could have imagined that 137 years later, the fleet that all but ended the Spanish Empire would be that of an independent America, with warships named for states and cities that had not even been thought of?

Historians who dismiss the Spanish-American War as a sad little affair ignore the unique psychological role it played in reuniting Britain and the United States, at least in strategic and collaborative terms. Spain was the old enemy, whose ships had landed soldiers in Scotland as late as 1719 and harassed Delaware Bay and Nantucket as late as the 1740s. In 1898, Methodist bishops out to curb the "Romish" threat in the Caribbean were as eager wardrummers as naval theorists out to cement Anglo-American cooperation. No other foe could have served so well. British support for the U.S. was so obvious that Spain began preparations to attack Gibraltar should war break out. When Lord Pauncefote, the helpful and highly regarded British ambassador during the war, died in 1902, President Theodore Roosevelt had his body taken back to England in the United States warship *Brooklyn*.

Sentiment was not the decisive factor on either side, of course. In the United States, the record waves of immigration from southern and eastern Europe in the 1880s and especially the 1890s and subsequent years up through 1914 were fueling another wave of nativism, this one taking a form of Anglo-Saxon ethnic pride. Portraits of the Progressive movement of 1900–1914 as partly a status revolt of old-stock Anglo-Saxon gentry and professional men threatened by the new rich and robber barons should note a related phenomenon. Rhetorical Anglo-Saxonism—the trumpeting of global Anglo-American destiny—was in part an indirect response of many of the same elites to the alleged perils of the new immigration, which were catalogued in books by leading scientists and eugenicists like Francis A. Walker, Charles Davenport, and William Z. Ripley. In the eastern wing of the Progressive movement, Theodore Roosevelt was by no means alone in his enthusiasm over Anglo-American greatness and destiny.

Greater New England also had an economic reason for imperialism and expansionism: the needs of regional commerce and industry. Some in New England, representing the region's peace and anti-expansion politics left over from the 1800–1850 period, had opposed the Spanish War in 1898. Several of the region's U.S. senators joined this opposition. By a broader range of calculations, however, the manifest destiny of the 1890s spoke with a Yankee accent. Between 1865 and 1898, American exports had expanded from $281 million to some $1,231 million, putting the United States third behind Britain and Germany. Equally to the point, the value of northern-produced manufactured exports to Asia and Latin America was fast overhauling the cotton, tobacco, and raw materials exported by the South to Europe. Details of 1898–1901 regional support in Congress for manufacturing and commerce-related imperialist policies—intervention in Cuba, annexation of Hawaii, construction of a Central American canal, and control of the Philippines—showed the most overwhelming backing in New England and the most lopsided opposition in the South.[106]

The same Republican politics and Greater New England support pattern showed up in 1890s commitment to naval expansion, which bolstered both imperialism and manufacturing. In 1890, the U.S. Navy ranked twelfth in the world behind Turkey and China, but by 1900, it was fourth in battleship strength, sixth in overall fleet size, and growing rapidly. The naval share of the federal budget jumped from just 7 percent in 1890 to over 20 percent in 1905 as the United States began bulding capital warships at a rate to match even Britain's. The names of the first three battleships authorized in 1890 mirrored the regionalism of the greatest enthusiasm for naval appropriations—the *Oregon,* the *Indiana,* and the *Massachusetts.*

The British government, preoccupied with naval power and battleship ratios, now saw, ever more fully, what Bismarck had grasped earlier: that English-speaking North America was the new key to world power alignments. War Office and Admiralty records detail the self-interest and tactical thinking that occurred. Few senior officers called for an outright U.S.-British alliance, but just as Britain had decided to remove its troops from Canada in 1871, the first decade of the new century saw the Admiralty withdraw most warships from the Western Hemisphere in favor of an assumption that war between the cousins was now unthinkable. The U.S. fleet would patrol those seas. Royal Navy strength would concentrate in European waters.

In 1904, the Earl of Selborne, first lord of the Admiralty, called friendship with the United States "the principal aim" of British policy and described "war with the United States of America as the greatest evil which could befall the British Empire."[107] Although the polyglot population of the United States was less sanguine about Britain, the ruling U.S. elites, many of them Greater New Englanders caught up in the notion of a shared Anglo-Saxon destiny, were ready to resume what would, in the twentieth century, become a partnership.

In 1791, John Jay, then chief justice of the United States, had warned British friends that the U.S. was undergoing an important generational change. The Americans who remembered the shared glories of 1759 and 1763, of Amherst, Wolfe, and triumph, years when they had been proud to be part of the empire, were dying off and being replaced by a generation "educated in a period of passion and prejudice."[108] Westward expansion, before the frontier was filled in during the 1890s, sustained those passions, prejudices, and memories. By 1905, however, the wheel had come full circle. Policy-makers who remembered the Aroostook War or British-built Confederate commerce raiders were themselves a vanishing breed. The more recent memory was of collaboration and shared values.

The last internal danger point in the evolution of Anglo-America—the pivotal importance of northern victory in 1861–1865—had come and gone. The rapprochement of the 1890s was about to give way to the twentieth-century alliance.

PART FOUR

The Triumph of Anglo-America— War, Population, and English Language Hegemony

12

THE COUSINS' WARS AND THE SHAPING OF ANGLO-AMERICAN POLITICS

The most important occurrence in the life of a nation is the breaking out of a war.
—Alexis de Tocqueville, *Democracy in America*, 1835

War is the extension of politics by other means.
—Karl Von Clausewitz, *On War,* 1831

The basis of (political) democratization is everywhere purely military in character. . . . Military discipline meant the triumph of democracy because the community wished and was compelled to secure the cooperation of the non-aristocratic masses and hence put arms, and along with arms political power, into their hands.
—Max Weber, *Essays in Sociology,* 1946

⌐

B Y 1910, BRITAIN AND THE UNITED STATES, though not yet open and official allies, were moving in that direction, with enormous consequences for great-power politics and the shape of the twentieth century. Two great wars later, Anglo-America and the incipient imperium of the English language were a reality.

This is the Anglo-America at the end of the twentieth century and the beginning of the twenty-first. To reach it, however, we must step out of the chronological presentation that has guided the first eleven chapters of this volume. One particular emphasis in the earlier sections—on Protestantism and religion—must be diminished in changing to a different framework to explain the rise of the English-speaking nations well into the twentieth century.

Part IV of this volume, which commences with these pages, will pursue three different threads: war, demography, and language. This chapter itself will emphasize the great impact of military conflict and its aftermath in shaping the electoral politics and even the character of the United States from the 1780s through two twentieth-century world wars, which were themselves cousins' fights of a very painful sort for German-Americans. War's recurring role, both as a label of generations and a shaper of U.S. politics, deserves more attention in its own right. In a new vein, four different conflicts have played a particular role in agitating but then also assimilating the U.S. Irish and German populations—the American Revolution, the U.S. Civil War, and both world wars of the twentieth century. Time after time, to reverse Clausewitz's famous saying, American politics has become a continuation of wartime internal divisions by other means. Nevertheless, the process ultimately produced the second of the English-speaking leading world powers.

The huge German and Irish populations of the United States—the Census of 1990 found nearly 100 million Americans out of 250 million claiming one or the other as their principal ancestry—could have proved large enough and ethnically sensitive enough to have kept U.S. public policy and diplomacy at arm's length from Britain instead of producing closeness. From time to time, British officials worried that would happen. Indeed, portions of this chapter will show how sensitive German-American voting became in the elections surrounding both world wars.

However, by putting a larger international framework around the emigration to the American Republic from 1790 to 1914, chapter 13 will show that its ultimate effect was quite different—to build a huge English-speaking country, one that wound up closely allied to Great Britain, and to do so in fair measure out of emigrant and refugee Celts and Germans. The massive Irish and Scottish exodus to North America, in turn, made it possible for England to dominate the British Isles, while the millions of Germans who crossed the Atlantic changed the ultimate balance of power in the twentieth century. Could any fleeing Palatine of 1710 or 1720 have even begun to imagine that a pair of descendants of such Rhenish emigrants—John J. Pershing in 1917 and Dwight D. Eisenhower in 1944—would command the New World armies in two wars that humbled the heirs of the Teutonic Knights and Frederick the Great?

The extraordinary expansion of the ranks of global English-speakers during the nineteenth and twentieth centuries, led by the New World, in turn becomes the framework for chapter 14. From the sixteenth century, if not earlier, English officials and policymakers advanced the English language in Wales, Ireland, and then Scotland as a weapon to expand English culture and power up and down the British Isles. American Anglo-Saxons were no less successful, Anglicizing all of French Louisiana save for the bayous near New Orleans, sweeping through what had been New Spain, and insisting in the years between 1917 and 1946 that the last midwestern redoubts of Teutonic settlement adopt English. At the end of the two world wars, the English language was perhaps the biggest winner of all, and by the advent of the millennium, on the shoulders of the post-industrial revolution, the tongue born of the Angles so many centuries earlier had created its own supranational, but Anglo-America–based, communications hegemony— from jet pilots requesting instructions from Singapore air control and round-the-clock traders arbitrating currencies for the big French, German, or Japanese banks, to a rock band taping for RCA in Budapest and India-based computer operators performing routine back-office work for New York insurance companies.

Chapter 14, even in its role as a conclusion, remains unfinished in a larger sense. The cultural and political saga of the English language itself is not over. For the moment, however, let us go back to the Britain and United States of an earlier day to trace the internal effects of war—its political and electoral pathologies—through two centuries. Had these not been managed successfully by the nations involved, the language opportunities might have been moot.

The Cousins' Wars and the
Genius of Anglo-American Politics

The three cousins' wars have been at the core of British and American national evolution. Rather than fading with the last echoes of gunfire, their memories instead became entrenched in their respective nations' psyches. Their terminologies and epithets then lived on to help shape further politics and subsequent wars.

The basis of the powerful politics generated by these civil wars can be summed up in three words: unusual public involvement. Ordinary folk were enmeshed, not just the political elites. The English-speaking communities took their religious and national roles—their task as a chosen people—too seriously for their major internal wars to be anything less than intense.

Popular participation in wartime British politics has rested on an unusual civic involvement that challenges theories of national deference. The "political nation" of England—the two hundred thousand voters and petitioners of 1640, the four hundred thousand of 1775, and the million or more active in 1861–1865—is no myth. An even more democratic and participatory politics unfolded in British North America and then in the United States.

In America, what some have called "the common language of liberty" first played its own transatlantic role in spurring the Harvard graduates of 1639 and 1640 as they took ship, a year or two later, for what had once been home and the Parliamentary side in the English Civil War. In 1775, shared seventeenth-century beliefs and memories, more than any unique nutrients in American soil, were the provenance of the associations, conventions, and committees of correspondence and safety in Boston, New York, and Philadelphia—and of the tea-party militance in such other spirited towns as Greenwich, New Jersey, and Annapolis, Maryland.

The American frontier was an effective incubator—the greater distance from authority, permissive colonial charters, and the absence of a local nobility combined to make yeomen, merchants, and ships' chandlers even more independent and politically active than those in England. The Ulster border had some of the same effect. Yet if frontier circumstances themselves were the key, why has no Frenchman, Portuguese, or Spaniard played Frederick Jackson Turner to a perception of some exalted nation-shaping contribution by the frontier of Quebec, Mexico, the Pampas, or São Paulo? Probably because in North America, the more than co-equal spur to participation was ethnocultural: the legacy transmitted by the Old World Essexes, Middlesexes, Hampshires, and Suffolks to their overseas progeny through books, pamphlets, sermons, coffeehouse plots, anti-Stuart tracts, and memories.

In the England of 1640 or 1775, the poorest half or third of the nation, illiterate and nonvoting, might have been a culture of forelock-tugging, grudged or otherwise. However, the middle-class and lower-middle-class population that included perhaps 150,000 eligible voters, some 50,000 nonvoters involved enough to sign petitions, and a further 50,000–100,000 through church halls, clubs, taverns, and coffeehouses ranked among Europe's most engaged and alert citizenries. The widely recognized periodic radicalism of London's artisans and shopkeepers of the seventeenth and eighteenth centuries is too easily described as unique and unmatched elsewhere in the nation. Kindred engagement in the 1770s, albeit on a smaller scale, has since been found for most of the ten principal urban centers. To call the literate 20 to 30 percent of the public apathetic to national affairs was as misguided as similar dismissals had been in the 1640s. The assertiveness of ordinary Englishmen—and English*women*—was a staple of wry continental comment from the tracts of Montesquieu to the operas of Mozart.

These pages must emphasize what the earlier chapters only touched upon collaterally: the relative intensity of English-speaking political interest. When the American Revolution broke out in 1775, activists in the northern English city of Newcastle, for example, plunged right into the controversy. The Constitutional Club of Durham, Northumberland, and Newcastle, established in 1772 to promote the cause of John Wilkes, applauded conciliation in America. Two local publications, the *Newcastle Chronicle* and the *Freeman's Magazine,* took up cudgels for the far-off colonies, and the Newcastle-based Philosophical Society debated the similarity of the civil war in the era of Charles I to the contest in America, with agreement on the parallel being carried unanimously. Activists even burned an effigy of John Wesley, who had written in support of coercion, after hanging the figure with placards likening Wesley to Sir

Robert Filmer and Thomas Hobbes, Royalist thinkers of the seven-teenth century.[1] Arthur Lee, who represented the Continental Con-gress in London circa 1775, was one of the few Americans to state that same lineage in a pamphlet: that the pro-coercion arguments of John Wesley and Dr. Samuel Johnson were indistinguishable from "those of Filmer, Mainwaring and Sacheverell and those in support of ship money."[2] Kindred portraits of activism and alert-ness circa 1775 have been drawn for Bristol, Norwich, Coventry, Manchester, Nottingham, and Cambridge.[3]

In both nations, interest was often fanned by resort to the com-mon vocabulary of the previous civil wars. Even in the 1860s, as we have seen, rhetorical assaults on cavaliers and Puritans still pa-raded across the U.S. political stage. "Puritan" was a curse word across the South and well into the Lower North. William Sumner, chairman of the Senate Foreign Relations Committee, on hearing that Queen Victoria had recognized Confederate belligerency, called her pronouncement the "most hateful act of English history since Charles II."[4] In 1861, after the pro-southern legislature of Missouri fled the state capital, federal forces ruled Missouri for four years with a convention—called the "Long Convention" as an analogy to the Parliament that ruled revolutionary England af-ter Charles Stuart fled London in 1642.[5] Henry Hotze, the resident Confederate propagandist in Britain, regretfully acknowledged that "the Lancashire (cotton) operatives were the only class which as a class continues actively inimical to us. With them the unrea-soning aversion to our institutions is as firmly rooted as in any part of New England."[6] The cotton-weaving part of Lancashire was old Puritan country, too.

Towns like Manchester, Bolton, and Bradford in nearby Yorkshire brought to the tables and meeting halls of the 1860s a unique tradi-tion of liberty. In the seventeenth century, these towns had been the Puritan Genevas of Lancashire. In the eighteenth century, when co-ercing the American colonies became an issue, the conciliatory counterpetitions were opened to public signature especially in the clothing towns—Manchester and Rochdale—where the first senti-ments of clothing workers and British manufacturers circa 1775 were pro-American.[7] After the Emancipation Proclamation, even when lack of southern cotton had shut mills in Lancashire, helping to cause huge unemployment, the English clothing towns could not have done other than rally overwhelmingly to the northern side.

Indeed, side-choosing during all three wars had considerable parallels with basic alignments of British and American politics. That was logical enough, because during the three centuries of the cousins' wars, British politics usually mirrored much the same issues that were visible in the wartime disagreements of 1642–1649, 1775–1783, and 1861–1865: a division between monarchy, aristocracy, and High Church views on one side and dissenting Protestantism and a more democratic ideology on the other. It would have been impossible for each of these wars—including the two principally fought on the other side of the Atlantic—*not* to cause major tensions within Britain's own political nation.

Wartime alignments also provided the principal architecture of politics in the late seventeenth-, eighteenth-, and nineteenth-century United States. The memory of who chose what side in the American Revolution, brought forward into peacetime politics after 1783, thereupon played a central role in shaping—and later, bluntly, *dooming*—the Federalist Party. No one doubts that the American Civil War, in turn, laid down the party system that guided the United States for a full century after the stillness at Appomattox.

Because of the intensity of popular involvement and the cumulative vocabularies shaped by each conflict, the cousins' wars, rhetorically and tactically, rise out of each other like philosophic ladders. Like the pueblos of the U.S. Southwest, they are houses built on each other. The American Revolution was scarcely under way before its perceived or exaggerated roots in the English Civil War became controversial. Patriots took up the old organizational forms of the 1640s: associations, committees, and conventions. New Englanders hurled the old epithets: The King's supporters were malignants and inimicals. The Royalists, in reply, damned the rebels as crop-eared Puritans, damned Presbyterians, and unrepentant Oliverians. The ghosts of Pym, Hampden, Sydney, and Harrington were seen guiding one side while the specters of Sacheverell, Filmer, and Hobbes—to say nothing of Charles I himself—prowled on the other.

As early as 1774, when Parliament shut down the port of Boston, Thomas Jefferson drew on Puritan precedents to convince the Virginia House of Burgesses to declare June 1 a day of fasting, humiliation, and prayer in support of its sister colony, Massachusetts. Fast days had become a regular event in the Long Parliament of the 1640s during the Puritan ascendency. As soon as the royal governor, Lord Dunmore, read of the fast day proclamation, he understood its incendiary political nature and dissolved the House of Burgesses. Loyalist Anglican clergymen such as Maryland's Jonathan Boucher retrospectively concurred. These events, he recalled, did as much damage in the early years of the American war as had been achieved by preachers and fast days in the early stages of the "Grand Rebellion" 130 years earlier.[8] Fast days recurred during the American Civil War, and once again, as we have seen, the role of religion and preachers was extraordinary.

In 1775, the rights of Englishmen were once more at issue, as were the privileges of monarchy and episcopacy. And like the Rump Parliament twelve decades earlier, the General Court of the Commonwealth of Massachusetts had little use for mere kings: Sovereignty, it announced, lay with the people under God. Another Chosen Nation had a Puritan destiny to fulfill—and, for that matter, would again in 1861.

The American Civil War bore an even more complicated historical burden: a frame of reference that reached back *two* centuries and *two* wars. This in addition to a new task of upholding an emerging set of Anglo-American rights—still very much at issue—for which perhaps half of the British Isles wound up looking to the young republic. The "Spirit of Seventy Six" itself was claimed by Yankees and Southerners alike. As the new Confederate states seceded in the winter of 1860–1861, their leaders insisted theirs was an imitation: to win independence from an increasingly oppressive North just as the thirteen colonies had separated from an increasingly tyrannical Britain. The South had earlier established its own minutemen, committees of correspondence, and Sons of Liberty. Even in the early 1850s, William F. Yancey of Alabama, a principal theorist of southern revolution and independence, was hoping for a southern Lexington and a southern Bunker Hill. By 1858, he called for "Committees of Safety" all over the cotton states to precipitate a revolution.[9]

To Southerners, the legacy of 1776 meant that the Union was consensual—a compact which, having been broken by the North, the Confederate states were even freer to abrogate. Many British, some of whose minds were also refighting the last war, agreed. The War for American Independence had indeed established the compact or states' rights theory. Now it was Dixie's turn. *The Times* of London concurred in the analogy that the Confederacy was opposing a war of aggression and an oppressive refusal to accept independence.[10] Some southern officials, taking this new goodwill further, suggested that allegiance to the former mother country might be restored as an alternative to Yankee tyranny. The future Confederate secretary of state, Judah Benjamin, himself British-born, was charged—he completely denied it—with hinting as much in a mid-1860 letter to the British Consul in New York.[11]

More often, however, New Englanders and southerners vied during the 1840s and 1850s to establish which side had been the more patriotic in the War for Independence. Massachusetts historian Lorenzo Sabine published a volume in 1847 alleging that New England had fewer loyalists than the South and that South Carolina, in particular, had been a hotbed of neutralism and loyalism. Congressman Lawrence Keitt of South Carolina later replied that in 1765, long before the Boston Tea Party, North Carolinians had seized a British ship loaded with stamped paper and burned the affixtures. Keitt also presented a list of one hundred Massachusetts soldiers who had been declared unfit for Revolutionary service.[12]

Once war started, even Confederate military strategy drew on that of the colonists in 1775. The Confederates, like the American colonists, thought that they could win independence in part by continuing to assert it—that as long as they could keep an army in the field and the loyalty of the southern people, sooner or later they would win. If the North had the navy and could capture cities at will, the British, with that same advantage, had failed because the patriots could outwait them.[13] That optimism might have succeeded had the Confederate government been able to complete the parallel by obtaining a major European ally.

In a sense, the older civil war was also being reenacted: the one between Cavaliers and Roundheads that matched manor lords against the advance agents of middle-class politics and industrial capitalism. The analogy was no longer to 1776 because the United States of 1860 was abandoning its loose federation to define a *national* approach to slavery and to emerge as an economic nation-state. And, of course, some in New England once again used English Civil War terminology to identify a new battle between Puritanism and malignancy. Prominent Yankees like Theodore Parker and Thomas Wentworth Higginson called John Brown, the antislavery radical, "a Cromwellian Ironside introduced in the nineteenth century for a special purpose."[14] Eighty-five years after Lexington and Concord, circumstances did indeed require the North American republic to resolve some of the same issues that wracked England in the seventeenth century. And this time, Britain's own constitutional evolution hung on the American outcome.

Few would disagree that these three were the most important English-speaking civil wars since the Reformation. However, the individual meaning of each war is still a matter of debate; the ultimate three-century connection and transatlantic impact are barely discussed.* Yet the emergence of Britain and the United States, as well as the forces that brought them back together in the twentieth century, are tied together with the effects and roles of these wars. Their recurring political importance mirrors the seamlessness of the oratory. If there is a shared genius of Anglo-American politics, a stability that has rarely required resort to internal warfare, the three reluctant but necessary conflicts have been part of it. And because these great internal wars have been so infrequent, they have also—usually, at least—been defining.

---

*This analysis is not the first to raise the possibility that a peculiar genius of American politics lies hidden in the continuities of the English Civil War, the American Revolution, and the American Civil War. Daniel Boorstin, in his own 1953 book, *The Genius of American Politics,* noted nineteenth-century French statesman and historian François Guizot's thesis that the English Revolution occurred twice, the second time in eighteenth-century America, as this book has detailed from some kindred and other different perspectives. Boorstin then added his own sound extension: that the English Revolution made its *third* appearance in mid-nineteenth century United States. This is because "the relation of the ancient rights of Englishmen to federalism, which was only partly redefined in the course of the American Revolution, was more extensively explored and settled in the American Civil War." This relationship is further discussed in the discussion of the overlapping names and roles of the three wars that appears in Appendix 1 on page 613.

War and Electoral Alignments in Britain and the United States

Less controversy attaches to a narrower question: How much have electoral politics in Britain and then the United States been shaped by wars and their issues? Probably, we must conclude, to a greater extent than by any other single factor.

To begin with Britain, politics and internal warfare were so commingled during the years from Edgehill to Yorktown that, despite inevitable oversimplification, the fights with steel and those with words were usually about the same things: royal versus legislative power, episcopacy, "popish plots," and Protestant political control. Even in the trough of worry over the Napoleonic Wars, following great French victories like Austerlitz and Jena, Britain fought the general election of 1807 in considerable measure over the issue of Catholic emancipation. Through the American Civil War, as we have seen, the basic divisions of the British party system continued to reflect the cleavage between the Church of England and the landed gentry on one side and the dissenters, reinforced by Low Church Anglicans, on the other.

Two very different conflicts, World Wars I and II, were necessary to shift the cultural and religious arena of British politics, partly superseding it with a class emphasis that came to the fore with the Labour Party. The American Civil War, with its stimulus to democracy and its working-class arousal, almost certainly helped to lay some groundwork.

In any event, the internal stresses of the years during and surrounding the First World War, arguably greater than any since the Stuart years, tore the old fabric of British culture and politics. The decline of the Liberal Party—well described in *The Strange Death of Liberal England* by George Dangerfield—provided the principal display. This chapter will not deal with the debate over the Liberal demise and whether it came with the Parliamentary crises of 1910–1914, as a result of World War I, or in the decades between the two world wars.[15] Suffice it to say that the war was obviously a catalyst, and its aftermath was also difficult. Official tabulations of the elections to Parliament in 1922 produced this unusual fragmentation: Conservative 36.7 percent; Labor, Co-op, and Socialist 29.4

percent; Asquith Liberal 14.6 percent; Lloyd George Liberal 9.2 percent; Prefix-less Liberal 9.2 percent; Independent Conservative 1.5 percent; and so on through five additional groupings. In the general election of 1924, even Winston Churchill ran on a transition party ticket called Constitutionalist.[16]

The effect of the three English-speaking wars on politics in the United States has been even more pervasive. Even the small encounters of the 1640s and 1650s between Puritans and Catholics in Maryland helped shape local politics. So did the Royalist–versus–old Cromwellian aspects of Bacon's Rebellion in Virginia in 1676. However, in most of the colonies, eighteenth-century legislative alignments were molded less by grand seventeenth-century acrimony than by local circumstances—the narrowness or breadth of the franchise, ethnic and religious polarizations, or the innate Whig bias of provincial legislatures obliged to square off against royal governors. Once politics put on a uniform in 1775, so did intrastate electoral alignments. As in the United Kingdom earlier, political alignments and loyalty issues became inextricably intertwined.

Tories who had not flown were commonly barred from voting by test acts, another legacy of the English Civil War. Neutrals, who were nonjurors (non-oathtakers), were often barred as well. In New York, Tories were disenfranchised by a test act in March 1778. A more severe one passed in May 1784 was said to disqualify "more than two-thirds of all of the inhabitants of the city and county of New York, of the county of Kings . . . nine-tenths of those of Queens and the whole of those of the Boro of Westchester."[17] As for Pennsylvania, its test act in place through the war years—strict enough to keep about half of the potential electorate disenfranchised—required voters to renounce fidelity to George III, pledge allegiance to Pennsylvania as an independent state, and promise to expose all traitorous conspiracies against the United States.[18]

Bitterness and acrimony were hardly relieved by the U.S.-British peace treaty, as chapter 8 has discussed, and survived well into the postwar decade. In many states, test acts aimed at ex-loyalists remained in place through 1787 and 1788. When the war ended, many farmers and backcountrymen, particularly those hostile to the coastal gentry or suspicious of their wartime leadership, wanted the new U.S. government to adhere to the egalitarian and anti-Tory commitment exemplified by the Pennsylvania and Georgia Constitutions of 1776. In some states, the test acts were important symbols.

Egalitarians and those favoring harsh test acts typically became anti-Federalists and, subsequently, supporters of Thomas Jefferson. Indeed, just as the winners of 1865 would "wave the bloody shirt" by urging northern veterans to vote as they had shot in the Civil War, the anti-Federalists of the 1780s groused about betrayal of the principles of the Revolution. Militia units in Pennsylvania and other states, rallying behind the exclusion mandates, opposed any civic reinvolvement of "Tories and traitors."[19] Besides complaining about how the Constitution promoted the stronger, British-style government favored by lawyers, merchants, and creditors, anti-Federalists felt strongly about a related cultural symbolism: the prominence of former Tories in the fight for its ratification. The politics of wartime acrimony, carrying over into peacetime, put down psychological roots that, in several new shapes, would dominate the nineteenth century and carry over into the twentieth. The subsections that follow will set out four powerful examples.

Federalists, Aristocrats, and Traitors

As ratification politics intensified in the mid-1780s, supporters of the federal Constitution had the most prominent martial and flag-based symbolism—backing from the former commander-in-chief, George Washington, as well as from the Society of the Cincinnati, a patriotic and fraternal organization limited to officers of the Continental Army. Founded in 1783 just before demobilization by General Henry Knox, who became Washington's secretary of war, the society's membership was made hereditary, with eligibility confined to eldest sons. The group took its name from Lucius Quinctius Cincinnatus, the former Roman official who came out of retirement in 439 B.C. to put down the plebeian revolt. Washington's officers, like Cincinnatus, went back to their farms in 1783, but many must have yearned for a further role. Members of the society were prominently represented in the state Constitutional Conventions of 1788–1789, invariably on the conservative side. All twelve who participated in New York, for example, were Federalists.

Yet partly because the order came under sharp attack for its thinly disguised factional purposes and apparent aspirations to provide an American nobility, its political effectiveness faded, and some of the same resentment attached to Federalism itself. The party's reunification of old colonial elites across wartime divisions, its seaboard biases, and pro-British sympathies all made it seem undemocratic. Criticism of Federalism's pro-English tendency—Thomas Jefferson enjoyed calling its adherents "Anglomen"—was especially damning, becoming the new republic's earliest pattern of postwar "bloody shirt–waving." An important U.S. political tradition (one that would later haunt Southerners and Germans) was in the process of forming.

In 1793, as Washington's first term was ending, Jefferson charged that Federalism had three defining bases of support: the "natural aristocrats" from the fashionable circles of Philadelphia, New York, Boston, and Charleston; the merchants who traded on British capital; and the "paper men," by which he meant bondholders, financiers, and investors.[20] The Federalist Party, he said, also "included all the old Tories" under one of these descriptions.

In fact, this was much oversimplified. Seafaring New England, the prosperous Congregationalist valleys, and the neat, orderly German farm districts from Lancaster, Pennsylvania, south to Virginia's Shenandoah Valley—Moravians and Mennonites, as well as Lutherans—were also part of the loose Federalist coalition. However, Jefferson could usefully have enlarged his analogy to include a broader Toryism—religious, cultural, and ethnic. The twentieth-century observer who pokes through old records in what were once colonial towns and courthouses from New Jersey to Charleston and Savannah will conclude that Federalism was indeed where the loyalists and neutrals of 1775–1783 found their second home. In the near term, such old Tory support broadened the Federalist electorate of the Washington and Adams years beyond the first president's own Virginia tidewater and the states dominated by the religious and commercial establishment of Congregationalist New England. To many Americans, though, it was a tainted politics.

After John Adams's narrow defeat in 1800, Federalism shrank back into what was a New England core region, augmented by Delaware, parts of New York and New Jersey, and a scattering of congressional seats and sympathetic counties in the plantation states. Wartime connotations clung to large portions of this geography. The noted military historian John Shy has correlated Toryism during the 1775–1783 period not simply with religion and ethnicity but with the penetration and occupation of British military forces. The aftereffects of wartime British occupation, neutralism, and loyalist sympathy, in turn, became strands of late eighteenth- and even early nineteenth-century Federalism.

Skeptics can validly say that most of the locales occupied by the British and later voting Federalist were also *commercial* centers. Many in New York, Newport, Philadelphia, and Charleston would have voted Federalist for cosmopolitan economic and cultural reasons. However, much of the Federalist support later discernible in areas of previous wartime loyalism and Toryism had little to do with cosmopolitanism or finance. Mountainous Vermont, one of the last Federalist strongholds after the War of 1812, had negotiated with the British off and on through the 1780s for independent and neutral status. John Simcoe, the British governor of Upper Canada, had even preened to London about turning the Green Mountain state into a North American Switzerland.[21]

Other examples of loyalist districts later Federalist in their politics included the agricultural Delaware, Maryland, and Virginia sections of the flat, fertile Delmarva Peninsula. John Adams, Thomas McKean, Caesar Rodney, and others during the war agreed that Delaware was the state with the highest ratio of loyalists, and the state's principal historian of that period has estimated that half the population were loyalists, 30 percent patriots, and the rest hesitants or neutrals.[22] It was no coincidence, as we will see, that Tory-leaning Delaware proved to be the most Federalist of states—the one non-Yankee jurisdiction that exceeded New England in its adherence.

Federalism on the eastern shore of Maryland also overlay areas of wartime Tory strength, and the two Virginia counties on the Delmarva Peninsula were sometimes Federalist. A more pointed example came in New Jersey, where Federalist strength persisted even after the War of 1812 in the two sections of the state most inclined to Toryism or neutralism in 1775–1783: the southern Quaker counties near Philadelphia and three northern counties with substantial Dutch populations (Bergen, Somerset, and Middlesex).[23] The close relationship between Federalism and wartime neutralism and Toryism became evident in Pennsylvania, too, as test act restrictions on voting were lifted in the 1780s. As the groups who had refused to take what was a very strict, even extreme wartime loyalty oath—Quakers, Anglicans, Lutherans, and Sectarians (Mennonites, Amish, Dunkers, Moravians, and Schwenkfelders)—streamed back into the late 1780s electorate, the conservative political faction that would be labeled Federalist started winning elections. The Scotch-Irish and German Reformed stalwarts of the Revolution, who had designed the test acts, were angry losers.[24]

Wartime loyalism or neutrality and British-occupation patterns also go a long way to explain the lesser spottings of Federalism in the South. Commerce alone would largely explain the Federalist politics of Charleston, but the occasional Federalism of backcountry South Carolina around Ninety-Six, Orangeburg, and the Dutch Fork presumably reflected wartime Toryism. In North Carolina, the principal backcountry Tory stronghold—the Scottish Highlander settlements of the Upper Cape Fear Valley—reemerged as the principal backcountry Federalist stronghold. In 1800, hundreds of Scots, led by pipers, paraded through Fayetteville on the party's behalf, causing the "Jacobins" (Jeffersonians) to take to their heels.[25]

No one doubts the all-powerful impact of the 1861–1865 war on subsequent U.S. voting patterns, whether in Maine or Mississippi. Wartime loyalties in the de facto civil war of 1775–1783 are equally logical major determinants of the politics of the 1780s and 1790s. In the last areas vacated by the British army—greater New York City (1783), part of eastern North Carolina (1782), Charleston and the South Carolina low country (1783), and the city and environs of Savannah (1783)—confiscations, amercements, test acts, and other loyalty-related issues burned fiercely for several years. Besides upper-income and commercial adherents, a further overlay of election support for Federalism would have come from wartime neutrals and Tories well aware that Federalists were the principal opponents of ongoing confiscations, penalties, or voting abridgements.

Scores of wartime loyalists did wind up serving in the legislatures of the new American states. Several found their way to Congress. Almost all seem to have been Federalists, although with no definitive tabulation, examples have to be gleaned from incidental mentions. As chapter 8 detailed, patriots from Ezra Stiles to

William Livingston decried the number of ex-Tories holding office. The loyalist and neutralist component of later Federalism is a neglected area of U.S. political history.

Federalism's Tory constituencies and pro-British leanings flared up as an issue in 1794 and 1795 during the controversy over how the Jay Treaty between the U.S. and Great Britain resolved problems left from the peace treaty twelve years earlier. A large number of voters in the United States, angered by simultaneous British provocations at sea, seem to have seen the treaty as too favorable to the British, and hostile demonstrations occurred in a number of U.S. cities.[26]

In the early years of the nineteenth century, as Federalism shrank back into New England and wartime loyalist strongholds, its intensifying opposition to another war with England enabled the party to increase its support from peace-minded Quakers and Germans.[27] After the War of 1812, however, the sweeping popular verdict outside New England in support of the war gave the politics of patriotism an anti-British cast, and left the Federalists associated with defeatism and perceptions of near treason. The Jeffersonians wound up presiding over a decade of virtual one-party rule.

Not surprisingly, the War of 1812 added new layers of Anglophobia to what already existed from the Revolution. This bitterness reflected the Indian atrocities in the West, the mistreatment of some twenty thousand Americans, mostly privateersmen, held in British prisons, and the wartime British depredations in the Chesapeake. William Henry Harrison, whose own military victories were on the buckskin frontier, dwelt on the "horrible species of warfare" practiced by British Indians. "Ages yet to come," he told one British officer, "will feel the effects of the deep-rooted hatred and enmity which (this warfare) must produce between the two nations."[28] It was an exaggeration, but an understandable one.

The Wartime Generations of U.S. Politics

Wars in the United States have had their own presidential generations.* The first five U.S. chief executives were prominently associ-

---

*This has not been true in Britain, despite the limited parallel in the quarter century after Waterloo when the Duke of Wellington served as prime minister from 1828 to 1830.

ated with the Revolution, although in James Monroe's case only as a young officer (an eighteen-year-old lieutenant wounded at the battle of Trenton, who thereafter rose to lieutenant colonel). Not until its sixth chief executive, John Quincy Adams, born in 1767 and elected in 1824, did the U.S. have a president too young to have been involved in the War for Independence.

Of the next three presidents, two—Andrew Jackson and William Henry Harrison—were among the most famous generals of the second British war. Jackson thrashed the Creek Indians at the Horseshoe Bend of the Tallapoosa River in Alabama in 1814, thereafter winning the most famous of his victories by beating the British at Chalmette, outside New Orleans. Harrison, in turn, took his political nickname—Old Tippecanoe—from the victory he won in 1811 over the British-incited Shawnee on the banks of the Wabash River in the Indiana Territory. Two years later, he defeated the British and Indians at the battle of the Thames in Canada. Van Buren, who came between Jackson and Harrison, spent the war politicking in New York. However, his vice president, Richard Mentor Johnson, had commanded the Kentucky Mounted Rifles, the troops that killed Tecumseh, the Shawnee chief, at the battle of the Thames and supposedly made razor strops out of his skin. So it is fair to call Jackson, Van Buren, and Harrison the War of 1812 generation.

If this war fatally embarrassed Federalism, its inflated symbolism was the making of a full generation of Jackson Democrats and Whigs. The Battle of the Thames became a second Bunker Hill of sorts, helping to create one president, one vice-president, three governors, three lieutenant governors, four U.S. senators, twenty congressmen, and a host of lesser officials.[29]

Even the Mexican War (1846–1847) empowered its own brief political generation. General Zachary Taylor, elected president as a Whig in 1848, had earned his nomination defeating the Mexicans in the battles of Palo Alto and Resaca de la Palma in 1846, before finally shellacking Santa Ana, Mexico's president, at the Battle of Buena Vista in 1847. The next elected president, Democrat Franklin Pierce, rose to brigadier general in Mexico, ironically serving under the very general, Winfield Scott, whom he would beat as the Whig nominee in 1852. The next president, James

Buchanan, was a political warhorse who had been secretary of state during the Mexican War. However, his vice-president, John C. Breckinridge, who would go on to be the presidential nominee of the southern Democrats in 1860, served below the Rio Grande as a major of Kentucky volunteers.

The opposition to the war by so many Whigs, especially in Greater New England, is one reason given for the party's collapse in the early 1850s. But at best that is a partial truth. The Whigs tried to cloak their wartime criticism by nominating victorious Mexican War generals in two straight presidential elections—Taylor in 1848, Scott in 1852—and Taylor, at least, put Whiggery in the White House. What the Mexican War *did* spotlight about Whig vulnerability was fourfold: the party's national attempt to straddle the slavery issue, its anti-expansionism, its opportunism, and its need to nominate successful generals to pretend to be something it was not. By 1852–1853, these weaknesses were becoming fatal.

The Civil War itself—in pounding the fault lines between Yankees and Southerners, Puritans and cavaliers—reintensified one of the strongest ongoing cultural divisions of the eighteenth- and nineteenth-century United States. The three cousins' wars also kept touching a central split within British society: Anglicans versus dissenters. These two political cleavages have been among the most sensitive on each side of the Atlantic. So powerful was the partisan split painted on the map by the U.S. Civil War that it remained vivid in 1936, seventy-one years after Appomattox, and only began to fade during the 1948–1964 period.

Civil War Loyalties: Tories and Patriots Revisited?

The duration and intensity of Civil War alignments and partisan loyalties almost certainly reflect how they tapped some of the same powerful cultural dislikes and polarizations important in the American Revolution. In places, grudges were piled on grudges. In the early years of the war, southern politicians and military officers frequently used the term "Tory" to describe dissidents in the new Confederate states who favored the old Union. The partial resemblance to the actual demographics of 1775–1783, while erratic, is also fascinating.

In New England, where the core of the Civil War was Yankee and Congregationalist, the (relative) soft spots of Republican voting and Union support bore some relation to the populations that had doubted or sidestepped the revolution three-quarters of a century earlier. These included quite a few rich merchants; part of upper-bracket Episcopal Boston, Newport, New Haven, and southwestern Connecticut; and a fair percentage of backcountry Baptist districts. Irish Catholics, naturalized in increasingly larger numbers in the years prior to 1860, provided a new population among the oldest suspicions of the "Puritans."

The middle states of New York, New Jersey, and Pennsylvania also repeated some of their internal divisions of the Revolutionary era. Some of those unenthusiastic about the New Englanders' war agitation in 1775 were dubious again in 1860 and 1861: Episcopalians, German Lutherans, the prosperous Dutch farmers of the Hudson Valley and New York City hinterland, and the northeastern Pennsylvania backwoodsmen and mountaineers rubbed wrong by expanding Yankee settlements. One analysis of New Jersey in the Civil War describes divided loyalties among factions in the Dutch Reformed Church not unlike the animosities so powerful among the Hackensack Valley Dutch in 1775–1783.[30] The geography of Dutch Copperheadism, in short, bore considerable resemblance to the earlier geography of Toryism.

Bergen County was a citadel both times. And in the northwest, New Jersey's Tory Moody gang that raided around Sussex County in the late 1770s also had its later Copperhead parallels on the Pennsylvania side of the Delaware River in Pike County and in the upper Susquehanna "Fishing Creek Confederacy." In this latter case, a thousand federal troops marched in 1864 to attack a fortified pro-Confederate mountaintop encampment that turned out not to exist.[31] The Episcopal discomfort with Republicanism and abolitionism circa 1860, documented in Connecticut, New York, Boston, Philadelphia, and Michigan, only partly parallels the Toryism of the 1770s, but it is another anti-Puritan reaction.[32]

Confederate officials, who enjoyed describing local Unionists as latter-day Tories, were pursuing a political point rather than a careful analogy. Even so, portions of the analogy work. The patriotic elites of Maryland, Virginia, and the Carolinas of 1775 and

1776 can be fairly described as Anglican plantation gentry whose greatest concentrations occurred in the tidewater and lowlands. To be sure, Tory ranks in the Revolutionary South included a High Church element among the Anglican plantation owners, but these were only a minority. In 1861–1865, the plantation elites were again the mainstays of Confederate sentiment.

What characteristics did many of the southern Tories of 1775–1783 and Unionists of 1861–1865 share? They largely came from the ranks of plantation-culture opponents or from cultural fringe groups. The Tories of the Revolution who were not Anglican, by way of quick review, came from a wide variation of outsider origins. In the Carolinas and Georgia, some were recently arrived Germans loyal to the House of Hanover, disinterested in the war, or both. Others were frontier drifters or refugees from the fighting (and conscription) near the coast. Still others were back-countrymen, ever at odds with the coastal gentry. In the late 1760s and early 1770s, as we have seen, considerable numbers of back-countrymen who participated in the Regulator movements in North and South Carolina subsequently declined to get involved in the gentry's war. A small minority supported the British. Several highland sections along the frontier were also known for Tory refugees or uprisings—the Peaks of Otter area of Bedford County, Virginia, and forks of the Yadkin region of North Carolina.

Another substantial group of loyalist districts of the 1770s fronted the coast from the Chesapeake south to the Outer Banks of North Carolina and the Sea Islands off South Carolina and Georgia. Toryism in such places had fed off trade, relationships to intermittent British occupation, the farmers' preference for selling produce for British gold, and the overawing impression made by naval guns and raiding parties. Finally, there were the southern cities and districts lengthily occupied and governed by the British, in particular Savannah, Charleston, Georgetown, and Wilmington. British authorities not only kept order but recruited militia and other loyalist military units.

A Confederate gazetteer of "Toryism" in early 1863, when the Confederacy was still optimistic about eventual victory, would have shown a considerable similarity. The plantation elites who dominated the Confederacy, like the Whig planters of 1775, commanded no great loyalty among the new nation's scattered ethnic peripheralists: the Mexicans of Texas's Rio Grande Valley, the French Cajuns of the Louisiana bayous, and the Germans of West Texas, New Orleans, Piedmont North Carolina, and the Shenandoah Valley of Virginia. The Germans, by and large, owned few slaves, disliked the war, and would have preferred to keep the Union—just as a large minority had also been leery of insurgency in 1775–1776.

Another nursery of Tories, 1861 vintage, lay in the poor sandhills, backcountry, and mountain districts of the South, where the slave economy was minor to nonexistent and the plantation elites were widely resented. Prominent locales ranged from Mitchell and Avery Counties, where the high peaks of North Carolina's Smoky Mountains poked into the clouds, to the "Free State of Winston" in upcountry Alabama and the "Free State of Jones," unreachable and unconquerable in the longleaf pineywoods and rattlesnake swamps of southern Mississippi. A full brigade was needed—and for unimportant Jones County, none could ever be spared. North Carolina, more than any other state, had backcountry counties, especially Randolph and Chatham in the Piedmont, that were cockpits of civil war, neighbor against neighbor, in *both* 1775–1782 and 1861–1865.[33]

Examination of these parallels suggests, tentatively at least, that civil war in the eighteenth- and nineteenth-century United States had a cultural geography and pathology that did not change as much as one might imagine. Ethnic, sectional, and denominational embroilments tapped ongoing animosities. Certain patterns would recur. Three or four prominent groups or factions set the allegiances and animosities in motion.

Military occupation was another powerful influence. By early 1863, the new confederation governed by Jefferson Davis had almost as high a ratio of its major towns in enemy hands as George Washington could have listed in 1780. The stars and stripes flew over ports like New Orleans (the biggest city below the Mason-Dixon line), Norfolk, and Portsmouth in Virginia, Galveston in Texas, Pensacola and Key West in Florida, New Bern and Beaufort in eastern North Carolina, and also the other Beaufort (pronounced *Byewfort*) in South Carolina. Interior cities under federal occupation included Baton Rouge, Little Rock, Fort Smith, Natchez, Vicksburg, Memphis, and Nashville. During the Revolution, once the British had effectively occupied a city, they could usually recruit loyalist troops. Ninety years later, so could the Yankees, whether it was in East Tennessee, coastal North Carolina, or New Orleans. This produced infuriated Confederate references to "Tory" troops—the Tory 1st Alabama, the Tory 3rd North Carolina, and so on.

Like the 1778–1782 fratricide in South Carolina, neighbor-versus-neighbor fighting produced some of the war's greatest cruelties. When Nathan Bedford Forrest, a former slave-trader turned southern cavalry general, captured Fort Pillow in his home state of Tennessee, in which the federal garrison included black Tennessee units and a white West Tennessee loyalist regiment, he executed two-thirds of the blacks and half of the whites—"the Tennessee Tories."[34] Confederate authorities were also livid, reminiscent of 1777, when the Federal 3rd North Carolina Mounted Infantry raided down from the mountains in the company of twenty-five Cherokee scouts—"Tory" epithets flew, even though the regiment wore regulation blue and flew U.S. flags.[35] Most of the other Cherokee were Confederate allies.

This is not simply a digression. The politics of loyalty, so intense that certain regional pathologies repeated, as did "Tory" terminology, was about to add another deep layer.

1861–1865 Wartime Embroidery on the Political Map

Any civil war that lasts four years creates enormous bitterness, which ensures its continuing acid effect on politics and elections. The U.S. wars of 1775–1783 and 1861–1865 also stirred an extraordinary array of ethnic and religious denominational enmities. Besides which, 1861–1865 memories gained additional staying power from the combination of bloodshed, far in excess of any previous English-speaking civil war, with economic penalization and prostration of the South arguably greater than what Prussia imposed on France in 1871 or France on Germany in 1919. Small wonder that such a war could shape U.S. electoral politics for virtually a century.

We have said that Lincoln's election painted the bulk of the canvas. That is true—but it did not paint all of it. The war added its own daubs and splotches of Yankee blue. A few were in the North—for example, in the far south of Illinois where Cairo, at the delta of the Ohio and Mississippi Rivers, became a major federal military base. Johnson, Pope, and Massac Counties, closer to Memphis than to Chicago, gave Lincoln less than a fifth of their vote for president in 1860. By 1864, fattened on greenbacks, graft, and contraband, they had a new presidential political loyalty: two-to-one Republican.

On the other hand, wartime events cost the Republicans support in Cass, Bates, and Vernon, the strip of Missouri counties just south of Kansas City. Local guerrilla activity was fierce enough to convince the federal military commander to issue General Order No. 11, clearing civilian inhabitants from their homes and forcing them to relocate elsewhere.[36] Resentment of wartime conscription also undercut Republican support, including declines in 1864 support for Lincoln in a considerable number of midwest German concentrations (as pp. 548–549 will discuss in more detail).

The soldier vote also made a big difference. By 1864, its loyalty was strong, and Lincoln was estimated to have received 78 percent support. With over a million men having worn Union blue, federal veterans quickly institutionalized as the Grand Army of the Republic; and supported by a network of other organizations including the National Tribune and Sons of Veterans Auxiliary, they remained a political force through the turn of the century.

Chapter 9 has discussed the Border state electoral patterns of Delaware, Maryland, West Virginia, Kentucky, and Missouri. From negligible backing in his first race, Lincoln won much stronger support in 1864, including solid victories in Maryland, West Virginia, and Missouri. However, this required the help of federal military occupying forces and the massive disqualification of Confederate sympathizers. The latter was achieved in most Border states—Maryland, West Virginia, and Missouri, in particular—by more of the test or loyalty acts so familiar from the seventeenth century and the years during and after the War for American Independence. Missouri's postwar "rebel disenfranchisement" constitutional clause required a would-be voter to swear to not having committed any one of eighty-six different acts of supposed disloyalty to the state or the Union. In Maryland, conservative Democrats were able to regain control and eliminate the test act in 1867, but the restrictions in West Virginia remained in place until 1870.[37] In Delaware, Republican supremacy was confined to a few years after the Fifteenth Amendment gave blacks the vote but before their participation was curbed by a Democratic registration law.

Elements of the wartime pattern persisted through 1872. However, from 1876 to 1892 the Republicans failed to carry the five states in any presidential election. Still, the postwar alignment made the Republican Party competitive where it had been impotent in 1860. Substantial support among four groups added up to give the Republicans 35 to 40 percent support in a typical election—the Germans (especially in Baltimore, Ohio River Kentucky, and the area around St. Louis), mountaineers, the old Whigs who remained Unionists, and black freedmen. The war forged a coalition at most dimly outlined in prewar election returns.

No such long-term benefit accrued in most of the former eleven Confederate states. While the votes of ex-slaves gave the party a 25 to 40 percent base for a decade or so, their importance declined in the 1880s and 1890s as the Democratic Party embraced poll taxes, literacy tests, and disenfranchisement. The three southern states where the Republicans remained competitive in presidential races, at least on occasion, were Virginia, North Carolina, and Tennessee, which had the most white Republicanism, mountain and piedmont, left from the Civil War era.

Unfortunately, no political gazetteer of the Confederacy has ever been assembled to describe each county's presidential vote in 1860, its stand on secession in 1860–1861, its slave data, local battles, skirmishes and uprisings during the 1861–1865 period, the local contribution of soldiers to the Confederacy and the Union, draft riots and resistance, casualties during the war, periods of occupation by troops of each side, citizen experience during Reconstruction, black and white electorates from 1866 to 1876, and presidential votes (as applicable) from 1868 to 1876. Lacking such detail, attempts to categorize the county-by-county impact of the war on subsequent elections involve many assumptions as well as facts.

That having been said, let us begin with the politics of military service: Confederate versus Yankee. By the 1920s and 1930s, when the top Democratic states in U.S. presidential elections were still the secessionist pacesetters from the winter of 1860–1861, the percentage of white southerners who cast ballots for Republican presidents was in the 15–18 percent range.* This level, ironically, is not too far above the 10–11 percent ratio of white southern males whose military service was in federal blue rather than Confederate gray.[38] Indeed, had North Carolinians and Texans remote and cut off from areas under federal control been freer to choose sides, the ratio of southern whites serving in the federal military might have been closer to 15 percent. Of the three principal states of the Upper South (Virginia, Tennessee, and North Carolina), the first two each contributed some 25,000–35,000 troops to the federal army. By contrast, North Carolina is credited with only 4,000, half in eastern coastal counties under federal occupation.[39] If its men had been as able to reach federal forces as Virginians and Tennesseans were, the piedmont and mountainous west of North Carolina would probably have produced 20,000–25,000 Union troops, an enlistment more in keeping with its postwar Republican ballots.

The impact of the Civil War and Reconstruction on southern elections, then, was to solidify a large majority of white voters dedicated to the Democratic Party as the instrument of racial supremacy and wartime Confederate memory. Ex-slaves were disenfranchised as quickly as possible, although less so in the Upper South, especially where a few black voters wouldn't matter. Even many whites who had taken the federal side shared local unhappiness over Reconstruction and black equality and moved back to the Democrats. Most of the whites willing to remain Republican after the 1870s lived in piedmont and upcountry districts where

---

*This excludes 1928, the year in which the Democratic nominee for president was the Catholic governor of New York, Alfred E. Smith. The result, predictably, was a very abnormal level of Republican support in the South. The two decades' other presidential elections were more normal.

ex-slaves were relatively few and where Reconstruction would have been mild. The vengeance of ex-Confederates on southern "Tories," another persistent practice of the late 1860s and 1870s, would also have kept wartime Unionist loyalties alive.

In short, most of the southern counties in which at least 25 to 30 percent of white voters cast Republican ballots during the first four decades of the twentieth century reflected one of these previous war-related circumstances: minimal dependence on slavery, opposition to secession, prickly relations with Confederate authorities, significant local enlistment with the federal armies, some occupation by the federal forces, or post-1865 difficulties with ex-Confederates, Klansmen, and others whose practices renewed old enmities. The southern counties that were at least 25 percent Republican in 1936, three generations later, were still little more than a portrait of wartime service done in northern blue or pro-Union sentiments that still dominated seven decades later.

This is not to say that blue-gray issues were all that mattered, or that politics in the North and South alike consisted of little more than a multidecade Gettysburg reenactment. Although the Civil War framework continued, even in the North, the issues that swept across it often involved economic protest: the agrarian Granger and Greenback movements of the 1870s; the Populist upheaval of the 1890s; the Progressive movement of the years before World War I; and the LaFollette insurgency of the 1920s, which tried to combine farm and labor dissent.

As the complaints of the Granger, Greenback, and Populist movements cumulated, they finally cost the Republicans a slew of plains and mountain states' electoral votes in 1892 and 1896. The hemorrhage of 1896, in fact, was staunched in pivotal midwestern states, though barely, by a tourniquet of Civil War nostalgia—a last round of "waving the bloody shirt"—wrapped in an unprecedentedly expensive and broad campaign of nationalism and symbolic use of the flag. William McKinley, the Republican presidential nominee, all but pinned his campaign buttons on the stars and stripes. Civil War veterans known as "patriotic heroes" toured the critical states with bugles and cannon mounted on a flatcar.[40]

Another disruption came in 1912, when ex-President Theodore Roosevelt mounted his Progressive or "Bull Moose" crusade, which dismissed the Republicans of President William Howard Taft as creatures of corporations and laissez-faire. This split the Republican coalition and put Woodrow Wilson and the Democrats in the White House for two terms. Twelve years later, progressive Republican senator Robert LaFollette's independent presidential campaign roared through the mid-twenties Midwest, winning Wisconsin, and coming close in Minnesota, Montana, and North Dakota. This, too, also previewed many of the issues and alignments that would develop under the New Deal in the 1930s, when economic indictments finally crumbled the Republican Civil War edge. However, even the New Deal era, as we have seen, reiterated the basic poles of sectionalism that had emerged in 1860.

Politicians on *both* sides worked hard to keep memories alive. From 1868 to 1896, the major party presidential candidacies drew upon the Civil War as baldly as the earlier parties had drawn on the great names of 1776, the heroes of 1812, and the conquerors of Santa Ana. The successful GOP nominee of 1868 and 1872, who would enjoy much less respect as president, was the commanding general of the million-man army of 1865: Ulysses S. Grant himself. The Republican standard-bearers of the next quarter century—all save the unsuccessful James G. Blaine of Maine in 1884—came from the swing states of Ohio or Indiana and held the following highest rank in the Union Army: Rutherford B. Hayes (1876), brevet major general of Volunteers; James A. Garfield (1880), major general of Volunteers; Benjamin Harrison (1888 and 1892), brevet brigadier general; and William McKinley (1896), brevet major of Volunteers.

The Democrats, who had not always distinguished themselves in wartime councils, imitated the Whigs' device for circumventing earlier lukewarmness toward the Mexican War. Twice the party nominated a well-known Civil War general for president: in 1864, George B. McClellan; and in 1880, Major General Winfield Scott Hancock, whose service record was further enhanced by a wound received in the front line at Gettysburg. Even James Weaver of Iowa, the Populist presidential nominee who received 8 percent of the national vote in 1892, had been a federal brigadier general.

Many midwest farmers who had been told to vote as they had shot were happy to do so: for populism, free silver, and faded Union blue.

This North-South division supplanted the anti-British, anti-Tory ethnocultural politics that had been so important for two generations after 1783. The great political imprints of the two wars should now be established. But another ethnocultural division, while already mentioned in earlier chapters, was already gaining importance for the Anglo-America of the twentieth century in ways that now require their own careful examination and amplification.

Irish and German Antiwar Politics

In addition to economic discontent, the second major blow that staggered the Civil War party system came during the twentieth century from a new set of combat-related events: the internal divisions caused by World War I and then by World War II, with a related echo in 1952 from an isolationist response to both the Cold War with the Soviet Union and the hot war with Korea and China. These wars turned loyalty politics ethnic—German and Irish, in particular.

In the United Kingdom, the era of the First World War realigned national politics. In the postwar United States, however, reaction to the war produced only a disillusionment in foreign policy: an isolationist triumph. In party patterns, this was compatible with a return to the basic post-1896 party cycle of nationalist Republicanism. The usual interpretation of World War II—that the German-Irish backlash in the elections from 1936 to 1952 represented a less powerful isolationism than the frenzy of 1920—is half true and half misleading. In *policy* terms, World War II internationalism did prevail over isolationism whereas it had lost two decades earlier. In the longer-term *electoral* scheme of things, however, the Democrats were significantly hurt by several war-related tides. The losses among Germans, in particular, but also among Irish and Italians, would be a secondary factor in dismantling the 1932–1968 Democratic majority presidential coalition.

Wars, as we have seen, have often threatened to overheat the American melting pot. Benjamin Franklin had worried in the

1750s about the number of Germans flooding into Pennsylvania. On the brink of war in 1754, Canadian officials and advisers to King Louis XV wondered along kindred lines: Could France disrupt Britain in the fight for western Pennsylvania and the Ohio Valley by stirring up German and Irish unrest in Pennsylvania and Maryland? Some of Germany's princes had been allies of the French during the prior seven decades of war with England. As for Irish Catholics, during the several French wars they had rebelled in several Caribbean islands and would do so again in Newfoundland when a French fleet stood offshore in 1760.

Several provinces took the possibility seriously. With New York and Pennsylvania being open to attack from Canada, both colonies acted. Catholics were disarmed, barred from the militia, burdened with added taxes, and kept under surveillance. In Pennsylvania, the assembly forbade Catholic settlement in a projected western colony planned to offset French influence on the frontier.[41] In Maryland, which had the mainland's largest Catholic population, officials went into a tizzy. The House of Delegates, accusing local Catholics and Jesuits of collaborating with the French, passed bills to prohibit Roman Catholics from owning weapons or serving in the militia. Incoming Irish Catholic servants were already taxed, but it was proposed to sharply increase the levy and apply it to all Catholic immigrants.[42] These hasty and hardly justifiable actions were an early sign of what would be a long-standing American pattern in wartime: suspicion of "hyphenate" loyalties.

Scholars who date the dilemmas faced by German-Americans and Irish-Americans only to 1916 and 1920 leave out a relevant earlier history: the religious politics of the seventeenth, eighteenth, and nineteenth centuries. From these, Irish Catholics learned to fear and hate English Protestants in general and Puritans in particular. Their wars were rarely Ireland's wars. Protestant Germans immigrating to England and America also brought bitter memories of European militarism, war, and devastation. To many, military service itself was an anathema. War itself, aggravated by the mobilization, conscription, and loyalty policies of 1754–1763, 1775–1783, and 1861–1865, rubbed nettle after nettle on these sensitivities. The following three subsections profile, separately, the circumstances of the Germans and the Irish, with an additional look at how their political dissent combined in the years leading up to both world wars.

St. Patrick's Battalions

Irish Catholics, as we have seen, had little loyalty to any English-speaking Protestant causes or armies during the eighteenth century. Two of the loyalist regiments the British organized after taking Philadelphia in 1777, the Roman Catholic Volunteers and the Volunteers of Ireland, were formed in part to hold Irish-born deserters from the rebel army and prisoners of war willing to switch sides. During the Mexican War, several hundred Irish emigrants deserted from the U.S. Army to join the Mexican army, in the famous San Patricio Battalion, fighting ferociously on behalf of their co-religionists at Churubusco and other way stations of the 1847 campaign for Mexico City.

In the U.S. Civil War, Irish Catholics fought on both sides. The huge majority of the recent arrivals from Ireland were in the urban North, where they disliked Yankees, ex–Know-Nothing Protestants, Republicans, abolitionists, blacks, and the National Conscription Act of March 1863—and not necessarily in that order. To be drafted into the army seemed bad enough, but the Irish were angrier at the idea of fighting to free slaves. Not only were blacks their principal rivals in the dock areas, labor gangs, and job queues, but northern free blacks were also exempt from the draft. With nearly 150 casualties, the Irish-dominated draft riots of July 1863 constituted the worst outbreaks of the war. But lesser eruptions, also largely Irish, broke out during that same period in Albany, Troy, and Boston.[43] Even as the famous Irish Brigade garnered commendations for horrendous losses at Fredericksburg, many Irish on both sides of the Atlantic voiced concern that Irish soldiers were being used as cannon fodder. Opinion in Ireland itself seems to have been pro-southern in 1862–1863 (as noted on p. 501).

Philadelphia's Irish were as ambivalent as those in New York. One wartime history of the city cites some Irishmen saying that if they had to fight, they'd rather fight for the Confederacy.[44] James McPherson, in his peerless war chronicle, noted that despite the attention to Irish-American and German-American soldiers in the U.S. Civil War, "the Irish were the most under-represented group in proportion to population, followed by German Catholics. Other immigrant groups enlisted in rough proportion to their share of the population."[45] Just as revealing, moreover, is the evidence that out of all captured Union soldiers, Confederate authorities regarded foreign-born Irish Catholics as the most likely to change loyalties and fight for the South, which several thousand did.[46] Their allegiance did not run deep, and getting out of death-ridden prison camps was a considerable incentive. Ironically, much the same thing had been true during the Revolution.

To Irish immigrants, the war and its need for soldiers were both opportunity and embitterment. The embitterment, obviously, was over being drafted to fight a war that southern and Copperhead opponents were calling "Puritan." Whatever the British practices in Ireland, they had not included military conscription. Soldiering for the Queen was voluntary. Not so, by 1862, in either the North or the South. While most of the anticonscription violence came in cities, the so-called Molly Maguires began their reign of terror in the anthracite coalfields of Pennsylvania's upper Schuylkill Valley about the time the first state-level draft procedures were set up. In October 1862, five hundred miners, mostly Irish-born, forcibly prevented a trainload of draftees from leaving Tremont and Pottsville.[47] For other Irish, however, service in the federal army was lucrative, much more so than taking the King's shilling in the British army during the Napoleonic Wars.

Conscription, with more loopholes than fangs, was actually a poor description of a system in which many draftees never served. Most of the new soldiers enlisted after mid-1863 were paid substitutes or bounty-seeking volunteers. By 1864, a clever bountyman could combine federal, state, and local enlistment payments into $1,000 or more—two to three times the average worker's annual wage in New York City. Thousands of Irish immigrants could and did enlist for bounties or to replace persons drafted in the North who had $300 or more to hire a substitute. Thousands more crossed the Atlantic for the opportunity: $1,000 was *4,000 shillings.*

Emigration from Ireland, thin in 1861–1862, tripled by 1864. The Irish were more pro-southern than pro-northern in sentiment, and unhappy with the reports of Irish casualties. Yet America's economic pull was strong, especially in the impoverished west of Galway and Connaught—Oliver Cromwell's alternative to hell in the civil war two centuries earlier. In addition to reporting employment opportunities at one to two dollars a day, young Irishmen wrote home about northern enlistment bounties of $700—more than ten years' wages for an Irish farm laborer—and many who joined sent a portion of their bounty back to mothers and wives. Hordes besieged U.S. consulates for passage money to enlist.[48] Thousands ultimately left bereaved widows and mothers, but the economy of post-famine Ireland received a major transfusion.

On the other hand, Irishmen in the United States were positioned to participate in another contest—the efforts of the Fenian Brotherhood, organized in 1858, which became the first North American–based movement for Irish freedom. Some emigrants came to the wartime United States simply for that reason: to get military training. One chronicle of the Irish emigration to America described the Fenian–Civil War interrelation this way:

> The Civil War freed many emigrants from financial concerns and provided a ready-made military framework for Fenian recruitment and training: over 150,000 Irish-Americans served in the Union armies, many in Irish-American companies easily converted into Fenian conventicles. At the war's end Fenianism had about 50,000 actual members, many of them trained soldiers, and hundreds of thousands of armed sympathizers.[49]

During the Civil War and its immediate aftermath, the Fenians raided Canada several times as part of their commitment to attacking Ireland's British occupiers. It is easy to imagine that for one-third to one-half of the Irish-born troops in the federal army, *this* was the preeminent cause. Service in federal blue, meanwhile, seems to have had little effect in turning Irish Catholics into Republicans. Fifty years later, just before the First World War, Irish Catholic America remained overwhelmingly Democratic in an anti-Yankee, anti-Calvinist way. And with no great military heritage in the United States, much of the patriotic focus was still fixed on support for Ireland and hostility to Britain.

The Colonial and Nineteenth-Century
Roots of German War Resentment

Pacifist sentiments among the German-Americans of 1917 often antedated the trauma of U.S. war with the Fatherland. Memories of how Germany, in particular the Rhineland, had been devastated by seventeenth-century wars weighed heavily on two important early and mid-eighteenth-century emigration streams: first, the refugees from the Rhenish Palatinate, with their hated memories of Louis XIV; second, members of the pietistic sects that shunned political and especially military participation—Mennonites, Amish, Moravians, Dunkers, and Schwenkfelders. In contrast to the Irish, who were war-minded but rarely committed to an English-speaking cause, the sects, in particular, were averse to wars and battlefields. They were drawn to Pennsylvania, where the Quaker Proprietary Party had similar views. Lutheran and Reformed "Church Germans," by no means all from the Rhineland, generally supported the Quaker regime in Pennsylvania until the 1760s. In several other provinces, they tried to live peacefully with the Indians—the Iroquois in New York's Mohawk Valley and the Shawnee in Virginia.

Ethnic historians have pointed to some pre-Revolutionary transformations—the increasing number of Pennsylvania Germans who sided with the more aggressive Scotch-Irish in the 1760s, as well as the recruitment of the famous Royal American Regiment during the Great French War from the German and Swiss districts of Maryland and Pennsylvania. South Carolina Germans formed a regiment in 1759 to fight in that colony's Indian wars. But even in the War for Independence, strands of German pacifism or noninvolvement were numerous. The behavior of the sects—mostly in Pennsylvania, but also in North Carolina—was especially overt. Their beliefs rejected war, in some cases grudging the power of governments, which is why, between 1717 and 1754, they had come to North America. The loyalty politics so familiar to English-speakers was alien to them.

Throughout the entire 1775–1783 war, the hinterland of Pennsylvania, in which the Plain People lived, was rebel-controlled, but most sect members refused to take oaths of support. As a contribution, however, the Moravians let towns like Bethlehem and Lititz be turned into hospitals, which they helped run and support—because of which, the Moravians also died by the score from illness and disease. The Anabaptists at the cloister in Ephrata cooperated with the new regime and took five hundred sick and wounded soldiers after the battle at Brandywine in 1777. Yet as two years lengthened into four and five, resentment built up over rebel demands for provisions and doubled or trebled taxes in lieu of military service. In some communities, this rekindled a preference for the British, for whose shelter the sects had been grateful as immigrants. Moreover, British wartime practices, also abusive, were many miles distant and thus unseen. The thrifty Germans were further soured by severe wartime inflation and the increasing worthlessness of the rebel state and continental currencies.

In 1780 and 1781, as we have seen, Pennsylvania Mennonites colluded with Philadelphia Quakers in helping British prisoners escape from prison camps in the Lancaster area and aiding their return to British lines (p. 218). The Dunkers, in turn, often leaned to the loyalist side, but were willing to give payments in lieu of taxes to rebel governments as long as they could observe a pretense that the contributions were to the poor and needy, not for munitions.[50]

Having come to the New World to escape intrusive governments and the tramp of unwelcome armies, many Church Germans, while doctrinally unbothered, also either resented the rebels or just wanted to be left alone. The famous tale of Lutheran minister Peter Muhlenberg shedding his clerical robes to stand before his Woodstock, Virginia, congregation in the uniform of a Continental army colonel—thereupon enlisting hundreds of them in his 8th Regiment—is only one part of a many-faceted story. In such Pennsylvania Church German strongholds as York and Northampton Counties, the lists of "nonassociators" in 1776 and 1777—persons who refused to take the test act oath of loyalty to the new government—were overwhelmingly German. In the "Little Pennsylvania" section of North Carolina south of Salisbury, the Rowan County Committee of Safety, mindful that the local Germans, during their midcentury migration, had been helped by the British government, did not press them for military service. Only in 1778 did the committee draw the line when residents in the Organ Church district signed a neutrality petition. That could be taken as opposition to public defense.[51]

The draft riots and antimilitary resentments of 1861–1865 reprised one of these eighteenth-century moods: the objections of a newly arrived German-speaking peasantry to military conscription they thought they had left behind in Oldenburg or Rhenish Prussia. The greatest anger seems to have been among Catholics, whose rural settlements were most likely to be transplanted Old World villages or farm districts, especially those in Wisconsin to which many south German Catholics had emigrated shortly before the war. They were also most likely to believe they were being treated unfairly. Wisconsin had to resort to a militia draft to fill its statewide quota for 1862, and the counties experiencing riots or other violence were recently settled and largely Catholic: Brown and Kewaunee (Belgian and Dutch), Washington and Milwaukee (German), and Ozaukee (Luxembourger and German). Rioters in Port Washington, the Ozaukee seat, stormed the courthouse, destroyed draft enrollment records, and beat loyal officials, obliging the governor to dispatch six hundred soldiers.[52] Lesser disturbances that year in Ohio and Indiana also included some German districts, Catholic and Protestant alike.

In mid-1863, after the National Conscription Act, further unrest occurred in German areas. But luckily, the draft was found to be unnecessary in Ohio, Indiana, and Illinois, three states where the portents for violence had been ominous. In New York City, though, the German immigrant population, after some initial gathering, drew back from prominent involvement in that city's July draft riots. There were, however, two sides to the story. By 1864, the draft in parts of the Midwest seems to have rested unfairly on the Germans. Professor Wood Gray's preeminent analysis of *The Hidden Civil War* in the Midwest notes that Democrats emphasized both the clumsiness of the draft and its conspicuous ethnic unfairness in the months leading up to the uncertain election of 1864.[53] A particularly pointed allegation appeared in a letter from a voter in Livingston County, Illinois, published by the pro-Democratic *Chicago Times* on October 4,

1864:

The draft is helping the Democratic ticket throughout this whole region. In the first place, the Germans are becoming very much excited, in Milwaukee there was scarcely any but Germans drafted. In St. Clair county, in this state, 700 Germans were drafted out of 900. In Woodford county about 100 Germans were drafted; about half the number drafted in Quincy. The Germans bear the brunt. The publication of the names in Chicago papers of drafted men in that city shows that almost every other man is a German. Why is this? It seems strange that, in a fair draft, nobody but Germans are called upon to do military duty. Is it because so many of them are turning Democrats and going for McClellan that they are drafted? . . . Very few of the Germans in Woodford County are responding. They have sold out their farms, their homes, the products of all their labor since immigrating to this county, including money brought by them from the old country. Thus they have realized a thousand dollars and purchased a substitute and are now homeless. These things are telling strongly against the Lincoln party . . .[54]

By election day, the draft had been more or less satisfactorily concluded. Northern military victories from Atlanta to the Shenandoah Valley helped by increasing popular belief that the war was almost over. Lincoln improved his 1860 margins in Illinois and Ohio, but his majority in Indiana shrank somewhat. At the county level, his biggest 1860–1864 declines were registered in many of the same areas most agitated by the draft—German and Butternut sections.

Like the military record of German settlers in the American Revolution, the German role in the U.S. Civil War had two faces. Each conflict had conspicuous German and German-American generals—Steuben, DeKalb, Herkimer, Muhlenberg, Heister, and Weedon during the 1775–1783 years, and a much longer northern list for 1861–1865 led by Rosecrans, Halleck, Sigel, Heintzelman, Schurz, Willich, Steinwehr, Wagner, Blenker, Kautz, Osterhaus, and Schimmelpfennig.

Of the senior officers actually born in Germany, many were Forty-Eighters, refugees from that year's failed republican revolution, to whom fighting and a New World cause also went hand in hand: Franz Sigel, who had been an officer in the Baden army and one of the leaders of Baden revolutionary forces fighting the Prussians in 1848; Carl Schurz, whose brief military service in Germany was as adjutant to the commander of Rastatt fortress; Louis Blenker, who had led the revolutionary forces of Hesse-Darmstadt against the Prussian occupation; August Willich, a Baden revolutionary; and many others.[55] Within the nonpolitical German immigrant community, however, some of the anger that bloomed so vividly in 1916 and 1920 and then again from 1936 to 1944 must have been abetted by memory of the conscription mismanagement, draft riots, and legitimate wartime resentments of the early 1860s. The process of Germans having to adjust to a civic-activist, loyalty-minded, and sometimes paranoid English-speaking political culture was often difficult.

The frustration among twentieth-century German-Americans brought on by two world wars has been captured best in a pair of books—to which we will return momentarily—by journalist Samuel Lubell. These were written in the 1950s, when wartime memories still smarted in heavily German counties like Stearns and Scott in Minnesota, Outagamie, Dodge, and Ozaukee in Wisconsin, Dubuque in Iowa, and Putnam and Mercer in Ohio, as well as others in Kansas and the Dakotas too new to have grudges from the Civil War era. Lubell's analyses also touch on the Irish, whose behavior was somewhat parallel even if the motivations differed.[56]

What his reconstructions of 1916 and 1940 miss, however, is that many of the same counties had been antiwar centers a half century earlier. The Mississippi River city of Dubuque could even have been called Copperhead. In states like Ohio, Indiana, Illinois, and Iowa, the several dozen counties in which Lincoln's ratios weakened between 1860 and 1864 were disproportionately Butternut and German. Many were specifically affected by war-related violence, draft disturbances, or conscription of the sort posed on the previous page. And however important German-American votes were to Lincoln in 1860, four years later in Indiana, Ohio, and to a lesser extent in Illinois, Germans were prominent in shifting against him.

In his home state, Lincoln's ratios shrank in the Illinois River Valley—not least in Woodford County, just mentioned, where the local Democratic vote surged. His support also weakened in the Teutonic counties and towns across the Mississippi from St. Louis. In Indiana, Lincoln's German losses came in the southern part of the state near Evansville and in the region centered on Fort Wayne. The German counties next door in northwest Ohio were another area where his support slipped, as were several of Ohio's Pennsylvania Dutch counties (for that matter, the anti-Lincoln trend also carried into the older German concentrations in Pennsylvania). Greater detail can be found in the endnotes. The import for the moment is simply one of backdrop. Many of the midwest locales that would show the greatest alienation from Democratic presidential nominees in 1916 and 1920 and from Franklin D. Roosevelt in 1940 had also been emphatic in reducing support for the Republican president three and a half years into the Civil War.[57] Their trauma was by no means new; neither was their acculturation process.

Ethnic War Resentment and Twentieth-Century Isolationism

Had election analysis been more advanced in 1916 and 1917, informed punditry on the political costs of U.S. war involvement might well have inhibited the Wilson administration. While the central Civil War–based frameworks of national politics were not affected—Yankee Republicanism and ex-Confederate fidelity to the Democrats—the collateral Democratic biases of Irish Catholics and Germans, bolstered by a different Civil War–related memory, were put at risk. Americans of German ancestry resented being forced to fight *their* European cousins. Irish Catholics seethed over aiding a Britain that was simultaneously throttling self-determination in Ireland.

In 1916, Woodrow Wilson had been generally believed when he promised the public that he would keep the United States out of war. Even so, German voters in several states fired small but significant warning shots in that year's election. Heavily German Catholic Stearns County, Minnesota, went Republican for the first time, narrowly costing Wilson the state. German counties also edged toward the Republicans in Iowa and Wisconsin.

Antiwar collaboration between the Irish and the Germans became significant between 1914 and 1916. Irish-German American
Leagues were organized around the country, and a Neutrality and
Peace Convention conjoining the representatives of German-
American and Irish-American groups called on President Wilson
to use all necessary force in protecting American commerce from
the British blockade. In 1915, the Germans even joined the Irish in
celebrating St. Patrick's Day, and subsequent joint celebrations
were held on the birthdays of Bismarck and Robert Emmett. Germans and Irish also made up most of the membership of the war
policy–linked American Truth Society.[58]

The next four years, however, led up to a political earthquake.
Once the United States declared war in 1917, its proponents,
echoing clumsy allied propaganda, tried to overcome popular reluctance with portraits of the evil Kaiser Wilhelm and barbaric
German soldiers, who were portrayed as Visigoths and Huns in
spiked helmets. Cultural anti-Germanism became a flood—German classes were canceled in high schools, Beethoven and
Brahms crossed out on concert programs, sauerkraut renamed
liberty cabbage, and children mocked for German names. Critics
of the war were arrested, especially if they had German accents.
German-language newspapers were shut down. Even well-known
historians vied to write tracts about "German Deviltries in Belgium." As Wilson's rhetoric heated, Americans were given a particularly unrealistic promise: that they were fighting "a war to
end all wars."

By 1919–1920, the actual results could not have been more different—a Communist revolution in Russia, Germany's prostration
and dismemberment, civil war in Ireland, and the familiar hag-
gling of European diplomacy. The furious "hyphenate" electorate
in the United States replied by devastating the Democratic Party,
which many of these voters had previously supported. The most
vengeful reaction came from the two large northern elements on
whom the Democratic Party was most dependent: Irish Catholics
and Germans. The trail of Gaelic political revenge can be followed—and has been—from the triple-decker houses of Boston to
Manhattan tenements and hardscrabble Irish farms in the cut-over
districts of northern Wisconsin.

The most vivid display of political fireworks came in the German Midwest. While Swedish Lutherans and Dutch Catholics might show a fifteen- or twenty-point swing, it is possible to find German counties—scores of them, in fact, between Ohio and the plains of Kansas and the Dakotas—where the Democratic share of the vote for president plummeted twenty-five to fifty points between 1916 and 1920. In Ohio, Indiana, Illinois, Iowa, Wisconsin, and Minnesota, counties like these, especially those with large Catholic populations, had been party mainstays. Nine German counties in Ohio, for example, had voted unbrokenly for Democratic presidents between 1836 and 1916.[59] Most showed substantial anti-Lincoln trends in the war election of 1864.[60] In 1920, seven of the nine voted for a Republican president for the first time.

Lubell has dwelt on the extreme volatility of the so-called Russian-Germans of the Great Plains—German farmers originally lured to Russia in the eighteenth century by Catherine the Great's promise of exemption from military conscription. When that promise was revoked a century later, many migrated to the United States, beginning in the 1890s. Their principal settlements—in Kansas, the Dakotas, and the Big Bend region of Washington State—have clung to the Germanism they maintained in Russia. This very ethnic intensity pushed them to the national extreme of anti-Democratic voting in 1920 and 1940. McIntosh County, North Dakota, produced Franklin Roosevelt's sharpest decline between 1936 and 1940—forty-eight percentage points.

Exotic as the Russian-Germans may be—their taste was for vodka, not pilsner—their vocation as wheat farmers led them to the prairie and electoral marginality. Midwestern Germans, by comparison, lived in pivotal states. For two decades, the election of 1920 was regarded as something of a fluke—a onetime flare-up of ethnic revulsion quickly lost in the subsequent presidential politics of Prohibition, anti-Catholicism (Al Smith), and the Great Depression. The resurgent ethnicity of 1936–1952 showed otherwise. The most important animosities, German and Irish, were anything but a fluke. Lubell, the electoral bloodhound, tracked them from World War I through the 1950s, finding war resentment an ongoing motivation. In 1924, for example, the highest support for the independent Progressive presidential candidacy of Senator Robert LaFollette of Wisconsin—his outspoken opposition to World War I was famous across the Midwest—did not come from Scandinavian progressives but from Germans anxious to cast another vote against their painful memories of 1916–1920.[61]

Further evidence came in 1936, when North Dakota congressman William Lemke, a Lutheran whose father had fought in the Prussian army in 1870, ran for president on the isolationist Liberty Party ballot line. He drew only 2 percent nationally, but took 5–13 percent in Wisconsin, Minnesota, and North Dakota. His support topped 10 percent in thirty-nine counties, twenty-eight of them German and twenty-one more than 50 percent Catholic, and he actually carried dozens of arch-German precincts in Ohio, Wisconsin, and Minnesota. In Boston, his citywide strength (8 percent) came mostly from Irish Catholics, who appear to have given him 15–20 percent of their local vote. The only two reasonably large cities where Lemke drew over 10 percent support—St. Paul (11 percent) and Dubuque (9 percent)—were heavily German and Irish Catholic.[62]

These between-the-wars grudge politics were also predictive. With Europe at war again in 1940, a substantial number of Germans and Irish, disbelieving Roosevelt's pledge not to intervene because of his pro-British diplomacy, again turned on the Democratic Party. Roosevelt was reelected, but this time he lost Kansas, Iowa, Nebraska, and the Dakotas, with what had come to be called the "isolationist vote" playing a major role. Such voters probably also made the difference in Indiana and Colorado. Figure 12.1 shows the German tide.

There is no need to revisit the map or to dissect how the same Ohio or Wisconsin county, over eighty years, soured on Lincoln's conscription, Wilson's war, and Roosevelt's pro-Allied diplomacy. What these interactions suggest is a larger political pathology: *World Wars I and II as a set of lesser cousins' wars,* traumatic in the German and Irish communities. Neither world war involved overt internal combat among English-speakers, unless civil war in Ireland circa 1916–1919 is counted. However, both great conflicts involved some internal violence, arrests, and prosecutions, and, arguably, a psychological equivalent of civil war for Americans of German and, to a lesser extent, Irish antecedents. Thus their powerful impact on

FIGURE 12.1   The Percentage Point Decline in the Roosevelt Share
of the Presidential Vote, 1936–1940

Number of Counties	Percentage-Point Decline	Number German*
20	35 or over	19
35	25–34	31
101	20–24	83

*Counties predominantly German in group with over 25-point decline;
counties with Germans as first or second strongest national origin in group
with 20–24-point decline.
Source: Lubell, *Future of American Politics*, pp. 133–134.

voting behavior. If most immigrants had not already been partially
assimilated, or if these wars had come a generation earlier, the outcome could have been more strained. The wartime alliances of
1917–1918 and 1941–1945 might never have been forged.

World Wars I and II:
Cousins' Wars for
German-Americans and Irish-Americans

Now we move to the crux: the testing of Irish and German assimilation in the two wars that made—rather than unmade—Anglo-
America. Assimilation won easily, although it might not have in
1890. Psychologies were torn, but rarely loyalties.

The troubled psychologies were understandable. Violence
against German and Irish immigrants had been at least a minor aspect of the Civil War. Troops were employed on a regimental scale
to put down Irish riots in New York City and German disorders in
Wisconsin. Both groups, inflamed by press reports, felt they were
being used as cannon fodder—and not without some justification.
Northern religious sensitivities undoubtedly added to wartime tension because, as we have seen, the Civil War was especially a Yankee, Puritan, Protestant cause led by the party heir to Whig and
Know-Nothing anti-Catholicism. With some exceptions, the Civil
War would not have made Irish and German Catholics feel like
full Americans. Just as often—perhaps more often—it would have
reinforced their hyphenate status and outsider self-perception.

Thus the provocation posed by two more wars fundamentally at odds with Old World loyalties. Neither future commitment of U.S. troops to Europe nor a wartime alliance with Britain—repressor of Ireland, foe of Germany—would have seemed possible as late as 1875 or 1880. Emigrants from Kildare or Cologne would have had no reason to expect either development. Lubell himself contended that both world wars were like civil wars to large parts of the U.S. population.[63] To be sure, most Americans, even those with battered homelands, were unaffected or strained only marginally. In 1940, for example, with Denmark and Norway occupied by Germany, the ethnicity of Danish- or Norwegian-Americans in Iowa was touched—some precincts showed a small shift to Roosevelt—but hardly traumatized.

Strongly Yankee coastal peripheries of New England, places where twentieth-century linguists still found traces of Devon or Cornish speech, showed a pro-Roosevelt, which is to say a pro-British, trend. So did Canadian-Americans, particularly in Maine. The South had a handful of heavily English coastal counties—also old-country speech-pattern sections in Virginia and the North Carolina Outer Banks—where the percentage of support for Franklin D. Roosevelt and his interventionist policies rose between 1936 and 1940.[64]

Yankee, Congregationalist, and Episcopal activism on behalf of Britain was itself considerable in both wars. During the First World War, one religious historian has noted how support for pro-war groups like the American Defense Society and the National Security League "flourished especially in the East among Americans of 'Anglo-Saxon' descent, and they won increasing support from clergy of the denominations with strong and clear British rootage—Presbyterians, Congregationalists, Methodists and, most outspokenly, Episcopalians." The Congregationalist minister at Henry Ward Beecher's old Plymouth Church in New York went so far as to call for "exterminating the German people . . . the sterilization of 10,000,000 German soldiers and the segregation of the women."[65]

Fortunately, ethnic vehemence was less severe in the early 1940s, condemnation concentrating on Adolf Hitler and the Nazis. The churches were also less mindless than in 1917–1918. But once again the warhawks—the pre–Pearl Harbor U.S. interventionists—concentrated among Americans of English descent, principally in the Northeast and Southeast.[66]

Assimilation held sway, but small wonder that the trauma of German communities and, to a lesser extent, Irish locales was a deep and lasting reaction. By Lubell's analysis, resentment over World War I might have dissipated if World War II hadn't come along twenty years later. The angers of the Second World War might have faded, in turn, if the rise of the Soviet Union, the descent of the Iron Curtain in Eastern Europe, and the fighting in Korea hadn't so quickly brought Communism to the fore. But old reactions came back into play, especially from 1949 to 1952, as many German, Irish, and to an extent Catholic voters concluded that the Soviet Union and Communism had been the principal enemies all along: We should not have fought Germany twice; those wars had paved the way for the Soviet emergence.[67]

The politics of indignation had continued to guide German-American voting in 1924 and 1936, even though the First World War was over, and the cumulative imprint of the two world wars carrying over into the Korean War elections of 1950 and 1952 helped to create a third wave of German-Irish support for the Republicans. Grassroots specialist Lubell, tracing his German and Irish counties, townships, and precincts like radioactive isotopes through the U.S. body politic, found 1952's victorious Republican presidential candidate Dwight Eisenhower to be the beneficiary of a tide that reached close to or even exceeded the highwater marks of 1920 and 1940. Of the 162 counties where Franklin Roosevelt dropped 20 percentage points or more, Eisenhower won 160. Of the 39 counties outside of North Dakota, where Lemke, the 1936 isolationist, won at least 10 percent of the vote, Eisenhower won 34, more than went Republican even in 1940–1944.[68] Four years later, Eisenhower generally kept and in some cases improved his 1952 German percentages. Of course, his name—German for "iron-hewer"—didn't hurt him. Yet, there was more to the growing Republican support pattern than onetime ethnic loyalty and temporary frustration.

By 1968, the Democrats had another unpopular war under way in Vietnam, and once again German sensitivities came into play, albeit in a reduced way. Across the Middle West, some of Republican presidential nominee Richard Nixon's largest improvements over his losing 1960 presidential race came in the German Catholic strongholds where wartime sensitivity now went back over a century. Lubell had seen the Democratic weakness among Germans and Irish beginning to undercut the New Deal coalition, and that process was further advanced by the late 1960s.* The strain of reaction to four wars begun by twentieth-century Democratic administrations had finally wiped out mid-nineteenth-century memories of Know-Nothings, temperance zealots, and discriminatory Yankee draft boards.

Indeed, realignment went a lot further than that. By 1984, in the peak presidential election of the later part of the Republican presidential cycle of 1968–1992, the German counties had displaced the Yankee bastions as the strongholds of midwest Republicanism. Lower-middle- and middle-class Irish districts in Boston and New York City showed some of the same pro-Republican transformation. Figure 12.2 shows the powerful reversal in the old nineteenth-century bellwether state of Ohio.

Can we call this century-long transformation a war-driven process? To a considerable extent, although in a different way than the stamp put upon U.S. voting patterns by blue-gray Civil War loyalties. In years like 1932, 1948, and 1960–1964, the German counties reverted to the old faith—if in some cases only partially. But the effects of so many negative cultural reactions kept building. The quiet consummation came with the extraordinary peacetime Republican support levels of 1984. The party could hardly have had a more appealing candidate for prospering midwest German-Americans than Ronald Reagan—Irish Catholic on his father's side, but nicknamed "Dutch"—raised in small-town Illinois and Iowa, an ex-Democrat, always a little distrustful of big banks and multinational corporations, a president who visited a German war cemetery and who called the Soviet Union the "Evil Empire" but who never drafted a single Cass County farmboy. In the once-Democratic German and Pennsylvania Dutch small

---

*These German trends were discussed in my own book, *The Emerging Republican Majority*, in 1969.

FIGURE 12.2   Republican Share of the Vote for President in Selected Ohio Counties, 1860–1984

	1860	1864	1920	1940	1952	1984
Yankee						
Geauga	80%	86%	77%	62%	68%	70%
Ashtabula	81	85	70	56	61	53
Medina	63	64	68	60	70	66
German						
Mercer	34	27	56	61	66	71
Putnam	40	39	52	71	69	78
Holmes						
(Pa. Dutch)	36	28	39	49	65	74

towns and farm districts, his drawing power was awesome. His three- and four-to-one sweeps in some of the German bellwether counties set Republican presidential records.

By any standard definitions of wartime, the effects of the major twentieth-century military conflicts on U.S. politics ended many years ago. The dead are long buried, the memories themselves dying. Yet if one ventures a different yardstick, hypothesizing the upheavals in the United States of the 1960s and early 1970s as a different kind of civil war—Washington itself had riots, and the army took up positions on Capitol Hill—fought amid a new stress-context of technology and culture, perhaps the old North-South animosity can be extended to the realignments of 1968–1972. The case has indeed been made.[69]

But such arguments aside, our chronicle of the rise of Anglo-America can now turn away from the direct subject matter of war and its alignments. Demographic and linguistic imperialism provide the other battlegrounds—victorious for the English-speaking peoples through the eighteenth, nineteenth, and twentieth centuries, uncertain for the twenty-first. It is these transformations to which we must turn. Without them, Anglo-America would have been much smaller and weaker. Gaelic might still be a major language in the British Isles and Greater Germany might have become the twentieth-century colossus of the West.

13

DEMOGRAPHIC IMPERIALISM

The Second Architecture of Anglo-American Hegemony

The struggle of pious Protestants to extend English religion and English civilization, first to the "dark corners" of England and Wales, then to Ireland and the highlands of Scotland, was a struggle to extend the values of London, and so to reinforce England's national security.

—Christopher Hill, *National Unification*, 1967

Nearly all of the growing preponderance of England within the United Kingdom can be explained by the decline in the population of Ireland. . . . had (it) grown in proportion to that of England, at the time of the 1916 insurrection against the Crown, it would have had about 12 million people. One third of all United Kingdom MPs would have been Irish.

—Richard Rose, *Governing Without Consensus*, 1971

Most of the peoples of Europe (besides the Germans) have at one time or another been exterminators. The French exterminated the Albigensians in the 13th Century and the Huguenots in the 17th; the Spanish exterminated the Moors; the English exterminated the North American Indians and attempted in the 17th Century to exterminate the Irish.

—A. J. P. Taylor, *The Course of German History*, 1946

To govern is to populate.

—Juan Bautista Alberdi, Argentine demographer, 1853

E MPIRES, IN THE END, rise or fall on population as well as war. In the year 1500, the English-speaking government in London had some 2 million subjects. By 1800, Scotland, Ireland, and Wales had been added and the population of Britain was now 16 million, with millions more in an empire that included a substantial part of India. The new English-speaking regime in the United States counted a population of 5.3 million. A century later, the population of Britain and Ireland was 41.4 million, with another 150 million in the rest of the empire. The United States held a further 76 million. After the nineteenth century, no other major Western power's linguistic bloc came close.

The Germans, by contrast, having chosen for centuries to look east into Slavic lands and only secondarily westward, had a nineteenth-century imprint spread too thin. Emigration from what would become Germany may have totaled nine hundred thousand in the eighteenth century, and less than 15 percent went to what is now the United States. Catholics, in particular, were not officially welcomed in the thirteen colonies, and most Catholic emigrants from Germany went east.[1] German expansion had been further handicapped by unification under Prussian auspices coming only in 1871. Little around the world was left to colonize. Both circumstances cost Germany strength in the upcoming wars for the domination of the twentieth century. Too much accumulated political, demographic, linguistic, and economic advantage favored the English-speaking peoples.

Anglo-America's usually favorable "God of Warr" was a principal shaper. So, however, was a factor so far only merely alluded to: *demographic imperialism*—the movement and redistribution of ethnic and religious groups among nations and alliances. Mankind's search for freedom has helped to spur immigration to tolerant lands. But at the other moral pole, few major nations have fully avoided temptations to ethnic or religious extermination. Professor Taylor is not the only historian to accuse the English of doing so in Ireland. And the stakes should not be underestimated: An England that had been stymied in or by seventeenth-century Ireland probably never would have come to dominate North America, with all that could have meant. This is what these pages will examine: how England, then Britain, and then the United States built the political, demographic, and linguistic imperium that reached across three centuries.

Anglo-America and the Winning of the West

The gradual "Winning of the West" between 1500 and 1900—the battleground in this case spanning Europe and North America—pivoted, as chapter 1 has argued, on England's gaining political, religious, and ethnic control of the British Isles, an undertaking completed during the eighteenth century. Establishment of English Protestant hegemony in North America, in turn, positioned the mainland colonies to become the principal receptacle for seventeenth-, eighteenth-, and early nineteenth-century emigrants from Protestant western Europe: English, Welsh, Scots, Ulster Irish, Germans, Dutch, French Huguenots, Swiss, Swedes, and Finns.

This gave the United States, still overwhelmingly Protestant, a population of 13 million people by 1830, the only large European national culture in the Western Hemisphere, as well as a gathering dominance of the Americas reflected in the grudging Old World acceptance of the Monroe Doctrine. Geographies, spellers, and school readers of the early nineteenth century all make the point: that the United States described itself as a Protestant nation.[2] Besides bolstering successful competition with Catholic Spanish and Portuguese America, this settlement pattern ultimately also shaped the independent United States around a relatively ecumenical political and religious culture able, in the mid- and late nineteenth-century explosion of European emigration, to attract—and in a generation or two assimilate—wave after wave of Catholic and Jewish emigrants from central, eastern, and southern Europe. For the contests of the twentieth century, this was a powerful preparation.

By 1914, German political geographers, looking at their war-shadowed maps of eastern Europe, could see millions of ethnic Germans beyond their own borders. Some were within the territory of their ally, the Austro-Hungarian Empire. Several million, however, were scattered under the jurisdiction of probable wartime foes: Russia, Rumania, and Serbia. Still another million or so were in South America—Argentina, Brazil, and Chile. The weightiest concentration of overseas German stock, however, was the nearly 15 million spread across what could be called *Mittel-Amerika*—the lost Germania of the New World, still significantly German-speaking, not entirely committed to assimilation, that stretched from central New York and eastern Pennsylvania west to the wheatfields of the Great Plains.

Across the entire United States of 1914, persons of German ancestry numbered about 20 million out of 100 million. In *Mittel-Amerika*, the ratio would have been higher—perhaps 30 percent of the population. Officials of the German Foreign Office would have had the data, probably mapped just as they had charted the Germanic contours of the Banat, Transylvania, or the borderlands of Slovenia and Alsace-Lorraine. Statistics for German immigrants in the United States, although not for persons of German stock or German speech, were readily available, county by county, in the census books for 1910. Map 13.1 on p. 565, which shows the principal concentrations in 1997 of the 58 million Americans (out of a total of 250 million) who listed German as their principal ancestry, would not have changed much from that of 1914. The New World Germania between the Delaware River and the Upper Missouri stretched roughly as far as the one in the Old World between the Niemen and the Rhine: eight hundred miles across.

The difference, of course, was that citizens in Bismarck, North Dakota, or the Over-the-Rhine section of Cincinnati pledged allegiance to English-speaking politicians. The impact of this ethno-linguistic transformation in the United States was massive. As Prussia's chancellor had grasped a generation earlier, North American settlement had irretrievably altered the European power balance. This, in a nutshell, was how the West—and the twentieth century—was won.

To paint its sweep requires transcending the narrow stereotype of the westward-moving U.S. frontier: the sagas of Daniel Boone, Lewis and Clark, Davy Crockett, and the rest in the adventure novels and Hollywood epics that begin with pioneers leaving Pennsylvania or Missouri in Conestoga wagons or taking flatboats down the Ohio River—or, in another interpretation, those that

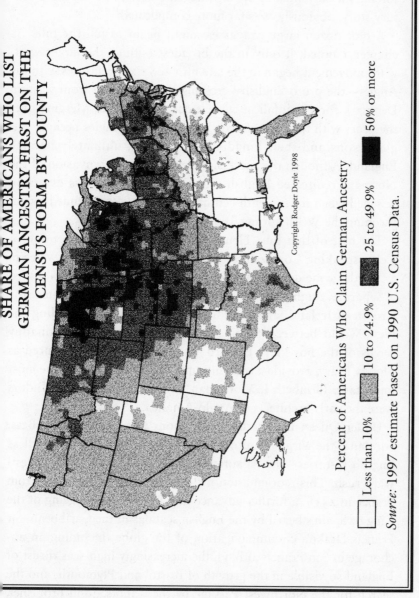

SHARE OF AMERICANS WHO LIST GERMAN ANCESTRY FIRST ON THE CENSUS FORM, BY COUNTY

Copyright Rodger Doyle 1998

Percent of Americans Who Claim German Ancestry

Less than 10% | 10 to 24.9% | 25 to 49.9% | 50% or more

Source: 1997 estimate based on 1990 U.S. Census Data.

Map 13.1

showed the West being won in the sixteenth- or seventeenth-century Caribbean by the sack of Cartageña or by English broadsides forcing the surrender of Spanish treasure fleets. The full three-century story, obviously, was far more complicated.

A half dozen large canvasses might begin to tell the tale. As chapter 1 noted, if only in the broadest outline, the larger westward movement began in the late fifth and sixth centuries with the Angles—the proto-English—crossing the North Sea from western Denmark for a landfall in current-day East Anglia. Merging over the years with their new Saxon neighbors, the Angles became Anglo-Saxons and their kingdom, Angle-land, ultimately became England. Although the successful eleventh-century invasion of the Normans redirected English attentions to France, this diversion lessened when the fifteenth-century War of the Roses ended by enthroning the Welsh-sprung Tudors.

The first of that line, Henry VII, completed the absorption of Celtic-speaking Cornwall. Henry VIII, his son, annexed Wales in 1536, the same decade in which he broke with Rome, established a separate, highly nationalistic English church, assumed the Crown of Ireland, and repudiated the Pope's edict dividing the New World between Spain and Portugal. The short, unhappy reigns of the boy-king, Edward VI, and his sister, caricatured as Bloody Mary, provide a brief intermission. But then came the most important: Elizabeth I. More than any other dynasty, the Tudors were the early architects of Anglo-America.

Under Queen Elizabeth—descriptions like Good Queen Bess, Gloriana, the Virgin Queen parade through American as well as English histories—the Atlanticization of England became a westward rush. This reorientation included the final withdrawal from France in 1558, a further advance into Ireland, the singeing of the King of Spain's beard by the English seadogs in the Caribbean, Sir Francis Drake's circumnavigation of the globe (including an anchorage in San Francisco Bay), the increasingly high-seas thrust of England so visible in the growth of Bristol and Plymouth, and the search for the Northwest Passage by the Cabots, John Frobisher, and Sir Humphrey Gilbert, which opened up Newfoundland.

Courtiers and advisers from the Welsh border and Wales, the country from which the Tudors themselves hailed, were important in convincing the Queen to look west, as well as in originating the idea of a *British* (not English) Empire. West Countrymen who had been prominent in colonizing Ireland—Gilbert, Walter Raleigh, and Richard Grenville—stretched their minds and ambitions across the Atlantic to Virginia. Finally, Elizabeth's decision to announce as her heir a cousin, James VI of Scotland, served to combine the two Crowns and to further accelerate the west-tilting unification of the British Isles.

Long before flatboats on the Ohio River, *this* movement was the beginning of the way west. Professor A. L. Rowse, in his book *The Elizabethans in America,* opined that "the discovery of America ultimately made the fortune of this island, transformed our situation in the world. . . . here was a very taut, efficient little society within an island lying athwart the main seaways from America to Northwestern Europe, a situation from which this country profited more and more. As America prospered and became important, so did we."[3] There is some exaggeration in these words, written in the years that followed World War II. Until the mid-eighteenth century, America's importance was more incipient than actual. Yet the proofs of Bismarck's thesis were already taking shape.

The first of the English settlements in what would become the United States—at Roanoke Island on the coast of North Carolina—had failed between 1587 and 1590. The aging Queen, however, gave Raleigh permission to name another colony after her: *Virginia.* This settlement, only begun in 1607, four years after her death, survived and for a decade or so gave its name to the entire coast. Captains Gosnald and Bartholomew Gilbert, navigating near Cape Cod and Martha's Vineyard in 1602, described that trip as sailing around north Virginia.[4] Captain John Smith, of the Puritan faction, called it New England in 1614, which stuck. The two great names of early Anglo-America were now in place.

The second tableau of Anglo-American emergence, which we have glimpsed in bits and pieces, should also be set out whole: the relentless interplay between war and imperial expansion. Each of the cousins' wars reaffirmed English-speaking expansionism and even millennialism: God's Protestant Kingdom had not only to be maintained but enlarged and made supreme. The last English war prior to

1640, the factional contest between the Houses of York and Lancaster from 1455 to 1485, had been a medieval affair and mostly English, save for the ties to Wales of the ultimate Tudor victor. The Civil War, a century and a half later, was arguably triggered by the rebellions of 1638–1640 in Scotland and 1641 in Ireland, setting out a widening scope. We cannot call the fighting of the mid-seventeenth century a full-fledged British civil war. Yet its confrontations included a major Scottish battle in Dunbar (1650) and a gorier series in Ireland: Drogheda (1649), Clonmel (1650), and a half dozen others. Minor encounters took place in Chesapeake Bay and Barbados. Even Boston had prepared to fight off Charles I.

The Puritans, by nature and faith, were arch-expansionists: first into Ulster, then to Massachusetts Bay and Connecticut, then to the Caribbean. In the mid-1640s, Puritans ejected from Cavalier Virginia established the town of Providence in next-door Maryland, opening a decade of off-and-on civil war with Catholic Marylanders. Cromwell's own expansion of the Royal Navy and the "Western Design" for an enlarged English presence in the New World produced an expedition against Hispaniola in 1654, which was unsuccessful, and another in 1655 that put Jamaica under the English flag. The Protector even broached a scheme in 1654 to settle English Surinam with Portuguese Jewish refugees from Brazil.[5]

Each of the three cousins' wars, moreover, generated its own westward migrations. Royalists fled Puritan England to take up lands in Cavalier Virginia, and the Restoration later pushed more dissenters to North America and hundreds if not thousands of malcontents to the Caribbean as pirates, where former Levellers and Ranters helped to harass Spain under the skull and crossbones. The American Revolution, even as it progressed, beckoned some of the politically uncomfortable westward, including the partly Tory families of Daniel Boone and his wife who preferred to fight the Shawnee in Kentucky. The wartime exodus was even greater during the 1861–1865 years, when men drifted overland to avoid the draft. In 1864, as the Confederate cause collapsed locally, tens of thousands of pro-southern Missourians took their wagons and families on the trail to Oregon. Mining camps from the Rockies to the high Sierras conjured up lesser migrations with pits and shafts named Jeff Davis or Bonnie Blue Flag.

In the American Revolution, as we have seen, early combat spread far beyond the thirteen colonies, exemplified by the rebels' prompt invasion of Canada in 1775. Within most of the thirteen colonies, the most militant expansionists—Yankees, Scotch-Irish Presbyterians, and Virginia planters—were also in the forefront of the Revolution. The coastal residents least interested in westward movement—Anglican lawyers, merchants, and clergy; Quakers; and long-established Dutch farmers—were especially likely to favor the Crown. The coming of peace in 1783 set its own expansionist agenda: States like Massachusetts, Connecticut, and Virginia were obliged to resolve their huge, but conflicting, western land claims. Usually they received grants in the new territories where old claims had been yielded. The wedges sliced into Ohio, to take just one example, included the Virginia Military Tract (for veterans), the Connecticut Western Reserve, and the Connecticut Firelands (for those burned out of homes along the Long Island Sound by British raids). So great was the emigration that Ohio, scarcely settled in 1790, had a population of 580,000 by 1820.

The American Civil War, itself a match between two rival designs for expansion, luckily avoided the further effect of British involvement. Even without the Royal Navy, conflict between English speakers was probably at its most global, ranging from the Bering Straits, off Siberia, where Confederate raiders sank much of the New England whaling fleet in 1865, and Cherbourg, France, scene of the great battle between the CSS *Alabama* and the USS *Kearsarge*, to the Yankee Canadian border town of St. Albans, Vermont, which Confederates briefly occupied after a cross-border raid. Pennsylvania, Maryland, and Virginia were only the vortex; the peripheries were global.

Peace brought its inevitable corollary: backed-up population pressure and a third wave of republican imperialism. The United States, at war's end, was thought to covet Cuba, Mexico, other portions of the West Indies, an isthmian canal route across Central America (or even Central America itself), all or part of Canada, Alaska, and the Hawaiian Islands. Secretary of State Seward was especially given to orating about any half-plausible annexation. Literary figures like Walt Whitman, James Russell Lowell, and

569

Herman Melville openly enthused over American empire. Even so, as this three-century wartime tableau ended in 1865, *internal* expansion took clear priority: westward filling-in within existing borders, rapid industrial growth, and absorption of the biggest immigrant wave to date: the almost 25 million Europeans who arrived from that continent and Canada in the half century between Appomattox and Sarajevo.

This quick trip through two museum rooms of Anglo-American expansion still leaves this chapter with four more to explore. We will begin with the attitudes and practices over three centuries by which England and its government made the British Isles inhospitable for Celts and Catholics, political troublemakers and felons, using them instead as the landfill of empire. Within the British Isles, this helped to secure an English—and generally conservative—ascendancy. The hamstringing of Ireland was the most important part of the story, but not the entirety.

The second panorama to be examined will be the eighteenth- and early nineteenth-century emergence of British North America as the political and European population center of the Western Hemisphere, originally ensured by attracting Protestants from many different parts of Europe. This was well under way before North America's later significance for the nineteenth- and twentieth-century European balance of power was understood.

The third watershed, from the 1840s to 1914, was when the United States added large numbers of Catholics and Jews, as well as Protestants from Germany, Scandinavia, and Britain. Despite many fears, this accomplishment left in place its Anglo-Saxon language and national identification. Here, then, as well as in the reach of the British Empire, is where a new English-speaking hegemony started to be defined.

Our fourth focus will be on the twentieth-century demographic and military resolution: the success of Anglo-America, already victorious over Spain and France, against Germany in two world wars. The Germans, in a sense, were the final losers of the cousins' wars, after the Irish, the black slaves and ex-slaves, and the Native Americans, although their defeat was of a different kind. Mid-nineteenth-century Britain had a vast empire and an independent North American cultural and linguistic outlier. Germany, on the other hand, was still mired in a unification stage that Britain and France had completed centuries earlier. The hopes of intellectuals and nationalists for new Germanias in eastern Europe and the Americas would come to naught. One can only surmise how different the industrial and military outcomes of the twentieth century could have been had the 25–30 million German-Americans of 1917 or 1941 still remained in Europe or had they controlled a German-flavored Upper Mississippi Valley Confederation created in an 1860s breakup of the previous United States. The deutschmark, not the pound sterling and then the dollar, could have been the lead currency of what would not have been the American Century. Tsingtao, not Hong Kong, might have become the financial center of the East Asian mainland.

The ethnic and immigration arena, in short, was almost as important as the military battlefields. For the English-speaking peoples, the rearrangements of global population, less widely studied, were just as successful.

The Subordination of Ireland and the Anglicization of the British Isles

A seventeenth- or early eighteenth-century England that had remained militarily and politically embroiled within the British Isles, facing an independent Ireland (and even a Scotland) allied with France or Spain probably would have been unable to turn westward to North America. It might even have been overwhelmed.

Secure English control of the British Isles, achieved by the pacification of the Scottish Highlands in 1746 and the defeat of the last French-aided Irish rebellion in 1798, can be too easily assumed during the twentieth century because of the lopsided population disparities: 48 million people in England, as opposed to 3 million in Wales, 5 million in Scotland, and 5 million in Ulster and the Irish Republic. That, however, was the finishing line. The seventeenth-century starting gate could not have been more different.

Englishmen of that era plausibly feared French and Spanish plots because the population of the British Isles in 1600 divided as follows: England—4 million; Wales—500,000; Scotland—1 million; Ireland—1.5 million. Within the British Isles as a whole, English-speakers would have been a none-too-large majority. As for religion, despite the Protestantism of Elizabeth I and her court, Catholics represented two-fifths of the combined population. Numbers must be guesswork, but the Catholic camp could have included 95 percent of the people in Ireland, 10–20 percent in Scotland (mostly in the north), 40–50 percent in Wales (mostly in the north), and perhaps a lingering 10–15 percent in England itself. Across the English Channel, the Counter-Reformation was reclaiming for Catholicism areas of the continent that Protestantism had earlier penetrated: Flanders, France, parts of Germany, and Bohemia. Enough Catholicism remained in the British Isles to encourage similar intervention and to explain Protestant nervousness.

Dismay among true-believing Protestants was a factor in the exodus of some eighty thousand Puritans between 1620 and 1640, representing about 2 percent of England's population. More than half crossed to New England, about a quarter to Holland, and some to the Ulster plantations. The English government, fearing the loss, had tried to restrain it, but for the most part unsuccessfully. As the revolutionary Parliamentary regime gained authority in the 1640s, Ireland and Irish Catholics were particularly singled out for retribution because of the massacre of 1641 and because of the several plans that had been made for an Irish Catholic Royalist army to descend on England. The danger was neither distant nor imaginary.

This is why assessments that England tried to exterminate the Irish during the seventeenth century have an element of truth. The first major wave of destruction under Lord Mountjoy in 1602–1607 and the second from 1649 to 1653 under Cromwell and his generals were estimated to have dropped Ireland's population from a million and a half at the beginning of the century to some nine hundred thousand. Tens of thousands more were deported to the West Indies. The third round came in the Williamite wars of the 1690s where excesses on both sides produced an Ulster landscape described by one French officer as "like traveling through the deserts of Arabia."[6]

By 1700, the population of Ireland was estimated at one to one and a half million—the same as a century earlier—despite a high fertility rate and a Protestant influx. But although just 14 percent of the land was still in Catholic hands, emigration among Catholics remained small, the common explanation being that Gaelic-speakers feared departure as exile and preferred to cling to archaic customs, to dependency, and to smallholdings subdivided into minute portions.[7] Nor did English suasion ever turn more than a small number of Native Irish to Protestantism. In consequence, despite the last considerable wave of Scottish, English, and Huguenot settlers following the Williamite victories of 1690–1691, the Protestant share of the Irish population peaked at 27 percent in 1715. Thereafter, as the Scotch-Irish became the principal emigrants to America, the Protestant ratio declined. The Welsh and Scottish transitions to Protestantism had been slow, too, yet both became solidly Protestant. But by 1750, English officials knew that any similar hope for Ireland was a pipe dream.

The strategic demography of the region, however, was already moving in England's favor. When Henry VIII had himself declared King of Ireland in 1541, that second largest of the British Isles was a little-developed country of no particular religious intensity, with about 1.25 million people.[8] This was almost half the English and Welsh population of 2.5 to 3 million people, hardly an unrecoverable lead. Yet Ireland wound up, by the mid-nineteenth century, as a supine, subordinate island reduced by famine, foreign occupation, and the legacy of earlier destruction. England soared on religious, military, and commercial wings, and by 1900, its population of 30 million was fully seven times that of Ireland. The sixteenth-century relationships of the British Isles, in a nutshell, had been crushed and rebuilt.

The geopolitics of the region had been altered just as significantly. Could an Ireland unbroken and free to develop have reached a population of 12–15 million and become a nineteenth-century political, religious, and economic competitor of England's? Would such a nation have stopped the future British Empire in the tracks of its home waters? No one can say. However, even the real-life Ireland of the seventeenth and eighteenth centuries, with its population of between 1.5 million and 4 million, but sometimes stirred by men ready to conspire with Spain and France, was believed in London to threaten the pro-English, pro-Protestant power balance in the British Isles. Indeed, in 1689, a prospering Ireland with 4 or 5 million people might have been a base for successful invasion of England.

This is why the lesser island was overwhelmed by the British, religiously coerced, industrially hobbled, and turned into a dependent agricultural plantation. The population that might have been Ireland's was sent away—in chains, in indentured servitude, or belowdecks in steerage. Dispersal, in the end, succeeded in breaking Ireland's Catholic numbers where compulsion and exile to Connaught had failed. Over a generation or two, the West Indies, Appalachia, the Hudson Valley, and the Carolinas made unchurched persons or vague Protestants out of the majority of Irish emigrants unable to find a Catholic church in Jamaica or the Blue Ridge Mountains or indisposed to try.

By the nineteenth century, Irish emigrants to the United States could remain communion-receiving Catholics. Yet the size and importance of the seventeenth- and eighteenth-century diaspora that arrived in North America directly or, in earlier years, indirectly through the West Indies can be gleaned from a few stark statistics. By 1990, Ireland (the Republic and Northern Ireland alike) counted only 5 million people to England's 48 million. These Irish numbers were scarcely above the 4.4 million of two centuries earlier. The United States alone had almost 40 million residents who reported Irish ancestry, as Map 13.2 illustrates. More than half of them, principally outside the cities in a broad arc from small-town Pennsylvania to Texas, were Protestants.

We have seen in chapter 5 how Scotch-Irish Protestants from Ulster accounted for 70 percent or so of eighteenth-century Irish emigration to the thirteen colonies and for an even lower ratio of those who had left Ireland or been transported to America in the seventeenth century. Among the remaining 30 percent, the considerable number of Native Irish and Catholics more or less disappeared. Except in Maryland and Pennsylvania by the 1750s and 1760s, the openly Irish Catholic population in the mainland colonies was negligible—overall, it did not exceed ten thousand. What the colonies included by the scores of thousands, of course, were people of Irish origins named Murphy or Barry who were lost to Catholicism. The faith of the Irish was looser in the eighteenth century, before the mid-nineteenth-century "devotional rev-

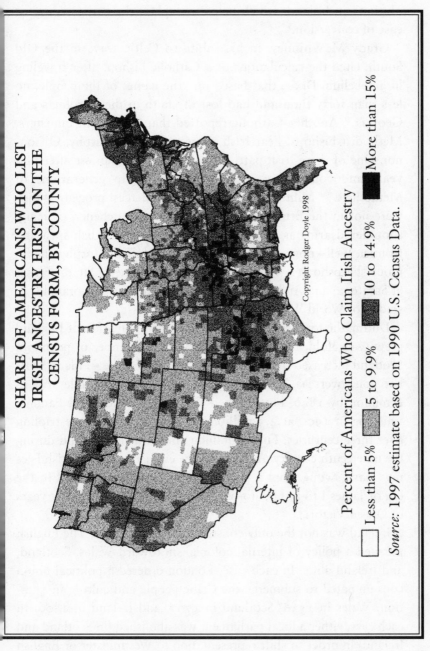

SHARE OF AMERICANS WHO LIST IRISH ANCESTRY FIRST ON THE CENSUS FORM, BY COUNTY

Copyright Rodger Doyle 1998

Percent of Americans Who Claim Irish Ancestry

☐ Less than 5% ▨ 5 to 9.9% ▦ 10 to 14.9% ■ More than 15%

Source: 1997 estimate based on 1990 U.S. Census Data.

Map 13.2

olution" in Ireland, which helps to explain the earlier laxity or ease of conversion.[9]

Grady McWhinney, in his salute to Celtic ways in the Old South, cited the calculations of a Catholic bishop, after traveling in antebellum Dixie, that based on "the names of the people, no less than forty thousand had lost the faith in the Carolinas and Georgia." Another Catholic reported that "Wesleyan ministers, Methodist bishops, bear Irish names—Healey, Murphy, O'Connor. One of these Irish patriarchs . . . did meet a priest after fifty years and could only present two grown-up generations of Methodists."[10] Militarily, many of Ireland's fiercest progeny, if they were not in the British army of Wellington, Kitchener, or Haig, shouldered arms as Protestants on America's English-speaking frontier. Well-known examples would include Tim Murphy, the famous sharpshooter who picked off British General Simon Fraser at Saratoga, and Audie Murphy of Texas, the most decorated U.S. soldier of World War II.

During the four centuries after 1600, the population of England grew twelvefold, that of Wales sixfold. The number of people in Scotland increased by a factor of only five, because so many Scots had gone overseas. The population of Ireland, meanwhile, rose to 8 million by 1840, but declined sharply after the Great Famine, finishing in 1900 at 4.5 million. The result was a mere tripling over three centuries. Fully 4 million emigrants left Ireland during the nineteenth century. As a result, the ethnicity of the British Isles may have swung from a potential English-Celtic standoff in the era of James I to a three-to-one English majority by the last years of Queen Victoria.

Ireland was not the only constrained Celtic culture. The English pursued a policy of internal colonialism toward Wales, Scotland, and Ireland alike. In each case, London ordered a political union consummated to submerge the Celtic people and culture in question: Wales in 1536, Scotland in 1707, and Ireland in 1800. In each case, either a local parliament was abolished (in Scotland and Ireland) in order to shift representation to Westminster or English law was simply imposed by statute, as with Wales.

What twentieth-century officials would call national security was usually part of the rationale: the Welsh preparing to assist Irish rebels in 1535, Ireland's own rebellion of 1798. Choking off economic rivalry was also a motivation, particularly in the case of Ireland. The latter had the beginnings of some industry in 1800—cotton textiles, in particular—but implementation of the Union in 1801 and thereafter allowed Lancashire to take the Irish clothing market while British capital steered Ireland away from industry toward agriculture and cattle-raising.[11] A century earlier, heavy-handed English import restrictions against Irish woollens, colored linen, and glassware had helped to spur Protestant emigration from Ulster to America. By the early nineteenth century, one-third of Ireland's agricultural produce went to the larger island next door, roughly the same percentage of Ireland's national income as was owed as rents and profits to absentee landowners residing in England.[12]

Even while the Great Famine of 1846–1849 caused Ireland's population to decline by one-quarter because of starvation, mortality, and emigration, greater than usual quantities of meat and produce were shipped to England. Nevertheless, the charge of genocide sometimes leveled again British policy-makers is excessive. Laissez-faire economics was too common during the nineteenth century to be transformed into abstract criminal responsibility. Callous neglect is a better description. Famine also spurred nineteenth-century emigrations to the United States from Germany and Scandinavia.

However, the English unmistakably regarded the Celtic-speaking peoples—the "mere Irish" especially, but also the Welsh and Scots of the Highlands—as biological inferiors. Even before the famine, Irish despondency and poverty were appalling. The Duke of Wellington, a native of County Meath, observed that "there never was a country in which poverty existed to the extent it exists in Ireland."[13] Charles Kingsley, a nineteenth-century Cambridge University historian, later chaplain to Queen Victoria, went so far in the 1840s as to describe the Irish as a biological subspecies: "I am haunted by the human chimpanzees I saw along that hundred miles of horrible country. I don't believe they are our fault. I believe that there are not only many more of them than of old, but they are happier, better fed and more comfortably fed and lodged under our rule than they ever were. But to see white chimpanzees is dreadful. If they were black, one would not feel it so much, but their skins, except where tanned by exposure, are as white as ours."[14] Kingsley, not surprisingly, was criticized for such statements.

Such was the English schizophrenia: on one hand, likening the Irish to chimpanzees, but on the other, regarding them as a political and economic threat. Even with only Protestants voting for the Irish Parliament in the 1790s, London still found the legislature's independence unacceptable. In the words of one official memo to Prime Minister William Pitt, elimination of the Dublin Parliament and submergence of Irish representation as a minority in Britain's Parliament through the Union "is the only answer to preventing Ireland becoming too great and powerful."[15]

For nineteenth-century England, keeping the Irish away from French and Spanish alliances was slowly replaced by a practical need to minimize the number of Parliamentary districts that might send Catholic nationalists to Westminster. As political scientists have pointed out, England, with 53 percent of the population of the British Isles in the early nineteenth century, enjoyed 74 percent of the seats in the pre-Reform House of Commons while Ireland had just 15 percent. Even after Catholic emancipation in 1829 and the first Reform Act in 1832, voting in public (rather than by secret ballot) and intimidation of Catholics made it possible to keep many Irish seats "loyal" and Protestant. Only in the later nineteenth century did the Reform Acts of 1867 and 1884 enlarge the electorate so that Catholics and nationalists carried the bulk of the Irish districts.

By this stage, however, emigration had shrunk the Irish count to just 10.8 percent of the nationwide population of 1901—down, we must remember, from fully 32.2 percent a century earlier. This kept the number of Irish MPs low enough to be dealt with in Westminster. British political scientist Richard Rose, who has tabulated these numbers, points out that had the Irish population grown in proportion to England's, then by the 1910–1914 period fully one-third of United Kingdom MPs would have been Irish, greatly complicating national governance.[16]

A parliament with this ratio of Irish Catholic and Nationalist MPs could have played havoc with British domestic politics, imperial emergence, and early twentieth-century diplomacy. Relations with the United States would have been affected, too, although fewer Irish emigrants to New York and Massachusetts would have left U.S. politicians less responsive to Irish arguments. A cynic can wonder: How many British policy-makers would have quietly understood, as the reports of Irish famine mounted in the late 1840s, that the rot turning Irish potato fields black almost overnight was a political godsend? Instead of having 9 million people in 1851 and 12 million in 1901, Ireland would have 6.5 million in 1851 and then 4.5 million in 1901—and English control of Parliament would be maintained.

Historians have not offered evidence of such cunning. Most Tory MPs of the late 1840s had the reputation of being to clever politics what most Irish peasants were to sophisticated farm management. Nevertheless, of all Europe's major nations, England and then English-dominated Britain were the most inclined to use forms of emigration—indentured service, transportation of rebels and criminals, and a large-scale exodus of Celtic peasants from Ireland and the Scottish Highlands—to clear its territory of the ethnically, politically, and socially undesirable. Statistics that show eighteenth- and nineteenth-century Britons emigrating in much higher ratios than French or even Germans—almost 11 million left between 1750 and 1900—are weighted by a two-thirds *Celtic* departure that helped to make Britain lopsidedly English.

The United States, in the meantime, took on the coloration of a very different English-speaking cultural and demographic success, to which we now turn.

Protestant Demography: The Thirteen Colonies and The Early Nineteenth-Century United States

The new republic of 1776 was not a land with doors open to the oppressed of Europe. It was a baker's dozen of provinces that with one principal exception—Pennsylvania—had given few or no political rights to Catholics and opened their doors to essentially the same Protestant nations and oppressed of Europe who already looked to Britain as a beacon light.

A related pattern prevailed among emigrants from *within* Britain. The Protestant oppressed or disfavored—religious dissidents, economic dispossessees, ethnic malcontents, and would-be

579

revolutionaries—had been the principal settlement group, flocking (or being transported) to the American colonies. Sometimes authorities in London tried to stem major emigration waves, as with the Puritans in the 1630s and the Ulster Scotch-Irish in the 1720s and 1760s. But in other ways, officialdom could be happy to see them go. The emigrants who fell into this political and religious category, even when their immediate spur was a failed harvest, plague, or particularly brutal winter, included Puritans, Baptists, Quakers, Scotch-Irish Presbyterians, Scots Covenanters, Scots Highlanders, and even Welshmen who sought to build a New Wales overseas in parts of Pennsylvania and the Carolinas. The thirteen colonies were also a haven for the German Peace sects that William Penn invited to his refuge on the banks of the Delaware.

The Europeans who had settled in the middle colonies before English rule—the Swedes and Dutch of Delaware, Pennsylvania, New Jersey, and New York—were fellow Protestants who could be easily absorbed. Some of the more conservative Swedish and Dutch congregations became virtual adjuncts of the Church of England, unsurprising because British policy was ecumenical in its collaboration with other Protestant state churches. The Swedes and Dutch were European allies of Britain, as were the dwindling ranks of French Huguenots. Jews, mostly Sephardic, were relatively welcome in the British Empire; Cromwell had reopened England to them in 1655.

The relatively large numbers of eighteenth-century German emigrants came as much to the realm of the King of England as to an abstraction called America. Even before the accession of the German-born Hanoverian monarchs, Protestants from the Rhenish Palatinate had looked to English rulers as protectors—an English princess had married the Elector Palatine during the seventeenth century. In response to a royal invitation from Queen Anne and a severe winter, thirteen thousand Palatine refugees poured down the Rhine to Holland and thence to England in 1708–1709. Some thirty-two hundred continued on to New York and Pennsylvania. Still others went to what became New Bern, North Carolina.

Some European Protestant refugees found haven in the British Isles themselves, but more crossed the Atlantic. Catholic Europeans, conversely, had little thought of migrating to English or British colonies. Among the Catholics who arrived in the eighteenth century, the Irish were mostly indentured servants or transported felons. However, among the German ironworkers and miners brought to Virginia and the middle colonies were substantial Catholic elements. A third Catholic element, dispersed through the colonies, included several thousand of the five to eight thousand French Acadians expelled from Nova Scotia in 1755. Some went to France or Louisiana, but others went to Maryland or drifted through the other mainland provinces, where they rarely felt at home.

After independence, prohibitions against Catholics were eased if not altogether eliminated.* And because the new United States was no longer British, it began to attract a larger number of Irish Catholics, especially after the abortive Irish rebellion of 1798. By 1800, the U.S. Catholic population was estimated at sixty thousand, and it grew again in 1803 when the Louisiana Purchase added some forty thousand—to the particular displeasure of New Englanders.

Through 1830, European emigration to the U.S. remained substantially Protestant. Even among the Irish, Ulstermen were still the principal arrival stream. But besides the Catholic need to flee after the rebellion of 1798, two other circumstances also worked to make the United States more appealing: the War of 1812, which renewed the U.S. image of hostility to Britain, and the success of Jacksonian Democracy in furthering the image of an America in which Protestants and Catholics could collaborate.

In 1815–1816, according to British data, twenty thousand Irish crossed the Atlantic, a majority from Ulster and most still Protestant. Even more came in the next two years. Between 1820 and 1827, another sixty thousand to seventy thousand went to Canada and the United States, mostly winding up in the latter. Between 1828 and 1837, an extraordinary four hundred thousand made the transatlantic crossing.[17] Even before the Great Hunger of 1847–1849, not only was Protestant Ireland being drained, but the old culturally and

---

*In many states, they were not allowed to hold office. New Hampshire voters, indeed, voted against letting Catholics hold office even in an 1850 statewide referendum.

religiously sealed container of Catholic Ireland was beginning to leak. The socioeconomic status of the emigrants conspicuously declined—in 1820, only a fifth had been ordinary laborers and servants, but by 1826, nearly two-fifths were. Even Gaelic-speakers from the impoverished west of Ireland, rarely able to afford passage and fearful of leaving home, were now contributing to the exodus. By the early 1830s, annual departures by Catholics were exceeding those by Protestants. For the entire 1827–1837 period, Catholics composed an estimated 50–60 percent of all Irish emigrants.[18]

By the 1830s, because of Irish arrivals, the Catholic population of the United States began doubling or trebling each decade, although the political and social effects of that change were still to come. Even before the first major rotted potato crop, the threat of a pivotal Irish bloc in Britain's own Parliament was receding. The future voters who could have paralyzed Westminster in 1898 or 1914 were moving to Boston, New York, and Philadelphia, although Irish populations were also rising in London, Manchester, Liverpool, and Glasgow.

In short, this represented the fading of America's older, colonial-type Protestant emigration from the same national groups that had fought alongside William of Orange or allied themselves with the Protestant Hanoverians. A different image, rooted in a European perception of the America of Thomas Jefferson and Andrew Jackson, of free worship and political democracy, was already taking hold, with enormous implications for the transformation of European migration. Those two centuries of overwhelmingly Protestant emigration, however, built the insurgent America, much of it dissenter- and refugee-fed, that achieved independence for the thirteen colonies and pushed what would be the United States far ahead of every rival colonial culture in the Americas. Even by the 1820s, as Spanish America was wracked by revolution, it was clear that an English-speaking republic would predominate in the Western Hemisphere.

Figure 13.1 shows the populations for the period from 1700 to 1820 in British North America and the United States compared with the two principal Iberian streams. These were the years during which English-speaking North America took the political and commercial lead.

Substantial numbers of Portuguese and Spanish also migrated to Central and South America in the eighteenth century, but their

FIGURE 13.1   Population Gains in the Western Hemisphere,
1700–1820

| | Population (Millions) by Year | | | | |
	Europeans	Blacks	Indians	Mestizos and Mulattos	Total
1700					
British America	0.3	0.1	0.03	0.02	0.45
Spanish America	0.7	0.5	9.0	0.1	10.3
Brazil	0.2	0.1	0.6	0.1	1.0
1820					
British N. America and U.S.	9.0	1.9	0.6	0.1	11.6
Spanish America	3.4	2.1	8.0	5.5	19.0
Brazil	0.9	1.9	0.4	0.7	3.9

Source: Max Savelle, *Empires to Nations: Expansion in America*, 1713–1824, p. 104.

ranks were necessarily capped by the plenitude of slave labor, black and Indian. European majorities were uncommon outside some major cities and the River Plate basin near what is now Buenos Aires. German movement to Latin America, in turn, virtually nonexistent in the eighteenth century, was kept relatively low in the nineteenth by two factors: the U.S. opposition under the Monroe Doctrine to foreign involvement in the hemisphere and the ebb after 1859 when the Prussian government banned emigration of its nationals to Brazil (through 1896) because of local mistreatment of German workers in the coffee plantations.

The first German colony in Brazil was Nova Friburgo, planted in 1819 near Rio de Janeiro, and other colonies followed in the temperate Brazilian states farther to the south and in the mountains near Rio. As late as 1867, there were only about forty thousand European farmers—predominantly German, with some Italians—scattered across Brazil in what amounted to transplanted European villages.[19] Without an equivalent of the U.S. Homestead Act, the need to purchase land was an obstacle. So was German distaste for Brazilian slavery, which remained legal until the 1880s.

Most of the German farm colonies were successful, not only maintaining the German language but imposing it on their environs. In Santa Caterina, even many blacks and Indians spoke German. However, although German-dominated southern Brazil became the most prosperous and modernized part of the country, the various drawbacks confined total nineteenth-century German emigration to Brazil to about one hundred thousand persons.[20] By World War I, there were about five hundred thousand Brazilians of German ancestry. German emigration to Argentina during the nineteenth century was a little larger, as was the German population by World War I.[21] This does not begin to compare to the more than four million German-speakers who chose the United States during the nineteenth century. Had half of those instead gone to Brazil and Argentina, approximating the Spanish, Portuguese, and Italian migrations, European Latin America would have gained size and importance relative to English-speaking North America, probably playing a greater role in both world wars.

A second characteristic of emigration to the British North American colonies in the seventeenth and eighteenth centuries—and a caveat to the emphasis put on political and religious refugees—was that less than half of the arrivals made their own arrangements. Not everyone was a self-supporting Puritan, Huguenot, Sephardic Jew, or third son of a Wiltshire baronet in flight from the Commonwealth. More than half came as indentured servants, redemptioners, or transported prisoners. Although rival colonial powers like Spain, Portugal, and France sent prisoners to their colonies, they were less systematic compared with the English practice of draining certain populations from the British Isles while building overseas territories.

Still another advantage lay with the unusual willingness of British officialdom to harness private enterprise. Commercial middlemen were allowed to handle indenturing, the arrangements by which would-be British and European emigrants would receive passage to America but then serve out a three- to seven-year term as servants, a status which could include anything from carpentry to field labor. Redemptioners, usually families, initially paid only part of their expenses, and then had two weeks or so after landing to arrange the additional money due, usually by one or more family members becoming servants for whatever time was necessary.

The result was that from New Jersey south to Georgia, between half and two-thirds of the pre-1775 emigrants came as redemptioners or indentured servants, especially those from Germany, Scotland, and Ireland.[22] Most of the German states were discouraging, although not absolutely barring, emigration. Without indenturing, British North America might not have outgrown Spanish and Portuguese America in terms of its European population. New England, as we have seen, wanted relatively few servants. But even in the southern colonies, indenturing produced a higher level of European arrivals—not just house servants, but white men to increase the militia, to serve as overseers and keep up white ratios in slave states, and to work in fields and mills—than the other colonizing powers generally managed.

Overall, England also surpassed the others in transporting a high ratio of newly convicted criminals and many of those incarcerated in its prisons, hospitals, and almshouses to the American colonies. Some two hundred different felonies in seventeenth-century England carried the death sentence. However, those convicted could usually opt for transportation: being taken to the colonies and sold into servitude. Between 1661 and 1700, about forty-five hundred were brought over this way, although the legislatures of Virginia and Maryland, two of the principal destinations, passed prohibitory statutes, which reduced the practice after the 1670s.[23]

Then, in 1717, Parliament passed transportation laws that overrode the objections of both provinces, and the traffic became heavier than ever. Between 1718 and 1775, some twenty thousand felons were brought to America this way from England, Scotland, and Wales. Somewhat over nine thousand more came from Ireland. Of all these, roughly twenty thousand wound up in just two colonies—Virginia and Maryland. According to the principal study, "over 70 percent of those convicted at the Old Bailey were sent to America."[24]

Because the middlemen who recruited indentured servants sometimes got them from houses of correction like Clerkenwell, institutions like Bridewell Hospital, brothels, and almshouses, some 15–20 percent of the four hundred thousand emigrants to the colonies between 1700 and 1775 must have been convicts, prisoners, or public charges.[25] Rebels captured in Monmouth's Rebellion and the Scottish risings of 1715 and 1745 were also transported.

Extraordinarily, when the War for Independence ended in 1783, the English appear to have thought that the old system could be resumed. One cargo of eighty felons was actually landed in Maryland. When rumors of more arrivals circulated in 1788, Congress urged the states to pass prohibitions, which was done, and Britain almost immediately established true penal colonies in Australia.[26]

Through all of these devices and circumstances—colonial charters for Protestant dissenters; occasional periods of Irish, Welsh, and Scottish ethnic persecution or flight; gathering of Europe's Protestant refugees; German recruitment; relentless transportation of felons, debtors, military prisoners, and vagabonds; and a private "emigrant agent" business that ranged from serious recruitment to kidnapping—Britain turned a late entry in New World colonizing into the largest and fastest-growing clump of European settlement in the Western Hemisphere, with remarkably dual success. We have seen how this exodus made the population and culture of the British Isles less Celtic and more English, less revolutionary and antisocial and more deferential. It also positioned the fledgling United States of 1820, with a very different population, and already set on a very different track, to become the preponderant demographic and political force in the new world.

The Nineteenth Century's
Massive Transformation

Few choruses figure more prominently in hymns to American exceptionalism than praise of "a nation of immigrants." True as this description was, we have seen how its seventeenth- and eighteenth-century origins owed much to the reputation of Britain in Protestant Europe and in democratic revolutionary movements from Corsica to Flanders.

By the 1830s and 1840s, however, the appeal of the United States of Thomas Jefferson and Andrew Jackson increasingly involved a new image of egalitarianism, freedom of religion, Catholic-Protestant collaboration in the Democratic Party, and a near-universal franchise among white males—attributes that smacked more of Revolutionary France than Whig or Tory England. As Jacksonian Democracy left colonial lineage behind in an era when Britain itself stood increasingly for aristocracy and

monarchy, the shores of the United States became more approach-
able by the cultures of European Catholicism, on the one hand,
and by refugees from nineteenth-century anti-monarchism and
revolution on the other.

The saga of pre-1914 American immigration—Ellis Island as a
hallowed entryway in the shadow of liberty's beckoning torch—
also has three less discussed corollaries. First, the centrality of the
Irish and German exodus to the United States in the late 1840s
and early 1850s in provoking the Know-Nothing movement,
which in turn helped to crystallize the new party system that
brought on the U.S. Civil War. Second, the pivotal role of U.S.
ability to attract and then to make English-speakers out of tens of
millions of Celts, Germans, Latins, Jews, and Slavs, changing the
cultural and geopolitical balance of power. And third, the inability
of Germany to keep a large block of German emigrants to North
America from being lost to the Fatherland and Americanized into
citizens and soldiers of the new Anglo-Saxon successor power, the
United States. Without these transformations, to which this subchapter will now turn, twentieth-century history would have been
altogether different.

Even during the last pre-famine years between 1838 and 1844,
351,000 Irish came to North America, most of them to the United
States, over half of them Catholic.[27] Then came the Great Hunger
and the Great Emigration. From the beginning of the famine in
1845 through 1855, nearly 1.5 million Irish sailed to the United
States, more than 300,000 went to Canada, and nearly that many
settled permanently in Great Britain. More Irish left home during
that period, according to one chronicler, than had left during the
preceding two and a half centuries.[28]

The flow from Ireland, which overlapped with the beginnings of
large-scale German emigration to the United States, also more or
less half Catholic, was the first of the huge immigration surges that
reconfigured nineteenth-century America as much as it reshaped
the British Isles. Not only did the outflow from Ireland reduce potential Catholic and Irish Nationalist power in Britain's Parliament
to levels that would be manageable during the Victorian and
pre–World War I years; but in the United States, one can fairly
doubt, as chapter 9 has pursued, whether the Republican-

FIGURE 13.2   The Four Waves of U.S. European Immigration,
1790–1914

Years	Size	Ethnic and Religious Makeup
1790–1830	350,000 (est.)	Largely Protestant British and German
1830–1860	4.5 million	Principally Irish, German, and British—at least half Catholic
1860–1890	9.1 million	Principally German, Irish, British, and Scandinavian—at least half Catholic
1890–1914	14.3 million	Predominantly Italian and eastern European—three-quarters Catholic and Jewish

Democratic party system and the Civil War could have come about without the immigrant flood, the settlement of the Great Lakes states, the rise of anti-Catholicism in the 1850s, and the role of the Know-Nothing movement in breaking up a Whig-Democratic system dedicated to straddling ideological and sectional divisions. Rotten potatoes in Clare and Galway did not spur the Confederacy to open fire on Fort Sumter, but immigration was a major catalyst of 1850s political behavior.

The chart above shows the four distinctive waves of emigration to the United States between 1790 and 1914. The last three were historical watersheds as well as demographic forces.

The huge Jewish influx of the late nineteenth and early twentieth centuries was also critical to the rise of Anglo-America. Although no one has ever prepared an authoritative tabulation of the worldwide distribution of Jews among the empires and kingdoms of 1775—British, French, Spanish, Portuguese, Prussian, Dutch, Hapsburg, Russian, and Ottoman—most were in central and eastern Europe, and it is unlikely that more than 15 percent were in British and Dutch lands. By the end of World War II, however, perhaps three-quarters lived in the territory of the United States or the British or Dutch Empire—all three Protestant and tolerant by political necessity. Parts of Britain and the United States, in paricular, were denominationally favorable rather than hostile to Jews because of biblical emphasis and Chosen Nation themes. Given the twentieth-century importance that Jews would attain in academia, science, communications, and finance, their relocation was a linchpin in the emergence of English-speaking global leadership.

These late nineteenth-century changes would have been unimaginable in the century's early years. In 1815, when Andrew Jackson defeated the British at New Orleans, the population of the United States was just over 8 million persons. Most Irish arrivals were Protestants. Southern and eastern Europeans were barely represented. The ability of the United States to affect the balance of power in a war fought in Europe was minor. A century later, however, when the German U-boat sinking of the liner *Lusitania*, drowning U.S. passengers, raised the possibility that U.S. soldiers might be headed for their first European war, the population of the United States had risen to 100 million, nearly as large as that of France and Germany together. Not a single European nationality went unrepresented on the sidewalks of New York and Chicago.

Did the nearly 25 million Europeans who emigrated to the United States between 1860 and 1914 leave a hole in the European population? Not necessarily, because the nineteenth century was one of huge population growth. *Fin-de-siècle* Europe could not have absorbed it. Greater problems might have built up without an emigration safety valve. Nevertheless, powerful effects were felt.

In the case of the United Kingdom, the huge nineteenth-century emigration of some 10 million people went overwhelmingly to the United States and Canada. Despite the obvious intermission of the War of 1812, along with the tensions of 1861–1865 that clouded transatlantic relations for another decade, this exodus built future linguistic, political, and military allies. Elsewhere in Europe, Spain and Portugal were no longer in the constellation of great powers. Relatively few emigrants left France, and of these, more went to French North Africa than to the United States.

The crumbling empires of eastern Europe—Austro-Hungarian and Russian—experienced large outflows of emigrants. But it is difficult to see that either notably gained or lost stability from the movement.

The greatest beneficiary, by far, was the United States, which leaped ahead of the major European powers in both population and industrial production. In doing so, it had also turned more

Gaelic-speakers into English-speakers than any eighteenth-century English lord lieutenant of Ireland could ever have imagined. Within another generation, the same would be said of Sicilians and Poles, Ruthenians, Yugoslavs—and even Prussians.

The secondary gainer, of course, was Britain. The emigration that had made the British Isles safe for England had created an American successor power and twentieth-century ally with an Irish-descended population four or five times that of Ireland, of whom half were assimilated Protestants. What hadn't worked in Cork or Kildare succeeded in rural America. Other New World outliers with large and politically sanitized Celtic populations actually flew the Union Jack: Canada, Australia, and New Zealand. In great power terms, the United States had used its democracy and disestablishmentarianism, the subjects of such disdain in the clubs of St. James circa 1861, not simply to build what would be the twentieth century's leading industrial economy, but to build a national culture and, ultimately, a military force that in 1917–1918 disembarked onto the quays of Southhampton and Le Havre shipload after shipload of English-speaking, khaki-clad soldiers just a generation or two from the coal mines of Silesia, the docks of Kronstadt, and the wheatfields of the Ukraine.

The principal loser, meanwhile, was the new and belated German Empire.

The German Empire: Defeated in North America?

When the English have crowned a foreigner as king, the country which he has left has been at some risk. When James VI of Scotland became James I of England in 1603, the union of the Crowns led, in another century, to the political union in which Scotland lost its Parliament. Then in 1689, the crowning of William of Orange, a Dutchman, was also handwriting on the European political and economic wall. Holland, Europe's fading great economic power, was about to be weakened in a series of wars between 1689 and 1713 that principally aggrandized England—and the Dutch found their global financial leadership also vanishing in that same direction.

The accession of the German-speaking House of Hanover to the British throne in 1714 had its own significance. The first large German settlements beyond Europe would be in the British North American colonies, and the Hanoverians in London would help to encourage them—from Lunenburg, Nova Scotia, and Waldoboro, Maine, south to the Saxe-Gotha towns in South Carolina and the Salzburger settlements in Georgia. To suggest that George I and George II suborned what could have been a Germania in North America would be foolish. But to suggest that their efforts—coming on the heels of William Penn's German sectarian recruitments of the 1690s and Queen Anne's encouragement of the Palatines—helped to give early German immigration to America a British predilection makes sense. The future Germany of the nineteenth century might look eastward through Prussian and Hapsburg eyes, but during the eighteenth century it looked westward, as we have seen, through the Protestant axis that joined London, Hanover, the great Lutheran University at Halle, and the emigration network centered on the Lutheran Chapel at the Court of St. James and the Society for the Propagation of Christian Knowledge.[29]

George II, Elector of Hanover as well as King of Great Britain, who helped redraw the political and military map of Europe in the 1740s and 1750s, is little remembered in U.S. history and scarcely overemphasized in British chronicles, for all that he was the last king personally to lead English (and Hanoverian) troops against the French in the Battle of Dettingen in 1743. Yet the great English-speaking victories over Prussian-built Germany, two centuries later, may have owed a little-recognized underpinning to eighteenth-century collaboration of London and Hanover in North American settlement.

The European Germans of the sixteenth and seventeenth centuries had been ready colonizers, but the bulk of their migrations followed eastward along the sea routes and footsteps of the Hanseatic League and the Teutonic knights. Those coming to North America during the eighteenth century—roughly one hundred thousand—were only a sixth of those exiting the German states for Poland, Hungary, Rumania, and the Russia of Catherine the Great.

If Tory squires in Staffordshire joked about lumpish German kings on the English throne, colonial Anglo-Saxons also had their qualms. Benjamin Franklin himself feared that the number of Teutons coming into mid-eighteenth-century Pennsylvania could turn that province German. "How good subjects they may make, and how faithful to the British Interest, is a Question worth considering," he said in 1751. Absent measures to stem immigration, "this will in a few years become a German colony: Instead of their learning our Language, we must learn theirs, or live as in a foreign Country."[30] Portions of that concern were plausible—elements in the rural southeastern part of the state continue to speak Pennsylvania Dutch, a patois with its origins in the German of the early eighteenth-century Rhineland. However, the larger frustration would lie with the nineteenth-century Germans whose hopes were for just what Franklin feared—a Germania in America.

Instructive detail on how so many Germans came to North America in the eighteenth and nineteenth centuries, yet failed to create any new ethnic homeland or independent republic, can be found in a book by an English social historian, John Hawgood, entitled *The Tragedy of German America*.[31] Many German intellectuals came to America with hopes and even plans for German-speaking states and independent republics. Ordinary Germans, by contrast, mostly came with a desire for farms, jobs, and an end to kings, margraves, and military conscription.

Philadelphia was an early center for German thinkers in America, and during the early nineteenth century some great plans were afoot. In 1813, one Lutheran magazine queried what Philadelphia would be like if local Germans maintained their culture and speech: "It would not be forty years until Philadelphia would be a German city, just as York and Lancaster are German counties. . . . what would be the result through Pennsylvania and Maryland in forty or fifty years? An entirely German state where, as formerly in Germantown, the beautiful German language would be used in the legislative halls and the courts of justice."[32] In 1836, the president of the German Society of Philadelphia, bolder still, called for "a union of the Germans in North America and as a result, the foundation of a New German Fatherland."[33] Through the mid-1840s, other meetings pursued the same broad idea—that one or more U.S. states would be German, or something even grander.

Hawgood, in documenting the unusual reluctance to assimilate among German immigrants in concentrated ethnic settlements, emphasized their use of the German language as a weapon to ward off Americanization during those years: "The Germans obtained favorable legislation in Ohio, in Pennsylvania and in Missouri in the thirties and forties as a result of their campaign to get state laws and constitutions published in both German and English, and everywhere they fought, often successfully, for permission to set up and maintain German language schools, or for the use of German in the public schools of the state."[34]

During these years, three sections beyond Pennsylvania became the principal focal points—the parts of Missouri and Illinois centered on St. Louis, Texas before it became a U.S. state, and Wisconsin. The German Society of Philadelphia rested its hopes on Gasconade County, Missouri, while the Germania Society of New York undertook to Teutonize Texas. Neither had much success, but the banner of Texas colonization was picked up in Germany by the Duke of Nassau, Prince Carl of Solms-Braunfels, and other noblemen. Between 1842 and 1857, enough emigrants arrived that a visitor in the later year estimated that Germans in Texas numbered thirty-five thousand, about one-sixth of the state population.[35]

Texas, then a remote frontier, might conceivably have become a New World Germania. Elsewhere, the German talent for choosing good farmland and identifying urban centers of opportunity served emigrants too well individually to serve the dream of a collective German-speaking polity: "Their hope of obliterating all signs of the earlier settlers by the overwhelming size of the German settlement was defeated by the fact that the lands they chose," as Hawgood saw them, "were among the richest and most potentially important in the whole of the United States," invariably crowded into by many other immigrants and native-born Americans.[36]

When these realities became clear, many German immigrants simply assimilated. Others, in districts with large German-speaking populations, already sensitized by the Know-Nothing movement and Civil War conscription, attempted to maintain themselves in a separate German-American culture. These areas, particularly in the Middle West, remained German enough into the early twentieth century to be traumatized by two U.S. wars with their homeland.

Official nineteenth-century German attitudes toward emigration to America also varied. Certain German state governments made attempts to curb emigration in the late 1820s, but individual departures rose steadily in the 1830s, 1840s, and 1850s because of failed revolutions, repression, flight from military conscription, and ecclesiastical disputes like the merger of the Lutheran and Reformed Churches in Prussia which sent many "Old Lutherans" to the United States. By the 1880s, emigration was again frowned upon. Then, after 1900, following the Spanish-American War and U.S.-British rapprochement, a period when prosperity and national consciousness were also rising in a united Germany, the imperial government and press took an unfavorable view of emigration to the United States, and although not actually prohibited, it declined sharply.[37] The United States would have increasingly looked like a possible wartime foe.

Probably few among the masses of German emigrants—over 5.5 million came to the United States between 1830 and 1914—would have cared that their personal success or assimilation undermined abstract ethnic politics. Had they seriously tried to create a new Germania, perhaps by attempting to make three or four midwestern states German-speaking, such attempts would almost certainly have been blocked. What remains now are mostly the vague ties of descent—the sprawling German-ancestry map of the Midwest, based on U.S. Census Bureau data (Map 13.1). Aside from a few historic towns, farm enclaves, and churches, and the Black Forest *Wursthaus* imitations of the Missouri *Weinstrasse*, little Teutonic imprint survives beyond the small-town newspaper morgues with their old German-language editions and the dusty courthouse records of the agonized electoral response to two world wars in precincts named for Westphalian saints and Holsteiner memories.

A political geographer might stretch and strain to hypothesize how this demographic strength could have been kept available to ally with a united Germany. Had the nineteenth-century immigrants gone to eastern Europe, several Slavic nations might have been German-run. Yet it is also easy to find, in German history from the late sixteenth century down through the nineteenth, ample reasons why many Germans would want to flee central Europe—and why America, in its different British colonial and then independent existences, would have beckoned and been able to perform its assimilation.

An early German-American, Christopher Ludwig, who became the "baker-general" of the U.S. Revolutionary army, understood the cultural dynamics as well as anyone. In speaking of the Hessians, Brunswickers, and other German mercenary soldiers captured by General Washington, he advised that they not be exchanged or sent back: "Bring the captives to Philadelphia, show them our beautiful German churches, let them taste our roast beef and homes, then send them away again to their people [German-speaking Pennsylvanians] and you will see how many will come over to us."[38]

He was prophetic. Sight of the rich Pennsylvania German farmland convinced many to volunteer for the American army. But these offers were declined. Instead, most of the Hessian defectors spent the war working for German farm families in Pennsylvania, New Jersey, and Maryland and never recrossed the Atlantic. In Frederick, Maryland, the cannon salute to the end of the war in 1783 was fired by Hessian gunners under a former Bayreuth artillery captain. In a larger sense, such was also the fate of Germania in America.

———

The Americanization of so many Germans between the early nineteenth and the early twentieth centuries—to say nothing of the German-American contribution in building U.S. technology and industry toward its strength in two world wars—was an important part of the shift in the balance of power that made the twentieth century an Anglo-American one. Yet the British, in particular, sometimes had a tin ear for who and what Americans were. In 1917, when the first U.S. troops started arriving in England, the chief of the Imperial General Staff, Sir William Robertson, suggested to the commander of the American Expeditionary Force, General John J. Pershing, that because of the common language, the Americans could most usefully be put into decimated British units as replacements. King George V, at a lunch with the two generals, took a different tack, arguing, "The Anglo-Saxon race must save civilization."[39]

Robertson's proposal, however, was quickly rejected by the American general, whose first ancestor in the New World had been Frederick Pfoerschin, a German-speaker who came to Pennsylvania from Alsace in 1749. Both the British Imperial General Staff and the German *Oberkommand Wehrmacht* must have also had their moments of irony in World War II with senior U.S. generals and admirals named Eisenhower, Nimitz, Eichelberger, and Spaatz. Indeed, Eisenhower's own forebears were refugee Swiss Mennnonites and German pietists who settled in Pennsylvania in the early 1730s. Subsequent generations refused to bear arms in either the American Revolution or the Civil War, and Dwight Eisenhower's parents in Texas were members of the pietist River Brethren sect. Between Pershing's ancestry and role in World War I and Eisenhower's in World War II, the descendants of the early eighteenth-century Rhenish refugees returned to the Old World in the most changed of circumstances.[40]

On the other hand, it was precisely this dissenter- and refugee-shaped Anglo-America, with these names and a score of other ethnicities—and speaking an English language that would be further flavored with words from Gullah, Spanish, and Yiddish—that had the democratic appeal and, with it, the armed might to prevail in the twentieth century. The reach of Britain and yesteryear's British North America, by themselves, would no longer have been enough. Such was the benefit, however, of the division brought about by the American Revolution. Without intending or expecting the result, the English-speaking peoples had two significantly different political cultures to become dominant great powers in two substantially different centuries.

By then, of course, the wars between the English-speaking cousins were long over. New rivalries partly over the hegemony of electronic and financial English—a sway not based on religion, political organization, or territory, but increasingly on a new communications primacy—were gathering force.

14

THE ENGLISH LANGUAGE
Words as Weaponry?

The world's language is English.
—*The Wall Street Journal*, 1997

The available data covering more than three decades (1958–1992) suggest ... that significant declines occurred in the proportion of people speaking English.
—Samuel Huntington, *The Clash of Civilizations and the Remaking of World Order*, 1996

T HE ENGLISH LANGUAGE was a weapon long before its reach became the stuff of silicon chips and satellites. From the fifteenth century to the millennium—from London's statutes governing late medieval Cornwall, Wales, and Ireland to the latter-day wizardries of computer software—the English language (spoken, written, and then electronic) has been not just a symbol of political hegemony but a powerful weapon in achieving and upholding it. The role of English in the twenty-first century is too complex (and uncertain) to conjecture in pages that are essentially political history. However, this being the end of a discussion about a time when language did, after all, follow and uphold two flags, British and American, that record deserves some amplification.

Do great languages *prolong*, or simply *outlast*, empires? The answer is unclear. Latin lived on in several of the legacies and vocations of Rome, especially Christianity, law, and history. Yet during Rome's late years of the fourth and fifth centuries, the importance of the imperial language may have disguised the rot of so much else that had been vital about Rome at its zenith. Perhaps a Roman senator of the period Edward Gibbon has stamped as decline also turned aside criticism by saying, "But our language is the world's." The role of French as a medieval lingua franca and then as the language of nineteenth- and even early twentieth-century diplomacy arguably did mirror France's own fortunes. On the other hand, the vastness of territory in which people spoke Spanish, Portuguese, or Chinese in 1900 meant little to the faded, tattered circumstances of Spain, Portugal, or China.

Still, the widespread use of a once-imperial language remains a potential lever of influence for a nation that, in bygone days, spread as well as spoke it. France nurtures a francophone bloc in world affairs, cherishing the hope that an independent Quebec may yet gnaw a hole in the map of English-speaking North America or that French may overwhelm English in West Africa. Spain approached the millennium with commercial ambitions in South America, plausibly premised on how much of that continent spoke Spanish. Portugal had its own hopes in Brazil, the last great mirror of its maritime reach. Mexico, in turn, sought to harness the large number of Spanish-speaking Mexicans—or ex-Mexicans—in the southwest United States for some form of *reconquista*. China, resurgent in the 1990s, was already reducing the use of English in Hong Kong. Despite these regional erosions and threats, English-speakers in business and finance approached the year 2000 with the expectation that in the twenty-first century, theirs would be the global language.

English, a Language of Victory

Time and expansion had already drawn a new English-language playing field. Five hundred years earlier, London's use of written and spoken English as a weapon had begun on a large scale on England's own volatile Celtic peripheries. English by then had replaced Norman-brought French in the royal court. In 1500, before the annexation of Wales, the British Isles would only have had a bare majority of English-speakers. After the union of the two in 1536, the Church of England was imposed, along with religious services in English that most of the population could not understand. English courts and judges were established, and only English-speaking Welshmen were permitted to hold administrative office.[1] By the era of Oliver Cromwell, who himself was partly Welsh, the Welsh aristocracy was almost entirely English-speaking even as the peasantry largely spoke Welsh (and would into the twentieth century).

In Scotland, English-speaking lowlanders took the lead in curbing highland culture and tribalism, which included the use of Gaelic. After the English and lowlander suppression of the clans following the final Stuart defeat in 1746, many highlanders emigrated, and by the end of the twentieth century, the ratio of Gaelic-speakers plummeted to only 3 percent of the population. As Scottish MPs of the late eighteenth century, along with a would-be attorney general, Alexander Wedderburn, found that their dialect produced snickers in Parliament, they took elocution lessons. By the nineteenth century, the Scottish gentry, like the Welsh aristocracy earlier, found it convenient to send their sons to Eton and Harrow, becoming almost completely Anglicized in speech and manner. Within the salons and anterooms of power, English conquered.

The English priority in Ireland was containing Catholicism rather than suppressing speech. Yet by the mid-1850s, the average Irish county was only 22 percent Gaelic-speaking. The more prosperous east spoke English, if not exactly the Queen's, while Gaelic remained predominant only in the west—Galway, Mayo, Sligo, and other counties to which earlier English policies had deliberately driven Gaelic-speakers. By World War I, the percentage of the southern Irish who spoke Gaelic had shriveled to 14 percent. Even late twentieth-century efforts for a Gaelic renaissance lifted it to less than a third.

Britain won primacy in North America, as we have seen, partly because its white settlers massively outnumbered those of the French and the Spanish, but within the British settlements, language conformity was not a major concern. Most of the local gentry were already English-speaking, and the Dutch and French Huguenot elites quickly became so. Lower-status Dutch and Germans of the Hudson Valley, Pennsylvania, and the Pennsylvania outliers in Virginia and North Carolina continued speaking Dutch and German, while after 1763, Quebeckers were allowed to retain their French. The Highland Scots of North Carolina's Upper Cape Fear Valley, in turn, kept their Gaelic.

With the independence of the United States, however, English-speakers became more demanding. Save in the bayous near New Orleans, English rapidly overwhelmed French in the new states carved from what had been Louisiana. Then its tidal movement through once-Spanish Florida and Texas helped to convince the southern expansionists of the 1840s and 1850s that they could Anglicize Cuba or northern Mexico almost as easily. Some linguistic residues were ignored. California became Anglophone following a single gold rush. But after largely Hispanic New Mexico was ceded by Mexico in 1848, it was kept a non-self-governing territory for six decades, becoming a state only in 1912 after English-speaking settlers had gained a majority (Anglos, for this purpose, already included Irish teamsters and Basque sheepherders). Most but not all German-speaking sections of the Midwest also surrendered during and after World War I.

Considering the Western and Eastern Hemispheres together, English-speaking expansion was phenomenal, especially in the nineteenth century. The United States rolled westward to the Pacific and then out into its islands, principally Hawaii and the Philippines. The British Empire spread over much of India and half of Africa. Figure 14.1 at least approximates the annexations and growth that were taking place.

The numbers of English-speakers should not be confused with statistics showing how many people were under the political or imperial control of English-speaking governments. Actual language is a different and less tractable measurement. Britain ruled hundreds of millions of people at the peak of empire. But the long-term significance remains unclear with respect to English becoming the lingua franca of Indians, Malayans, Nigerians, and other colonies whose territories included diverse tribes or peoples other-

FIGURE 14.1 The Expansion of the English-Speaking World, 1600–2000 (excluding Australasia)

	English-Speakers in British Isles	English-Speaking Population of North America	Population of British-Governed Nations Where English Was Lingua Franca
1600	4–5 million	—	—
1700	8 million	500,000	—
1800	12 million	6 million	10 million
1900	32 million	75 million	300 million
2000	55 million	300 million	1 million

wise unable to communicate with each other. The critical linguistic momentum of the twentieth century, arguably, has come from the weight of native English-speakers in militarily victorious and economically developed European and North American countries—about 200 million in 1945 and some 350 million in 2000. Their population, wartime prowess, and influence are what established English—not French, German, or Spanish—as the language of twentieth-century communications, finance, global business, entertainment, and travel. If it became a language of convenience, that was because it was first and foremost a language of *victory*.

Theories widespread at the century's end assumed that post-industrial circumstances in which communications and knowledge were, increasingly, the key to economics and wealth would give linguistic dominance an importance lacking in earlier years. Governance in the broad sense, to be sure, had been a principal export of third- and fourth-century Rome. Seventeenth-century Holland thrived—or its finance and commercial sector did—on being the chief entrepôt of the world. Latin lingered by being the language of belief, chronicle, and statute; Dutch (briefly) by being the language of commerce. The twenty-first century, however, stands to be one in which forms of language—the speech of broadcasting, the image-making of entertainment, the software of computers, the formulae of finance, the electronics of communications, navigation, and avionics—constitute a more integral equation of success.

The benefits to Americans or Britons of English becoming the language of global business or finance, standing by itself, could be as limited as the benefits to ordinary Frenchmen of theirs being the eighteenth-century tongue of diplomacy. What difference did that make in Tours or Besançon? The interaction of linguistic hegemony with the communications revolution, however, appears to be more rewarding. The United States and, to a lesser extent, Britain have developed major exports around language and communications preeminence: computers, software, entertainment, broadcasting, travel services, brokerage, shipping, air service and airliners, banking, financial services, insurance, advertising, law, and so on. However, even as the wealthier, better-educated English-speakers profit from these enterprises, English-speakers with fewer skills and less education and capital may lose out, in contrast to the breadth of the benefits that British manufacturing hegemony in 1890 or American industrial supremacy in 1950 extended to each nation's basic workforce.

Against this backdrop, the evidence that English-speakers are already losing ground as a percentage of the world population may be irrelevant on the upper-class dimension yet prophetic for the humdrum. By one plausible calculation, the burgeoning Spanish-speaking populations of Latin America and the Chinese-, Hindi-, and Bengali-speaking masses of Asia have already dropped English-speakers from their relative worldwide share of 1958. Back then, Mandarin-speakers were 15.6 percent of the total, English 9.8 percent, Hindi and Bengali 7.9 percent, and Spanish 5.0 percent. By 1992, the levels were Mandarin 15.2 percent, Hindi and Bengali 9.6 percent, English 7.6 percent, and Spanish 6.1 percent.[2] The English-speaking share is expected to keep dropping because of Third World birthrates, even if English becomes the second language of educated Swiss or Saudis.

Among the world's masses, then, the ratio of those using English is probably *declining*—a far cry from its escalation in the years between 1800 and, say, 1950. At the same time, during the last three decades of the twentieth century, usage was undoubtedly *rising* among the world's better-educated elites, although the numbers involved must be almost as imprecise.

The implications of such a duality can be left to twenty-first–century textbooks. So, too, for the relationship of global English to broader Anglo-American economic and cultural well-being.

Back in the years of the cousins' wars and the great expansion of the English-speaking community, doubts were few. English within the American colonies or the home culture itself was still a people's language—among those of European descent, at least, a popular medium unlike Latin, Greek, or French. The translation of the Bible into English, for example, was an event with democratic political and religious repercussions. The ordinary Briton or ordinary American was at least as likely as the aristocrat, banker, or government official to think and boast that he or she belonged to a chosen people or nation—and the industrial zeniths of the late nineteenth century in Britain or the 1950s in the United States seemed to prove that was true. The elite role of English in the twenty-first century could turn out to be quite different.

The Idea of an English-Speaking Imperium

The notion of a cousinship between the so-called Anglo-American nations—the United States, Canada, Britain, Australia, and New Zealand—has owed as much to sentiment and crisis as to ongoing realpolitik. It soared during both twentieth-century world wars, thereafter ebbing as peacetime or prosperity brought more relaxed views and opportunisms: the United Kingdom deciding to become part of Europe, Canada and the United States opting to join with Mexico, and Australia deciding to merge itself into Asia.

The intensity of relationships during the three great English-speaking civil wars, however, suggests that the English-speaking "cousin" nations may have too great a shared history and cultural and linguistic bond to split apart in such a fashion. Moreover, important elements in the populations of the United States and Britain still think of themselves somewhat as they did in the 1640s, 1770s, and 1860s: as chosen peoples. The notion that the relationship between the United States and Britain can be assessed through English-Speaking Union niceties and anecdotes about Roosevelt-Churchill wartime collaboration—and without any attention to the underlying religious and cultural bonds apparent in three civil wars that divided *both* sides of the Atlantic—is, in a word, unrealistic.

The shared economic stakes of a mutual language are easily set out. Airlines, advertising agencies, investment firms, and entertainment companies in London have a common interest with those in New York, Sydney, and Toronto: that the world continue to travel, communicate its information, and deal with money principally in English.

What has been understated on both sides of the Atlantic are the cultural and historical underpinnings that Britain shares with all of English-speaking North America. The point can be made, as one British newsweekly has, that it's all very well to talk about becoming part of Europe, but on Christmas and birthdays, when Britons dial family far away, there are precious few calls to Brussels or Turin—and a flood to Nova Scotia, New York, and New South Wales. About 50 million people of British (including Irish) ancestry lived in the British Isles in 1990, whereas roughly 150 million with that ancestry lived in the United States, Canada, Australia, and New Zealand.

The country with the largest number of persons of English ancestry is the *United States*. The greatest concentration of Britons outside the home islands is not in Singapore, Melbourne, or Majorca but in southern California, where as many as five hundred thousand people identify themselves or a member of their family as British. And in New York City, the press have regularly catalogued the succors of the city's large British population—the pubs that carry English soccer league matches and the stores that sell Marmite, a vegetable extract once described by the *New York Times* as summoning up powerful English childhood memories and tapping deeply into "a thousand-year heritage of bad food."[3] And the turn-of-the-century United States also counted more or less as many Irish bars and pubs as Ireland and as many Scottish festivals as Scotland. This ongoing reweighting of the English-speaking community should give history itself some new twists.

Geopolitically, moreover, Atlanticization in the sixteenth and seventeenth centuries, not French ambitions and adventures in the fourteenth and fifteenth, made Britain a great world power. The European continent has since often been a neighbor to be kept at arm's length by the Royal Navy. What is less obvious, until American history itself is viewed through the wider lens of three civil

wars over three centuries—which is to say through a broader English-speaking context—is how much U.S. evolution and character
bear a British stamp that most Fourth of July orators ignore or do
not realize. But the considerable continuities of the two nations
are little claimed in Britain, either.

American colonials got their sense of being a chosen people
from their antecedents in English Protestantism and in the
covenanting Presbyterianism of Scotland and Ulster. Few doubt as
much. The extent to which the thirteen colonies became a beacon
of liberty in 1776 was foreshadowed by England and then Britain
playing the same role over two centuries—attracting Dutch,
French Huguenots, Flemings, Palatines, and Salzburgers. Even in
the 1770s, London, not Philadelphia, played haven to the refugee
leader of the ill-fated Corsican Republic. On the other hand, just
as the price of liberty in both nations has been eternal vigilance,
the concomitant of eternal vigilance has been periodic political
paranoia—the episodes in the nineteenth- and twentieth-century
United States having roots aplenty in seventeenth- and eighteenth-
century Britain, not least the repeated invocations of "Popish
plots."

The American colonies, in turn, became a melting pot of sorts
during the eighteenth century, not because the mystique of Ellis Island was already taking dim shape, but because they flew the
British flag. British cities and towns like London, Norwich, Canterbury, and Colchester had become seventeenth- and eighteenth-
century havens and had Dutch, French Huguenot, and Jewish
districts to prove as much. Even the American Revolution succeeded, in part, because it was a very British revolution that
touched shared issues—radical London rallied round, as more quietly did much of East Anglia and many of England's nonconforming Protestants. Important English generals, as we have seen,
either refused to serve against the colonists or moved cautiously
and reluctantly because they had no taste for suppressing fellow
Englishmen.

The interplay between the British and American populations, so
often understated in largely separate historiographies, became especially important in wartime. In the War of 1812, New England
had largely been opposed to hostilities with Britain, and during the

American Civil War, the possibility of British intervention on behalf of the Confederacy and against the North was unacceptable to the nonconformists, working-class, and lower-middle-class populations who had the greatest family connections with the United States. Wars or threatened wars between the two countries were unusually divisive because of the bonds between the two populations. And when the dust had settled at Appomattox in 1865, the North's victory—and the democratic political forces thereby emboldened in Britain—all but ensured the further expansion of the franchise in the Reform Act of 1867. The alliances so prominent in the two world wars had many earlier foundations.

The unplanned success of the English-speaking peoples in their unique process of splitting into two national political cultures, one egalitarian and the other more deferential and traditional, has rarely been analyzed and dissected, perhaps because the split has become so ingrained—two nations divided by a common history as well as by a common language. However, we can reasonably wonder: Is the common language, now that it is becoming more unifying and vital because of its high communications-age stakes and corollaries, about to mandate a greater attention to a common history?

Quite conceivably. The beginning of the twenty-first century looks to be a time when ethnocultural alignments—overseas Chinese joining with mainlanders, Islamic collaboration from the Balkans to the Malay Straits, both Iberian nations courting their New World progeny—are reemerging. To call Anglo-America, the English-speaking world of holiday telephone calls, another likely grouping is an understatement.

The notion of this "Anglo-America" as a creature of monarchic or aristocratic connotation is erroneous. Belief in English-speaking destiny was especially strong among Puritans and Yankees, bespeaking roots equally, if not more, on the evangelical and republican side. In 1899, when Britain was about to dedicate a monument to Oliver Cromwell in Parliament Square (opponents succeeded in keeping the statue out of Westminster Abbey), the prime minister at the time, Lord Rosebery, rightly identified the Lord Protector of England's only republic as "a raiser and maintainer" of imperial power.[4] The pursuit of political and linguistic empire by the United States, while usually rejecting that name, was just as relentless and ecumenical: Sometimes Southerners and cavaliers were the principal proponents, sometimes Yankees and Puritans, often the larger population. William H. Seward, the outspoken foe of aristocracy who was secretary of state from 1861 to 1869, was arguably nineteenth-century America's most vehement expansionist.

Indeed, whatever political and religious differences put England and the United States on different—and successfully different—tracks with respect to egalitarian politics, religious conformity, and nineteenth-century immigration, both nations pursued expansion and global influence. This has been especially true in the Pacific, the ocean coming under English-speaking sway during the late nineteenth and twentieth centuries when Britain and the United States, increasing allies with diminishing differences, were usually on the same side. In the communications age, and with the English language coming to the fore, the separate cultural tracks have lost much of their significance. The shared ones have gained importance.

All in all, the communications, commercial, and military reach of the English-speaking people as the millennium turned was little short of extraordinary. Seward and Rosebery would have been astounded. George III and George Washington would have been awestruck. The cousins' wars of the seventeenth, eighteenth, and nineteenth centuries were an integral part of the expansion process, as were the Napoleonic Wars and the two world conflagrations of the twentieth century. Even the latter have begun to fade from personal memory and to join the three cousins' wars as soldiers and sailors, ships and cannon in museum displays and toy store windows.

Whether the sentiments of cultural community and available political tools of the English-speaking peoples can continue the successes of the earlier centuries, to say nothing of the twentieth, is enigmatic. But although the history of these periods is not a reliable guide to the future, and has stains to tarnish its glories, there are still enough statues and triumphs to support a simple but truthful closing: *Not since Rome . . .*

AFTERWORD

E VEN TRIUMPH, OF COURSE, cannot fully lionize three civil
wars or their formative role in English-speaking history. Including
as they did the two bloodiest one-day battles ever fought on British or
American soil—Marston Moor in Yorkshire in 1644 and Antietam in
Maryland in 1862—the three conflicts generated great bitterness and
unhappy memories.

There is also a certain disrepute simply in elevating war. To call campaigns and battles the principal building blocks of militarist Persia,
Sparta, Rome, or Prussia will provoke no great debate in Britain and
the United States. But as architects of English-speaking political emergence, we would like to hold up some better angels: liberty, democracy,
the rights of man.

Perhaps, but the barons of England went armed to achieve the Magna
Carta at Runnymede, the Declaration of Independence came from a
wartime meeting, and the Gettysburg Address was delivered at the conse-
cration of an army cemetery. Force is not always aimed at bloodshed.
Even the better angels often require military escort. Such are the realities.

In any event, it was fascinating to have viewed history anew through
the prism of these three great confrontations. Few historians have embraced the idea of an important interrelationship and partial continuity
amongst them. One English historian, J. G. A. Pocock, published a
book after the U.S. bicentennial that conjoined the English Civil War,
the Glorious Revolution of 1688, and the American War for Independence as three British revolutions. The English historian and novelist
John Buchan earlier drew a parallel between aspects of the English Civil
War and the U.S. Civil War. A few U.S. historians have noted, in the
years between 1861 and 1865, how High Church Southerners and Low
Church Congregationalist and Unitarian Yankees saw the Civil War as
a continuation of the battles over the Reformation fought in the 1640s,

1688, and 1775. And these aspects, we have seen, are only a part of the interconnection.

But however great or debatable the linkage, for the English-speaking peoples these internal wars were unique evolutionary events. And it is sad to see the dereliction of their campaign grounds and battlefields in both the British Isles and the United States. This does not apply to the U.S. Civil War, which from Gettysburg south to Richmond has become a centerpiece of historical tourism. However, it certainly does apply to the great battlegrounds of the English Civil War. Naseby, the most decisive, remains a barely marked oatfield divided by a major road. Marston Moor and Edgehill are little better commemorated. Their importance to the evolution of Anglo-America deserves much better.

In the United States, to be sure, the major Revolutionary battle sites are set aside as monuments or historic parks. Even so, Yorktown, the best marked and explained, is atypical. The Saratoga battlefield in itself is well preserved, and Forts Ticonderoga and Stanwix have been accurately reconstructed, but much of the rest of the Mohawk, Hudson, and Champlain Corridor is being lost as facilities close and upstate New York continues a decline in which the historylands of two centuries ago are too often framed—and in a sense, diminished—by the side effects of the decline of the Adirondack paper industry and the old factory towns of the Mohawk Valley. In 1947, *National Geographic* could still run an article entitled "Drums to Dynamos Along the Mohawk." A half century later, the better alliteration would be drums to decay.

An equal embarrassment lies in the failure to mark the battlefields where Native Americans and blacks played a prominent role on the patriot side. Despite attempts in recent decades to elevate the role of minorities in U.S. history, the tale has only begun to be told of their contribution in the Revolution: the Massachusetts Stockbridge Indians who were cut down fighting British dragoons in what is now New York City's Van Cortlandt Park, for example, or the Battle of Rhode Island in 1778, in which the substantially black First Rhode Island Regiment distinguished itself defeating the Hessians around Bloody Brook. Manufacturing false history is inadvisable; pushing aside what genuinely exists is inexcusable.

There is equal room for improvement on both sides of the Atlantic. Britain should develop the Edgehill, Marston Moor, and Naseby battlefields to approach the commemoration and explanation available at Bosworth Field and Culloden. Oliver Cromwell himself deserves a prominent statue or monument at Naseby, and—one would think—in New England. However, if the battle sites of Ireland are developed, as they should be, Cromwell's memory will be justifiably stained by any major signposting at Drogheda. In the United States, there is no excuse for not establishing a Champlain-Hudson-Mohawk National Historical Corridor reaching from the Canadian border at the northern end of Lake Champlain down to Saratoga itself and through southwest Vermont to the great ironworks in Salisbury, Connecticut, south to the forts of the Hudson highlands, then back up the Hudson valley, past the brief (burned) capital at Kingston, to the Mohawk corridor and west to Lake Otsego, Oriskany, Fort Stanwix, Wood Creek, and the Oneida towns.

These, after all, are not simply unrelated historic sites. They are the reaches of a great and pivotal battlefield. They are the sites of events in the late summer and autumn of 1777 that eventually and uniquely divided the English-speaking world into two great powers and a remarkable future.

Appendix 1

THE PARALLEL
NAMES OF THE
COUSINS' WARS

THE OCCASIONAL BOOKS that assemble the various names that have been applied to one of the wars come up with a surprising number. But why not? If people, and not just academicians, can't entirely agree on what the wars were about, that makes it difficult to agree on terminology. In a way, even the choice of names is still political, still side-choosing, still ideologically participatory.

Indeed, several turn-of-the-century British books and articles described the U.S. Civil War as the Second American Civil War because the Revolution was actually the first. In particular, see Henry Belcher, *The First American Civil War* (London: Macmillan, 1911). I have included these variations even though they are rare usage. In a similar vein, some seventeenth-century observer is bound to have called the English Civil War the Second Civil War because the Wars of the Roses (1455 to 1485) were the first. However, the dynastic struggle of the House of Lancaster versus the House of York involved times that were still feudal and little public involvement. I have left it out.

Daniel Boorstein, in his book *The Genius of American Politics,* called the American Civil War "The Second War for Independence." This was because he thought it completed elements of the nation's evolution left unresolved in the First American Revolution or War for Independence. Charles A. Beard had earlier called the U.S. Civil War the Second American Revolution.

The names commonly applied to these conflicts share three streams of recurring perception: (1) that of civil war, (2) that of revolution or rebellion, and (3) that of war for independence or secession. This last does not fit the English Civil War, unless one thinks of independence or secession from the monarchy, which certainly did have its protagonists (but became an open early goal only in the American Revolution). Of the English-speaking wars, our three alone have this sweep. The Glorious Revolution of 1688 does not, but draws its historical stature from being a second, more moderate and satisfactory, consummation of the English Civil War.

War	Civil War–related Names	Rebellion or Revolution–related Names	Independence or Secession–related Names
English Civil War	English Civil War, the Civil War, the British Civil War, the First Civil War (1642–1645), the Second Civil War (1647–1648)	The Great Rebellion, the English Revolution	None in normal use
American Revolution	Civil war phraseology was used in some states, but the term "First U.S. Civil War" was only applied in retrospect.	The Rebellion, the American Rebellion, the American Revolution	War for American Independence
U.S. Civil War	The American Civil War, the Second Civil War, the War Between the States	The Southern Rebellion, the War of the Rebellion, the Confederate Rebellion, the Southern Revolution, the Second American Revolution (applied only in retrospect)	War for Southern Independence, the War for the Confederacy, the War of Southern Secession, the Second War for Independence (applied only in retrospect)

Although French historian François Guizot, as noted, described the American Revolution as a second version of the English Civil War, neither American nor British historians have done so.

Appendix 2

THE COUSINS'
WARS AS A
CONSPIRACY
CHAIN

THESE THREE WARS constitute the principal framework through which the twin and sometimes related fears of seventeenth-, eighteenth-, and even nineteenth-century Anglo-America—that liberty was at risk to tyranny, and that true Protestantism and the Reformation were threatened by Catholicism and even episcopacy—found political and military expression on both sides of the Atlantic. Indeed, these fears of Catholics, Catholic plots, and alleged tyrannies, which verged on paranoia, constitute an important linkage between the three confrontations.

Many historians have developed these interpretations for each of the individual wars, but this appendix will try to pull them together using two mainstreams: political liberties and tyrannies and "Popish" plots and anti-Catholicism.

War	Popish Plots, Fear of Catholicism and Episcopacy	Political and Constitutional Liberties at Risk and Fear of Tyranny
English Civil War	Concern about Charles I and his Catholic queen plotting with France or the Pope or to bring an Irish army to England had a real basis; so did concern about Archbishop Laud persecuting Puritans. Protestant fear of Popish plots and royal arrange-	In England circa 1640, Catholicism and autocratic government were thought to go together, and the Grand Remonstrance of late 1641 complained about both Catholicism and constitu-

(continues)

War	Political and Constitutional Popish Plots, Fear of Catholicism and Episcopacy	Liberties at Risk and Fear of Tyranny
	ments with France or the Pope repeated in the 1680s, especially under James II.	tional abuses that spanned a range from extralegal taxation to Star Chamber practices and monopolies. The period of eleven years when the King governed without Parliament was described as his "personal tyranny."
American Revolution	Many historians agree that Protestant colonists' fear over the Quebec Act of 1774 recognizing Catholicism in Quebec and extending Quebec territory to the Ohio River at the expense of claims by the colonies was a major context of the Revolution. So was colonial concern over episcopacy: the possibility that Anglican bishops would be appointed in North America, putting Congregationalism and Presbyterianism at risk. In Britain itself, the nearest thing to insurrection during 1775–1783 involved the anti-Catholic riots of 1780 led by the erratic but pro-American Lord George Gordon.	Colonists who feared British plots took up the old rhetoric; George III as a "tyrant," foes as "malignants and inimicals," and multiple conspiracies. Even Washington, Adams, and Jefferson saw conspiracies putting liberty at risk. In the foreword to his book *The Ideological Origins of the American Revolution*, Bernard Bailyn went so far as to say that "in the end, I was convinced that the fear of a comprehensive conspiracy against liberty throughout the English-speaking world—a conspiracy believed to have been nourished in corruption, and of which, it was felt, oppression in America was only the most visible part—lay at the heart of the Revolutionary movement."
American Civil War	Spurred by huge Irish and German Catholic immigration, fear of Catholicism became a major political force in the United States of the 1850s. New Hampshiremen, in a statewide ballot, even voted in 1850 against letting Catholic hold political office, and the anti-Catholic and anti-immigration sentiment that came to the fore as the Know-Nothing movement helped break up the old Democratic-Whig party system and create the new one that brought on the Civil War. New Englanders, in particular, were inclined to see the Catholic Church and the slavery interests as allies and kindred malign powers. It is also appropriate to repeat here the quote from David Brion Davis in Chapter 9 that	Both sides, North and South alike, saw the other conspiring against liberty. In the North, the Slaveocracy became the culprit—the Southerners who used their political power to dominate government on behalf of slavery and against free soil, free men, and free labor. To the South, the threat to liberty came from black Republicans and Yankees who were trampling on southern honor and and liberty by trying to end compact of 1787. Abolitionism, as seen by the South, was a conspiracy against property and southern equality; the plot seen by the North was against human freedom. In Britain, some in the pro-northern

many in New England considered themselves to be carrying on the precepts of the Reformation as in 1642 and 1775 and that "repeatedly the opponents of slave power likened their stand to that of Protestant reformers from Luther to Wesley and thought of their crusade as a reenactment of sacred struggles against the Kingdom of Darkness."

working class saw the British upper classes conspiring in a favor of the South because northern triumph would ensure a new wave of reform and democratization of voting in Britain itself.

Conspiracy theory was potent in Greece and Rome. However, it particularly seems to have come into its own in the seventeenth- and eighteenth-century circumstances of embattled English-speaking Protestantism, in which Stuart kings and Stuart pretenders were indeed plotting with popes and foreign kings. The cousins' wars, being the principal civil wars of the English-speaking peoples, were for all practical purposes a three-ladder interconnection of politico-religious sensitivities, accusations, and paranoias.

Appendix 3

THE COUSINS'
WARS: A SHORT
TIMELINE

The Chronology Surrounding
the English Civil War

March 1625   Charles I becomes King of England and King of Scotland.

May 1625   Charles I marries Catholic Princess Henrietta Maria of France.

July 1628   High Churchman William Laud, opponent of Puritans, is appointed Bishop of London.

March 1629   Parliament passes three resolutions against royal fiscal and religious policy, is then dissolved, and will not meet again for eleven years—the beginning of what has been called "personal rule" by Charles I.

June 1630   The first large group of settlers (400) arrives in Massachusetts.

August 1633   Laud becomes Archbishop of Canterbury, primate of England.

Autumn 1634   The Royal Commission for the Plantations tries to stop emigration to Massachusetts Bay by Puritans.

June 1635   Controversial ship money (taxes) levied for the first time on all English counties.

May 1637   Court of the King's Bench rescinds the Charter of Massachusetts Bay and the King announces that he is assuming management of New England (but does not).

July 1637   Scots begin petitioning movement against English (Anglican) prayer book imposed on Scotland by Charles I.

February to November 1638   The Scottish National Assembly draws up a National Covenant abolishing the (English-imposed) Book of Common Prayer. In November, the assembly also abolishes bishops, prompting both countries—Scotland and England—to prepare for war.

June 1639 Charles I, unable to get adequate Parliamentary backing for a war, negotiates a truce with the Scots at Berwick.

April 1640 The King convenes Parliament for the first time in eleven years. This session—the Short Parliament—is dissolved in May after refusing to give the King subsidies for another Scottish war.

August to October 1640 The Scottish army crosses the border, and after some fighting at Newburn, occupies Newcastle. The King is told in September that he will get no funding in England without calling Parliament, so, in October, he makes another truce with the Scots (to temporarily accept their occupation army and pay it £850 a day) and issues writs for a new Parliament.

November 1640 The new Parliament convenes—the famous Long Parliament that will sit, in various forms, for twelve years—and it quickly moves to attack royal tax, monopoly, and religious policy and to impeach the King's two principal advisors, Lord Strafford and Archbishop Laud.

February to August 1641 Parliament acts to (1) pass a law against dissolving the Long Parliament without its own consent; (2) set out a protestation oath against popery; and (3) pass laws abolishing the courts of star chamber and high commission and to abolish ship money, the King's most controversial extralegal tax. But the House of Lords rejects Commons-passed legislation to exclude bishops from Parliament and signals opposition to a root-and-branch bill proposing the abolition of bishops.

October 1641 Outbreak of Catholic-led rebellion in Ireland, in which several thousand Protestants are killed. Several leaders of the rebellion claim to act in the name of King Charles.

November 1641 The radical "Grand Remonstrance" to the King—which stated the political, fiscal, and religious grievances (and Catholic plot fears) of Parliament—passes the House of Commons by 159 votes to 148.

January 1642 Charles I fails in his attempt to arrest five members of the House of Commons—John Pym, John Hampden, William Strode, Arthur Hazelrigg, and Denzil Holles—and leaves London.

February 1642 Queen Henrietta Maria goes to the continent to seek assistance for her husband's cause.

March to May 1642 Parliament issues militia ordinance without King's consent and takes control of the militia and raising troops. The King is blocked from taking control of ammunition stored at Hull.

June 1642 Parliament sets out the Nineteen Propositions, including major constraints on the monarchy and Catholicism, as a basis for negotiating with the King, who rejects them.

August 1642 The King raises his standard at Nottingham, marking the official beginning of the Civil War.

October 1642 The first actual battle of the war is fought at Edgehill in Warwickshire.

December 1642 to April 1643   December sees agreement to hold negotiations between Parliament and the King, which begin in Oxford in February, but then collapse in April.

April to July 1643   Royalists take the lead on the battlefield as the Earl of Newcastle subdues Yorkshire and northern Lincolnshire, while Sir Ralph Hopton prevails in southwest England. July sees Royalist forces victorious at the Battle of Roundway Down in Wiltshire and in capturing Bristol. Some begin to see the possibility of an unconditional Royalist victory that would restore the King.

August 1643   Parliament turns to military conscription to raise forces.

August to September 1643   Parliament and the Scots negotiate an alliance, with Parliament accepting the "Solemn League and Covenant" in England.

January 1644   A Scottish Presbyterian army enters England to join with the forces of Parliament.

August 1644   The allied army of Scottish and Parliamentary forces defeats the Royalist armies at Marston Moor, Yorkshire, the bloodiest battle ever fought in England.

Autumn 1644   Factionalism intensifies within the Parliamentary camp because of religious disagreements with the Scots and antagonism between political Presbyterians (moderates) and political Independents (the more radical group in which Oliver Cromwell was a rapidly emerging leader).

January to February 1645   Royalist-Parliamentary peace negotiations resume in January and then break off in February.

June 1645   Parliamentary forces led by Sir Thomas Fairfax and Oliver Cromwell defeat the King's forces in the most decisive battle of the war—at Naseby in Northamptonshire, on June 14. The King's captured papers reveal his unpopular negotiations with the Irish, the French, and the Pope. Parliament's "New Model Army," soon to be controversial for its power and its political and religious radicalism, proves itself in battle.

July to September 1645   Defeats for the Royalists at Longport, Bristol, Rowton Heath, and Philiphaugh in Scotland underscore the rising victory prospects of Parliament.

May to June 1646   Charles I surrenders to the Scots, and Oxford, the Royalist headquarters since 1642, surrenders to Parliament, marking the end of the war.

Late 1646 to early 1647   Disagreements intensify between Parliament and the increasingly radical New Model Army, and Oliver Cromwell moves to the political forefront.

June to August 1647   Soldiers of the New Model Army seize the King from his Parliamentary guards, and the army occupies London.

March to August 1648   The New Model Army defeats revolts in South Wales, Kent, and Essex, and Cromwell defeats an invading Scottish army at Preston, Lancashire.

December 1648   The New Model Army reoccupies London. The army undertakes what is called "Pride's Purge" of Parliament—Colonel Thomas Pride and Lord Grey physically exclude about 110 members from Parliament with another 260 voluntarily withdrawing. This ensures radical control of Parliament, which is now called the "Rump Parliament."

January to March 1649   Parliament tries and executes the King, thereafter in March passing acts to abolish the monarchy and the House of Lords.

May 1649   The Rump Parliament passes an act declaring England a republic.

August to October 1649   Cromwell goes to Ireland to suppress rebellion there. He succeeds, but his victories are stained by the massacre of Irish Catholics at Drogheda.

September 1650   Cromwell defeats the Scots at the Battle of Dunbar.

September 1651   Cromwell follows up with a defeat of Charles II, son of the executed Charles I, at the battle of Worcester, and Charles flees to the continent, to remain there until 1660.

April 1653   Cromwell dissolves the Rump Parliament, which is followed by the Barebones Parliament, an assembly of representatives of England, Wales, Scotland, and Ireland, nominated by the Council of State and the army.

December 1653   Cromwell accepts the new republican Instrument of Government and is installed as England's first Lord Protector.

April 1655   Cromwell orders the readmission of Jews into England.

June 1657   Cromwell is installed for the second time as Lord Protector.

September 1658   Cromwell dies and is succeeded as Lord Protector by his son, Richard.

January 1660   Amid growing chaos, General George Monk, in Scotland with a major English army, marches southward in support of a new parliamentary arrangement reincluding those Members of Parliament excluded by the army in the purge of 1648.

March–April 1660: New elections are called, and the "Convention Parliament" passes a resolution to return to government by King, Lords, and Commons.

May 1660   The return and Restoration of the monarchy under Charles II.

January 1661   Bodies of Oliver Cromwell and other regicides exhumed, hanged, and decapitated.

The Chronology Surrounding the American Revolution

February 1763   Britain and France sign the Treaty of Paris, which concludes the Great French War. Britain gains Florida from Spain and Quebec and the rest of North America east of the Mississippi from France.

October 1763   The King's Proclamation establishes the royal "Proclamation Line" along the crest of the Allegheny and Appalachian Mountains and forbids settlement west of those points.

April 1764   The British government's American Duties Act, often called the Sugar Act, replaces the old Molasses Act duty with a new 3d per gallon levy, but the legislation also provides for improved customs enforcement.

March 1765   Parliament passes the Stamp Act, which in effect imposes taxes on the colonies, and the Quartering Act, which requires the colonies to provide quarters and provisions for locally stationed British soldiers.

October 1765   As opposition to the Stamp Act spreads, a Stamp Act Congress, with delegates from eight colonies, meets in New York.

March 1766   Parliament repeals the Stamp Act, but also passes the Declaratory Act, which asserts Parliament's right to legislate for the colonies "in all cases whatsoever."

October 1766   Anglicans in New Jersey petition the Archbishop of Canterbury and the Bishop of London to establish bishoprics in the American colonies.

June 1767   Townshend Acts impose revenue tariffs on goods imported into the American colonies. By the end of the year, nonimportation agreements are established within and between a number of colonies.

June 1768   Seizure by Boston royal customs officials of John Hancock's sloop causes a riot, and Bostonians attack customs-men who withdraw to Castle William in the harbor.

January to March 1770   Confrontations between colonials and British soldiers in Manhattan—the so-called Battle of Golden Hill in January—and in March's so-called Boston Massacre raise political tension. Five colonials die in the Boston confrontation.

April 1770   The Townshend Acts are repealed.

April 1770   The first committee of correspondence is formed in Boston, with the idea spreading to the other colonies.

April 1772   Rhode Islanders burn the Royal Navy sloop *Gaspee*.

May 1773   Parliament passes the Tea Act, giving the East India Company a monopoly in the colonies so it can sell tea in the colonies at low prices—a device unacceptable to many colonial leaders.

December 1773   In the famous Boston Tea Party, the Sons of Liberty board tea ships and dump 90,000 pounds of tea into the harbor.

March to May 1774   Parliament replies with the Coercive Acts closing the port of Boston, suspending local government in Massachusetts, and requiring colonists to furnish quarters and supplies to (occupying) British troops as needed.

June 1774   George III approves the Quebec Act, accepting bishops and Catholicism in Quebec and extending Quebec's western boundary south to the Ohio River. This rejects claims to the same land by Massachusetts,

Connecticut, Virginia, and other colonies, based on their charters, putting in place another major spur to rebellion.

September 1774   The First Continental Congress, with representatives from twelve colonies (all except Georgia), meets in Philadelphia.

October 1774   Massachusetts organizes an extralegal provincial assembly to govern the towns and counties outside of occupied Boston. The First Continental Congress in Philadelphia approves a Declaration of Rights and Grievances and calls for an economic boycott of British goods.

December 1774   Patriots in Rhode Island and New Hampshire seize British ammunition and ordnance.

February 1775   Parliament declares Massachusetts in a state of rebellion.

March 1775   The Virginia Convention resolves that the colony should go into a posture of defense.

April 18–19, 1775   British troops marching from Boston to Concord to seize munitions are drawn into an engagement with patriot militia in Lexington and Concord. British troops suffer heavy casualties from the sniping fire of militia gathering by the thousands, and the British forces returning to the main army in Boston are promptly encircled and besieged by fast-gathering militiamen.

May 10, 1775   Second Continental Congress assembles in what will become Independence Hall in Philadelphia.

May 10–12, 1775   Patriot forces capture the sparsely manned British forts at Ticonderoga and Crown Point, New York.

May 25, 1775   Generals William Howe, Henry Clinton, and John Burgoyne arrive in Boston to assist the embattled British commander, General Thomas Gage. They did not know the Revolution was starting when they sailed from England.

June 17, 1775   British forces in Boston take Bunker Hill in the third wave of a frontal assault, but suffer heavy casualties.

June and July 1775   Congress organizes the Continental Army and names George Washington of Virginia as its commanding general.

August 1775   George III rejects an "Olive Branch" petition from the colonies and proclaims them "in open and avowed rebellion."

September 1775   Americans begin the invasion of Canada, reaching Montreal in December.

October 1775   General William Howe succeeds Gage as British commander-in-chief.

December 1775   Parliament passes the Prohibitory Act against trade with the colonies.

December 31, 1775   With the short enlistments of some soldiers expiring, American forces are defeated in an assault on Quebec City and settle into a winter siege.

January 1776   Britain begins to arrange for German states to provide twenty thousand mercenary troops to help suppress the rebellion.

February 1776 Loyalist Scots Highlanders are routed by rebel Whigs at the Battle of Moore's Creek Bridge in eastern North Carolina.

March 1776 American cannon on Dorchester Heights force the British to evacuate Boston and shift their military forces to Halifax, Nova Scotia.

May 1776 Congress adopts John Adams's resolution for the thirteen colonies to form their own governments, adding a preamble that calls for the suppression of executives holding office under Crown authority.

June 1776 British forces are repulsed in an attempt to capture Charleston, South Carolina. But American forces in Canada, defeated, abandon that campaign.

July 2–12, 1776 The Howe brothers, General William Howe and Admiral Richard Howe, arrive in New York Harbor with their huge army and fleet.

July 4, 1776 Congress accepts Thomas Jefferson's Declaration of Independence, and on July 12, a committee presents draft Articles of Confederation.

August–November 1776 General Howe defeats Washington in a series of engagements—in Long Island, Manhattan, and Westchester (White Plains), culminating in the captures of Forts Washington and Lee in Manhattan on November 16–18—and takes complete control of what is now metropolitan New York City, Long Island, and nearby New Jersey. Washington and the Americans, pursued by Howe, cross the Delaware from New Jersey into Pennsylvania.

October–November 1776 To the north, General Guy Carleton defeats a hastily built fleet of small American ships on Lake Champlain at the Battle of Valcour Island and recaptures the fort at Crown Point, but ends his expedition for the winter without making a serious attempt to recapture Fort Ticonderoga.

December 26, 1776 Washington surprises the British at Trenton and captures one thousand Hessian troops. He follows up with another victory at Princeton on January 3, somewhat restoring rebel morale.

June 18, 1777 General John Burgoyne's Champlain-Hudson expedition sets out from St. John, reaching Crown Point on June 27 and capturing Fort Ticonderoga on July 6.

July 23, 1777 Much of the British army and fleet under the Howe brothers departs from New York to capture Philadelphia instead of going north to join up with Burgoyne in Albany.

August 16, 1777 Part of Burgoyne's force is defeated and some nine hundred captured at the Battle of Bennington.

August 19, 1777 General Horatio Gates takes over the rebel command against Burgoyne from General Philip Schuyler.

September 11, 1777 George Washington fails to stop Howe's advance on Philadelphia at the Battle of the Brandywine.

September 19, 1777 Burgoyne and Gates fight a bloody but more or less drawn first engagement at Freeman's Farm on what is now the Saratoga battlefield.

September 26, 1777   The British occupy Philadelphia.

October 6, 1777   In a diversionary movement to help Burgoyne, British forces from New York capture the highland fortifications, Fort Clinton and Fort Montgomery, guarding the Hudson River narrows. But they do not make a major effort to reach Albany.

October 7, 1777   Burgoyne's forces are defeated at Bemis Heights, the second major engagement in the Saratoga vicinity. This makes surrender almost inevitable.

October 17, 1777   Burgoyne officially surrenders his army to General Gates.

November 1777   The British consolidate their control of the Philadelphia area, and in December, Washington begins withdrawing to nearby Valley Forge, where the American troops will spend the winter.

December 17, 1777   The French, who received news of Burgoyne's defeat on December 4, promise American commissioners in Paris that France will recognize American independence and make a treaty.

February 6, 1778   France and the United States sign a treaty of alliance, amity, and commerce. France and Britain go to war.

February 17, 1778   Britain appoints the Earl of Carlisle to head a peace commission to America, but Congress rejects any negotiations and says that no terms are acceptable short of British withdrawal and recognition of U.S. independence.

May 8, 1778   Sir Henry Clinton replaces Sir William Howe as British commander-in-chief and shifts British strategic emphasis to the southern colonies.

June 18, 1778   Clinton orders the evacuation of Philadelphia to concentrate forces in New York.

December 1778   New British strategic emphasis on the South starts to bear fruit with British capture of Savannah, Georgia.

June 1779   Spain joins France in the war against Britain.

October 1779   Clinton evacuates Rhode Island in order to concentrate British efforts in New York and the South.

May 1780   Clinton captures and occupies Charleston, South Carolina.

September 8, 1780   A British army under Earl Cornwallis invades North Carolina.

September 25, 1780   American General Benedict Arnold turns to the British side, but fails in his plot to betray and deliver the key fortress at West Point.

March 1781   Cornwallis loses one-quarter of his force at an indecisive battle at Guilford, North Carolina, and heads to Virginia, arriving at Yorktown in August.

September–October 1781   The French fleet turns back the British fleet off the Virginia Capes, denying Cornwallis naval support, while U.S. and French forces under General Washington and the Comte de Rochambeau encircle Yorktown. Cornwallis's surrender on October 19 ends the principal course of the war.

February 1782 After the news of Cornwallis's surrender, Parliament votes to discontinue offensive operations in America.

March 1782: A pro-American ministry headed by Lords Rockingham and Shelburne replaces the government of Lord North, and in April opens informal peace talks with American representatives in Paris.

May 1782 The British evacuate Savannah, Georgia, and Charleston, South Carolina.

November 29, 1782 A provisional peace agreement is reached in which Britain recognizes American independence and cedes all lands between the Great Lakes and the Mississippi River.

April 11-15, 1783 Congress proclaims the cessation of the war and ratifies the provisional treaty.

April 26, 1783 Some seven thousand loyalists leave New York, the last of the one hundred thousand who relocate to Britain or Canada.

November 25, 1783 British troops finally evacuate New York.

Note: The chronologies set out here draw, in particular, on the timelines in Barry Coward's *The Stuart Age (England 1603–1714)*, *The Blackwell Encyclopedia of the American Revolution*, and *The War of the American Revolution* (Center of Military History, United States Army).

The Chronology Surrounding the U.S. Civil War

December 1845–January 1846 Texas formally admitted to the Union. President Polk orders General Zachary Taylor to the Rio Grande.

March–May 1846 Mexican troops attack U.S. detachment. Battles of Palo Alto and Resaca de la Palma. U.S. declares war on Mexico.

March–April 1847 Taylor wins Battle of Buena Vista; General Winfield Scott captures Vera Cruz, begins advance inland.

August–September 1847 U.S. troops win Battles of Churubusco and Chapultepec, then go on to occupy Mexico City. Santa Ana relinquishes the Mexican presidency.

March–June 1848 U.S. and Mexico ratify Treaty of Guadeloupe-Hidalgo, in which Mexico relinquishes all claims to Texas and cedes to the U.S. territory including all of the present states of Arizona, Nevada, California, and Utah and parts of New Mexico, Colorado, and Wyoming, with the U.S. paying just $15,000,000. But the terms did not include cession or U.S. purchase of any of the half dozen Mexican states Southerners were becoming interested in. U.S. soldiers evacuate Mexico City.

May–November 1848 Whigs nominate General Taylor for president; Democrats nominate Lewis Cass of Michigan, while antislavery Democrats nominate ex-President Martin Van Buren on the Free Soil ticket. Taylor prevails easily, the last Whig to win a national election.

Summer–Autumn 1850   Congress votes to admit California as a free state, but also enacts the Compromise of 1850, which includes a fugitive slave law favorable to the South and unpopular in the North. On paper, California tilts the balance among the states to the antislavery side, but in fact its politics are Democratic, spurred by the high ratio of Southerners in the population.

1851–1852   Controversy over the fugitive slave law grows, while meetings and conventions in southern states ponder secession possibilities. Fugitive slave rescues rise. Harriet Beecher Stowe's antislavery tract *Uncle Tom's Cabin* achieves huge popularity and sales in the North. Irish and German immigration to the United States reaches several hundred thousand arrivals a year, setting records and stirring anti-immigrant and anti-Catholic feeling as the influx seems to correlate with rising crime, squalor, and drunkenness.

Summer–Autumn 1852   The Whigs nominate General Winfield Scott for president while the Democrats nominate New Hampshireman Franklin Pierce. John Hale runs as the Free Soil nominee. Pierce wins easily as the Whig party begins to fade in the South and Hale diverts antislavery Whig votes in the North. Anti-Catholicism becomes an issue as the Catholic hierarchy attacks Protestants while the latter mobilize against Catholics and foreigners. Many Northern Whigs stay home or decline to vote for High-Church Episcopalian Scott because he is called pro-Catholic. Religious politics build in intensity along with racial and sectional tensions.

November 1853   Frustration politics emerges as a major force in state and local elections as turnout slumps. Anti-immigrant, temperance, and Free Soil candidates gain at the expense of Democrats and Whigs. The outlines of the new American Party begin to emerge.

December 1853   The U.S. negotiates the Gadsden Purchase with Mexico, paying $15 million for a rectangular strip of territory in what is now southern Arizona. But southern hopes for larger territorial acquisitions in Mexico and the Caribbean continue to fail because of northern opposition in Congress.

May 1854   Congressional passage of the Kansas-Nebraska Act, overturning previous compromises and opening the western territories to slavery (or free-state status) based on popular sovereignty, infuriates antislavery Whigs and Democrats in the North, adding to the pressure for new political alignments.

February to July 1854   Meetings of Whigs, Free-Soilers, and antislavery Democrats in Wisconsin, Michigan, Vermont, Ohio, and Indiana lead to the organization of a new party, named "Republican," opposed to the extension of slavery into the territories.

November 1854   Old Democratic-Whig party system falls apart in the state and Congressional elections, but the Whigs find themselves embarrassed by two new parties—the Republicans and the Americans (Know-Nothings).

The latter run ahead of the Republicans in state elections in Massachusetts, New York, and Pennsylvania. The results in the House of Representatives are 108 Republicans, 83 Democrats, and 43 others.

1855 The "Kansas Question"—whether proslavery or antislavery forces will win control of the state—moves to the forefront of national politics, continuing into 1856.

February to November 1856 The Democrats nominate James Buchanan for president, who wins with 45 percent of the vote, Republican John C. Frémont coming in second with 33 percent, and Millard Fillmore, the American (Know-Nothing) Party nominee, drawing 22 percent. Sectionalism is pervasive, with Buchanan carrying the South and a few northern states, Frémont taking Greater New England, and Fillmore doing best in the border region. Despite Fillmore's 22 percent, the Know-Nothing Party is clearly losing out to the Republicans in the race to become the principal opposition to the Democrats.

March 1857 The U.S. Supreme Court, in the famous Dred Scott case, holds that for Congress to ban slavery in the territories was unconstitutional under the Fifth Amendment, angering Northerners and widening the cleavage between the sections.

August to September 1858 Debates between Abraham Lincoln and Stephen A. Douglas in their contest for an Illinois U.S. Senate seat emphasize the slavery issue and mark Lincoln's emergence as a national figure

November 1858 Lincoln fails to win the Illinois Senate seat—the state legislature elected Douglas—but Republicans dominated the northern elections, carrying all the state races save in Illinois and Indiana. The Republicans also gain 18 House seats, enabling them to take control of the U.S. House from the Democrats who had regained it in 1856.

October–December 1859 The raid by abolitionist radical John Brown on the federal arsenal in Harper's Ferry, Virginia, fails. He is tried, convicted, and hung in December, becoming a hero and a martyr to antislavery groups.

February to May 1860 In state legislatures and on the floor of Congress, cotton states politicians begin to talk more and more about secession, saying that the election of a Republican president would be just cause for dissolving the Union. Voters and leaders in the Upper South, by contrast, favor compromise and staying in the Union.

April to June The presidential election of 1860 escalates to four parties and nominees instead of three as the Democrats nominate Stephen Douglas of Illinois, the Republicans, Abraham Lincoln, the largely southern residue of the Whigs and Americans picks John Bell of Tennessee on the so-called Constitutional Union ticket, and and proslavery Southern Democrats nominate John C. Breckinridge of Kentucky.

November 1860 Abraham Lincoln wins 39.8 percent of the popular vote, taking all the northern states but New Jersey for a broad margin in the

Electoral College. Douglas wins 29.5 percent, Breckinridge takes 18.1 percent, and Bell 12.6 percent. The South faces just what it has been afraid of—a "black Republican" in the White House.

December 1860 to February 1861   South Carolina votes to secede on Dec. 20, and the rest of the lower South follows suit: Mississippi on January 9, Florida on January 10, Alabama on January 11, Georgia on January 19, Louisiana on January 26, and Texas on February 1. On February 8, the seven hold a secession conference in Montgomery, Alabama, to frame a constitution and form a provisional government. The states of the Upper South continue to remain in the Union.

March 1861   Lincoln is inaugurated in Washington, but promises not to interfere with slavery in the states where it already exists. He also says that the South has no right to secede.

April 6–12, 1861   Lincoln notifies South Carolina on April 6 that a federal expedition is en route to provision the federal garrison of Fort Sumter in Charleston Harbor. On the morning of April 12, Confederate shore batteries open fire on Sumter.

April 15 to May 1861   On April 15, Lincoln says that an "insurrection" exists and calls for 75,000 troops. A wave of patriotism sweeps the North, but the Upper South decides to cast its lot with the Confederacy. Virginia secedes (April 20), then Arkansas (May 6), Tennessee (May 7), and North Carolina (May 20). The spotlight swings to Maryland, Kentucky, and Missouri, where opinion is divided. Kentucky tries to be neutral, while Federal troops dominate Maryland and Missouri.

July 21, 1861   Confederate troops win the first major battle at Bull Run in northern Virginia, cheering the South and bringing home to northern opinion that it could be a serious and lengthy war. Irwin McDowell, the northern general defeated at Bull Run, is replaced by General George B. McClellan who becomes commander-in-chief of the Federal armies in November.

November 1861   The federal warship *San Jacinto* causes a major furor when it stops the British steamer *Trent* and removes John Mason and James Slidell, two Confederate commissioners on the way to England. Washington officials are angry with the British because in May, the latter had declared their neutrality in a statement that recognized the belligerency of the Confederacy. Nevertheless, Mason and Slidell are released in December.

January–August 1862   The war heats up with northern forces making gains in the West—the capture of Forts Henry and Donelson on the Tennessee River in February, and the fall of New Orleans in April. But the war in the East goes badly for the North—defeats and stalemates in Virginia. By August, Confederate forces have won at the Second Battle of Bull Run and are ready to advance into Maryland.

September 1862   On September 17, Antietam becomes the bloodiest battle of the war, winding up as a draw. But the Confederates under Robert E.

Lee withdraw to Virginia, giving the North a badly needed technical victory. This causes Britain and France to delay recognition that might otherwise have taken place. Lincoln also takes advantage of the Confederate retreat to announce his Preliminary Emancipation Proclamation: that on January 1, 1863, he will free the slaves in all areas still in rebellion against the United States.

November 1862   The Congressional elections go poorly for the Republicans, especially in the Middle West—Ohio, Indiana, and Illinois. But luckily for Lincoln, those states were not electing governors that year or the Union cause could have been in some danger in those states by January.

December 1862   Despite a much larger Union army, northern forces are badly beaten by the Confederates at the Battle of Fredericksburg in Maryland. Commanding General Ambrose Burnside is replaced.

January 1, 1863   Lincoln issues the Emancipation Proclamation, angering Southern Unionists but laying the framework for northern victory in the battle for British public opinion.

March 1863   The first Conscription Act spurs draft protests and riots in the North, especially in Irish, German, and Ohio Valley butternut districts. The Confederacy's resort to conscription is no more popular.

May to July 1863   The siege of Vicksburg, in Mississippi, and the battle of Gettysburg in Pennsylvania, produce the two most important northern victories of the war. Vicksburg's surrender on July 4, the same day Lee begins his retreat back to Virginia, marks a major turn in the war's fortunes—in restropect probably pivotal.

September to November 1863   Further northern victories at Chickamauga and Chattanooga, in Tennessee, confirm the Union tide.

May to June 1864   Once again, Virginia helps the Confederacy to overcome northern gains to the west. But despite the Confederate victories in the Battles of the Wilderness, Spotsylvania, and Cold Harbor, the Confederacy is also being worn down—and Lee's army is much less able to replace its losses.

May to September 1864   While Grant is bogged down in eastern Virginia, General William Tecumseh Sherman captures Atlanta, and General Philip Sheridan takes control of the Shenandoah Valley. These armies are now positioned to consolidate victory outside of the eastern Virginia theater.

November 1864   After being afraid of going down to defeat as late as early August, Lincoln decisively defeats the Democratic presidential nominee, former general George McClellan. Southerners correctly interpret Lincoln's re-election as meaning that the North will maintain and intensify its now increasingly successful war effort.

January to February 1865   Riots and demonstrations against the Confederate government break out in southern cities. Sherman's troops sweep through the Carolinas.

April 2 TO 9, 1865   Lee abandons Richmond, the Confederate capital. By April 7, Lee's army is surrounded, and on April 9, he surrenders.

April 14, 1865   Abraham Lincoln is assassinated while he attends Ford's Theater in Washington.

NOTES

Chapter One

1. Christopher Hill, *The English Bible and the 17th Century Revolution* (New York: Penguin, 1993), pp. 264, 274.

2. Christopher Hill, *Puritanism and the Revolution* (New York: St. Martin's, 1997), pp. 37–40.

3. A.L. Rowse, *The Expansion of Elizabethan England* (New York: St. Martin's, 1955), pp. vii and 158–159.

4. Ibid., pp. 176–177.

5. Linda Colley, *Britons* (New Haven: Yale University Press, 1992), p. 330.

6. Barry Coward, *The Stuart Age: England 1603–1714* (London: Longman, 1994), p. 199.

7. Patricia U. Bonomi, *Under the Cope of Religion* (New York: Oxford University Press, 1986), p. 157.

8. Carl Bridenbaugh, *Vexed and Troubled Englishmen* (New York: Oxford University Press), p. 465.

9. William Hunt, *The Puritan Moment: The Coming of Revolution in an English County* (Cambridge: Harvard University Press, 1983), p. 87.

10. Christopher Hill, *Society and Puritanism in Prerevolutionary England* (1964), pp. 1–2.

11. George M. Trevelyan, *England Under the Stuarts* (London: Methuen, 1949), p. 50.

12. Coward, op. cit., pp. 83–87.

13. David Hackett Fischer, *Albion's Seed: Four British Folkways in America* (New York: Oxford University Press, 1989), p. 46.

14. Bridenbaugh, op. cit., pp. 472–473.

15. Trevelyan, op. cit., pp. 150–151.

16. Penelope Corfield, "Economic Issues and Ideologies," in Conrad Russell, ed., *The Origins of the English Civil War* (London: Macmillan, 1980), p. 213.

17. Bridenbaugh, op. cit., pp. 468–469.

18. Richard C. Dunn, *Puritans and Yankees* (Princeton: Princeton University Press, 1962), pp. 34–35.

19. Bridenbaugh, op. cit., pp. 69, 77, 213; Fischer, op. cit., p. 57.

20. Bridenbaugh, op. cit., pp. 244–247; Fischer, op. cit., pp. 196–197.

21. Fischer, op. cit., 130–132; Bridenbaugh, op. cit., p. 347.

22. Fischer, op. cit., pp. 44–48.

23. Bernard Bailyn, *The Ideological Origins of the American Revolution* (Cambridge: Harvard University Press, 1992), pp. 79–83.

24. Bridenbaugh, op. cit., p. 402.

25. R. H. Tawney, *Religion and the Rise of Capitalism* (New York: Mentor, 1954), p. 165.

26. Hunt, op. cit., p. 161.

Chapter Two

1. Alfred A. Young, "English Plebeian Culture and 18th Century American Radicalism" in Margaret Jacob and James Jacob, eds., *The Origins of Anglo-American Radicalism* (New Jersey: Humanities Press International, 1991), p. 195.

2. Dunn, op. cit., p. 67.

3. Ibid., pp. 66–68.

4. John Buchan, *Oliver Cromwell* (Boston: Houghton-Mifflin, 1934), p. 84.

5. Lawrence Stone, *Social Change and Revolution in England, 1540–1640* (New York: Barnes & Noble, 1965), p. xviii.

6. C. V. Wedgwood, *The King's Peace* (New York: Macmillan, 1956), p. 45.

7. David Underdown, *Revel, Riot and Rebellion* (New York: Oxford University Press, 1987), pp. 44–72.

8. Trevelyan, op. cit., p. 41.

9. In 1642, and again in 1643, 1647, and 1648, over a thousand books—excluding newspapers—were published on political or religious topics; and the beginnings of the English newspaper in the 1620s led into its fuller emergence in the 1640s, with as many as ten journals a week appearing. Derek Hirst, *Authority and Conflict: England, 1603–1658* (Cambridge: Harvard University Press, 1986), p. 194.

10. Puritan civic involvement was especially intense. While tenants on the fat manor lands of Wiltshire or Worcestershire celebrated a saint's day or paused for autumn Michaelmas events, the townspeople of Puritan centers like Dorchester, Stroud, and Norwich, besides condemning drunkenness and immorality, did have their own celebrations: Guy Fawkes Day (the exposure of the Catholic Gunpowder Plot) doubled as the Protestant Halloween; Dorchester rang its bells in 1631 for the victory of the Swedish Protestant warrior-king, Gustavus Adolphus, at the Battle of Breitenfeld; and Norwich, less hospitable to mere entertainment, had no objection to a waxworks featuring an effigy of King Gustavus. Underdown, op. cit., p. 71.

11. Tawney, op. cit., p. 152.

12. Wedgwood, op. cit., pp. 159–161.

13. The tin mines in Cornwall, the iron and coal belt in Derbyshire, the coal mines of Durham, Northumberland, and Wales all provided income for the King and, oftentimes, soldiers for his army. The coal miners of Cannock Chase, whose descendants would be red-tinged Socialists three hundred years later, served in 1643 as sappers to help Prince Rupert mine the walls of Parliamentarian Lichfield. Richard Cust and Ann Hughes, eds., *Conflict in Early Stuart England* (New York: Longman, 1989), pp. 239, 242; *Civil War in England*, p. 66; John Morrill, *The Nature of the English Revolution* (New York: Longman, 1993), p. 218.

14. Christopher Hill, *The Century of Revolution 1603–1714* (New York: Norton, 1982), p. 30.

15. Ibid., p. 22; Cust and Hughes, eds., op. cit., p. 242.

16. Tawney, op. cit., p. 169.

17. Max Weber, in *The Protestant Ethic and the Spirit of Capitalism,* argues that Calvinism and, in particular, English Puritanism, played an essential part in creating the moral and political conditions favorable to the growth of capitalist enterprise. Tawney, in his notes to Chapter 4 of *Religion and the Rise of Capitalism,* agrees with much of

what Weber wrote, but criticizes Weber's skipping over the extent to which capitalism also had roots in the Catholic commercial cultures of Flanders and Italy, Weber's insufficient acknowledgment of the various strands of Calvinism and Puritanism, and his minimal attention to the further impact of phenomena like the Renaissance and Machiavellian realpolitik. My analysis, in turn, would be that Tawney, too, may have somewhat overplayed the Puritans relative to the Tudors and the larger maritime culture of Britain. Nor does Tawney do more than touch on the role of New England in carrying forward the rise of capitalism, but then his time frame doesn't really go beyond the sixteenth and seventeenth centuries.

18. John Morrill, op. cit., pp. 69–89.

19. Austin Woolwych, *Battles of the English Civil Wars* (London: Pan Books, 1966), pp. 37, 90.

20. The interpretive tide of British historiography in the 1980s and 1990s has been in the direction of attributing more rather than less importance to religion as a cause and source of alignments of the English Civil War. New books and articles by historians like John Morrill (*The Nature of the English Revolution,* 1993), Conrad Russell (*The Causes of the English Civil War,* 1990), and Barry Coward (*The Stuart Age,* 2nd ed., 1994), as well as contributions by religious specialists like Nicholas Tyacke and Robin Clifton, have made, variously, a number of points. They are that anti-Catholicism permeated English Protestantism, that it influenced High Church Anglicans as well as Puritans, and that besides the inevitable local quarrels, the best yardsticks for measuring activism on each side were religious—by 1642 and 1643, the King's supporters tended to be pro-episcopacy, pro-Laudian Anglicans, and mostly Catholics (who were a small minority overall, but more important among the aristocracy), while Parliament drew heavily on the other side, Puritans and the Low Church Anglicans suspicious of bishops, High Church Anglicans, Catholic plots by the King and Queen, and the threat Catholicism posed to English institutions. At the local or county level, studies that have shown the people or the nobility and gentry dividing substantially along these lines include a group of analyses of northern counties, most Royalist in which the polarizations were between Puritan-minded supporters of Parliament and disproportionately Catholic Royalists, while in the south of England, where Catholics were fewer, the essential division was usually between Puritans and adherents of a more ceremonial, ritualistic, and arguably more easygoing Anglicanism. The findings for six northern shires—Shropshire, Cheshire, Lancashire, Yorkshire, Cumberland, and Westmorland—are summarized in Morrill, op. cit., pp. 204–206. Ann Hughes, in *Conflict in Early Stuart England,* op. cit., p. 231, notes that in Essex, Wiltshire, and other southern counties, the split was between Puritans and ceremonial Anglicans. For the purposes of *The Cousins' Wars,* this underscores the heritage lurking in the background for the American rebels of 1775—and following beyond them into the nineteenth century. Morrill, op. cit., p. 68.

21. Ibid., p. 153.

22. J. P. Kenyon, op. cit., p. 84.

23. Christopher Hill, *The World Turned Upside Down* (New York: Viking Press, 1972), pp. 59–69.

24. Ibid., p. 64.

25. Dunn, op. cit., p. 48.

26. Ibid., pp. 54–55.

27. Trevelyan, op. cit., pp. 283–284.

28. The first rising to follow Charles's restoration was a three-day bout of London street fighting in 1661 led by New England–born Thomas Venner, a former Puritan who had become a Fifth Monarchist committed to launching a thousand-year reign of "King Jesus" by a popular rebellion. This was followed in 1663 by the Derwentdale Plot of 1663, a north-of-England conspiracy of Presbyterians and Anabaptists. J. C. D.

Clark, *The Language of Liberty, 1660–1832* (Cambridge: Cambridge University Press, 1994), pp. 225–227.

29. Hill, *Century of Revolution,* op. cit., pp. 205–206.

30. K. Merle Chacksfield, *Glorious Revolution 1688 (*Somerset: Wincanton Press, 1988), pp. 55–56.

31. David S. Lovejoy, *The Glorious Revolution in America* (New York: Harper Torch Books, 1974), pp. 354–361.

32. Stephen Saunders Webb, *1676: The End of American Independence* (Syracuse: Syracuse University Press, 1995), pp. 6, 27–28.

33. Richard L. Bushman, *King and People in Provincial Massachusetts* (Chapel Hill: University of North Carolina Press, 1992), p. 101.

34. David S. Lovejoy, "Two American Revolutions, 1689 and 1776," in J. G. A. Pocock, ed., *Three British Revolutions* (Princeton: Princeton University Press, 1980), p. 253.

35. Ibid., p. 249.

36. Lawrence Stone, "The Results of the English Revolutions of the 17th Century," in Pocock, ibid., pp. 57–62.

37. C. G. Robertson, *England Under the Hanoverians* (London: Methuen, 1923), p. 23.

Chapter Three

1. See Douglas Leach, *Roots of Conflict: British Armed Forces and Colonial Americans, 1677–1763* (Chapel Hill: University of North Carolina Press, 1986) and John Shy in *Toward Lexington: The Role of the British Army in the Coming of the American Revolution* (Princeton: Princeton University Press, 1965).

2. Bailyn, op. cit., pp. 61–66.

3. Don Cook, *The Long Fuse* (New York: Atlantic Monthly Press, 1995), p. 34.

4. Ian Christie and Benjamin Labaree, *Empire or Independence, 1760–1776* (New York: 1976), pp. 31–34.

5. Theodore Draper, *A Struggle for Power* (New York: Times Books, 1996), p. 208.

6. Christie and Labaree, op. cit., p. 92.

7. Cook, op. cit., p. 120.

8. Draper, op. cit., p. 324.

9. Gary Nash, *The Urban Crucible* (Cambridge: Harvard University Press, 1986), pp. 205, 231, 238.

10. William Warren Sweet, "The Role of the Anglicans in the American Revolution," *Huntington Library Quarterly,* vol. II, 1947–1948, pp. 70–71.

11. Pauline Maier, *The Old Revolutionaries* (New York: Norton, 1980), p. 204.

12. Sydney Ahlstrom, *A Religious History of the American People* (New Haven: Yale University Press, 1972), p. 34.

13. Carl Bridenbaugh, *Mitre and Sceptre* (New York: Oxford University Press, 1962), p. 313.

14. Bailyn, op. cit., p. 257.

15. Bonomi, op. cit., p. 4.

16. Harry S. Stout, *The New England Soul* (New York: 1986), pp. 6, 260, 277; Clark, op. cit., p. 44.

17. Bonomi, op. cit., p. 176.

18. Ibid., p. 195.

19. Ibid., p. 5.

20. Reginald Stuart, "For the Lord Is a Man of Warr," *Journal of Church and State* (Autumn 1981), p. 519.

21. Bonomi, op. cit., pp. 152–153.

22. J. C. D. Clark, op. cit., p. 275.

23. Bonomi, op. cit., pp. 206–207.

24. Ibid., p. 187.

25. Whereas the Whig historians of the nineteenth century blamed George III and the "Tories" around him for provoking and losing the thirteen colonies, the British imperial school that has since emerged has found little that was tyrannical in the Crown's behavior. More blame is attached to the fiscal pressures that followed the Great French War, to poorly thought-out ministerial policies, and to the way in which the interests of the rapidly growing colonies and the increasingly imperially minded mother country were diverging. A few British historians—J. C. D. Clark at Oxford is one—have argued that religion was very much involved because the dissenting Protestantism and Low Church Anglicanism of the colonies was central to the widening gap and to the rebellion.

26. See, for example, Esmond Wright, *Causes and Consequences of the American Revolution* (Chicago: Quadrangle, 1966), p. 4.

27. Horace Walpole, *Memoirs of the Reign of George III*, Vol. 2, p. 243.

28. The tendency to downplay the intellectual influence upon the American Revolution of the Seventeenth Commonwealth theorists—so-called Commonwealthmen like James Harrington and Algernon Sidney—comes from several directions. The first, more indirect, is Bernard Bailyn's emphasis instead on a more radical pre-1775 literature of pamphlets, sermons, and jeremiads. See Bailyn, op. cit., pp. 1–21. The second is from the analysis by J. C. D. Clark that the works of Harrington, Sidney, and their colleagues were simply not reprinted in the colonies, although that hardly means that they were unavailable. See Clark, *The Language of Liberty 1660–1832*, pp. 23–27.

29. James C. Spalding, "Loyalist as Royalist," *Church History* 45 (September 1976), pp. 329–340.

30. Alfred Young, "English Plebeian Culture and 18th Century American Radicalism," Jacob and Jacob, eds., op. cit. (NJ: Humanities Press, 1991), p. 195.

31. Ibid., p. 194.

32. Ibid., p. 196.

33. Ibid., pp. 198–199.

34. In *The Causes of the English Civil War* (1993), Conrad Russell has compiled a list of the twenty-two towns and villages that gathered volunteers for the Parliamentary army before the standard was actually raised in August 1642. His list—see Appendix—begins with Nottingham and ends with Bridport, and has an extraordinary overlap with towns and boroughs that had "pro-American" Members of Parliament during the 1775–1782 period, held serious debates over policy in America, or signed conciliatory petitions as discussed in chapter 6.

35. Max Savelle, *Empires to Nations* (Minneapolis: University of Minnesota Press, 1974), p. 38.

36. Eric Robson, *The American Revolution* (London: Batchworth, 1955), p. 15; Savelle, op. cit., p. 213.

37. Wright, op. cit., p. 128.

38. Ibid., pp. 162–163.

39. Steven Watson, *George III* (London: Oxford University Press, 1960), p. 92.

40. Robson, op. cit., p. 7.

41. Christie and Larabee, op. cit., p. 43.

42. Robinson, op. cit., p. 8; Draper, op. cit., p. 128.

43. Ibid., p. 118.

44. J. H. Plumb, *England in the 18th Century* (Harmondsworth, England: Penguin, 1966), p. 126.

45. Ibid., p. 126.

46. Robson, op. cit., p. 52.

47. Marc Egnal, *A Mighty Empire* (Ithaca: Cornell University Press, 1988), p. 304.
48. T. H. Breen, *Tobacco Culture* (Princeton: Princeton University Press, 1985), p. 128.
49. Chard P. Smith, *Yankees and God* (New York: Hermitage House, 1954), p. 114; Egnal, op. cit., p. 26.
50. Egnal, op. cit., pp. 1–15.
51. Ibid., p. 299.
52. Jack P. Greene, *Understanding the American Revolution* (Charlottesville: University Press of Virginia, 1995), p. 153.
53. John Shy, *A People Numerous and Armed* (Ann Arbor: University of Michigan Press, 1990), p. 24.

Chapter Four

1. Thomas Raddell, *Path of Destiny* (New York: Popular Library, 1957), p. 19.
2. Alison G. Olson, "Parliament, Empire and Parliamentary Law, 1776," in J. G. A. Pocock, ed., op. cit., pp. 315–316.
3. The two articles in question are: George W. Kyte, "Some Plans for a Loyalist Stronghold in the Middle Colonies," *Pennsylvania History*, Vol. 16, 1949, pp. 3–16, and George W. Kyte, "A Projected British Attack on Philadelphia in 1781," *Pennsylvania Magazine of History and Biography*, Oct. 1952, pp. 379–393.
4. Analyses of how the American rebels might have invaded Nova Scotia in late 1775 usually go little further than to note the disinterest of Massachusetts leaders like John Adams—the British were still occupying Boston at the time—or the cautious attitudes of the transplanted New Englanders who made up about one-half of the Nova Scotia population. However, if Benedict Arnold, instead of taking his force up Maine's Kennebec River that autumn to join in investing Quebec, had taken a small Yankee fleet with a thousand men to raise the Nova Scotia New Englanders and to capture the weakly defended capital and military base at Halifax, it might have succeeded. If Halifax had fallen in late October, the Royal Navy probably could not have recaptured it until the spring, which would have greatly complicated their ability to relieve and resupply Quebec and Montreal. Halifax was the critical base until the St. Lawrence thawed in May.
5. In his book *Path of Destiny*, (pp. 50–51), Canadian historian Thomas Raddell notes that in February 1776, "the *congressistes* were still actively recruiting among the population. General Wooster had given them a good talking point this month when he commanded free elections in the Canadian parishes, cutting away the last traditional authority of the *seigneurs* and of the governor. The *congressiste* merchants of Montreal were busy supplying Arnold's army from their own stocks and with provisions gathered in the countryside. At Three Rivers the ironworks of Christophe Pélissier were casting mortars and bombshells and making various military tools for Arnold's use. These forges, employing four hundred to eight hundred Canadians, remained an arsenal for the Americans during the whole period of the occupation."
6. Allan S. Everest, *Moses Hazen and the Canadian Refugees in the American Revolution* (Syracuse, NY: Syracuse University Press, 1976), p. 39.
7. General Frederick Haldimand, who took over as Canadian commander-in-chief in June 1778, ordered the construction of a new fort at the eastern end of Lake Ontario to protect the St. Lawrence and improved the British defenses at St. John's, and at Quebec itself. He also ordered the Loyal Block House built as an advance post on North Hero Island, in what is now the northernmost Vermont portion of Lake Champlain. In early 1782, following Cornwallis's capitulation at Yorktown, the British had a brief final scare from reports of a joint Franco-American invasion force gathering. But it never took place.

8. G. A. Rawlyk, "The American Revolution and Canada," in *The Blackwell Encyclopedia of the American Revolution* (Oxford: Blackwell Publishers, 1994), pp. 499–500.

9. Henry C. Wilkinson, "They Built Small Ships of Cedar," in C. W. Toth, ed., *The American Revolution in the West Indies* (Port Washington, NY: Kennikat Press, 1975), p. 165.

10. Selwyn H. Carrington, "The American Revolution and the Sugar Colonies," in *The Blackwell Encyclopedia,* op. cit., pp. 514–515.

11. Ibid., p. 513.

12. Max Mintz, *The Generals at Saratoga* (New Haven: Yale University Press, 1990), p. 74.

13. Russell Bellico, *Sails and Steam in the Mountains: A Maritime and Military History of Lake Champlain* (New York: Purple Mountain Press, 1992), p. 152.

14. Piers Mackesy, *The War for America, 1775–1783* (Lincoln, NE: Bison Books, 1993), p. 96.

15. Mintz, op. cit., p. 114.

16. Ibid., p. 161.

17. Colin Haydon, *Anti-Catholicism in 18th-Century England* (London: 1993), p. 76.

18. Colley, op. cit., p. 52.

Chapter Five

1. South Carolina historical markers and tourist brochures illustrate the dilemma of America's two civil wars. It's almost possible to smell the gunpowder on Charleston's famous Battery, where *the* Civil War started on the morning of April 12, 1861, when artillery aimed opened fire on Fort Sumter. Yet the prior civil war of eighty years earlier is indisputable. South Carolinians circa 1860, more than most other Americans, should remember its neighbor-versus-neighbor character. Local historian Edward McCrady counted an extraordinary 137 battles, actions, and engagements of the Revolution in the Palmetto State, of which 103 were fought by South Carolinians alone on *both* sides. In twenty others, South Carolinians took part with troops from other states. Few, if any, states could match that awful measure in 1861–1865. Missouri, torn by guerrilla warfare down the Missouri-Kansas border below Kansas City, probably came closest.

2. Five hundred miles to the north, on Route 15 heading into Gettysburg, Pennsylvania, the nation's greatest concentration of historical markers and monuments also describes how *the* Civil War climaxed a few miles away. There are no markers to describe how, in the 1770s, when the future Cemetery Ridge and Little Round Top were still part of next-door York County, a York militia colonel, William Rankin, came close to starting an earlier civil war in that part of Pennsylvania. After two years of ostensibly suppressing British sympathizers, in 1778 he began *enlisting* some of them in clandestine loyalist units. These men, he wrote secretly to Sir Henry Clinton in New York, were ready to rise in support of a British invasion of Chesapeake Bay and its Pennsylvania hinterland. Between 1778 and 1781, Rankin or one of his associates promised from 1,800 to as many as 7,000 potential adherents. Earlier, in August 1777, when General Howe had landed in northern Chesapeake Bay to march to Philadelphia, lower Pennsylvania from Croghan's Gap to Lancaster County hummed with talk of a loyalist rising. The Rankins were said to have 500 men, the sheriff of Lancaster 800. Cattle and grain were being gathered for Howe's army. But five days before the Battle of Brandywine, informants notified the rebel authorities. At least one conspirator was arrested—and the rising never took place. Even so, Rankin's name was well-known to Tory leaders in New York. Former New Jersey governor William Franklin and John Graves Simcoe, commander of the Queen's Rangers, both believed Rankin enough in 1780 to

make separate proposals to lead invasions that would link up with his forces. The most comprehensive discussion appears in Carl Van Doren, *A Secret History of the Revolution* (New York: The Viking Press, 1941).

The broad region that Rankin hoped to convulse included the eastern shore and Upper Chesapeake Bay areas of Maryland and the southern three-quarters of Delaware, as well as the German-dominated districts of Pennsylvania (from Lancaster, Lebanon, and Ephrata west to York and Hanover) and western Maryland (between Baltimore and Frederick). Its potential explosiveness, never tested, remains one of the war's great unknowns. Tories were numerous among the substantial Anglican population. Would-be neutralism was the rule among Quakers and pacifist German sects like the Amish, Mennonites, and Moravians. Even many of the Lutheran and Reformed "Church Germans," recent immigrants, refused to break oaths sworn earlier to the British Crown. In York County the non-oathtakers to the new government, called nonjurors, were mostly Germans. Some were outright Tories. The Pennsylvania-Maryland region also included the colonies' only significant Catholic subculture: Maryland tobacco gentry, plus German and Irish immigrants, former indentured servants, and runaways. It was well known that Maryland had America's harshest indentured-servant laws. Maltreated white servants, many Irish, had been identified as possible insurrectionists by the French in the Great War. They would be again by the British in 1775–1776.

Rankin's civil war could have been a fierce one, although Pennsylvania historians shrug. Secret meetings and cabals notwithstanding, no rising ever occurred. The chief plotter himself finally fled to British-occupied New York in 1781. Yet American historian Carl Van Doren, working from British documents and records, has described these machinations at length, and *Pennsylvania History Magazine* published a detailed article in 1949 entitled "Some Plans for a Loyalist Stronghold in the Middle Colonies." Half a dozen senior British officers, at one time or another, urged a major invasion through the Upper Chesapeake. If so, the unimportant hamlet of Marsh Creek, the future Gettysburg, might have been a battlefield eighty-five years earlier. Nearby Hanover, the town in which the first Civil War engagement north of the Mason-Dixon line was fought on June 30, 1863, could have seen an important skirmish in 1779. Rankin reported to New York that a Hanover resident named Scherrop had organized a loyalist regiment of six hundred, mostly Catholics, then a significant local minority in that area. Had this region erupted during those years, the latter-day signposting around Gettysburg would be more complicated: *The Civil* War? Which civil war?

3. Henry S. Young, *The Treatment of Loyalists in Pennsylvania* (Ph.D. thesis, Johns Hopkins University, 1955), pages unnumbered in copy.

4. John Shy, op. cit., p. 178.

5. All forty-seven Nantucket Quakers who served in the war were disowned by Nantucket's other Quakers. One, Paul Hussey, was read out of the island's Quaker meeting for simply going onboard an armed ship to negotiate a prisoner exchange. Because of these attitudes, Congress and the Massachusetts House of Representatives bluntly identified the island as a nest of Tories. Indeed, Quaker anger at the war involved more than religious beliefs. Nantucket's commerce was temporarily ruined. See Edwin P. Hoyt, *Nantucket* (Brattleboro, VT: The Stephen Greene Press, 1978), p. 28. In Rhode Island, where Quakers were a tenth of the population, few would fight and prosperous Newport merchants cooperated with the British occupation. But the state's most prominent general, Nathaniel Greene, was a fallen-away Quaker, dropped from membership when he joined the militia.

6. Independent-minded Vermonters even negotiated for separate recognition from the British during the period from 1779 to 1782, although the talks were partly designed to help them stave off claims by New York and New Hampshire. The western towns of New Hampshire were themselves semi-independent during the 1776–1782 period. When, at one point, three dozen tried to break away and join Vermont, congres-

sional intervention was necessary to avert civil war. British success in occupying Maine's lower Penobscot Valley after 1779 led Whitehall to consider establishing a new loyal province, New Ireland, to be a southern buffer between Nova Scotia and New England, just as an independent Vermont would have been a buffer state along the Champlain-Hudson Corridor.

7. *Greenwich: A Tea Party Town,* local pamphlet.

8. *The Tea-burners of Cumberland County,* local pamphlet, p. 20.

9. When Georgia meetings could not agree on sending delegates to the Continental Congresses in 1774 and 1775, the disgusted Congregationalists cut off trade with the rest of Georgia and tried to join South Carolina. The royal governor, Sir James Wright, condemned politics in St. John's as "Oliverian," but the impatient parish elected Dr. Lyman Hall as its own delegate to the Continental Congress and sent him north with £100 worth of food and £50 in currency for the relief of the port of Boston. For these pains, in 1779, St. John's (Midway) Congregational meetinghouse became one of the first southern churches to be burned by the British army.

10. David N. Doyle, *Ireland, Irishmen and Revolutionary America* (Cork: The Mercier Press, 1981), pp. 109–112.

11. Kerby A. Miller, *Emigrants and Exiles* (New York: Oxford University Press, 1985), pp. 137–149.

12. In the decades after 1717, as the Scotch-Irish began to leave Ulster for America, their fierce Protestantism was often that of persecuted refugees. Besides the Covenanters, fleeing from dragoons in southwest Scotland, the Ulster stock even included several thousand French Huguenots uprooted after the revocation of the Edict of Nantes in 1685. Two men of such antecedents would play prominent military roles on the American Revolutionary frontier: General John Sevier—"Nolichucky Jack" to his Holston settlers—who won at Kings Mountain in 1780, and General Andrew Lewis, who commanded in western Virginia.

13. The Ulster Scots who came to America were a unique breed. Unlike Scots who stayed in Ayr or Lanark, those moving to Ulster left feudalism behind and assumed control over their own lives, vocations, and residences. No lairds came along. Second, after two or three generations on a rugged frontier that was mixing Protestant ethnic strains, even the Scots lost some of their identity. They recognized a shared heritage with Scotland, but *Ulster* became the place to which they were loyal. Third, the Puritanical, covenanting Presbyterianism of the Scotch-Irish was unlike the religion of most of the rest of Scotland—poles apart from the old Catholicism of the highlands, altogether unlike the Jacobite Anglicanism of the northeast, and different enough from the more cosmopolitan Presbyterianism of Edinburgh, soon to come under the Enlightenment. The other Scots that Ulstermen resembled most were the old Covenanters of the southwest, which was fitting. James G. Leyburn, *The Scotch-Irish* (Chapel Hill: University of North Carolina Press, 1962), pp. 140–143.

14. The economic provocations and tribulations encouraging emigration were multiple: the Woollens Act of 1699, which forced Irish producers to export all their cloth through England and Wales, denying them foreign and colonial markets; the droughts of the "teen years"; the pain and provocation of widespread rack-renting (rent increases) by landlords; famine winters like the legendary "black frost" of 1739–1740; and, by the 1770s, hard times in the hitherto successful linen industry. In the early years of the eighteenth century, religious discrimination added to these discontents. The established Church of Ireland, a replica of Anglican worship and backed by English authority, took umbrage at the growth of the Presbyterian church the Ulster Scots had brought with them. Marriages performed by Presbyterian clergymen were declared illegal. The Test Act of 1704, enacted against Ulster Presbyterians in particular, excluded Protestant dissenters from all civil and military offices under the Crown. Officeholders

were required to take Anglican communion. In Belfast and Londonderry, large numbers of Presbyterian magistrates and town councilmen were forced to resign. Some relief for dissenters came in 1719. After that, emigration was principally economic.

15. Leyburn, op. cit., p. 169.

16. Hubertis M. Cummings, *Scots Breed and Susquehanna* (Pittsburgh: University of Pittsburgh Press, 1974), pp. 293–298.

17. Henry S. Young, op. cit. (pages not numbered).

18. Thomas Fleming, *New Jersey* (New York: Norton, 1984), p. 62.

19. Emory G. Evans, "Trouble in the Back Country," in Ronald Hoffman and Thad Tate, eds., *An Uncivil War: The War in the Southern Back Country* (Charlottesville, University of Virginia Press, 1985), p. 179.

20. The Waxhaws would become notorious to British officials. In 1758, the congregation of Sugar Creek Church called the Reverend Alexander Craighead a man of highly controversial religious beliefs akin to those of the Cameronians. This radical Scottish sect rejected not only the Stuarts but the English settlement of 1689 and even the Hanoverian kings in their roles as heads of the Church of England. Anglican missionaries reported this radicalism to London: that Mecklenburg was populated by "dissenters of the most rigid" kind hostile to England and its church. The Presbyterian ministers and congregations of Mecklenburg and adjacent Rowan County bred much of the vehemence that would be voiced years later, following the confrontation at Lexington, in the famous Mecklenburg Resolves of May 1775. These declared the authority of king and Parliament annulled and vacated, much like the language of Scotland's Presbyterian Convention in 1689 in arguing that James II had "forfaulted" the Crown. Rowan, next door, passed the boldes of North Carolina's local resolves, calling for an "indissoluble union" of the colonies, and becoming the first county to form a committee of safety. A Rowan town caught up in the *rage militaire* was another of those that changed its name to Lexington. Colonel Banastre Tarleton, Lord Cornwallis's cavalry commander, observed, "The counties of Mecklenburg and Rohon [Rowan] were more hostile to England than any others in America." Their contribution to America's frontier spirit could also be said to include Andrew Jackson, born nearby, and Daniel Boone, a brief resident, along with the ancestors of Davy Crockett and Kit Carson.

21. Billy Kennedy, *The Scots-Irish in the Shenandoah* (Belfast: Causeway Press, 1996), p. 94.

22. "Patriots and Tories in Piedmont Carolina" (Salisbury, NC: *Salisbury Post*), p. 49.

23. Bonomi, op. cit., p. 209.

24. Ahlstrom, op. cit., p. 320.

25. Data from Alamance Historic Site; also cited in Leyburn, op. cit., p. 307.

26. Jack Greene, "Independence, Improvement, and Authority," in Hoffman and Tate, eds., op. cit., p. 14.

27. Philip R. Katcher, *Encyclopedia of British Provincial and German Army Units, 1775–1782* (Harrisburg, PA: Stackpole Books, 1973), pp. 99–101.

28. Breen, op. cit., p. 69.

29. Ibid., p. 141.

30. Jacob M. Price, *Capital and Credit in British Overseas Trade* (Cambridge, MA: 1980), p. 137.

31. Thomas J. Wertenbaker, *Torchbearer of the American Revolution* (Princeton: Princeton University Press, 1940), p. 211.

32. Kenneth Coleman, *The American Revolution in Georgia* (Athens: University of Georgia Press, 1958), p. 58.

33. Roger Fink and Rodney Stark, *The Churching of America* (New Brunswick, NJ: Rutgers University Press, 1992), pp. 277–279.

34. John F. Woolverton, *Colonial Anglicanism in North America* (Detroit: Wayne State University Press, 1984), p. 89.

35. Bridenbaugh, *Mitre and Sceptre,* op. cit., p. 256.

36. Loyalists in Connecticut were lopsidedly from the ranks of Anglicans, especially in Fairfield County where—as in neighboring Westchester County, New York—Anglicans constituted about one-third of the population. According to court records, Tory cases were most common in the following towns: Norwalk, Stamford, Fairfield, Ridgefield, Newtown, Greenwich, Stratford, and Redding, in that order. Robert A. East, *Connecticut's Loyalists* (Chester, CT: Pequot Press, 1974), pp. 14–15.

37. Bonomi, op. cit., p. 199.

38. Philip Ranlet, *The New York Loyalists* (Knoxville: University of Tennessee Press, 1986), pp. 186–187.

39. Wallace Brown, *The Good Americans* (New York: William Morrow, 1969), p. 243.

40. Richard McCormick, *New Jersey* (Newark: New Jersey Historical Society, 1981), pp. 127–128.

41. Carol E. Hoffecker, ed., *Readings in Delaware History* (Newark: University of Delaware Press, 1973), p. 54.

42. W. W. Manross, *A History of the American Episcopal Church* (New York and Milwaukee, 1935), pp. 173ff.

43. According to church historian William Warren Sweet, "The proportion of loyalists among colonial Anglicans was in inverse relationship to their numbers in the several colonies. Thus, in Virginia and Maryland, where the Anglicans were most numerous, there was the smallest proportion of Tories. In the middle colonies, where they were less strong, but where there was relatively little hostility to them, their allegiance was about equally divided. In New England, however, where the Episcopal church was bitterly opposed and where the Anglicans were weaker than anywhere else, they were almost a hundred percent loyalist." Sweet, "The Role of the Anglicans," op. cit., p. 52.

44. Despite the general pattern of greater Anglican support for the rebels in the plantation colonies, Tory Anglicans were common on the Delmarva Peninsula, where Maryland, Delaware, and Virginia join together. Members of some old Virginia families like the Byrds and Carters, unhappy with the Revolution and with religious disestablishmentarian upstarts like Patrick Henry and Thomas Jefferson, took the King's side—William Byrd of Westover is the principal example.One of his sons served Royal Governor Dunmore as colonel of the Queen's Loyal Virginia Regiment. North Carolina historians have described the Llewellyn Conspiracy of 1777, in which a group of Anglican planters in the eastern counties, aroused by the religious disestablishment article in the state constitution of 1776, briefly plotted to seize the rebel arsenal and Halifax and rally to any invasion by General Howe. Jeffrey Crow, "Tory Plots and Anglican Loyalty," *North Carolina Historical Review,* Vol. 55 (1978), pp. 1–17.

45. Fink and Stark, op. cit., p. 74.

46. "Some Plans for a Loyalist Stronghold in the Middle Colonies," *Pennsylvania Magazine of History and Biography,* 1949.

47. Adele Hast, *Loyalism in Revolutionary Virginia* (Ann Arbor, MI: 1982), p. 11.

48. Ibid.

49. The population of North Carolina was growing so fast in the 1760s and early 1770s that any estimate of the number of highlanders in the state—15,000 or otherwise—has to be taken with a grain of salt. While it may not be far off, the second caveat, also substantial, is that North Carolina also had a considerable Scotch-Irish population in areas close to the Scots district, and that would have produced at least some confusion on the margins. Many loyalist highlanders left North Carolina between 1775 and 1783, so that the numbers may have been less after the war.

50. J. Leitch Wright, Jr., *Florida in the American Revolution* (Gainesville: University of Florida Press, 1975), p. 11.

51. Hugh Douglas, *Flora MacDonald* (London: Mandarin, 1994), p. 241.

52. Robert S. Lambert, *South Carolina Loyalists in the American Revolution* (Columbia: University of South Carolina Press, 1987), p. 26.

53. Kenneth Coleman, op. cit., p. 75.

54. Ibid., pp. 45–46.

55. Ibid., p. 200.

56. Lambert, op. cit., p. 295.

57. Barbara Graymont, *The Iroquois in the American Revolution* (Syracuse: Syracuse University Press, 1972), p. 146.

58. Brant, the assiduous Anglican, and Sir William Johnson both knew in 1773–1774 that the strongest influence pulling the Oneida to the rebel side was that of Samuel Kirkland, their Presbyterian minister.

59. The best known of the Tory Indian officials—the Johnsons, McKees, Elliotts, Campbells, Frasers, and Butlers in New York; the Stuarts, Camerons, and McGillvrays in the South—were all Scots or Irish. The vivid Scots role has been chronicled often enough. The southern Indian superintendent, John Stuart, had a different Scot handling each of four tribes, the Cherokees, Creek, Choctaw, and Chickasaw. The Irish parallel should also be noted. A Dublin historian has pointed out that relatives and fellow countrymen of Sir William Johnson, mostly also ex-Catholics from the Irish midlands, surrounded him in the Northern Indian Department: George Croghan, John Connolly, and Daniel Clark. Most would be Tories in 1775–1776. Doyle, op. cit., p. 39.

60. Henry S. Young, op. cit.

61. Fink and Stark, op. cit., pp. 277–281.

62. Sydney G. Fisher, *The Quaker Colonies* (New Haven: Yale University Press, 1921), p. 115.

63. Delaware, in turn, was originally part of Pennsylvania until the lower three counties broke off in 1703. West Jersey came under Quaker control in 1673 and remained that way until East Jersey and West Jersey merged in 1702. Nonsectarian Rhode Island was the only part of New England where Quakers felt welcome, and their communities in Newport and Narragansett Bay were able to elect two seventeenth-century governors—William Coddington and Nicholas Easton. Even North Carolina was Quaker-led during the period from 1672 to the first decade of the new century, when their settlement, Hertford, was the provincial capital and John Archdale and another Quaker served as governor.

64. Cecil B. Currey, "Eighteenth Century Evangelical Opposition to the American Revolution: The Case of the Quakers," paper delivered at the Conference on Faith and History, Dallas Baptist College, Dallas, Texas, October 3, 1970, p. 20.

65. Ibid., p. 25.

66. Ibid., pp. 25–26.

67. Ibid., p. 26, citing E. F. Humphrey, *Nationalism and Religion in America, 1774–1789* (Boston: Chapman Law Publishing Co., 1924), p. 133.

68. The Quakers of Perquimans County, North Carolina's first capital a century earlier, turned Methodist; many in Nantucket, Massachusetts, became Methodists and also Baptists. Others of the fallen-away and falling-away went west. Despite their sect's earlier dislike of the frontier Scotch-Irish, sons of Quaker families heeded the same wilderness call: Daniel Boone went from Pennsylvania to North Carolina to wartime Kentucky. After the war, James Fenimore Cooper went with his family from Quaker-run Burlington, New Jersey, to Cooperstown, New York, which he would make famous as the heart of the Leatherstocking Country of Hawkeye and Chingachgook. Both Quaker families, biographers have made clear, had tinges of Toryism during the Revo-

lution. See John M. Faragher, *Daniel Boone* (New York: Henry Holt, 1992) and Alan Taylor, *William Cooper's Town* (New York: Knopf, 1995).

69. Henry M. M. Richards, *German-Americans in the Revolution* (Bowie, MD: Heritage Books, 1992), pp. 339–359.

70. Henry S. Young, op. cit.

71. Ibid.

72. Graham Hodges, *Slavery and Freedom in the Rural North* (Madison, WI: Madison House, 1997), p. 95.

73. Benjamin Quarles, *The Negro in American Revolution* (New York: Norton, 1973), p. 113.

74. Richard S. Dunn "Black Society in the Chesapeake," in Ira Berlin and Ronald Hoffman, eds., *Slavery and Freedom in the Age of the American Revolution* (Charlottesville: University Press of Virginia, 1983), p. 58.

75. Philip D. Morgan, "Black Society in the Low Country," in Berlin and Hoffman, ibid., p. 111.

76. Lambert, op. cit., p. 254.

77. Ronald Hoffman, "The Disaffected in the Revolutionary South," in Alfred Young, ed., *The American Revolution* (DeKalb: Northern Illinois University Press, 1976), p. 281; Quarles, op. cit., p. 153.

78. Quarles, op. cit., pp. 74, 87.

79. Jeffrey J. Crow, *The Black Experience in Revolutionary North Carolina* (Raleigh: North Carolina Department of Cultural Resources, 1977), pp. 56–63.

80. Ibid., p. 63.

81. Quarles, op. cit., pp. 72–73.

82. Ibid., pp. viii–ix.

83. Ibid., p. 70.

84. Hodges, op. cit., pp. 95–107.

85. Quarles, op. cit., p. 78.

86. See Owen S. Ireland, *Religion, Ethnicity and Politics* (University Park: The Pennsylvania State University Press, 1995).

87. See Adrian C. Leiby, *The Revolutionary War in the Hackensack Valley* (New Brunswick, NJ: Rutgers University Press, 1992), pp. 18–23, 112–115, and 226–231.

88. Randall Balmer, *A Perfect Babel of Confusion* (New York: Oxford University Press, 1989), p. 149.

89. Leiby, op. cit., p. viii.

90. Charles H. Glatfelter, *The Pennsylvania Germans* (University Park: Pennsylvania Historical Association, 1990), p. 18.

91. Van Doren, op. cit., p. 221.

92. Abbott E. Smith, *Colonists in Bondage* (New York: Norton, 1971), pp. 262–263.

93. Doyle, op. cit., p. 149.

94. Lynn W. Turner, *The Ninth State* (Chapel Hill: University of North Carolina, 1983), p. 88.

Chapter Six

1. Thomas Fleming, *1776: Year of Illusions* (Edison, NJ: Castle Books, 1996), pp. 83–84.

2. Sympathizers included one of the King's brothers, the Duke of Gloucester, as well as prominent Whig peers from the Dukes of Grafton, Rutland, and Richmond to the Marquess of Rockingham and the Earls of Chatham, Effingham, Abingdon, and Shelburne. Other doubters included a bishop or two, a number of prominent military officers, fifty or sixty MPs, and a contingent of bankers and merchants.

3. According to one study, more than half of the eighty county MPs voted this way, a total which represented nearly one-quarter of the pro-American members. Mary Kinnear, "Pro-Americans in the British House of Commons in the 1770s" (University of Oregon Ph.D. dissertation, 1973), p. 71, quoted in James Bradley, *Religion, Revolution and English Radicalism* (Cambridge: Cambridge University Press, 1990), p. 363.

4. Like the counties, the large boroughs were to other constituencies too big to be (easily) bought. The cities of Bristol and Norwich, with about 5,000 voters each, were two of the largest, and another dozen boroughs included 2,000 to 3,000 voters each. One political scientist has calculated that the thirty-two boroughs in which he could find evidence of national issues being discussed—from London, Bristol, and Norwich down to much smaller Beverley, Bridgnorth, and Sudbury—represented a combined electorate in 1780–1784 of 62,400. This was roughly half of the estimated late eighteenth-century borough total. Fleming, 1776, op. cit., pp. 83–84.

5. Christie and Labaree, op. cit., p. 257.

6. James Bradley, *Popular Politics and the American Revolution in England* (Macon, GA: Mercer Press, 1986), p. 144.

7. Bradley has two books on this subject matter: *Popular Politics*, op. cit., and *Religion, Revolution and English Radicalism*, op. cit. Both have great detail and neither is easy reading.

8. Bradley, *Popular Politics*, op. cit., p. 59.

9. Ibid., pp. 59, 235.

10. Ibid., p. 236.

11. Ibid., pp. 79–81.

12. Ibid., p. 137.

13. Ibid., pp. 53–77.

14. Ibid, p. 127.

15. The numerical ups and downs of English dissent are an issue in themselves. Well-recommended books include A. D. Gilbert, *Religion and Society in Industrial England: Church, Chapel and Social Change, 1740–1914* (London: 1976) and Michael Watts, *The Dissenters* (Oxford: 1978). Puritanism and dissent had reached a peak in the mid-seventeenth century, and nonconformity kept declining through at least the middle of the eighteenth century. It began a resurgence amid the emergence of the Industrial Revolution and the political tensions of the American and French Revolutions and popular reaction against the reassertion of aristocratic conservatism in the United Kingdom, but how important this turnaround was in the 1770s as opposed to the more obvious renewal of nonconformity in the 1780s and 1790s remains unclear. As chapter 9 discusses, however, English nonconformity was surging again in the early nineteenth century, and it was a major source of support for the North in the U.S. Civil War. The relative low point of nonconformity in the United Kingdom of the 1760s—after it had been lulled by a half century of tolerant or latitudinarian Anglican government under the Whigs—was part of the context that permitted the breach between London and the colonies.

16. J. C. D. Clark, op. cit., p.10.

17. Bradley, *Religion Revolution and English Radicalism*, op. cit., pp. 360–409.

18. Ibid., see especially pp. 372–385.

19. David Cannadine, *G. M.Trevelyan: A Life in History* (New York: Norton, 1992), p. 202.

20. John Sainsbury, *Disaffected Patriots* (Kingston and Montreal, 1987), p. 141.

21. Bradley, *Religion, Revolution and English Radicalism*, op. cit., pp. 325, 357.

22. Ibid., p. 386.

23. Richard B. Sher and Jeffrey R. Smitten, eds., *Scotland and America in the Age of Enlightenment* (Edinburgh: Edinburgh University Press, 1990), p. 91.

24. R. B. McDowell, *Ireland in the Age of Imperialism and Revolution* (Oxford: Clarendon Press, 1979), pp. 241–242.

25. Owen Dudley Edwards, "The Impact of the American Revolution on Ireland," in *The Impact of the American Revolution Abroad* (Washington, DC: Library of Congress, 1976), p. 135.

26. McDowell, op. cit., p. 249.

27. Mary Beacock Fryer, *Allan Maclean, Jacobite General* (Toronto: Dundurn Press, 1987), pp.148–150.

28. Paul Langford, "Old Whigs, Old Tories and the American Revolution," *Journal of Imperial and Commonwealth History* (January 1980), pp. 124–126.

29. Sainsbury, op. cit., p. 92.

30. Ibid., pp. 92–93.

31. Ibid., p. 94.

32. Colley, op. cit., p. 142.

33. Ibid., pp. 138–139.

34. Huntingdon was the Lord Protector's former home—its tourist brochures, come full circle, now advertise "Cromwell Country"—but in 1775, amid all the court and church condemnation of Oliverians, that connection must have been dismaying. Local authorities must have thought it wise to send in affirmations of loyalty akin to those volunteered by the Jacobite Scottish Highlands and Lancashire towns still embarrassed by the Forty Five. Perhaps more to the point, Huntingdon was also a pocket borough of the Earl of Sandwich, the first lord of the Admiralty. Sudbury was simply what chroniclers have called a "venal borough." The mayor and aldermen usually sold the Parliamentary seat to the highest bidder. Bradley, *Popular Politics,* op. cit., p. 58; Bradley, *Religion,* op. cit., p. 396.

35. Bradley, *Popular Politics,* op. cit., p. 130.

36. John Phillips, *Electoral Behavior in Unreformed England* (Princeton: Princeton University Press, 1982), p. 120.

37. Bradley, *Religion, Revolution and English Radicalism,* op. cit., pp. 132–133.

38. Bradley, *Popular Politics,* op. cit., p. 177.

39. George Rude, cited in Bradley, *Popular Politics,* op. cit., p. 125.

40. Colley, op. cit., p. 139.

41. F. T. McGlynn, *The Jacobite Army in England, 1745* (Edinburgh: John Donald, Publishers, 1983), p. 80.

42. McDowell, op. cit., p. 241.

43. Owen Dudley Edwards, "Ireland and the American Revolution," in Owen Dudley Edwards and George Shepperson, eds., *Scotland, Europe and the American Revolution* (New York: St. Martin's, 1978), p. 124.

44. The bicentennial of the American Revolution became something of a moment of truth for Irish historiography. The weight of the evidence that Catholics in Ireland in 1775–1777 had favored the Crown while Presbyterians had cheered the colonists had to be faced. The University of Edinburgh held a Conference on Scotland, Europe, and the American Revolution, and published a book of the papers delivered under that same title: Edwards and Shepperson, eds., ibid. In his own paper on *Ireland and the American Revolution,* Edwards noted that at the Irish American Bicentennial Summer School, under the auspices of Cumann Merriman, "a range of scholars as divergent in other respects as Professor John Murphy, Dr. Conor Cruse O'Brien, Dr. David Doyle and myself acknowledged that our independent investigations had all moved to the same conclusion of Irish Catholic hostility to the American Revolution" (ibid., p. 124).

45. McDowell, op. cit., pp. 242–243.

46. Besides the Irish historians cited in endnote 44, other prominent historians have portrayed Irish Catholics as lopsided backers of George III and the American war while Presbyterians empathized with the rebels. Professor R. B. McDowell, in *Ireland in the Age of Imperialism and Revolution,* op. cit., p. 241, notes that before France entered

the war, Protestants mostly supported the Americans while "the Irish Catholics, in so far as they were politically articulate, supported the government's American policy" and the war. Professor J. H. Plumb has also indicated, "Ironically, the major support for the British policy in America came from the Catholics. . . . Catholic regiments were dispatched to America, much to the bitter fury of Protestants, who howled in the press that 'Irish Papists are being permitted to murder American Protestants'" (Plumb, "The Impact on Great Britain," in *The Impact of the American Revolution Abroad* [Washington, DC: Library of Congress, 1976], p. 71).

47. McDowell, op. cit., p. 247.

48. Colley, op. cit., p. 130.

49. Robert Kent Donovan, "The Popular Party of the Church of Scotland and the American Revolution," in Sher and Smitten, op. cit., p. 81.

50. Ibid., p. 84.

51. Ibid., p. 83.

52. Ibid., p. 86

53. Bradley, *Religion, Revolution, and English Radicalism*, op. cit., pp. 360–409.

54. Lewis Namier, *England in the Age of the American Revolution* (London: Macmillan, 1961), pp. 200–202.

55. Langford, op. cit., p. 123.

56. Clark, op. cit., p. 10.

57. Bradley, *Religion, Revolution and English Radicalism*, op. cit., p. 369.

58. David Smurthwaite, *Battlefields of Britain* (Exeter, UK: Webb and Bower, 1984), pp. 174–175.

59. Sir Robert Rait and G. S. Pryde, *Scotland* (London: Ernest Benn, 1954), p. 99.

60. Herbert Butterfield, *George III and the Historians* (New York: Macmillan, 1959).

Chapter Seven

1. Dorothy Smith, *Staten Island* (Philadelphia: Chilton Press, 1970), p. 70.

2. John H. G. Pell, "Phillip Schuyler," in George A. Billias, ed., *George Washington's Generals and Opponents* (New York: DaCapa, 1994), p. 56.

3. See Mackesy, op. cit., p. 112.

4. See Chester M. Destler, *Connecticut: The Provisions State* (Chester, CT: Pequot Press, 1973).

5. Katcher, op. cit., pp. 137–139.

6. Mackesy, op. cit., p. 34.

7. Mintz, op. cit., p. 56.

8. Mackesy, op. cit., p. 133.

9. Graymont, op. cit., pp. 118, 129.

10. George A. Billias, "John Burgoyne," in Billias, ed., op. cit., p. 166.

11. Mintz, op. cit., p. 145.

12. Billias, op. cit., p. 177.

13. Mackesy, op. cit., p. 132.

14. Mintz, op. cit., pp. 160–161.

15. Mackesy, op. cit., p. 127.

16. Graymont, op. cit., p. 129.

17. Ibid., p. 136.

18. Mackesy, op. cit., p. 123.

19. Mintz, op. cit., p. 165.

20. Ibid., pp. 180–183.

21. Ibid, p. 170.

22. Ibid., p. 175.

23. Ian Graham, *Colonists from Scotland* (Ithaca: Cornell University Press, 1956), p. 49.

24. Mintz, op. cit., p. 172.

25. Ketchum, *Saratoga* (New York: Henry Holt, 1997), pp. 292–313.

26. Jeremy Black, *War for America* (Stroud, Gloucestershire: Alan Sutton, 1991), pp. 132–135.

27. Paul Smith, "Sir Guy Carleton," in Billias, ed., op. cit., pp. 122–123; and Mackesy, op. cit., p. 94.

28. John Shy, "Thomas Gage," in Billias, ed., op. cit., pp. 23–26.

29. Ibid., p. 32.

30. Admiral Augustus Keppel, who refused a naval command in America but took one against the French, was from a famous family of whom a number had pro-American leanings. His relation, the Duke of Richmond, flaunted them to the point of sailing his pinnace near the British fleet flying American colors. Even the King's younger brother, H.R.H. The Duke of Gloucester, had been loudly pro-American in foreign visits (see J. H. Plumb, "The Impact of the American Revolution on Great Britain," in *The Impact of the American Revolution Abroad*, op. cit., pp. 65–66). These were exceptions, not the rule, but they provide an interesting subtext to the civil war aspect of the conflict even within the United Kingdom.

31. Mintz, op. cit., p. 23.

32. Fryer, op. cit., pp. 148–150.

33. Mitz, op. cit., p. 28.

34. Ibid., p. 55.

35. George A. Billias, "John Burgoyne," in Billias, ed., op. cit., p. 160.

36. Mintz, op. cit., p. 28.

37. John Hyde Preston, *A Short History of the American Revolution* (New York: Pocket Books, 1952), p. 138.

38. Ibid., p. 139.

39. Maldwyn Jones, "Sir William Howe," in Billias, op. cit., p. 48.

40. Ibid., p. 50.

41. Ibid., p. 43.

42. Ibid., p. 66.

43. Ira Gruber, *The Howe Brothers and the American Revolution* (Williamsburg: Institute of Early American History and Culture, 1972), pp. 57–62.

44. Ira Gruber, *Blackwell Encyclopedia*, op. cit., p. 784.

45. Gruber, *The Howe Brothers*, op. cit., p. 47.

46. Ibid., pp. 54–55.

47. Ibid., pp. 51–52.

48. Ibid., pp. 56–57.

49. Jones, "Sir William Howe," in Billias, op. cit., p. 49.

50. Gruber, op. cit., p. 63.

51. Edwards and Shepperson, eds., op. cit., p. 26.

52. Simon Schama, *Patriots and Liberators: Revolution in the Netherlands, 1780–1813* (New York: Vintage, 1992).

53. R. R. Palmer, "Introduction," in *The Impact of the American Revolution Abroad*, op. cit., p. 9.

54. Ian Christie, *Wars and Revolutions: Britain 1760–1815* (Cambridge: Harvard University Press, 1982), p. 140.

55. Christie, op. cit., p. 200.

56. Plumb, "The Impact on Great Britain," in *The Impact of the American Revolution Abroad*, op. cit., p. 73.

57. David Brion Davis, *The Problem of Slavery in the Age of Revolution* (Ithaca: Cornell University Press, 1975), p. 55.

58. Christie, op. cit., p. 190.
59. Colley, op. cit., p. 193.
60. Plumb, op. cit., p. 74.
61. Charles Ritcheson, *Aftermath of the Revolution* (New York: Norton, 1971), p. 31.
62. Plumb, op. cit., p. 76.
63. Bradford Perkins, *Prologue to War* (Berkeley: University of California Press, 1968), p. 382.
64. John Brewer, *The Sinews of Power* (New York: Knopf, 1989), p. 114; Christie, op. cit., pp. 185–186.
65. Christie, op. cit., pp. 185–186.
66. Mackesy, op. cit., p. 537.
67. G. J. Marcus, *A Naval History of England* (Boston: Little, Brown, 1961), pp. 461–462.
68. Mackesy, op. cit., p. 517.
69. Davis, op. cit., p. 56.
70. Perkins, op. cit., p. 1.

Chapter Eight

1. Ritcheson, op. cit., p. 34.
2. Roger Brown, *The Republic in Peril: 1812* (New York: Norton, 1971), p. 5.
3. Ritcheson, op. cit., p. 18.
4. Don Higginbotham, *The War of American Independence* (New York: Macmillan, 1971), p. 375.
5. *South Carolina*, American Guide Series (New York: Oxford University Press, 1949), p. 305.
6. Quarles, op. cit., p. 174.
7. *Georgia*, American Guide Series (Athens: University of Georgia Press, 1946), p. 42.
8. Ritcheson, op. cit., p. 60.
9. Ibid., p. 2.
10. Ahlstrom, op. cit., p. 368.
11. After Saratoga, when British strategists forsook expectation of military victory in the northern colonies and soon became preoccupied by war with the old French enemy, their attentions shifted to the Carolinas and Georgia for a number of reasons: (1) These areas produced the commodities—tobacco, rice, indigo, etc.—that were most important to British mercantile interests; (2) the three colonies had established Anglican churches and high ratios of Tories; (3) the expectation was that once they were occupied, loyalist troops could be recruited in large numbers, so that subsequent fighting could pit American against American, enabling British troops to be largely withdrawn for service elsewhere; and (4) the Carolinas, Georgia, East Florida, the Bahamas, and Bermuda were seen as a plausible postwar British colonial grouping even if the colonies between Virginia and New England were lost. In 1779 and 1780, temporary British military success in Georgia and the Carolinas made these hopes seem plausible.
12. Jackson Turner Main, *The Anti-Federalists* (New York: Norton, 1974), pp. 31–35.
13. Robert A. Becker, "Salus Populi, Suprema Lex," *South Carolina Historical Magazine* (January 1979), pp. 67–68.
14. *Georgia*, American Guide Series, op. cit., p. 43.
15. Philip D. Morgan, "British Encounters with Africans and African-Americans" in *Strangers in the Realm* (Chapel Hill: University of North Carolina Press, 1991), pp. 186–195.
16. Ibid.

17. The question of whether blacks in the future United States, most still slaves, were helped or hurt by the American Revolution has been widely pursued, but usually in article rather than book length and with some disagreement. In the northern colonies, especially New England, emancipation sentiment flourished, but in the South, the war's effects were more negative. Scholars who see the Revolution as a favorable watershed for blacks usually emphasize its impact in promoting emancipation and abolition sentiment in the North or, like Benjamin Quarles, describe the Revolution as a "black Declaration of Independence" in the sense that it spurred black Americans to seek freedom and equality. Critics like David Brion Davis or Sylvia Frey, writing in the *Blackwell Encyclopedia of the American Revolution,* emphasize the entrenchment and expansion of slavery in the South. The overall legacy included a mass of contradictions.

18. *North Carolina,* American Guide Series (Chapel Hill: University of North Carolina Press, 1955), p. 76.

19. Davis, op. cit., p. 89; Richard S. Dunn, "Black Society in the Chesapeake," op. cit., p. 62.

20. Benjamin Quarles, "The Revolutionary War as a Black Declaration of Independence" in Hodges, op. cit., pp. 299–300.

21. Ira Berlin, "Introduction," in Hodges, op. cit., p. xv.

22. Davis, op. cit., p. 273.

23. Duncan J. Macleod, "Toward Caste," in Hodges, op. cit., pp. 230–231.

24. David Brion Davis, "American Slavery and the American Revolution," in Berlin and Hoffman, op. cit., p. 264.

25. Staughton Lynd, "The Conflict over Slavery," in Allen Davis and Harold Woodman, eds., *Conflict and Consensus in Early American History* (Lexington, MA: D.C. Heath, 1976), p. 131.

26. Lisle A. Rose, *Prologue to Democracy* (Lexington: University of Kentucky, 1968), p. 7.

27. George Novack, "Slavery in Colonial America," in Novack, ed., *America's Revolutionary Heritage* (New York: Pathfinder Press, 1976), p. 148.

28. Davis, *The Problem of Slavery,* op. cit., p. 124.

29. Philip F. Gura, *A Glimpse of Sion's Glory* (Middletown, CT: Wesleyan University Press, 1984), pp. 229–230.

30. See Jackson Turner Main, *Political Parties Before the Constitution* (Chapel Hill: University of North Carolina Press, 1973).

31. Ibid., pp. 14–15.

32. Ibid., see pp. 365–407.

33. Ibid., p. 378.

34. Wright, op. cit., p. 261.

35. Leiby, op. cit., p. 306.

36. The wartime bargain struck between Virginia's pro-Revolutionary and mostly Low Church Anglican gentry and the Baptists resulted in immediate freedom of religion and subsequent (1786) Anglican disestablishment. In fact, from Virginia south to Georgia, the effect of the Revolution and the expansion of the backcountry and frontier over the next two generations produced a massive Baptist numerical edge. North Carolina historians, as noted, believe that Baptists (of all varieties) had together become a plurality within that colony even in 1775. By 1820, Baptists led in all four states by wide margins. However, the first statistics are available for 1850 when the ratio of Baptists to Episcopalians showed a huge upheaval compared with 1776, based on data from *The Churching of America, 1776–1990,* op. cit. By 1850, Baptists dwarfed Episcopalians below the Mason-Dixon line, but Episcopalians were still an important religious and political elite in Virginia and South Carolina—and as a result, in the future Confederacy.

	Virginia	*N. Carolina*	*S. Carolina*	*Georgia*
1776				
Anglican				
Congregations (%)	34.6%	14.5%	22.9%	13.0%
Baptist				
Congregations (%)	29.9	25.5	24.7	30.4
1850				
Baptists per				
1,000 population	96	129	136	202
Episcopalians per				
1,000 population	13	4	12	3

37. William N. Chambers, *Political Parties in a New Nation* (New York: Oxford University Press), p. 182.

38. This is the most widespread view—that the Federalists were not democratic enough for the new century. By 1805—or, more vividly, by 1815—their strength had shrunk back into mostly coastal and commercial enclaves from New England to New Jersey, Delaware, and Maryland, and a few locales farther south. This shrinkage is compatible with the argument of insufficient democracy and egalitarianism. However, the fading of earlier Federalist support that had been based on voters' 1775–1783 neutralism or Toryism is also important—and will be pursued further in chapter 12 and its examination of the impact of wars on U.S. electoral behavior and voting patterns.

39. Too often, the British seizure and impressment of U.S. seamen in the years leading up to the War of 1812 is treated without sufficient reference to the backdrop of maritime commerce after 1783. American ships had large numbers of British-born seamen for three major reasons: (1) Large numbers of American citizens were themselves British born; (2) service in U.S. vessels was so much easier and better paid than service in the wartime Royal Navy of 1793–1814 that many British sailors and merchant seamen ran to American ships, draining the all-important navy; and (3) U.S. maritime interests had also found it profitable in the 1780s and 1790s to have American ships pass for British to take advantage of opportunities in the West Indies and elsewhere. The arrogance of British naval officers has been widely chronicled, but much less attention has been given to what Charles Ritcheson, in his *Aftermath of Revolution,* op. cit., described as a great "network of smuggling, collusion, clandestine partnerships and other illicit practices" (see pp. 212–214). American ships of the 1780s and early 1790s would use old or forged British Registers, as well as seamen born in Sussex or Devon, to pass in British or British colonial ports, especially the West Indies. With this kind of interaction, impressment from U.S. ships was inevitable; the Royal Navy was not much more abusive in taking seamen than the Yankee ships were in sailing into Kingstown or Bridgetown with false registration, the Union Jack flying and Londoners conversing on deck.

40. Perkins, op. cit., p. 345.

41. James M. Banner, Jr., *To the Hartford Convention* (New York: Knopf, 1970), pp. 342.

42. Donald R. Hickey, *The War of 1812* (Urbana: University of Illinois Press, 1990), p. 279.

43. See Avery Craven, "The 1840s and the Democratic Process," *Journal of Southern History,* XVI (1950), pp. 161–176; James G. Randall, "A Blundering Generation," *Mississippi Valley Historical Review,* XXVII (1940), pp. 3–28; and Thomas N. Bonner, "Civil War Historians and the 'Needless War' Doctrine," *Journal of the History of Ideas* (April 1956), pp. 193–216.

44. William R. Taylor, *Cavalier and Yankee* (New York: Doubleday Anchor, 1963), p. 42.

45. Howard Jones, *Union in Peril* (Chapel Hill: University of North Carolina Press, 1992), p. 32.

46. James McPherson, *Battle Cry of Freedom* (New York: Oxford University Press, 1986), p. 2.

47. Lynd, op. cit., p. 133.

48. Ibid., p. 136.

49. Michael F. Holt, *The Political Crisis of the 1850s* (New York: John Wiley, 1978), p. 223.

50. Davis, *The Problem of Slavery,* op. cit., p. 57.

51. Robert E. May, *The Southern Dream of a Caribbean Empire* (Athens: University of Georgia Press, 1989), pp. 136–162.

52. Ibid., pp. 142, 155–162.

53. Ibid., p. 267.

54. Ibid., p. 251.

55. Ibid., p. 147.

56. Ibid., p. 9.

57. Richard W. Van Alstyne, *The Rising American Empire* (New York: Norton, 1974), p. 149.

58. Ibid., p. 149.

59. May, op. cit., p. 160.

60. Ibid., p. 156.

61. Ibid., pp. 205, 221–244.

62. Van Alstyne, op cit., p. 151.

63. Frederick Jackson Turner, *The United States, 1830–1850* (New York: Norton, 1965), p. 148.

64. *Southern Literary Messenger* 30 (June 1860), pp. 401–409.

65. John W. Thomason, *Jeb Stuart* (New York: Charles Scribner, 1930), p. 16.

66. Abbott E. Smith, *Colonists in Bondage* (New York: Norton, 1971), pp. 131–132.

67. See Grady McWhiney, *Cracker Culture* (Tuscaloosa: University of Alabama Press, 1988).

68. Turner, op. cit., p. 152.

69. Taylor, op. cit., p. 183.

70. May, op. cit., pp. 150–151.

71. Robert East, "The Massachusetts Conservatives in the Critical Period," in Richard B. Morris, ed., *The Era of the American Revolution* (New York: 1939), pp. 349–391.

72. Perkins, op. cit., pp. 13–14.

73. Taylor, op. cit., p. 3.

74. David Brion Davis, *The Slave Power and the Paranoid Style* (Baton Rouge: 1969), p. 16.

75. Joseph Charles, *The Origins of the American Party System* (New York: Harper Torch Books, 1961), p. 23.

76. Ibid., p. 18.

77. Chard Smith, op. cit., see pp. 291–420.

78. Vernon Parrington, *The Romantic Revolution in America 1800–1860* (New York: Harcourt Brace/Harvest Books, 1954), p. 334.

79. Ibid., p. 335.

80. Ibid., p. 337.

81. See especially Christopher Hill, *The World Turned Upside Down,* op. cit.

82. Chard Smith, op. cit., p. 321.

83. Ibid., p. 361.

84. Ibid., pp. 356–359.

85. George M. Frederickson, *The Inner Civil War* (New York: Harper Torch Books, 1968), pp. 65–83.

Chapter Nine

1. Daniel Walker Howe, *The Political Culture of the American Whigs* (Chicago: University of Chicago Press, 1979), p. 162.

2. Lynd, op. cit., p. 138.

3. Madison's fascination with Pennsylvania had a solid footing. During the 1790s, the state emerged as the pivot between New England, New York, and New Jersey on one side and the South on the other both in Congressional votes on commerce and finance and in presidential elections. Its swing presidential role was especially apparent in the 1796 and 1800 elections, but it remained a fair mirror through the first quarter of the nineteenth century and then again became a bellwether—Pennsylvanians thought of themselves as a "Keystone"—in the 1830s. It played that role very successfully from 1836 to 1856 and then swung decisively to the new Republican Party (and a de facto alliance with New England) in 1860.

4. Daniel W. Crofts, *Reluctant Confederates* (Chapel Hill: University of North Carolina Press, 1989), p. 336.

5. William C. Wright, *The Secession Movement in the Middle Atlantic States* (Rutherford, NJ: Fairleigh Dickinson Press, 1973), p. 143.

6. C. Vann Woodward, *American Counterpoint* (Boston: Little, Brown, 1964), p. 27.

7. Even during the War for Independence, some British officials thought that the differences between the southern colonies and those to the north were great enough that they could be split apart. Richard Oswald, a British peace commissioner who had lived in Virginia, advised Lord North that the South had an aristocracy with great family connections that deplored the "mob of northern yeomen" (Robson, op. cit., pp. 90–91). During the 1860–1862 period, similar sentiments and analyses led British conservatives, in particular, to say that the North and South were really different countries, which made their splitting apart reasonable.

8. Allan Nevins, quoted in Kenneth M. Stampp, ed., *The Causes of the Civil War* (New York: Simon and Schuster/Touchstone, 1991), p. 220.

9. Social histories of mid-seventeenth-century England—Christopher Hill's *The World Turned Upside Down*, for example—often make some mention of the Puritan-era revolution in the position of women. Hill even points out that divorce was easier in Puritan New England than in Old England (Hill, op. cit., chapter 15 and p. 250). During the seventeenth century, the Puritan centers, especially Greater London and East Anglia, were the sections of England where women had their greatest role beyond the household. Greater New England played the same forward role in the nineteenth century. Thus the English and U.S. Civil War eras have another parallel that might be examined: their comparative impact on women.

10. Abbott Smith, op. cit., pp. 3, 4, 337.

11. Ibid., p. 27.

12. Ahlstrom, op. cit., p. 670.

13. Ibid., p. 667.

14. See Christopher Hill, *The World Turned Upside Down*, op. cit.

15. See Ahlstrom, op. cit., pp. 654–655.

16. Chard Smith, op. cit., p. 340.

17. Two of the more prominent attempts to present the South as different from the North because of its greater ancestral roots in the north and west of England and Scotland and Ireland are David Hackett Fischer, *Albion's Seed*, op. cit., and Grady McWhiney, *Cracker Culture: Celtic Ways in the Old South*, op. cit. The argument

clearly has some merit. The question is whether both take the ancestral and ethnic component in its own right too far. The different regional cultural developments may have been as important. The North and South were very different cultures in different climates and perceived themselves as different, which presumably increased their divergence beyond what the original ethnic distinctions might have accomplished.

18. Bridenbaugh, *Vexed and Troubled Englishmen*, op. cit., pp. 365–366.

19. Underdown, op. cit., p. 49.

20. McPherson, op. cit., p. 29.

21. The nineteenth-century economic and commercial differences between the South and the North have been discussed in many books and textbooks. Less attention has been paid to how full-blown some of these divisions—and the perceptions of them— were in the 1780s and 1790s. Visible at the Constitutional Convention, they were even more striking in the early congressional voting on Alexander Hamilton's economic program providing a major early signal of sectionalism. See Charles, op. cit., p. 23, for details.

22. Stampp, op. cit., p. 92.

23. Ibid., p. 93.

24. Algie M. Simons, *Class Struggles in America* (Chicago: 1906), pp. 32–36, quoted in Stampp, op. cit., p. 98.

25. Fleming, *New Jersey*, op. cit., p. 116.

26. See Michael Holt, *Forging a Majority: The Formation of the Republican Party in Pittsburgh, 1848–1860* (New Haven: Yale University Press, 1969).

27. The thrust of the studies of voting in the industrial Northeast during the 1848–1860 period suggests that such areas were Whig-inclined, especially in New England and around Philadelphia. Religion seems to have been the best gauge. Irish Catholics would have been lopsidedly Democratic when they became voters. Young Protestant artisans and industrial workers, meanwhile, were especially likely to support nativist movements in the late 1840s and early 1850s because of their anxiety about competition from low-income immigrants, the Irish in particular. This was true in New England, New York, and Pennsylvania, and may have been truest in the state that was most industrialized: Massachusetts. The anti-Irish, plague-on-the-old-parties vote for the Know-Nothings in 1854 on the part of Yankee mechanics, factory workers, clerks, and tradesmen was extraordinary, fueled by a sense that the politicians and wealthy elites had blocked true reform and forced native-born people into disadvantaged circumstances. So many workers rushed into anti-establishment Know-Nothing lodges that it produced talk of a labor uprising. See John R. Mulkern, *The Know-Nothing Party in Massachusetts* (Boston: Northeastern University Press, 1990), pp. 67–70.

28. Woodward, op. cit., pp. 124–125.

29. Peter Laslett, quoted in ibid., pp. 136–137.

30. Ibid., p. 127.

31. Ibid., p. 138.

32. Howe, op. cit., pp. 152–153, 168.

33. Davis, *The Slave Power*, op. cit., pp. 75–76.

34. Thomas J. Pressly, *Americans Interpret Their Civil War* (New York: Free Press, 1965), p. 14.

35. Ahlstrom, op. cit., p. 672.

36. McPherson, op. cit., p. 318.

37. *Guide to U.S. Elections* (Washington: Congressional Quarterly, 1975), p. 271.

38. Bart Talbert, *Maryland: The South's First Casualty* (Berryville, VA: Rockbridge Publishing, 1995), p. 16.

39. Fleming, *New Jersey*, p. 116.

40. Stampp, op. cit., pp. 42–43.

41. Ibid., pp. 60–62.

42. Vernon L. Parrington, *The Romantic Revolution in America, 1800–1860* (New York: Harcourt Brace/Harvest Book, 1954), p. 364.

43. Merrill Jensen, *The Articles of Confederation* (Madison: University of Wisconsin Press, 1976), p. 187.

44. David Thomson, *England in the Nineteenth Century* (Harmondsworth, UK: Penguin Books, 1950), p. 89.

45. Ahlstrom, op. cit., pp. 675–676.

46. Howe, op. cit., p. 42.

47. Ibid., p. 37.

48. Lynn L. Marshall, "The Strange Stillbirth of the Whig Party," *American Historical Review*, vol. 72–72 (January 1967), p. 446.

49. Holt, *Political Crisis*, op. cit., p. 123.

50. Ibid., p. 235.

51. Howe, op. cit., p. 167.

52. A wide range of historians have taken very seriously the role of the Second Great Awakening in mobilizing New England and helping to crystallize its political reemergence in the 1850s. Ahlstrom, in his *A Religious History of the American People*, op. cit., pp. 419–428 and 637–638, explains how the Second Great Awakening roused New England, stirred abolitionism, and gave rise to the "vision of a great Christian republic stretching westward beyond the Appalachians as a beacon and example for the whole world." James McPherson sets the success of Harriet Beecher Stowe's book *Uncle Tom's Cabin* in the context of its appeal to evangelical Protestants drawn into abolitionism by the Second Great Awakening (McPherson, *Battle Cry of Freedom*, op. cit., p. 88). Eric Foner states that "the intense individualism of the abolitionists, historians are agreed, derived from the great revivals of the Second Great Awakening, which identified moral progress with each individual's capacity to act as an instrument of God.... Religious benevolence was, it seems clear, the primary root of antebellum reform" (Foner, *Politics and Ideology*, op. cit., pp. 64–65). Foner correctly points out that much abolitionist and reform sentiment was also bred in deist and freethinker circles unhappy with the prominence of the evangelical role. But in the United States, the role of the religious evangelicals in reform movements has often been what has given them political success.

53. Banner, op. cit., p. 91.

54. Holt, *Political Crisis*, op. cit., p. 120.

55. Howe, op. cit., p. 164

56. Ibid., p. 35.

57. Eric Foner, *Free Soil, Free Labor, Free Men* (New York: Oxford University Press, 1970), p. 242.

58. Bruce Maizlish, *The Triumph of Sectionalism* (Kent, OH: Kent State University Press, 1983), pp. 192–227.

59. Foner, op. cit., p. 242.

60. Chard Smith, op. cit., p. 379.

61. Ahlstrom, op. cit., p. 380.

62. This particularly applies to Connecticut, New Hampshire, and Massachusetts.

63. Parrington, op. cit., p. 351.

64. Howe, op. cit., p. 18.

65. Foner, op. cit., p. 231.

66. McKay, op. cit., p. 150; see also Ahlstrom, op. cit., p. 566 and Kleppner/Luebke, op. cit., p. 168.

67. Foner, op. cit., p. 78.

68. Ibid., p. 246.

69. Eric Foner, *Politics and Ideology in the Age of the Civil War* (New York: Oxford University Press, 1980), p. 84.

70. William W. Sweet, *The Story of Religion in America* (Grand Rapids, MI: Baker House, 1979), p. 312.

71. Ahlstrom, op. cit., p. 673n.

72. Ibid., p. 668.

73. Christie, op. cit., p. 282.

74. Bradley, *Religion, Revolution,* op. cit., p. 20.

75. "Nineteenth Century Cromwell," *Past and Present,* vol. 40 (1968), p. 187.

76. J. P. Parry, *Democracy and Religion* (Cambridge: Cambridge University Press, 1986), pp. 7 and 39.

77. Ibid, p. 11.

78. Ibid., p. 11.

79. Ibid., p. 4.

Chapter Ten

1. Stewart Holbrook, *The Yankee Exodus* (New York: Macmillan, 1950), p. 5.

2. Turner, op. cit., p. 98.

3. Maizlish, op. cit., p. 15.

4. Foner, *Free Soil,* op. cit., p. 22.

5. Ibid., p. 30.

6. Fink and Stark, op. cit., p. 282; James L. Sundquist, *Dynamics of the Party System* (Washington, DC: Brookings Institution, 1973), p. 75.

7. Revolutionary-era political tensions between Connecticut Congregationalists and Anglicans, later Episcopalians, flamed up again in the years between 1815 and 1818 when Episcopalians joined with Baptists, Methodists, and freethinkers to win control of the governorship and end the statewide establishment of the Congregational Church. Most of the active Connecticut Congregationalists were Federalists, while most of the other groups used the state Democratic Party as a vehicle. The ill will during this period, widely noted in local histories, carried over into the Democratic-versus-Whig politics of the 1830s and 1840s. The emergence of the new Republican Party in the mid-1850s, taking much of the previous Whig constituency, saw Congregationalists, Unitarians, and antislavery activists in the lead. This, in turn, ensured that many or most members of the anti-Congregationalist denominations would remain Democrats, while the Democrats also attracted social conservatives opposed to abolition and the other Yankee "isms." In most elections during the 1856–1864 period, Connecticut Democratic strength was greatest in some Methodist and Baptist sections of the east and in Fairfield and New Haven Counties in the southwest, where Episcopalians were most numerous and the pull of New York and commerce with the South was greatest. In 1860, Fairfield was the only county not to give Lincoln a majority.

8. The distaste for New Englanders among old New Yorkers (Knickerbockers) and Pennsylvanians—against whom Connecticut had contested for late eighteenth-century settlement of the area that is now Wilkes-Barre—is less recognized than the anti-Yankeeism among Southerners, but it was widespread. New Yorkers grumbled as New Englanders took over much of the upper portion of the state in the 1820s and 1830s, and pushed into New York City commerce. In the three months after the 1860 election, when sympathy for the South had yet to be cut short by April's cannonade on Fort Sumter, pro-southern comments in New York and Philadelphia were often coupled with derogations of the Yankees and suggestions that even the middle states would be better off cutting clear of them.

9. For all that Dutch German and East Anglian Protestants served together on many seventeenth- and eighteenth-century European battlefields, there were New World undercurrents of animosity between the Pennsylvania Germans and New York Dutch and the New England Yankees. Boston-born Benjamin Franklin's several-times-expressed

doubts about the Germans will be cited in chapter 12, but fellow Massachusetts man John Adams was even more outspoken. He was critical of the Dutch in the summer of 1777 when New Englanders wanted to push aside New York general Philip Schuyler as the rebel commander in the North and replace him with Horatio Gates. But the fuller measure of Adams's candor came in describing Germans: "In politics," he wrote to his wife in 1777, "they are a breed of mongrels, or neutrals, and benumbed with a general torpor" (Belcher, op. cit., p. 247).

10. Wood Gray, *The Hidden Civil War* (New York: Viking Press, 1964), p. 25.

11. Ibid., pp. 45–46.

12. Maizlish, op. cit., pp. 7–8; Foner, *Free Soil*, op. cit., p. 286.

13. Ibid., p. 218.

14. Turner, op. cit., p. 50.

15. Richard O'Connor, *The German-Americans* (Boston: Little, Brown, 1968), p. 132.

16. Gray, op. cit., pp. 113–117.

17. Frank Klement, *The Copperheads in the Middle West* (Chicago: University of Chicago Press, 1960), pp. 3–9.

18. Gray, op. cit., p. 108.

19. Ibid, p. 13.

20. Ibid., p. 108.

21. Walter Dean Burnham, *Presidental Ballots 1832–1896* (Baltimore: Johns Hopkins University Press, 1955), p. 510.

22. Ibid., p. 512.

23. Ibid., p. 318.

24. Ernest A. McKay, *The Civil War and New York City* (Syracuse: Syracuse University Press, 1960), pp. 14–15; Iver Bernstein, *The New York City Draft Riots* (New York: Oxford University Press, 1990), pp. 145–146.

25. McKay, op. cit., p. 18.

26. Ibid., p. 26.

27. Ibid., pp. 34–35.

28. Bernstein, op. cit., pp. 11–12.

29. John T. Cunningham, *This Is New Jersey* (New Brunswick, NJ: Rutgers University Press, 1953), pp. 109–110.

30. Data from John F. Coleman, *The Disruption of the Pennsylvania Democracy, 1848–1860* (Harrisburg: Pennsylvania Historical and Museum Commission, 1975), appendix.

31. Andrew Crandall, *The Early History of the Republican Party* (1930) cited in Sundquist, op. cit., pp. 68 and 83.

32. Gray, op. cit., p. 38; McKay, op. cit., p. 29.

33. Shane White, *Somewhat More Independent* (Athens: University of Georgia Press, 1991), p. 16.

34. Ibid., p. 16.

35. Ibid., p. 18.

36. Hodges, op. cit., p. 172.

37. Fleming, *New Jersey*, op. cit., p. 118.

38. Sundquist, op. cit., p. 86.

39. Owen S. Ireland, "Germans Against Abolition, a Minority's View of Slavery in Revolutionary Pennsylvania," *Journal of Interdisciplinary History* 3 (1973), pp. 685–706.

40. Wright, *The Secession Movement in the Middle Atlantic States* (Rutherford, NJ: Fairleigh Dickinson Press, 1973), p. 126.

41. William Dusinberre, *Civil War Issues in Philadelphia, 1856–1865* (Philadelphia: University of Pennsylvania Press, 1965), p. 88.

42. Fleming, *New Jersey*, op. cit., p. 121.

43. The name of Millard Fillmore, the vice-president who became president in July 1850 on the death of Zachary Taylor, lingers on mostly as a shorthand for the minor stature and relative anonymity of four or five nineteenth-century U.S. presidents. But the vote Fillmore received in 1856 as the presidential candidate of the American (Know-Nothing) Party is more intriguing than his accomplishments in the White House. In the North, Fillmore's best showings were rarely among Protestants close to the greatest Catholic and immigrant concentrations. For example, Wisconsin, which had the nation's highest percentage (35) of foreign-born, gave Fillmore only one-half of 1 percent; New Hampshire, which had voted in 1850 to continue to bar Catholics from statewide office, gave him just six-tenths of 1 percent. The highest Fillmore levels in the North came in non-Yankee rural and small-town areas suspicious enough of foreigners in the cities but probably even more suspicious of Yankees, abolitionists, and the idea of pulling the country apart over slavery: in southern New Jersey, southern Pennsylvania, and downstate Illinois. Most of Fillmore's best northern counties were in these areas. Even higher support came in California, then the only state in the Far West, which gave Fillmore 32.8 percent—his best showing outside the slave states. California, settled from North and South alike, would be torn again in 1860.

44. The point made in note 43 can be pursued in the Ohio Valley, which included most of the Midwest's best Fillmore counties. In Illinois, Indiana, and Ohio, Fillmore support peaked in the southern sections, principally along the Ohio River. Although immigrants were coming into the Ohio Valley, most of the top Fillmore counties were rural, southern-settled, and presumably anxious to try to look away from the slavery issue and to keep any war from developing.

45. See especially Holt, *Political Crisis*, op. cit., pp. 163–169. Holt's point about the anitparty and reformist aspect of the Know-Nothing movement is especially well detailed for Massachusetts in John R. Mulkern, *The Know-Nothing Party in Massachusetts: The Rise and Fall of a People's Movement* (Boston: Northeastern University Press, 1990).

46. For Cincinnati, see Maizlish, op. cit., pp. 178–192; for Pittsburgh, see Holt, *Forging a Majority: Pittsburgh,* op. cit.

47. Frederick Luebke, editor, *Ethnic Voters and the Election of Lincoln* (Lincoln: University of Nebraska Press, 1971), p. 11.

48. The strong influence of religion on American politics, voting patterns, and wars is one that gives many historians and political scientists problems. Civic-spiritedness and melting-pot exaggerations suggest that things should not be this way, which does not encourage such interpretation. Moreover, voting patterns for 1830–1860 are not the easiest to study. At the presidential level, party upheaval was relentless—from a Democrats–versus–National Republicans race in 1832 to a Democrats-versus-Whigs election framework from 1836 to 1852 (with major Free Soil splinterings) and then to a three-way race in 1856 and a four-way split in 1850. Emigrants from Europe were redrawing the political map in the East, and emigration from both Europe and the East was changing politics in the Midwest. Voting returns, as a result, are less Mozart than Moussorgsky—few orderly restatements of themes and more cacophony. Even so, I would place some faith in the basic conclusions of a half dozen historians and political scientists who have found ethnic and religious striations everywhere. Daniel Walker Howe laid out the latter for the Whig-Democratic rivalry in his *The Political Culture of the American Whigs*, op. cit. Academicians more devoted to scripting ethnic and religious divisions in different states and circumstances during this period include Michael Holt (in *Forging a Majority: Pittsburgh*, op. cit.), Lee Benson (in *The Concept of Jacksonian Democracy: New York as a Test Case* [Princeton: Princeton University Press], 1961), Ronald Formisano (*The Birth of Mass Political Parties: Michigan, 1827–1861* [Princeton: Princeton University Press], 1971). Michael Jensen ("The Historical Roots

of Party Identification," paper delivered to the annual meeting of the American Political Science Association in September 1969), James Bergquist (Luebke, op. cit.), Paul Kleppner (*Cross of Culture*, op. cit.), and others. Based on some forty years of my own study, in which I have looked at religious and ethnic underpinnings of political behavior in the United States from the late eighteenth century down to the late twentieth—and have done so in actual national election campaigns, as well as in theory—these examinations are substantially correct in the importance they claim for such divisions. The problem, of course, is that the Irish, German, or Yankee district that is concentrated and intense enough to isolate as a barometer probably overstates the (looser) behavior of others of that background living in a more cosmopolitan or ecumenical milieu. Groups that seem to be 85–95 percent cohesive behind Democrats, Whigs, or Republicans in their archetypal villages or neighborhoods will probably drop to 65–80 percent when the behavior of those outside the concentrations is factored in. But the basic emphasis is warranted, even if the polarizations are somewhat overstated.

49. Foner, *Political Ideology,* op. cit., p. 18.

50. Bergquist, in Luebke, op. cit. By 1855–1856, he estimated that Illinois Germans were voting 55 to 60 percent Rebublican.

51. Anyone who doubts that the so-called Pennsylvania Dutch, whose forebears first came to the present-day United States in the early and mid-eighteenth century, still thought of themselves as German in the mid-nineteenth century—and to some extent still do—should look at the map of self-identified German ancestry in the United States of 1990. Pennsylvanians rank close to Iowa and Wisconsin in self-perceived Germanness. And between 1856 and 1860, Abraham Lincoln made major gains over John C. Frémont in the state's principal German counties (including partly Mennonite and abolitionist Lancaster County, which had given Frémont considerable support in 1856). The chart below shows the increase in three major Protestant Church German counties: Berks (Reading), Northampton, and York (the statistics are taken from John F. Coleman, *The Disruption of the Pennsylvania Democracy,* op. cit., appendix):

Frémont Share of Total Vote for President, 1856		*Lincoln Share of Total Vote for President, 1860*
Berks	7%	42%
Northampton	14%	44%
York	5%	44%

Thus, even though Lincoln won Pennsylvania easily, the massive German gains he made over the more abolitionist Frémont were important. The German vote remained Democratic in 1860 but the margins were narrow.

52. Counting the Pennsylvania Germans, who do not show up in nineteenth-century immigrant statistics, increases the importance of the 1856–1860 German swing in both Ohio and Indiana. Even today, both states feature their Pennsylvania Dutch and Amish settlements in tourist literature. The cover story in the August 1998 issue of *Ohio Magazine* blazoned: "Welcome to Amish Country." And a map inside showed the attractions in Wayne, Stark, Holmes, and Tuscarawas Counties, where Pennsylvania Germans settled after the Revolution, immediately south of the Yankee districts of the old Connecticut Western Reserve. However, Holmes County, the atypical Amish core, gave Lincoln a slightly lower minority of the vote than it had given Frémont in 1856, which is counter to the Pennsylvania tide. Indiana had fewer Pennsylvania Germans, but Lincoln's majority there was so thin that the old Pennsylvania emigrants could have provided a vital boost.

53. See, for example, Richard O'Connor, *The German-Americans* (Boston: Little, Brown, 1968.), p. 126.

54. Kleppner, *Cross of Culture,* op. cit., pp. 40–52.

55. Ibid., pp. 40-52.

56. Ibid., pp. 44-49.

57. Ibid., pp. 48-49.

58. William Gillette, *Jersey Blue: Civil War Politics in New Jersey* (New Brunswick, NJ: Rutgers University Press, 1994), p. 210. See also Kleppner, op. cit., pp. 59-60.

59. Peter A. Munch, The Norwegians," *Harvard Encyclopedia of American Ethnic Groups* (Cambridge: Harvard University Press, 1980), pp. 754-757.

60. Pease and Pease, *Ends, Means and Attitudes*, p. 111.

61. Richard N. Current, *Lincoln's Loyalists* (New York: Oxford University Press, 1992), p. 164.

62. *Mississippi*, American Guide Series (New York: Viking Press, 1943), p. 50.

63. Current, op. cit., pp. 107-110.

64. *Alabama*, American Guide Series (New York: Richard R. Smith, 1941), p. 50.

65. McPherson, op. cit., pp. 831-838.

66. Faragher, op. cit., pp. viii–ix, notably the map of "Daniel Boone's America" emphasizing Pennsylvania, Virginia, North Carolina, Tennessee, Kentucky, and Missouri.

67. I am not aware of any comparisons of the loyalist or "Tory" troops raised by the British between 1775 and 1783 and the loyalist or "Tory" troops—or so Confederates named them—raised by the federal government in the South during the 1861–1865 period, but useful ones can be made. Especially after 1778, loyalists constituted a much larger percentage (one-third to two-fifths) of the Crown's forces in the thirteen colonies than they would have of federal troops in the South in 1864–1865 (under 10 percent). Roughly one-quarter of Americans in 1775–1783 were loyalists and perhaps one-fifth of those Americans who wore uniforms during the entire period were loyalists. By the end of the Civil War, only about 11 percent of Southerners in uniform wore Yankee blue. However, the British in 1775–1783 and the federals in 1861–1865 made some of the same points. Many who might have sympathized or joined up were unreachable in territory occupied by the foe. The opportunity to get enlistments came when a nonhostile territory was occupied: the British of 1775–1783 in and around New York, New Jersey, Philadelphia (during the 1777–1778 occupation), Charleston, Savannah, and the Cape Fear region of North Carolina, the federals of 1861–1865 in western Virginia, Tennessee, coastal North Carolina, northern Arkansas, and the area around New Orleans. Neither the British in 1775–1783 nor the federals in 1861–1865 were inclined to restore civil government in occupied territory, which might have spurred loyalist recruitment; they preferred to keep authority in military hands.

68. Talbert, op. cit., pp. 39–51.

69. McPherson, op. cit., p. 284.

70. The extent to which occasional to substantial Republican election victories in the Border states during the 1861–1865 period depended on federal bayonets, martial law, or disenfranchisement of Confederate sympathizers is noted in Talbert, *Maryland*, op. cit., pp. 67–83; Richard O. Curry, ed., *Radicalism, Racism, and Party Realignment: The Border States During Reconstruction* (Baltimore: Johns Hopkins University Press, 1969), pp. 6 (for Missouri), 112 (for Kentucky), and 194 (for Delaware).

71. Alvin Josephy, Jr., *The Civil War in the American West* (New York: Knopf, 1991), p. 238.

72. Ibid., p. 264.

Chapter Eleven

1. Cullen Murphy, "History's Parallel Universe," *The Atlantic* (August 1995), p. 20.

2. Kenneth Bourne, *Britain and the Balance of Power in North America* (Berkeley: University of California Press, 1967), pp. 235, 240.

3. Had adverse politico-military circumstances in 1861–1863 broken up the United States into regional confederacies, adding new ones in the Midwest and the Pacific, the

British government would have been particularly interested in the latter. British and U.S. troops had almost come to blows in Puget Sound in 1859 during the so-called Pig War, the Oregon boundary had been hotly disputed in the 1840s, and some British maps had claimed southward from Oregon as far as San Francisco in the 1820s. A "Western Confederacy" would have almost certainly gotten considerable British investment and attention, not least because London was busy during these years creating British Columbia (1858), merging it with Vancouver Island in 1866, and helping the combined colony to join the Canadian Confederation in 1870–1871. Had the 1860s seen a breakup of the United States, who can say what Pacific confederations would have emerged and where? See Van Alstyne, op. cit., p. 119.

4. See Bourne, op. cit., p. 240 for the weakness of a British fleet attempting a U.S. blockade.

5. The Confederacy, in keeping with its plumed cavalier image, had been home during prewar years to occasional jousts and medieval tournaments, and some even hankered after a return to monarchy. Judah Benjamin, the British-born politician who became the Confederate secretary of state, was rumored to have raised with a British diplomat the idea of the South coming back under the Crown, but Benjamin denied this. In the early days, when Montgomery, in the heart of cotton plantation country, was the Confederate capital, several chronicles mention vague talk of having something like a European court.

6. Foner, *Political Ideology*, op. cit., p. 49.

7. McPherson, op. cit., pp. 859–860.

8. Hirst, op. cit., pp. 330–331.

9. Some history books occasionally suggest that in the loose decade or two after the Revolution, when free blacks were allowed to vote in some states, women might have also have done so in a few places. The *Blackwell Encyclopedia of the American Revolution,* however, makes no mention of such participation (Betty Wood, "The Impact of the Revolution on the Role, Status and Experience of Women").

10. The Thirteenth, Fourteenth, and Fifteenth Amendments to the U.S. Constitution were proposed and ratified during and after the Civil War to free those blacks remaining in slavery and to secure their voting rights. The Fifteenth Amendment was proposed specifically to secure black voting because so many northern and Border states were rejecting it in legislatures and in statewide popular votes. Indeed, Maryland, Delaware, New Jersey, New York, and Ohio voted at least once to *reject* the Fifteenth Amendment or to withdraw a prior approval.

11. Frederickson, op. cit., p. 118.

12. William B. Hesseltine, "Reconstruction," in Davis and Woodman, op. cit., p. 405.

13. Frederickson, op. cit., pp. 138–141.

14. Ibid., pp. 161–164, 184.

15. Ibid., p. 185.

16. Robert E. May, ed., *The Union, the Confederacy and the Atlantic Rim* (Lafayette: Purdue University Press, 1995), p. 116.

17. J. P. Kenyon, op. cit., pp. 2–4, 126–127.

18. Higginbotham, op. cit., p. 313.

19. Ibid., p. 311.

20. Ibid., p. 251.

21. Bruce D. Porter, *War and the Rise of the State* (New York: The Free Press, 1994), p. 258.

22. Porter, op. cit., p. 259.

23. Ibid., pp. 258–262.

24. Ibid., p. 265.

25. Ibid., p. 262.

26. Milton Friedman and Anna Schwartz, *A Monetary History of the United States 1867–1960* (Princeton: Princeton University Press, 1963), pp. 20, 34–37.

27. Kennedy, op. cit., p. 242.

28. Crofts, op. cit., p. 21.

29. Matthew Josephson, *The Robber Barons* (New York: Harcourt Brace/Harvest Book, 1962), p. 80.

30. Frederickson, op. cit., p. 197.

31. James McPherson, "Reconstruction: A Revolutionary Manque," in Davis and Woodman, eds., op. cit., p. 419.

32. Ibid.

33. William E. Parish, *Missouri Under Radical Rule* (Columbia: University of Missouri Press, 1965), p. 252.

34. Library of Congress, *Constitution of the U.S. Annotated*, pp. 62–66.

35. Frederickson, op. cit., pp. 128, 191.

36. Paul Buck, *The Road to Reunion* (Boston: Little, Brown, 1937), p. 155.

37. Porter, op. cit., p. 267.

38. C. Vann Woodward, *Reunion and Reaction* (New York: Doubleday Anchor, 1956), p. 246.

39. Robert R. Russel, *History of the American Economic System* (New York: Appleton-Century-Crofts, 1964), pp. 273–274.

40. Albert B. Moore, "One Hundred Years of Reconstruction of the South," *Journal of Southern History*, May 1943, pp. 153–180.

41. McPherson, op. cit., p. 818.

42. Moore, op. cit., pp. 153–180.

43. Roy F. Nichols, *The Stakes of Power* (New York: Hill and Wang, 1961), p. 171.

44. Charles P. Roland, *The Confederacy* (Chicago: 1960), pp. 194–195.

45. Moore, op. cit., p. 491.

46. Fischer, op. cit., p. 863.

47. McPherson, op. cit., pp. 818–819.

48. Report of the National Emergency Council (Washinton, DC: Government Printing Office, 1937).

49. Stephen Vincent Benet, *John Brown's Body* (Holt, Rinehart and Winston: 1956).

50. Roger Chauvire, *A History of Ireland* (New York: Mentor Books, 1964), p. 94.

51. Kerby Miller, op. cit., p. 18.

52. Leyburn, op. cit., p. 125.

53. Kerby Miller, op. cit., p. 139.

54. G. A. Hayes-McCoy, ed., *The Irish at War* (Cork: The Mercier Press, 1965), p. 69.

55. Kerby Miller, op. cit., pp. 21–22.

56. Doyle, op. cit., p. 149.

57. Bailyn and Morgan, op. cit., pp. 157–219.

58. Duncan Macleod, op. cit., in Berlin and Hoffman, eds., op. cit., p. 225.

59. Hickey, op. cit., pp. 154, 204.

60. Leyburn, op. cit., p. 191.

61. Bailyn and Morgan, op. cit., pp. 295–296.

62. Bruce E. Johansen, *Forgotten Founders* (Boston: Harvard Common Press, 1982), p. 16.

63. Colin G. Callaway, *The American Revolution in Indian Country* (New York: Cambridge University Press, 1995), p. 124.

64. Ibid., p. 126.

65. Ibid., pp. 293–301.

66. Laurence M. Hauptman, *Between Two Fires* (New York: Free Press, 1995), p. 46.

67. Ibid., pp. 87–102 and 103–122.

68. Ibid., pp. 22, 30.

69. Bourne, op. cit., p. 235.

70. H. C. Allen, *Great Britain and the United States* (New York: St. Martin's, 1955), p. 456.

71. Ibid., p. 453.

72. Howard Jones, op. cit., p. 230.

73. Three useful books on the period or covering it are E. D. Adams, *Great Britain and the American Civil War* (London: Longmans, 1925); H. C. Allen, *Great Britain and the United States,* op. cit.; and, of much more recent vintage, Howard Jones, *Union in Peril,* op. cit.

74. *The Life and Times of Charles James Fox,* 3 vols. (London: Richard Bentley, 1859), vol. 1, p. 82.

75. D. P. Crook, *The North and South and the Powers* (New York: John Wiley, 1974), p. 10.

76. W. D. Jones, "The British Conservatives and the American Civil War," *American Historical Review* 58 (April 1953), p. 529; R. G. May, ed., op. cit., p. 137.

77. See Philip Foner, *British Labor and the American Civil War* (New York: Holmes and Meier, 1981), especially chapter 8.

78. *Times* of London, quoted in McPherson, op. cit., p. 551; *New York Times,* November 8, 1662, quoted in Foner, ibid., p. 74.

79. Donald Bellows, "A Study of British Conservative Reaction to the American Civil War," *Journal of Southern History* 51 (November 1985), pp. 510–520.

80. W. D. Jones, op. cit., p. 536.

81. W. C. Wright, op. cit., p. 155.

82. R. E. May, ed., op. cit., p. 70.

83. D. G. Wright, "Bradford and the American Civil War," *Journal of British Studies* 8 (May 1989), p. 83.

84. R. E. May, ed., op. cit., p. 74.

85. The Census of 1860 enumerated 431,692 English-born persons in the United States. I could not find Welsh Census data for 1860, but as of 1870, there were 74,533 natives of Wales in the United States. The problem for Scots and Ulster (Scotch-Irish) Protestant data is the confusion between the two, but there were almost certainly 250,000 Scottish and Ulster-born Protestants in the U.S. as of 1860. That would make about 750,000, of whom 650,000 to 700,000 would have been in the northern and western states.

86. Kleppner, op. cit., pp. 76.

87. "The Welsh," *Harvard Encyclopedia of Ethnic Groups* (Cambridge: Harvard University Press, 1980), p. 1015.

88. Bradley, *Popular Politics,* op. cit., p. 179.

89. R. E. May, ed., op. cit., p. 93.

90. Kerby Miller, op. cit., p. 359.

91. Ibid., p. 359.

92. P. Foner, *British Labor,* op. cit., p. 45.

93. Ibid., p. 71.

94. Ibid., p. 59.

95. Allen, op. cit., p. 496.

96. See especially Ritcheson, op. cit., and Perkins, op. cit., for the earlier period and Bourne, op. cit., on the latter.

97. George Dangerfield, *The Awakening of American Nationalism* (New York: Harper Torch Books, 1965), p. 257.

98. Turner, op. cit., p. 93.

99. Van Alstyne, op. cit., p. 95.

100. Ibid., p. 196.

101. Allan Nevins, *War for the Union*, vol. 2, p. 242.

102. John Trumbull, *Autobiography*, p. 169.

103. Fischer, op. cit., p. 845.

104. Michael Kammen, *A Season of Youth* (Ithaca: Cornell University Press, 1978), pp. 168–172.

105. Allen, op. cit., p. 577.

106. Peter Trubowitz, in his book *Defining the National Interest: Conflict and Change in American Foreign Policy* (Chicago: University of Chicago Press, 1998), includes a useful chart showing the extent to which imperialist policies during the 1890s were supported in Congress by the North—and New England, in particular—over the objections of the South:

Support of Members of the House of Representatives for Imperialist Policies by Regions, 1898–1900

	Intervention in Cuba	Annexation of Hawaii	Isthmian Canal	Control of Philippines	Puerto Rican Tariff
North					
New England	95.8%	95.7%	91.3%	85.7%	82.6%
Middle Atlantic	87.8	92.9	63.9	66.7	61.4
Great Lakes	73.7	91.3	77.1	73.9	70.4
South					
Southeast	20.3	32.8	36.5	14.3	14.7
Southwest	4.0	4.5	15.8	4.5	0.0

Details on the regions and the legislative topics and votes appear on p. 54 of his book. Western members of the House fell in between in their support.

107. Bourne, op. cit., p. 381.

108. Ritcheson, op. cit., pp. 121–122.

Chapter Twelve

1. Bradley, *Religion, Revolution*, op. cit., pp. 340–341.

2. Clark, op. cit., p. 10.

3. Both of James Bradley's books on English politics during the period of the American Revolution have considerable detail about these major towns, many drawn from specific studies done by other academicians. Political activism among the middle classes was widespread—and with respect to occasional national as well as local issues.

4. Howard Jones, op. cit., p. 27.

5. McPherson, op. cit., p. 293.

6. Howard Jones, op. cit., p. 156.

7. Plumb, *In the Light of History* (Boston: Houghton Mifflin, 1973), p. 77.

8. Spalding, op. cit., pp. 329–330.

9. Emory Thomas, *The Confederacy as a Revolutionary Experience* (Columbia: University of South Carolina Press, 1991), pp. 28 and 35.

10. R. E. May, ed., op. cit., p. 55.

11. Allen, op. cit., p. 460.

12. Kammen, op. cit., pp. 53, 56.

13. Emory Thomas, op. cit., pp. 43–51.

14. McPherson, op. cit., p. 204.

15. See, for example, George Dangerfield, *The Strange Death of Liberal England, 1910–1914* (New York: G. P. Putnam's, 1961).

16. Michael Kinnear, *The British Voter* (Ithaca: Cornell University Press, 1968), pp. 40–46.

17. Oscar Zeichner, "The Loyalist Problem in New York," *New York Historical Association,* vol. 21 (1940), pp. 286, 294.

18. Robert L. Brunhouse, *The Counter-Revolution in Pennsylvania* (Harrisburg: Pennsylvania Historical and Museum Commission, 1971), pp. 40–41.

19. See, for example, Owen Ireland, *Religion, Ethnicity, and Politics* (University Park: Penn State Press, 1995), p. 251.

20. William Chambers, *Political Parties in the New Nation* (New York: Oxford University Press, 1963), p. 25.

21. The ties between Vermont and Switzerland these days involve skiing instructors and Alpine village motifs in some of the winter resorts, but two hundred years earlier, John Graves Simcoe, the future British governor of Upper Canada, had a different Swiss analogy in mind. Without an alliance between an independent Vermont and Canada, he argued in 1789, Canada's security would be at risk. With such an arrangement, he told the British government, Vermont, inhabited by "a brave, virtuous and English race of people," could become "another Switzerland" between Canada and the United States (Ritcheson, op. cit., p. 155).

22. Harold Hancock, *Delaware Loyalists* (Wilmington: Historical Society of Delaware, 1940), p. 46.

23. Rudolph Pasler and Margaret Pasler, *The New Jersey Federalists* (Rutherford, NJ: Fairleigh Dickinson University Press, 1975), p. 115.

24. Owen Ireland, op. cit., Introduction and chapter 7.

25. Rose, op. cit., p. 260.

26. Ibid., p. 337.

27. This was true in Pennsylvania; in Massachusetts, the big Federalist gains came among Quakers (see Banner, op. cit., pp. 212–213).

28. Quoted in Hickey, op. cit., p. 305.

29. Quoted from Hickey, ibid., p. 307.

30. Gillette, op. cit., pp. 209–211; Leiby, op. cit., pp. 227–231.

31. Carl Carmer, *The Susquehanna* (New York: David McKay, 1955), p. 221.

32. Northern Episcopal discomfort with Republicanism and abolition is not hard to conjecture. To begin with, the prewar church, as noted in chapter 9, did not take a position against slavery. In Connecticut (1818) and Massachusetts (1833), Episcopalians had been arrayed with the Democrats against the Whigs—who largely became the Republicans—in disestablishing the Congregational Church. In Pennsylvania, the Democrats of 1860–1861 absorbed a considerable number of Whigs from old-line Episcopal families and from Philadelphia's Market Street Cottonocracy (see Dusinberre, op. cit., and Sundquist, op. cit., p. 83). In Michigan, data for the party affiliations of the economic elite in Detroit, Michigan, circa 1860, cited by Ronald Formisano in his book *The Birth of Mass Parties: Michigan, 1827–1861,* op. cit., p. 346, set out the following split: Presbyterians 4:1 Republican, Catholics 3:1 Democratic, Episcopalians 2:1 Democratic. This cursory analysis and data don't prove much of anything, but the findings of a detailed investigation of the entire North might be revealing.

33. There are only a handful of U.S. counties that experienced a serious local civil war and fratricide in *both* the Revolution and the War Between the States—and two of the prime examples are Randolph and Chatham in east-central North Carolina. In January 1984, the *North Carolina Historical Review* published an article by William T. Auman entitled "Neighbor Against Neighbor: The Inner Civil War in the Randolph County Area of Confederate North Carolina." What Randolph almost uniquely offers is a chance to compare the dynamics of two such inner civil wars: the one of 1861–1865 and the one of 1775–1783.

34. Current, op. cit., pp. 141–142.

35. Ibid., p. 71.

36. McPherson, op. cit., p. 786.

37. Curry, ed., op. cit., pp. xvi–xxv.

38. Richard Current, in *Lincoln's Loyalists*, op. cit., estimates on p. 218 that at least 100,000 Southerners served in the Union armies, with 850,000 to 900,000 fighting for the Confederacy.

39. Current, op. cit., pp. 61–73.

40. Lawrence Goodwyn, *The Populist Moment* (New York: Oxford University Press, 1978), p. 281.

41. Ray A. Billington, *The Protestant Crusade* (New York: Macmillan, 1938).

42. Timothy Bosworth, "Anti-Catholicism as a Political Tool," *Catholic Historical Review*, vol. 61 (1975), pp. 554–559.

43. Gray, op. cit., p. 219.

44. Dusinberre, op. cit., p. 47.

45. McPherson, op. cit., p. 606.

46. Current, op. cit., pp. 129–132.

47. Gray, op. cit., p. 216.

48. Kerby Miller, op. cit., pp. 360–361.

49. Ibid., p. 336.

50. Donald F. Durnbaugh, "The Brethren and the Revolution: Neutrals or Tories?," in *Brethren Life and Thought*, vol. XXII (Winter 1977), p. 16.

51. *Patriots and Tories in Piedmont North Carolina*, op. cit., p. 6.

52. Gray, op. cit., p. 111.

53. Ibid., pp. 190–193.

54. Ibid., pp. 192–193.

55. O'Connor, *The Germans* (Boston: Little, Brown, 1968), pp. 123–158.

56. The two Lubell books, in which the noted grassroots political journalist probed German, Irish, and isolationist voting patterns between 1916 and 1952, are *The Future of American Politics* (New York: Harper & Row, 1952) and *Revolt of the Moderates* (New York: Harper, 1956). While German war-related voting patterns get the most attention, the Irish are tied in both as voters and through the particular examples of Father Charles Coughlin and Senator Joseph McCarthy.

57. This yardstick works for the principal German concentrations in Ohio, Indiana, Wisconsin, and northern Illinois.

58. O'Connor, op. cit., pp. 394–395.

59. Lubell, *Revolt*, op. cit., pp. 67–68.

60. For example, of the nine German counties in Ohio that were solidly Democratic from Andrew Jackson's day through World War I, all showed major trends against the Democratic presidential nominee again in 1940—and most were among the relatively small group of Ohio counties to trend away from Lincoln between 1860 and 1864. War sensitivity did not begin with World War I.

61. Lubell, *Revolt*, op. cit., pp. 70–71.

62. Lubell, *Future*, op. cit., p. 143.

63. Lubell, *Revolt*, op. cit., pp. 68, 78.

64. Comparing the 1940 results with those of 1936, Roosevelt made significant gains in parts of Yankee coastal New England and the Canadian-settled reaches of Maine. He also increased his support in some of the oldest-settled areas of coastal Virginia and North Carolina. In the overwhelmingly white and English-descended Outer Banks of North Carolina, Franklin D. Roosevelt raised his support between 1936 and 1940 by eight points in Dare County, two in Carteret, and one in Currituck. In the first-settled part of Virginia, where the old English dialects survived the longest—in Matthews, Gloucester, and York Counties—FDR's gain was one to five points. These changes may not seem like much, but the norm almost everywhere was a loss, not an increase, in comparison with 1936.

65. Ahlstrom, op. cit., pp. 883–885.

66. Warhawks, pp. 19–23.

67. Lubell, *Revolt*, op. cit., pp. 73–74; Lubell, *Future*, op. cit., pp. 150–152.

68. Lubell, *Future*, op. cit., pp. 135, 201–202.

69. This question of whether or not the United States might have had a third civil war of sorts in the late 1960s and early 1970s doesn't strike some prominent observers of the period as foolish. On the contrary, on May 1, 1968, I moderated a panel for the Washington-based Newseum on the thirtieth anniversary of 1968 that included political journalists Pat Buchanan, Robert Novak, and Jules Witcover; and with this chapter on my mind, I asked all three whether they thought those years did amount to a kind of political and cultural civil war. The transcript carries their answers as follows: Buchanan: "I do agree that it was a civil war in American politics"; Witcover: "Well, I guess you could call it a civil war"; Novak: "There was a civil war." So in a sense, perhaps the emerging Republican majority that elected a president for twenty years out of twenty-four between 1968 and 1992 was also the product of a "war."

Chapter Thirteen

1. Aaron Fogelman, *Hopeful Journeys* (Philadelphia: University of Pennsylvania Press, 1996), p. 31.

2. Martin Marty, *Righteous Empire* (New York: Dial Press, 1970), p. 15.

3. Rowse, *The Elizabethans and America* (New York: Harper, 1989), p. 1.

4. Ibid., p. 92.

5. John Buchan, op. cit., p. 100.

6. Leyburn, op. cit., p. 130.

7. Kerby Miller, op. cit., pp. 167–173.

8. No one knows what the population of Ireland was in that year, but it was probably somewhat lower than the 1.5 million often used as an estimate for the year 1600.

9. Emmet Larkin, "The Devotional Revolution in Ireland," quoted in McWhinney, op. cit., p. 5.

10. Ibid., p. 7.

11. Michael Hechter, *Internal Colonialism* (Berkeley: University of California Press, 1975), pp. 80–85.

12. Ibid., pp. 85–86.

13. Cecil Woodham-Smith, *The Great Hunger* (New York: Signet Books, 1964), p. 14.

14. Hechter, op. cit., p. xvi.

15. Ibid., p. 73.

16. Richard Rose, *Governing Without Consensus* (Boston: Beacon Press, 1971), pp. 71–73.

17. Kerby Miller, op. cit., pp. 179–199.

18. Ibid., p. 198.

19. Rollie Poppino, *Brazil* (New York: Oxford University Press, 1968), pp. 185–186.

20. Ibid., pp. 192–193.

21. Argentina was the Western Hemisphere nation most impacted by immigration during the period from 1880 to 1914, according to N. S. Albarnoz, *The Population of Latin America* (Berkeley: University of California Press, 1974). Germans trailed far behind Italians and Spaniards, but their net arrivals would have exceeded 100,000.

22. A. E. Smith, op. cit., chapter 1.

23. Ibid., p. 104.

24. Ibid., p. 117.

25. Ibid., pp. 140–142.

26. Ibid., pp. 123–124.

27. Kirby Miller, op. cit., p. 199.

28. Ibid., p. 281.

29. See especially A. G. Roeber, "The Dutch-Speaking and German-Speaking Peoples of Colonial America," in *Strangers Within the Realm*, pp. 244–247.

30. Francis Jennings, *Benjamin Franklin, Politician* (New York: Norton, 1996), p. 70.

31. John A. Hawgood, *The Tragedy of German America* (New York: 1940).

32. H. Richard Niebuhr, *The Social Sources of Denominationalism* (New York: Meridian Books, 1957), p. 227.

33. O'Connor, op. cit., p. 73.

34. Hawgood, op. cit., p. 39.

35. O'Connor, op. cit, p. 93.

36. Hawgood, op. cit., p. 85.

37. Ibid., p. 63.

38. O'Connor, op. cit., p. 60.

39. Brian Morton, *Americans in London* (New York: William Morrow/Quill, 1986), p. 281.

40. Fischer, *Albion's Seed*, op. cit., p. 881.

Chapter Fourteen

1. Hechter, op. cit., p. 57.

2. Samuel P. Huntington, *The Clash of Civilization and the Remaking of World Order* (London: Simon and Schuster, 1997), p. 60.

3. "Britons Abroad," *The Economist* (December 26, 1992), p. 86.

4. Fraser, op. cit., p. 699.

BIBLIOGRAPHY

THIS BIBLIOGRAPHY IS ORGANIZED to some extent by chapter, which means largely chronologically, but also by nation, culture, and general focus (religion, for example). In part, this reflects the book's organization. However, in some respects it also reflects how the book evolved: from a (brief) beginning stage in which it was to focus on the American Revolution and its 1776–1777 pivot in the Hudson-Champlain Corridor, then into a second stage in which that Revolution would be revisited as a civil war within English-speaking North America with some parallel divisions in the British Isles. From there, the subject matter—the war's meaning and alignments—pushed both backward into the meanings and constituencies of the English Civil War and forward into the meanings and constituencies of the U.S. Civil War. Important relationships and continuities began to fall into place. And, in the meantime, the book's aim also pushed outward from its core of war, religion, and politics into showing how the three wars added up to a vital governmental, cultural, and linguistic ladder by which the English-speaking community divided into two related but different nations—the two principal "cousins"—and achieved nineteenth- and twentieth-century global hegemony under two flags.

This explanation underpins an obvious bibliographical caveat. When I set out in 1994, I did not have in mind the scope that the finished book of 1998 has been drawn into encompassing. Some books that seemed important in early 1995—on the history of late seventeenth- and eighteenth-century warfare in the Mohawk Valley, the navigability of the Hudson River, or the battle of Bennington—are not even cited. My interest in the British politics and constituencies of the 1775–1783 war ballooned after I visited Oxford to give a speech on U.S. politics in April 1995 and left with a detailed eighteenth-century reading list.

It began to fall into place that the divisions within Britain over the War for American Independence bore a considerable relation to the divisions within the thirteen colonies. In short, that many of the 1775–1783 alignments within the thirteen colonies—especially the dominant ones involving religion, ethnicity, and culture—echoed those visible in the English and British wars and risings of the 1640s, 1688, 1715, and 1745. I had already seen a similarity between some of the U.S. alignments of the 1770s and some of those of the 1860s. Now I would have to go back into a century and a half of pre-1775 British history.

In 1995, it had become reasonably clear in my mind that my book on the Hudson-Champlain pivot of 1776–1777 was partly transitioning into a political analysis: the Emerging Republican Majority of 1776 (backstopped by important minorities in the British Isles). Maybe I would also have a final chapter or two on some of the continuities visible between the eighteenth-century pattern and the first Emerging Republican Party Majority (Plurality) of 1860. I had been working on aspects of that for nearly forty years.

By 1996, it was clear that I would have to go back into seventeenth- and early eighteenth-century British wars and politics in so much detail that I might as well do a three-part book about three English-speaking civil wars and the formation of three vital political alignments: the emerging (and short-lived) Republican plurality of 1640s England, the emerging Republican plurality (but soon majority) of 1770s America, and the emerging Republican plurality (but soon majority) of the United States of 1860. It also promised to be more interesting than spending that year thinking about Bill Clinton, Al Gore, Bob Dole, and Jack Kemp.

At this point, having spent a year immersed in seventeenth- and eighteenth-century British history, I found myself repeating my old technique of the 1960s in writing *The Emerging Republican Majority* that had predicted the coming quarter century of U.S. presidential politics: Find out as much as possible about the different voting streams and constituencies and why they take sides as they do—history, religion, ethnicity, economics, and localism. The voting patterns and wartime loyalties will tell you a lot about what issues and themes really mattered.

My reading was designed to do this for both the 1640s and the 1770s, each time on *both* sides of the Atlantic, and it involved readings in geography, economics, religion, shire and county localisms, and suchlike, as well as political and wartime histories. The U.S. patterns, at least, of the 1860s were already reasonably well known to me. For the U.S., I could immediately pursue county-level detail with a good framework of political and geographic knowledge. That was less true for Britain. The most useful books and articles for the latter were those that spelled out political and wartime alignments on local, religious, or economic levels—in Ireland and Scotland, as well as in England.

By 1997, I was further afield, pondering other patterns such as the prime moving group's close similarity, almost identity, in each of the three wars: Puritans from eastern England (East Anglia) in the 1640s, and then their Yankee descendants in New England in 1775 and 1860. Not only were all three wars about an aggressive, dissenting Protestant interpretation of liberty, but they spread English-speaking power around the world, overwhelming rival national cultures. This last English-speaking victory pulled me into twentieth-century world political geographies, books analyzing German emigration and the Irish and Scottish overseas diasporas, as well as chronicles of the U.S. ethnic voting patterns in World Wars I and II and studies of Latin America's failure to rival the United States as a receptacle for European emigration between 1865 and 1914.

The bibliography set out here is in no sense exhaustive. For the most part, it consists of books and articles that have beeen cited in this volume's many footnotes. But I have added several score others that I paid close attention to.

What are rarely cited are the materials from local historical societies; county and township voting data from long-ago elections (and yellowing World Almanacs); battlefield guides; histories of Cheshire, England, or Westchester, New York, that produced some political equivalent of local color; tourist guides to East Anglia or eighteenth-century Charleston; and map compilations ranging from the *Macmillan Atlas of Irish History to the Atlas of Early American History* published by the Institute of Early American History and Culture.

The following sources are grouped by subject-matter cluster.

1. The Expansion of Sixteenth- and Early Seventeenth-Century England and the Seventeenth-Century Colonial United States

Sacvan Bercovitch, *The Puritan Origins of the American Self* (New Haven: Yale University Press, 1975).

Carl Bridenbaugh, *Vexed and Troubled Englishmen* (New York: Oxford University Press, 1968).

Richard C. Dunn, *Puritans and Yankees* (Princeton: Princeton University Press, 1962).

David Hackett Fischer, *Albion's Seed: Four British Folkways in America* (New York: Oxford University Press, 1989).

Philip F. Gura, *A Glimpse of Sion's Glory* (Middletown, CT: Wesleyan University Press, 1984).

David S. Lovejoy, *The Glorious Revolution in America* (New York: Harper Torch Books, 1974).

A. L. Rowse, *The Elizabethans and America* (New York: Harper, 1989).

A. L. Rowse, *The Expansion of Elizabethan England* (New York: St. Martin's Press, 1955).

Stephen Saunders Webb, *1676: The End of American Independence* (Syracuse: Syracuse University Press, 1995).

Thomas J. Werterbaker, *Torchbearer of the American Revolution* (Princeton: Princeton University Press, 1940).

2. The Seventeenth-Century British Isles, the English Civil War, the Glorious Revolution, and the Risings of 1715 and 1745

Maurice Ashley, *The Greatness of Oliver Cromwell* (New York: Collier, 1962).

John Buchan, *Oliver Cromwell* (Boston: Houghton-Mifflin, 1934).

Richard L. Bushman, *King and People in Provincial Massachusetts* (Chapel Hill: University of North Carolina Press, 1992).

K. Merle Chacksfield, *Glorious Revolution 1688* (Somerset: Wincanton Press, 1988).

Linda Colley, *Britons* (New Haven: Yale University Press, 1992).

Barry Coward, *The Stuart Age: England 1603–1714* (London: Longman, 1994).

Richard Cust and Ann Hughes, editors, *Conflict in Early Stuart England* (New York: Longman, 1989).

Antonia Fraser, *Cromwell: The Lord Protector* (New York: Knopf, 1973).

Christopher Hill, *The Century of Revolution 1603–1714* (New York: Norton, 1982).

Christopher Hill, *The English Bible and the 17th Century Revolution* (New York: Penguin, 1993).

Christopher Hill, *Puritanism and the Revolution* (New York: St. Martin's Press, 1997).

Christopher Hill, *Society and Puritanism in Prerevolutionary England* (1964).

Christopher Hill, *The World Turned Upside Down* (New York: Viking Press, 1972).

Derek Hirst, *Authority and Conflict: England, 1603–1658* (Cambridge: Harvard University Press, 1986).

William Hunt, *The Puritan Moment: The Coming of Revolution in an English County* (Cambridge: Harvard University Press, 1983).

J. P. Kenyon, *The Civil Wars of England* (New York: Knopf, 1988).

David S. Lovejoy, *The Glorious Revolution in America* (New York: Harper Torch Books, 1974).

John Morrill, *The Nature of the English Revolution* (New York: Longman, 1993).

John Morrill, *The Revolt of the Provinces* (London: Longman, 1980).

J. G. A. Pocock, editor, *Three British Revolutions: 1641, 1688, 1776* (Princeton: Princeton University Press, 1980).

C. G. Robertson, *England Under the Hanoverians* (London: Methuen, 1923).

Conrad Russell, *The Causes of the English Civil War* (Oxford: Clarendon Press, 1990).

Conrad Russell, editor, *The Origins of the English Civil War* (London: Macmillan, 1980).

Lawrence Stone, *The Causes of the English Revolution 1529–1642* (New York: Harper Torch Books, 1972).

Lawrence Stone, *Social Change and Revolution in England, 1540–1640* (New York: Barnes & Noble, 1965).

R. H. Tawney, *Religion and the Rise of Capitalism* (New York: Mentor, 1954).

George M. Trevelyan, *England Under the Stuarts* (London: Methuen, 1949).

David Underdown, *Revel, Riot and Rebellion* (New York: Oxford University Press, 1987).

Stephen Saunders Webb, *1676: The End of American Independence* (Syracuse: Syracuse University Press, 1995).

C. V. Wedgwood, *The King's Peace* (New York: Macmillan, 1956).

Austin Woolwych, *Battles of the English Civil Wars* (London: Pan Books, 1966).

John R. Young, editor, *Celtic Dimensions of the British Civil Wars* (Edinburgh: John Donald, 1997).

3. The Eighteenth-Century Background and Origins of the American Revolution

Bernard Bailyn, *The Ideological Origins of the American Revolution* (Cambridge: Harvard University Press, 1992).

Patricia U. Bonomi, *Under the Cope of Heaven* (New York: Oxford University Press, 1986).

T. H. Breen, *Tobacco Culture* (Princeton: Princeton University Press, 1985).

Carl Bridenbaugh, *Mitre and Sceptre* (New York: Oxford University Press, 1962).

Ian Christie and Benjamin Labaree, *Empire or Independence, 1760–1776* (New York: 1976).

J. C. D. Clark, *The Language of Liberty, 1660–1832* (Cambridge: Cambridge University Press, 1994).

Don Cook, *The Long Fuse* (New York: Atlantic Monthly Press, 1995).

Theodore Draper, *A Struggle for Power* (New York: Times Books, 1996).

Marc Egnal, *A Mighty Empire* (Ithaca: Cornell University Press, 1988).

Lawrence H. Gipson, *The Coming of the Revolution, 1763–1775* (New York: Harper Torch Books, 1962).

Jack P. Greene, *Peripheries and Center* (New York: Norton, 1986).

Jack P. Greene, *Understanding the American Revolution* (Charlottesville: University Press of Virginia, 1995).

Jack P. Greene and J. R. Pole, editors, *The Blackwell Encyclopedia of the American Revolution* (Oxford: Blackwell, 1994).

Douglas Leach, *Roots of Conflict: British Armed Forces and Colonial Americans, 1677–1763* (Chapel Hill: University of North Carolina Press, 1986).

Pauline Maier, *The Old Revolutionaries* (New York: Norton, 1980).

Gary Nash, *The Urban Crucible* (Cambridge: Harvard University Press, 1986).

Eric Robson, *The American Revolution* (London: Batchworth, 1955).

Max Savelle, *Empires to Nations* (Minneapolis: University of Minnesota Press, 1974).

John Shy, *A People Numerous and Armed* (Ann Arbor: University of Michigan Press, 1990).

John Shy, *Toward Lexington: The Role of the British Army in the Coming of the American Revolution* (Princeton: Princeton University Press, 1965).

Chard P. Smith, *Yankees and God* (New York: Hermitage House, 1954).

James C. Spalding, "Loyalist as Royalist," *Church History* 45 (September 1976).

Harry S. Stout, *The New England Soul* (New York: 1986).

Reginald Stuart, "For the Lord Is a Man of Warr." *Journal of Church and State*, (Autumn 1981).

William Warren Sweet, "The Role of the Anglicans in the American Revolution," *Huntington Library Quarterly* II (1947–1948).

Steven Watson, *George III* (London: Oxford University Press, 1960).

Gordon Wood, *The Radicalism of the American Revolution* (New York: Knopf, 1992).

Esmond Wright, *Causes and Consequences of the American Revolution* (Chicago: Quadrangle, 1966).

Alfred F. Young, editor, *The American Revolution: Explorations in the History of American Radicalism* (DeKalb: Northern Illinois University Press, 1976).

Alfred F. Young, "English Plebeian Culture and 18th Century American Radicalism," in Margaret Jacob and James Jacob, editors, *The Origins of Anglo-American Radicalism* (NJ: Humanities Press International, 1991).

4. The Great French War and the War for American Independence as a Civil War Across Much of the British North Atlantic

Russell Bellico, *Sails and Steam in the Mountains: A Maritime and Military History of Lake Champlain* (New York: Purple Mountain Press, 1992).

Selwyn H. H. Carrington, "The American Revolution and the Sugar Colonies," in Greene and Pole, editors, *The Blackwell Encyclopedia of the American Revolution* (Oxford: Blackwell, 1994).

Allan S. Everest, *Moses Hazen and the Canadian Refugees in the American Revolution* (Syracuse: Syracuse University Press, 1976).

Lawrence Henry Gipson, *The Triumphant Empire* (New York: Knopf, 1956).

Colin Haydon, *Anti-Catholicism in 18th Century England* (London: 1993).

Wilfrid B. Kerr, *The Maritime Provinces of British North America and the American Revolution* (New York: Russell and Russell, 1970).

D. W. Meinig, *The Shaping of America, Volume 1: Atlantic America, 1492–1800* (New Haven: Yale University Press, 1982).

Alison G. Olson, "Parliament, Empire and Parliamentary Law, 1776," in J. G. A. Pocock, editor, *Three British Revolutions: 1641, 1688, 1776* (Princeton: Princeton University Press, 1980).

Thomas H. Raddell, *Path of Destiny* (New York: Popular Library, 1957).

G. A. Rawlyk, "The American Revolution and Canada," in Greene and Pole, editors, *The Blackwell Encyclopedia of the American Revolution* (Oxford: Blackwell, 1994).

C. W. Toth, editor, *The American Revolution in the West Indies* (Port Washington, NY: Kennikat Press, 1975).

George J. Varney, "Acadia in the Revolution," *Magazine of American History* 8 (1882), pp. 486–495.

5. Background to the Hudson-Champlain Corridor and the Military Side of the American Revolution

George A. Billias, editor, *George Washington's Generals and Opponents* (New York: DaCapa, 1994).

Jeremy Black, *War for America* (Stroud, Gloucestershire: Alan Sutton, 1991).

Chester M. Destler, *Connecticut: The Provisions State* (Chester, CT: Pequot Press, 1973).

Ian Graham, *Colonists from Scotland* (Ithaca: Cornell University Press, 1956).

Ira Gruber, *The Howe Brothers and the American Revolution* (Williamsburg: Institute of Early American History and Culture, 1972).

Don Higginbotham, *The War of American Independence* (New York: Macmillan, 1971).

Richard Ketchum, *Saratoga* (New York: Henry Holt, 1997).

Piers Mackesy, *The War for America, 1775–1783* (Lincoln, NE: Bison Books).

Max Mintz, *The Generals at Saratoga* (New Haven: Yale University Press, 1990).

John Hyde Preston, *A Short History of the American Revolution* (New York: Pocket Books, 1952).

John Shy, *A People Numerous and Armed* (Ann Arbor: University of Michigan Press, 1990).

John Shy, *Toward Lexington: The Role of the British Army in the Coming of the American Revolution* (Princeton: Princeton University Press, 1965).

6. The Thirteen Colonies: Religion, Ethnicity, Politics, and the Wartime Alignments of 1775–1783

Bernard Bailyn and Philip Morgan, editors, *Strangers Within the Realm: Cultural Margins of the First British Empire* (Chapel Hill: University of North Carolina Press, 1991).

Randall Balmer, *A Perfect Babel of Confusion* (New York: Oxford University Press, 1989).

Lucy Bittinger, *Germans in Colonial Times* (Bowie, MD: Heritage Books, 1986).

Wallace Brown, *The Good Americans* (New York: William Morrow, 1969).

Colin G. Callaway, *The American Revolution in Indian Country* (New York: Cambridge University Press, 1995).

Kenneth Coleman, *The American Revolution in Georgia* (Athens: University of Georgia Press, 1958).

Jeffrey J. Crow, *The Black Experience in Revolutionary North Carolina* (Raleigh: North Carolina Department of Cultural Resources, 1977).

Jeffrey J. Crow, "Tory Plots and Anglican Loyalty," *North Carolina Historical Review,* Vol. 55, 1978, pp. 1–17.

Hubertis M. Cummings, *Scots Breed and Susquehanna* (Pittsburgh: University of Pittsburgh Press, 1974).

Cecil C. Currey, "18th Century Evangelical Opposition to the Revolution: The Case of the Quakers," in *Conference on Faith and History,* Dallas Baptist College, October 3, 1970.

Robert O. DeMond, *The Loyalists in North Carolina During the Revolution* (Hamden, CT: Archon Books, 1964).

Hugh Douglas, *Flora MacDonald* (London: Mandarin, 1994).

David N. Doyle, *Ireland, Irishmen and Revolutionary America* (Cork: The Mercier Press, 1981).

Richard S. Dunn, "Black Society in the Chesapeake," in Ira Berlin and Ronald Hoffman, editors, *Slavery and Freedom in the Age of the American Revolution* (Charlottesville: University Press of Virginia, 1983).

Robert A. East, *Connecticut's Loyalists* (Chester, CT: Pequot Press, 1974).

Emory G. Evans, "Trouble in the Back Country," in Tate and Hoffman, editors, *An Uncivil War: The War in the Southern Back Country* (Charlottesville: University Press of Virginia, 1985).

Sydney G. Fisher, *The Quaker Colonies* (New Haven: Yale University Press, 1921).

Thomas Fleming, *New Jersey* (New York: Norton, 1984).

Charles H. Glatfelter, *Pastors and People, Volume II—The History* (Breiningsville: The Pennsylvania German Society, 1981).

Barbara Graymont, *The Iroquois in the American Revolution* (Syracuse: Syracuse University Press, 1972).

Robert V. Haynes, *The Natchez District and the American Revolution* (Jackson: University Press of Mississippi, 1976).

Graham Hodges, *Slavery and Freedom in the Rural North* (Madison, WI: Madison House, 1997).

Carol E. Hoffecker, editor, *Readings in Delaware History* (Newark: University of Delaware Press, 1973).

Ronald Hoffman, "The Disaffected in the Revolutionary South," in Alfred Young, editor, *The American Revolution* (DeKalb: Northern Illinois University Press, 1976).

Owen S. Ireland, *Religion, Ethnicity and Politics* (University Park: Pennsylvania State University Press, 1995).

Philip R. Katcher, *Encyclopedia of British Provincial and German Army Units, 1775–1782* (Harrisburg, PA: Stackpole Books, 1973).

George W. Kyte, "Some Plans for a Loyalist Stronghold in the Middle Colonies," *Pennsylvania Magazine of History and Biography* (October 1952).

Billy Kennedy, *The Scots-Irish in the Shendandoah* (Belfast: Causeway Press, 1996).

Robert S. Lambert, *South Carolina Loyalists in the American Revolution* (Columbia: University of South Carolina Press, 1987).

James S. Leaman, *Revolution Downeast* (Amherst: University of Massachusetts Press, 1993).

Adrian C. Leiby, *The Revolutionary War in the Hackensack Valley* (New Brunswick, NJ: Rutgers University Press, 1992).

James G. Leyburn, *The Scotch-Irish* (Chapel Hill: University of North Carolina Press, 1962).

W. W. Manross, *A History of the American Episcopal Church* (New York and Milwaukee: 1935).

Richard McCormick, *New Jersey* (Newark: New Jersey Historical Society, 1981).

Jacob M. Price, *Capital and Credit in British Overseas Trade* (Cambridge, MA: 1980).

Benjamin Quarles, *The Negro in American Revolution* (New York: Norton, 1973).

Philip Ranlet, *The New York Loyalists* (Knoxville: University of Tennessee Press, 1986).

George Raynor, "Patriots and Tories in Piedmont Carolina," *Salisbury Post,* Salisbury, NC (1990).

Henry M. M. Richards, *German-Americans in the American Revolution* (Bowie, MD: Heritage Books, 1992).

John E. Selby, *The Revolution in Virginia, 1775–1783* (Williamsburg: The Colonial Williamsburg Foundation, 1988).

Lynn W. Turner, *The Ninth State* (Chapel Hill: University of North Carolina Press, 1983).

Carl Van Doren, A *Secret History of the Revolution* (New York: The Viking Press, 1941).

J. Leitch Wright, Jr., *Florida in the American Revolution* (Gainesville: University of Florida Press, 1975).

Henry S. Young, *The Treatment of Loyalists in Pennsylvania* (Ph.D. thesis, Johns Hopkins University, 1955).

Oscar Zeichner, *Connecticut's Years of Controversy* (Chapel Hill: University of North Carolina Press, 1949).

7. British Politics and the American Revolution

James Bradley, *Popular Politics and the American Revolution in England* (Macon, GA: Mercer Press, 1986).

James Bradley, *Religion, Revolution and English Radicalism* (Cambridge: Cambridge University Press, 1990).

Herbert Butterfield, *George III and the Historians* (New York: Macmillan, 1959).

David Cannadine, *G. M. Trevelyan: A Life in History* (New York: Norton, 1992).

Ian Christie and Benjaman Labaree, *Empire or Independence, 1760–1776* (New York: 1976).

J. C. D. Clark, *The Language of Liberty, 1660–1832 (Cambridge: Cambridge University Press,1994).*

Linda Colley, *Britons* (New Haven: Yale University Press, 1992).

Robert Kent Donovan, "The Popular Party of the Church of Scotland and the American Revolution," in Richard B. Sher and Jeffrey E. Smitten, editors, *Scotland and America in the Age of Enlightenment* (Edinburgh: Edinburgh University Press, 1990).

David Doyle, *Ireland, Irishmen and Revolutionary America* (Cork: The Mercier Press, 1981).

Editor?, Library of Congress, *The Impact of the American Revolution Abroad* (Washington, DC: 1976).

Owen Dudley Edwards, "The Impact of the American Revolution on Ireland," in *The Impact of the American Revolution Abroad* (Washington, DC: Library of Congress, 1976).

Owen Dudley Edwards, "Ireland and the American Revolution," in Edwards and Shepperson, editors, *Scotland, Europe and the American Revolution* (New York: St. Martin's Press, 1978).

Owen Dudley Edwards and George Shepperson, editors, *Scotland, Europe and the American Revolution* (New York: St. Martin's Press, 1978).

Thomas Fleming, *1776: Year of Illusions* (Edison, NJ: Castle Books, 1996).

Mary Beacock Fryer, *Allan Maclean, Jacobite General* (Toronto: Dundurn Press, 1987).

A. D. Gilbert, *Religion and Society in Industrial England: Church, Chapel and Social Change, 1740–1914* (London: 1976).

Paul Langford, "Old Whigs, Old Tories and The American Revolution," *Journal of Imperial and Commonwealth History* (January 1980).

R. B. McDowell, *Ireland in the Age of Imperialism and Revolution* (Oxford: Clarendon Press, 1979).

McGlynn, *The Jacobite Army in England, 1745* (Edinburgh: John Donald, 1983).

Lewis Namier, *England in the Age of the American Revolution* (London: Macmillan, 1961).

John Phillips, *Electoral Behavior in Unreformed England* (Princeton: Princeton University Press, 1982).

J. H. Plumb, *England in the 18th Century* (Harmondsworth, England: Penguin, 1966).

J. H. Plumb, "The Influence of the American Revolution on Great Britain," in Library of Congress, *The Impact of the American Revolution Abroad* (Washington, DC: 1976).

Sir Robert Rait and G. S. Pride, *Scotland* (London: Ernest Benn, 1954).

John Sainsbury, *Disaffected Patriots* (Kingston and Montreal: 1987).

Richard B. Sher and Jeffrey R. Smitten, editors, *Scotland and America in the Age of Enlightenment* (Edinburgh: Edinburgh University Press, 1990).

Michael Watts, *The Dissenters* (Oxford: 1978).

8. Saratoga and the British Generals

In focusing on Saratoga and the qualities and politics of the British generals involved in one way or another, the most useful major books were these: Max Mintz, *The Generals at Saratoga* (New Haven: Yale University Press, 1990), is helpful partly for the battle itself but more for the larger British and American background on John Burgoyne and the American commander, Horatio Gates; Richard Ketchum, *Saratoga* (New York: Henry Holt, 1997), is particularly good on the details of the battles in and around Saratoga, but does not have as much detail on what shaped the two generals; *The Howe Brothers and the American Revolution,* op. cit., by Ira Gruber, provides the best focused material on General William Howe, Admiral Richard Howe, and why they did what they did. Of the books on the military side of the Revolution from the British point of view, Piers Mackesy, *The War for America, 1775–1783,* op. cit., is an authoritative and comprehensive chronicle. As for the other commanders involved, the anthology by George A. Billias, editor, *George Washington's Generals and Opponents* (New York: DaCapa, 1994), includes portraits of British generals Thomas Gage, William Howe, Henry Clinton, John Burgoyne, Charles Cornwallis, and Guy Carleton, as well as profiles of two admirals: Thomas Graves and Richard Lord Howe. These five books provide a good framework for the campaign, on which other specific political and military detail can be hung.

9. The Aftermath of the American Revolution in Britain and the United States

James M. Banner, Jr., *To the Hartford Convention* (New York: Knopf, 1970).

Robert A. Becker, "Salus Populi, Suprema Lex," *South Carolina Historical Magazine,* vol. 80, no. 1 (January 1979).

John Brewer, *The Sinews of Power* (New York: Knopf, 1989).

Roger Brown, *The Republic in Peril: 1812* (New York: Norton, 1971).

William N. Chambers, *Political Parties in a New Nation* (New York: Oxford University Press, 1963).

Ian Christie, *Wars and Revolutions: Britain, 1760–1815* (Cambridge: Harvard University Press, 1982).

George Dangerfield, *The Awakening of American Nationalism* (New York: Harper Torch Books, 1965).

David Brian Davis, *The Problem of Slavery in the Age of Revolution* (Ithaca: Cornell University Press, 1975).

Elisha P. Douglas, *Rebels and Democrats* (Chicago: Ivan R. Dee, 1989).

Georgia, American Guide Series (Athens: University of Georgia Press, 1946).

Donald R. Hickey, *The War of 1812* (Urbana: University of Illinois Press, 1990).

Don Higginbotham, *The War of American Independence* (New York: Macmillan, 1971).

Merrill Jensen, *The Articles of Confederation* (Madison: University of Wisconsin Press, 1976).

Michael Kammen, *A Season of Youth* (Ithaca: Cornell University Press, 1978).

Staughton Lynd, "The Conflict over Slavery," in Allen Davis and Harold Woodman, editors, *Conflict and Consensus in Early American History* (Lexington, MA: D.C. Heath, 1976).

Piers Mackesy, *The War for America, 1775–1783* (Lincoln, NE: Bison Books, 1993).

Jackson Turner Main, *The Anti-Federalists* (New York: Norton, 1974).

G. J. Marcus, *A Naval History of England* (Boston: Little, Brown, 1961).

Philip D. Morgan, "British Encounters with Africans and African-Americans," in *Strangers Within the Realm: Cultural Margins of the First British Empire* (Chapel Hill: University of North Carolina Press, 1991).

North Carolina, American Guide Series (Chapel Hill: University of North Carolina Press, 1955).

George Novack, "Slavery in Colonial America," in Novack, editor, *America's Revolutionary Heritage* (New York: Pathfinder Press, 1976).

Bradford Perkins, *Prologue to War* (Berkeley: University of California Press, 1968).

Charles Ritcheson, *Aftermath of the Revolution* (New York: Norton, 1971).

Lisle A. Rose, *Prologue to Democracy* (Lexington: University of Kentucky Press, 1968).

Simon Schama, *Patriots and Liberators: Revolution in the Netherlands, 1780–1813* (New York: Vintage, 1992).

South Carolina, American Guide Series (New York: Oxford University Press, 1941).

10. Sectionalism and the Political Geography of the U.S. Civil War

Lee Benson, *The Concept of Jacksonian Democracy: New York as a Test Case* (Princeton: Princeton University Press, 1961).

Walter Dean Burnham, *Presidental Ballots 1832–1896* (Baltimore: Johns Hopkins University Press, 1955).

Joseph Charles, *The Origins of the American Party System* (New York: Harper Torch Books, 1961).

"Civil War Historians and the 'Needless War' Doctrine," *Journal of the History of Ideas* (April 1956).

John F. Coleman, *The Disruption of the Pennsylvania Democracy, 1848–1860* (Harrisburg: Pennsylvania Historical and Museum Commission, 1975), appendix.

David Brian Davis, *The Slave Power and the Paranoid Style* (Baton Rouge: Louisiana State University Press, 1969).

William Dusinberre, *Civil War Issues in Philadelphia, 1856–1865* (Philadelphia: University of Pennsylvania Press, 1965).

Robert East, "The Massachusetts Conservatives in the Critical Period," in Richard B. Morris, editor, *The Era of the American Revolution* (New York: 1939).

Eric Foner, *Free Soil, Free Labor, Free Men* (New York: Oxford University Press, 1970).

Eric Foner, *Politics and Ideology in the Age of the Civil War* (New York: Oxford University Press, 1980).

Ronald Formisano, *The Birth of Mass Political Parties: Michigan, 1827–1861* (Princeton: Princeton University Press, 1971).

George M. Frederickson, *The Inner Civil War* (New York: Harper Torch Books, 1968).

Guide to U.S. Elections (Washington, DC: Congressional Quarterly, 1975).

Stewart Holbrook, *The Yankee Exodus* (New York: Macmillan, 1950).

Michael Holt, *Forging a Majority: The Formation of the Republican Party in Pittsburgh, 1848–1860* (New Haven: Yale University Press, 1969).

Michael F. Holt, *The Political Crisis of the 1850s* (New York: John Wiley, 1978).

Daniel Walker Howe, *The Political Culture of the American Whigs* (Chicago: University of Chicago Press, 1979).

Owen S. Ireland, "Germans Against Abolition, a Minority's View of Slavery in Revolutionary Pennsylvania," *Journal of Interdisciplinary History* 3 (1973), pp. 685–706.

Howard Jones, *Union in Peril* (Chapel Hill: University of North Carolina Press, 1992).

Frederick Luebke, *Ethnic Voters and the Election of Lincoln* (Lincoln: University of Nebraska Press, 1971).

Bruce Maizlish, *The Triumph of Sectionalism* (Kent, OH: Kent State University Press, 1983).

Lynn L. Marshall, "The Strange Stillbirth of the Whig Party," *American Historical Review* 72:2 (January 1967).

Robert E. May, *The Southern Dream of a Caribbean Empire* (Athens: University of Georgia Press, 1989).

James McPherson, *Battle Cry of Freedom* (New York: Oxford University Press, 1986).

Grady McWhiney, *Cracker Culture* (Tuscaloosa: University of Alabama Press, 1988).

Vernon Parrington, *The Romantic Revolution in America 1800–1860* (New York: Harcourt Brace/Harvest Books, 1954).

Abbott E. Smith, *Colonists in Bondage* (New York: Norton, 1971).

Southern Literary Messenger 30 (June 1860).

Kenneth M. Stampp, editor, *The Causes of the Civil War* (New York: Simon and Schuster/Touchstone, 1991).

James L. Sundquist, *Dynamics of the Party System* (Washington, DC: Brookings Institution, 1973).

William R. Taylor, *Cavalier and Yankee* (New York: Doubleday Anchor, 1963).

John W. Thomason, *Jeb Stuart* (New York: Charles Scribner, 1930).

Frederick Jackson Turner, *The United States, 1830–1850* (New York: Norton, 1965).

Richard W. Van Alstyne, *The Rising American Empire* (New York: Norton, 1974).

Shane White, *Somewhat More Independent* (Athens: University of Georgia Press, 1991).

C. Vann Woodward, *American Counterpoint* (Boston: Little, Brown, 1964).

William C. Wright, *The Secession Movement in the Middle Atlantic States* (Rutherford, NJ: Fairleigh Dickinson Press, 1973).

11. Loyalties and Alignments of the U.S. Civil War

Annie H. Abel, *The American Indian as Slaveholder and Secessionist* (Lincoln: University of Nebraska Press, 1992).

Iver Bernstein, *The New York City Draft Riots* (New York: Oxford University Press, 1990).

John F. Coleman, *The Disruption of the Pennsylvania Democracy* (Harrisburg: Pennsylvania Historical and Museum Commission, 1975).

Daniel W. Crofts, *Reluctant Confederates* (Chapel Hill: University of North Carolina Press, 1989).

John T. Cunningham, *This Is New Jersey* (New Brunswick, NJ: Rutgers University Press, 1953).

Richard N. Current, *Lincoln's Loyalists* (New York: Oxford University Press, 1992).

Richard O. Curry, editor, *Radicalism, Racism, and Party Realignment: The Border States During Reconstruction* (Baltimore: Johns Hopkins University Press, 1969).

William Gillette, *Jersey Blue: Civil War Politics in New Jersey* (New Brunswick, NJ: Rutgers University Press, 1994).

Wood Gray, *The Hidden Civil War* (New York: Viking Press, 1964).

Lawrence M. Hauptman, *Between Two Fires: American Indians in the Civil War* (New York: The Free Press, 1995).

Michael F. Holt, *The Political Crisis of the 1850s* (New York: John Wiley, 1978).

Alvin Josephy, Jr., *The Civil War in the American West* (New York: Knopf, 1991).

Frank Klement, *The Copperheads in the Middle West* (Chicago: University of Chicago Press, 1960).

Ernest A. McKay, *The Civil War and New York City* (Syracuse: Syracuse University Press, 1960).

James McPherson, *Battle Cry of Freedom* (New York: Oxford University Press, 1986).

Thomas J. Pressly, *Americans Interpret Their Civil War* (New York: The Free Press, 1965).

Bart Talbert, *Maryland: The South's First Casualty* (Berryville, VA: Rockbridge Publishing, 1995).

12. Britain and the American Civil War and U.S.-British Relations in the Late Nineteenth Century

E. D. Adams, *Great Britain and the American Civil War* (London: Longmans, 1925).

H. C. Allen, *Great Britain and the United States* (New York: St. Martin's Press, 1955).

Donald Bellows, "A Study of British Conservative Reaction to the American Civil War," *Journal of Southern History* 51 (November 1985).

Kenneth Bourne, *Britain and the Balance of Power in North America* (Berkeley: University of California Press, 1967).

D. P. Crook, *The North and South and the Powers* (New York: John Wiley, 1974).

Philip Foner, *British Labor and the American Civil War* (New York: Holmes & Meier, 1981).

Howard Jones, *Union in Peril* (Chapel Hill: University of North Carolina Press, 1992).

W. D. Jones, "The British Conservatives and the American Civil War," *American Historical Review* 58 (April 1953).

Robert E. May, editor, *The Union, the Confederacy and the Atlantic Rim* (Lafayette: Purdue University Press, 1995).

"Nineteenth Century Cromwell," *Past and Present* 40 (1968).

J. P. Parry, *Democracy and Religion* (Cambridge: Cambridge University Press, 1986).

David Thomson, *England in the Nineteenth Century* (Harmondsworth: Penguin Books, 1950).

"The Welsh," in *Harvard Encyclopedia of Ethnic Groups* (Cambridge: Harvard University Press, 1980).

D. G. Wright, "Bradford and the American Civil War," *Journal of British Studies* 8 (May 1989).

13. The United States in the Decades After the American Civil War

Paul Buck, *The Road to Reunion* (Boston: Little, Brown, 1937).

Richard O. Curry, editor, *Radicalism, Racism, and Party Realignment: The Border States During Reconstruction* (Baltimore: Johns Hopkins University Press, 1969).

Milton Friedman and Anna Schwartz, *A Monetary History of the United States 1867–1960* (Princeton: Princeton University Press, 1963).

Matthew Josephson, *The Robber Barons* (New York: Harcourt Brace/Harvest Books, 1962).

Library of Congress, *Constitution of the U.S. Annotated* (Washington, DC: 1968).

Allan Nevins, *War for the Union*, vol. 2. (New York: 1959–1971), p. 242.

Roy F. Nichols, *The Stakes of Power* (New York: Hill and Wang, 1961).

William E. Parish, *Missouri Under Radical Rule* (Columbia: University of Missouri Press, 1965).

Bruce D. Porter, *War and the Rise of the State* (New York: The Free Press, 1994).

Charles P. Roland, *The Confederacy* (Chicago: 1960).

Robert R. Russel, *History of the American Economic System* (New York: Appleton-Century-Crofts, 1964).

C. Vann Woodward, *Reunion and Reaction* (New York: Doubleday Anchor, 1956).

14. The Role of War in U.S. Politics and Elections

Ray A. Billington, *The Protestant Crusade* (New York: Macmillan, 1938).

Timothy Bosworth, "Anti-Catholicism as a Political Tool," *Catholic Historical Review* 61 (1975).

Robert L. Brunhouse, *The Counter-Revolution in Pennsylvania* (Harrisburg: Pennsylvania Historical and Museum Commission, 1971).

George Dangerfield, *The Strange Death of Liberal England, 1910–1914* (New York: G. P. Putnam's, 1961).

Aaron Fogelman, *Hopeful Journeys* (Philadelphia: University of Pennsylvania Press, 1996).

Lawrence Goodwyn, *The Populist Moment* (New York: Oxford University Press, 1978).

Samuel Lubell, *The Future of American Politics* (New York: Harper & Row, 1952).

Samuel Lubell, *Revolt of the Moderates* (New York: Harper, 1956).

Martin Marty, *Righteous Empire* (New York: Dial Press, 1970).

Richard O'Connor, *The Germans* (Boston: Little, Brown, 1968).

Rudolph Pasler and Margaret Pasler, *The New Jersey Federalists* (Rutherford, NJ: Fairleigh Dickinson University Press, 1975).

Emory Thomas, *The Confederacy as a Revolutionary Experience* (Columbia: University of South Carolina Press, 1991).

Oscar Zeichner, "The Loyalist Problem in New York," *New York Historical Association* 21 (1940).

15. The Demographic Rise of the English-Speaking Peoples

N. S. Albarnoz, *The Population of Latin America* (Berkeley: University of California Press, 1974).

John A. Hawgood, *The Tragedy of German America* (New York: 1940).

Michael Hechter, *Internal Colonialism* (Berkeley: University of California Press, 1975).

Francis Jennings, *Benjamin Franklin, Politician* (New York: Norton, 1996).

Emmet Larkin, "The Devotional Revolution in Ireland," quoted in Grady McWhinney, *Cracker Culture* (Tuscaloosa: University of Alabama Press, 1988).

Brian Morton, *Americans in London* (New York: William Morrow/Quill, 1986).

H. Richard Niebuhr, *The Social Sources of Denominationalism* (New York: Meridian Books, 1957).

Rollie Poppino, *Brazil* (New York: Oxford University Press, 1968).

A. G. Roeber, "The Dutch-Speaking and German-Speaking Peoples of Colonial America," in *Strangers Within the Realm: Cultural Margins of the First British Empire* (Chapel Hill: University of North Carolina Press, 1991).

Richard Rose, *Governing Without Consensus* (Boston: Beacon Press, 1971).

Cecil Woodham-Smith, *The Great Hunger* (New York: Signet Books, 1964).

16. The English-Speaking Peoples and the Global Language Battle

"Britons Abroad," *The Economist*, December 26, 1992.

Michael Hechter, *Internal Colonialism* (Berkeley: University of California Press, 1975).

Samuel P. Huntington, *The Clash of Civilization and the Remaking of World Order* (London: Simon and Schuster, 1997).

Robert McCrum, William Cran, and Robert NcNeil, *The Story of English* (New York: Viking Penguin, 1986)

17. The History of Religion in the United States

Sydney Ahlstrom, *A Religious History of the American People* (New Haven: Yale University Press, 1972).

Patricia U. Bonomi, *Under the Cope of Religion* (New York: Oxford University Press, 1986).

Roger Fink and Rodney Stark, *The Churching of America* (New Brunswick, NJ: Rutgers University Press, 1992).

Martin Marty, *Righteous Empire* (New York: Dial Press, 1970).

H. Richard Niebuhr, *The Social Sources of Denominationalism* (New York: Meridian Books, 1957).

Peter H. Odegard, *Religion and Politics* (New Brunswick, NJ: Rutgers/Oceana Press, 1960).

William W. Sweet, *The Story of Religion in America* (Grand Rapids, MI: Baker House, 1979).

INDEX